AF579060

ITALIAN RENAISSANCE PAINTING

John Hale

ITALIAN RENAISSANCE PAINTING

from Masaccio to Titian

Phaidon · E. P. Dutton
OXFORD NEW YORK

PHAIDON PRESS LIMITED,
Littlegate House, St Ebbe's Street, Oxford
Published in the United States of America by
E. P. DUTTON & CO., INC.

First published 1977

ISBN 0 7148 1599 3

Library of Congress Catalog Card Number: 76-5355

Printed in Great Britain.
Text and monochrome illustrations by W & J Mackay Limited, Chatham.
Colour plates by J. Howitt & Son Limited, Nottingham.

Contents

Preface

In the interest of telling a coherent story and presenting an unfaltering series of masterpieces, this book starts, after a brief prelude, with the work of Masaccio (1401–*c.* 1428) and ends with that of Federigo Barocci (*c.* 1535–1612).

Its scope, then, is not precisely that of the period associated with the phrase 'Italian Renaissance', which has come to mean a period of cultural achievement spanning the careers of Giotto (1266?–1337) and Michelangelo (1475–1564). The phrase, in any case, is better suited to a title than to a text; it suggests values—humanistic, individualistic, paganizing, sceptical, exploratory, and so forth—that are so glamorously subjective that they should be kept to one side when looking at individual paintings. It is convenient to divide our period into two parts, and in each to follow an introductory section which sets the scene, with interpretive descriptions of a series of key works. To use 'Fifteenth Century' and 'Sixteenth Century' would be to carry objectivity too far. So I have used the Italian equivalents Quattrocento and Cinquecento, words which carry enough cultural flavour to make the chronological implications less rigid.

'Italian', too, is a word to treat with caution. The Italian peninsula was not politically one country, and its inhabitants had no notion that it should be. They spoke versions (not always mutually comprehensible) of the same language, they shared a pride in being the inheritors of the civilization of ancient Rome, a confidence that they were culturally superior to lesser breeds beyond the Alps or across the Mediterranean. But in day-to-day terms they were the subjects of independent and frequently competing units, and saw themselves first and foremost as Florentines, Venetians, Milanese, Romans or Neapolitans or, to name some of the smaller city states, men of Urbino, Ferrara or Siena. Although painters crossed these frontiers to study or to fulfil commissions 'abroad', art retained a strongly regional flavour even while absorbing influences from elsewhere.

In the sphere of politics, Machiavelli travelled widely as a diplomat and saw the necessity for at least some of the Italian states combining together against the 'barbarian' powers—France, Germany and Spain—whose wars brought havoc to the peninsula in the first quarter of the sixteenth century. But at heart, and in his 'style' as a writer, he remained doggedly a Florentine. And so did his contemporary Michelangelo, in spite of long residence in Rome and of works that forced themselves into the consciousness of artists all over Italy. Independent states and their changing alliances; 'schools' of painting and their varying interactions: the parallel is close enough to forbid a unitary treatment of the history of either Italian politics or art.

In tracing the development of painting through so long a period the temptation, to which I have yielded, is to concentrate on those painters of genius whose work was innovative or influential, or both. And this imposes a pattern—a heavily Florentine Quattrocento, a Cinquecento first Roman-Florentine and then Venetian—which does far less than justice to the full range of accomplishment, the staggering total of visual and intellectual pleasure offered by these two centuries as a whole.

I should like to record my gratitude to members of the publisher's staff, who have written the captions to the plates, and to Keith Roberts, who chose the illustrations; and also to Lucia Wildt, who wrote the Biographical Notes.

The text has benefited from the generous vigilance of Michael Levey. The opinions and emphases, however, and any errors that remain, are my own.

Venice–London 1976 J. R. HALE

Part one The Quattrocento

The painters' world

'In this splendid, noble art,
So many have been famous in our century,
They make any other age seem poor.'

THIS CONFIDENT ASSERTION of the dignity of painting and the high reputation of its practitioners was written in about 1490 by Giovanni Santi, himself a competent, if platitudinous, painter, in a rhyming chronicle designed to commemorate his patron, the *condottiere* Duke of Urbino, Federigo da Montefeltro. The chronicle did not achieve its purpose. Federigo is remembered through the work of a greater artist, Piero della Francesca (Plates 58, 59, 65). Moreover, Giovanni Santi had a son, Raffaello, whose fame is so great that it has all but obscured the work of his father. All the same, obscure, provincial, almost forgotten, Giovanni is an important witness to the stimulus to painters provided by the interest men took in their careers; and, what is more, if he had been entrusted with selecting the artists to be included in this book, his choice would have been uncannily close to that of our own day.

These are the painters he goes on to list as having been 'famous in our century':

	Plates
GENTILE DA FABRIANO (*c.* 1370–1427)	6, 82
ANTONIO PISANELLO (*c.* 1395–1455)	36
PAOLO UCCELLO (*c.* 1397–1475)	26, 28, 32, 37
FRA ANGELICO (*c.* 1399–1455)	12, 20, 23, 24, 41
MASACCIO (1401–*c.* 1428)	3, 5, 7, 8, 18, 22, 127
FRA FILIPPO LIPPI (*c.* 1406–69)	12, 16
DOMENICO VENEZIANO (*c.* 1410–61)	10, 56
PIERO DELLA FRANCESCA (before 1420–92)	21, 25, 29, 31, 34, 35, 58, 59, 65, 77
PESELLINO (*c.* 1422–57)	
ANDREA DEL CASTAGNO (*c.* 1421 ?–57)	30, 101
ANTONELLO DA MESSINA (*c.* 1430–79)	42, 52, 62
GENTILE BELLINI (*c.* 1429–1507)	
GIOVANNI BELLINI (*c.* 1430–1516)	45, 54, 79, 84, 92, 103, 136
COSIMO TURA (before 1431–95)	69
ANTONIO POLLAIUOLO (*c.* 1432–98)	50, 83, 97
ANDREA MANTEGNA (*c.* 1430/1–1506)	27, 46–9, 51, 112
MELOZZO DA FORLI (1438–94)	66
PIERO POLLAIUOLO (*c.* 1441–96)	50, 83
SANDRO BOTTICELLI (*c.* 1445–1510)	11, 38, 55, 57, 71, 72, 75, 76
ERCOLE DE' ROBERTI (*c.* 1450–96)	44
DOMENICO GHIRLANDAIO (1449–94)	53, 64, 91

LUCA SIGNORELLI (*c.* 1441–1523)	74, 96
LEONARDO DA VINCI (1452–1519)	63, 80, 85, 102, 125, 128, 129
PIETRO PERUGINO (*c.* 1445–1523)	81
FILIPPINO LIPPI (*c.* 1457–1504)	17, 67, 68

Only two of these artists are not included here, Pesellino and Gentile Bellini, and that is purely for reasons of space. Among the chief Quattrocento Italian painters most sought after by modern museums, Giovanni only omitted perhaps five:

	Plates
SASSETTA (*c.* 1392–1450)	15, 43
GIOVANNI DI PAOLO (*c.* 1399–1482)	14
BENOZZO GOZZOLI (*c.* 1421–97)	13
CARLO CRIVELLI (*c.* 1435–93)	70
ANDREA VERROCCHIO (*c.* 1435–88)	39, 40

Of these, Verrocchio was better known as a sculptor when Giovanni was writing his chronicle. The Sienese Sassetta and Giovanni di Paolo, the Venetian Crivelli and the Tuscan Gozzoli were predominantly local artists and may not have been known to him; but all four had something in common which might reasonably account for their omission: they contributed nothing by way of technique, nor by the means adopted to achieve illusion or expressiveness, to the mainstream of what was above all an innovative, even a restlessly experimental, period in the history of art.

No comparable list was compiled elsewhere in Europe. This is not because there was no painting of comparable merit north of the Alps. From Jan van Eyck and Rogier van der Weyden in the first half of the Quattrocento, to Dürer at its close, works by Netherlandish and German painters were known to Italians and influenced them, especially in portraiture. But nowhere outside Italy were painters so conscious of the status of their craft or so interested in the fame of their predecessors and contemporaries. From his hill-top town near the Adriatic, Giovanni was well aware that Florence was the chief artistic centre, supplying a new and forceful direction to art (thirteen of his twenty-five painters were born or spent most of their working lives there); and the very insipidity of his own altarpieces strengthens the tribute he pays to artists of such widely differing energies as Masaccio, Uccello, Piero della Francesca and Castagno. From Giovanni's list alone one can surmise that it was above all in Italy that painters of genius, whatever their approach to art, could rely on their individuality being recognized, and on the support of a public that had a measure of real understanding of what they were trying to achieve.

By itself, the mere demand for paintings does little to explain the characteristics of outstanding artistic achievement, though certainly, at this purely quantitive level, Quattrocento artists were fortunate. Italian churches and palaces, with their emphasis on slabs of wall rather than expansive fenestration, offered a sizeable area for decoration to the fresco painter. In addition to chapels at the east end, churches provided for rows of altars, and thus of altarpieces, along the sides. There was also a lively demand for smaller devotional paintings for chapels in private houses or to hang in bedrooms. Prestige objects, like the chests given to brides to contain their trousseaux, the circular trays presented to mothers on the birth of a child (possibly the origin of the *tondo*, or round painting, that became fairly common), or the shields and banners carried in processions or at jousts: these all provided employment for the painter as well as for the carpenter, armourer and embroiderer. And it was during the Quattrocento that the individual portrait became one of the major challenges to an artist's skill.

Italian humanists had pioneered the rediscovery of classical texts, and had prompted an awareness of the pre-Christian societies of Greece and Rome. They had also done something to quicken men's belief in the value of their own careers and characters. But for reasons of tradition and prestige in the eyes of others, as well as of personal devotion, the demand was overwhelmingly for paintings with a religious content. The striking changes that took place in Quattrocento art can be described without any reference to the challenge of new subject matter—a Mars and Venus (Plates 73 and 75) or a family group (Plate 47)—and entirely within the context of those innumerable Madonnas, martyrdoms and 'sacred conversations' that fill, one might feel almost to weariness, the churches of Italy and our own museums. The demand was for works of art dealing with the mysteries of the Christian faith, but that art itself became a revelation was not due to the number of orders, which could have led to mere repetition, but to the fact that painters of genius wanted to treat old subjects in new ways and were to a large extent given their heads by a sympathetic public.

This sympathy was of crucial importance at a time when artists painted not to please themselves, nor to assemble works for future exhibition and sale, but to fulfil specific orders. A painter could only develop freely if the patron was receptive to changes and surprises. And because so many paintings were designed for display in churches or town halls, the innovative painter needed a public that would not be upset by an unfamiliar approach. In fact we know of extremely few instances of commissioned paintings being rejected, and none of public outcry.

There is plenty of evidence, besides Giovanni Santi's chronicle, to show that the acceptance of innovation was not just the result of indifference, of pioneer artists railroading a passive public. At the very beginning of the Quattrocento an educational treatise stressed that an ability to discuss and appreciate works of art was appropriate for the man with a liberal education. Although subjective expressions of opinion remain rare, the words and phrases used to describe paintings become steadily richer through the century. It became more common to compare one artist with another, to value the imprint of a painter's hand, rather than the value of the pigments he used (previously a factor much stressed in commissions) or the speed with which a contract could be fulfilled with the aid of collaborators in the painter's workshop. In the 1470s a Florentine patrician noted with pride that he possessed works by Filippo Lippi, Uccello, Domenico Veneziano, Castagno, Pollaiuolo and Verrocchio—by no means a conservative assembly. A ready appreciation of the difficulties painters set themselves and solved—foreshortened figures (e.g. Plate 32), a graphically 'life-like' setting (e.g. Plate 51)—encouraged them to continue to experiment. Not all purchasers were enlightened. Many shopped around for the cheapest or most expeditious painters, but there was enough recognition of what 'art' was about to encourage artists to follow their own preoccupations in a personal style. Interest was also spread by the system whereby chapels and altars in churches were allocated to families, guilds and lay religious confraternities. Here, as with commissions placed by monastic orders or cathedral chapters, the choice of a painter was the result of a degree of consensus.

Known as individuals through their faces and manners, as they walked the streets of what were, after all, very small cities, as well as through the open nature of their workshops, painters were, literally, public figures. Some were prominent enough to be called upon to work far afield, as, for instance, Uccello and Castagno, who went from Florence to work in the Basilica of San Marco in Venice, and Fra Angelico and Botticelli, who were called to work in Rome. And there was another element in the support given by society to the artist, though a trickier one to assess because it comprised habits of mind, points of view and intellectual concerns. The extent to which any of these affected the painter can only be guessed at, but that, taken as a whole, they influenced the development of Quattrocento art may be taken as certain.

Let us look at Florence, whose artists, from Masaccio to the young Leonardo, acted as pacemakers throughout the century. An intense civic pride had included painters as part of the city's patriotic roll-call ever since Dante in the *Divine Comedy* had pointed out that the fame of Giotto had eclipsed that of his predecessor Cimabue. The habit of celebrating painters along with statesmen and scholars may have spurred them on to forge a distinctive style. This desire to stand out, to be remembered, also encouraged patrons to have their own faces and families commemorated in paint, and thus led them to choose painters that would make them appear as real, as recognizably individual, as possible. This worship of the secular 'real presence' was nourished by two other concerns: a belief in the inherent dignity of human beings, and the almost faddish respect paid to classical sculpture (no figure paintings having as yet been unearthed), with its emphasis on the realistic nude and the portrait bust.

The forces making patrons want an art that was a recognizable, if selective, version of real life included other factors. Humanism itself was taken up by the well-to-do in Florence because classical moral philosophy (the key figure being Cicero) offered a justification for active participation in civic councils and counting houses and provided an honourable supplement to primarily contemplative and other-worldly ethics. The Saints, after all, were men like us before sanctity etherealized them: so let them be made to look like the men they were. And the Church agreed; preachers stressed that religious paintings should be memorable and readily understood: realistic after-images to aid private devotion. The painter's task of achieving a semblance of things seen involved a rigorous analysis of how to render depth in order to make pictorial space look like the real space in which men moved and through which rivers meandered, and how to give a sense of the real volume of solids. Here, too, support was forthcoming from a society of merchants, bankers and shopkeepers, men used to counting, weighing, measuring and calculating, men likely to understand the purpose of the artist's preoccupation with perspective, and to be tolerant if mathematics at times seemed to take over from nature, as in the work of Uccello (Plates 26, 32).

If it is no accident that the most advanced painting in fifteenth-century Europe was produced in an unusually well-educated and rational society, it is also no accident that so many of the artists who contributed to that advance grew up in Florence. With few exceptions, Quattrocento painters who were not themselves the sons of painters, like Filippino Lippi or Giovanni Bellini or Raphael, were the sons of artisans and shopkeepers: cobblers, tanners, poulterers—the occupations respectively of the fathers of Piero della Francesca, Botticelli and the Pollaiuolo brothers. The largest pool of recruits to the painter's calling was thus provided by large cities, and apart from the Netherlands (the other chief centre of painting at the time), Italy was by far the most heavily urbanized country in Europe.

By itself, a city, for all its potential recruits and its potential patrons, has no more than a statistical likelihood of producing artists of genius, let alone an innovative, exploratory art. But given the atmosphere of support we have described, children with an artistic bent had the best chance of becoming painters, and of being encouraged to reveal their genius, in cities or within their sphere of influence. In addition, cities, once established as art centres, attracted the few men of genius whose talent first flowered in the provinces, as Gentile da Fabriano was drawn to Florence and Antonello da Messina to Venice. Piero della Francesca was unique in deciding to pass almost the whole of his long life in the unchallenging provincialism of Borgo San Sepolcro. For those boys who, between the ages of seven and thirteen, joined a painter's workshop to begin an apprenticeship lasting from seven to ten years, the life was challenging. Vasari, whose mid-sixteenth-century biographies of painters are our chief source of information about them, records that when Andrea Mantegna, a talented peasant boy, was taken to Padua and placed in the workshop of Francesco Squarcione, 'he was given no little help and incentive by the competition he met from the pupils of his master.' The more workshops—as in Florence—the greater the pressure to excel. And this competition grew as purchasers increasingly distinguished between the individual's and the workshop style, and came to value the artist whose knowledge and temperament, as well as skill, could make the commissioning and the production of a work of art as close a collaboration as possible. The team spirit that enabled Masaccio to leave the face of Christ, in the very middle of his *Tribute Money* fresco, to his colleague Masolino (Plate 7) did not die—masters as different as Domenico Veneziano and Castagno could work together on occasion—but by the end of the century the variety of different approaches, encouraged by competition between artists and the 'support' of patrons, came to produce a sensitiveness to style that meant that men like Perugino, who could not keep abreast of change, found themselves neglected in the art centres and were forced to seek commissions in the provinces.

Before turning to the painters themselves and their works we have looked at some of the factors that combined to make Quattrocento Italy a place uniquely receptive to vitality and change in the arts. And we must make a further point. These factors supported innovation among sculptors and architects as well, and no account of Quattrocento painting can ignore the importance of cross-fertilization among the arts, especially the influence of sculpture.

Medieval painters had not been shy about signing their works. But none had shown the confidence that made Nicola Pisano inscribe himself, on a pulpit finished in 1260, as being the greatest sculptor of his day—a claim for which he was outbid by an inscription of about 1300 trumpeting the fame of his son Giovanni. In the early Quattrocento the same combination of self-esteem (and it is worth remembering that sculpture was far more expensive than painting) and sensitivity to the relevance of classical models made contemporary sculptors at least as great a challenge to painters as was the work of their own predecessors. By the mid-1420s, when Masaccio was working on frescoes (Plates 5 and 7) whose novelty and superb assuredness inaugurated a new era in the history of painting, sculptors like Ghiberti and Donatello had prepared the way for rendering human figures, both nude and draped, with a life-like solidity and expressiveness, and, in their reliefs, for conveying a believable sense of distance. Again and again painters turned to sculptors for inspiration and guidance. If it was from Florence that the influence came to stress monumentality at the expense of pattern, energy rather than elegance, overall optical realism rather than fragmentary allusions to reality—in a word, the humanistic rather than the Gothic—it was partly due to works in the round and in relief by the city's sculptors. Painters like Verrocchio and Antonio Pollaiuolo were themselves sculptors, and the sculptural strain in Tuscan painting was to culminate in the towering master of both arts, Michelangelo.

Without the challenge of the three-dimensional quality of sculpture, neither painters nor their patrons might have continued to press towards imposing the full illusion of a third dimension on flat walls and panels. In life, men fight real men, make love to real women, criticize the finer points of real horses and hunting dogs, and trudge along real roads. But they do not necessarily want to find more than hints of, or allusions to, the actual appearance of these things in art.

Dante had observed shadows. In a moving passage in the *Divine Comedy* he is recognized as being alive because he alone, of all the multitude of those he encounters, casts a shadow. Yet nowhere in the work of his great contemporary, Giotto, does a human figure cast a shadow This was not from ignorance, or technical inexperience, but from choice. When Giotto chose to show things as they really were, he did. But while his sense of what degree of realism was appropriate to an episode from the Bible could include such novel 'touches of life' as characters shown casually from the back, it stopped short of attempting complete illusionism. Neither he, nor as yet his public, really wanted that. Indeed, no great artist, nor any sensitive class of patrons, wants an art that is merely a substitute for reality.

Because the business of art is not to copy life but to enhance it, the route to deception is never a straight one. Some Quattrocento painters planned their groups of figures by making little stage sets (or by getting sculptors like Ghiberti to make them for them), or drew from models posing in the workshop, or froze the play of drapery for closer study by arranging dampened linen on clay figures. There was a move from treating light as though it came from an arbitrary source, or a number of sources, and was simply a handy device for giving figures or buildings an appearance of relief, to using one source—in frescoes, often coming from the same direction as real light came through a chapel's windows—and thus increasing the appearance of reality in the scene as a whole. But reliance on convention, on allusion rather than illusion, remained a possible idiom for the artist's transference of things seen (or read about) to paint. Just as in the thirteenth century heads were frequently represented as bigger, because more 'significant', than bodies, and in the fourteenth century human figures tended (for the same reason) to be rendered very large in proportion to buildings, a Quattrocento painter could depict clouds that were only symbols of real clouds over carefully observed people; landscape backgrounds that were descriptions of real places remained rare. The love of making patterns, of thinking along with the brush or pencil, linearly; the instinct to idealize: these perennial aspects of an artist's make-up remained potentially very strong.

Although a consciousness of the techniques and choices involved in recording things seen was a dominant preoccupation, and although the means whereby paint could be made to give an illusion of reality were constantly being refined, we must not interpret the history of Quattrocento painting as a steady march towards realism. Both the temperaments of artists and the expectations of patrons broke up the march into a series of diversions. Uccello used perspective, one of the chief means of reproducing observed reality, with an emphasis, an impassioned playfulness, that makes his world strikingly at odds with the real world. Again, the freedom and the realistic vitality of many preparatory under-paintings for frescoes was stiffened and sobered in the finished work: a reminder that there can be a difference between a painter's natural vision and his commissioned one.

Thanks to the tradition—however dimly remembered—of classical sculpture, and the Christian tradition of illustrating biblical figures and the Saints, in medieval Europe the demand for art as a supplement to nature was constant. The degree of actual correspondence between the two varied according to the impulses of artists and the mood of the public. Giotto's fame, which led to his being called to work in Padua, Rome, Assisi and Naples, as well as Florence, showed that in the early fourteenth century there was a desire to bring art and nature closer together. Then the generally decreased emphasis on verisimilitude during the following generations (although there were exceptions) showed that realism was only one of the functions men found satisfying in works of art. All the same, it was this aspect that Boccaccio, writing a generation after Giotto's death, was to stress. 'The painter exerts himself to make any figure he paints—actually just a little colour applied with skill to a panel—similar in its actions to a figure which is the product of nature and naturally has that action, so that it can deceive the eyes of the beholder, either partly or completely, making itself be taken for what it really is not.'

'Partly or completely': the range of options between an art that alludes to nature and one that strives to reproduce it is kept open. And they remained open even when Masaccio had, as it were, reached back to Giotto's figures and given them an ampler naturalism and placed them against buildings and hills that echoed real streets and landscapes. But the Quattrocento saw a crucial and permanent change of emphasis. However urgently a painter wanted to create a world that was prettier, nobler, more harmonious, or more intellectually organized than the real world, he started from the assumption that his personal vision must arise from the deliberate observation of actual appearances. Instead of taking convention as his starting point and merely reaching out towards nature in order to incorporate a real tree, or rabbit, or human expression, he took his stand in nature and filled in the gaps (what he had not seen, or could not accurately render) from traditional formulations. And this change of stance, although it was fairly generally shared, produced an unprecedentedly vivid variety of achievement.

Painters, encouraged by descriptions in Pliny's rediscovered and immensely prestigious *Natural History* of painted grapes that birds swooped to peck at, or of painted mares at which real stallions neighed, might strive to imitate nature. But their quest is hopeless. The retina itself has a confusion of memories which deny the eye complete objectivity at any given moment. Light changes, expressions flicker:

nature is too complex to allow it to be transposed on to a panel or a wall. In any case, many Quattrocento artists, growingly conscious of their role as creators, rather than as copiers or the passers-on of tradition, used the means of coming to terms with what they saw (perspective, anatomy, slurred outlines) with increasing arbitrariness. An exception was Leonardo, who strove to paint everything true to nature: the evanescence of expression, the growth of leaves, the strata of mountains, the seething of falling water. Nevertheless, the vision of reality he has left us is—Leonardesque.

Italian painters, moreover, lacked the patient curiosity that enabled northern artists, like Masaccio's contemporary, Jan van Eyck, to render every inch of a scene with minute, loving verisimilitude. The Italians were more inclined to say: that is reality, this is what I can do with it. So, although there was a tendency on the part of many of those who supported the arts to prefer paintings that referred directly to phenomena of real life, and although painters experienced a increasing excitement in discovering the rules whereby this might be done, the shift from convention-based to observation-based art, far from producing a century of uniform realism in the sense of grimly recorded slices of life, released scores of individual visions: radiant, truculent, analytical, obsessive, documentary, decorative, rapt.

The Quattrocento rooms of an art gallery do not provide an accurate illustrated social and natural history of the period. This is partly because the largest number of works treat subjects the painter could never have seen: the end of the long safari of the three Kings, the birth of the goddess of love. Leaving aside a portrait here, there the stuff of a bodice or the slow curves of the river Arno, what they provide is not so much a record of what things were like as a celebration of the multitudinous ways in which they could be painted.

The painters' work

None of the paintings illustrated in this book was meant to hang in a gallery or museum. Some—portraits, mythological scenes, a few small religious paintings, historical decorations like Uccello's *The Battle of San Romano* (Plate 32)—were designed for private houses. Here they hung in significant isolation. In the Quattrocento, at least, walls were covered with tapestries, painted with patterns, or left bare. Pictures were not bought for their decorative effect (there were no landscapes, still-lifes or other *genre* subjects), but for their significance. They were commissioned to aid devotion, foster family pride or to refer, however playfully, to intellectual interests. But the great majority were intended for churches, and their removal to a secular setting, with its almost inevitable air of didacticism, or of a *concours d'élégance*, makes it difficult to recapture the potency of their religious function. Moreover, away from their original architectural setting and seen in a uniform light at a uniform level (the effect also given by photographs), we often forget the allowance made by painters for individual lighting conditions and perspective viewpoints.

A collection of photographs does less injustice to the spirit in which the originals were painted than to the mood in which they were looked at by the public. Artists were, as we have seen, competitive. Even the saintly Fra Angelico was alert to changing styles and techniques he could incorporate into his work. Artists and their assistants did not paint an altarpiece on their knees, but once removed from workshop to church, it became part of the lives of those who did kneel before it, who believed that St. Luke himself had been a painter, who walked in procession behind certain specially sacred paintings that were thought to bring rain after a long drought or have the power to turn away an invading army. At the deepest level of religious need the clumsiest or the most vulgar of paintings can suffice to comfort or terrify. The paintings illustrated here were ordered by well educated, even sophisticated, men for the purpose of guiding the prayers and meditations of the ordinarily devout during an era which was, in contrast with the panic produced by the Black Death, reasonably tranquil. And the worshipper's desire to feel at home in the company of Christ, his Mother and the Saints was eagerly seconded by painters who saw a humanized religion as the perfect excuse for rendering human figures and the space through which they moved in ways which, if not purposefully lifelike, were at least based on what life was like.

All too little is known about the hopes and fears of those who knelt to look up at these paintings. It is difficult to sense the priority of the painter's religious or artistic instinct in some thrilling rush of line, some specially poignant effect of colour or foreshortening. But each work comes to us charged both with the sensibility of its painter and the sentiment of its audience, and if the latter is irrelevant to a purely aesthetic judgement of the work, we must remember the painter took account of it.

If peacocks had not been generally accepted as symbols of immortality, lilies of purity, rabbits of unthinking natural fecundity, there would be fewer of them in Quattrocento art. Nativities were set in shattered classical architectural settings not because these were interesting to paint but because they signified the superseding of the old, graven Law of Moses by a gentler era of Grace. The Christ Child reaches towards grapes, or a scarlet-flecked goldfinch, or a lamb, because these are symbols of the blood he must shed for man's salvation. If his mother seems oddly grave when he is a playful infant, unnaturally young when he is a man lying dead across her knees, it is because to the worshipper the Child is potentially the ebbing Saviour nailed on a Cross; the 'dead' Saviour is a reminder of the Child whose birth was the precondition of every Christian's rebirth. If Eve is shown being expelled from the garden of Eden while the angel of the Annunciation appears to Mary, that illustrates a familiar tag: *Quos Evae culpa damnavit, Mariae gratia solvit,* Mary's grace redeems whom Eve's sin had damned. And if in the background there is an enclosed garden, it is both a garden and a symbol of Mary's virginity. Everything can stand for itself and yet mean more, and that 'more' is a link we must understand between those who executed and those who looked at religious paintings. What appears realistic in effect may not have been purely realistic in intent. The spectator's desire to identify himself with religious scenes through psychological and physical realism was catered for without alienating the mystical temperament that sought for deeper meanings, messages from and to the spirit.

It is also difficult to gauge from photographs the effect on the spectator of chapels whose walls were entirely covered in frescoes. The first impulse of the modern visitor, often hurried, is to switch on the light, to see them fully and evenly illuminated. At the time, however, their dimness was only relieved by shafts of sunlight striking now here, now there, according to the time of day, or partially and flickeringly by lamps and candles. Awareness of them was built up from a mosaic of separate impressions; they were learnt, rather than seen as a whole. But once so learnt, the worshipper, now able to sense the whole from the part, was in a comfortingly small but still mysterious version of the universe, where everything proclaimed the power of God but not everything could be seen at the same time. It is, perhaps, a mistake to stress (and to some extent necessary to guess at) the subjective reactions of contemporaries. But it is a worse error to leave them out of account. Patron, painter, public: an understanding of Renaissance art involves them all. And all, with degrees of intensity that varied from personality to personality, from day to day, believed themselves to be in the hands of a God who would ultimately judge them.

Gentile da Fabriano's *Adoration of the Magi* (Plate 6), signed and dated May 1423 (a precision probably called forth more by pride in meeting a contract deadline than by the solemnity of completing a religious masterpiece), is the earliest Quattrocento painting in this book. A sense of Judgement is not altogether lacking. In the central roundel, Christ blesses with one hand, excludes with the other. But overwhelmingly this painting is a jostling, encyclopedic celebration of the joyousness of Christianity. A tense and mysterious birth has been accomplished (left-hand predella panel). The fearful trek to Egypt for refuge (centre predella panel; Plate 82) is in the unguessed-at future. A saviour is born. A star blazes and moves. An eastern caravanserai discharges its exotic cargo of men and beasts at the doorstep of Bethlehem. Monarchs, denying their own proud but erroneous religion, come to adore the child of a humble craftsman's wife and acknowledge a new faith.

It is the only really carefree moment in the Christian story, the most naively self-congratulatory. Gentile, probably the most famous Italian painter of his day, newly come to Florence (his birthplace, Fabriano, is north of Ancona, on the Adriatic, and he had been working previously in Venice), and commissioned by the richest man in the city, Palla Strozzi, to produce a work for one of its most fashionable churches,

Santa Trinità, excelled himself. At the top of the painting, within the arches, a curlicue of narrative; on the left the three kings sight the star from a mountain top; in the middle they and their energetic entourage wheel towards one of the cities they passed through by day; on the right they file into one of the towns they came to at dusk. Then, as though they had riotously slid downhill, there, abruptly, they are, in the right-hand foreground, gesturing, grimacing, trying to remember the importance of the occasion. Birds fly and fight, monkeys gibber, a camel looks down his nose, a lion's head looks like a man in a lion mask.

With sheer fashion-plate elegance the standing king quiets without sobering this mood. From his central axis his colleagues fall, like stills from a stroboscopic film, into attitudes of deepening adoration. They fall into what is almost another picture. Isolated by the rock which shelters the ox and the ass, Joseph and Mary look gravely down at the gestures in which the work's meaning culminates, the reciprocal acts of homage and blessing. And it is a mark of Gentile's genius that this moment is both ritualistic and natural. The child is doing what no newborn baby could do, yet his hand touches the old man's head with something of an infant's automatic exploratoriness, and while one foot goes forward dutifully to be kissed, the other curls up as though afraid of being tickled.

The picture is so full of inventiveness that it comes as a surprise to see that in the central predella panel Gentile has copied the pose of the two midwives who discuss the old king's present behind the Virgin's back. It is so consistently exotic that the presence of the two ladies dressed in the height of early Quattrocento fashion in the right-hand panel comes as something of a shock. But though the surface is held together by the restrained splendour of its colour, this is not a work to be read as a whole but to linger over, detail by detail. Much of the detail (for instance, the David-like page holding the horse and the huge sword, with his sturdy legs-apart stance and eager expression) has so much energy, incorporates so much fresh observation, that it casts doubt on the acceptability of the conventions that contain it. Gentile continues the old double standard for the size of buildings and human beings. The distant landscapes have an unnatural clarity and end against an unvarying gold sky. The figures on the right are less a crowd than a pile of faces. Much has been observed. Nothing has been rethought.

All the same, it is difficult to repress an initial pang of disappointment when turning from Gentile's superabundance and cajolery to a work where almost everything has been rethought, to Masaccio's rigorous *Tribute Money* (Plate 7), which was probably finished only two years after the *Adoration*.

Little is known about Masaccio as a person. He was born in a small town in the valley of the Arno, and such local tradition as Vasari could pick up about him led him to conclude that 'he was very absent-minded and erratic, and devoted all his mind and thoughts to art and paid little attention to himself, and still less to others'.

This rings true. For though something of the broadness of approach in the *Tribute Money* may be due to its being a fresco, forcing Masaccio to work speedily to cover each day's portion of fresh plaster before it dried out, and though he must have studied the new three-dimensionality of sculptors like Nanni di Banco and Donatello, and though, again, like his scholarly humanist contemporaries, he felt the urge to 'go back to the sources' (in his case, to Giotto), his work has a revolutionary completeness that only intense single-mindedness can bring about.

Like the *Adoration*, the painting was commissioned by a layman, Felice Brancacci, for his family's chapel in the church of Santa Maria del Carmine (Plate 3). Like the *Adoration*—and after this point any resemblance ceases—it is a multiple narrative. Christ and the Apostles have arrived at Capernaum. It is a Roman city and they are asked to pay an entrance toll or tribute. As Jews, in their own homeland, they argue —in the central episode—about the rights and wrongs of this imperialist imposition with the gate-keeper, whose back and arms eloquently declare his surprise at their obstinacy. Christ, intent on his mission, cuts the argument short. He tells the indignant Peter to cast a line in the lake of Galilee—as he does in the episode on the left, flushing with the exertion—'and when thou hast opened his mouth, thou shalt find a piece of money: that take, and give unto them for me and thee' (Matthew 17:26). In the third episode Peter angrily dumps the coin in the gate-keeper's hand.

The resemblance to the *Adoration* ceases because we are brought to the outskirts of a credible town, where buildings soar up beyond the picture's frame. We watch a group whose expressions all follow the same argument and whose bodies are spaced believably over a firmly imagined tract of ground; in spite of the damaged condition of the fresco, we look past buildings and figures into a landscape of trees, hills and cloudy sky which do not just hint at reality but show it. The painting is not without oddities. The relationship between Christ's and the gate-keeper's left feet, for instance, precisely defines the plane on which the ground rises away from us, yet when the gate-keeper reappears on the right, facing us, his right leg, seen from the back, has become his left leg seen from the front. Nevertheless, the painting's power depends on the substitution of rules and logic for fancy and convention. All lines not parallel to the picture's edges recede to a common vanishing-point. The landscape does not take a series of leaps backwards from one equally clearly defined zone to another but recedes evenly, changing in tone and clarity. Figures are defined not just by outline but by the play of light and shade which builds up a sense of their volume. The application of these rules, plus a personal taste for simple, naturally falling drapery (unlike the Gothic bravura of Gentile's Virgin) and rugged but unquirkish faces, gives Masaccio's *Tribute Money* a 'reality' heightened by the intellect above the reality perceived by the normally restless eye.

What is more, by giving his figures an ample dignity, and by planting them so firmly in the world they inhabit, Masaccio illustrates a favourite theme among contemporary humanists: the moral responsibility accruing to a man conscious of his own worth and social standing. This overtone is perhaps all the stronger here because the subject had a practical application. Florence was at war. A new tax had been introduced to raise defensive armies. Not only Christ's, but every Florentine's opportunity to live according to the values he cherished depended on paying cash to the state in order to preserve his private freedom of thought and action.

The same fusion of the appreciation of human dignity with intellectual rigour is present, and with even greater force, in another fresco by Masaccio, the *Holy Trinity*, in the church of Santa Maria Novella in Florence (Plate 5). For the lay Christian, the good life is a thoughtful and active preparation for a good death. Calmly and resolutely, the donor and his wife kneel before an enactment of the central doctrine of the Christian Church. God, unalterable Being, is also omnipresent Spirit and, for a chosen time, suffered and died as a man. This—the figure of St. John suggests—is the most sublime of all subjects for meditation. But it is also the central guide for everyday life, and the Virgin, who has suffered and understood, invites us to sustain our lives with the promise of the sacraments. Both for what it was, and for what it promised, the Trinity is a doctrine of perfection. And Masaccio has placed it in a 'perfect' setting, a mathematically faultless version of his friend Brunelleschi's newly discovered formulation of the rules governing classical architecture; both men believed this to be as much 'better' than Gothic as the age of Christian grace was 'better' than the previous age of Mosaic law.

It would be too simple to say that, for most of the rest of the Quattrocento, painting swung between the extremes represented by two such masters as Gentile and Masaccio, between delight, decoration and line on the one hand, and rigour, analysis and volume on the other. It can serve as a rough guide, but allowance must be made for the influence of the great Florentine sculptors, especially Donatello and Ghiberti, and for the, admittedly weaker, traditions of non-Florentine painting centres. It was, as we have suggested, a period of strong individual styles and a great variety of experiment and adaptation, not a time when an admired work was treated as a new orthodoxy, a convention to be passed on.

Of the Quattrocento painters illustrated in this book, Vasari lists the following among those 'who have become wonderfully proficient and famous by studying in that [Brancacci] chapel': Fra Filippo Lippi, Fra Angelico, Filippino Lippi, Baldovinetti, Castagno, Verrocchio, Ghirlandaio and Botticelli. There is no reason to doubt this statement, surprising as it may seem when confronting the at times almost winsomely elegant charm of Filippo, the occasional surrender of Fra Angelico to the sheer loveliness of all things, the workmanlike pleasure taken by Ghirlandaio in recording the here and now, the deceptively simple linear style of some of Botticelli's most intensely felt paintings. Masaccio's work acted more as a conscience than as a practical guide, until, with Leonardo, Raphael and Michelangelo, a generation arrived who wanted to take stock of the present state of art by turning to a prodigy (Masaccio was only twenty-six when he died) who had seen too much and re-considered it too clearly to be altogether congenial to his immediate successors.

The working of that conscience can be seen in Fra Angelico's *The Deposition from the Cross* (Plate 20). Born within a year of Masaccio, Fra Angelico started this painting only two or three years after the completion of the *Trinity*. Though markedly individual in effect, it contains homage to the contrasting approaches of both Masaccio and Gentile. It was commissioned by the latter's patron, Palla Strozzi, to complement the *Adoration*, and Fra Angelico only got the commission after the death of Strozzi's first choice, Lorenzo Monaco, a painter working within the idiom employed by Gentile. Lorenzo had already designed the 'Gothic' frame and completed the paintings in the pinnacles and end columns. Fra Angelico pitched his tonality to sustain the sweet-sharp brilliance of Lorenzo's blues, pinks and orangey reds, and shared Gentile's belief that each degree of distance should be rendered with the sharp detail observable by someone who was actually there.

But here the homage stops. Its pendulum swings across an area peculiar to Fra Angelico: a sense of everything being newly minted, a humanization of symbols that make the passive grave-cloths a concern of the women on the left, the active instruments of pain (crown of thorns, nails) a rueful centre of attention among the men on the right. Then it moves towards the influence of Masaccio. The view of Jerusalem in the left-hand arch is based on a real flair for the analysis of geometrical solids, a flair enhanced by the device of storm clouds casting shadows that draw attention to their three-dimensionality. There is a suggestion of mathematics, too, in the symmetrical grid formed by the two ladders on either side of the Cross in the centre; and as the topmost man stoops to let Christ down, his halo stoops with him. The landscape, once we have crossed the stage area of flowery grass, moves uninterruptedly back to the horizon, and there, as in nature, the sky darkens. Among the figures, there is a shared, intent concentration on the central tragedy or—for this painting is an aid to meditation, not an attempt to record an event as it actually might have been—the symbols associated with it. And, finally, the faces (Plates 23 and 24) are moulded into relief by the light that falls across them from a common source on the left. Everything is gentler, prettier, more insinuating than in Masaccio, but the hints of analytical rigour and consistency are Masaccio's.

Moving to the middle of the century, we find the balance of influences has gone. Within the general framework of ideas provided by Masaccio, painters produced work of outstanding quality not by rethinking the relationship between art and nature as a whole, but by pushing one or two components of picture-making to extremes.

Domenico Veneziano's *St. Lucy Altarpiece* (Plate 10) of about 1445, bland as it may seem today, was a pioneering work because he saw it primarily as a pattern of colours. There is much else here: the surprise of seeing Renaissance niches through

Gothic arches, the emphasis on decorative strips and bands, the contrast between the indicated shadows and the use of a suffused light to mould the figures, the not-quite-achieved but moving sense of concentration that the figures share. But all these are subordinate to, and controlled by, a shy revelling in the discovery of a new role for colour, and the pretence of depth is only a pretence, because the colour pattern is felt more as a treatment of the panel surface, than as a means of describing what lies behind it.

It was probably in the same year that Uccello was commissioned to paint three episodes from a Florentine victory over the Sienese, the so-called *Battle of San Romano* of 1432, for a bedroom in the Medici palace. Plate 32 shows the painting in London; its companion panels are in Paris and Florence. The artist rendered the landscape backgrounds, planned to run across the top of a wall above cupboards, in flat slabs of colour, with a hint of vegetation and a few small figures. But if the landscape is casual, in the foreground Uccello rides his (it is difficult to avoid the phrase) hobby-horses into action with a bizarrely effective passion.

This is not the sober reporting of a battle. It is a heraldic celebratory replay in the form of a tournament, one of those mêlées which delighted the spectator with their combination of pageantry, risk, and the opportunity to gaze at newsworthy men. Reportage is out of place in a near-princely bedroom, and Uccello was tactful enough to offer instead the fantastic helmets not of real war but of parade and mock-combat; a close-up (on the right) of what could be seen to happen in the mêlée but was never reported of an actual battle; the open features of the hero of the occasion and of his bare-headed page—who is having no difficulty whatever in controlling his horse—represent a moment from a triumphal procession to the tournament ground. True to chivalric tradition, life on horseback is elegant in form and noble in action, while death (and death did haunt the tournament) is best thought of as a litter of stage-properties.

The convention works as a masterpiece because Uccello's tact was seconded by his zeal to analyse space and form. The shattered weaponry on the ground represents the unrubbed-out parts of the orthogonals and transversals that were used as the guidelines for contemporary perspective construction. The lances (and the commander's baton) slice the surface into sections and they stick out from carapaces more curved and pouting than were the actual armours of the day. The way the horses are rendered gives them a wooden, toy-like appearance because Uccello was less concerned with lifelikeness than with obtaining a satisfying relationship between the curves and edges of a surface, and the volume they enclose. The frozen quality this gives the picture is enhanced by the adamant way in which he insists on decorative effects to strengthen individual forms. The two white horses prance against dark backgrounds; as though their shoes were not enough to end their hooves off crisply, he gives the left-hand horse a scrap of dark carpet from which to rear.

While Uccello was using the device of perspective so obsessively that it became almost a subject in its own right (see also Plate 26), and was pressing an inherently rational way of creating volumes into the service of fantasy, another Florentine painter, Andrea del Castagno, was turning a signpost into a destination, and forcing elements of the fantastic into the service of expressive realism.

The signpost pointed to sculpture. Many painters had looked in that direction, partly because, as an aid to achieving the semblance of solidity, a statue could be more suggestive than the live model, and partly because sculptors in low relief were 'drawing' in stone and bronze with a new springiness and verve from which painters had much to learn. In his *Last Supper* (Plate 101) Castagno has gone so far as to give the illusion of a vast niche of variegated marble in which thirteen polychrome statues have been inserted. Their clothes hang in harsh folds. The discs of their haloes are so highly polished that they reflect the crowns of their heads, emphasizing their weighty separateness. Some exchange glances, others are sunk in reverie. Only the large hands maintain a flow of eloquence up and down the table: it is as though we were watching an assembly of deaf mutes. The joyous mystery of the sacraments has not yet been announced. Judas has taken the sop, the theme of treachery broods heavily. Next it will be Peter. Who else—among the nuns for whom the work was made—will betray their God? The fantastic elements, the violently veined marble panels, the harpy bench-ends, the archaic pose of the last disciple but one on the right, Judas's weirdly pointed ears, all help to create a sense of disturbance that yet has the stony ring of truth.

A streak of eccentricity, an emphasis on one over-riding element within a painter's interests, can still be seen if we move from Florentine works of the mid-1440s to those of the mid-1470s.

At first sight, Antonio Pollaiuolo's *Martyrdom of St. Sebastian* (Plate 50) demonstrates an unusual range of strongly felt interests. Once the eye is clear of the stagey hilltop in the foreground, it drops down and is led back into the most convincing panorama of the period. It is guided, with deliberate assiduity, by the dwindling size of the groups of horsemen on the right (so much nearer to the horses of Velazquez than to those of Uccello) and the architectural perspective of the building on the left (the first Renaissance, as opposed to Roman, ruin), and nudged, too, by the weir-like barriers across the Arno and the diminishing scale of the cypresses (Plate 83). Only a foreground composition of unusual strength could hold our interest against the competition of this landscape. Pollaiuolo achieves this with an astonishingly symmetrical pyramid of gymnasts, starting in the very bottom corners of the painting, and ending at the very top and, in spite of the tree, to all intents and purposes hollow in the middle, as though the key performer had walked away, a hollowness increased by the stooping position of the two nearest figures which fully reveals the two above them. The pyramid is also symmetrical in its parts. The man fixing the cocking thong to his cross-bow on the left has been turned round through some 130 degrees to become the man on the right, and he has lost most of his clothes en route to increase the sense of antithesis. The standing archer on the left has been rotated through a full half-circle to become, literally, his own opposite number. The poses of the bowmen at the back are more varied (they are using different weapons) but they, too, have the air of being two versions of the same figure.

The lack of interest in his figures as individuals (it is probable that Antonio asked his brother Piero, a weaker painter, to supply St. Sebastian's painedly pious face) is more than compensated for by their confident but unfailingly sensitive outlines (Plate 97). As a sculptor, Antonio was familiar with that medium's ability to reveal volume by rotation (as the spectator walks round it) while always maintaining a hard edge. Here he combines both qualities, and to follow his line as it now defines an edge, now suggests a curve or hollow that continues 'round the corner', is one of the most exhilarating experiences that Quattrocento painting can offer. But this mastery springs from his over-riding interest: anatomy; not the anatomy of actual dissection, perhaps, but a studied sympathy for the actual contents of the human body, especially when muscle and sinew are brought up to the surface or clenched back towards the bone in positions of strain. Hence the pyramid of seven detached figures, hence the comparative weakness of St. Sebastian himself, who is restricted by his bonds to mere isometrics, hence the groups of horses, only second to man as a challenge to the Quattrocento anatomist, and treated here, as are the bowmen, in a way that demonstrates the painter's knowledge. The group on the left, one pacing, one rearing, turned through 180 degrees becomes the group on the right. Indeed, if we want a detail to serve as Pollaiuolo's 'signature', it lies within the inverted triangle (or pyramid section) formed by arrow, string and bow on the left: a running, semi-nude man, overlapped by a prancing horse.

The work of Sandro Botticelli is another example of the beauty that can arise from specialization. For him this was drawing. Whereas Pollaiuolo's draughtsmanship was an immensely gifted adjunct to his passion for anatomy, Botticelli's has the absolute assurance of a natural gift. Where Pollaiuolo's line broke off or gouged out in order to demonstrate weight and volume, Botticelli's outlined an unbroken silhouette (Plate 75) and relied on colour and shading to produce an appearance of volume; weightiness did not preoccupy him.

He could do, and do well, the other things that were expected of painters: get his perspective right, achieve a likeness, tell a story, prettify a scene with the fruits, flowers and foliage that contemporary taste, nourished by decorative tapestries imported from northern Europe, found so pleasing. But essentially he was an artist whose flair for drawing and eagerly sensitive temperament gave him an unusual ability to enter the imaginative world of his patrons, to realize their programmes, however esoteric, as though they were his own dreams.

His *Primavera* (Plate 72) was painted for the fourteen- or fifteen-year-old Lorenzo di Pierfrancesco de' Medici, a second cousin of Lorenzo the Magnificent. The youth was apparently intellectually precocious and was festooned with tutors, who, in turn, were kept on their toes by correspondence with the doyen of Italian Neoplatonic philosophers, Marsilio Ficino. He was brought up, that is, in a circle which believed that classical mythology, if interpreted correctly, represented an inspired poetic fiction dealing with the nature of the world and man's place in it, and with his aspirations to rise above its limitations. Although it was fiction, it was irradiated with the truth that had partially informed the prophets and sibyls, before God's whole purpose had been made clear to all by Christ. Botticelli was asked to share both the poetry and the pedagogy of this credo and provide a visual gloss for the benefit of the young Medici. It is a bookish subject, and Botticelli starts with a mild joke, inviting us to 'read' his painting from the right.

There the wind-god Zephyr comes in through the trees. At his touch, the nymph Chloris is transformed; flowers come from her lips, a moment later she has become Flora, goddess of Spring, glowingly conscious that of all goddesses she is the one most ardently, most universally desired. When nature wakes, love can appear. But the Venus of this picture is not the wan, toppling sea-maid of the *Birth of Venus* (Plate 38). While approving, and gently welcoming us to a world now suitably decked for her appearance, her gaze has a monitory, 'think on these things' quality. She stands alone, a tutoress weighing our response. Behind her the orange trees have been prised apart to make an arch filigreed with branches of juniper, itself a monitory form of vegetable life. All the same, as Lorenzo the Magnificent had written: 'The juniper's sharp leaves will not offend / The hands that take their branches as a friend.' But how to take the deity they enhalo? Not just with fleshly love. She discards that over-simplification with the hand that holds her cloak across her sex. Instead, she quietly urges us to assess the Graces, three versions of three emanations from her, joined in harmonious but enigmatic dance. The enigma is a real one, so various were the explanations of what the Graces stood for among contemporary mythologizers. Let us assume that Botticelli selected (surely discussion with scholars was an essential preliminary to this work) the triad of meanings that was easiest to paint: love that cherishes, love that represents beauty, love that lusts. The first is the Grace who gravely dances with her back to us; the second, artless and open, marks time on the left; the third, the most masculine in feature, completes with her forefinger the gesture known to Shakespeare as the fig of Spain and to Botticelli's contemporaries as a symbol of sexual intercourse. All are linked. It is not a question of choosing one exclusively but of selecting an emphasis. And until we (or, rather, Lorenzo di Pierfrancesco) choose, Cupid is blindfold, hovering in anticipation. On the left, Mercury supplements Venus's tutorial role by pointing to the heavens, where all is known and all will be judged.

To control this blend of narrative and didacticism into a whole that has become almost the symbol of the beauty attained by Quattrocento painting was a task so complex that its success must remain mysterious. But that the chief element in achieving this control was draughtsmanship becomes clearer when we look at Botticelli's later paintings, more personal and (due to the agitating influence of the great preacher-evangelist, Savonarola) more frenetic (Plates 55, 57). Here, from his wide repertory of accomplishments, line, now dogged and harshly rhetorical, is his chosen weapon, and it is brandished in the face of a generation that took up again the problem of how *all* a painter's talents could be enlisted in the cause of restating the relationship between what man felt about nature and what he wanted from art.

This involved a reappraisal of the extent to which man, by destiny and in terms of day-to-day experience, was in harmony with the world around him. To a Christian, even if not in a very energetically Christian age, this presented difficulties. But a solution was being worked out by scholars and philosophers whose sense of balance between the human, the natural, and the divine was nourished by their increasing knowledge of earlier civilizations, Greek and Roman, which appeared to have accepted life fully without ceasing to respond to the promptings of a higher order of being. Humanism, the study of these civilizations, fostered a sense of wholeness, of harmony, of human dignity that was capable of being transmitted to art. But that transmission did not happen at once. Masaccio had responded to the noble lucidity of classical Roman architecture, Botticelli, for a while at least, to the teasingly esoteric significance of gods and goddesses. But painters had to catch other aspects, among them respect for learning itself, and for the quality of life that had flourished among what were now the cracked statues, decayed arches and tarnished coins that conveyed only irregular pulses from the classical past. And the transmission was haphazard. It depended on the sympathies and working needs of individual painters, their degree of education, their closeness to humanist patrons. Although the humanistic world view was reasonably well formed in the early Quattrocento, it is not surprising that it was not meaningfully reflected in art until the Cinquecento.

Respect for scholarship and antiquarian fervour was best exemplified by painters working outside the Florentine ambience, respectively by Antonello da Messina and Mantegna.

In Antonello's *St. Jerome in his Study* (Plate 62), painted about 1450–5, the spectator looks through a spacious stone doorway into a great vaulted hall. Its top half looks ecclesiastical, but the effect of the bottom half is domestic: gay rectangular windows (one with seats) and a delicate colonnade. Into this hall a most ingenious piece of carpentering has been inserted, a study for the scholar who has everything. Raised to give a little dignity and freedom from draughts, it is condensed and practical: enough shelves, desk at the right height and slope, plenty of room to push the books back before writing. Potted plants, a sleepy cat, a few ornaments: a wonderful sense of self-containment. The scholar has kicked off his shoes, climbed those few steps and is in a little world, a world within two worlds: inside, a world of architecture, sacred and secular, and outside a world of nature, hills, a town, a river. For this study is not the isolated cell of a recluse. The late afternoon sun—to judge from the shadow of the finial—strikes almost full on the warm stone of the door and across the floor, and the glow over the countryside beyond reaches back along the roof of the colonnade and through the unglassed upper windows where the birds glide in to land.

Antonello has rendered the scene with great particularity. Though a southern Italian, he had clearly learnt from the Netherlandish painters who were known in Sicily and Naples in the middle of the fifteenth century. There is an Italian rigour about the perspective; the tiles, the door mouldings, the shelf edges all cant to a common vanishing-point. But the minute attention paid to each tile, the neat asymmetry of the patterns they form, the way in which they enhance the sense of depth by becoming paler and vaguer towards the back of the hall, the constant care to give the eye more information about each object than it really needs, these derive from, and are worthy of, Jan van Eyck. We would expect so realistic a doorway to have inner doors to keep the wind and rain out. Yet the briefest counting of the tiles shows that the study is too close to allow them to shut. So we are not just looking at an accurately cut slice of reality, but also at a point that is being made. The vanishing-point itself provides the clue, for the structural centre of the painting is not the scholar's face, nor his books, but lies half-way between them. The act of reading, that is the central point, and the reader, burly and intelligent, suggests the dignity and the strong humanity of the occupation.

The cardinal's hat on the shady bench, the lion in front of the arcade, reticently identify him as St. Jerome, though almost certainly this is a portrait. Previous Italian paintings of St. Jerome had concentrated on his breast-beating penitence after a vision in which he had seen himself at the Judgement Seat, accused by God of putting Cicero before Christ. Antonello shows the man who, after five years in the wilderness, had returned to civilization, mastered Greek and translated the Bible into Latin, the Vulgate of the Catholic Church. Quattrocento humanists were convinced that their work was morally supportive and actively useful to Christianity, and Jerome putting his classical learning at the service of religion perfectly represents this belief. That it was expressed with such sympathetic assurance by Antonello—and echoed later by Carpaccio (Plate 61), who introduced classical statuettes into the study of another Father of the Church, St. Augustine—shows a respect for scholarly activity that made it easier for painters to enter the flow of humanistic values and ideas.

For some humanists, and for many of those who patronized humanists and painters alike, an interest in the civilization of ancient Rome was helped by the visible remains of it, here an arch still standing, there an inscribed marble waiting to blunt a plough and be heaved with curses into the present. Of all Quattrocento painters it was the farmer's son, Andrea Mategna, who expressed both the archaeological and the antiquarian aspects of humanism most trenchantly. He was apprenticed to the Paduan painter Squarcione, and what he was taught there can be deduced from a document in which Squarcione undertook to teach another boy 'the system of the floor [i.e. paving in perspective] . . . and to put figures on the said floor here and there at various points, and to put objects on it . . . and he is to be taught a head of a man in foreshortening . . . and the method for a nude figure, measured before and behind'.

One of Mantegna's earliest works, the *St. James Led to Execution* (Plate 27), shows an energetic mastery of the theory of perspective. It also shows that at the age of about twenty-five he knew enough about the principles of classical Roman architecture to paint a triumphal arch he had never seen. While his interest in classical remains was stimulated by an informal academy he belonged to (which made field trips in search of antiquities), the *St. James* shows the degree to which his approach as a painter had been influenced by the statues and reliefs Donatello was making at the chief Paduan church, Sant' Antonio. This stony style—dropped by the time he came to paint the unprecedentedly relaxed family scenes in the Camera degli Sposi in the Palazzo Ducale in Mantua (Plates 47 and 51) and its humorously illusionistic ceiling (Plate 48)—appears again, and with renewed assurance, in the *Martyrdom of St. Sebastian* (Plate 49), which was painted at about the same time. The broken arch, the fig tree burgeoning among the cracks: these are conventional references to the collapse of an old pre-Christian era and the growth of a spiritually more fruitful one. All the same, trussed and skewered as he is, Sebastian's rapt expression (for he survived this preliminary ordeal) seems less concerned with the faith for which he is suffering than with the passing of an age that had produced works as beautiful as the capital above him. In this painting Mantegna has progressed beyond the urge to reconstruct an ancient monument as it might have been, to a more sophisticated delight in classical remains. Another triumphal arch, this time in the form of a gateway, appears in the background, but in the foreground, and emphasized by the juxtaposition of real foot and marble foot (Plate 112), is a pile of antique fragments for which there was a growing demand among collectors; such a heap, indeed, as Mantegna might have seen in the yard of Squarcione, who was, among other things, a dealer in antiquities. They are painted with the stonemason's eye of a man for whom nature itself could appear in the guise of a gigantic quarry (Plate 46), but they are also resonant with a sense of history: Mantegna has caught the classical scholar's awareness of the continuity between his day and that earlier civilization, of clouds sailing over century after century of falling keystones, collapsing architraves and splitting statues. The painting combines two moods of pathos, Christian and humanistic, and two sorts of time, the gap between suffering and eternity, and the slow, measurable wasting of the things of this world, between God's time and man's.

What it does not do is provide an environment in which saints and centaurs, marbles and fallen fruit, man and nature, exist together in a shared and binding light and in an overall sensitivity that suspends all incompatibilities in the harmonizing atmosphere of an idyll. This magic (for though analysable it defies analysis) was almost achieved by Mantegna's brother-in-law Giovanni Bellini in his *Religious Allegory* (Plate 79), painted about 1485. A comparison between his *Agony in the Garden* (Plate 45) of about 1465 and Mantegna's slightly earlier treatment of the same subject (Plate 46) shows certain features in common. The general idea of Christ at prayer on a rocky platform above three sleeping disciples was probably derived by both of them from a drawing by Giovanni's father Jacopo, but the two men also striate their giant prie-dieu in a comparable way, and Giovanni has echoed Mantegna's treatment of the Apostles' robes and the strong foreshortening in which one of them is shown. Where the painters abruptly part company is in the backgrounds. Mantegna's precipitous landscape winds upward through its pale cincture of fantastic architecture at the impulse of a powerful imagination. Giovanni's, unsensational even to the point of dullness (Plate 84), derives from the close observation of familiar views, and with it painting takes another step into the real countryside. Mantegna's landscapes continued to rely on his imagination and its formidable powers of assembly, while Giovanni Bellini pursued his instinct to remember how particular tracts of country looked at specific times of day. The setting of the *Religious Allegory* is real only in the sense of being possible. But through light and tone Bellini persuades us that the wall between reality and poetry is so thin that we can pass through with only a mild surprise at the odd company we find ourselves keeping on the other side.

The artist has spread out the participants in a *sacra conversazione* on a geometrically paved classical terrace giving on to an inhabited landscape of water, rocky hills and woods. The Virgin adores the child seated on a cushion looking at the oranges the *putti* have shaken down for him. St. Joseph meditates with closed eyes. St. Sebastian, charmingly awkward in his extreme youth, is contrasted with a grizzled elder. St. Paul shakes his sword at the retreating infidel. St. Anthony Abbot, first of monks, is about to encounter one of the denizens of his wilderness life, a wise monster from the still-pagan world he was born in. Across the water life goes on, men drowse, converse, walk, threaten a flagging donkey. The identity of other characters and the key to Bellini's programme have been lost, and, along with them, a full knowledge of the work's intellectual significance. It hardly seems to matter. Forming his own gentler vision without being influenced by the chiselled pertinacity that was part of

Mantegna's, and by absorbing Antonello's (who came to Venice in 1475) coolly authoritative treatment of light and colour gradation, Bellini pioneered a way in which the most diverse elements could be absorbed into a harmony which, if dreamlike, is sufficiently close to nature to be readily shared with the spectator.

It is not surprisng that the *Religious Allegory* used to be attributed to Giorgione (see Plate 86), nor that Titian could rework parts of Bellini's *Feast of the Gods* (Plate 103) so naturally. Bellini was already at work before 1460. His last work illustrated here (Plate 92) dates from 1515, the year before his death. The length of his career, his ability to use the ideas of others while steadily expressing deeper feelings of his own, his continuing compositional inventiveness, his range of subjects, religious, classical, portraits: all these do much to explain how painting in Venice passed unfalteringly from the Quattrocento to the Cinquecento, while painters in Florence, or under Florentine influence, felt the need to take stock of their talents by seeking a new synthesis.

Let us, too, take stock, turning from painting in Quattrocento Florence itself to the work of a painter who first came to Florence to work there as a young man and revisited it from time to time, but who for most of his career stayed in his provincial south Tuscan home to work out the consequences of what he had seen in a metropolis which he may have found too raucous and aggressive.

Piero della Francesca's mid-century *Flagellation of Christ* (Plate 29) represents Florentine emotion recollected in Tuscan tranquillity. The passion for perspective shown in the architecture and pavement; the delight in creating a sense of volume by seeing bodies in terms of columns and spheres weighted by heavy, simply-falling materials; the energetic purity of the linear envelope within which each mass is built up; the diffused, and thus predominantly bright blonde light that defines the mass; the indebtedness to sculpture (the staircase behind Herod is rendered as if it actually was a sculptural relief): all reflect the Florence of Masaccio and Brunelleschi, of Domenico Veneziano and Donatello. But Piero subordinates the varied experimentation of the city to a lucid stillness of his own; at the back a blow that will never fall, in the front a mouth that opens but will not utter. The stillness is, of course, relevant to the subject, a meditation on the significance of the scourging of Christ. As an allegory of injustice or sacrilege, as an allusion to assaults on the Church, which, in a mystical sense, is Christ's body, the flagellation was a theme rich in motives for contemplation. The three figures, so impressively near the spectator, and spanning the three ages between childhood and senility during which man is a responsible, thinking being, have been variously and inconclusively identified. As with Bellini's *Religious Allegory*, the key to an understanding of the imagery has been lost. And as with the *Religious Allegory*, uncertainty of meaning hardly maims the power of a painting so totally uniform in mood. But whereas Bellini's figures could change their positions without breaking the mood, Piero's have been manœuvred according to a formula based on colour, light and, above all, proportion (he wrote three treatises on mathematics) which locks them into place. Even when he has to show a scene of desperate violence (Plate 31) he not only eschews an impression of instantaneousness but avoids giving any gesture a sense of 'before' and 'after', and instead of fleeting expression he chooses the timelessness of grimace. Piero's last great painting, the *Virgin and Child with Angels and Saints, Adored by Federigo da Montefeltro* (Plate 65), with its serious adolescent angels, its firmly planted barefoot saints, raptly unconscious of one another's presence, the Madonna's face as clearly modelled as the ostrich egg above it (symbol at once of eternity and of purity), and its mathematically precise light-filled architectural setting, is a perfect summary of the artist's ability to synthesize his means into an effect of radiant trance.

The work can also be seen as a magical dead-end. Piero had little influence. His reputation itself lay dormant until, with Post-Impressionism and Cubism, the cool logic of his structures and his committed impassiveness in face of the temptations of mere surface prettiness was 'discovered', and made him possibly the most respected of all Quattrocento painters. But his contemporaries in Florence did not want his sort of completeness. They—or the most earnest and talented of them—wanted grace, flexibility, movement, faces less brusquely earthy, harmonies more philosophical and less like equations, in fact a new basis from which to re-create or reconsider nature, not to cast a spell on it.

Part two The Cinquecento

The painters' world

THE WORLD in which patrons coaxed and bargained, painters sketched bored apprentices in order to turn them into angels, and men posed for portraits that would quietly show their private thoughts, has to be seen through the smoke and blood of war. From 1494 the Italian peninsula was marched across and shot over by French, German and Spanish armies and those Italian forces who happened to be their allies of the moment. Territories were lost, regained and lost again; governments and constitutions had change forced upon them until a culmination of violence came in 1527 with the ruthless sack of Rome itself. Even then war threatened, and at times broke out, until the general peace settlement of 1559. Politically, diplomatically and militarily it was a time of such confusion that the local scenes of action have never been plotted into a coherent historical panorama. Nevertheless, painting, though stirred and dinted by war, displays a complex but comprehensible pattern of its own.

Except for peasants on a line of march, or citizens during the aftermath of a successful assault, war at that time was not total. Battles were fought, constitutions changed, but painters were neither soldiers nor politicians, though they could be forced to move from place to place.

Michelangelo grew up in a Florence which was a republic. In old age he refused to work for its absolutist duke, Cosimo I. But he was rare among artists in professing a political faith. Concerned primarily with one another and their common aim of finding new ways of translating nature into art, they were like gamblers intent on discovering a 'system' even when in the basement of a collapsing building.

It is not that art was unresponsive to the preoccupations of society, but it reflected values, not events, Nor were prominent artists asked to illustrate the wars they lived through. The historian, indeed, is all too grateful for the few homespun attempts at pictorial journalism that try to show what a contemporary battle or siege was like. Leonardo and Michelangelo were asked to paint battle scenes, but these were battles fought in the past, excuses not for documentation but for artistically ideal performances by horsemen and nudes.

Crisis by crisis, patrons continued to commission artists and to demand familiar fare: portraits, religious scenes and, still in a minority, mythological subjects. However, between 1495 and 1515 a change took place great enough to justify the later invention of new labels—'Classic Art', 'High Renaissance'—and to explain the long centuries of neglect to which 'Pre-Raphaelite' painters were to be condemned.

In the 1520s yet another change in style occurred. Divergencies from the lofty harmoniousness, the relaxed but dignified celebration of man associated with the 'High Renaissance' style became so marked as to call into being a more contentious modern label: Mannerism, a word calling attention to a tendency to let emotion dominate in composition and colour, to treat space and human proportion with a certain irrationality, and to make the determination to achieve a 'style' a deliberate part of a painting's impact. The temptation to connect these changes with political circumstances is strong. But great art is never fully part of the world it comments on, never an immediate witness in the sense that a seismograph can be. And least of all can painting respond directly to day-to-day events when there exist aesthetic challenges that seem more relevant to the painter's specialized activity, and, moreover, appeal to (or, at least, do not put off) the men who pay him.

Between Ghirlandaio's loving portrait (Plate 53) of about 1480 and the *Mona Lisa* (Plate 125) of 1503, between Signorelli's *Kingdom of Pan* (Plate 74) of about 1490 and Titian's *Fête Champêtre* (Plate 87) of about 1510 a profound and irreversible change has taken place: a style softer but grander, more psychologically complex, nobler yet more at ease. The term Cinquecento is dyed with the impression of that style at its maturity and of the subsequent variations to which it continued to provide a major theme, but it also reaches back to include the style's origin in Leonardo's work of the 1480s (Plates 63 and 80). For Vasari it was in the last decades of the Quattrocento that what he calls 'the dry, hard, harsh style' of Piero della Francesca, Baldovinetti, Castagno, Mantegna and Ghirlandaio gave way to the gentler, more unifying colour sense of Perugino (Plate 81) and to the knowledge and 'inspired grace' of Leonardo, which enabled him to paint 'figures that moved and breathed'. Vasari adds that the change was so great that it made 'the people run like mad to gaze on this new, realistic beauty'.

This was the challenge, anticipating the wars by a decade, that determined the direction painting was to take. The thrust towards change, and the excitement that attended it, acquired all the more momentum for the extraordinary talent of its principal agents, Leonardo, Michelangelo and Raphael. Radically different in temperament, they shared an instinct to restudy nature and to look back to Masaccio (all of them pondered in the Brancacci Chapel) as the last reliable base for such a study. The freedom with which they then worked out their ideas was helped by their absorbing the notion, already in the air of Florence, that the artist was different in kind from other men, able, like a priest, but without the need for the ceremony of ordination, to work miracles. The concept of creative genius fostered originality, and it was shared by enlightened patrons, whose encouragement at times even took the form of accepting 'anything', rather than insisting on a commission scrupulously fulfilled. Moreover, under the influence of humanism, and, to a lesser extent, of chivalry, wealthy patrons had come to have an image of themselves and their style of life which was close to the aims of the new style in art. It was an image which played down purely vocational roles, and emphasized a spacious hospitality to ideas, an imperturbable confidence in the face of adversity and a calculated ease of manner, a carrying lightly of varied social accomplishments. And this helped them find congenial the effects sought by painters: a broad spatial coherence, an absence of fussiness, a concealment of the means whereby the overall impression had been gained, portraits that represented expression in terms of the state of mind that produced it, an idealization of man and his setting, whether landscape or architecture, that rang true because it was refined from a close study of the actual.

Patronage itself rose to the level of genius in the person of the most militant and earthily spoken of popes, Julius II (1443–1513, pope from 1503). Infected by the artists' own conviction that anything produced in this new phase was bound to be better than what had gone before, he ordered the destruction of Europe's most hallowed edifice, St. Peter's, and asked Bramante to design a worthier successor. He commissioned the twenty-five-year-old Raphael, after the briefest of trials, to paint over the work of earlier masters in the Vatican. He let Michelangelo, unproven as a fresco painter, loose across the vast ceiling of the Sistine Chapel. Taken together, these actions constitute the most emphatic and the most productive vote of confidence in the arts ever cast.

As in the Quattrocento, then, painting responded to and was supported by the values and interests of those who commissioned works of art. The influence of architecture and sculpture, too, remained strong. Indeed, even allowing for the encouragement of Julius, it is doubtful whether the years spent by Raphael and Michelangelo in Rome (a place where Leonardo, who shrank from being urged beyond the pace set by the multitudinous preoccupations of his intellectual curiosity, did not feel at home) would have resulted in work quite so confidently noble had it not been for the presence of the greatest of humanist architects, Bramante, and the discovery of ancient statues like the Laocoön and the Apollo Belvedere. Besides the careful study of the effect of atmosphere on the colours and shapes of nature, and endless preparatory studies of faces and bodies in the studio, painters were able to imagine marble figures of an ideal beauty in buildings of ideal symmetry and grace.

Thanks to the increasing use of engravings and the circulation of drawings, painting in Italy became less regionally differentiated as the Cinquecento wore on. But it never became uniform; Raphael's and Michelangelo's own art changed to a revolutionary degree, multiplying the models available to those who looked to their work for guidance. Venice gave more to Lombardy than it took from Rome. Leonardo's more copyable inscrutabilities lingered on among the frailer talents of the Milanese. The paintings we shall look at represent a variety of approach as rich as that of the Quattrocento. But however much the 'classical' ideal of an enhanced reality was relaxed, prettified, parodied and distorted, or, up to a point, jettisoned, no return to the manners of the previous century was possible: nature had been looked at too closely, man too entirely, and both had been interrelated too convincingly.

The painters' work

Castagno's static *Last Supper* (Plate 101) was finished in about a month. Leonardo's (Plate 102) took between two and three years (about 1495–8). He was chided for delay. There were stories of his coming into the refectory, climbing the scaffolding and staring at the unfinished painting for hours, and then departing without having made a brush-stroke. Yet the immediate effect, even in its present battered and decayed state, is of the liveliest animation, a vivid sense of something electrifying having been said or done. Nothing could be more normal than the table, with its pleasantly patterned cloth, littered with pewter plates and the remains of what was obviously a solid meal. Yet the diners have been thrown into a state of agitation that makes them rise, gesticulate, lean or huddle into groups. The agitation centres on Christ, and there is only one thing he said on that occasion that could have caused it: the announcement that 'One of you which eateth with me shall betray me' (Mark 14:18). And because Leonardo wrote that 'music is not to be called anything other than the sister of painting', we may liken the Apostles' reactions to the aghast 'Is it I?' in Bach's *St. Matthew Passion*. Only two of the Apostles have no need to question themselves or their neighbours: John, secure in the knowledge that he is the Apostle whom Christ loves, and Judas, equally sure that he is the betrayer.

But this immediate reading of the scene in dramatic human terms becomes overlaid by the conviction that something more is intended. Why is the table jammed so close against the picture plane? Not to give the monks the impression that it is on a dais—the doorway (cut when the painting was barely decipherable) shows that it is too far above the ground for that; nor to give the effect of being at the edge of a raised continuation of the refectory, for the painted architecture is quite different. Nor, indeed, is the viewer tempted to imagine the possibility of entering the room portrayed by Leonardo in order to puzzle out why the table has been placed in so unlikely a manner across one end—its evasive perspective issues no such invitation. Leonardo is not evaporating a wall in Milan to show us a room in Jerusalem, but forcing us to reappraise a frieze of action otherwise so spontaneous and natural in human terms that its importance as a milestone on the route to Calvary might be ignored.

The reappraisal is guided by two elements more readily recognized by Leonardo's contemporaries than by ourselves: the sign language of gesture (evolved by monks under a vow of silence, preachers, professional rhetoricians and the actors in *tableaux vivants*) and the numerical significance of groups.

Christ's left hand rests open on the tablecloth. This just works as a gesture of resignation within the context of 'One of you which eateth with me shall betray me', but, read upwards through the profile hand above it and the pointed index finger of the hand above that, it forms the prefix of a code directing the attention to the heavenly, or spiritual, significance of what is seen. His other hand makes the opposite gesture: facing downwards, it is mirrored—across John's neutrally intertwined fingers—by Judas's. Both of Christ's hands indicate pieces of bread, symbol of a body ritually eaten by every one of the fresco's observers, bread which if taken in a mood of betrayal remained food merely for the body, but which if taken in a mood of faith directed the soul towards Heaven. The hands play a spiritual accompaniment to the theme of treachery established by bodily pose and facial expression.

The arrangement of the Apostles into four groups accentuates Leonardo's intention to treat two subjects simultaneously: the announcement of betrayal and of the eucharistic significance of the bread, to combine the quick human response to the one with the meditative impression of the other. It was a commonplace that the scriptures contained four layers of meaning: literal, allegorical, moral and mystical, and no passages in the gospels were so frequently expounded in this way as those concerned with the institution of the sacraments. Again, the efficacy of the sacraments depended on Christ's human perfection as well as on his divinity. So pervasive was the belief that a man's physical condition was determined by another four-fold formula, the humours, that it is possible that many of those who saw the fresco would sense that the groups represented phlegm, melancholy, blood and choler, which could only be perfectly balanced in the perfect man sitting in their midst. Leonardo's intention was to present a theological argument within the context of an immediate, if ennobled, vision of actuality.

The 'accompaniment' to the betrayal theme in the *Last Supper* is the sole subject of the first fresco Raphael painted (in 1509), when he was employed by Julius II in the Vatican, the '*Disputa*', or discussion of the sacrament (Plate 123). The mystic bread stands in a monstrance on the altar, like a motion posted for debate. That Christ's life as a man constituted the most important of all biographies in a literal sense and the most relevant in a moral sense is the chief concern of the figures on the left, who stand against a landscape of grassy slopes, trees, a road and a village. The theologians and seers (including a laurel-crowned Dante) on the right are more concerned with the allegorical and mystical significance of the host, which was the vital link between men and the realm of saints, prophets, and angels (Plate 122). To establish their identity, the figure beside the altar points to heaven with the gesture Leonardo gave to the Apostle next to Christ. Behind them is not a landscape, but the slabs of a now empty tomb.

Turning our backs on this work and looking across the quite small Stanza della Segnatura, we face a fresco, painted immediately afterwards, that has entirely lost the air the '*Disputa*' has of being a little too dutiful in its anxiety to spell everything out. It is not just that with the '*School of Athens*' (Plate 124) we turn our backs on a world half of which hovers on an air cushion of cherubs, to consider a well organized gathering of figures all of whom have their feet firmly planted on the ground. As with Masaccio's *Trinity* (Plate 5), we confront a 'perfect' architecture—in this case suggested by Bramante, whose role in the early Cinquecento repeats that of Brunelleschi in the early Quattrocento—which has a symbolic as well as a structural function. We have moved from Christian theologians to classical philosophers, but, as with the '*Disputa*', half are of a mystical bent (the bearded Plato's heavenward gesture mirrors that of his theological opposite number) and half are involved with the worldly application of knowledge. While neither Plato nor his companion and mental complement Aristotle are gods, they and their disciples are associated respectively with statues of gods—with Apollo, whose music moved the soul, and Minerva, the representative of practical wisdom.

The radiant certainty of the '*School of Athens*' comes from other sources. One is Raphael's unique ability to learn, to remember all he had seen in art and life and incorporate his memories instantaneously into the working needs of the moment. Another is the unparalleled nimbleness with which his brush and mind moved together, a nimbleness which enabled him to give grace and nobility to a dozen pages torn, as it were, from an encyclopedia. For here we have almost the full roll-call of famous thinkers from antiquity, whose works were so deeply studied and admired at the time. An artist, a man of lines and colours, has (doubtless with scholarly advice) hit the essential point of humanism: that it enabled a man surrounded with classical texts to time-travel into the world that had produced them. A couple of years later, in 1513, Machiavelli provided a prose equivalent to the spirit of Raphael's fresco.

> 'When evening comes, I return home and go into my study. On the threshold I strip off my muddy, sweaty, workaday clothes, and put on the robes of court and palace, and in this graver dress I enter the antique courts of the ancients and am welcomed by them, and there I taste the food that alone is mine and for which I was born. And there I make bold to speak to them and ask the motives of their actions, and they, in their humanity, reply to me. And for the space of four hours I forget the world, tremble no more at death: I pass indeed into their world.'

With Raphael we too pass into another world and feel, if not welcomed to (for they are intent on their own concerns), at least given the liberty of, the antique courts of the ancients. Gone are the '*Disputa*' devices (bottom left and right) for prodding the painter's world back into ours. He now has the confidence simply to say, with the most authoritatively spacious of gestures, 'enter'. And as we do we respond not only to the pull of arch beyond arch, but to a sensation, among the first provided by painting, of actual atmospheric pressure. Only, on closer inspection, the throng of ancients themselves disappoint, separating out into a series of tableaux that bring a whiff from the artist's workshop in the world we have just left.

One figure, indeed, belongs wholly to the whirl of impressions that Raphael's genius was constantly absorbing into his own vision. On a stretch of fresh plaster, when the rest of the work was finished, he painted the 'Heraclitus' in the foreground and slightly to the left. In 'Platonic territory', the figure is hunched and brooding, separated as much from the others by his introspection as by his rough boots and contemporary workman's smock. It is a portrait of Michelangelo, whose hitherto closely guarded work in the nearby Sistine Chapel Raphael must just have seen and which was already, as the knees and clothing of this figure show, beginning to move him towards a new strength.

By now (1511) Michelangelo had moved his scaffolding to the third and last zone of the ceiling and was about to begin the compartments that start with the *Creation of Adam* (Plate 105) and continue to the altar wall (Plate 4).

Looking up at the ceiling (Plate 109) we can see how Michelangelo used, as had Leonardo and Raphael, a fictive architecture to support and bind together the whole scheme. Between each of the triangular vaults over the windows two ribs sail across from side to side, each pair forming three compartments. The lower compartments form thrones for prophets and sibyls, inspired figures from the classical and Old Testament worlds who, by study or inspiration, had foretold how God the Creator would have to enter the world as Christ the re-Creator. The throne compartments are topped by cornices, which run continuously from one end of the ceiling to the other, supported alternately by corbels shaped like rams' heads (the sacrifice acceptable to God in lieu of Isaac), and by short projecting pillars carved into pairs of *putti*. The thickness of each pillar forms a seat above the cornice for a nude youth, one of a race of unchosen Adams, responsive to every mood save those induced in a soul wakened by God and burdened by that knowledge, free, restless witnesses to the artist's chosen raw material (even the sibyls were studied from male models). The scenes, alternately large and small, in the central compartments can only be properly looked at when walking down the axis of the chapel towards the altar. The ceiling cannot be read from any one point of view: the observer is forced both to move along and to twist from side to side.

He has to move, moreover, against his sense of chronology, for these central scenes begin at the entrance with Noah's Ark and the Flood and end, over the altar, with the first act of Creation, the separation of light from darkness. This is the direction in which Michelangelo painted, bay by bay from 1508 to 1512, and it also determined the direction he was to follow as an artist, for as he moved from the crowded scene of the Flood to scenes where God was alone with the elements, his sense of each figure's significance for the human condition made him work on a scale ever grander and more impetuously original. Bay by bay the prophets and sibyls filled their thrones more hugely, the nude youths grew to more enrapturing states of energy and beauty: swaying and swelling figures progressively obscured the architectural grid they lived amongst as the energy in the central panels grew more thunderous. Practice in the new medium, changing subject-matter, deepening commitment: these factors spurred Michelangelo's creativity as he moved towards the central moments of Creation itself.

The greatest change comes between the *Creation of Eve* and the *Creation of Adam* (Plate 105). In the first, God appears as an amply cloaked and decently bearded wizard drawing Eve out of Adam's side with a gesture of urbane gravity. Adam, portrayed with the utmost tenderness, sleeps the last sleep of human innocence, while above him, parallel to Eve's back, there is a branch prefiguring that other, later branch to which, as a consequence of this act, Christ will have to be nailed. In *The Creation of Adam* (earlier in the chronology of Creation), God has produced the shape of a man visibly in his own image, a relaxed, perfect, just sentient form, already infused with a love that reaches for the final irradiation with divine energy. God, no longer an earth-bound wizard, but the sky-borne tamer of chaos, stretches out a bare arm from the vehicle he rides in, uterine in shape and redness, and prepares to charge him with the destiny of mankind. With two individual male bodies, one nude, the other as good as nude, Michelangelo has expressed the idea that haunted him for the rest of his life: that beyond physical perfection lies perfectibility. He has achieved the never-before-attempted feat of portraying the Creation not of the body, but of the soul.

In the refectory of Santa Maria delle Grazie, in the Stanza della Segnatura, and in the Sistine Chapel, we have been breathing an air tense with intellectual power and expository determination. The sensuous appeal of objects and bodies is there, but it has been subordinated to the desire to organize and to teach. We have been shown miracles but have been deprived of magic.

Paintings had usually provided moments of relaxation, an animal (Plate 73) or bird expression, an unpedagogic invitation to step into a room (Plate 61) or view (Plate 59), but hitherto the passages allowing the spectator to ruminate or indulge in a flight of fancy were details that had escaped the central argument. Whole paintings charged with invitations to daydream were introduced by the Venetians, and works like Giorgione's *Tempest* (Plate 86) of about 1506, and the *Fête Champêtre* (Plate 87) of about 1510 (variously given to Giorgione or Titian), came, significantly, to be called *poesie*, invented, fictional situations that induced a mood hitherto associated with poetry rather than with painting. The magic in both cases, is, of course, partly the result of a certain enigmatic quality: we are there, we are happy to be there, but why are we there, what is, or has been, going on?

Why is the woman in the *Tempest* sitting in that pose, so protective towards the child, so open towards the spectator? Who is the informally but expensively dressed young man on the left, and what is the relationship between them? The eccentric placing of the two broken columns on their plinth seems to be recalling something, but what? Why does the building on the left end so deliberately at a point where no real building would end—just beyond the mid-point of an arch? Why do the very Venetian chimney-pots in the back lead to the dome and square shoulders of a mosque? The search for a literary source that would finally explain these puzzles has been ingenious, but so far unconvincing. The discovery through x-ray photographs that in place of the clothed young man was originally a nude woman bathing suggests that if there was a source, Giorgione treated it with some casualness. If we did know the answer to the riddle it would not quench the power of that still, green world, quietly poised on the edge of thunder, to posit endlessly the proposition that thought is free.

Much of that power comes from the new (or, at least, newly expressed) feeling for nature explored by Bellini and, above all, by Leonardo. It is not that previous artists had just used 'nature' because a narrative—a Flight into Egypt, for instance—called for it, or to fill in the interstices in a figure composition. There had been a love of growing things, a pleasure in the shapes of hills and river courses, even, with Leonardo, a severe fascination with the physical forces that had moulded the surfaces men walked on and looked at. But in the *Tempest* and the *Fête Champêtre*, nature is, simply, there. Men and women will enter, sit on the grass and crush it. But when they leave, it will spring back, ready for sheep to munch. The latter painting also poses its riddles. Those naked women (how marvellously un-Florentine is their soft, blurred massiveness!): what is their relationship to the clothed, mutually attentive young men? Why is the woman on the left pouring water *into* a well? We do not know, but perhaps it is not important that we should know. The shepherd comes in, and will pass through. The leaves turn brown, and will fall. The music pauses, and will sound again. Saints, virgins, apostles and prophets are restless beings, always hinting at what we ought to do or ought to think about doing. Pagan deities have a nagging quality, for they incorporate appetites or qualities with which we have to come to terms. Nature soothes because it cannot preach. Nothing that happens to it is (until comparatively recently) our fault. These paintings liberate because they are non-committal, and they start a tendency which, eventually jettisoning gods and humans, will establish landscape as a recognized *genre* of its own.

To turn to the dervish-like intensity of the Florentine Rosso's *Moses and the Daughters of Jethro* (Plate 147), painted in 1523–4, is to leave the quiet evolution introduced by Giovanni Bellini to the Venetian lagoon for an atmosphere of almost strident professional earnestness. The text from Exodus that Rosso was called on to illustrate seems to be a fairly mild one: 'Now the priest of Midian [Jethro] had seven daughters: and they came and drew water, and filled the troughs to water their father's flock. And the shepherds came and drove them away: but Moses stood up and helped them, and watered their flock.' (Exodus 2:16, 17) It is true that anyone who grew up during the cut-throat Wars of Italy might realize that the driving away could not be done without some show of force. All the same, to show Moses wrenching and pounding, berserk with blood-lust, casts a doubt on the respect in which Rosso held his Old Testament. And to show him straddling the top of a pyramid rising from a base comprising the logical extreme of Pollaiuolo's two contrasted foreground bowmen (Plate 97) leaves none about his self-consciousness as an artist. This is one of the first paintings that can properly be dubbed academic. Unlike other works by Rosso (Plate 158), its intention is less to explore new means of expression than to demonstrate an almost feckless redeployment of the means used by others. The fallen figure in the right foreground is deliberately difficult: the parallel arm and thigh, the pelvis heaved up by the crossed legs to provide a previously unattempted vista of belly and inner thigh seen beyond an escarpment of ribcage. The difficulties here, and in the other nude figures, are solved with an almost ruthless (though not unsensual) professional fervour, while the parody of their axes provided by the cluster of sheep's heads shows the emotional distance between the painter and his subject. The shepherd storming in from the left, hand histrionically outflung in a gesture of 'look what you have been responsible for' and cloak artificially stiffened upwards, is another academic exercise, eliciting, foreseeably enough, the frozen 'don't' of the marvellously balanced figure of Jethro's better-than-naked daughter. Her face is doll-like, the hands mincing, the coiffure jauntily out of keeping with the theme, but the exposed breast, the shoulder and extended arm proclaim the Florentine tradition of defining by outline and modelling by light. In spite of the over-elegances, the shrilly unnatural colours and the almost divinatory quality of certain passages, such as the rendering of the two daughters in the top right-hand corner—all elements that stamp Rosso's personality upon the work—the painting is a tribute to the humanistic, sculptural, rationally analytical strain Rosso had absorbed as a 'Fiorentino'.

Two years later, Jacopo Pontormo began his *Meditation on the Body of Christ* (Plate 155). Because of its vertical composition it is commonly referred to as *The Deposition*. As Christ's wounds have already been washed, it is sometimes called an Entombment. But the depictment lies outside the chronology of the Passion, nor does it focus attention on the Passion's eucharistic significance: the nail holes in the hand and the lance thrust are mere flecks, the feet are unblemished. Pontormo, in the self-portrait on the right (and Plate 153), is staring in ecstasy neither at the event nor at us. He has painted an entirely personal vision (it was said later that he had forbidden access to the chapel in Santa Felicita while he was working there). Its starting point is the dead, beautiful body of an incarnate God, at the same time visible but insubstantial—Christ is 'lifted' without strain by one youth, his weight, transferred through the stooping youth, does not dent the puff of drapery on the ground. Nor, apart from St. John (recognizable as a male from the preliminary drawing—Plate 152), does any of Pontormo's cast of figures look directly at Christ; they see him through Mary or in their own minds. The stooping youth, involved so closely only at Pontormo's bidding, for he represents no gospel character, asks the spectator what he thinks, and this invitation to meditate is supported by the quietly circling drive of the composition. At the centre of this movement is a cloth. To wipe the sweat and blood from the Creator of All Things: what does this mean?

Apart from the cloud, the hint of hillside in front of his self-portrait, and the suggestion of depth given by the feet in the foreground, Pontormo is not concerned to present a sense of place. Nor, though the posture of Christ and the youthfulness of the Virgin would seem to refer to Michelangelo's *Pietà* sculpture in St. Peter's, is he concerned to show what he could do with the mastery of line and modelling shown in the preliminary drawings (e.g. Plate 151). There is plenty of virtuoso quirkishness here: an arbitrary use of colour, clothing at times almost indistinguishable from dyed skin. But while the painting reflects impatience with the rationality of the Florentine tradition, and much that is purely idiosyncratic, these elements fuse into so urgent a desire to communicate truth through beauty that in its underlying feeling it remains closer to Fra Angelico (Plate 20) than to a deliberately 'artful' work like Parmigianino's '*Madonna of the Long Neck*' (Plate 167), which was painted less than ten years later (1535).

This work could with equal justice be called the Madonna of the Long Fingers, or of the Extended Torso, or, more briefly, of the Nipple or of the Navel, so many are the features that distinguish her from other Madonnas, let alone from real women. There is nothing ultra-personal or undescriptive about the colour here. The child is scarcely winning, but his size is a conventional reminder of the dead Christ, who will be supported on that same lap. The Bacchus-Baptist youth, whose wine jar will then be replaced by the new wine of the Redeemer's blood, represents a concept hardly more far-fetched than was a good deal of contemporary religious imagery, nor is the contrast between the B.C. background, with its reference to a time of refined paganism and Old Testament prophecy, and the foreground, unduly strained, though it almost over-aestheticizes the contrast between an age of Law and the age of Grace. But here the more-or-less conventional comes to a stop, to be overtaken by the urge, at any cost to the reality of appearance or the truth of feeling, to be exquisite. And if a touch of the bizarre helps draw attention to that exquisiteness, so much the better.

The painting looks towards a portrait of a type not yet invented. In its centre, an attractive young matron in elegant undress. On the left, a group of young persons belonging to her family. Behind them all, rich draperies hang down from an unknown support. On the right, classical architecture in a landscape. How frequently, from van Dyck to Reynolds and beyond, is this formula going to be repeated! But this is not a portrait, not yet a formula. As the young people are not ordinary children, the painter can produce here a face of ideal beauty, there a moment of cool eroticism, as where foot, urn and forefinger play against the glimpse of flesh above the Bacchus-Baptist's thigh. As the distant view is not that from the sitter's country estate, the painter can slide its fore-stage up to the Madonna's dais without increasing the scale of the figure, who seems more intent on memorizing than proclaiming his prophecies. Behind him are the bases of a row of columns, but only the first soars up to its full height, so perfectly proportioned and smoothly rendered that its lack of a concluding capital is realized only after a jarring double-take. The others blend into a strip of brownish underpaint, which extends blankly to the curtain and the Virgin's neck and shoulder. Why Parmigianino left a work of such consummate finish uncompleted is not clear. It has been suggested that the columns set a problem he could not solve without destroying the balance of the painting. Yet never had a painting been more completely artful, for point by point he brings off brilliantly contrived moments of dislocation, moments when to see is not to believe, as where the Virgin's right foot, if measured against the nearness of the cushions its heel rests on, 'must' extend out of the picture altogether. It is more likely that Parmigianino had exhausted a mood than run out of skill.

Ten years later, Michelangelo finished *The Conversion of Saul* (Plate 163), the last but one of his paintings. The artist whose range of invention had offered a whole new vocabulary to his younger contemporaries has passed into a phase so solitarily combative that it could be drawn on by nobody. No other masterpiece so conspicuously fails to communicate the pleasure of being a master. Faces of great beauty, poses of extraordinary daring, memories of fellow painters like Leonardo and Raphael, all come unbidden, unsought-for into the heavy convulsion of this sternly felt work. Between clumps of spirits enrolled almost at random from Michelangelo's vast repertory of forms, Christ rams down a pulse of light. All see it. The horse bolts. Saul's attendants flee, fall, shrink back, peer aghast or bemused, huddle, exclaim. Only one did not see it but feels it. Momentarily blinded, Saul's face records the inner devastation that must precede a spiritual resurrection (Plate 165). The face of the Father, who on the Sistine ceiling thirty years before so confidently created the first man, is now enlisted agonizedly to enact the creation of the new man, as an example to all those who must, in order to rejoin him, re-create themselves. Michelangelo's poems of these years drag with a sense of sin, a conviction of inescapable bondage. The painting's theme is conversion. But how can a mind clogged with a lifetime's preoccupation with limbs and faces clear itself and let in the light? The figures stumble and run as though Saul must exorcize them before the new life can begin. Ill-clad, almost loutish, they owe as little to any ideal of beauty or refinement as the folds that stand out from his body like varicose veins.

'Saul, Saul, why persecutest thou me?' asks Christ, and Saul's face turns the question back upon him.

The tension between the figures plunging away and the sensation that Saul is about to roll slowly towards us is forceful because it was forced out of a state of mind. In the *Removal of the Body of St. Mark from Alexandria* (Plate 181), painted between 1562 and 1566, the Venetian Tintoretto uses a similar tension to enhance the dramatic quality of a story he simply watches—from beside the camel's neck. The group supporting the body of Venice's patron saint looms towards the spectator all the more powerfully because so much of the rest of the composition is devoted to making his eye race towards the depths of the picture: up the perspective grid of the piazza (though set in Alexandria, there is clearly a reference to the piazza of San Marco in Venice), along the terrified pagans plunging for safety into the arcade. They had killed St. Mark and were preparing to burn him before his fellow Christians could secure the body (cleaning has revealed a vast bonfire almost obscuring the central and right-hand arches of the building in the background). But God has sent a storm. Dark clouds ride out under the moon. Lightning coats the scene with a phantasmagoric glare. The rain that has quenched the fire pours on, slopping over the roof on the right and forming a flood in the piazza (a phenomenon with which Venetians were already well acquainted), quivering under the impact of gusts of wind that leave the draperies of the Christian rescue party unmoved, though their feet stir the waters. The unnatural lighting, the swift, sketch-like quality of the background, make the painting appear at first glance to be one of actors moving across a stage set. But while intensely dramatic, Tintoretto was never theatrical. We are at the beginning of a long journey: St. Mark's body will be buried, forgotten, miraculously found again and, centuries after the moment portrayed here, brought across the sea to ensure the glory and sustain the piety of Venice. The piazza in Alexandria, the discomfiture of the infidels: these are no more than points of departure for the journey of that heavy, reverently tended body into the devotions and sense of history of a people for whom St. Mark was associated with every battle they fought, every profit (his image was on the ducat) they made, every Mass they knelt for. That is what is real. That is what Tintoretto concentrates on.

Tintoretto's profound sense that his art should be primarily in the service of religion, his habit of freeing his imagination through a preliminary, rapid bout of re-examining the point of view from which traditional subjects should be seen and the compositional setting in which they should appear, forced him, in the main, outside the sensuous, slow-moving, colour-based love of real appearances that was the hallmark of Venetian painting. *Susannah and the Elders* (Plate 174) shows that he could, on occasion, be susceptible to the cherishing of tone and texture habitual to Veronese. *St. George and the Dragon* (Plate 171) shows that he sometimes looked outside his almost claustrophobically busy studio at the work of his chief, and much older, rival in public esteem, Titian.

In its range of greens that modulate up from the dark foreground, through grass, sea and trees to stain the castle walls and be reflected among the clouds, this is the most romantic landscape of the Cinquecento, painted freely and blithely from the imagination. Though unruined, univyed, with neither keep nor tower, the castle, so practical in its shape, is painted into the world of chivalry and fairy tale. And the clouds piled above it with so telling a blend of meteorology and evocativeness: what a pity, one may think, that they house a counter-atmosphere of supernatural light radiating from an insubstantial God the Father. But reading the story down again, past the dashing knight, to the princess saved from a dreadful death, we stop, on that hint from the clouds, to look more closely at the victim that did not escape death, and see that he is like Christ, arms outstretched and feet together between the bare and the broken trees that could symbolize his Cross. This reference to the divine significance of a combat usually treated in a mood of picturesque derring-do was presumably asked for by Tintoretto's patron, and to direct attention to it the dominating figure of the princess is used to invite us to re-enter the picture and look again. Hitherto, in representations of this legend, she had been shown in flight, in prayer, or merely watching the combat. Tintoretto has combined all three reactions in one pose: she appears to flee, she actually kneels, and she casts a glance, part fearful, part grateful, at her deliverer's joust with Satan. The pose is achieved with a Parmigianinesque ingenuity. The superb *contrapposto* of the body, arms and shoulders swaying against face and hips, makes us think she is running until the eye is forced to notice that her knees are on the ground. Her outstretched hand and arm draw attention to her backward glance with another device. Assuming her right shoulder to be in the same plane as her left knee, then, measured against the distance between knee and picture ledge, her hand must be touching the surface of the space she is pictured in, if not actually puncturing it. Yet with her firmly normal face and body she is not a Mannerist figure. The devices are used solely to help us feel the presence of God without turning a romance into a sermon.

If Tintoretto's personal indifference to comfort and money and his intense empathy with every turn in the long story of man's salvation made him the ideal depictor of the more fervent aspects of Venetian religious life, Veronese, dignified and comfort-loving if a shade parsimonious, perfectly represented the moral values of the patrician class which patronized him. Highest in the scale of those values was magnanimity. As Aristotle and Cicero had taught, magnanimity could only be displayed by the possessors of wealth and authority: without these, it was impossible to show generosity or mercy. For a society based on commerce, a class which shared a monopoly of legal and political power, the concept was at once a justification of the monopoly and an apology for it.

In, probably, the late 1560s Veronese was commissioned to exemplify the concept by the wealthy and influential Pisani family. That he shows them in the guise of donors being introduced into the divine presence under the auspices of a patron Saint witnesses the importance given to magnanimity as a virtue. Nor could anyone better represent this virtue than the god-like Alexander the Great, ruler of the widest and richest of empires—an empire looking eastwards, as did Venice's own. *The Family of Darius before Alexander* (Plates 168, 169) illustrates an episode that followed the battle of Issus. Alexander had defeated the army of the Persian King Darius, who fled with the survivors, leaving his family in the Emperor's hands; they begged for mercy, and he let them go. During a century racked with vengefulness, moralists had time upon time cited this episode as a way of restraining the powerful without irritating them with references to the gospel. And Veronese shows a version of the story which enables him to refer to the modesty and good manners that should accompany an act of magnanimity. Darius's dependants address a figure whose outward gorgeousness persuades them that he is the Emperor. But this is Alexander's young comrade in arms Hephaestion; he stills their pleading and refers them to the sterner faced and more practically armoured monarch behind him, who shows no resentment at the misidentification.

It is a theme that justified an emphasis on the attributes of wealth and position, and Veronese lets the delicately pungent raciness of his colour sense, his delight in what is firm and splendid, clothe the occasion. Although carefully drawn, the architectural setting is little more than a pale indication of the Asian setting: the native inhabitants pass by below or chatter on the balustrade with as little interest in the event as we are expected to show in them. The moral is to be brought home to Venice, and its protagonists are spread along close to the gaze of the Venetian spectator, dressed in the brocades, furs and velvets worn in Venice; and the showpiece armours and weapons could have come from the Council of Ten's armoury, which was one of the sights of Venice. Though the monkey, the dwarfs and the two slave girls with 'Asiatic' features on the left reflect the taste of courts, this dignified assemblage has none of the rhetoric or preciosity associated with princely art. Veronese was the Master of Ceremonies of Venetian painting, but a factual eye and a sober understanding of social values enabled him to show the Venetians, in expression, bearing and costume, as paragons among patricians, not as would-be dukes and courtiers.

Of the three long-lived masters of Venetian Cinquecento painting, Titian had the longest life (the late 1480s to 1576), the most international reputation, and the most consistently wide range of commissions: mythological scenes, great altarpieces, small religious paintings, and single and multiple portraits. For all his fame, property (a palace in Venice, farms and woods on the mainland), warm friendships, travels and passports to high places (court-painter to the Emperor Charles V, who, it was widely rumoured, once in Augsburg stooped to pick up a brush he had let fall), Titian was the most constantly exploratory of the means whereby visual experience can be recorded. To take very different styles spaced between 1510 and 1546, he would have been a great and sought-after painter if he had clung to the vein of soft transitions and lyric melancholy shown in the *Fête Champêtre* (Plate 87), or the soaring wholesome ecstasy of the *Assumption of the Virgin* (Plate 99), or the flash-light immediacy of *Pope Paul III with his Grandsons* (Plate 148). But as he aged, the impetus to reduce the distance between art and nature grew. Inevitably this led to his leaving aside the *reductio ad absurdum* of attempts at complete reproduction and, instead, to his opting for the impression. Not the instantaneous impression, which does not give the mind time to analyse what the eye registers, not the structural and tonal simplification which can be art's revenge on nature, but a reliance on patches of colour to do the work of line in defining and modelling, and a determination to leave room, as it were, for those sounds and breaths of air without which nature falls mute and ceases to live. Titian was the first painter to invite a spectator to have all his senses, not just his eyes, about him. This is not to say that he took a camp-stool into the countryside. A painter who knew him in the last years has described his working methods.

> 'He laid in his pictures with a mass of colour which served as a groundwork . . . With the same brush dipped in red, black or yellow he worked up the light parts and in four strokes he could create a remarkably fine figure . . . Then he turned the picture to the wall without looking at it, until he returned to it and looked critically at it, as if it were a mortal enemy . . . Thus by repeated revision he brought his pictures to a high state of perfection . . . Sometimes he used his finger to dab a dark patch in a corner as an accent, or to heighten the surface with a bit of red like a drop of blood. He finished his figures like this, and in the last stages he used his fingers more than his brush.'

So for Titian an impression was the result of a somewhat lengthy process, in which he combined what he had seen with his reaction to the episode he had been asked to represent, and in which he re-considered the means of fusing the optical and emotional components of a subject together. And always he maintained an invigorating steadiness of purpose. Only for sentimentalists, or for those who read too much 'impressionism' into the many paintings left unfinished at his death, has Titian a 'late period', in which the role of art is extended in the darkness of introspection.

In *Diana and Actaeon* (Plates 172 and 175), painted in 1559, the sleeping nude in '*The Andrians*' (Plate 104), of about 1520, has aquired a fullness of life and potential movement and expression that puts her nearer to Rembrandt than to the works of Titian's own youth. The pearl-like application of colour within areas of clear drawing has gone, as has the reliance on light chiefly as a tool for the analysis of volume. Diana and her attendants, bodies already sensed as round and warm and breathing on the empty canvas, are revealed in terms of the colours wakened by light. Just how far art had been inhibited by a preoccupation with the ideal can be seen by contrasting the nymph of '*The Andrians*', not so much with Diana as with the more similarly built attendant holding up the curtain with such casual naturalness. Behind the figures, nature, tranced in the earlier painting, has also come alive. This almost audible wildness adds to the tension of the moment when the hunter Actaeon stumbles unawares on the virgin goddess naked after her bath. In that moment, too short for the woman drying her mistress's leg to realize what is happening, Actaeon drops his bow and Diana snatches up a cloth to conceal not her sex nor her breast but the emblems of godhead on her brow, and in this reversal of human instinct she is seconded by her black attendant. It is a gesture of deadly flirtatiousness; he sees her body and so is condemned to the death announced by the skeleton stag's head on the pillar. It is dramatically, and mysteriously, at odds with all the gestures of outraged modesty displayed by dozens of Cinquecento Susannahs and Bathshebas.

When, some five years later, Titian completed the consequence of this moment in the *Death of Actaeon* (Plate 170), the pitilessness with which he invests the story is still more marked. The punishment of being transformed into a stag will ensure Actaeon's death at the jaws and claws of his own hounds; there is no need for Diana to be there at all, let alone loosing her bow. Indeed, her disproportionate size shows that she is not 'there' as an actress in the scene but as one of those celestial influences (she was, after all, also goddess of the moon) that decide men's fate and were conventionally shown in the sky. The deliberately ugly killing in a lonely woodland brutally states the fact that man lives in a world where not only deliberate but also involuntary offences are punished. The existence of undeserved cruelty is the cruellest problem of Christian theism, and Titian has been moved by his story to turn a pantheistic rage upon it.

His dauntless originality was to ensure him a hearing in the future, from Rubens and Rembrandt to Turner, but his withdrawal from sweetness and his contempt for the display of skill isolated him from the painters maturing in Italy during his last years. Their most sensitive and, for a while, most influential representative was Federico Barocci, a native, like Raphael, of Urbino, and like him, a painter equally swift to respond to the qualities of others, including Raphael himself but especially Correggio (Plate 139), and to enlist them among his own.

In *The Circumcision* (Plate 186) of 1590, the godfather, in accordance with Jewish ritual, supports the child on a cushion on his knee. The *mohel* places the foreskin in a dish while he checks the bleeding with a wad. God has already been born as a man; the shepherd in the foreground, the dimly seen ox and ass in the distance, Mary and

Joseph on the right, all allude to this. But born in Jewry, he only becomes part of a people, in a religious sense, through this ceremony; only at this moment does he receive his name, Jesus. No wonder the angels rejoice and bestow light on this particular surgical operation. After it, Christ is fully part of the world he has come to save. For all its winsome moments, it is a painting of great compositional ingenuity and has a swift sureness of technique that can bring off passages as different as the crumpled bell of an angel with its clapper-like feet, and the lucid still-life on the floor. In its overall lightness of touch and unstrenuous complexity, it, too, points far beyond the century; not, as with Titian, because of power or novelty, but because it gathers together the defter achievements of the Cinquecento in a way which was to prove congenial to artists of the Rococo. Meanwhile, all it had to offer the rising generation of Caravaggio (Plate 188) was the shepherd boy with his hoarse bagpipe and slouch hat: pointers to a new approach to the relationship between art and reality—an approach that lies beyond the compass of this book.

It is fitting that this survey should end, as it began, at Urbino. It is a reminder of the vitality of the smaller places which have been passed by as we have moved with the main stream of development during two hundred years. In the Quattrocento, Cosimo Tura (Plate 69) and Ercole de' Roberti (Plate 44) were only two of the painters that made Ferrara a brilliant provincial centre, Carlo Crivelli (Plate 70) only one of the many artists who, constantly on the move from commission to commission, have left works that draw visitors away from the great cities to hill towns and remote monasteries all over central and northern Italy. In the Cinquecento Rome, Florence and Venice have diverted us from Parma, the home not only of the extremely influential Correggio (Plates 132, 139, 140) but of Parmigianino (Plate 156, 161), and from Brescia, the base of an outstanding school of painters of portraits and religious subjects (Plates 138, 150). Barocci is also a reminder of painters such as Lotto (Plates 90, 115) and Dosso Dossi (Plate 173), whose highly personal vision absorbs so much, from so many sources, that no survey based on 'centres' can readily accommodate them.

Barocci, finally, reminds us that while the reputations of few, if any, of the painters discussed here is likely to be seriously devalued, some may wane, others come to glow even more brightly. Our judgement nowadays accords with the list drawn up by Giovanni Santi. But only a hundred years ago many, if not most, of the artists he praised were looked on chiefly as curiosities. Barocci himself had become little regarded until a generation ago; the first exhibition devoted to his work was as recent as 1975. Taste changes. To some extent we make 'The Renaissance' as we go along by populating it with the works that appeal to us. Books on art can formulate, inform, explain, but they can never keep up with the eye.

List of Plates

List of Collections

The Plates

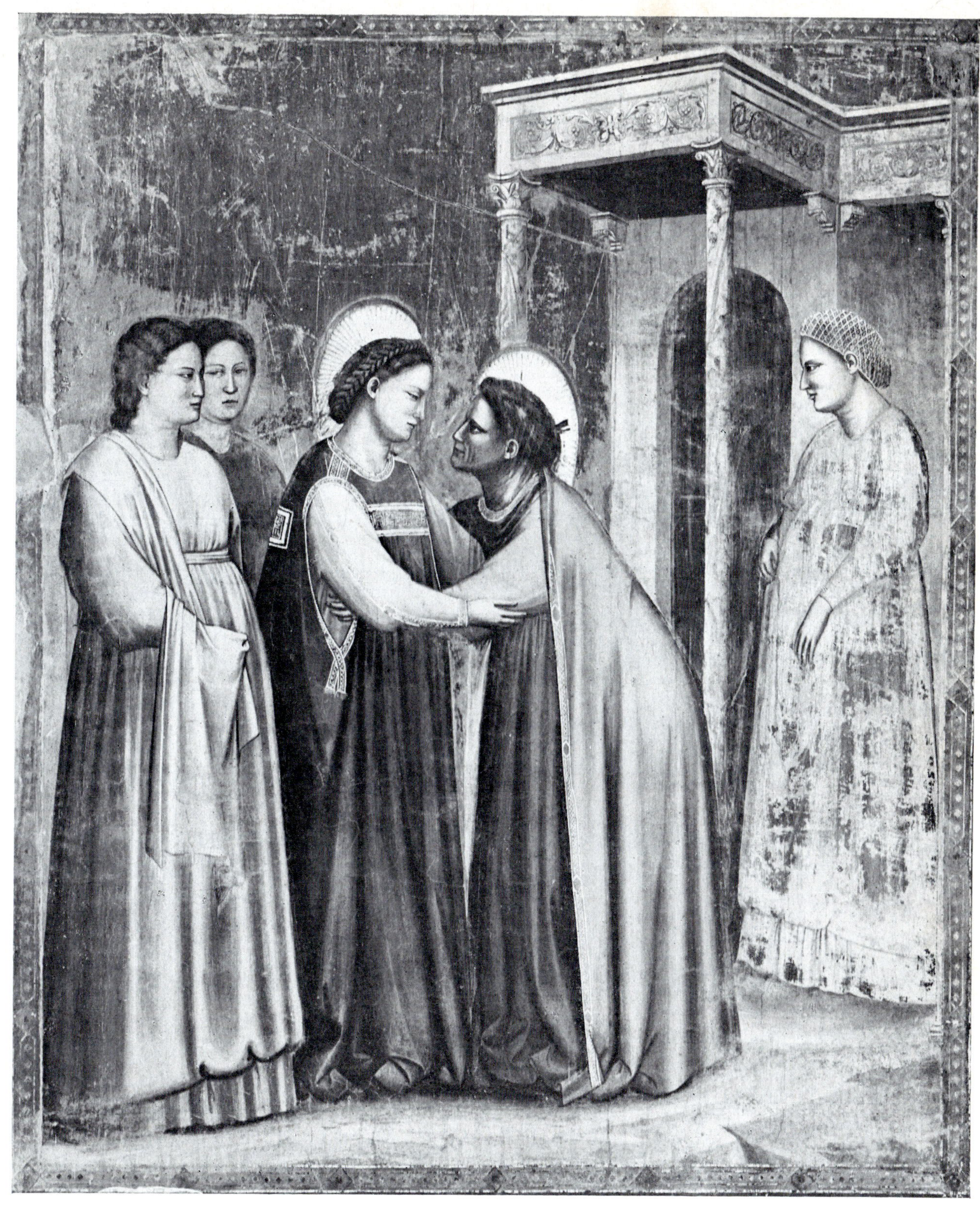

1. GIOTTO (1266?–1337): *The Visitation*. About 1310. Fresco. Padua, Arena Chapel

The Virgin Mary visits her aged cousin, St. Elisabeth, the former bearing the Christ Child and the latter St. John the Baptist (Luke 1:39ff.). The fresco forms part of an extensive cycle (see Plate 2) and shows the striving for naturalism and clarity of narrative which were to be taken up and developed by Masaccio.

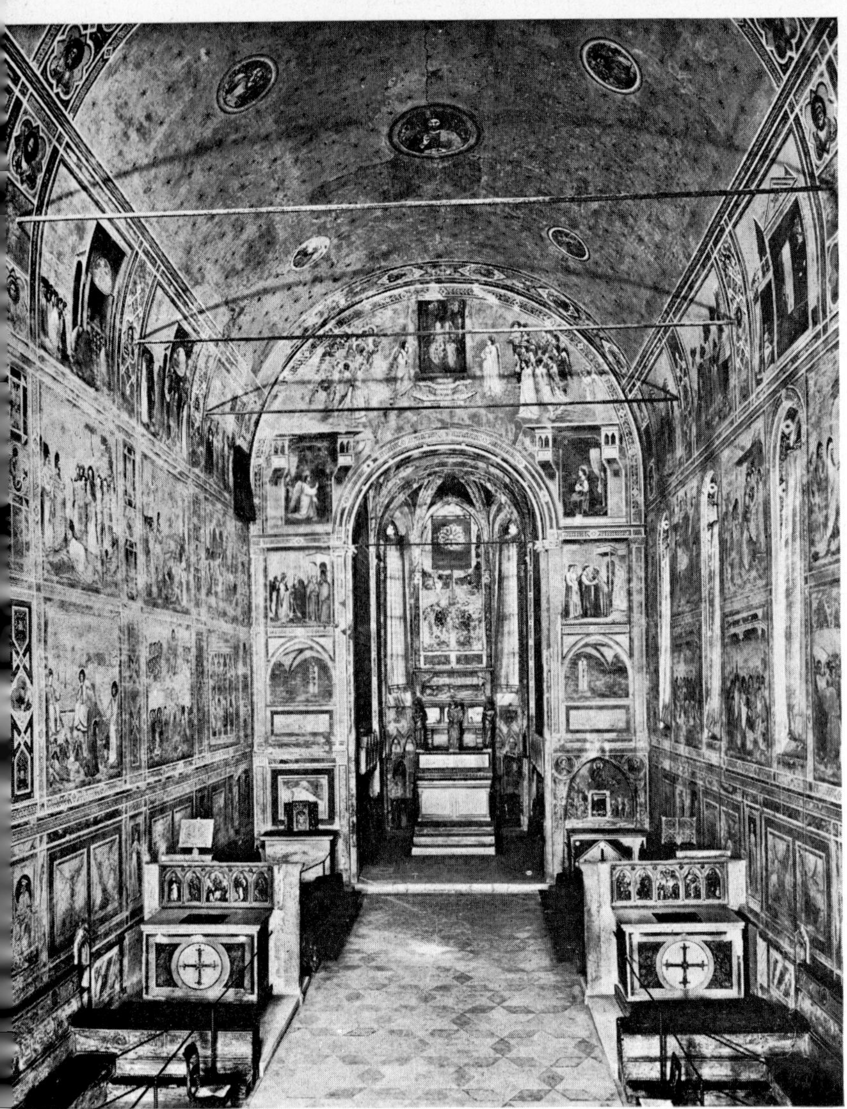

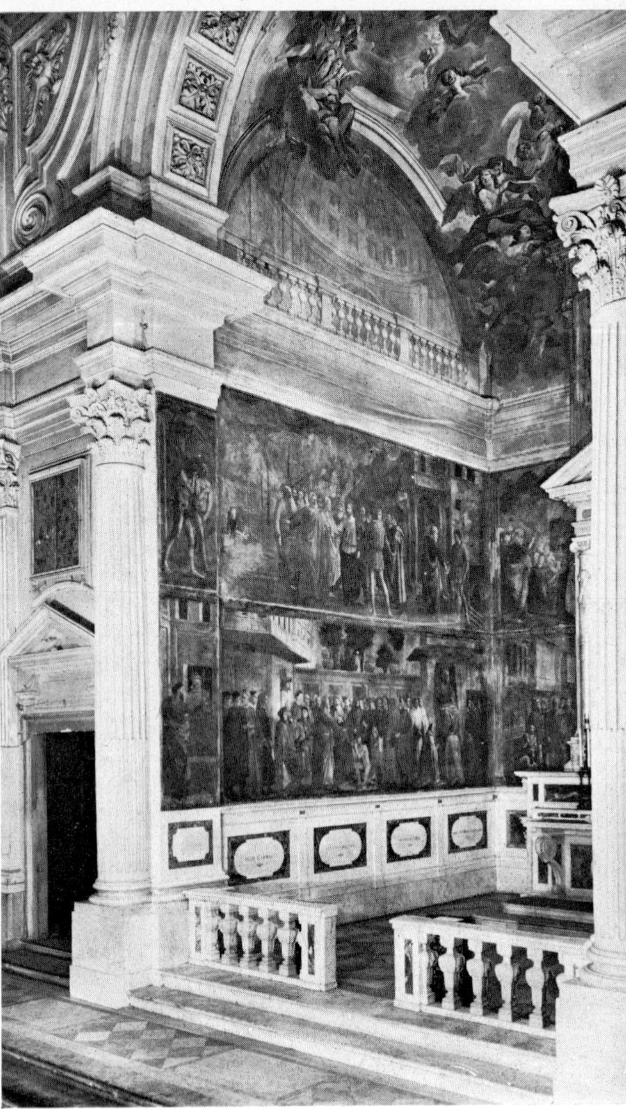

2. The Arena Chapel, Padua. Decorated by GIOTTO (1266?–1337)

3. The Brancacci Chapel in Santa Maria del Carmine, Florence. Decorated by MASACCIO (1401–*c.* 1428), MASOLINO (*c.* 1383–after 1432?), and FILIPPINO LIPPI (*c.* 1457–1504)

4. The Sistine Chapel in the Vatican

The Church was by far the most important patron of Italian Renaissance artists. Popes, monastic communities and pious donors commissioned countless altar-paintings and mural decorations (many of which have suffered much damage in succeeding centuries). These three examples of fresco cycles by Florentine artists are widely separated in time. Giotto's frescoes of scenes from the lives of Christ and the Virgin were painted about 1310. Over a century later, in 1425–7, his great successor, Masaccio (assisted by Masolino), decorated the Brancacci Chapel with scenes from the lives of the Apostles Peter and Paul (Plates 7, 18, 19, 22). Unlike this small family chapel, the huge Sistine Chapel, built by Pope Sixtus IV (see Plate 66), has no such unified scheme. It is 133 ft. long, 43 ft. wide and 68 ft. high. The frescoes on the side walls representing the life of Moses and the life of Christ were painted in 1481–2 by Botticelli, Ghirlandaio, Perugino and Rosselli; the ceiling (Plates 105, 108, 109) was executed in 1509–12 by Michelangelo, who thirty years later also painted the altar wall (Plate 162). The tapestries after Raphael's celebrated cartoons (see Plates 116–18) were also displayed here.

The Sistine Chapel and the adjacent *Stanze* decorated by Raphael are the greatest surviving schemes of Italian Renaissance painting. The content of the elaborate frescoes was often supplied by learned churchmen or intellectuals; but the programme of the Sistine ceiling, originally much simpler, was planned and developed by Michelangelo himself.

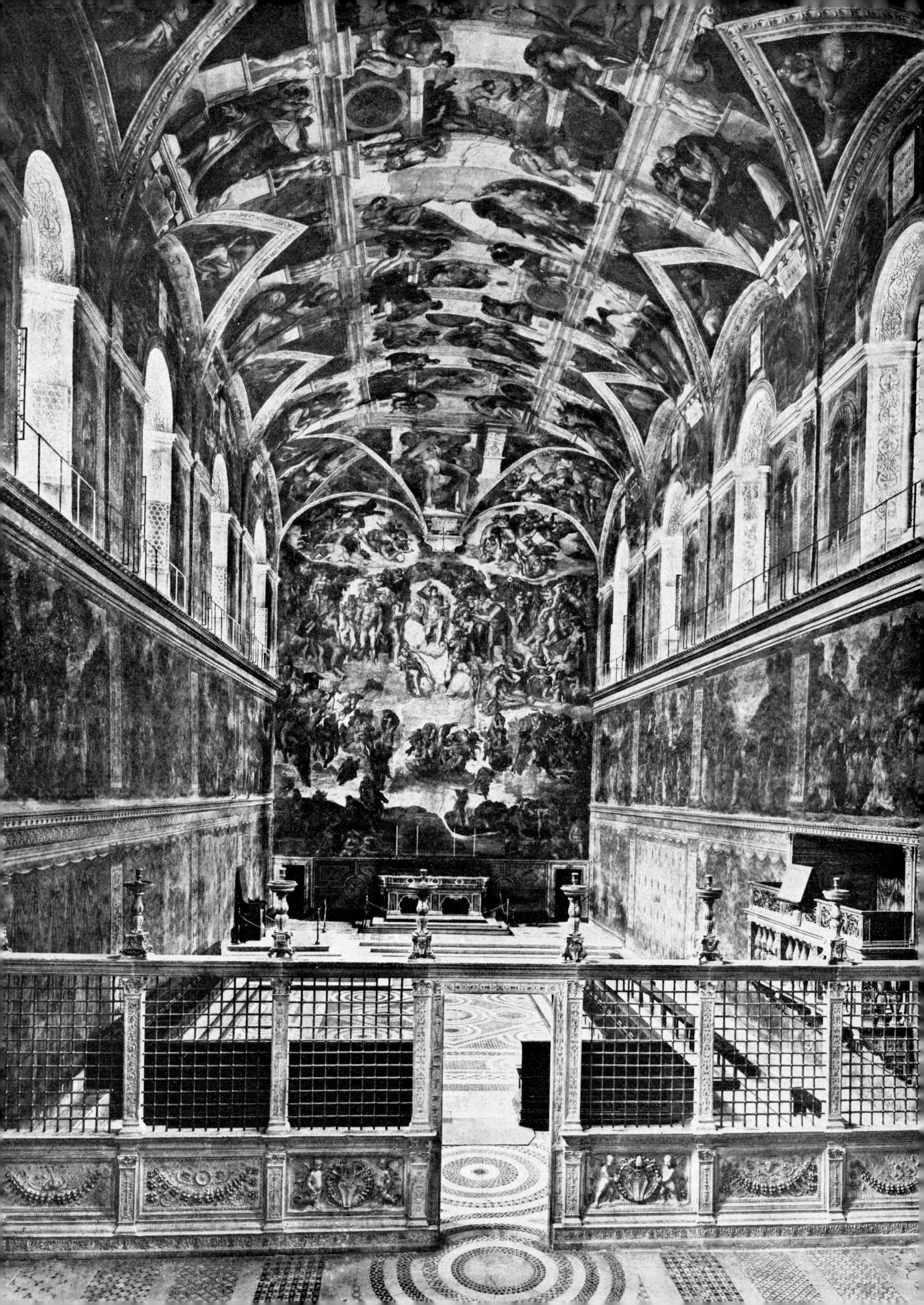

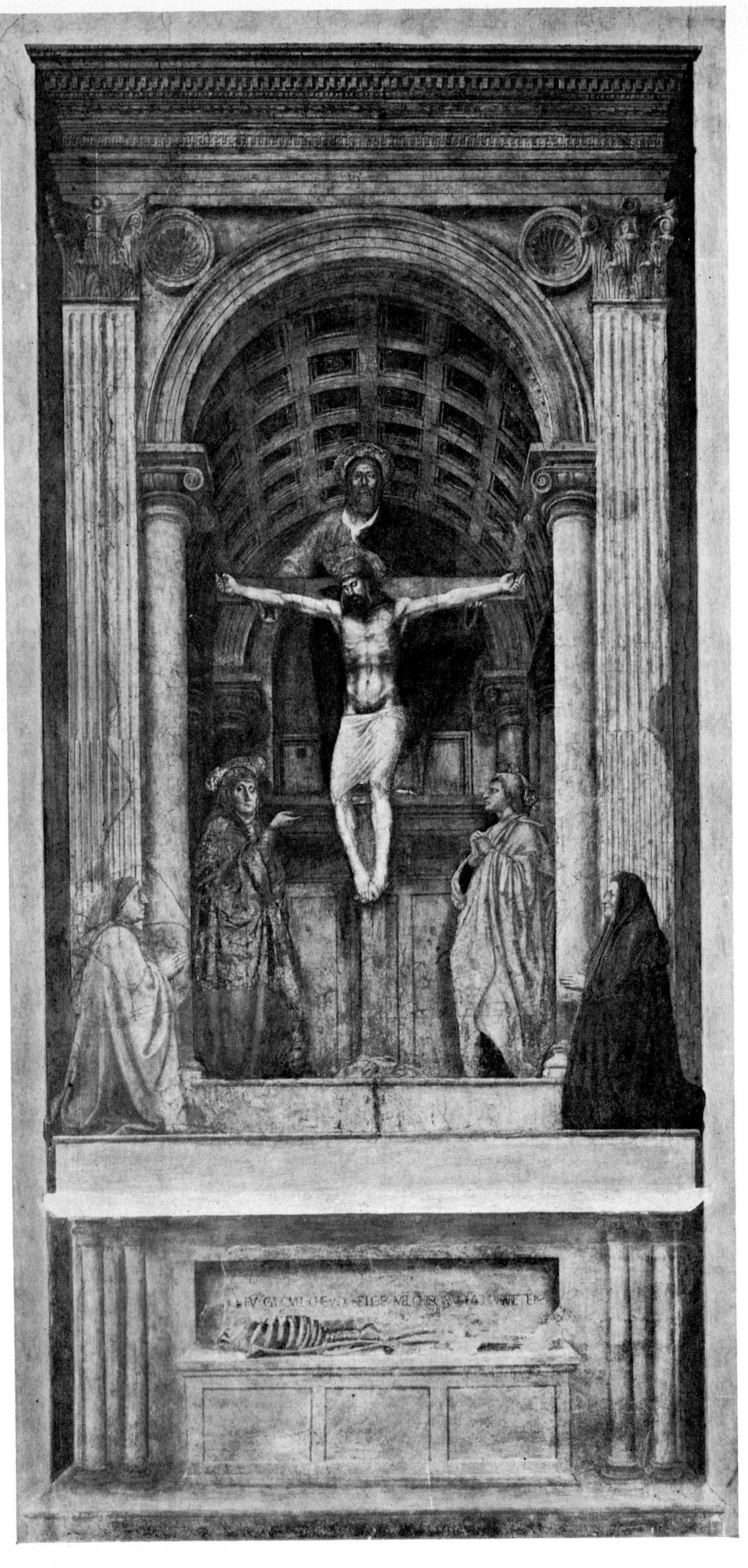

5. MASACCIO (1401–*c.* 1428): *The Holy Trinity with the Virgin and St. John the Evangelist, Adored by the Donor and his Wife.* 1426–7. Fresco. Florence, Santa Maria Novella

6. GENTILE DA FABRIANO (*c.* 1370–1427 *The Adoration of the Magi.* 1423. Pane 118 × 111 in. Florence, Uffizi

Painted in the same city and in the same decade, these two pictures sho the transition, in style and in spirit, t the Renaissance. Gentile's altarpiece looks back to the medieval vision of terrestrial happiness: a gorgeous cavalcade come to do homage to a prince. Masaccio sets the divine mystery in a Renaissance chapel. Th Father is a hieratic icon, the Son's human nature is conveyed by the naturalistic rendering of the nude body, triumphing over death in the tomb-chamber beneath. The noble dignity of the sacred personages is shared by the kneeling donors.

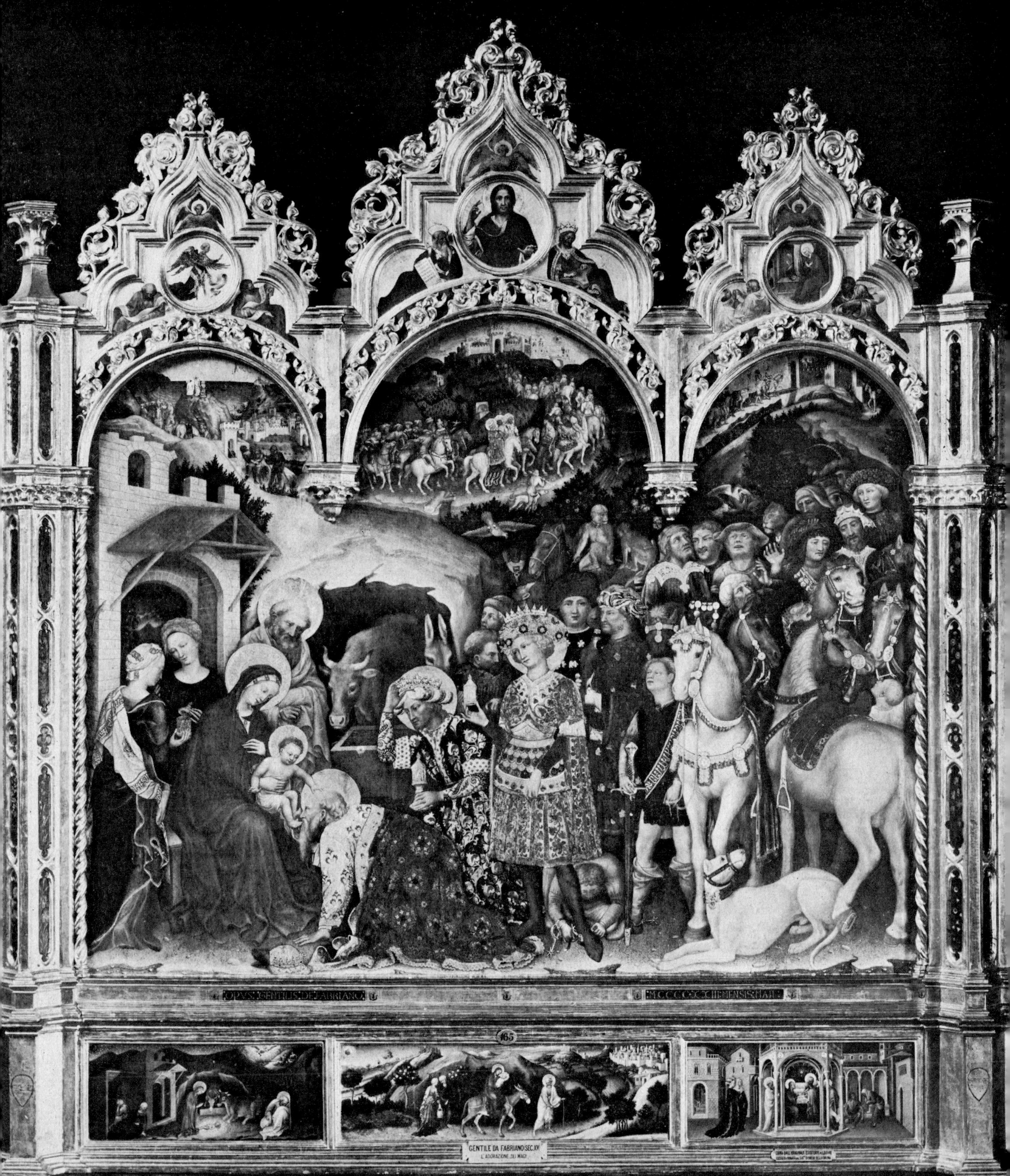
165
GENTILE DA FABRIANO SEC.XV
L'ADORAZIONE DEI MAGI

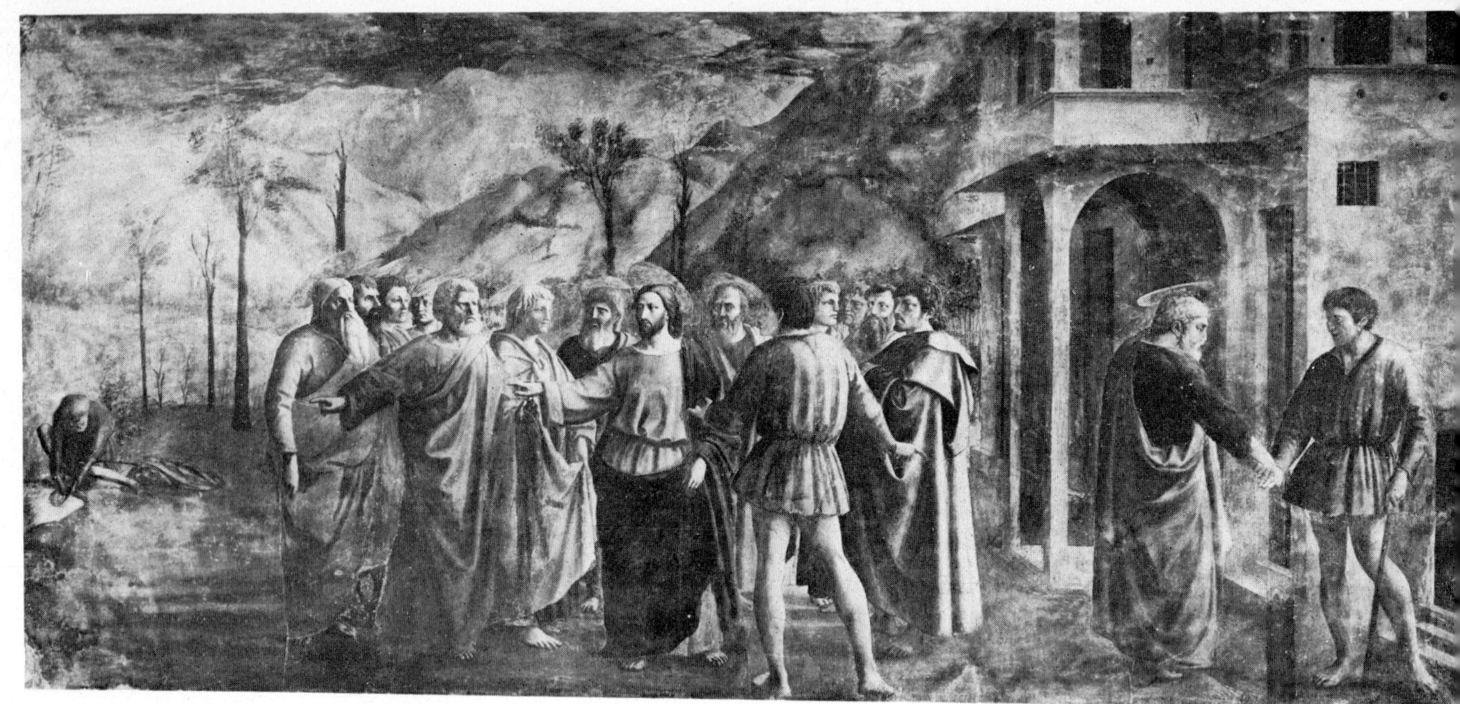

7. MASACCIO (1401–*c.* 1428): *The Tribute Money*. About 1425. Fresco. Florence, Santa Maria del Carmine, Brancacci Chapel

In the centre the gate-keeper of Capernaum, clad in a short tunic, demands payment of the dues. Christ is accompanied by the twelve Apostles and tells Peter to catch a fish in the lake of Galilee (Matthew 17:27). His hand and that of Peter point to the lakeside at the left, where the miracle is to take place, and where Peter is seen again, opening the mouth of the fish and finding a coin. On the right Peter is seen for the third time, paying the dues to the gate-keeper. The grave demeanour and statuesque poses of the central group are accentuated by the strong modelling in light and shade, which gives each figure weight and conviction, so that the spectator seems confronted, for the first time in the history of Italian painting, by idealized images of himself. Masaccio's fresco forms part of the decoration of the Brancacci Chapel (Plate 3). The series was painted, in collaboration with Masolino da Panicale, between 1425 and 1427; and eventually completed by Filippino Lippi in the mid-1480s.

8. MASACCIO (1401–*c.* 1428): *Head of the Virgin*. Detail from Plate 5

The bereaved Virgin, standing under the Cross, turns to the beholder with an expression of restrained grief. Her gaze (like the pointing gesture of her hand) mediates between us and her divine Son.

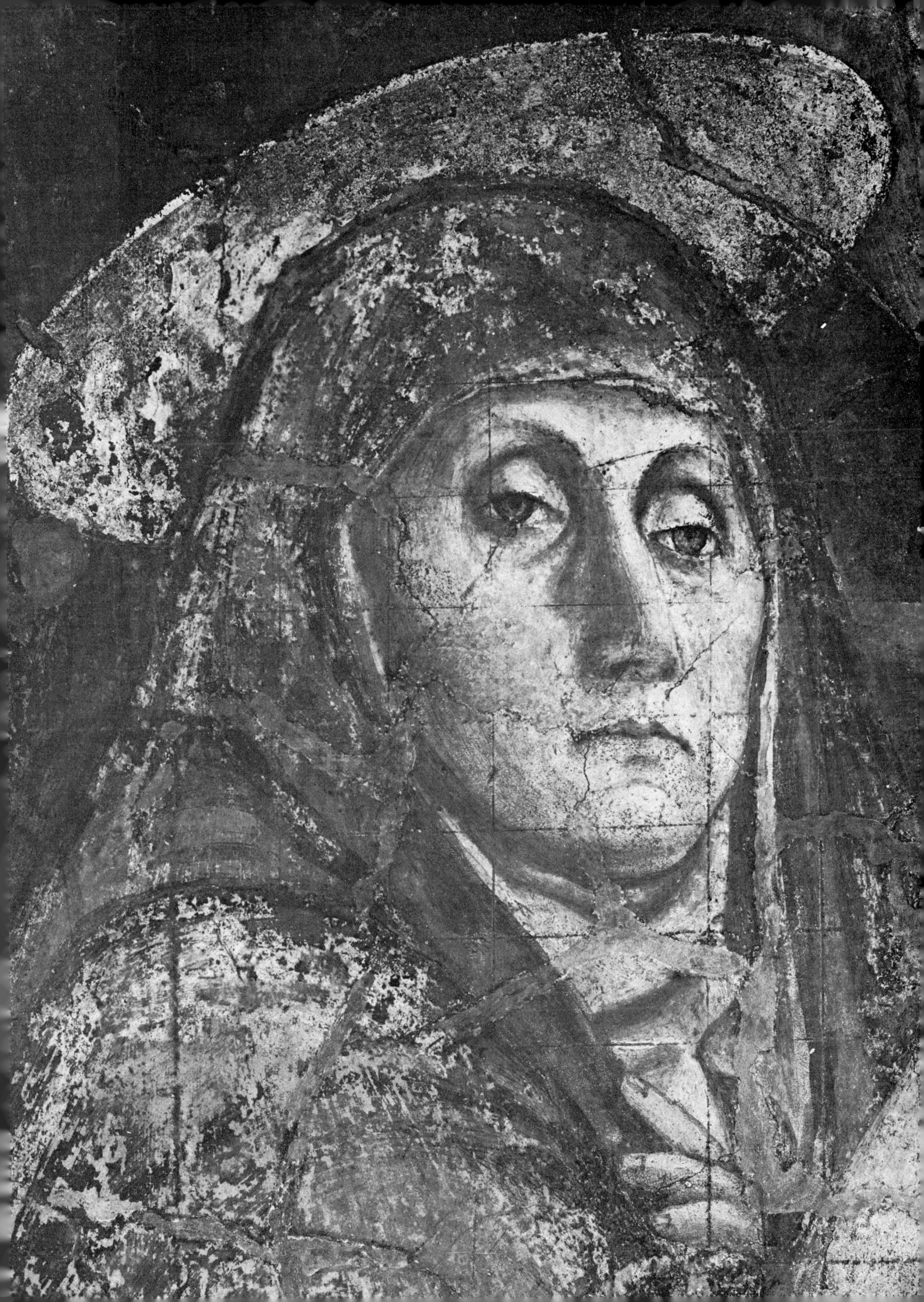

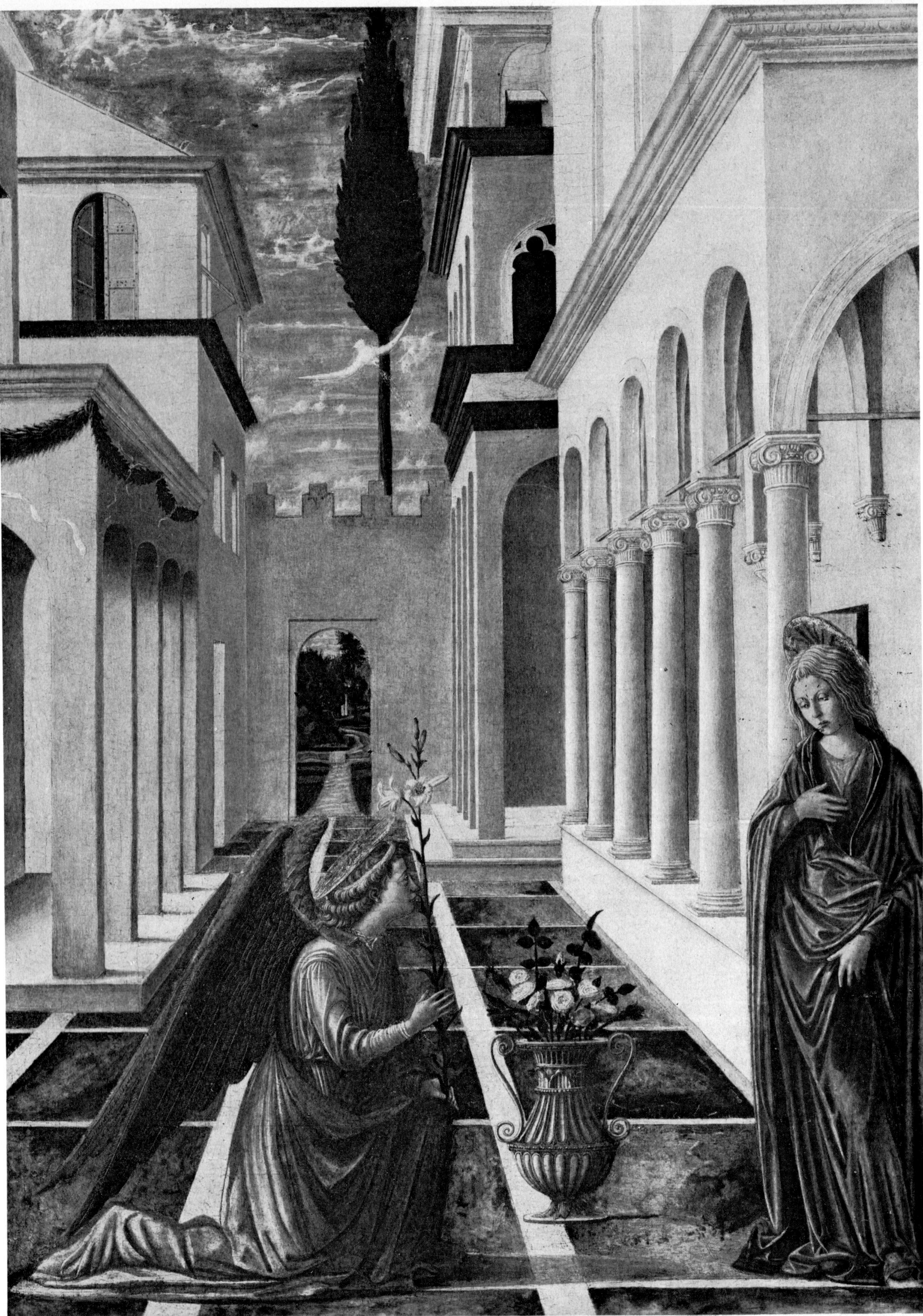

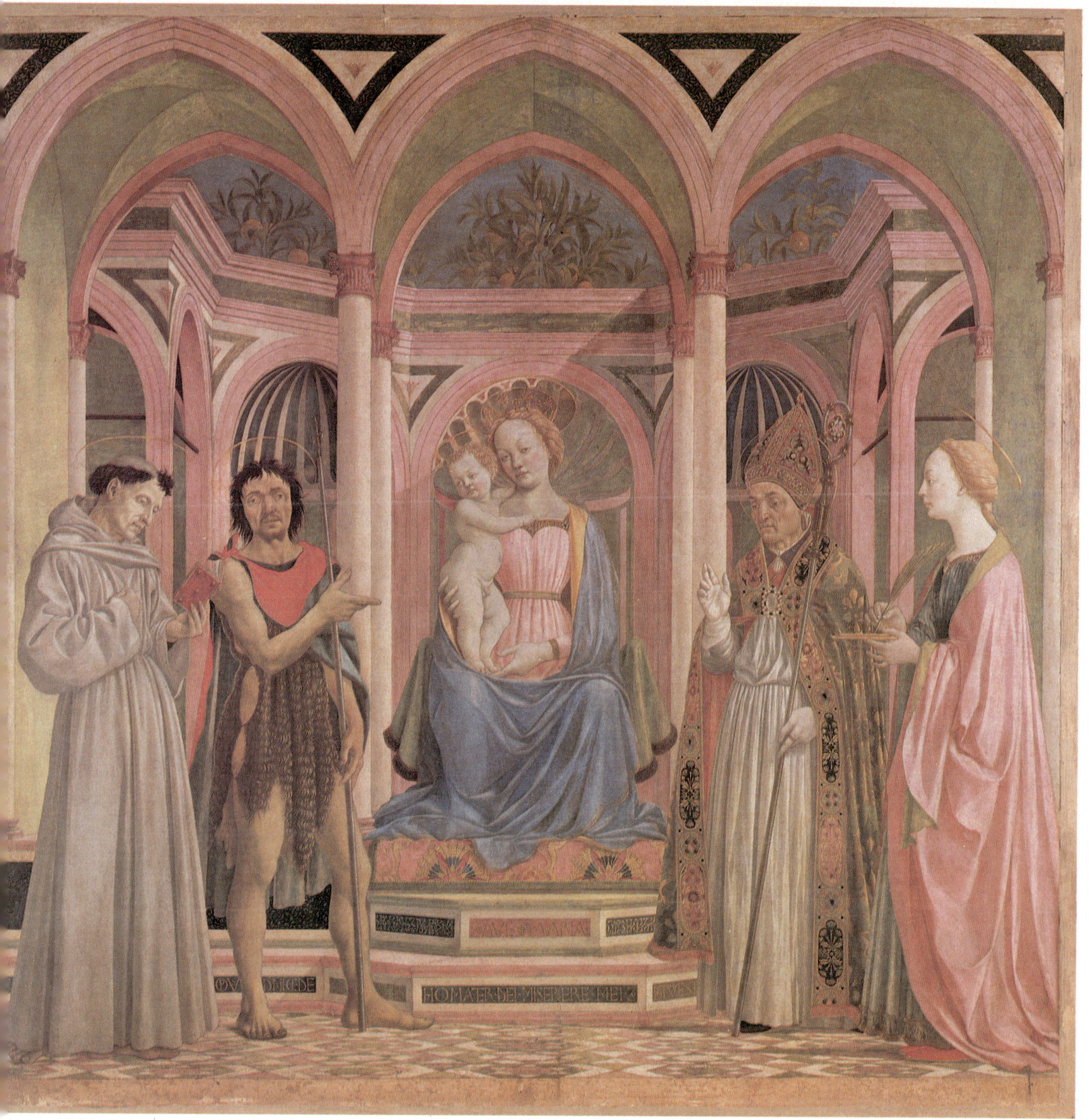

DOMENICO VENEZIANO (*c.* 1410–61): *The St. Lucy Altarpiece*. About 1445. Panel, 82¼ × 84 in. Florence, Uffizi

The Madonna holding the Christ Child is seated on a throne and flanked by St. Francis, St. John the Baptist, the bishop St. Zenobius (who enjoyed special veneration in Florence, see Plates 56, 57), and St. Lucy. St. John's gesture, pointing to the Redeemer, echoes his role in the gospels. The symmetry of the group is matched by the centralized perspective of the sumptuous setting, which reflects the achievements of contemporary architecture.

THE MASTER OF THE BARBERINI PANELS (active *c.* 1450–70): *The Annunciation*. About 1450. Panel, 34½ × 24½ in. Washington, D.C., National Gallery of Art (Samuel H. Kress Collection)

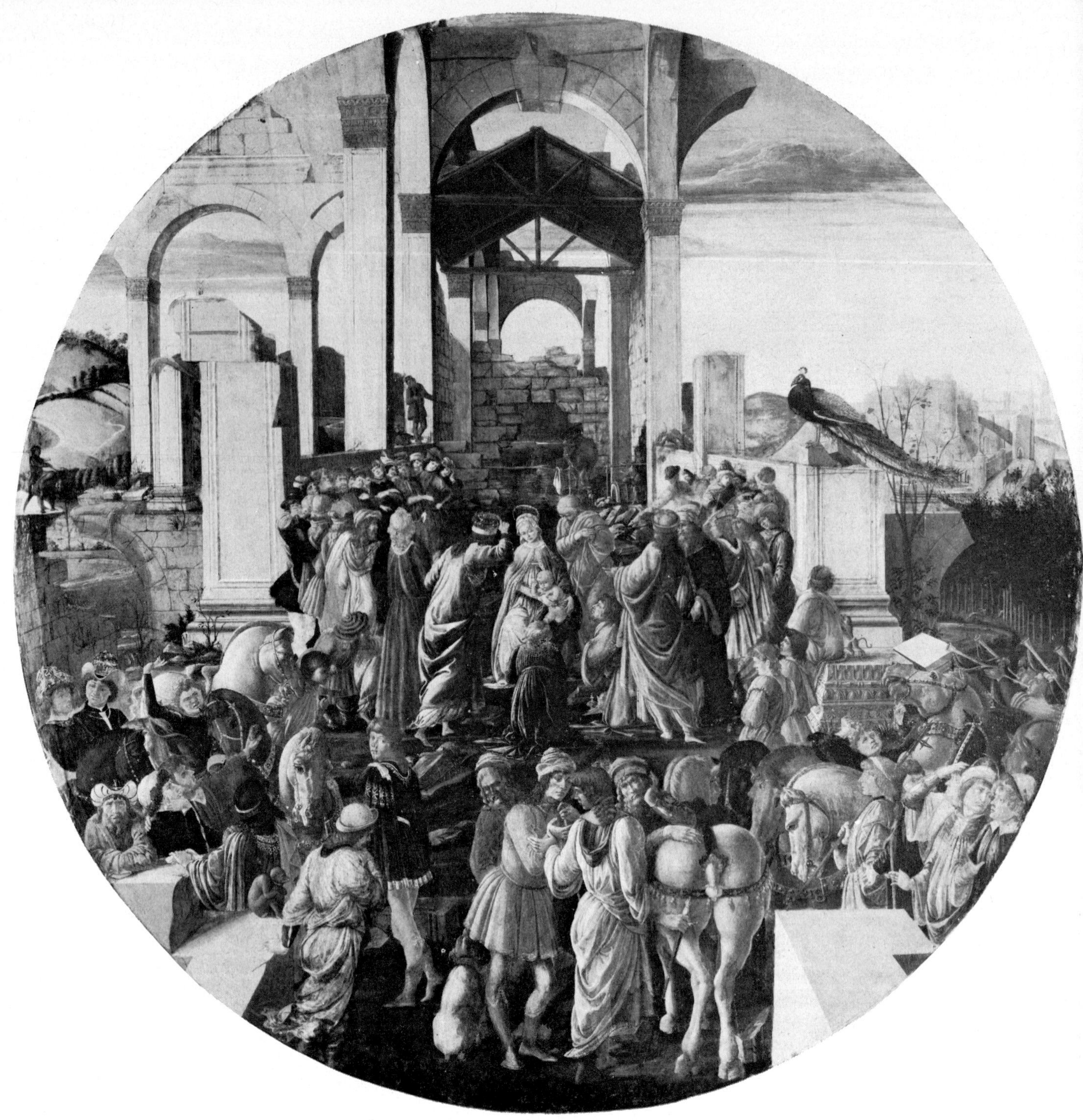

11. SANDRO BOTTICELLI (*c.* 1445–1510): *The Adoration of the Kings*. About 1472–6. Panel, 51½ in. diameter. London, National Gallery

The basic simplicity of the biblical narrative, and its want of incidental detail, has meant that artists, in addition to depicting a biblical scene, have felt free to embroider on it in their own way. Botticelli was obviously interested in Renaissance architecture, perspective and bodily movement. Note the way the lines of the perspective meet in the central group of the Holy Family.

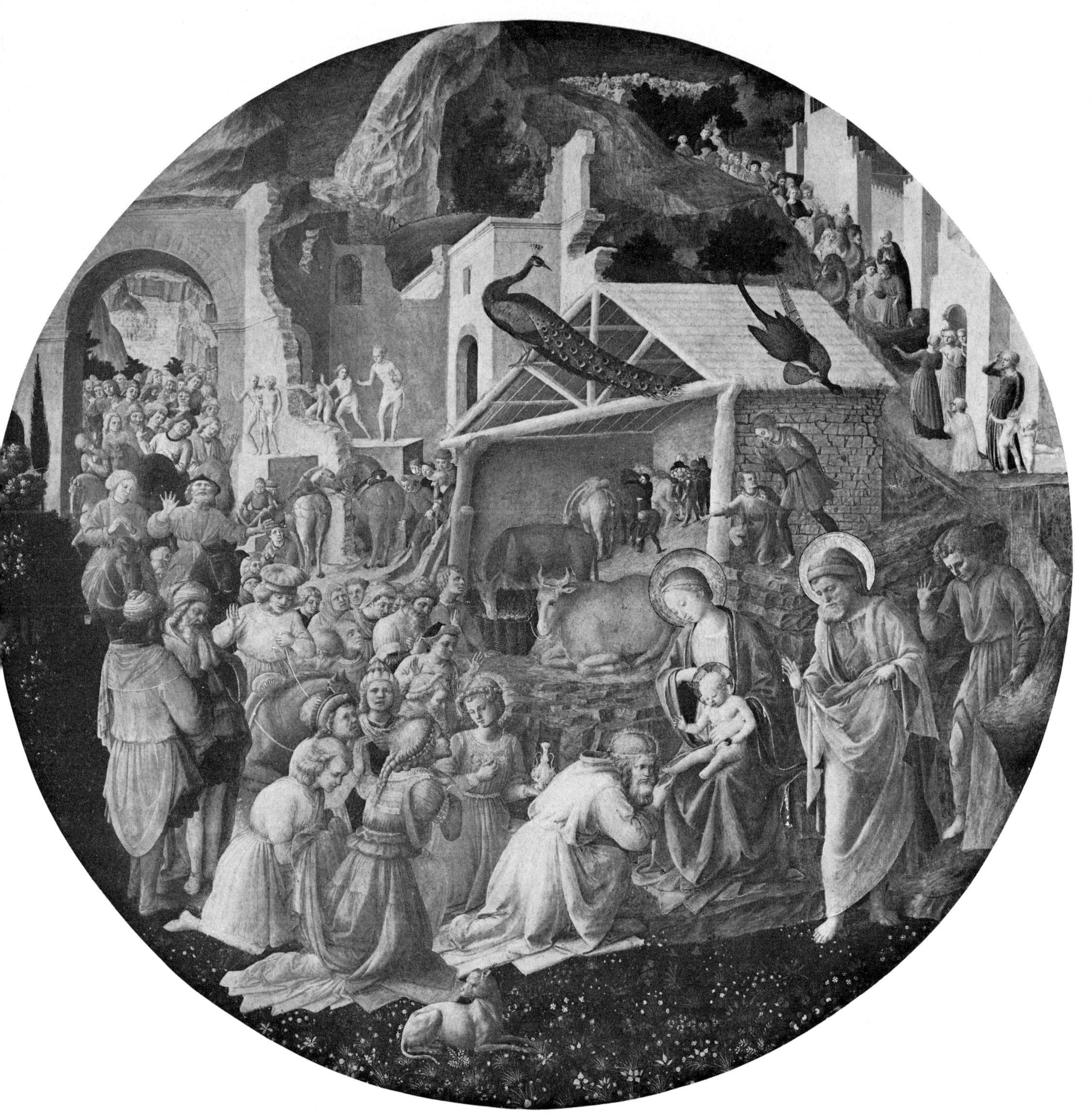

12. FRA ANGELICO (*c.* 1399–1455) and FRA FILIPPO LIPPI (*c.* 1406–69): *The Adoration of the Magi.* 1525–5. Panel, 54 in. diameter. Washington, D.C., National Gallery of Art (Samuel H. Kress Collection)

The throng of the kings' retinue is in marked contrast to the calm of the sacred group on the right, and is echoed in the crowd of curious spectators along the city wall. Delightful details, such as the boys climbing on the masonry, the small children clinging to their mother, the pair of pheasants, the bulldog, and the grooms in the stable, show a vivid and loving observation of daily life. The peacock with its gorgeous plumage is a symbol of the immortality of Christ.

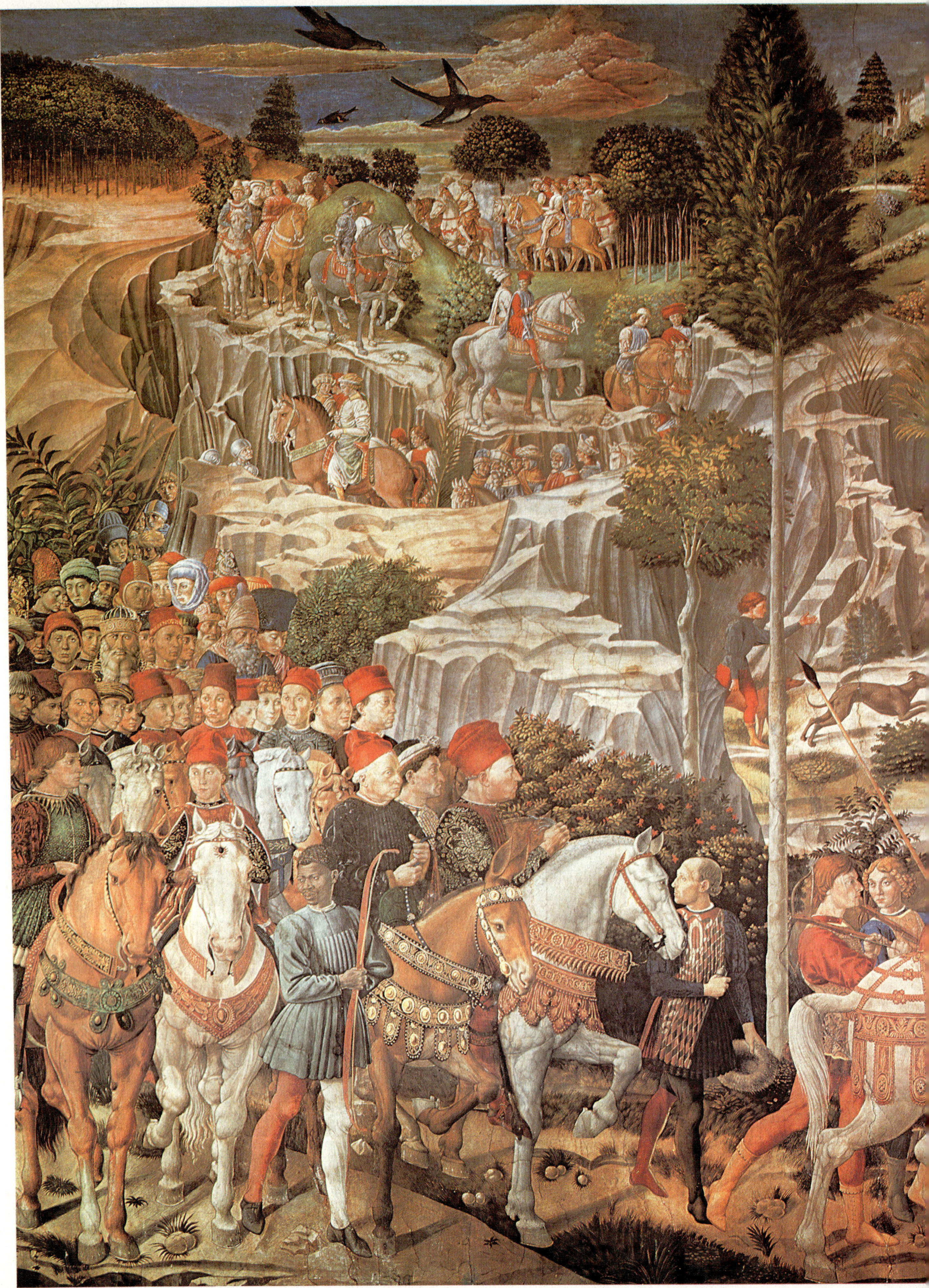

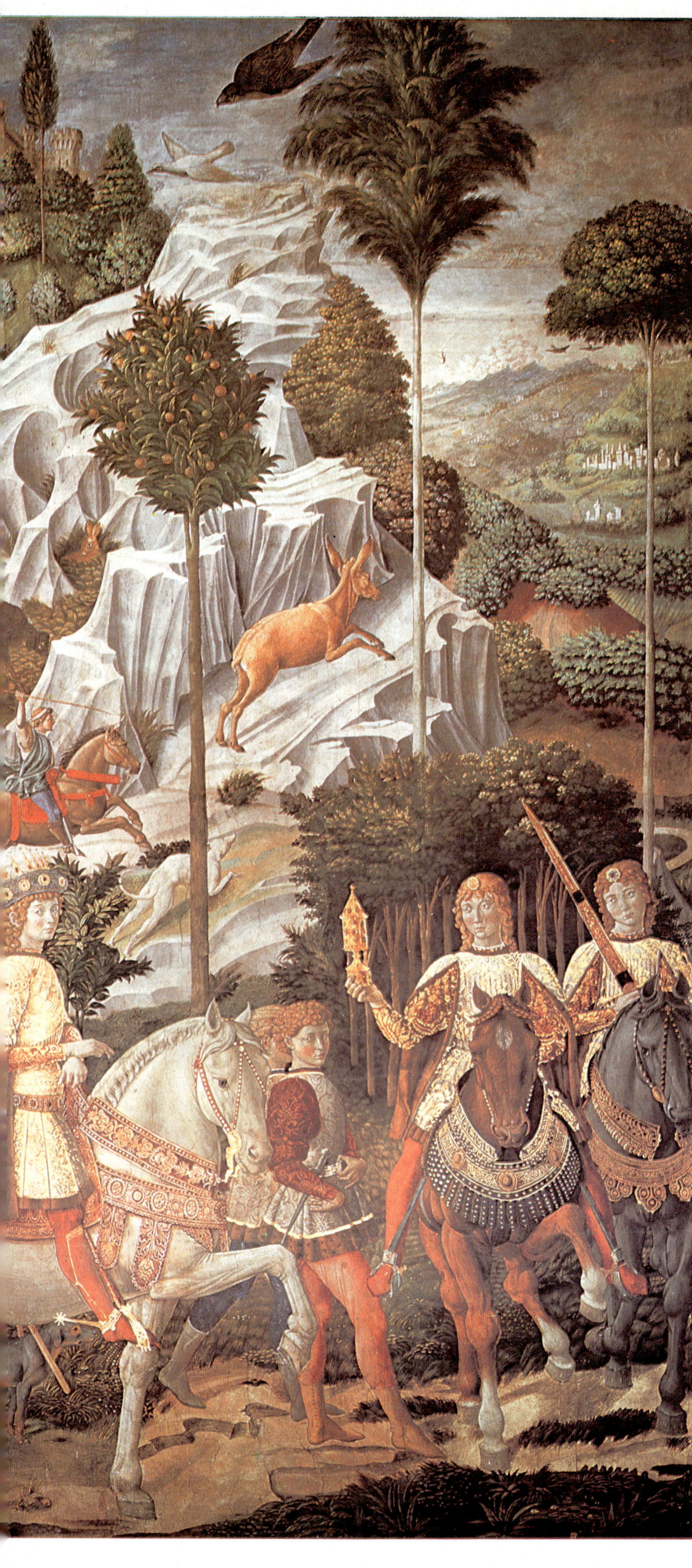

13. BENOZZO GOZZOLI (*c.* 1421–97): *The Journey of the Magi*. 1459–61. Fresco. Florence, Palazzo Medici-Riccardi

The king rides at the head of his resplendent retinue on the way to Bethlehem, where he will adore the new-born King of the Jews. The procession moves along the winding road on a rocky hillside, into a gorge, and emerges in the open country in the foreground.

Like Gentile's altarpiece (Plate 6), the fresco evokes an age of colourful chivalry and courtly splendour, but for all its 'medieval' features (such as the schematic rocks and the size of the deer fleeing from huntsman and hounds) the space is now more convincingly organized. The fresco covers one of three walls which Gozzoli painted in the private chapel of the Medici, the richest merchants in Florence; the four horsemen in the left foreground are portraits of members of the family.

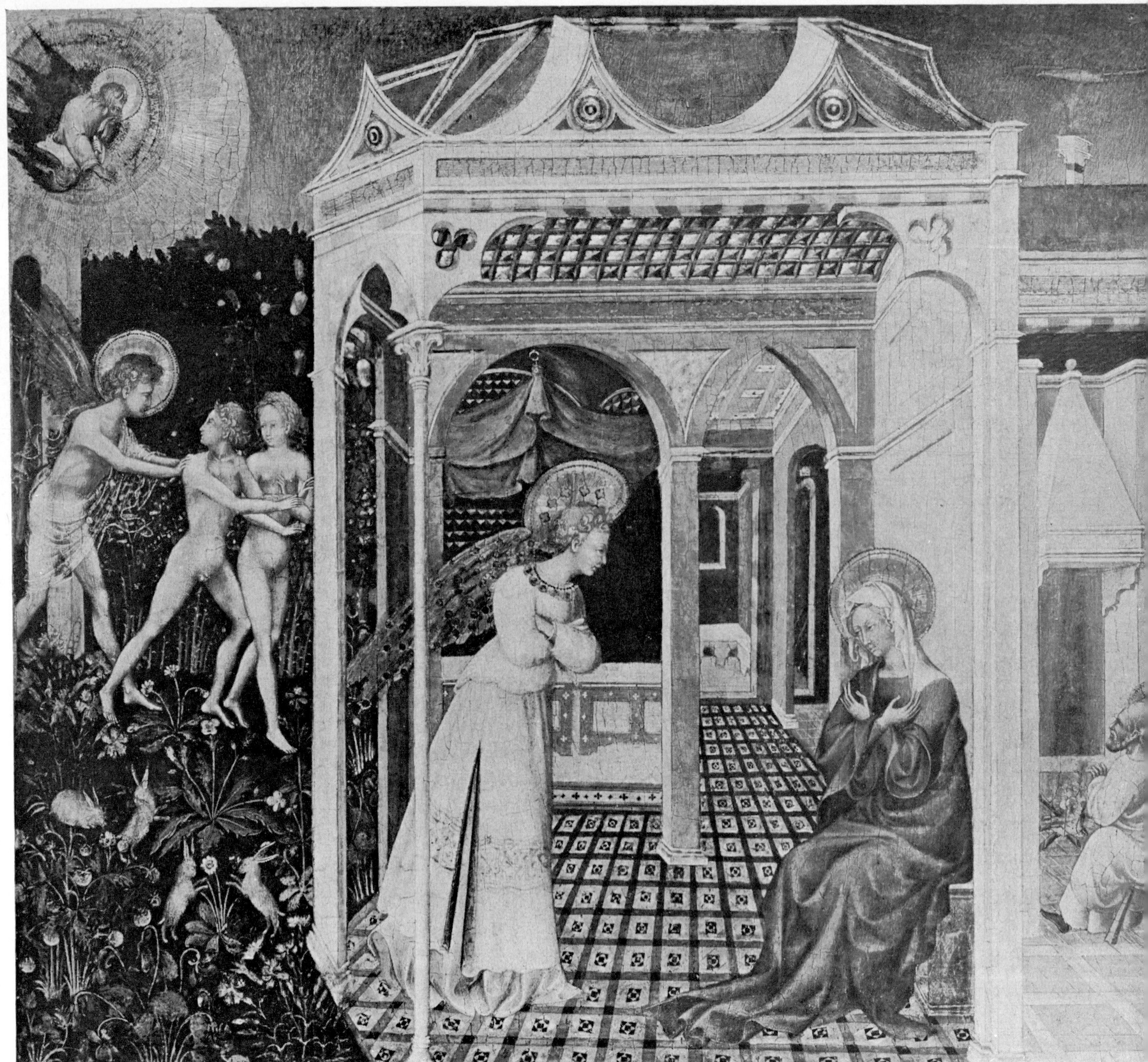

14. GIOVANNI DI PAOLO (*c.* 1399–1482): *The Annunciation.* About 1445. Panel, $15\frac{3}{4} \times 18\frac{1}{4}$ in. Washington, D.C., National Gallery of Art (Samuel H. Kress Collection)

The principal scene is set in a schematically rendered building, where the angel Gabriel gives the Virgin Mary the divine message of the birth of Christ. God the Father looks down from on high. On the left the building opens onto a spring meadow (the feast of the Annunciation is celebrated on 25 March), where the angel drives Adam and Eve from the garden of Paradise. On the enchanting carpet of flowers gambol two pairs of rabbits, symbolizing the temptations of the flesh to which the human race is henceforward subject. The scenes of the Fall and the Redemption lead the eye to the narrow strip at the right: here it is winter, the season of the Nativity, and St. Joseph warms his hands over a blazing fire.

Giovanni di Paolo belonged to the Sienese School, which in the fifteenth century was much less advanced than its Florentine counterpart.

15. SASSETTA (*c.* 1392–1450): *The Journey of the Magi*. About 1449. Panel, $8\frac{1}{2} \times 11\frac{3}{8}$ in. New York, Metropolitan Museum of Art

A particularly good example of Sassetta's style, with its emphasis on linear pattern and sweetness of mood. His pictures are seldom dramatic and he was never very interested in the realistic rendering of anatomy pioneered in Florence. However, he was fascinated by perspective, which he obviously worked out with care, especially in some of the scenes in his best known work, the polyptych illustrating the life of St. Francis, of which seven panels are now in the National Gallery, London. Sassetta was the major figure in fifteenth-century Sienese painting.

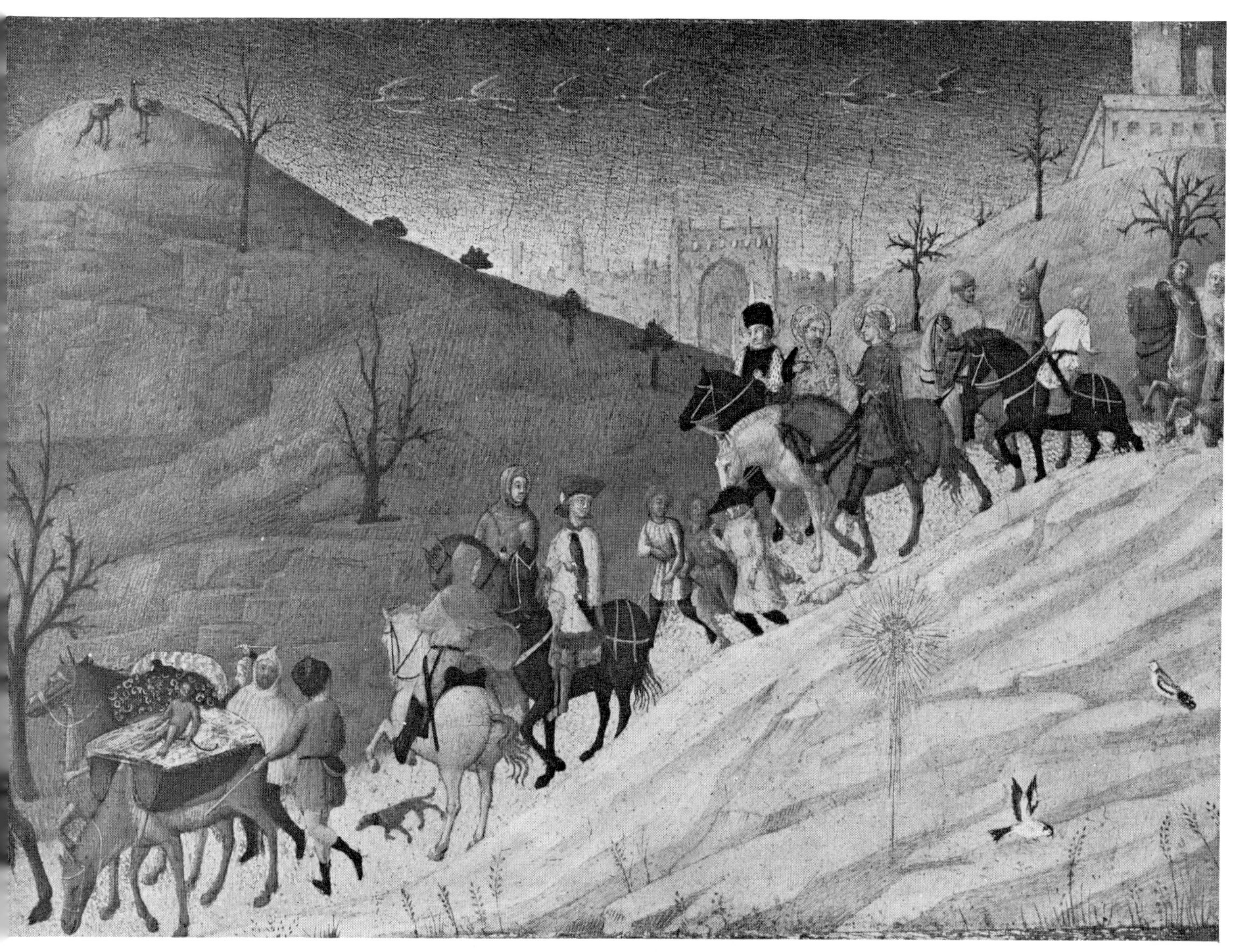

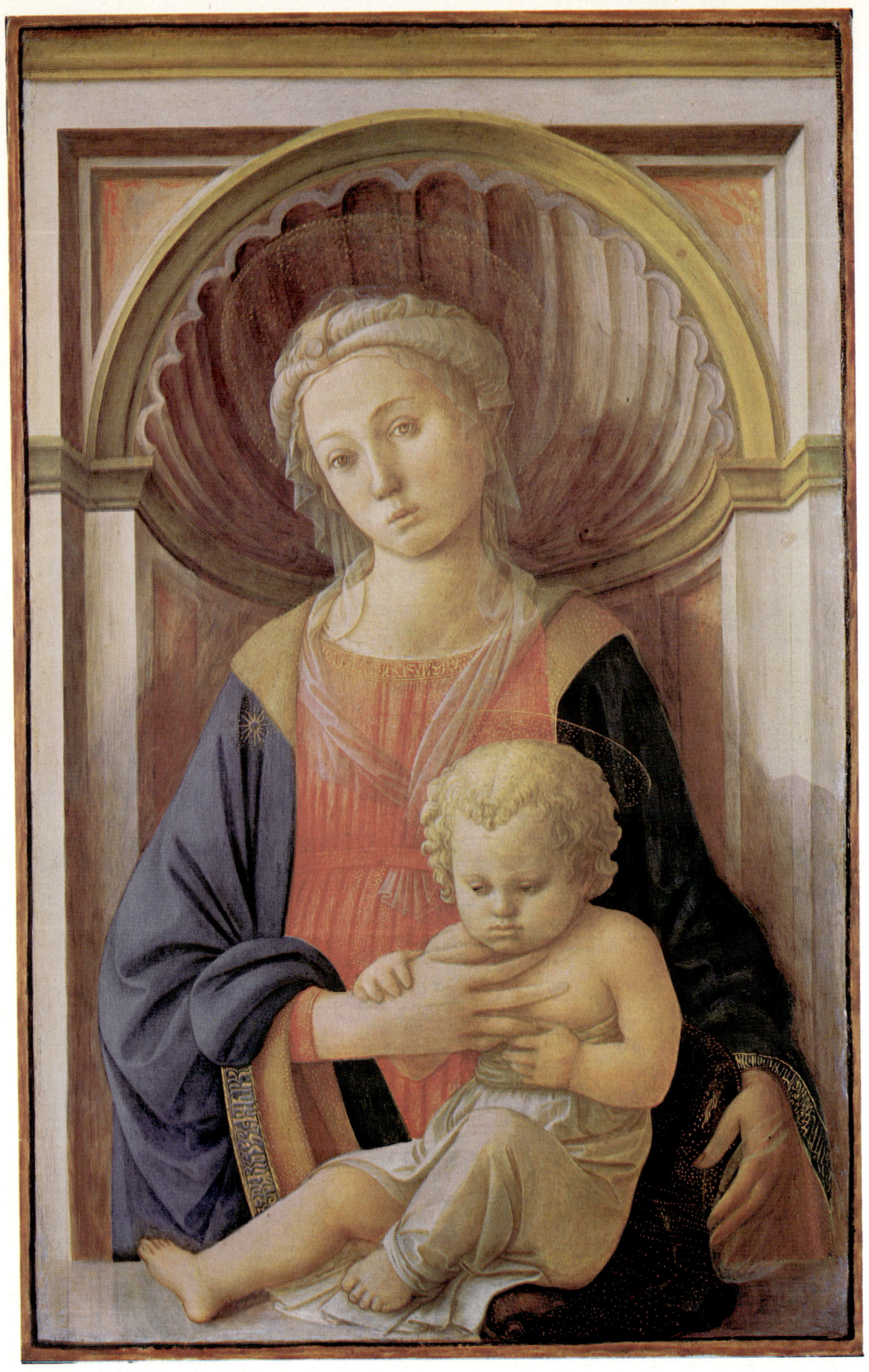

16. FRA FILIPPO LIPPI (*c.* 1406–69): *The Virgin and Child*. 1440–5. Panel, 31½ × 20¼ in. Washington, D.C., National Gallery of Art (Samuel H. Kress Collection)

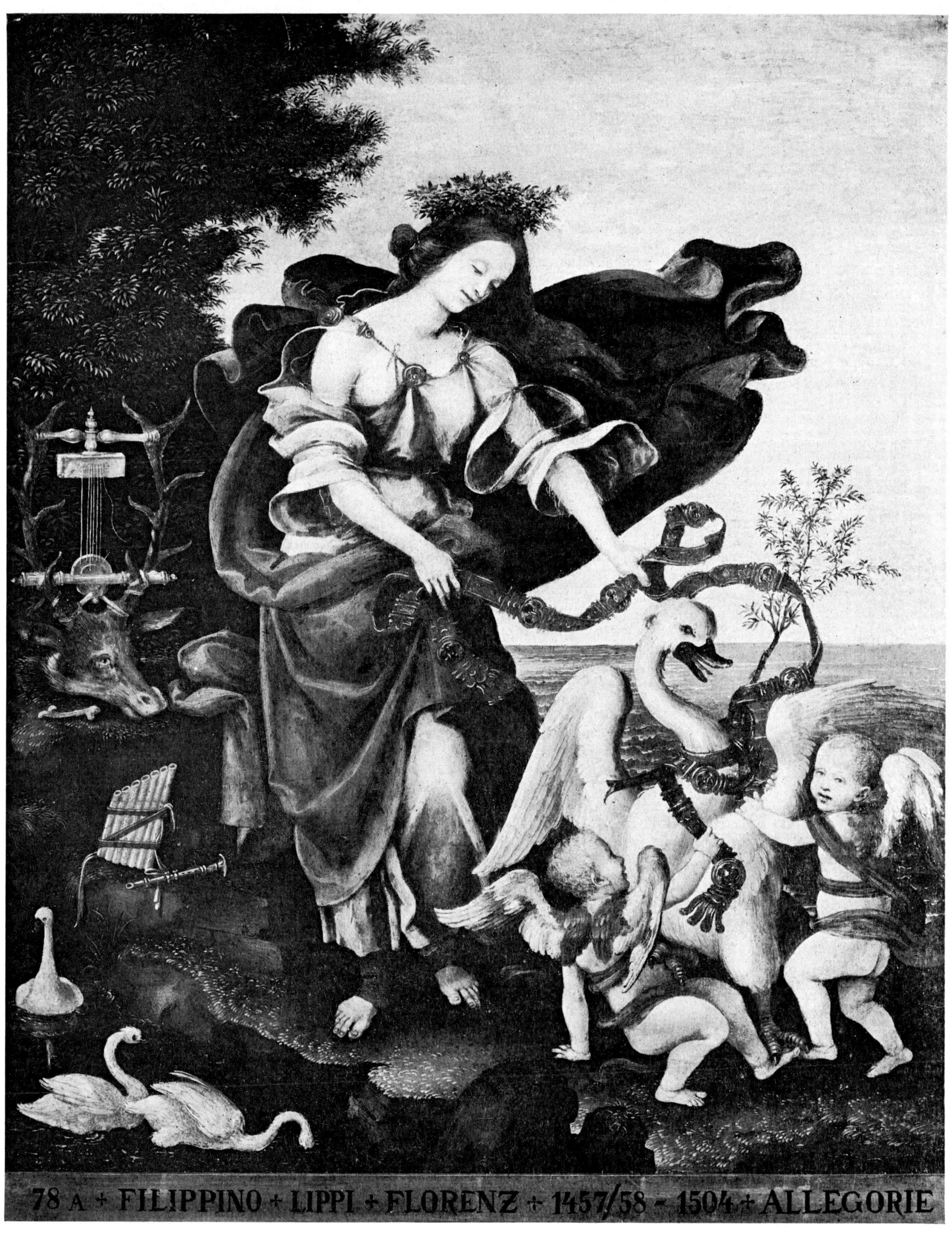

17. FILIPPINO LIPPI (*c.* 1457–1504): *Allegory of Music*. About 1500. Panel, $24\frac{1}{4} \times 20$ in. Berlin–Dahlem, Staatliche Museen

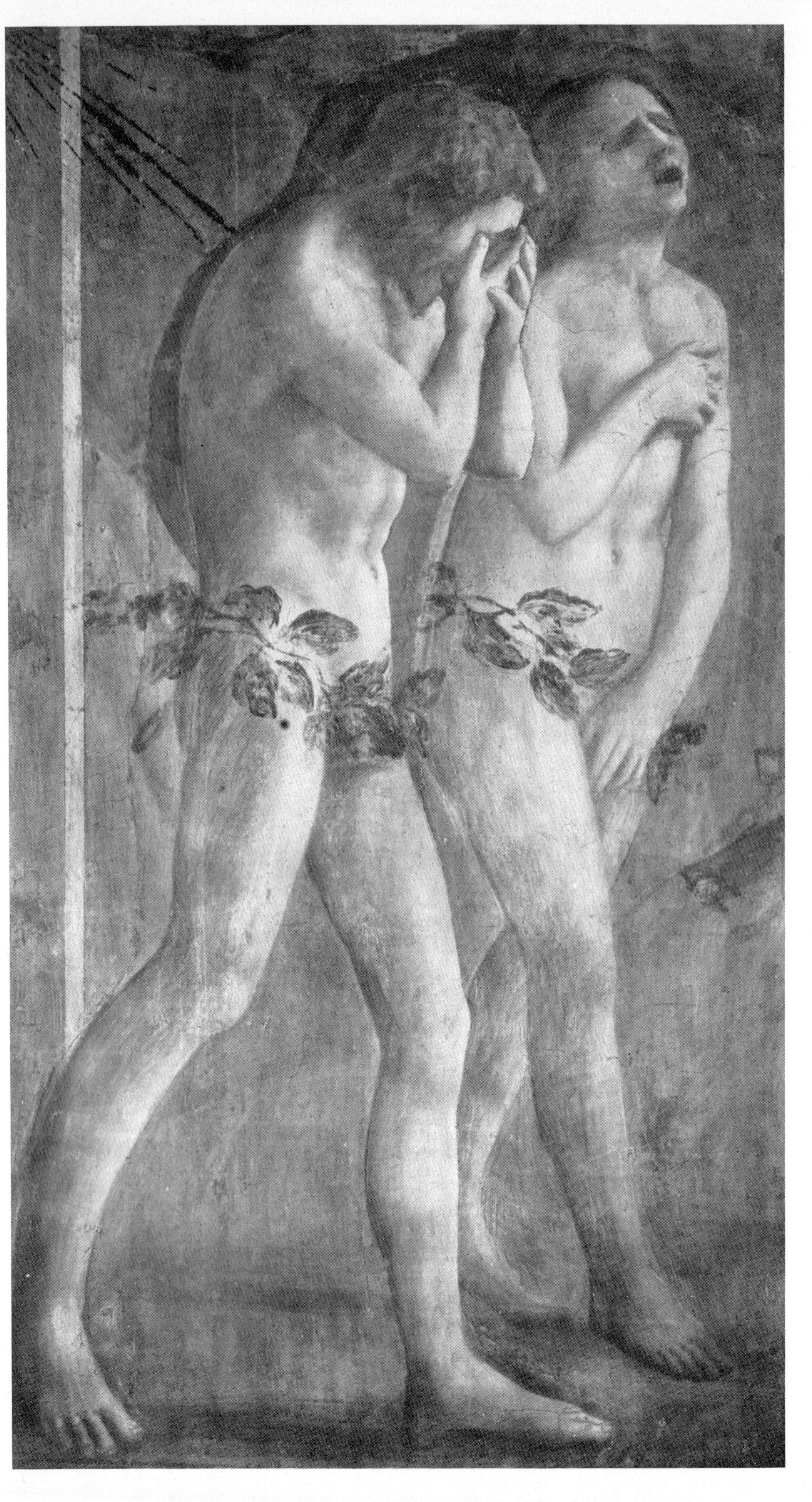

18. MASACCIO (1401–c. 1428): *Adam and Eve being Expelled from Paradise*. Detail. 1425–8. Fresco. Florence, Santa Maria del Carmine, Brancacci Chapel

'Adam and Eve stride away from Eden heart-broken with shame and grief, hearing, perhaps, but not seeing, the angel hovering high over-head, who directs their exiled footsteps.' (B. Berenson) This fresco is on the pier to the left of the *Tribute Money* (see Plate 3). A later, yet much more 'medieval' rendering of the subject appears in Plate 14.

19. MASOLINO (*c.* 1383–after 1432?): *The Temptation*. 1423–30. Fresco. Florence, Santa Maria del Carmine, Brancacci Chapel

Eve has taken a fruit from the Tree of Knowledge and shares it with Adam, while the Tempter, a human-headed serpent, looks down at them. Masolino worked in the Brancacci Chapel at the same time as Masaccio (Plates 3, 7, 18, 22), but his figures are much stiffer and more awkwardly posed, and he had no share in the stylistic revolution initiated by his younger colleague.

Masolino is in fact a somewhat mysterious artist, about whom very little is known. It is possible that he worked in the studio of the sculptor Ghiberti, at the time when the latter was engaged on the first set of doors for the Baptistry at Florence (1403–7); but his career remains shadowy until 1423, when he became a member of the Florentine Painters' Guild. In 1427 he went to Hungary, after a short phase in the Brancacci Chapel assisting Masaccio, by whom he was undoubtedly influenced.

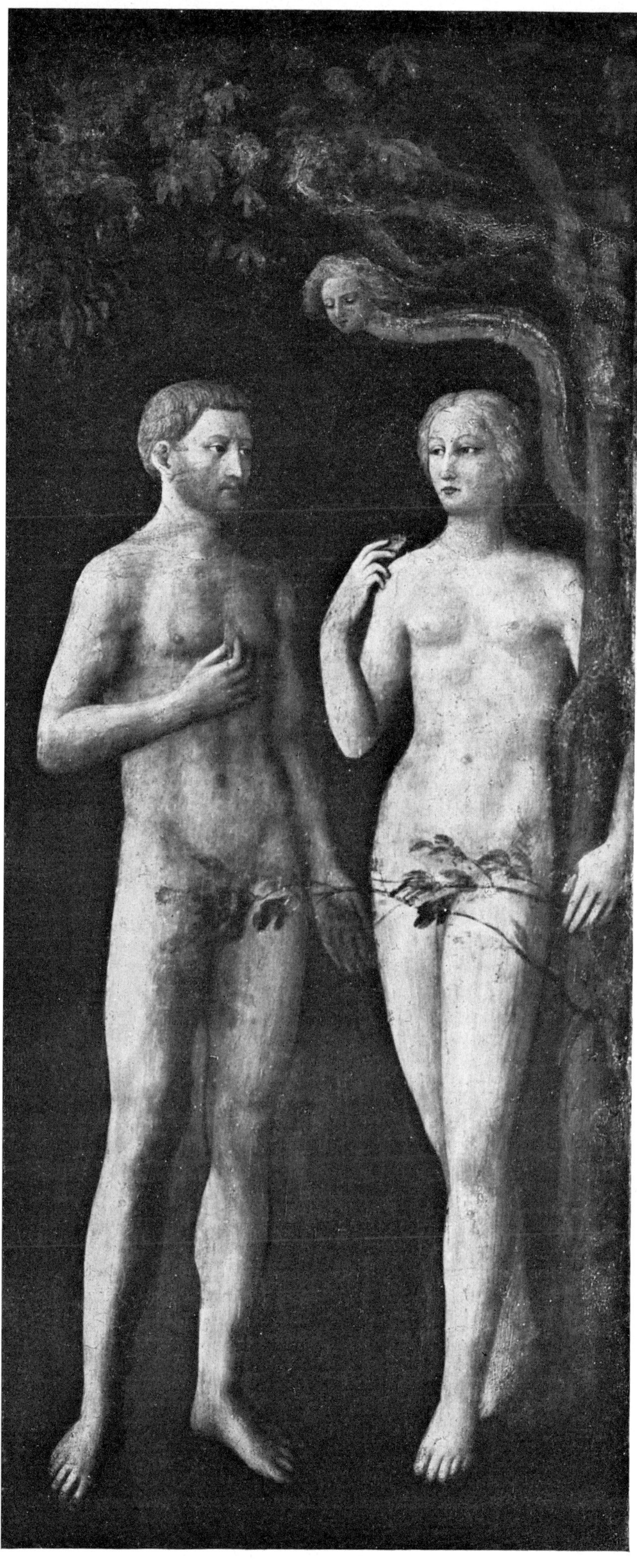

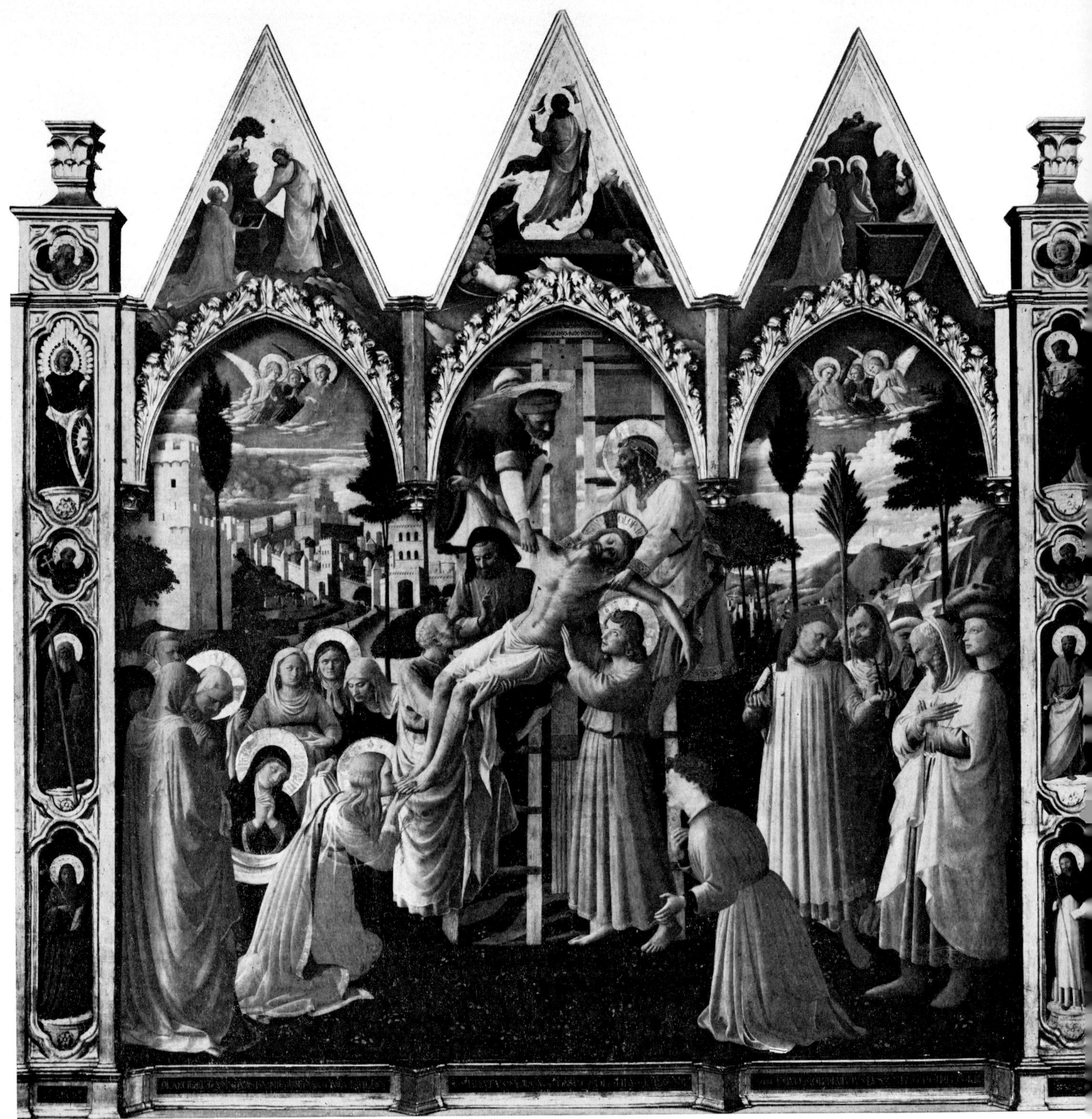

20. FRA ANGELICO (*c.* 1399–1455): *The Deposition from the Cross.* About 1443. Panel, $69\frac{1}{4} \times 72\frac{3}{4}$ in. Florence, Museo di San Marco

The kneeling figure in the foreground invites us to take part in an elaborately organized Easter meditation. As the dead Christ is tenderly lowered from the Cross, the young St. John reverently touches the body and St. Mary Magdalene kisses the feet. The other holy women surround the bereaved Virgin, and male mourners close the composition on the right. The idealized Tuscan landscape, bathed in the light of spring, gives the sorrowful scene an added immediacy. The three pinnacles at the top and the pilasters at the sides had been painted almost twenty years earlier by Lorenzo Monaco.

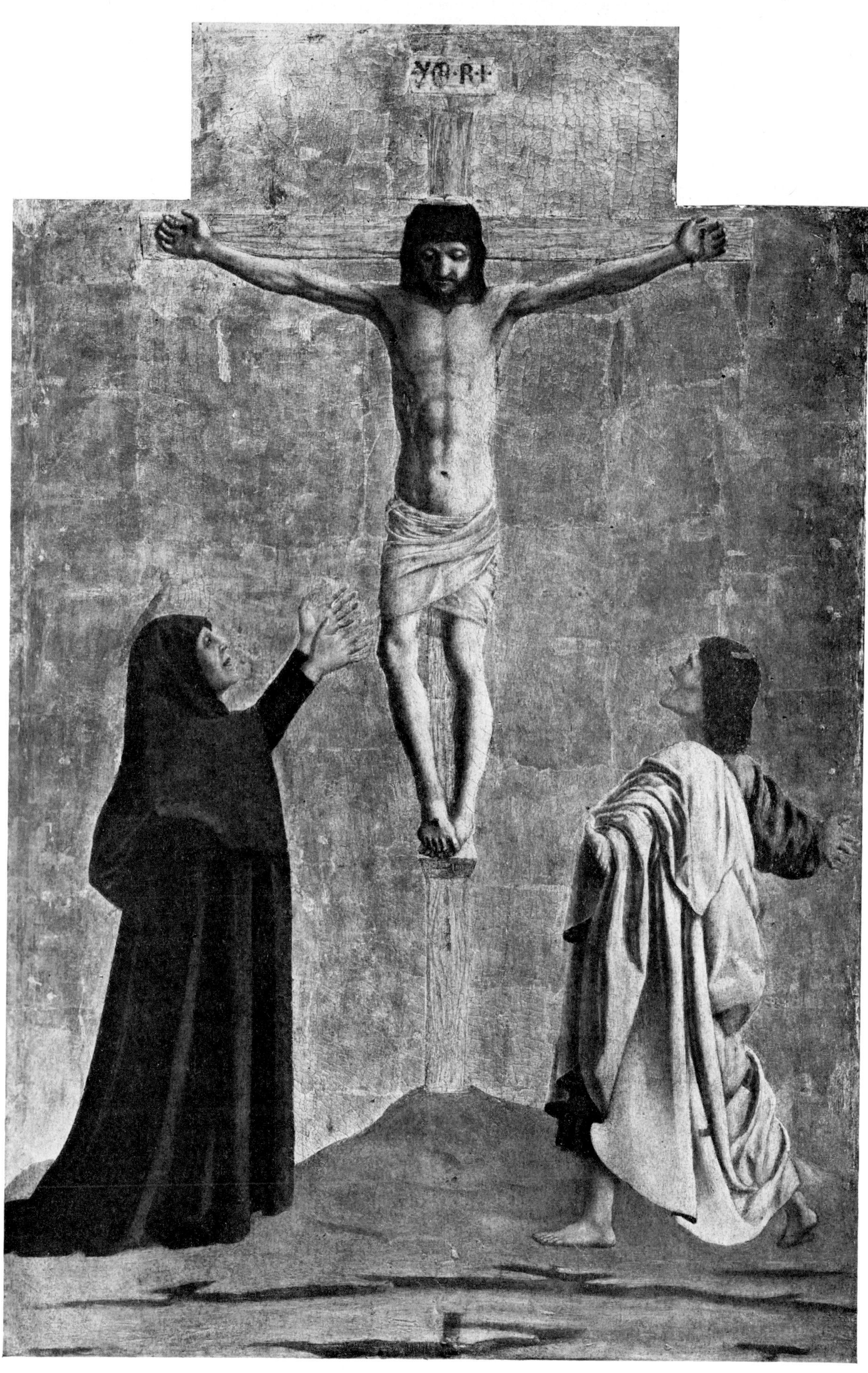

21. PIERO DELLA FRANCESCA (before 1420–92): *Christ on the Cross with the Virgin and St. John the Evangelist.* 1446–9. Panel, $32\frac{3}{4} \times 21\frac{1}{2}$ in. Borgo San Sepolcro, Palazzo Comunale

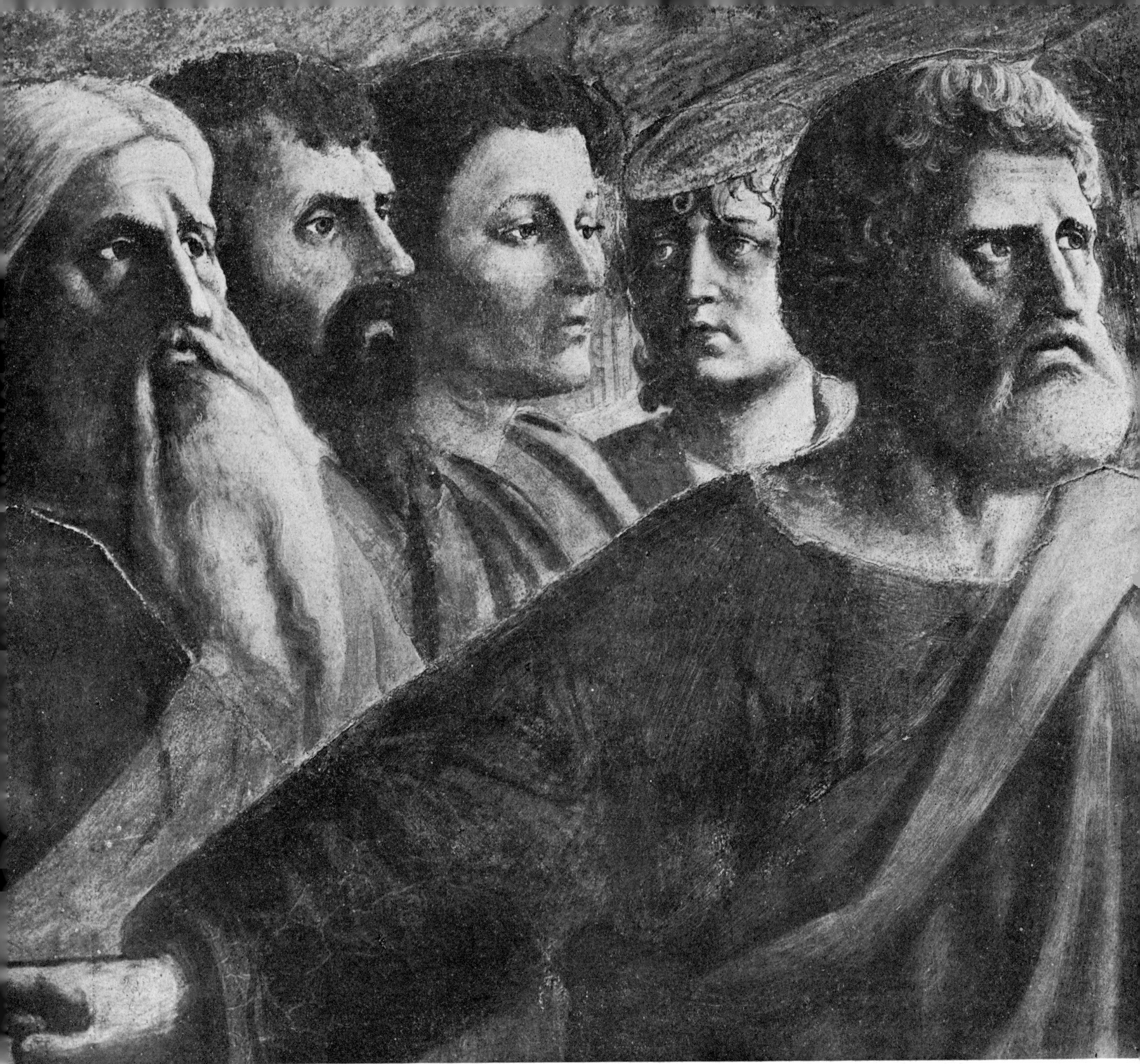

22. MASACCIO (1401–c. 1428): *St. Peter and four other Apostles*. Detail from Plate 7

A strong light lends a sculptural solidity to the features of the Apostles. Those of the bystanders at the Deposition (opposite) are bathed in the softer light of a spring day.

23. FRA ANGELICO (c. 1399–1455): *A Group of Onlookers*. Detail from Plate

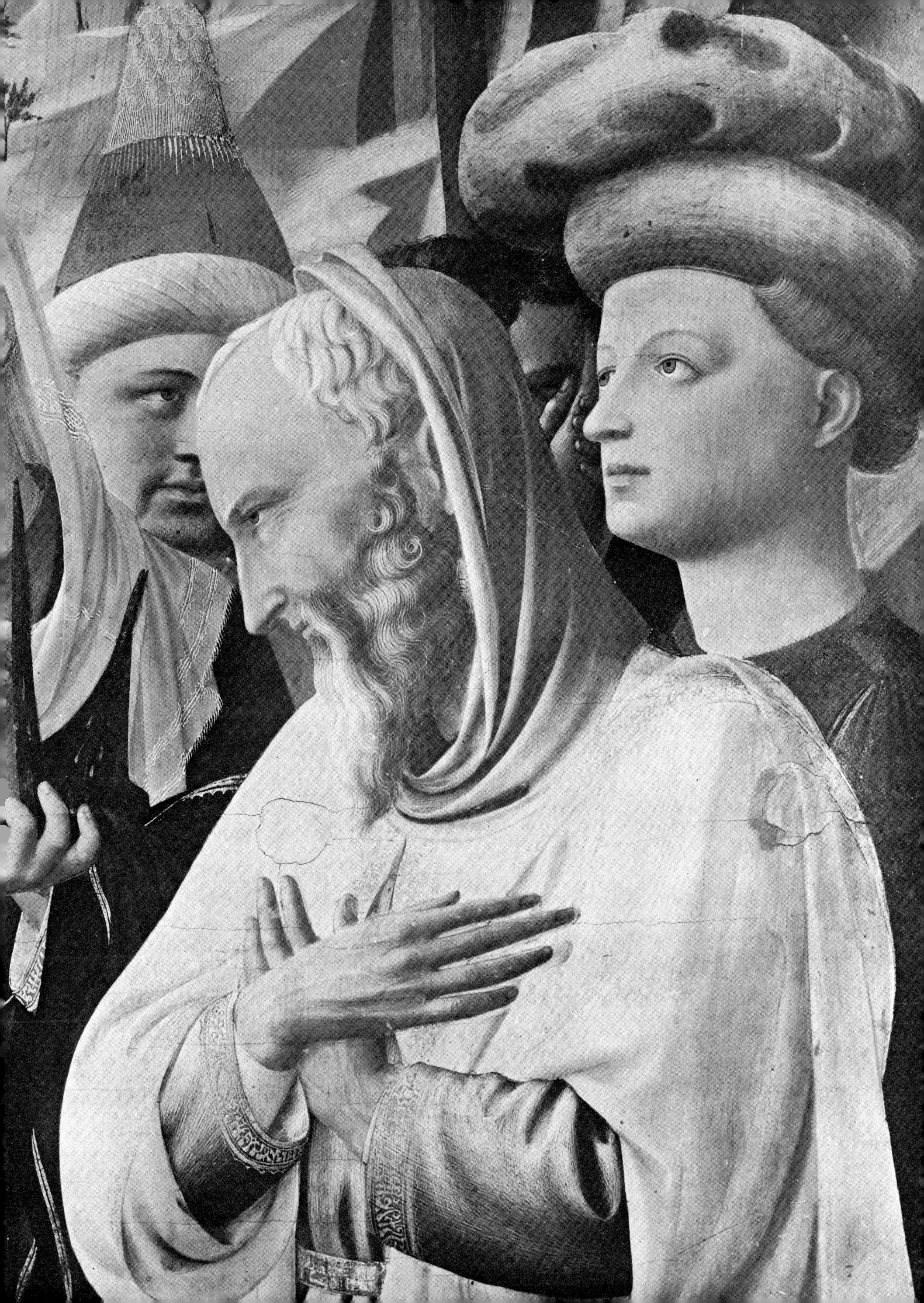

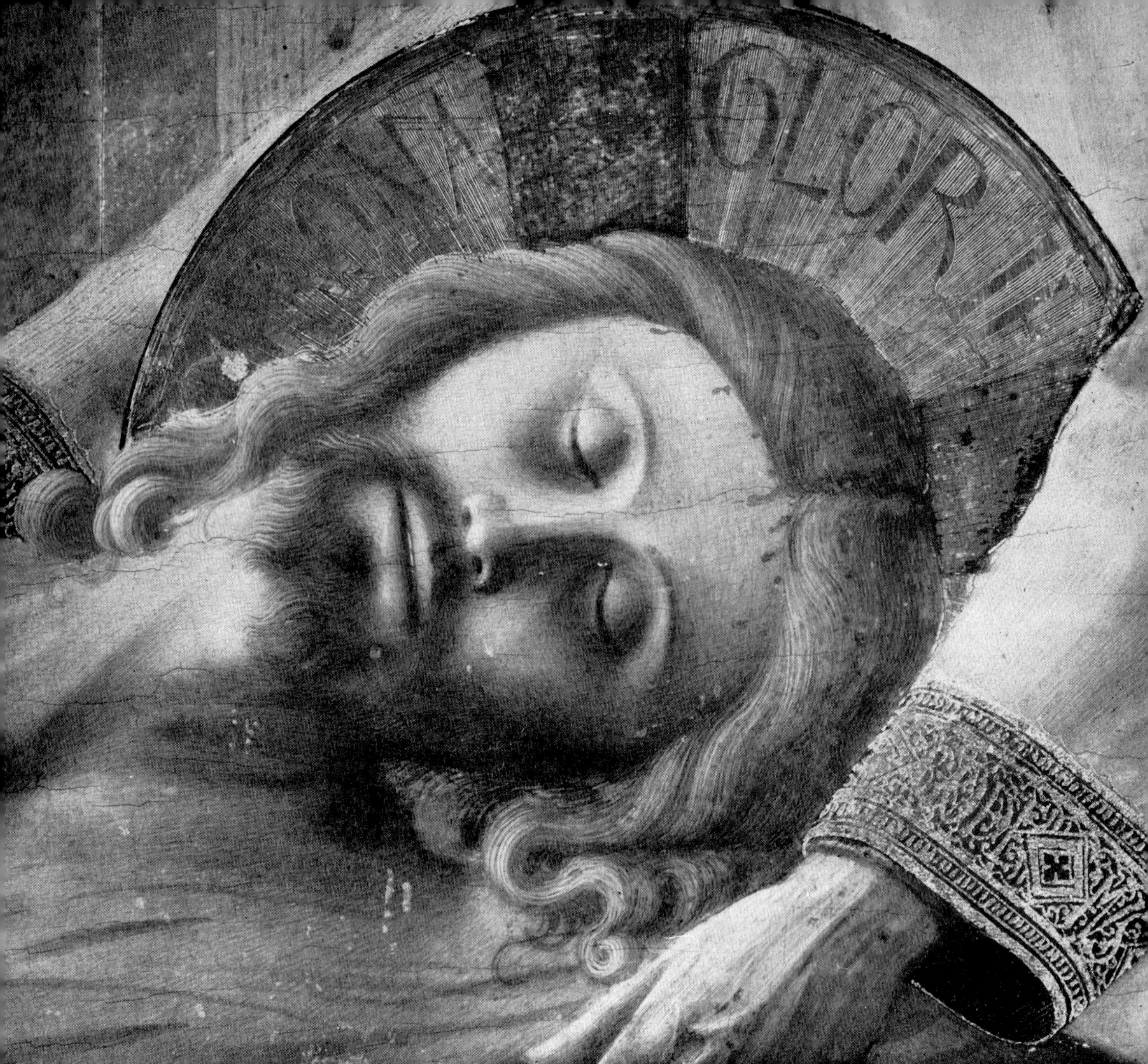

24. FRA ANGELICO (*c.* 1399–1455): *Head of Christ.* Detail from Plate 20

25. PIERO DELLA FRANCESCA (before 1420–92): *Head of Christ.* Detail from the fresco of the *Resurrection*
About 1463. Borgo San Sepolcro, Palazzo Comunale

The Passion has been consummated and the head of the dead Redeemer wears 'the crown of glory'. Having risen on the third day, he now confirms his promise that we may share in his triumph over death. 'This *Resurrection*', says Kenneth Clark, 'is one of the supreme works of painting in the worl . . . Before Piero's risen Christ we are suddenly conscious of values for which no rational statement adequate; we are struck with a feeling of awe, older and less reasonable than that inspired by the Blessed Angelico. . . . The head of Piero's Christ is outside and beyond his ordinary range, and shows . . . how he had come to discover in himself new depths of spiritual understanding.'

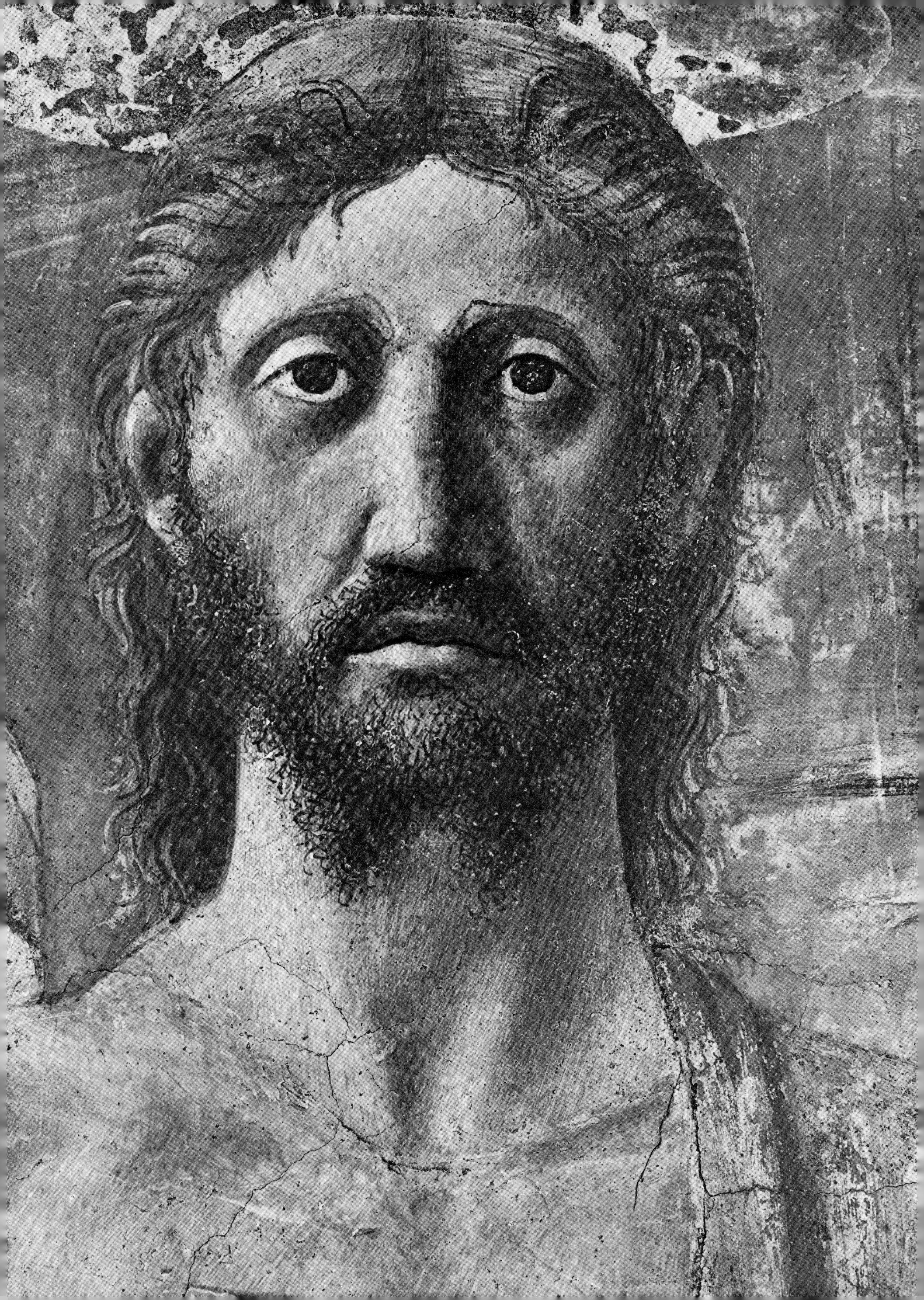

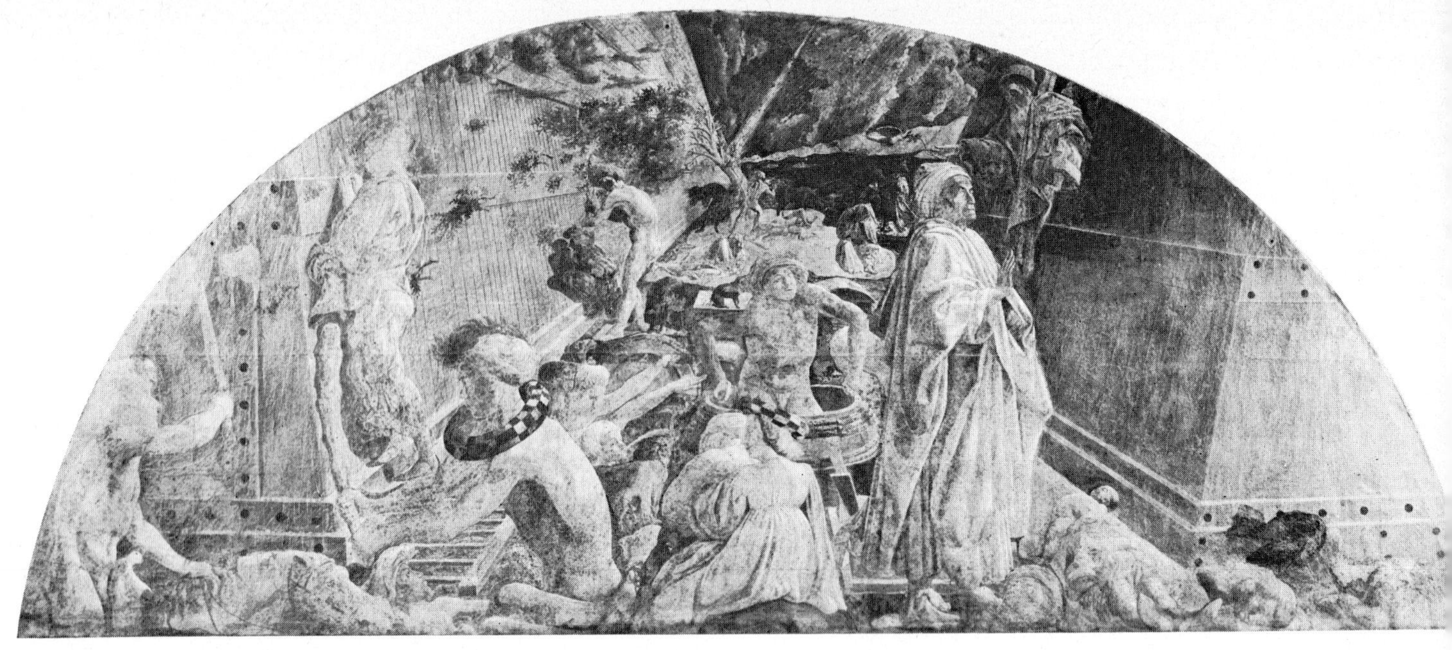

26, 28. PAOLO UCCELLO (*c.* 1397–1475): *The Deluge*. About 1445. Fresco. Florence, Santa Maria Novella

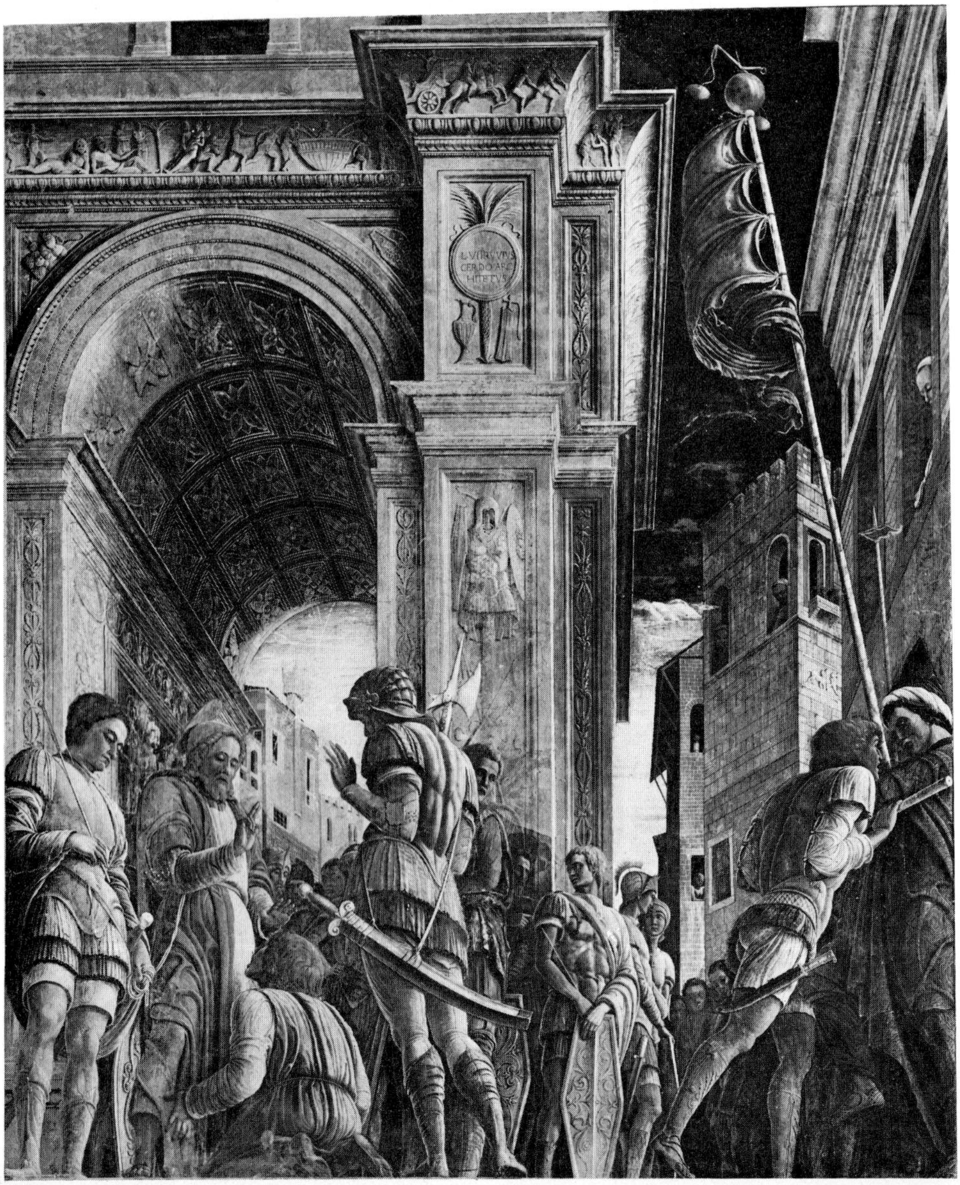

27. ANDREA MANTEGNA (*c.* 1430/1–1506): *St. James Led to Execution*. About 1456. Fresco. Formerly Padua, Eremitani Church. Destroyed in 1944

Uccello shows, on the left, the rising of the waters and the vain struggle of those outside the ark, and on the right the abating of the Flood and Noah at the window of the ark greeting the returning dove. His pioneering use of perspective and foreshortening extends even to the cloth-covered hoops, which were part of Florentine headgear. Mantegna was, of all Renaissance painters, the most eager student of ancient sculpture and architecture, which here almost overwhelms the moving scene of the aged Apostle blessing, on his way to execution, a man whom he has just converted. In scenes such as this Mantegna would have been influenced by the compositions in relief on the sides of ancient sarcophagi and on triumphal columns and arches.

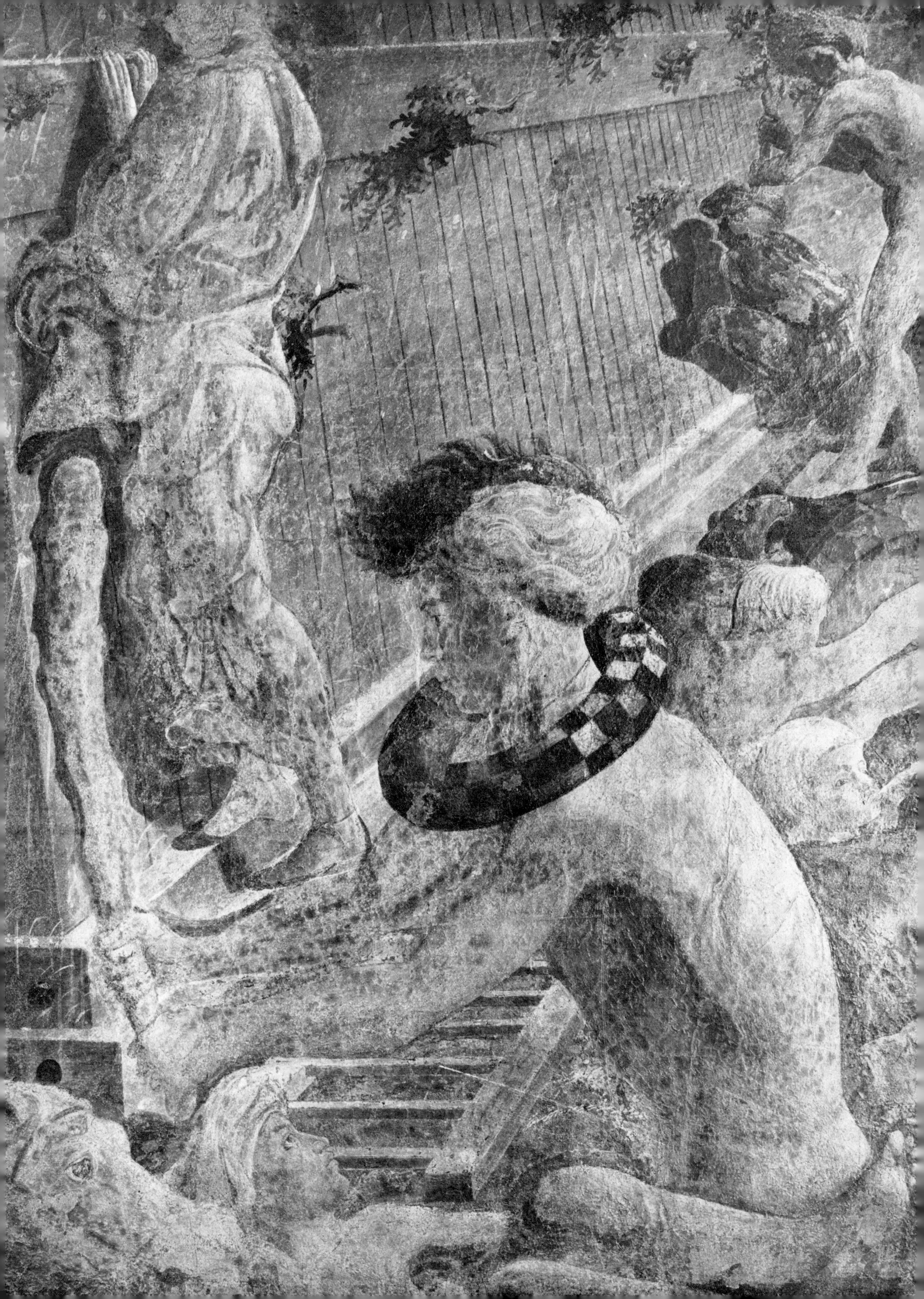

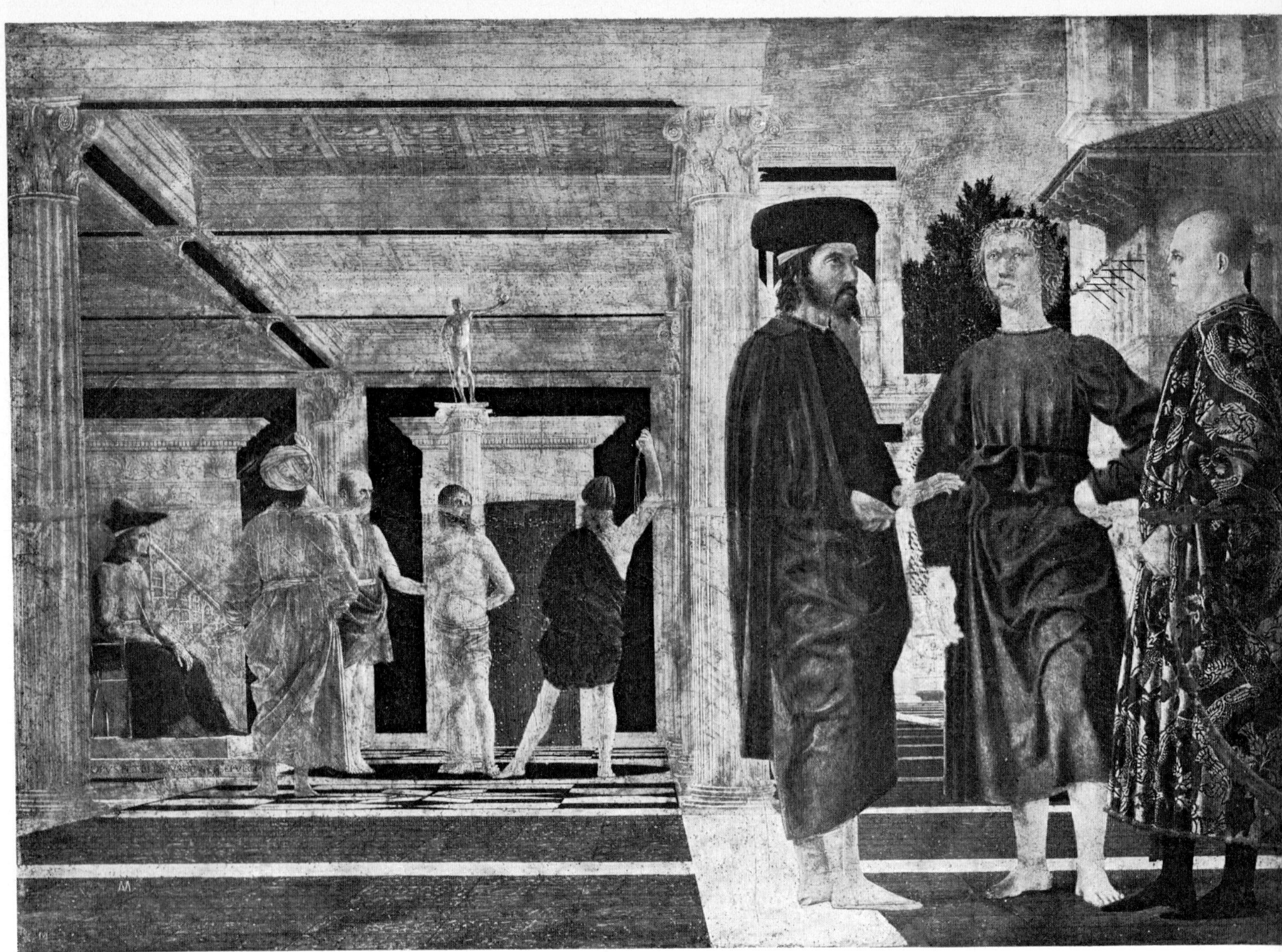

29. PIERO DELLA FRANCESCA (before 1420–92): *The Flagellation of Christ.* About 1456–7. Panel, $23\frac{1}{4} \times$ 32 in. Urbino, Galleria Nazionale delle Marche

Pontius Pilate, seated at the left, looks on as Christ, bound to a column, is about to be scourged. At the right three noble figures stand in the foreground, 'as unconcerned as the everlasting rocks'. They are clearly portraits of Renaissance personages, but their identities (though their strikingly different clothes may conceal a clue) and their association with the scene from the Passion have not been determined. What gives this small picture its unique quality among Renaissance masterpieces is the subtlety with which the new architectural principles have been transmuted into visual poetry—not unlike the way a great Renaissance sonnet turns to account the rules of metrics. The governor's marble hall is truly palatial, and its magnificent pavement, fluted columns with Corinthian capitals, inlaid beams and coffered ceiling are all interlocked in a perspective design of breathtaking perfection. But Piero has used a second means to unify the architecture: the diffused light, which models the marble surfaces as well as the bodies and draperies and perfectly countervails their severity.

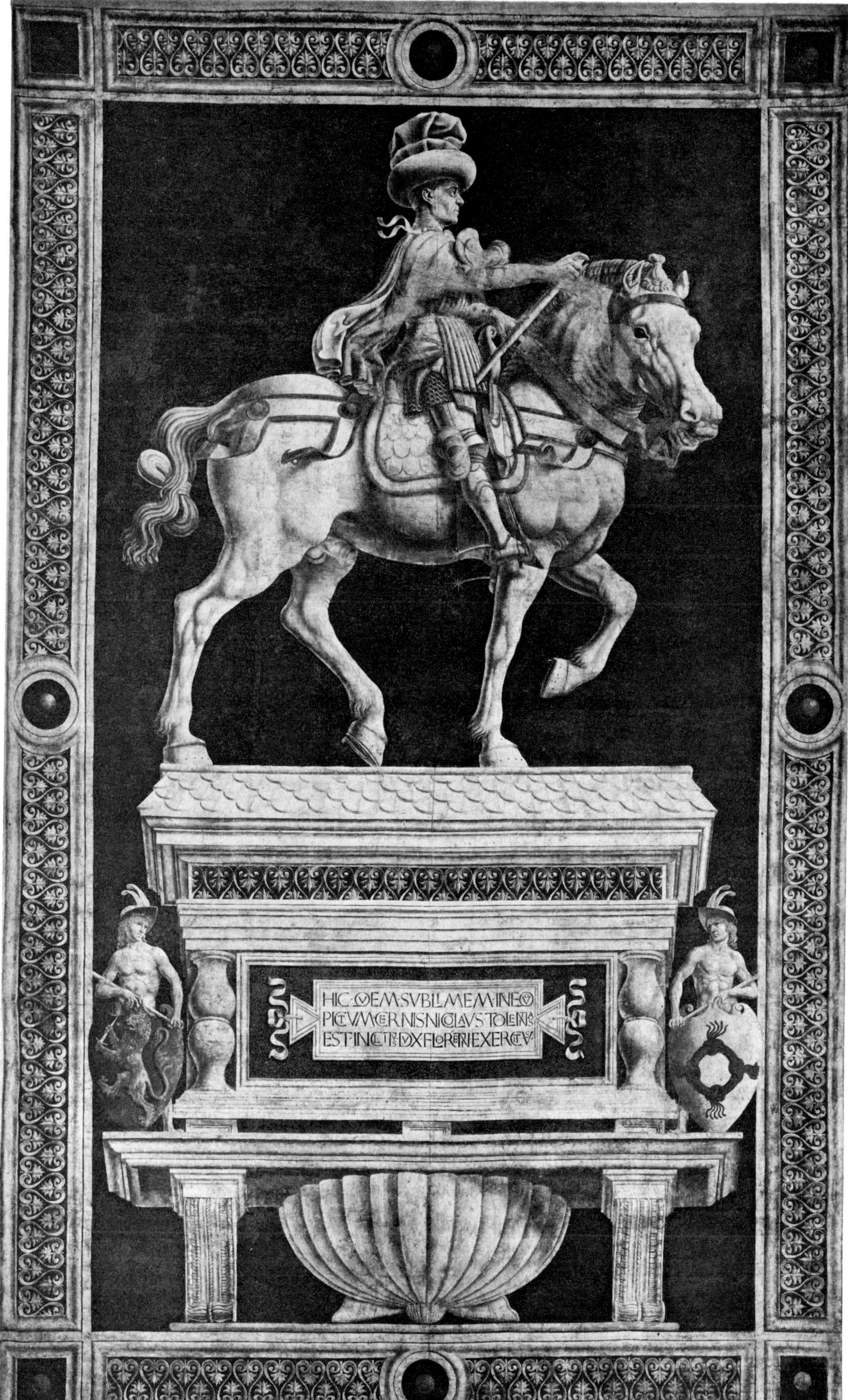

30. ANDREA DEL CASTAGNO (*c.* 1421?–57): *Niccolò da Tolentino*. 1456. Fresco. Florence, Cathedral

Niccolò da Tolentino had led the Florentine forces against Sienese invaders in 1432. This painted monument recalls Donatello's great equestrian statue in Padua, which in turn was inspired by the famous Marcus Aurelius on the Capitol in Rome. Niccolò's device, 'Solomon's knot', appears prominently here as well as on the banner in Uccello's fresco commemorating his victory (Plate 32).

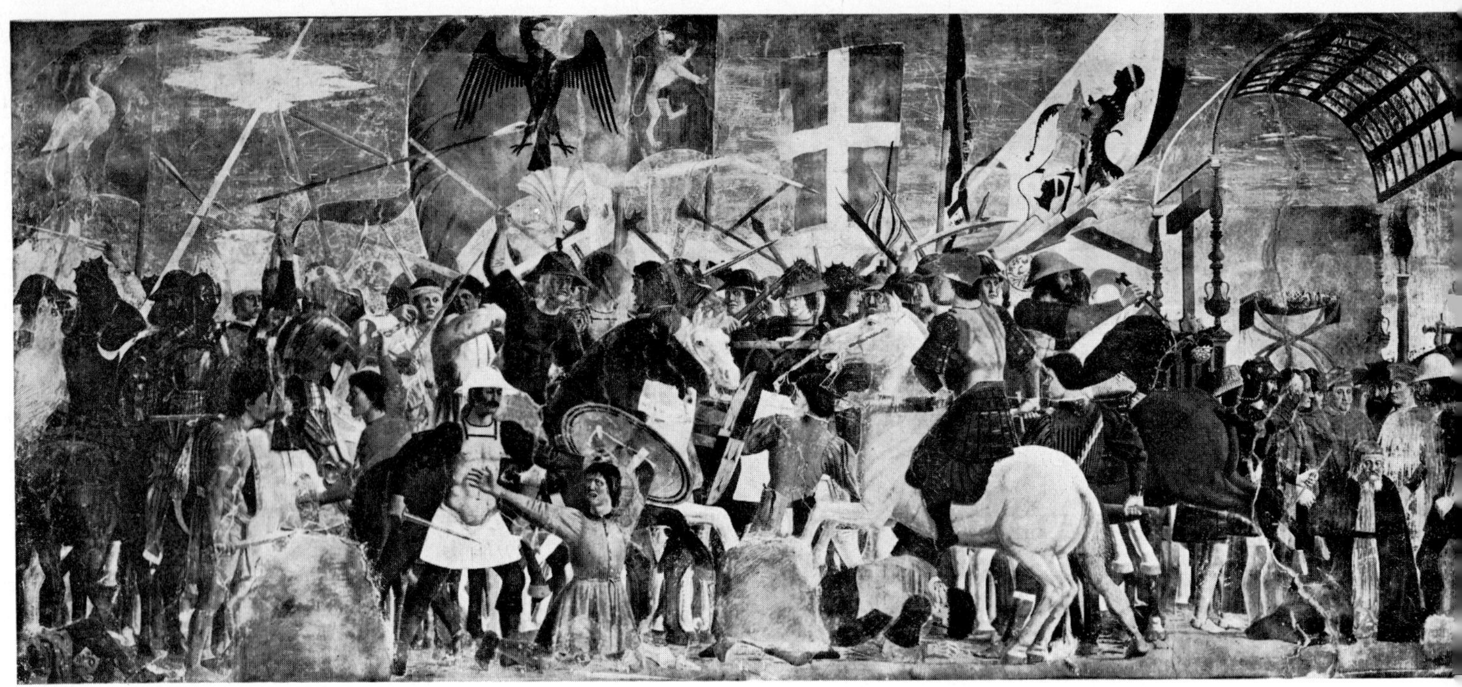

31. PIERO DELLA FRANCESCA (before 1420–92): *The Victory of the East Roman Emperor Heraclius over the Persian King Chosroes*. 1452–8. Fresco. Arezzo, San Francesco

32. PAOLO UCCELLO (*c.* 1397–1475): *The Battle of San Romano*. About 1457. Panel, $71\frac{1}{2} \times 126$ in. London, National Gallery

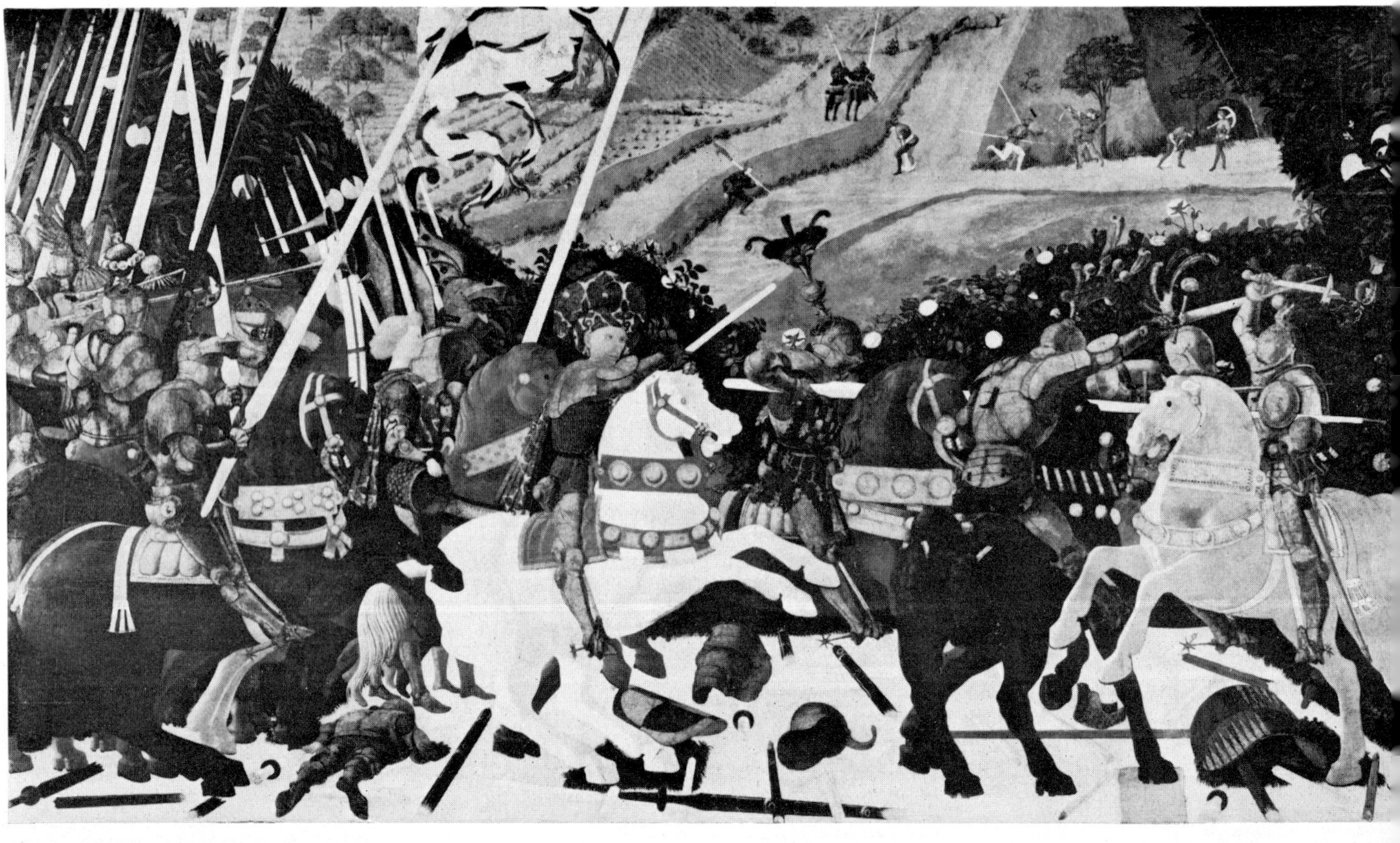

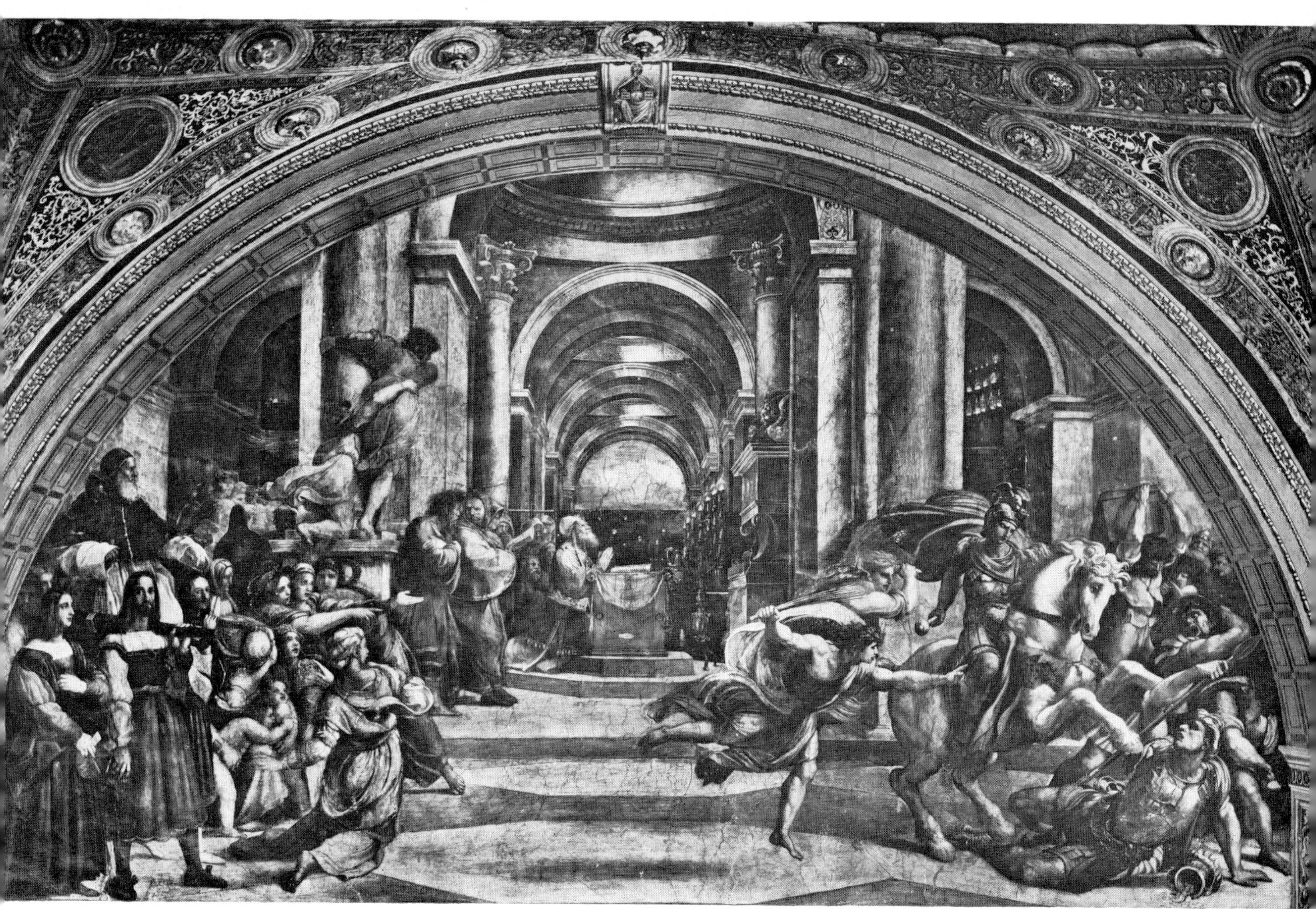

33. RAPHAEL (1483–1520): *The Expulsion of Heliodorus from the Temple*. 1513. Fresco. Vatican Palace, Stanza d'Eliodoro

Piero's fresco forms part of his great cycle depicting the Legend of the True Cross and shows the defeat of the Persian king, who had seized the precious relic, in A.D. 625. Amid the carnage and confusion the king's son is stabbed in the throat and near him the dignified figure of Chosroes himself is about to be beheaded below his throne. The battle depicted by Uccello (opposite, below) had been fought in his own lifetime, but his principal interest was not in the action itself. He displays his mastery of foreshortening and his love of decorative patterns in the prancing horses, the knightly armour and the fantastic arabesques of the helmet-plumes set in front of a flat backdrop. Raphael's fresco, set in the Temple of Jerusalem, shows how the high priest's prayer was answered by the divine punishment of the Syrian general, who had sacrilegiously looted the money of widows and orphans and is about to be trampled down by the heavenly rider in golden armour. The biblical scene is watched at the left by Raphael's patron, Pope Julius II, borne on a litter and attended by a secretary.

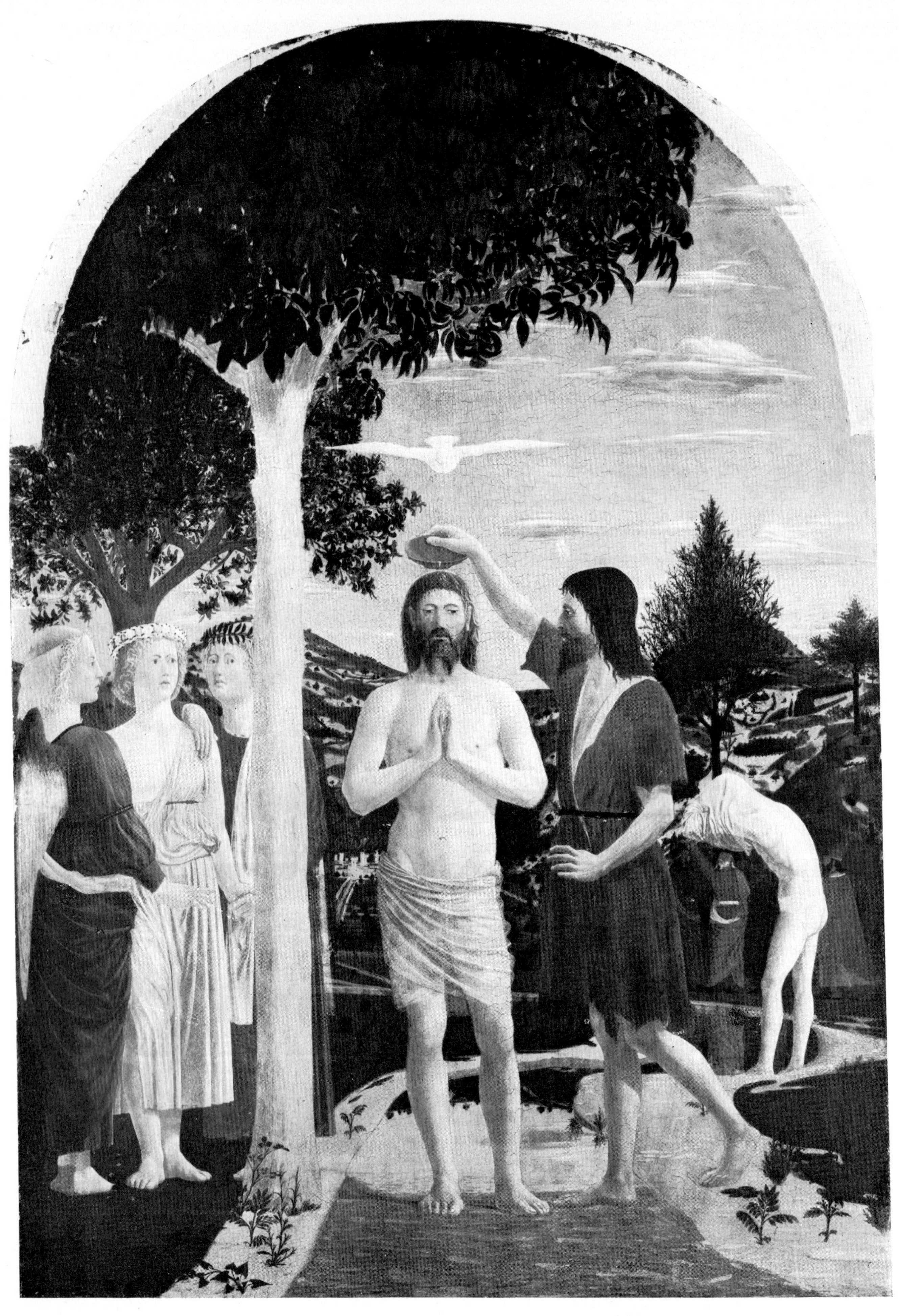

34. PIERO DELLA FRANCESCA (before 1420–92): *The Baptism of Christ*. 1448–50. Panel, $66 \times 45\frac{3}{4}$ in. London, National Gallery

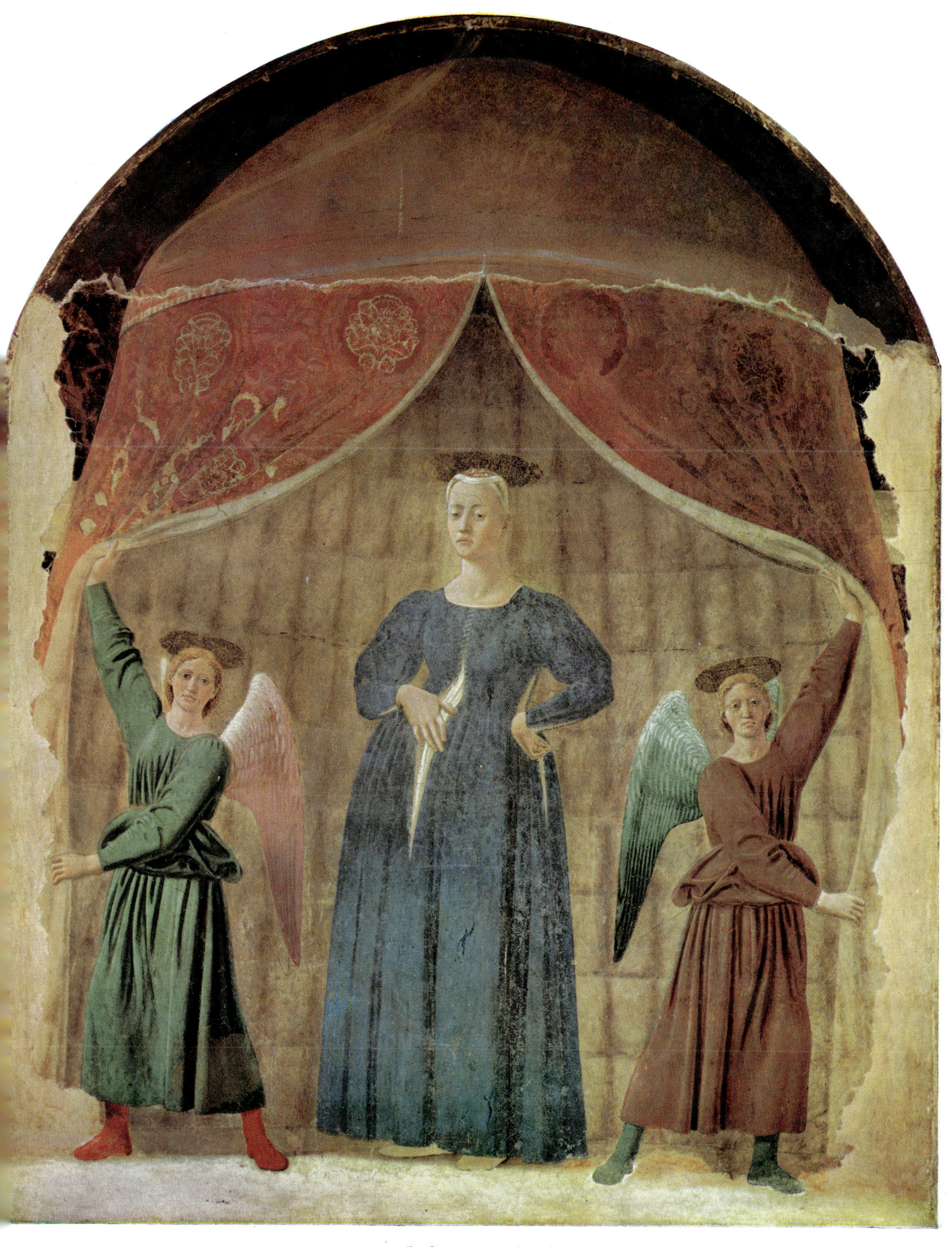

35. PIERO DELLA FRANCESCA (before 1420–92): *The Madonna Pointing to her Pregnant Womb* (*'Madonna del Parto'*). About 1461. Fresco. Monterchi, near Arezzo, Cemetery Chapel

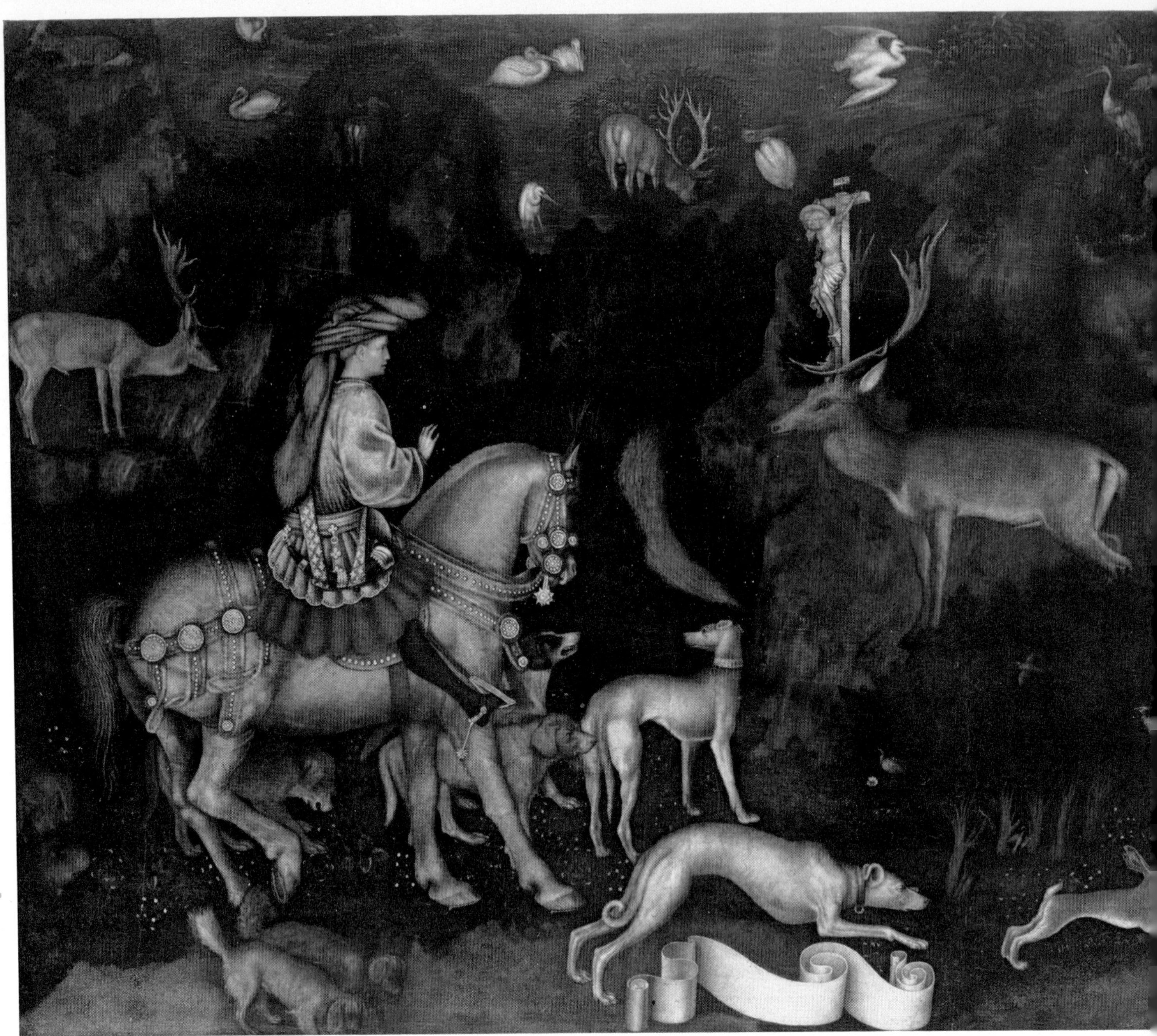

36. ANTONIO PISANELLO (*c.* 1395–1455): *The Vision of St. Eustace.* 1436–8. Panel, $21\frac{1}{2} \times 25\frac{3}{4}$ in. London, National Gallery

Pisanello was the last major Italian artist to work in the International Gothic style. He was possibly born at Pisa but soon moved to Verona, which became his centre of operations. He is known to have worked on several important fresco cycles, and, on the basis of pictures like *The Vision of St. Eustace*, must have developed a style for individual, small-scale paintings; much of his painted work now survives. What does remain is a superb series of medals and a great many drawings, which reveal a sharply observant eye for details of ordinary life. Many of them are of animals and some even correspond with beasts in *The Vision of St. Eustace.*

37. PAOLO UCCELLO (*c.* 1397–1475): *St. George and the Dragon.* About 1460. Canvas, $22\frac{1}{4} \times 29\frac{1}{4}$ in. London, National Gallery

Very few paintings on canvas survive from the mid-fifteenth century. Uccello is chiefly remembered as a pioneer of perspective, which he liked to work out with great ingenuity and care, often to the detriment of a theme. This is one of his most charming works.

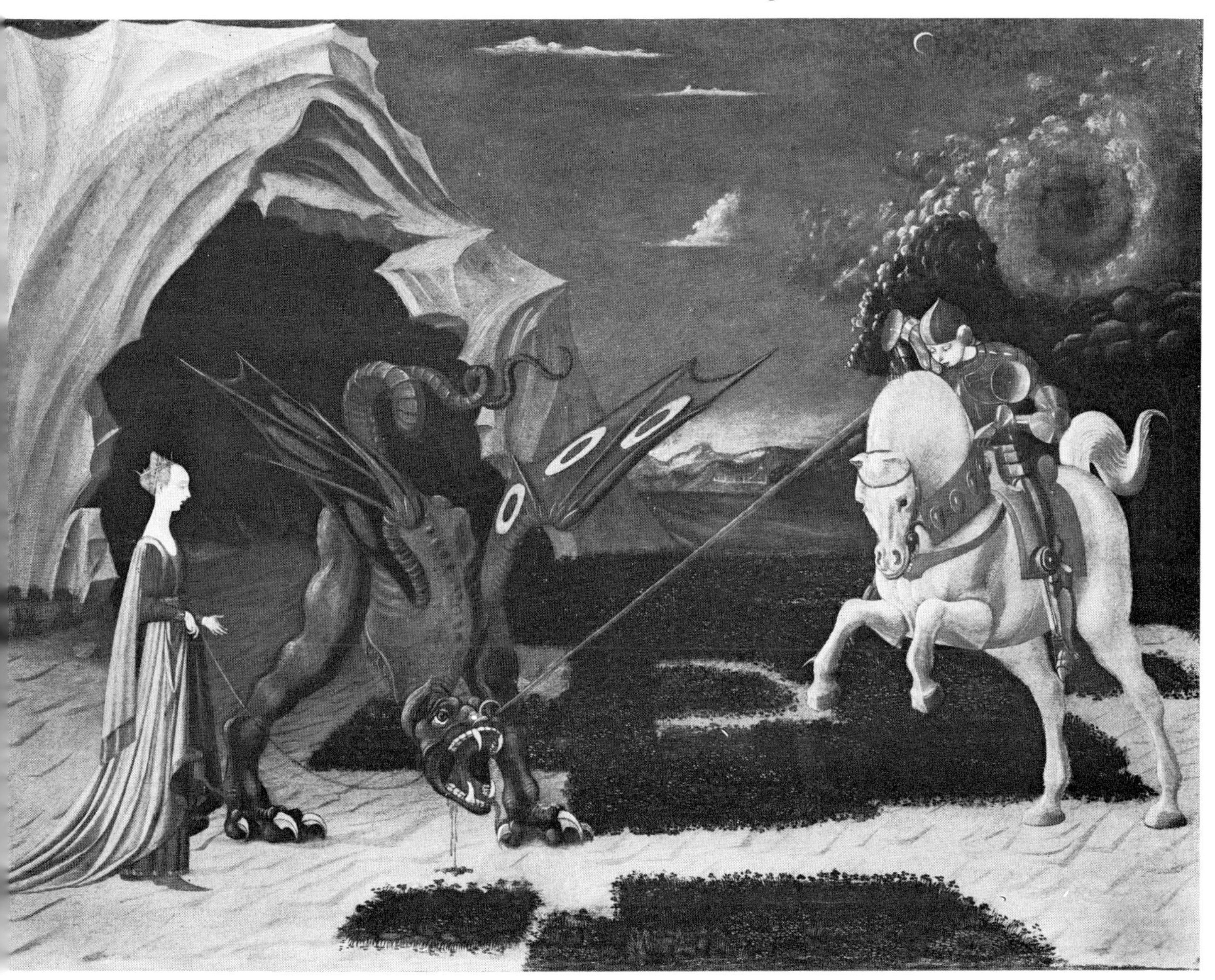

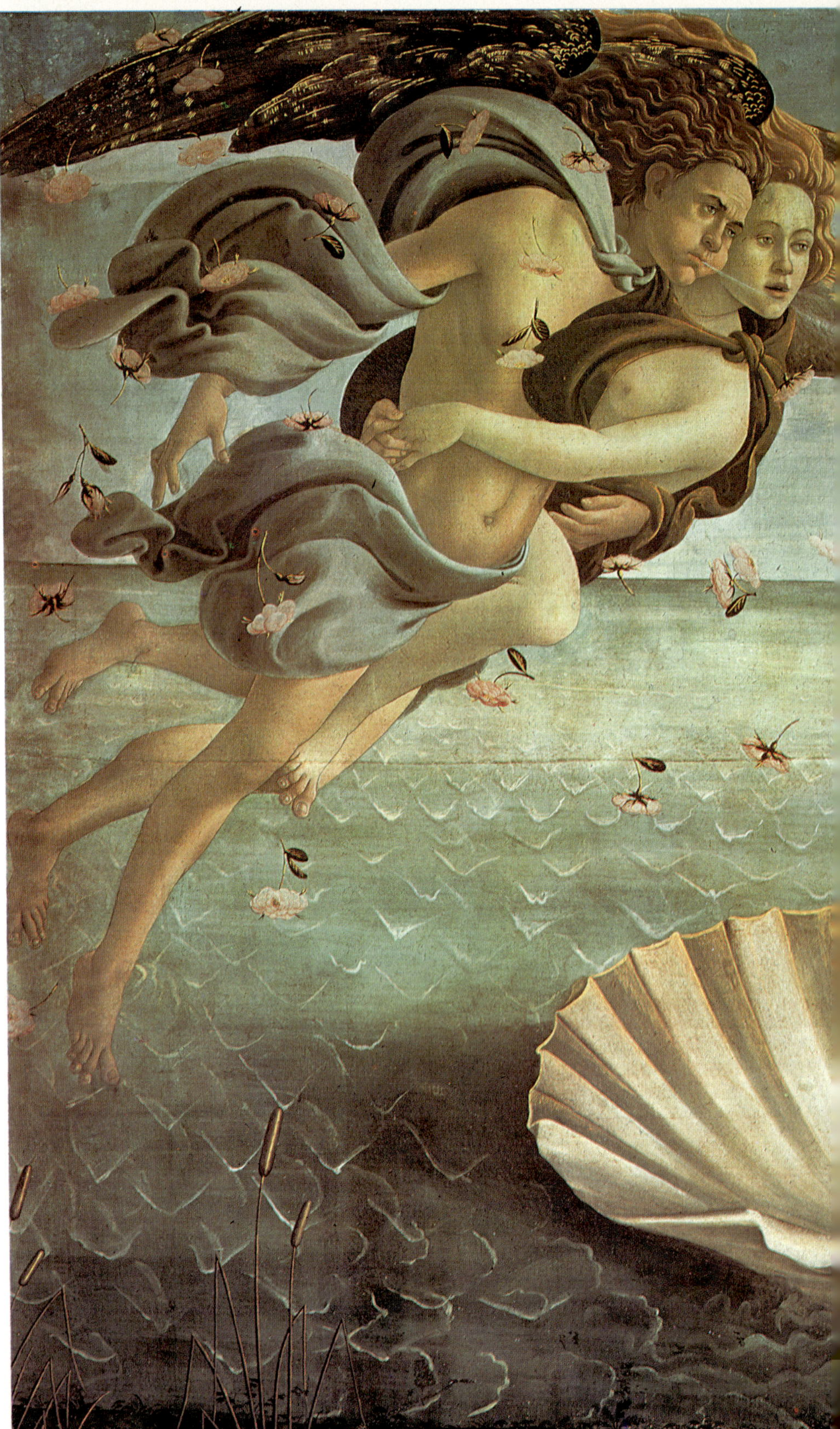

38. SANDRO BOTTICELLI (*c.* 1445–1510): *The Birth of Venus*. About 1485–90. Tempera on linen, 70 × 111 in. Florence, Uffizi

The goddess of love was said to have risen from the sea and to have been blown by the west wind towards the coast of Cyprus. The melodious beauty pervading this famous picture is enchanting: the pair of winged wind-gods with fluttering draperies, the roses scenting the breeze, the ripples on the crystalline water, the nymph of the shady grove holding out the sumptuous red cloak to Venus, her graceful body, and her gestures of modesty.

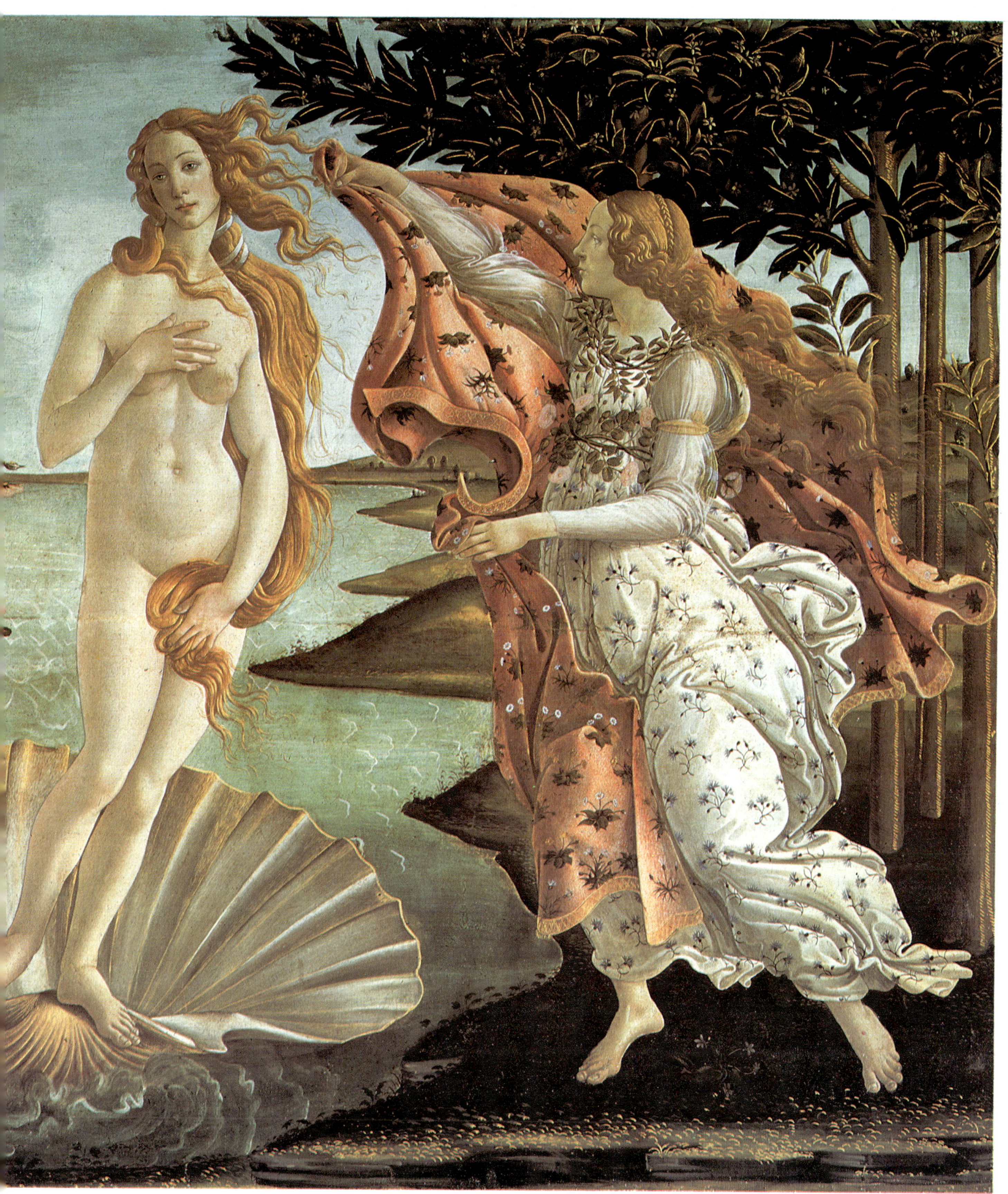

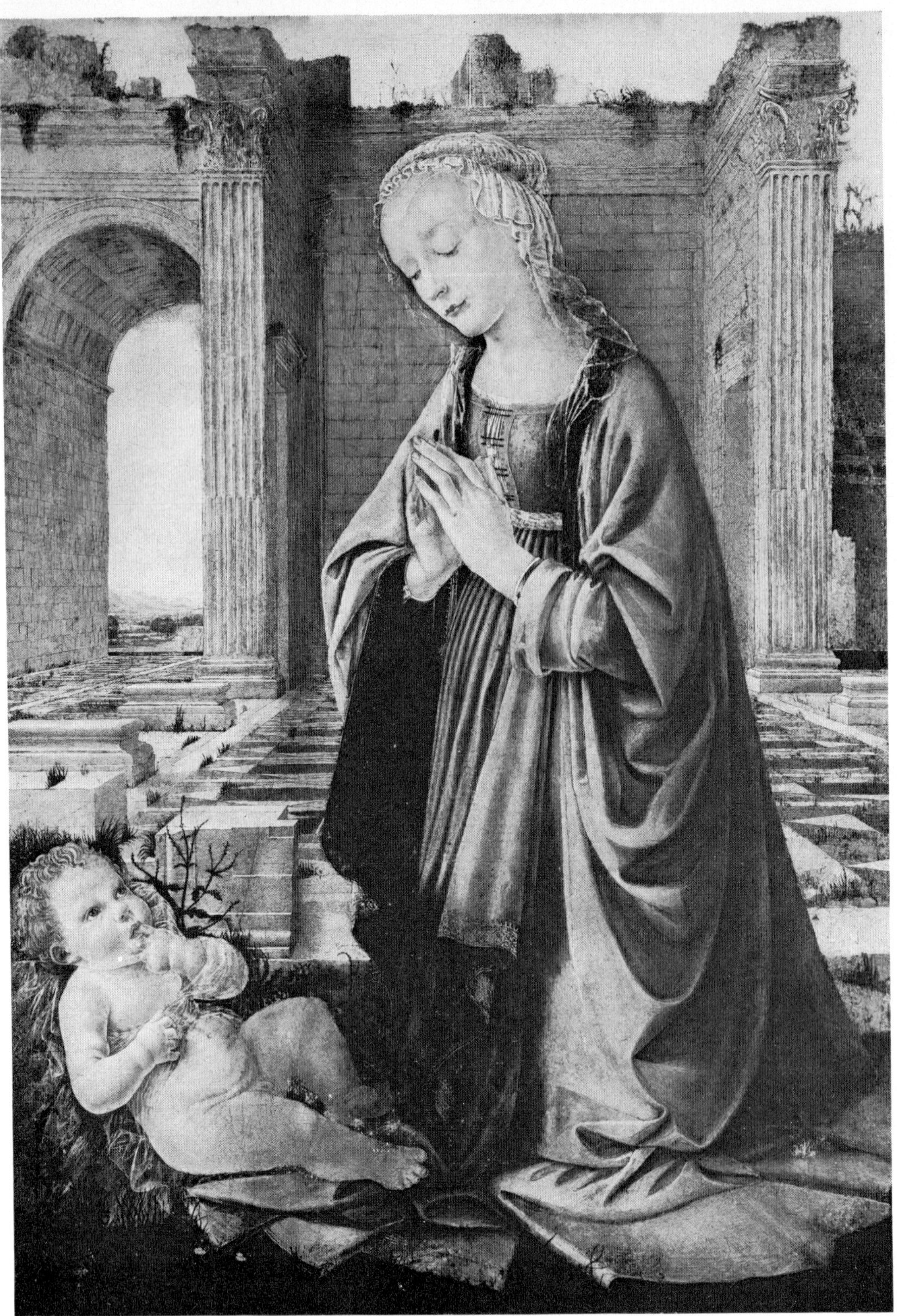

39. ANDREA VERROCCHIO (*c.* 1435–88): *The Virgin and Child* ('*The Ruskin Madonna*'). About 1470? Canvas, transferred from a panel, $42\frac{1}{2} \times 30$ in. Edinburgh, National Gallery of Scotland

This damaged but important picture is usually attributed to Verrocchio, who ran a busy studio in Florence that produced sculpture and decorative work as well as paintings. It has recently been suggested that, in part, it might even be by the young Leonardo da Vinci, who was a pupil in Verrocchio's studio in the 1470s. There is, for example, an authentic drawing by Leonardo (now in the British Museum) of drapery that is very close to the arrangement of the Virgin's mantle in the Edinburgh work, which is often known as '*The Ruskin Madonna*', after its former owner, the great Victorian critic, John Ruskin.

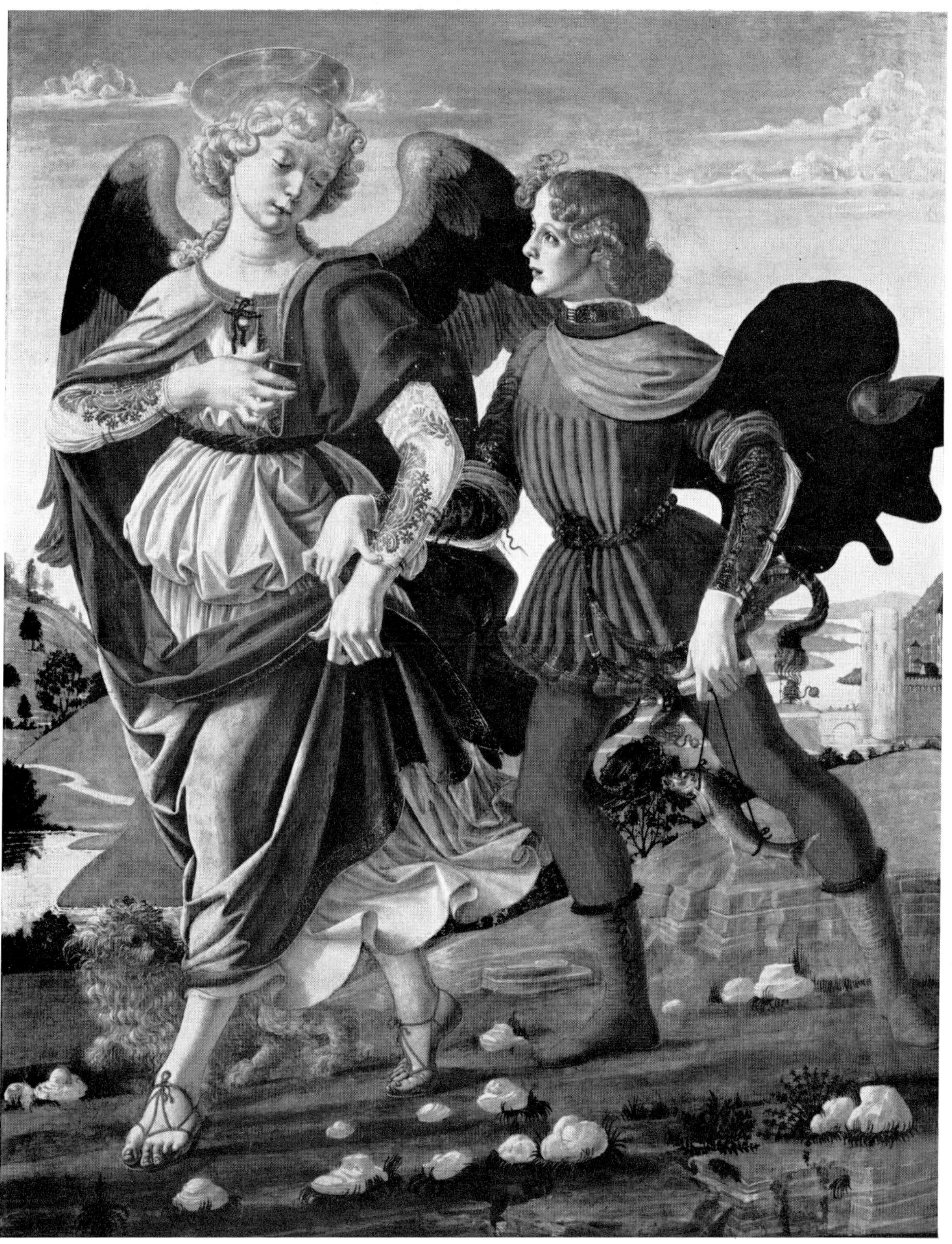

40. ANDREA VERROCCHIO (*c.* 1435–88): *The Archangel Raphael with Tobias*. About 1467. Panel, 33 × 26 in. London, National Gallery

Raphael, in human shape, guided the young Tobias to Media and taught him how to use the entrails of a monstrous fish to exorcize the devil from his bride Sara and later to cure his father's blindness. But the artist has not followed the details of the biblical story, for this is a devotional picture: the young wayfarer shows, by glance and gesture, that he places his trust in his heavenly guardian—and the spectator is bidden to follow his example.

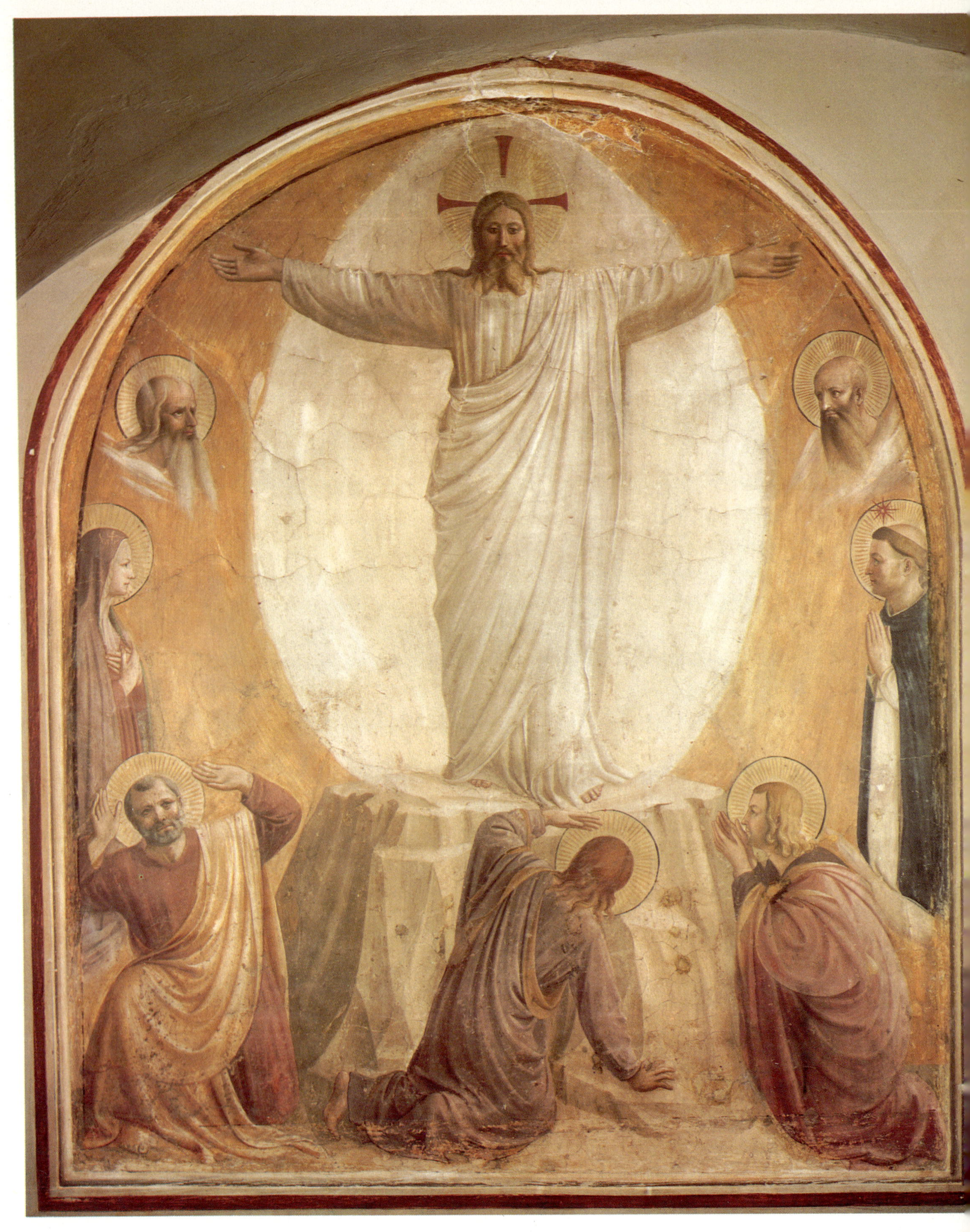

41. FRA ANGELICO (*c.* 1399–1455): *The Transfiguration of Christ*. 1444–5. Fresco. Florence, Convent of San Marco

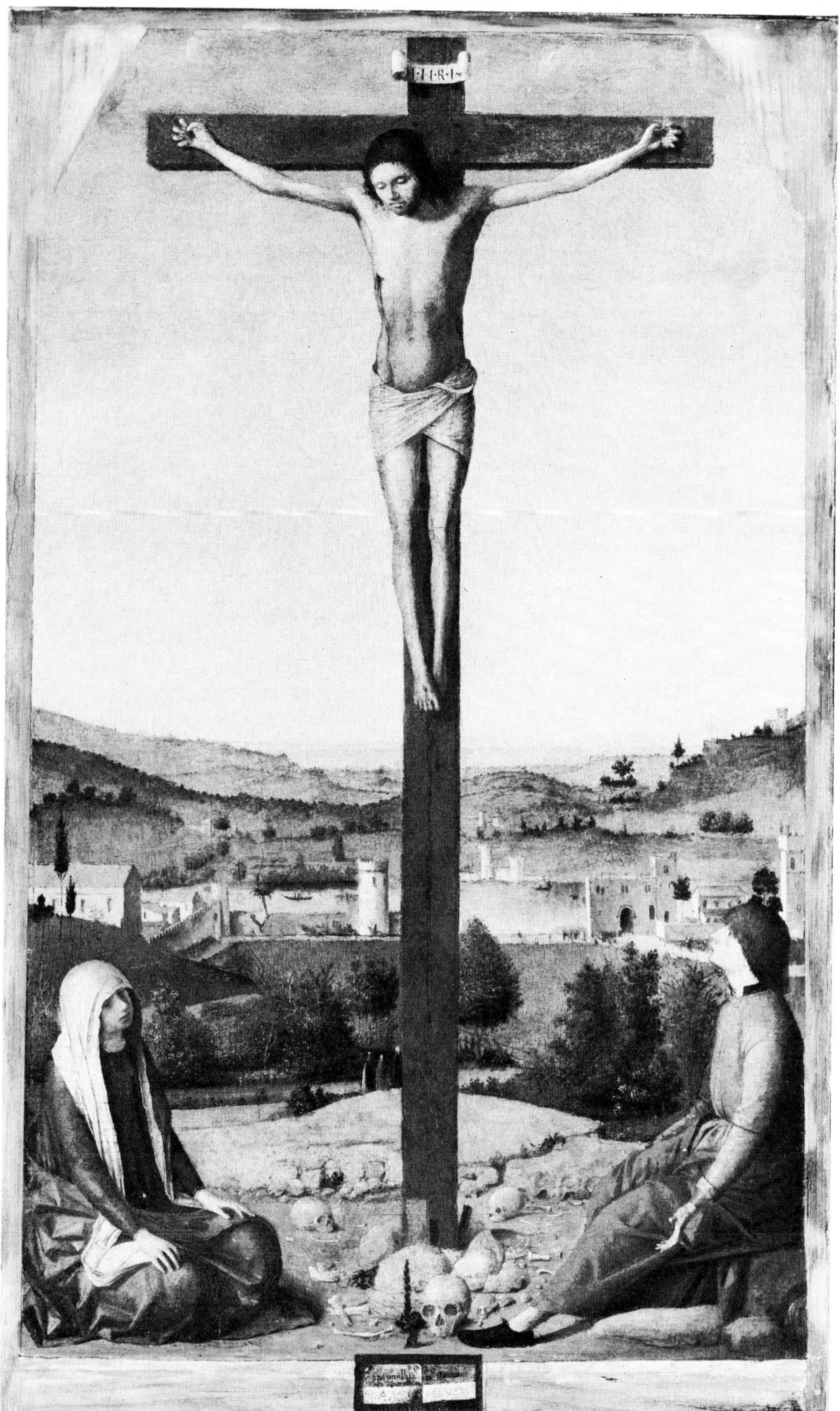

42. ANTONELLO DA MESSINA (*c.* 1430–79): *Christ Crucified.* About 1475. Panel, $16\frac{1}{2} \times 10$ in. London, National Gallery

As his name implies, Antonello worked in southern Italy, where he was the most important Italian artist of his day. He pioneered the use of the oil technique, derived from Northern masters such as Jan van Eyck, and, when he worked in Venice (1475/6), influenced Venetian artists, notably Giovanni Bellini.

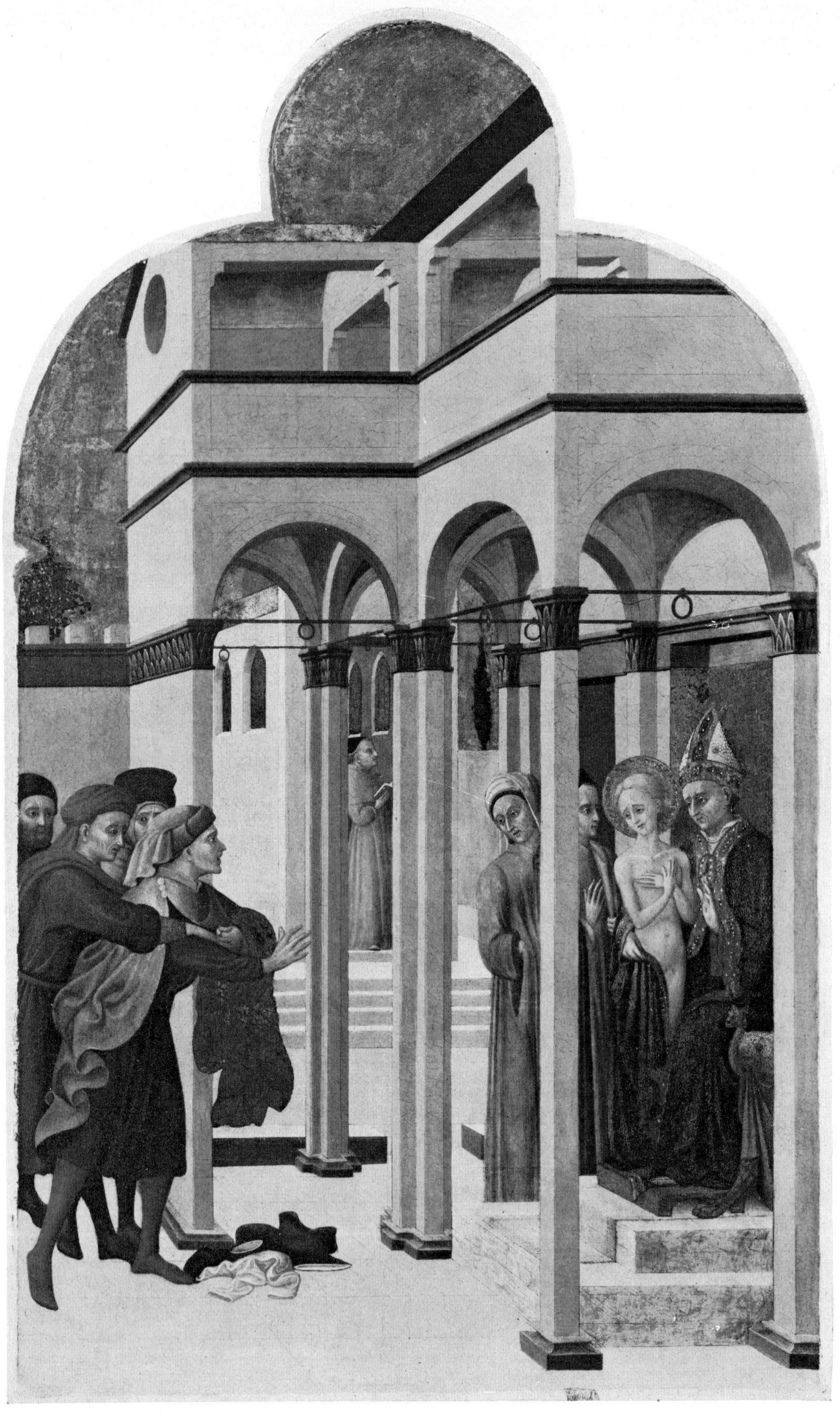

43. SASSETTA (*c.* 1392–1450): *St. Francis Renounces his Earthly Father.* 1437–44. Panel, $34\frac{1}{2} \times 20\frac{3}{4}$ in. London, National Gallery

This is one of the panels from a polyptych painted between 1437 and 1444 for the high altar of the church of S. Francesco at San Sepolcro. Six other panels are now in the National Gallery, London.

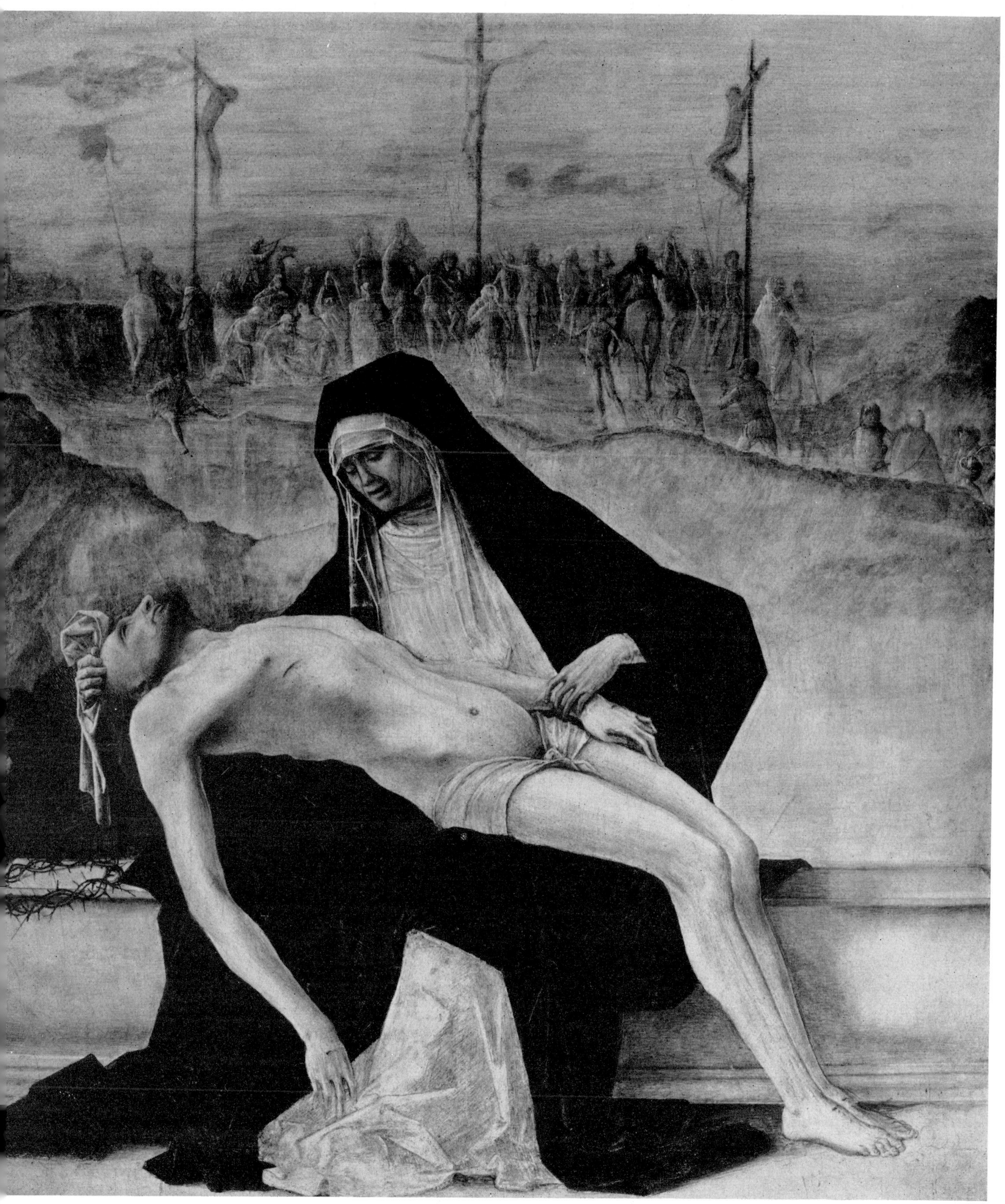

44. ERCOLE DE' ROBERTI (*c.* 1450–96): *Pietà*. About 1485. Panel, $13\frac{1}{2} \times 12\frac{1}{4}$ in. Liverpool, Walker Art Gallery

45. GIOVANNI BELLINI (*c.* 1430–1516): *The Agony in the Garden*. About 1465. Panel, 32 × 50 in. London, National Gallery

The day of the Crucifixion is dawning. Christ kneels in prayer on the Mount of Olives, while an angel holds out to him the chalice of suffering. His loneliness is emphasized by the silhouette of his head above the trough of the largely featureless skyline. Peter, John and James, too weary to watch with him, have fallen asleep, and the soldiers, led by Judas, are drawing near. The beauty of the lovingly rendered landscape enhances, rather than softens, the sense of spiritual desolation which pervades this moving and poetic picture. It is this poignancy which, together with the depth of the landscape and the early morning sky above a gentle horizon, distinguishes Bellini's picture from a smaller version of the same subject (opposite) painted, perhaps a few years earlier, by his brother-in-law, Andrea Mantegna.

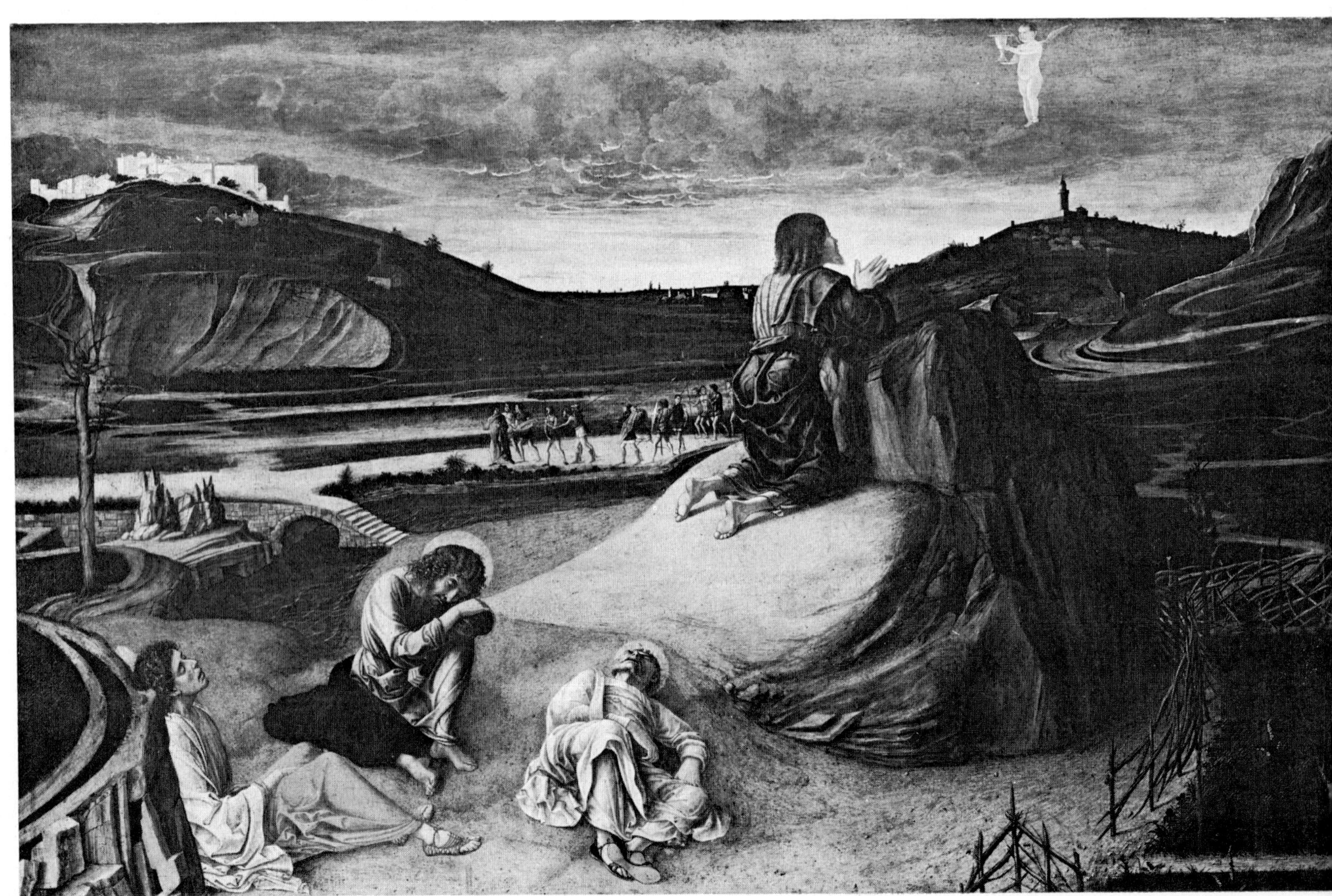

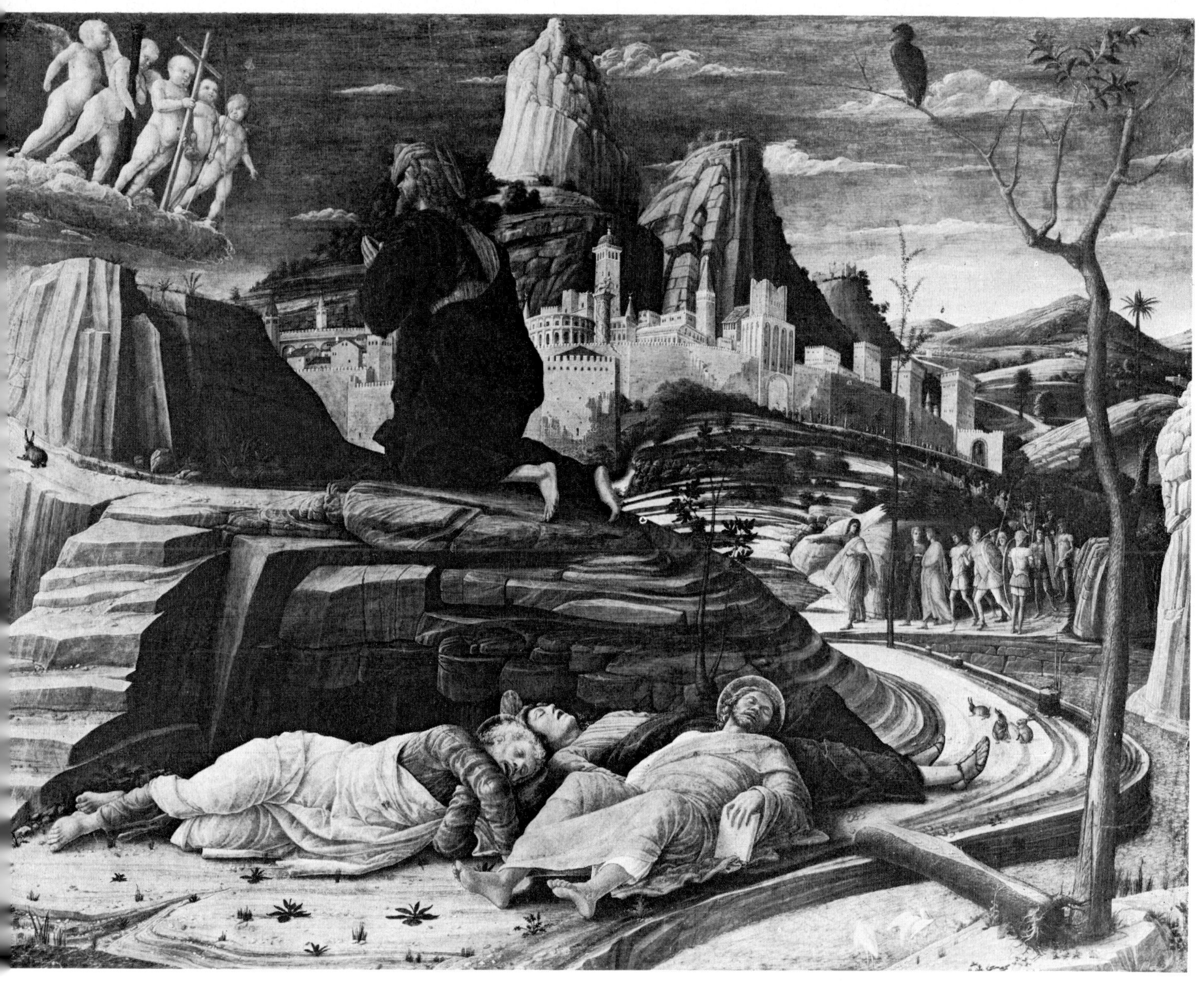

46. ANDREA MANTEGNA (*c.* 1430/1–1506): *The Agony in the Garden*. About 1460. Panel, $24\frac{3}{4} \times 31\frac{1}{2}$ in. London, National Gallery

Having prayed, 'Father, not my will, but thine be done', Christ has a vision of five angels holding instruments of his Passion: the column, the Cross, the sponge and the lance. This is a world of stone: between the rocky hillock on which he kneels and the craggy peaks towering in the distance nestles the walled city of Jerusalem with a strange medley of medieval and quasi-Roman buildings. The sublimity of the composition and the conviction it carries are not impaired by the striking lack of depth in the space construction. Compared with Bellini's picture (opposite), the planes seem shallow and the effect somewhat crowded; even the sleeping Apostles are huddled together. But if it is less spacious in effect, it has some vivid details, which might seem out of place in Bellini's version: the frisky rabbits, the pelicans wading in the stream and the uprooted tree trunk bridging it, and the vulture on the bare tree foreshadowing Christ's death.

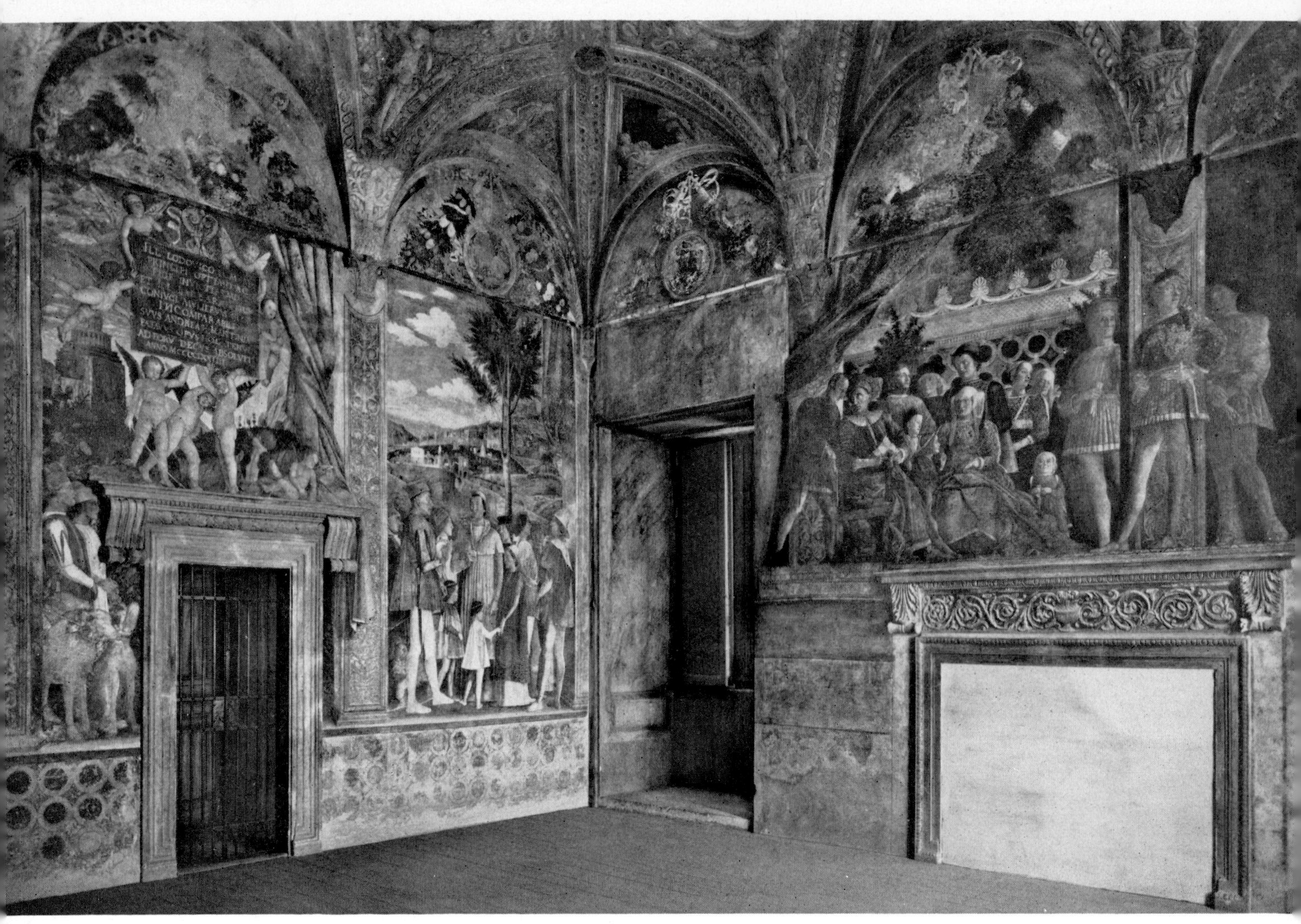

47. The Camera degli Sposi in the Palazzo Ducale, Mantua. Decorated by ANDREA MANTEGNA, 1473–4

48. ANDREA MANTEGNA (*c.* 1430/1–1506): *Putti and Spectators Looking down*. 1473–4. Ceiling fresco. Mantua, Palazzo Ducale, Camera degli Sposi

Mantegna was court-painter to the ruler of Mantua, Marchese Lodovico Gonzaga, and created for him the greatest private decorative scheme of the fifteenth century. Frescoes and real architecture a interlocked in a singularly ingenious way. The spandrels articulating the vault spring from stone capitals crowning painted pilasters, and this fusion, which appears to give solidity to the figure groups, is enhanced by the simulated rods and curtains, which produce the impression that the spectator looks through windows into open-air reality. This illusionism was to find its spectacular culmination in the art of the Baroque. Mantegna's frescoes show the Gonzaga court (Plate 51): on th left wall Lodovico greeting his son, Cardinal Francesco Gonzaga, in the countryside outside Mantua huntsmen with hounds; and *putti* holding a tablet glorifying Lodovico and his wife: and on the ceiling, a balcony open to the sky, with five girls, boldly foreshortened *putti* and a pheasant looking down.

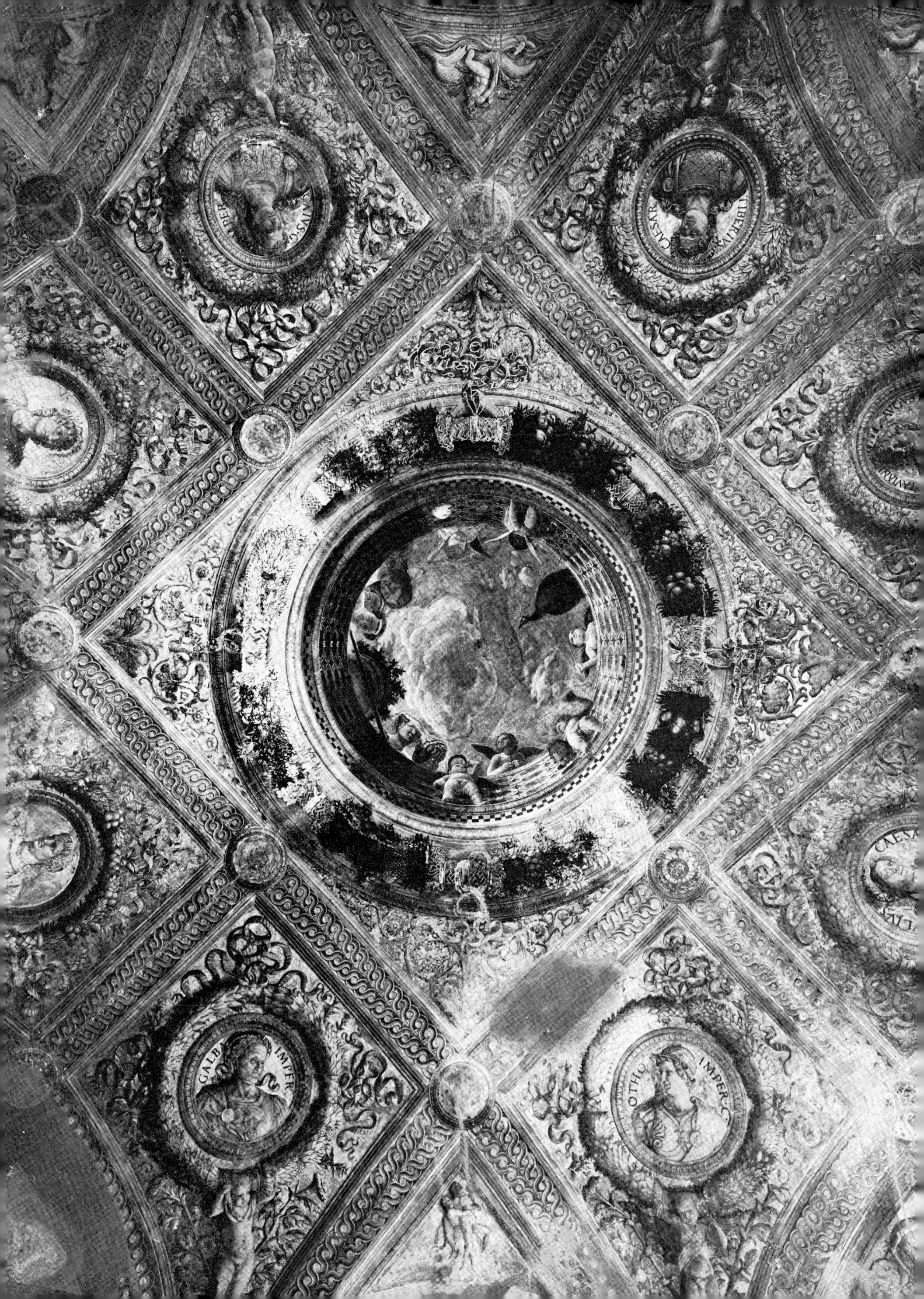
GALBA IMPER
OTHO IMPER C

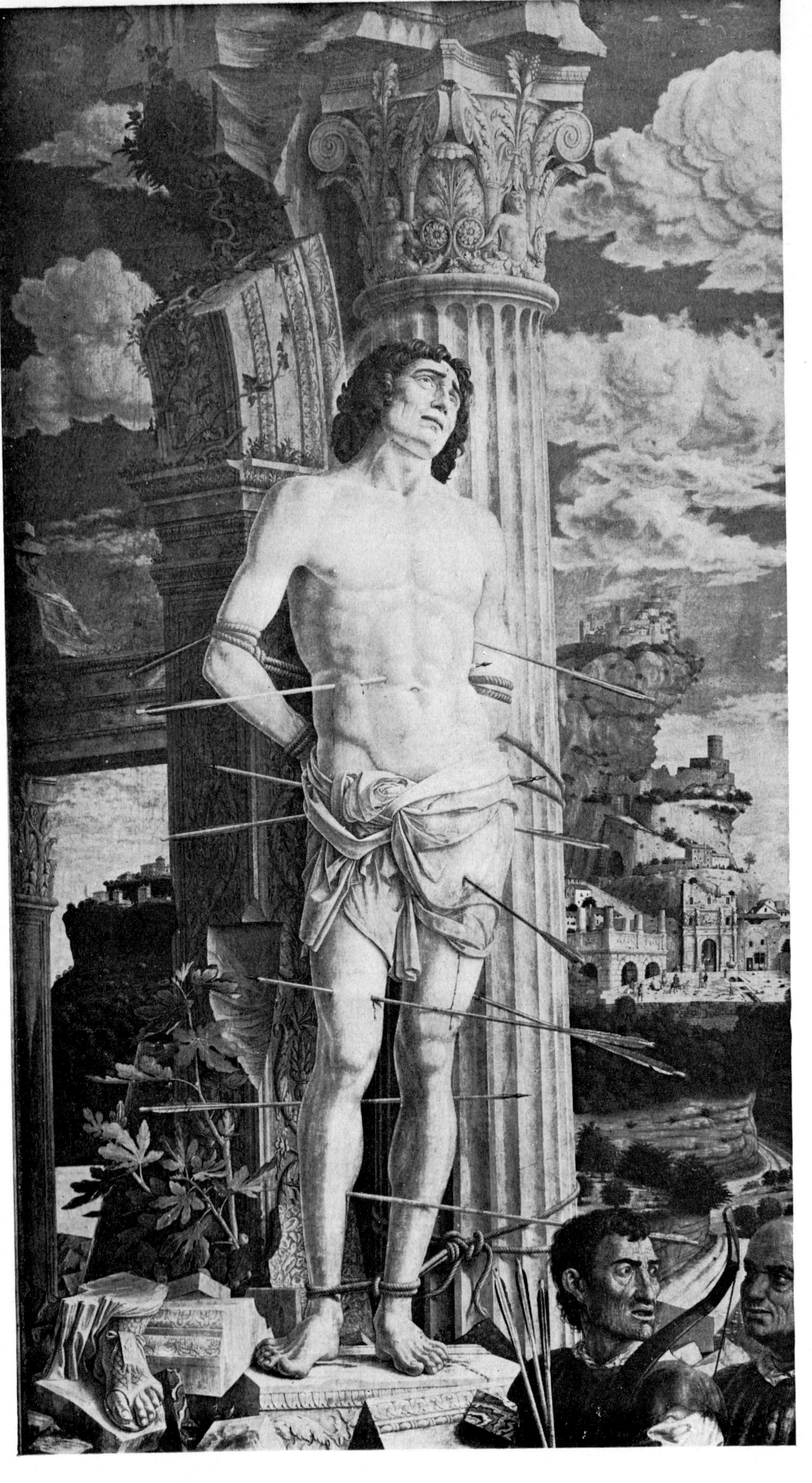

49. ANDREA MANTEGNA (*c.* 1430/1–1506): *The Martyrdom of St. Sebastian*. About 1474. Canvas, $101\frac{1}{2} \times 56$ in. Paris, Louvre

Sebastian, a Roman who had suffered in the persecutions of the Emperor Diocletian, was invoked throughout Italy for help against the all too frequent outbreaks of the plague, and his martyrdom by arrows was a popular subject of large votive pictures. These two contemporary altarpieces offer an interesting comparison. Mantegna shows only the head of two archers and concentrates attention both on the sufferings of the saint and on the antique sculptural fragments, which evoke ancient Rome. The Pollaiuolo brothers (opposite), in contrast, evoke ancient Rome by showing an imposing architectural ruin, and give pride of place to the grouping and skilfully varied poses of six muscular executioners.

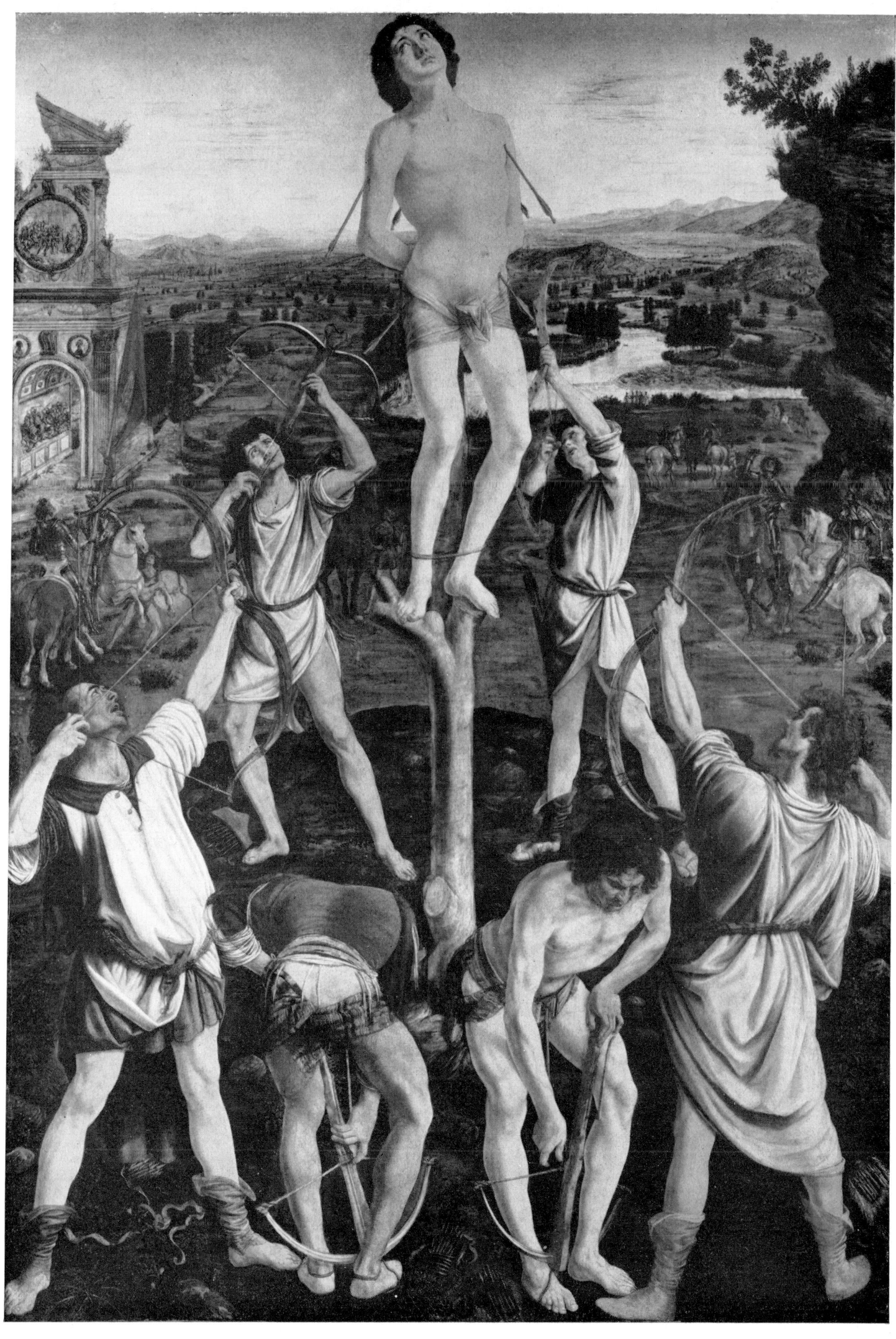

50. ANTONIO (*c.* 1432–98) AND PIERO (*c.* 1441–96) POLLAIUOLO: *The Martyrdom of St. Sebastian*. 1475. Panel, $114\frac{3}{4} \times 79\frac{3}{4}$ in. London, National Gallery

51. ANDREA MANTEGNA (*c.* 1430/1–1506): *Marchese Lodovico Gonzaga with his Family and Courtiers.* 1473–4. Fresco. Mantua, Palazzo Ducale, Camera degli Sposi

This great portrait group, placed above a fireplace (see Plate 47), shows the ruler of Mantua with his wife and small children, attended by members of his entourage and his court dwarf. Several compositional devices are used to produce an illusion of reality. The simulated curtain hanging from a rod and looped at the left seems to have been drawn back to admit the spectator to a view of the terrace. Lodovico, his favourite dog under his chair, has just turned to discuss a document with his secretary. The latter and the courtier with the sword seem to stand in front of the fictive pilasters, which are thus made to appear real and this, in turn, extends the illusion of reality to the fine screen behind the principal group. All the figures are painted in a great variety of informal poses, except the dwarf, the only figure to look straight out at the spectator.

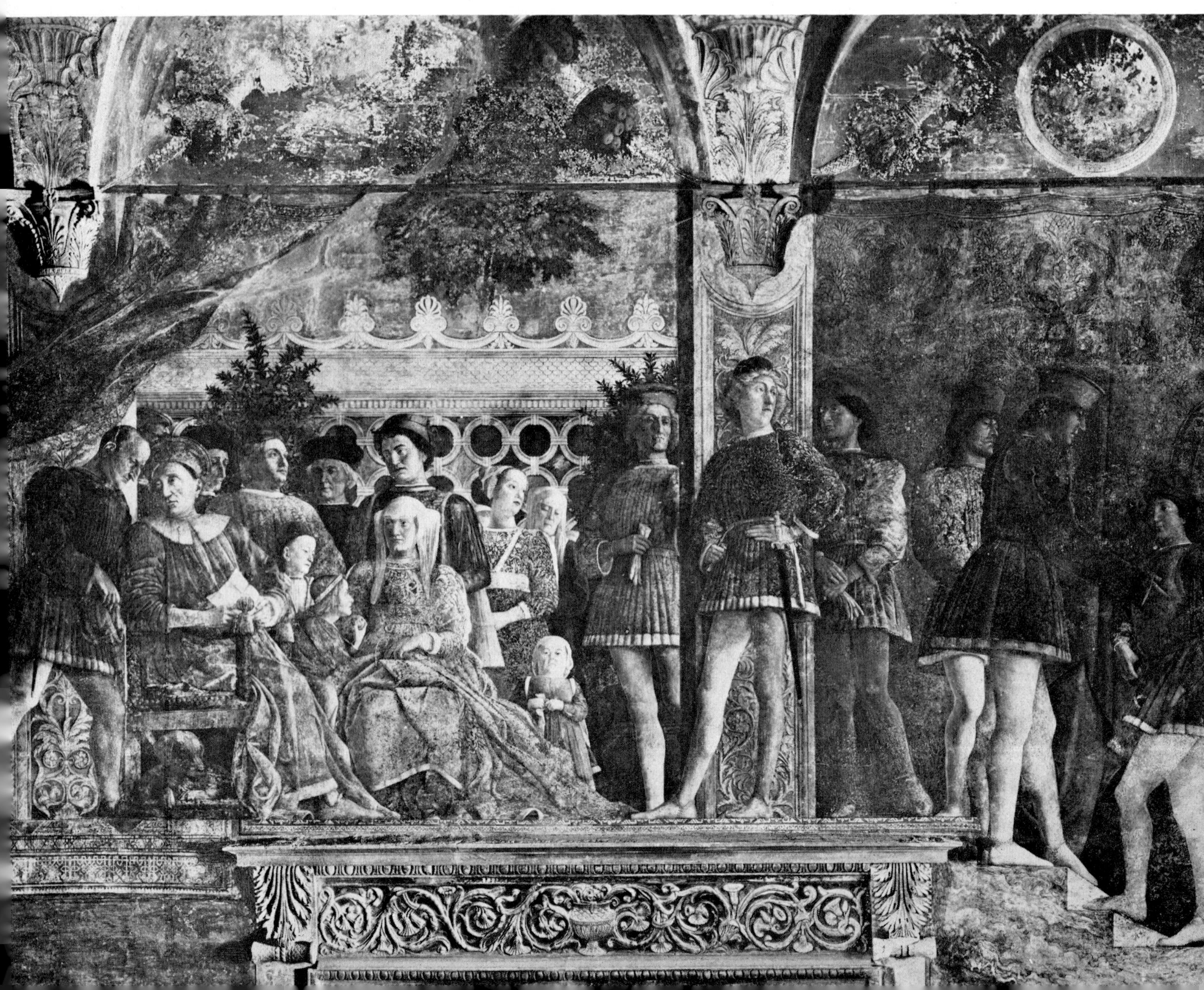

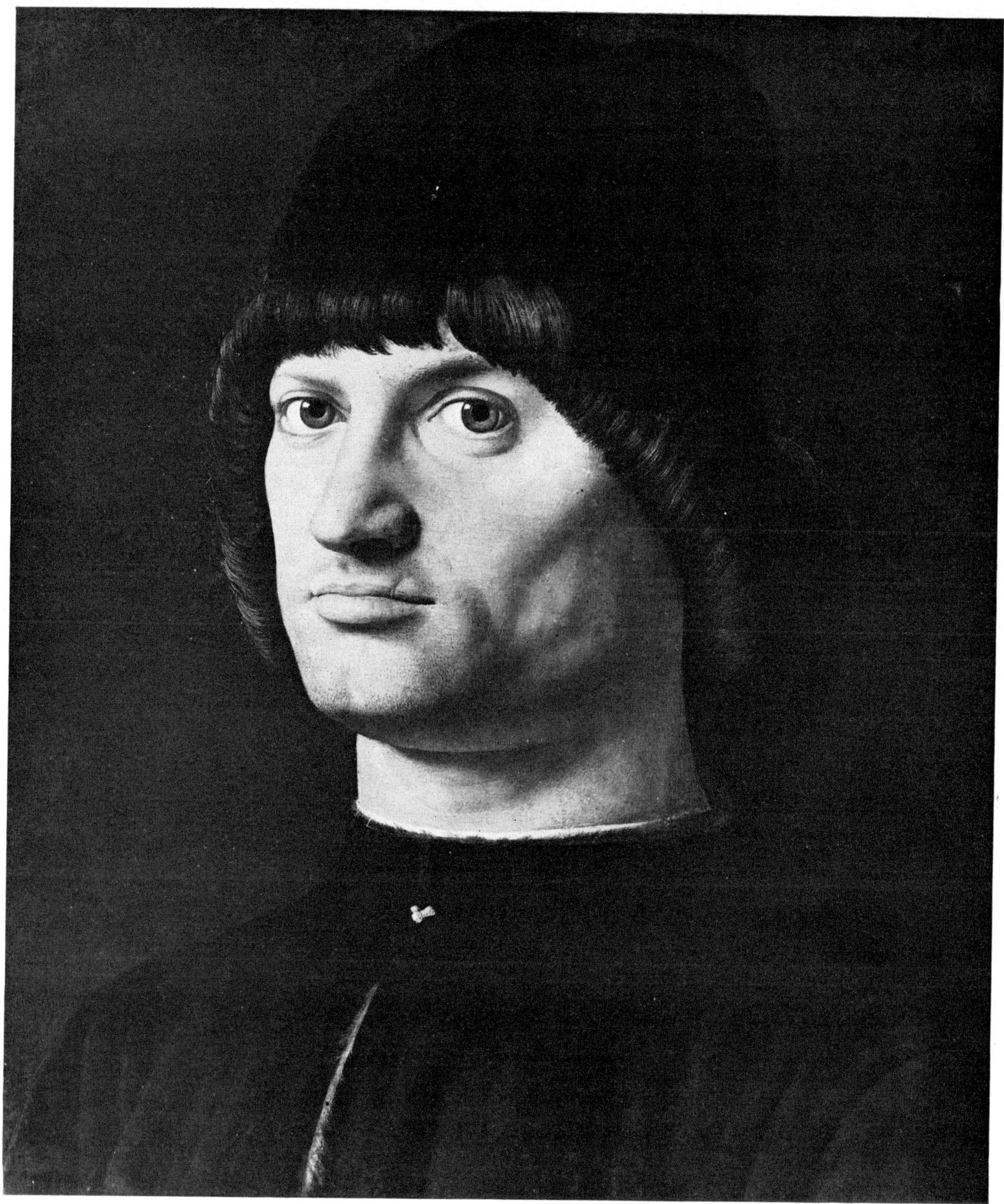

52. ANTONELLO DA MESSINA (*c.* 1430–79): *Portrait of a Condottiere.* 1475. Panel, $13\frac{3}{4} \times 11$ in. Paris, Louvre

Antonello, the only major South Italian painter of the century, adopted, probably in Naples, the technique of early Netherlandish oil painting. He is best known for his vivid head-and-shoulders portraits. Here the head of the stern man of action, slightly turned, is strongly modelled in light and shade and his eyes, 'the mirrors of the soul', are fixed firmly on the spectator.

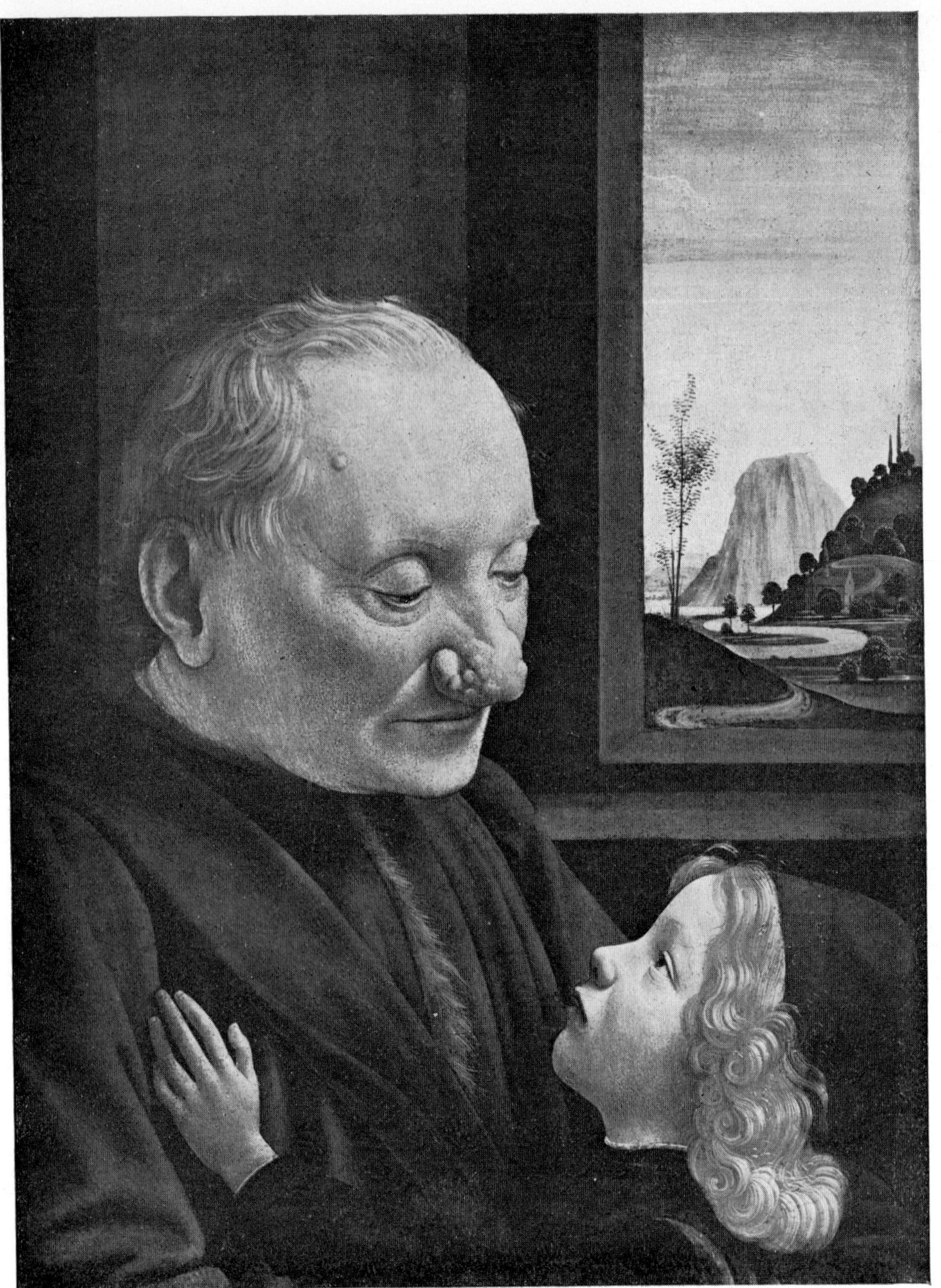

53. DOMENICO GHIRLANDAIO (1449–94): *Portrait of an Old Man and a Boy*. About 1480. Canvas, $24\frac{3}{8} \times 18\frac{1}{8}$ in. Paris, Louvre.

Among the Florentine painters of his time, Ghirlandaio was probably the one who most keenly observed his fellow citizens (see also Plates 64 and 91). In this touching portrait the fresh, curly-headed boy looks up at an old man with wispy hair, whose spongy nose shows the ravages of disease. They seem to offer one another loving reassurance: the old man seems to say, 'I shall look after you as long as I can', and the boy, 'You can lean on me when your weak eyes begin to fail'. The old man was, in fact, adapted from a drawing which Ghirlandaio had made of the head of a corpse lying on a bier. A church is the only building in the mountainous river landscape seen through the window.

54. GIOVANNI BELLINI (*c.* 1430–1516): *Portrait of Doge Leonardo Loredan*. About 1503–4. Panel, $24\frac{1}{4} \times 17$ in. London, National Gallery

The republic of Venice was the first state to commission and preserve portraits of its chief rulers. Bellini's superb state portrait shows Loredan, who had been elected doge in 1501, in his richly embroidered skull-cap and robe of office. The concept of the figure cut off by a ledge, or sill, was derived from Flemish painting.

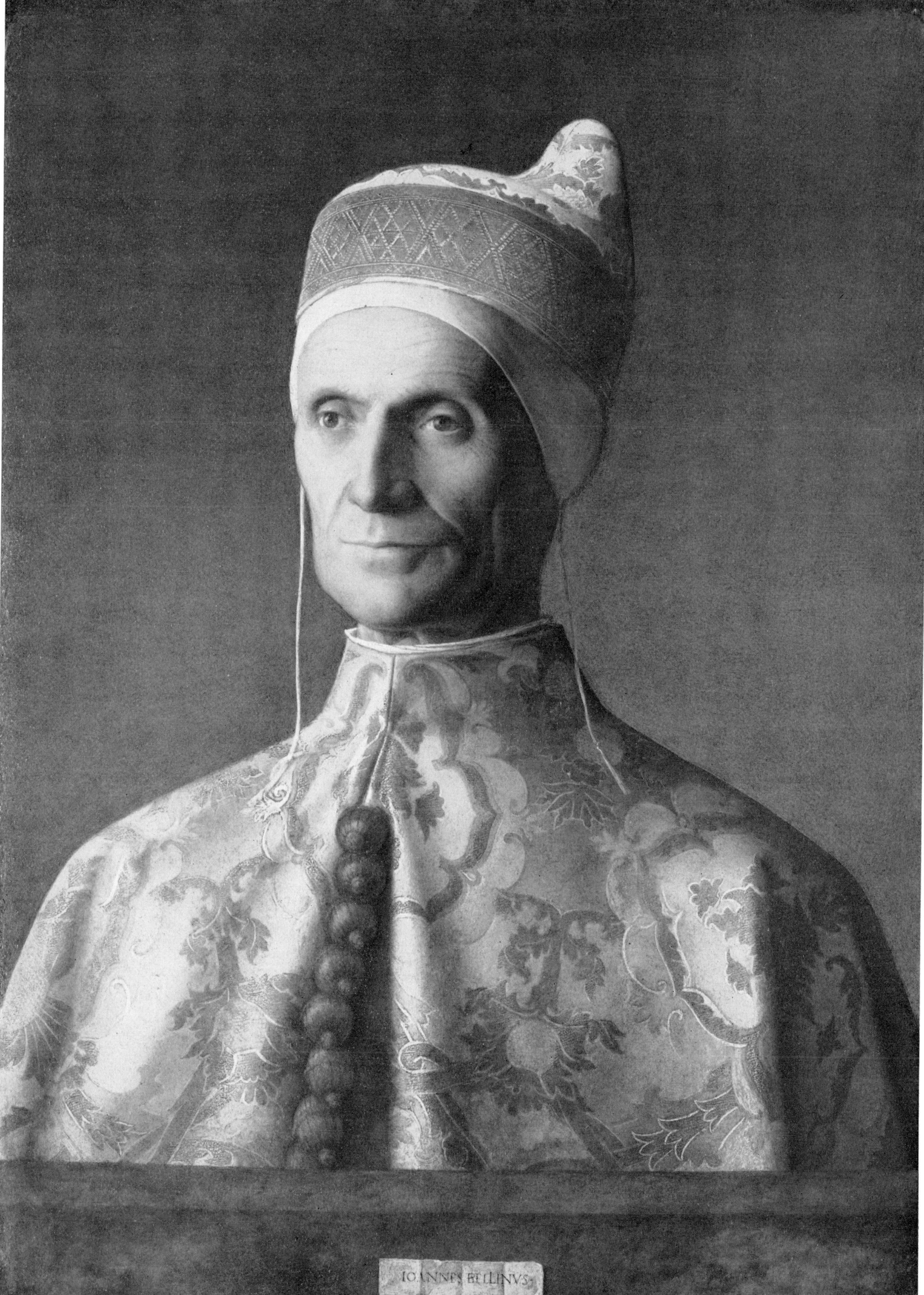
IOANNES BELLINVS

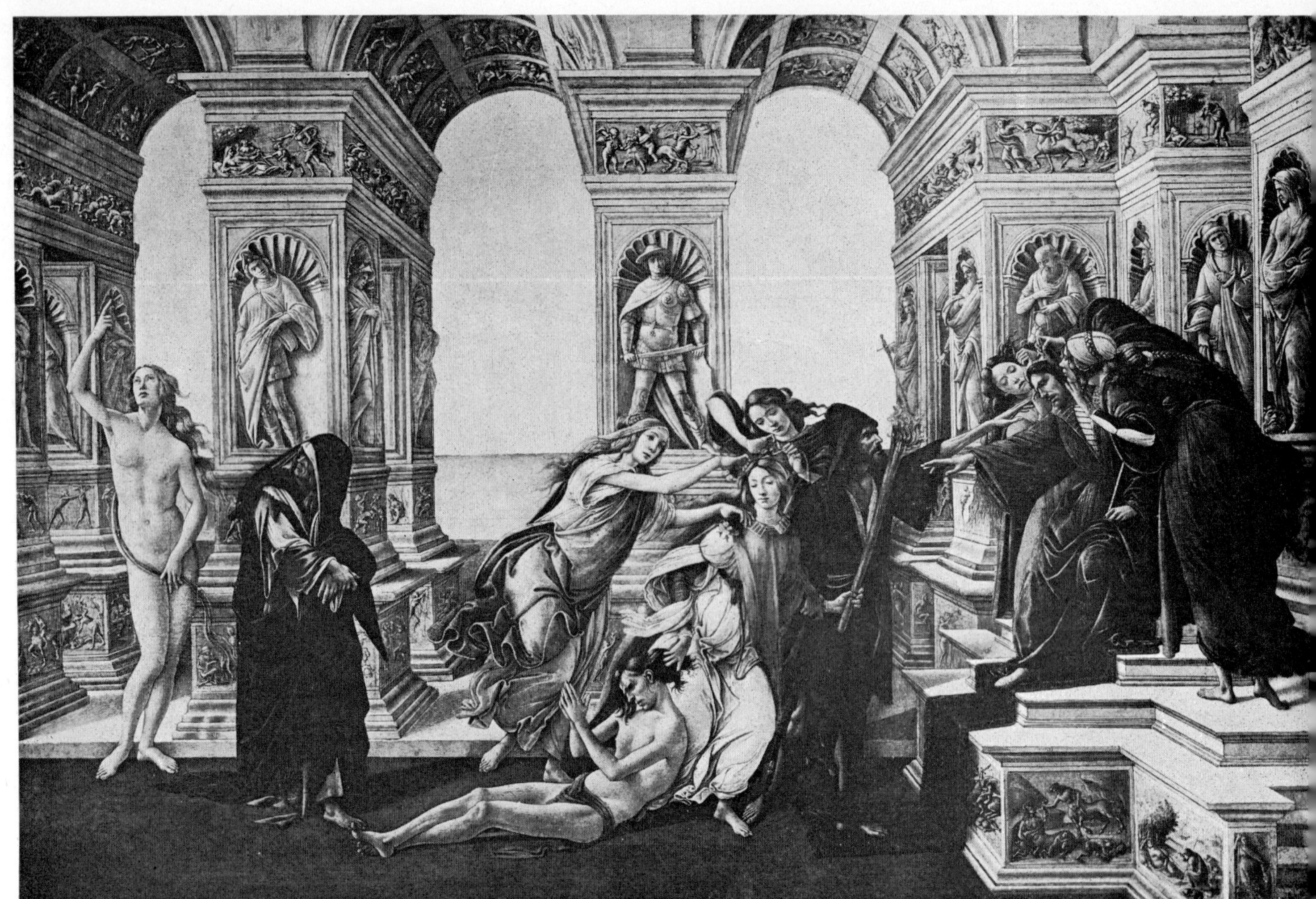

55. SANDRO BOTTICELLI (*c.* 1445–1510): *The Calumny of Apelles.* 1494–5. Panel, $24\frac{3}{8} \times 35\frac{7}{8}$ in. Florence, Uffizi

Florentine humanists were keenly interested in the lost paintings of antiquity and this allegory, like *The Birth of Venus* (Plate 38), sets out to recreate a masterpiece of the Greek painter, Apelles. In a richly decorated Grecian hall, the credulous judge listens to Prejudice and Ignorance, while Envy, Intrigue and Deception attend Calumny and try to make her appear attractive. She holds a torch (signifying that gossip spreads like fire) and drags along her hapless victim, who has been stripped of his good name. Repentance, an old crone bowed down in mourning, turns to look at Truth, who calls Heaven to witness. In her posture and nakedness, she and Botticelli's Venus are divine sisters: the painter seems to tell us, like Keats evoking the ideal world of ancient Greece, that 'Beauty is truth, truth beauty.'

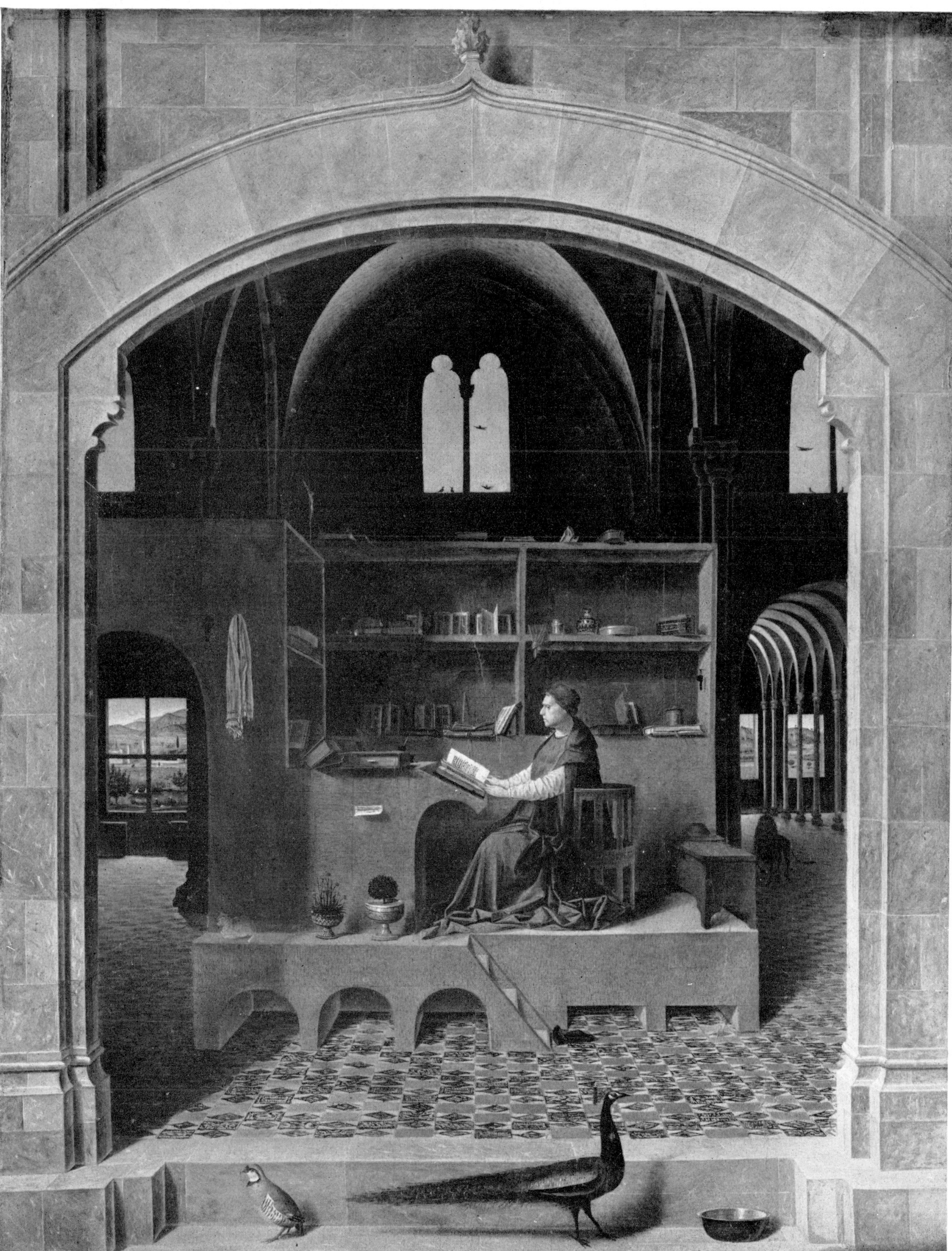

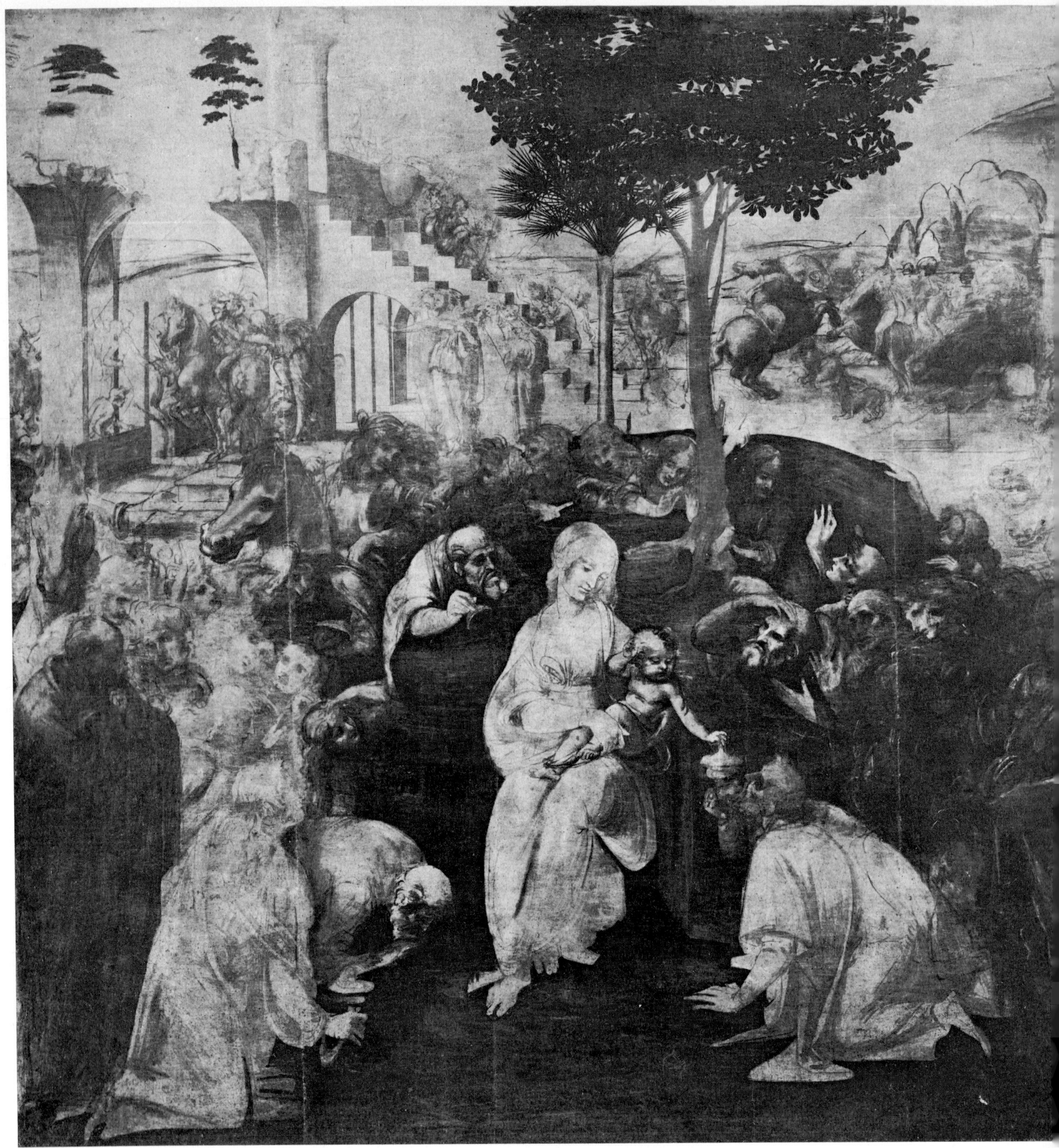

63. LEONARDO DA VINCI (1452–1519): *The Adoration of the Magi*. 1481. Panel, 96 × 97 in. Florence, Uffizi

Leonardo abandoned work on this large altarpiece at an early stage, but the underdrawing alone is a miracle of boundless inventiveness subordinated to a masterly design. In the background, studies of horses in movement and of strongly lit architecture, and notations of mountains, nudes and drapery; in the foreground, the semicircle of worshippers, sharply characterized in expressions and gestures, surround the serenely relaxed Virgin, a maternal smile hovering on her lips.

64. DOMENICO GHIRLANDAIO (1449–94): *The Birth of the Virgin.* 1486–90. Fresco. Florence, Santa Maria Novella

The religious subject is here treated, very engagingly, as an event in the everyday life of a rich Florentine family. St. Anne sits up in bed while a bath is being prepared for her new-born daughter, who is being held by a nurse. The visitors who have entered to pay their respects are grave Florentine matrons, preceded by an elegant younger woman. She seems to bear some resemblance to Giovanna Tornabuoni, whom Ghirlandaio portrayed about the same time (Plate 91) and who was the daughter-in-law of the patron who commissioned the cycle of frescoes (to which this wall-painting belongs), depicting the lives of the Virgin and St. John the Baptist. The principal subject is combined with that of the 'Visitation': on top of the steps, St. Elisabeth, the mother of the Baptist, greets the Virgin Mary (Luke 1:42).

It used to be thought that the setting of religious subjects in fifteenth-century contexts was merely typical of the secular tendencies of Renaissance thought. But this is not true. The real purpose of this approach was to emphasize the sitters' and donors' piety by associating them directly with the biblical characters in contemporary settings that stressed the modern relevance of the Christian faith.

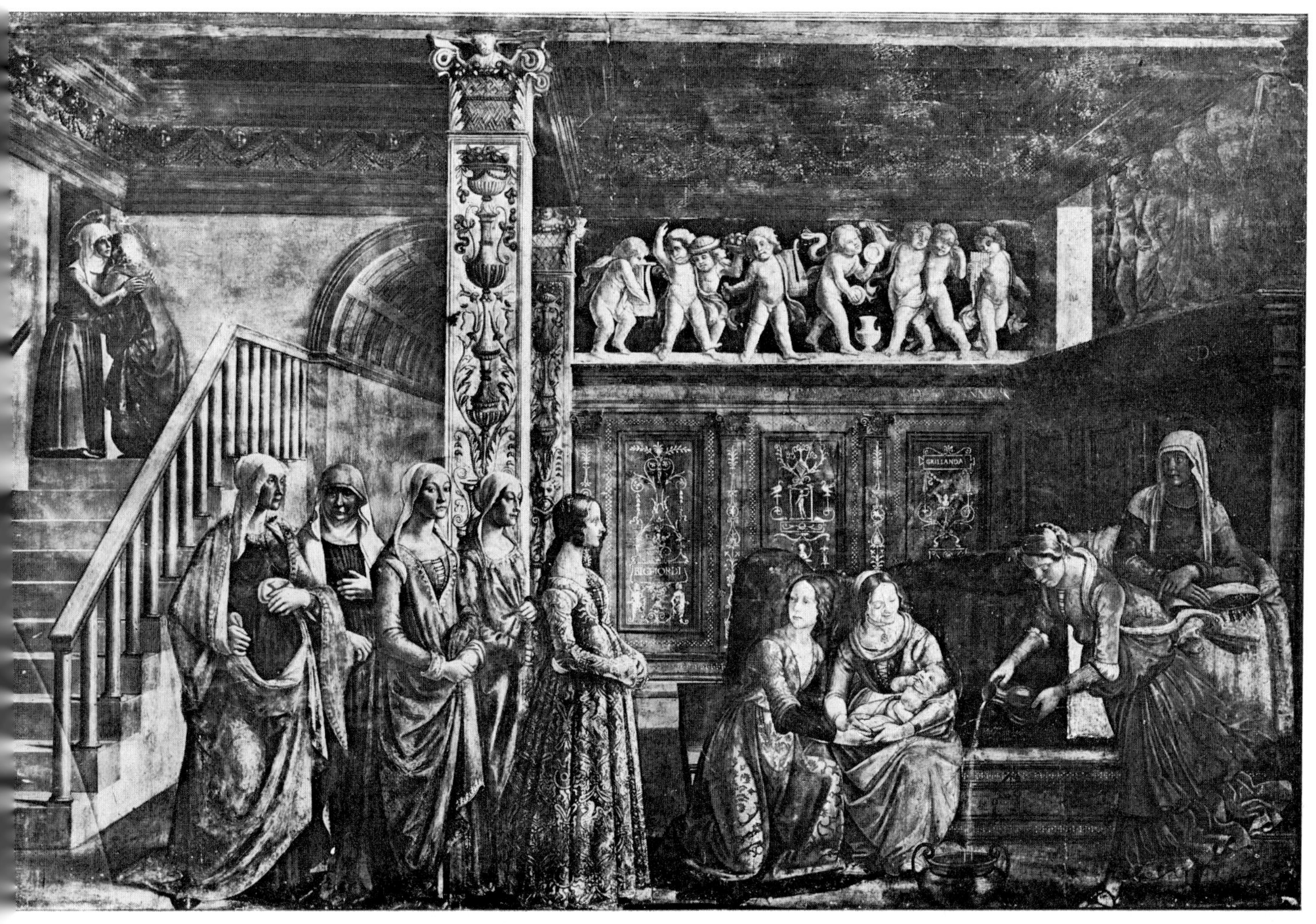

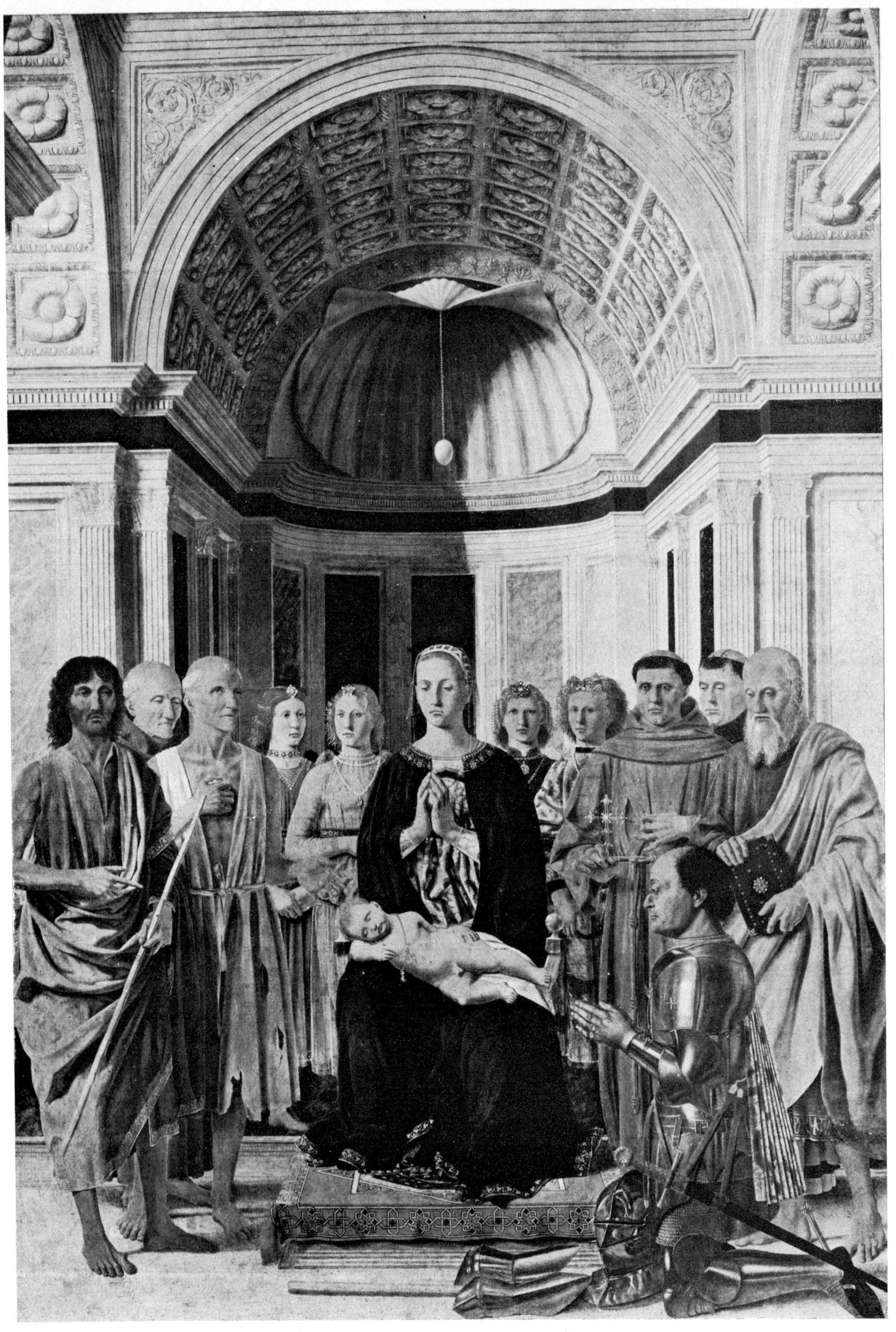

65. PIERO DELLA FRANCESCA (before 1420–92): *The Virgin and Child with Angels and Saints, Adored by Federigo da Montefeltro, Duke of Urbino.* 1472–5. Panel, $97\frac{1}{2} \times 66\frac{3}{4}$ in. Milan, Brera

66. MELOZZO DA FORLI (1438–94): *The Inauguration of the Vatican Library*. 1477. Fresco. Vatican, Pinacoteca

Both these paintings are notable for the sumptuous and magnificently painted architecture. In Piero's altarpiece the egg suspended in the apse is a symbol of eternity and purity, and the Duke, in gleaming armour, is now ten years older than in Piero's earlier portraits of him (Plates 58, 59). In Melozzo's fresco Pope Sixtus IV, who built both the papal library and the Sistine Chapel (Plate 4), appoints his first librarian.

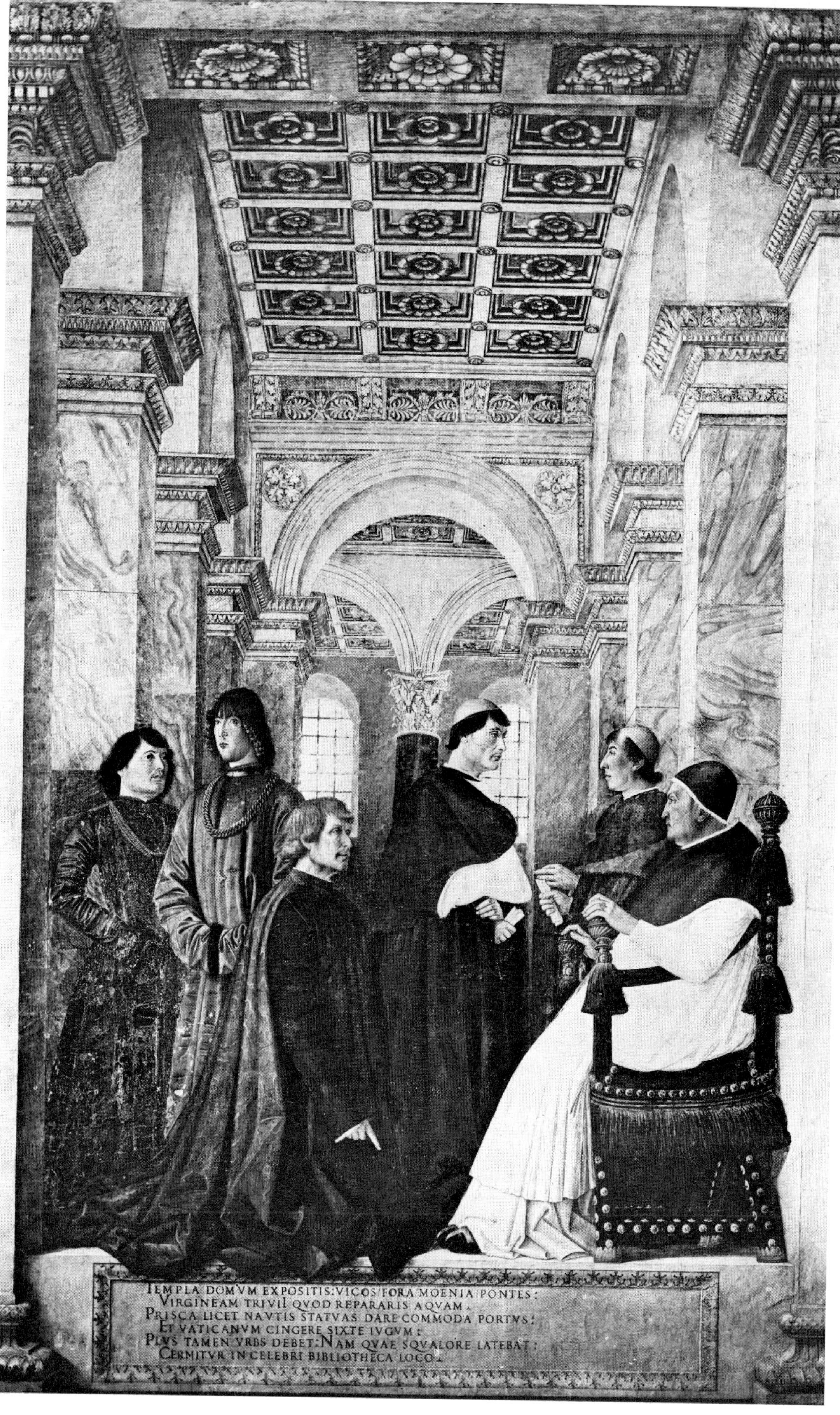

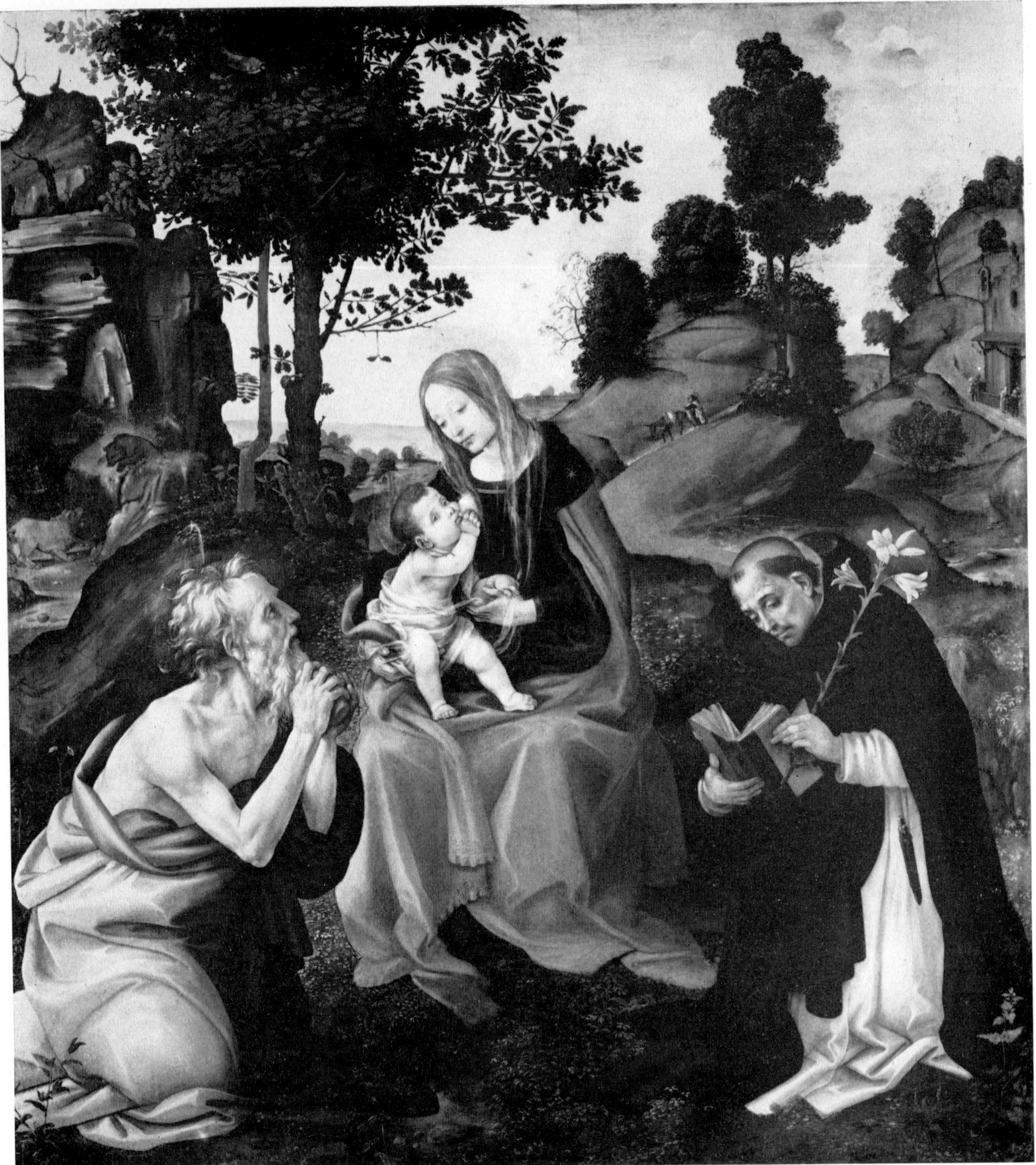

67, 68. FILIPPINO LIPPI (*c.* 1457–1504): *The Virgin and Child with St. Jerome and St. Dominic.* About 1485. Panel, 80 × 73¾ in. London, National Gallery

St. Jerome is usually represented as a scholar in his study (see Plate 62) or as a penitent mortifying himself in the desert. Here he has the features of an emaciated ascetic and clutches the stone with which he beat his breast; behind him, his tamed lion threatens a bear. St. Dominic is clad in the black and white habit of his Order and holds a stalk of lilies symbolizing purity. The prominence of St. Jerome is explained by the fact that the picture was painted for a chapel dedicated to the saint in the church of S. Pancrazio, Florence.

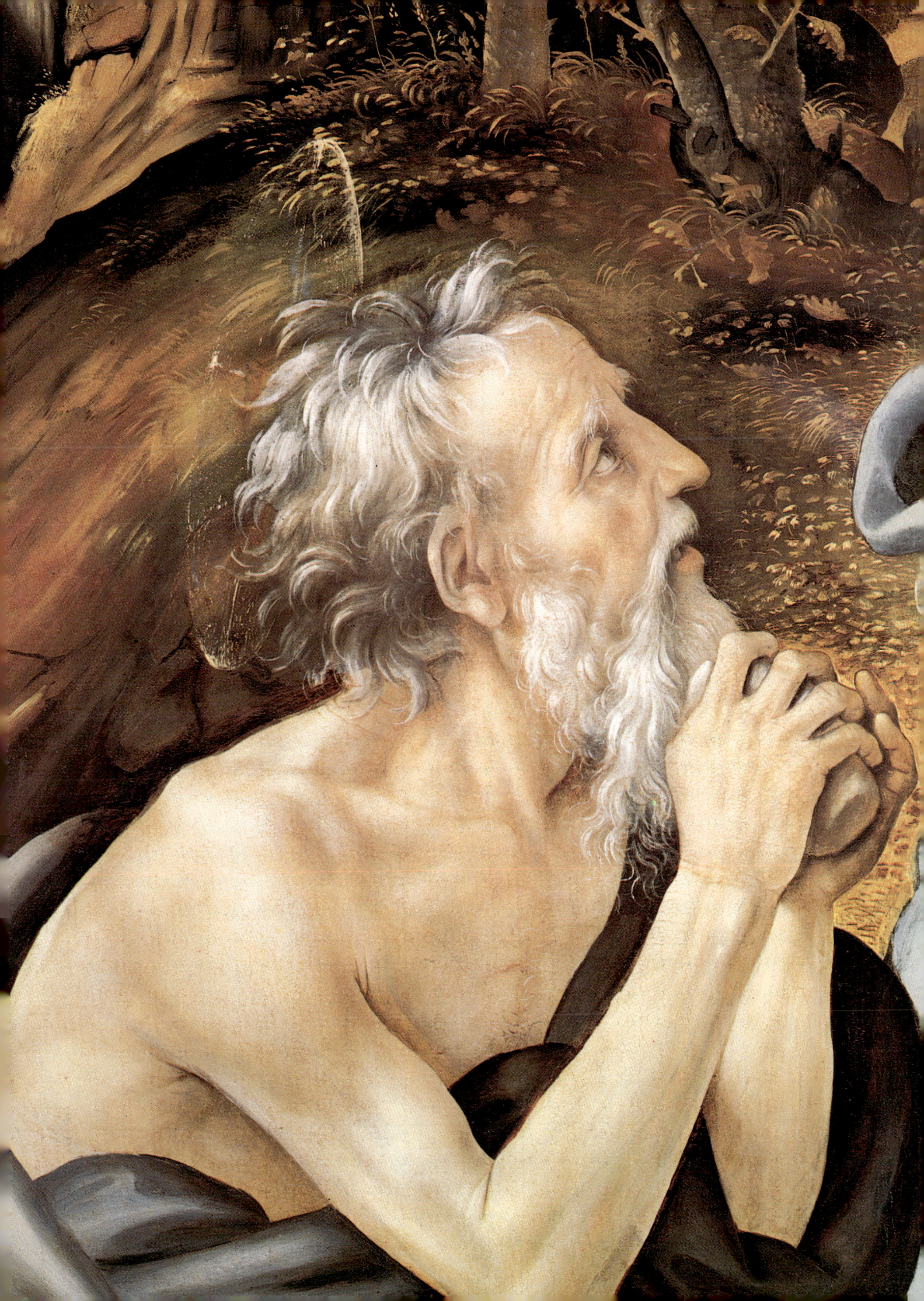

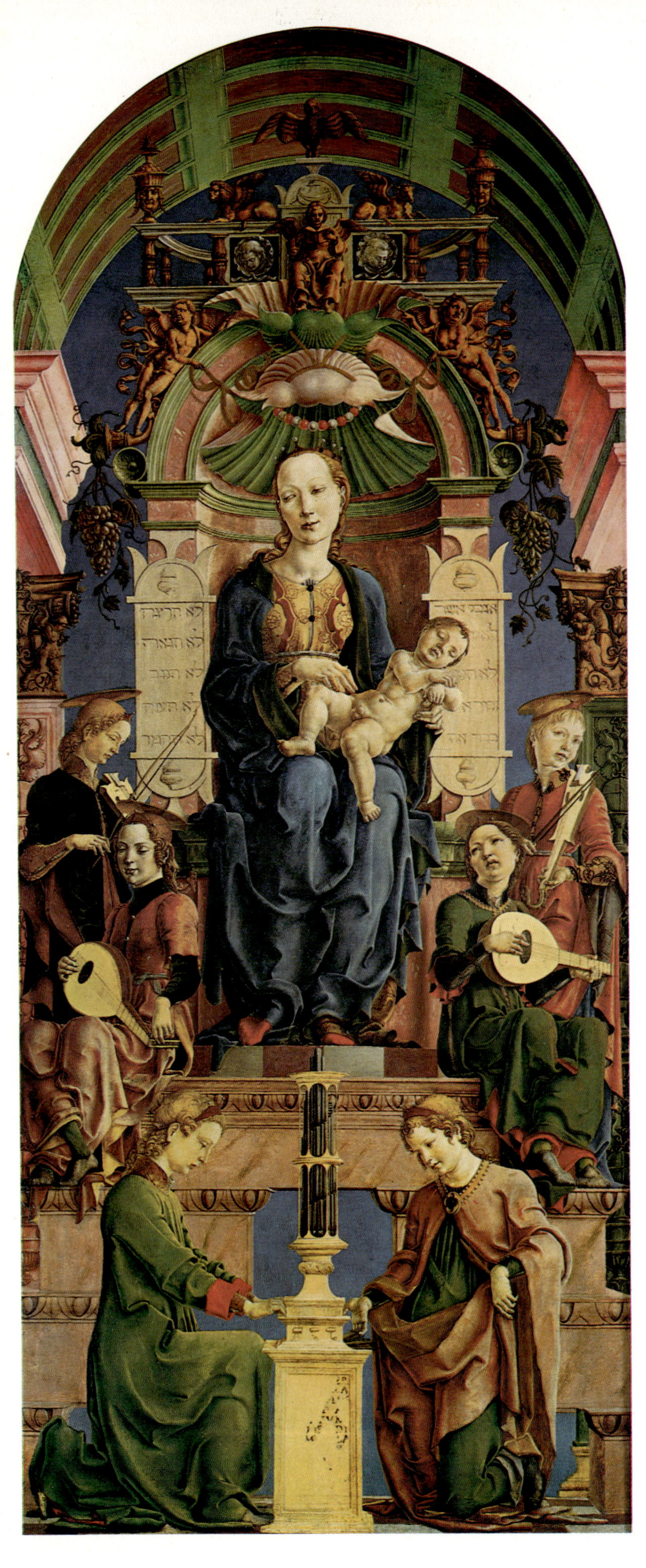

69. COSIMO TURA (before 1431–95): *The Virgin and Child Enthroned*. About 1480. Panel, $94\frac{1}{4} \times 40$ in. London, National Gallery

The elaborate top of the Virgin's throne, with its profusion of fantastic ornaments, testifies to Tura's 'brittle and metallic sense of form'. Among its decorations are the symbols of the four Evangelists: the angel of St. Matthew, the winged lion of St. Mark, the winged ox of St. Luke and the eagle of St. John. On the pillars are inscribed, in Hebrew, some of the Ten Commandments. Paintings such as this have contributed much to our knowledge of Renaissance music. The two angels in the foreground play a small organ, while the other four play a variety of stringed instruments.

The National Gallery picture is the main panel from a now dismembered altarpiece formerly in the chapel of S. Maurelio in S. Giorgio, Ferrara. The linear, decorative and even fantastic style is characteristic of Ferrarese painting.

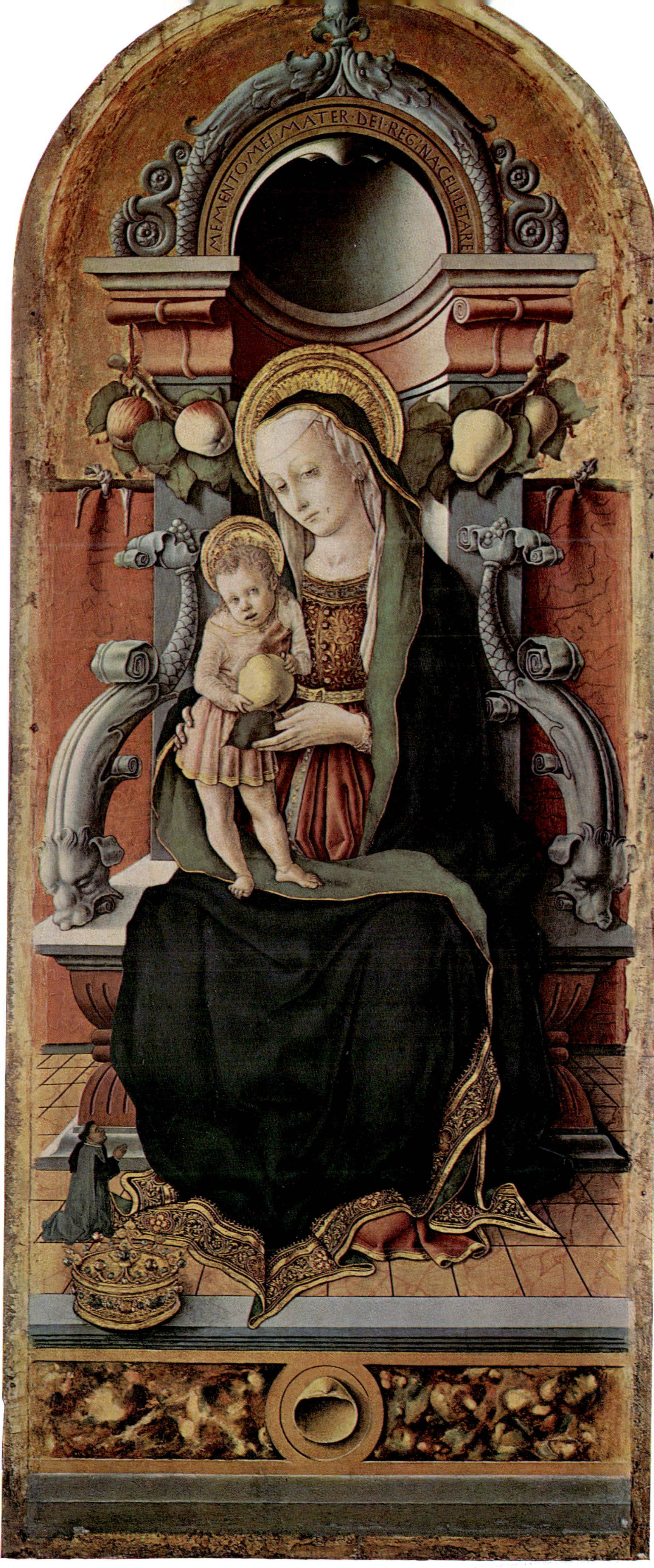

70. CARLO CRIVELLI (*c.* 1435–93): *The Virgin and Child Enthroned, Adored by a Donor*. 1470. Panel, $51 \times 21\frac{1}{4}$ in. Washington, D.C., National Gallery of Art (Samuel H. Kress Collection)

Like Tura's large altarpiece (opposite), Crivelli's small picture reveals delight in decorative accessories. His scroll shapes have a seductive 'strength of line and metallic lustre', which give the Virgin's ornate throne the quality of a craftsman's masterpiece. The dolphins, which form the arms of the throne, are symbols of eternal life, and the fruits, too, have symbolic significance. The Latin inscription means: Remember me, Mother of God, Queen of Heaven, rejoice. The spectator's eye tends to adjust itself to the scale of the sacred group and the luxuriance of the setting before he discovers the tiny figure of the kneeling donor.

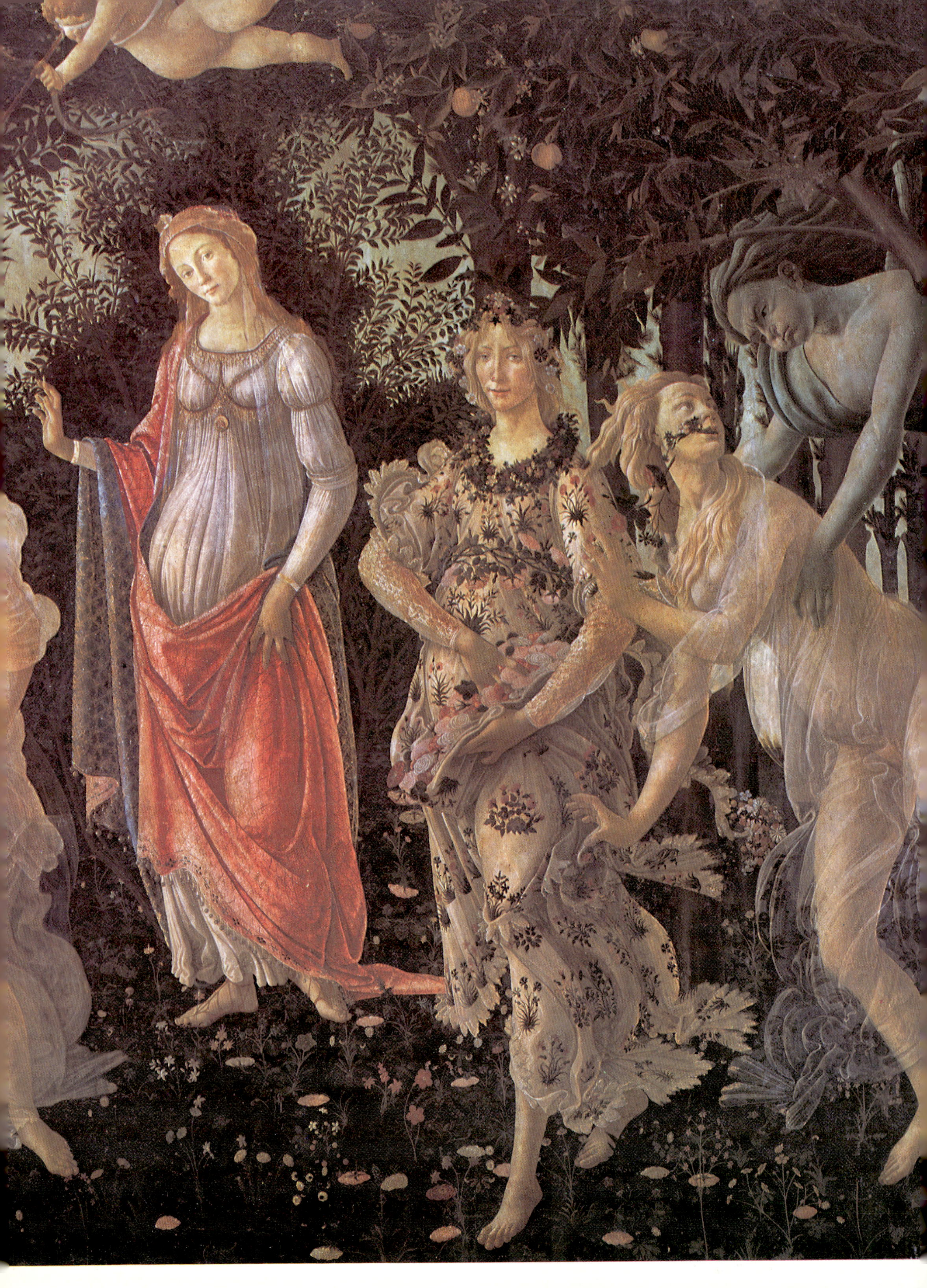

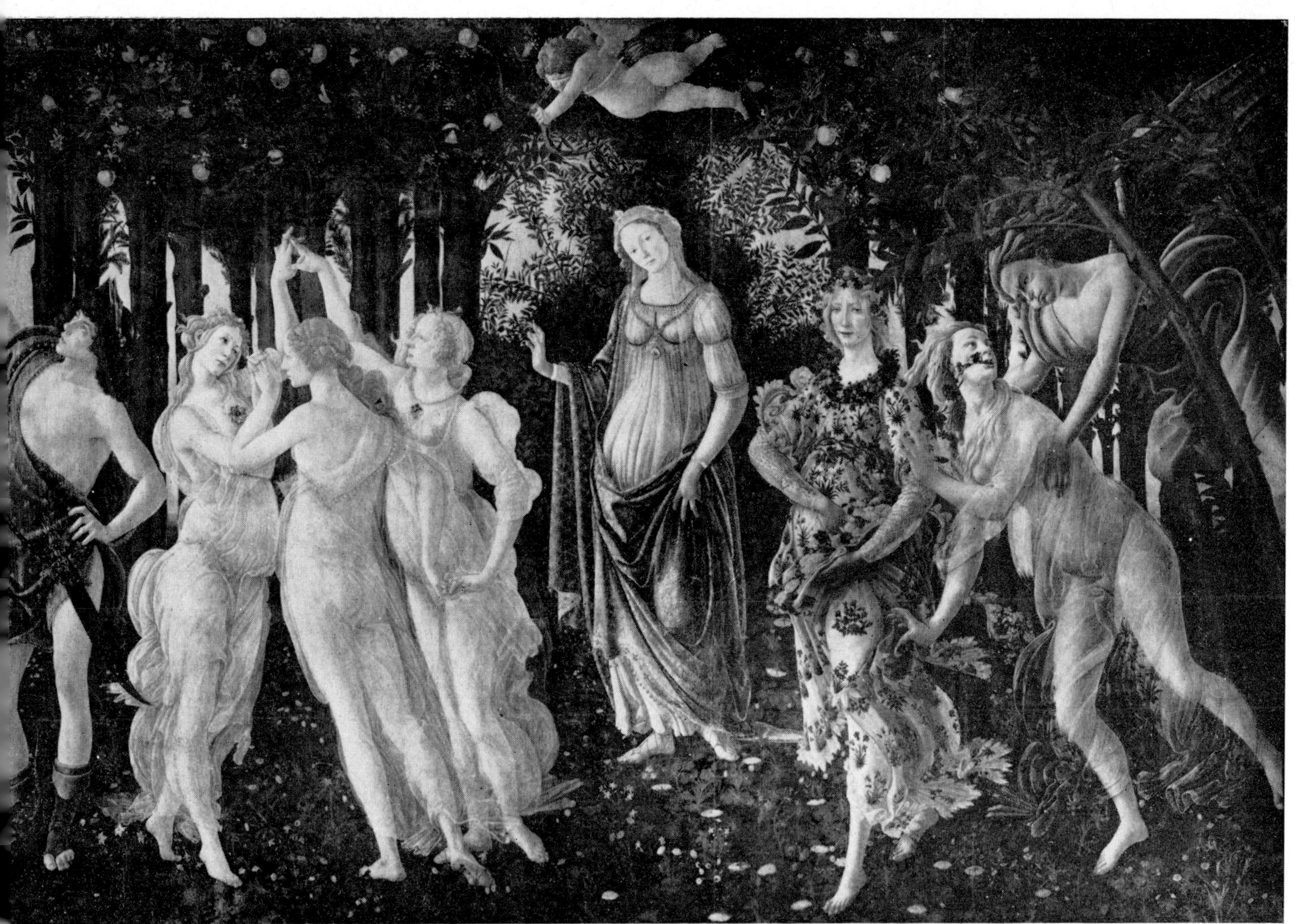

72. SANDRO BOTTICELLI (*c.* 1445–1510): *Spring* ('*La Primavera*'). 1477–8. Canvas, 80 × 124 in. Florence, Uffizi

At the left Mercury, in a charmingly relaxed posture, points upwards. Next to him the three Graces, with hands interlaced and billowing draperies, perform a slow dance, while, above, a blindfolded Cupid with bow and arrow aims a barb of fire at them. At the right the wind-god Zephyr pursues the fleeing nymph, Chloris, who is dressed in a clinging transparent veil. At his touch, she is transformed into Flora, goddess of Spring, gorgeously arrayed in an embroidered gown. The centre of the stage is held by Venus herself, in a relaxed stance and inclining her head. The poetry of this idealized tableau is echoed by the leafy orange grove and the flowery meadow. Like Botticelli's other large mythological painting (Plate 38), the '*Primavera*' was painted for the young Lorenzo di Pierfrancesco de' Medici and its allegorical significance once carried an educational exhortation. The classical goddess has here become a personification of Christian love and humanity, which the young man is to strive after—'beauty is a gateway to the divine'. But neither its underlying seriousness nor the antique cast of figures impair our enjoyment of its magical enchantment.

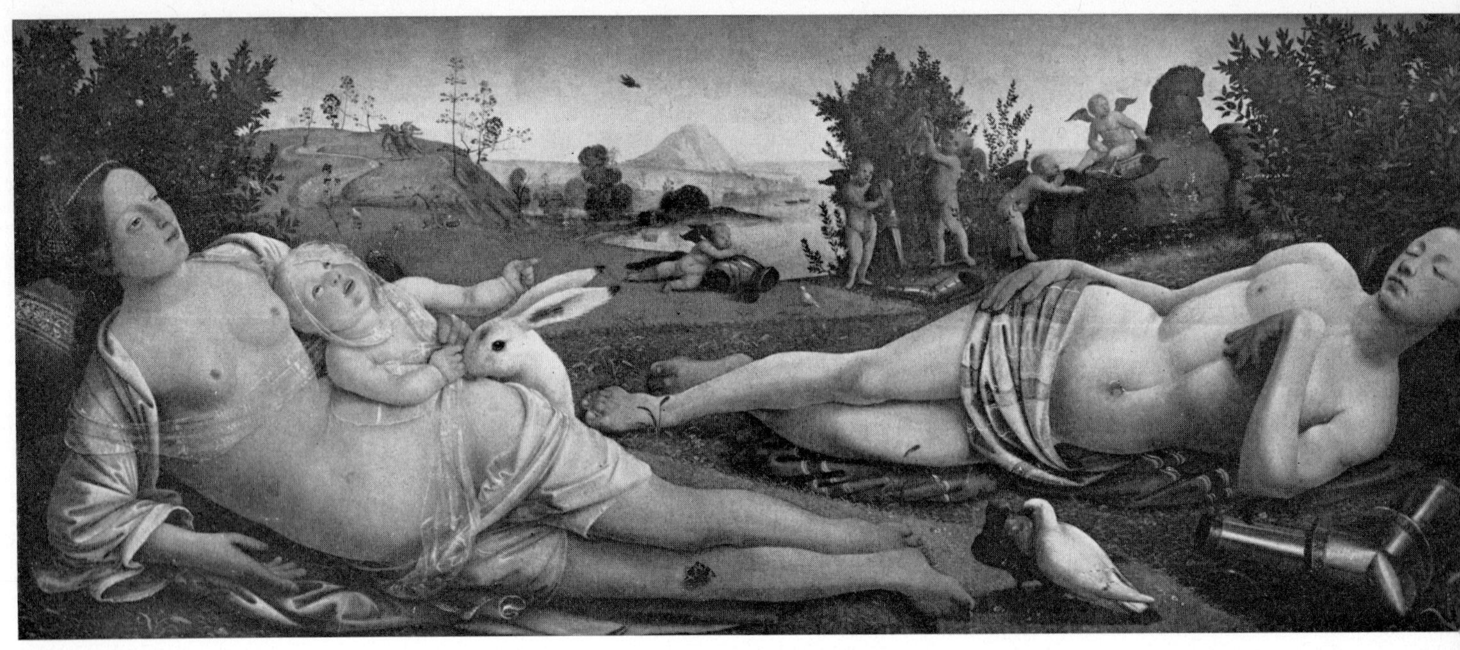

73. PIERO DI COSIMO (*c.* 1462–after 1515): *Mars and Venus*. About 1490. Panel, $28\frac{1}{4} \times 72$ in. Berlin-Dahlem, Staatliche Museen

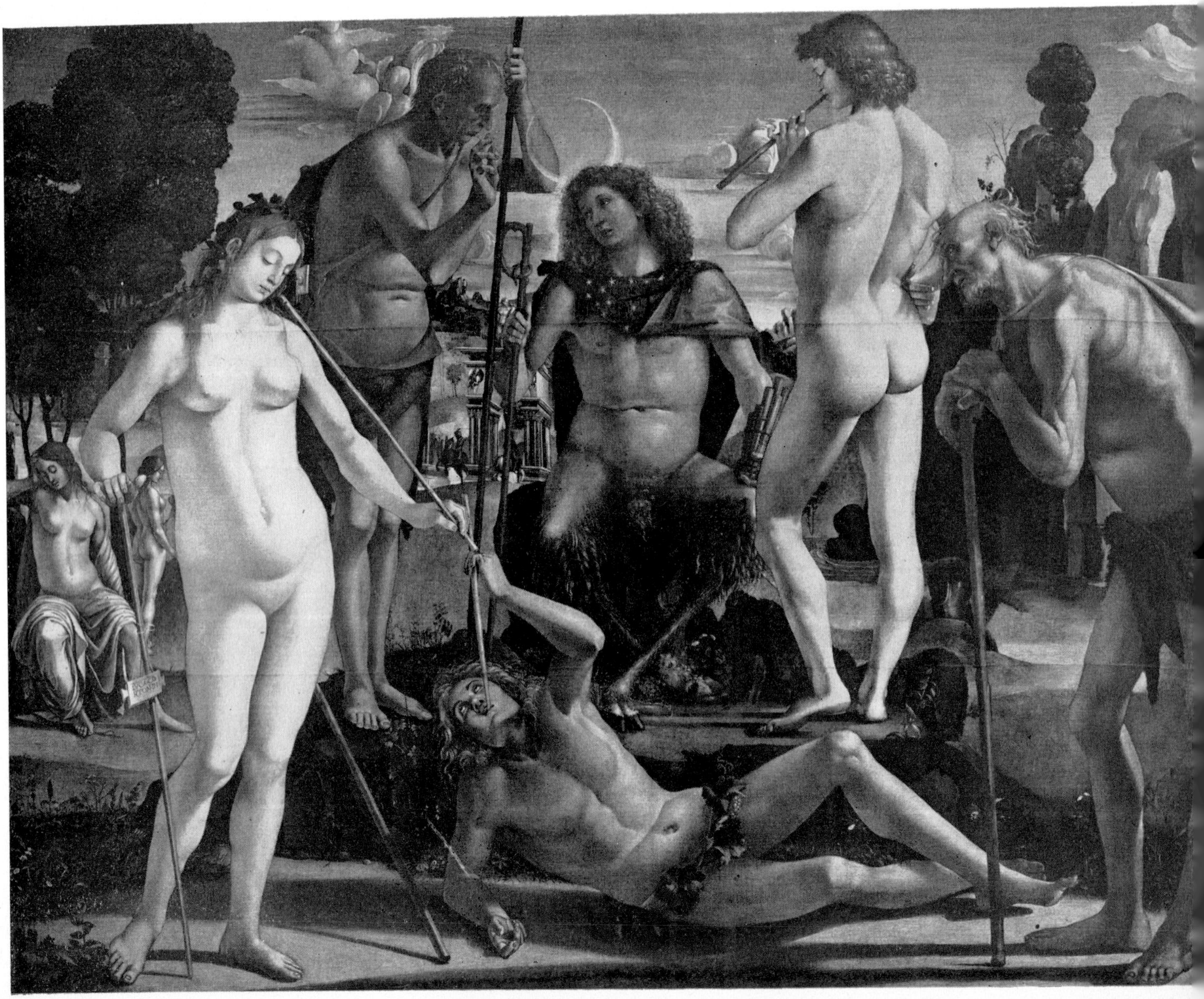

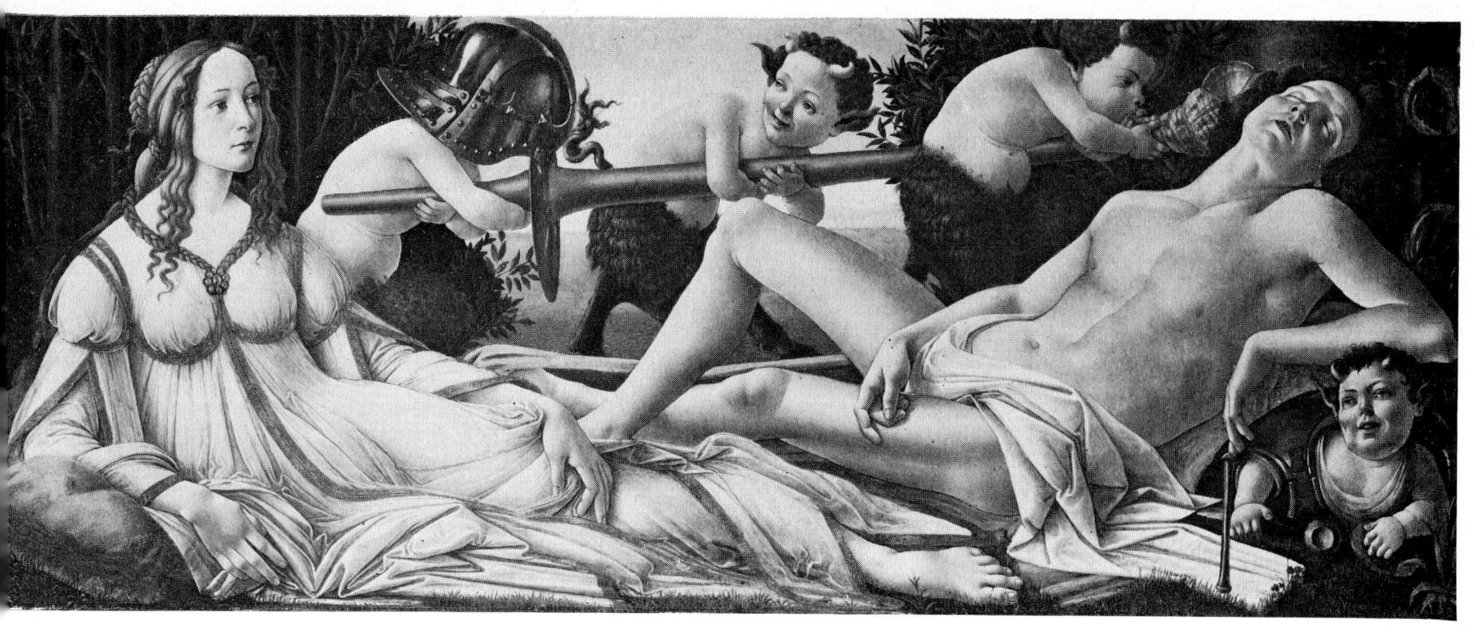

75. SANDRO BOTTICELLI (*c.* 1445–1510): *Mars and Venus*. 1483–5. Panel, $27\frac{1}{4} \times 68\frac{1}{4}$ in. London, National Gallery

Venus watches her lover, who has fallen asleep. In Piero's picture (opposite, above) the erotic significance is made doubly clear by the two billing doves. A large Cupid, less attractive than the large rabbit, points at his brothers, who play with the armour they have stolen from the defenceless god of war. In Botticelli's version, Mars is so exhausted that not even the satyr blowing at a shell can waken him. Two other young satyrs, one of them wearing his helmet, carry his heavy lance, and a fourth has donned his cuirass. The wasps at the top right of the painting may refer to the Vespucci family, who were among Botticelli's patrons.

4. LUCA SIGNORELLI (*c.* 1441–1523): *The Kingdom of Pan*. About 1490. Canvas, $76\frac{1}{2} \times 101$ in. Formerly Berlin, Kaiser Friedrich Museum. Destroyed in 1945

'The goat-footed Pan, with the majestic pathos of Nature in his aspect, sits in the hushed solemnity of the sunset, the tender crescent moon crowning his locks. Primevally grand nude figures stand about him, while Olympus is piping, and another youth lies at his feet playing on a reed. They are holding solemn discourse and their theme is "The Poetry of Earth is never Dead". The sunset has begotten them upon the dew of the earth, and they are whispering the secrets of the Great Mother.' (B. Berenson)

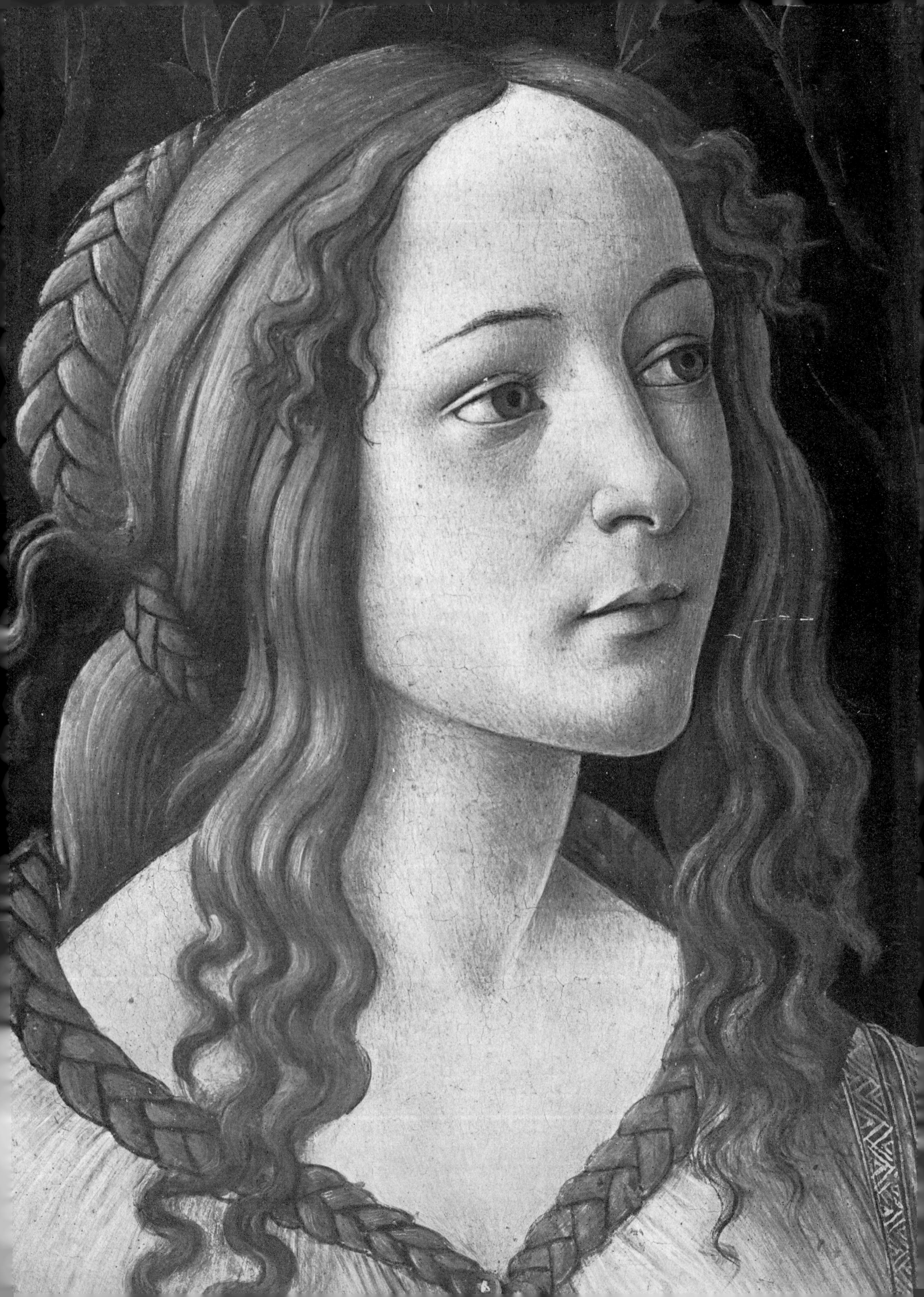

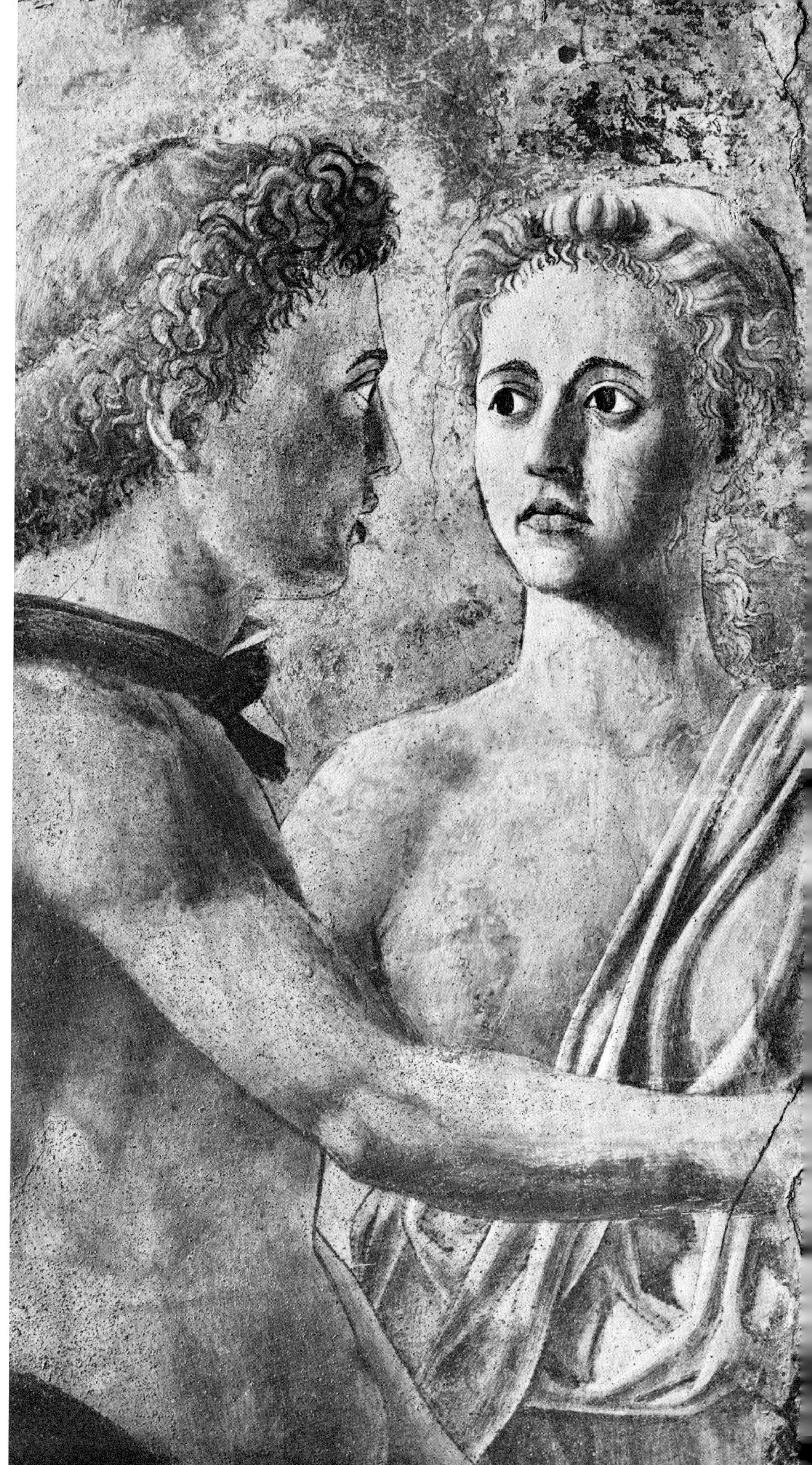

77. PIERO DELLA FRANCESCA (before 1420–92): *Two Children of Adam*. About 1458. Detail of a fresco. Arezzo, San Francesco

One of the frescoes in the cycle of 'The Legend of the True Cross' (see Plate 31) depicts the death of Adam. Here, two of his children look at one another fearfully and uncomprehendingly, trying to understand that from now on death will be inseparable from life.

76. SANDRO BOTTICELLI (*c.* 1445–1510): *Head of Venus*. Detail from Plate 75

A Florentine ideal of womanly beauty.

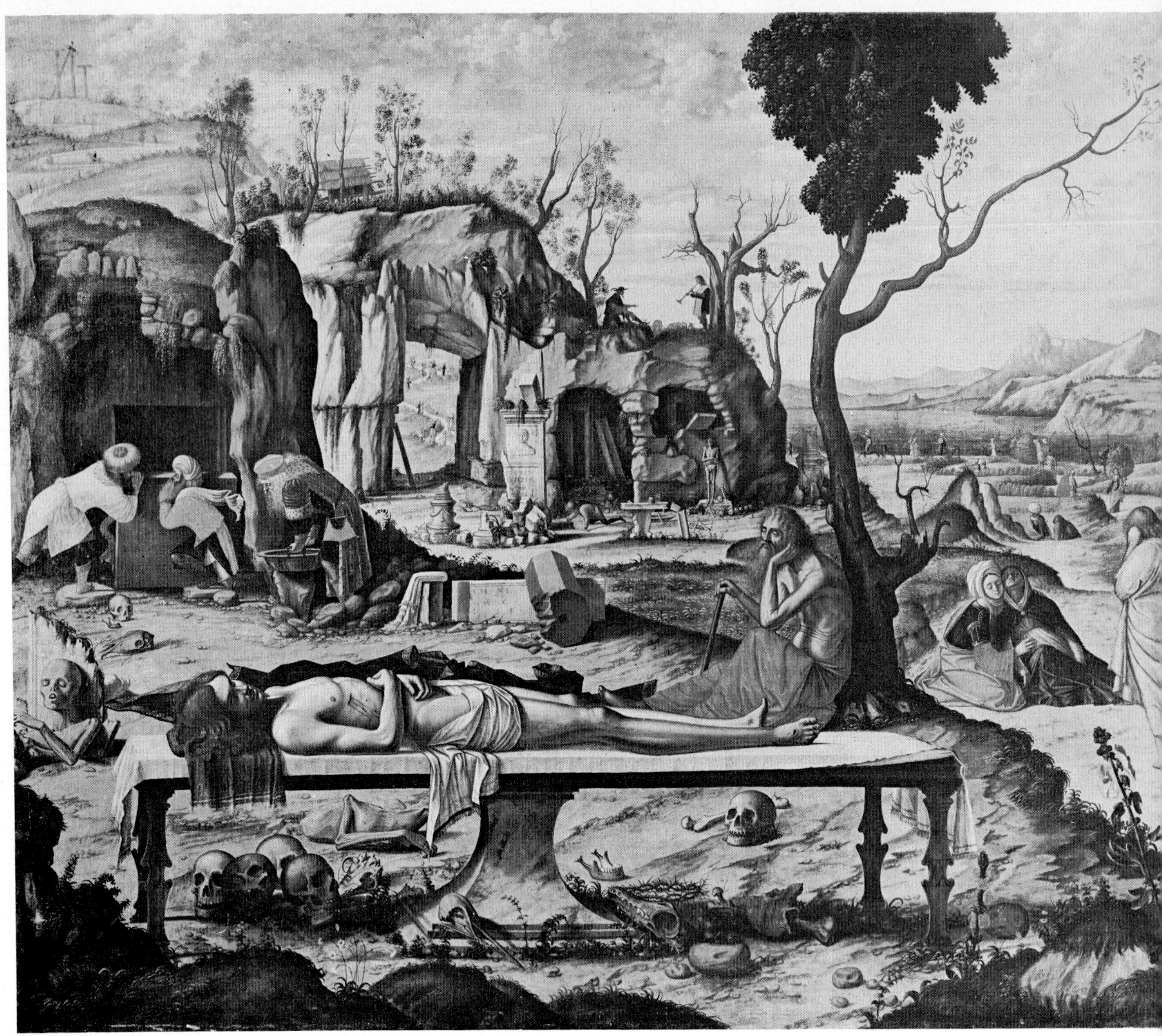

78. VITTORE CARPACCIO (*c.* 1460–1523/6): *Meditation on the Death of Christ.* About 1502–7. Canvas, $57\frac{1}{2} \times 73$ in. Berlin, Staatliche Museen

The body of Christ is stretched out on a marble bier and at his feet sits an old man in meditation, perhaps representing the patriarch Job. At the right the fainting Virgin is supported by a companion and St. John turns away, unable to bear the harrowing sight. At the left three men in Turkish costume open up a sepulchre for the burial. The ground is littered with skulls, bones and severed limbs and, further back, with fragments of antique sculpture. The two shepherds on the rock and the landscape idyll in the distance have no part in the mournful tableau, but on the left the ground rises to the three crosses on Calvary.

79. GIOVANNI BELLINI (*c.* 1430–1516): *Religious Allegory*. About 1485. Panel, $28\frac{3}{4} \times 46\frac{3}{4}$ in. Florence, Uffizi

The Christ Child is seated on a cushion (exactly in the centre of the elaborate marble pavement) and plays with oranges shaken down from a tree by *putti*. He is being adored by the Virgin, who is enthroned on a dais under a graceful canopy, and by five saints, among them Joseph, leaning on the balustrade, and Sebastian, whose hands are tied behind his back. St. Paul, with drawn sword, threatens a Turk. On the far side of the water St. Anthony Abbot is about to encounter a centaur, and beyond rises a more familiar landscape with farm buildings and a castle.

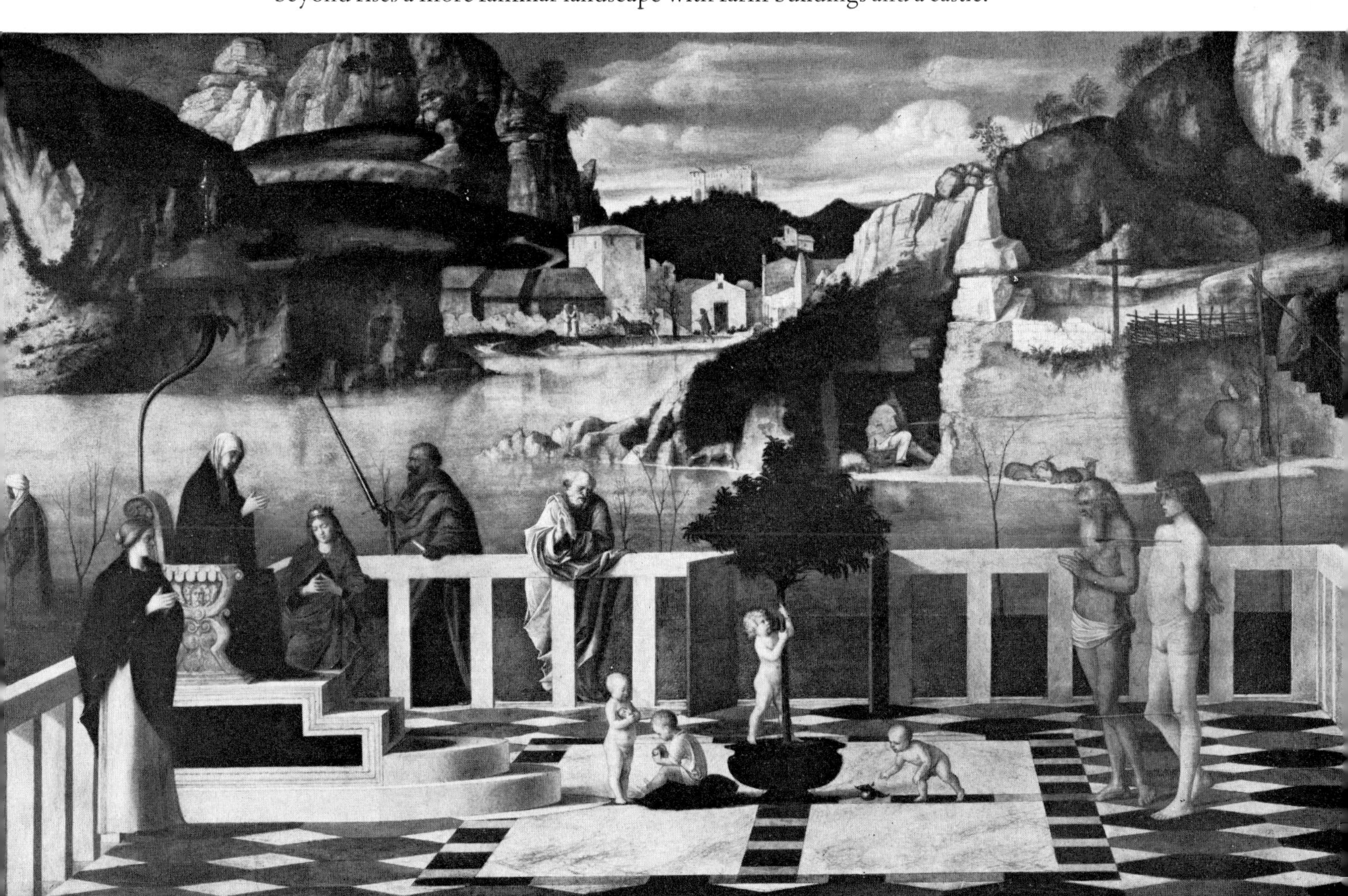

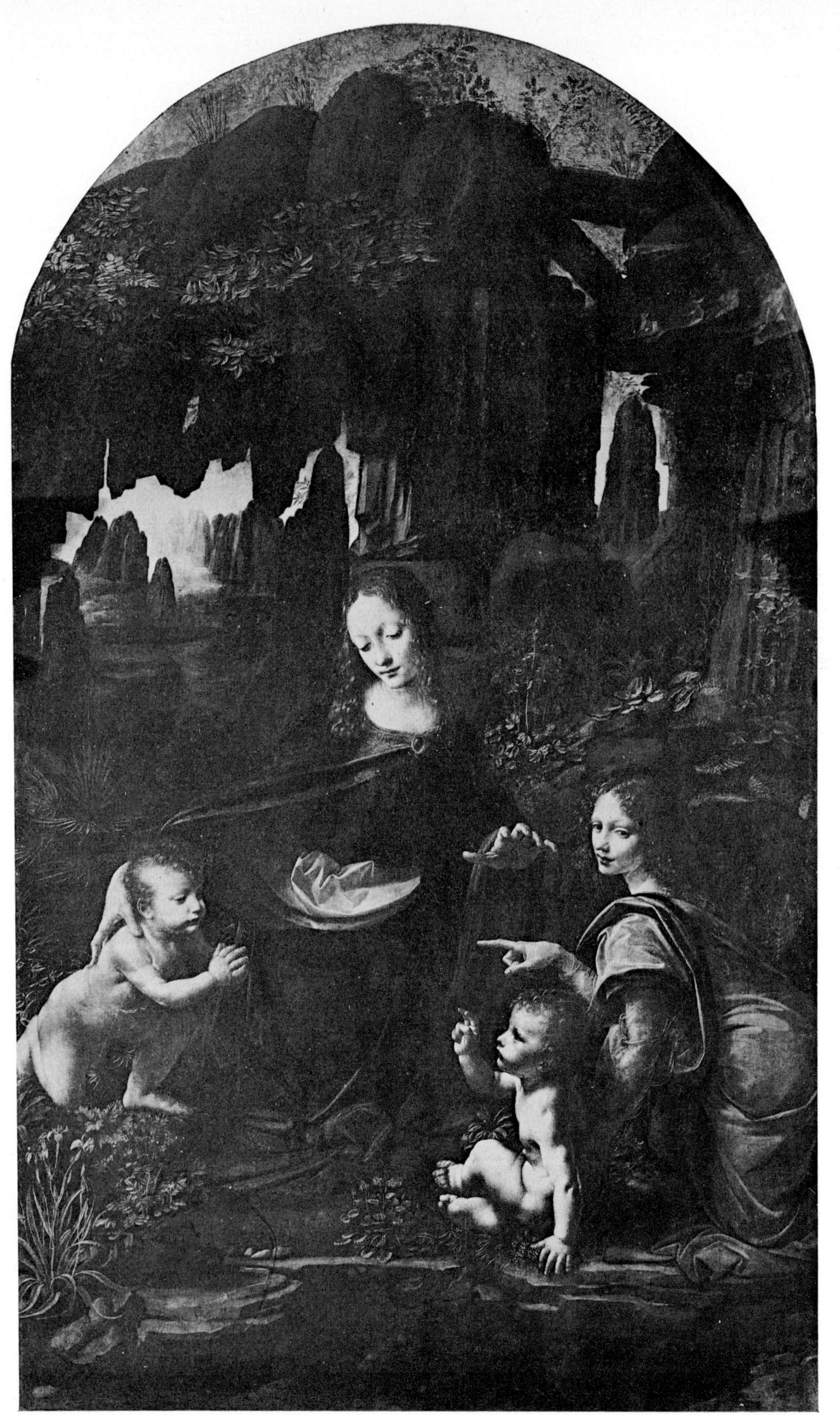

80. LEONARDO DA VINCI (1452–1519): *The Virgin of the Rocks*. Between 1483 and 1506. Panel, $74\frac{5}{8} \times 47\frac{1}{4}$ in. London, National Gallery
In the mysterious solitude of a fantastic rocky shelter the Christ Child, held by an angel, blesses the young John the Baptist, who kneels in adoration. Details such as the angel's sleeve, the Virgin's drapery, the plants and flowers, and the distant view add to the beauty of the composition.

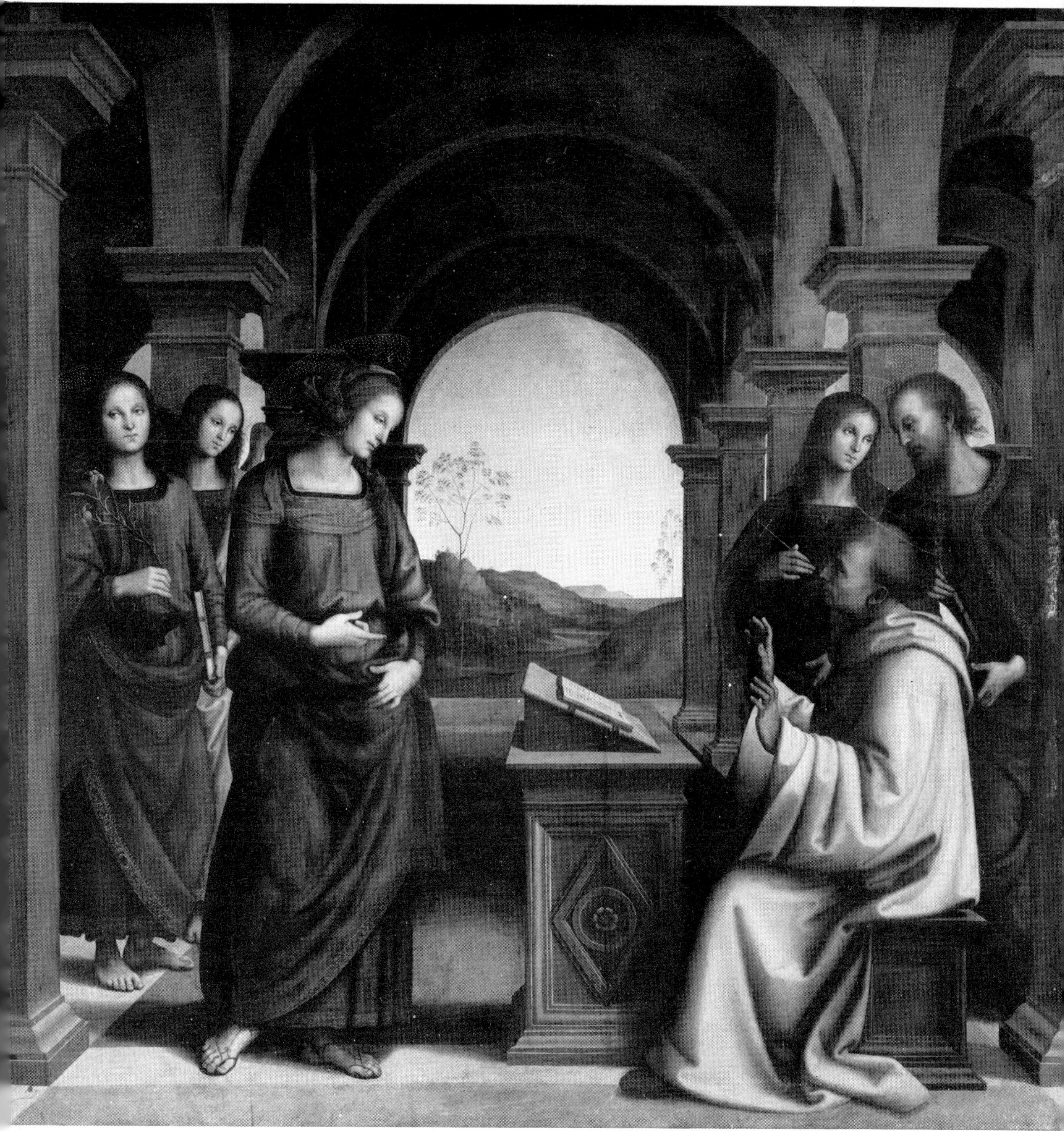

1. PIETRO PERUGINO (*c.* 1445–1523): *St. Bernard's Vision of the Virgin.* 1489. Panel, 68 × 67 in. Munich, Alte Pinakothek

St. Bernard, a Doctor of the Church and Abbot of Clairvaux, is shown in the white habit of the Cistercian Order. The centralized architecture in perspective recession and the refined, if stereotyped, figures were among those elements in Perugino's work that were absorbed and reshaped by the genius of his pupil Raphael.

83. ANTONIO (*c.* 1432–98) and PIERO (*c.* 1441–96) POLLAIUOLO: *Landscape*. Detail from Plate 50

The predella of Gentile's resplendent altarpiece (Plate 6) has three panels showing scenes from the childhood of Christ: the Nativity, the Flight into Egypt, and the Circumcision. The painter made good use of this choice of subjects to vary his backgrounds: the first is a night scene, the last has an is architectural setting, while the group of the Virgin and Child seated on the donkey led by St. Joseph is set in a landscape which seems to echo the hills and castles at the top of the main panel. In each of the three panels the sacred event is watched by two elegant ladies in Renaissance costume. The pair in the *Flight* is somewhat awkwardly posed and their hands are difficult to 'read'. But the beauty of nature is delightfully caught in the orange trees and flowering shrubs.

In the next two generations this schematic rendering of landscape gave way to more atmospherically rendered views: the Pollaiuolo brothers' panorama leads the eye convincingly from the carefully observed wooded river landscape in the foreground over the hills to the hazy and featureless mountain in the distance. This and the high viewpoint are links with the landscape in Piero della Francesca's '*Triumphs*' (Plate 59).

82. GENTILE DA FABRIANO (*c.* 1370–1427): *The Flight into Egypt*. 1423. Detail from a panel, 10 × 34¾ in. Florence, Uffizi

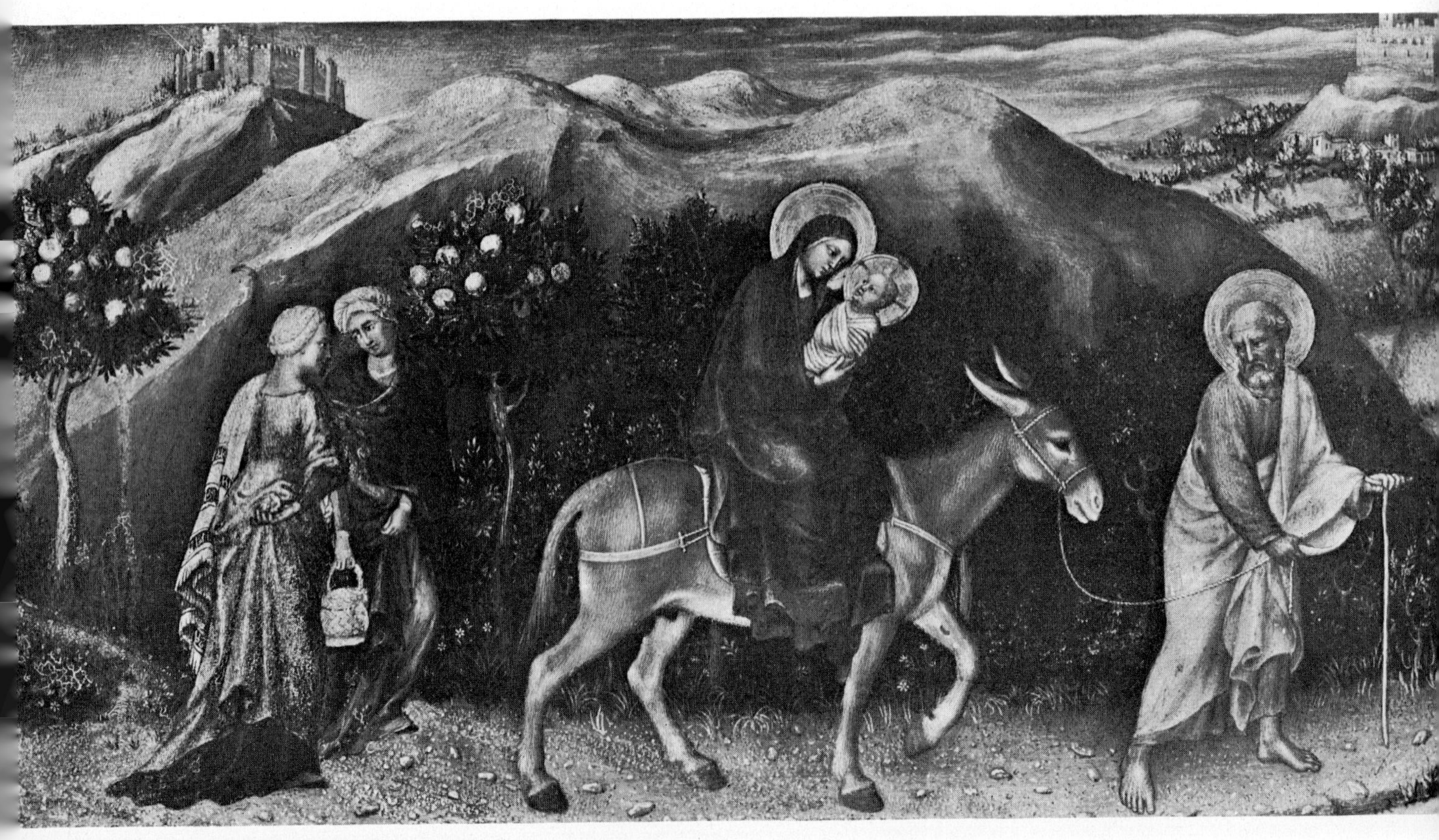

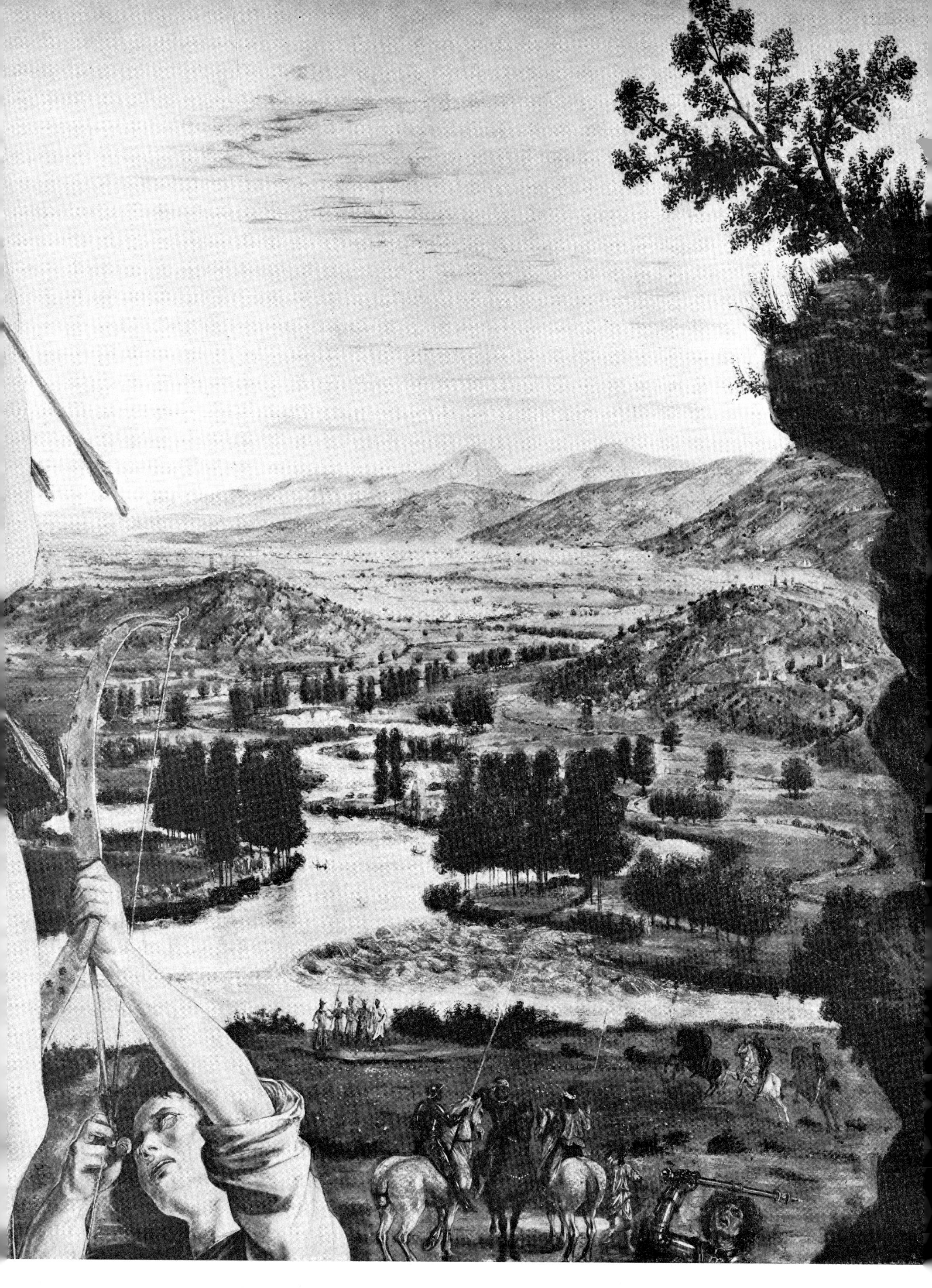

84. GIOVANNI BELLINI (*c.* 1430–1516): *Town on a Hill*. Detail from Plate 45

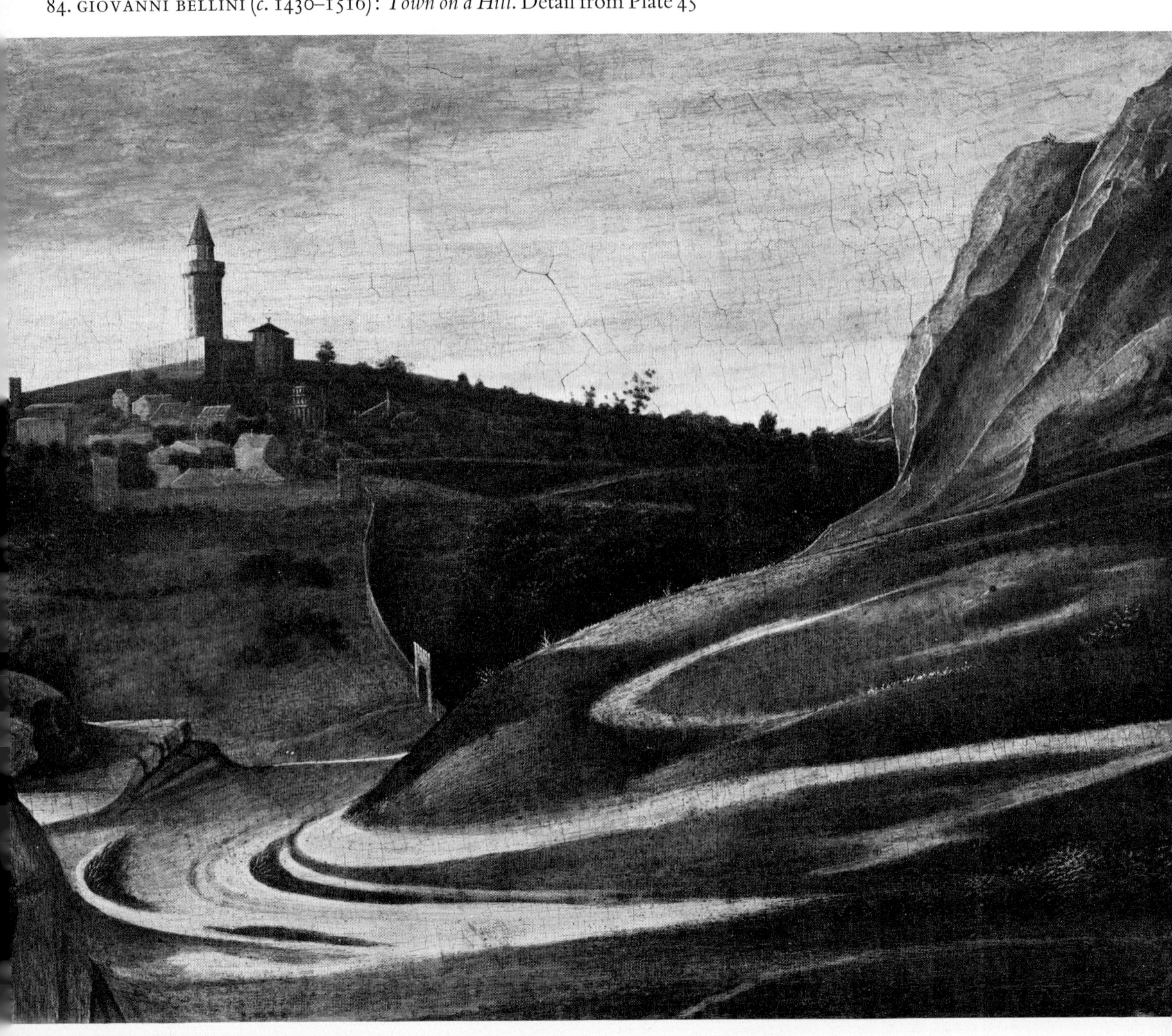

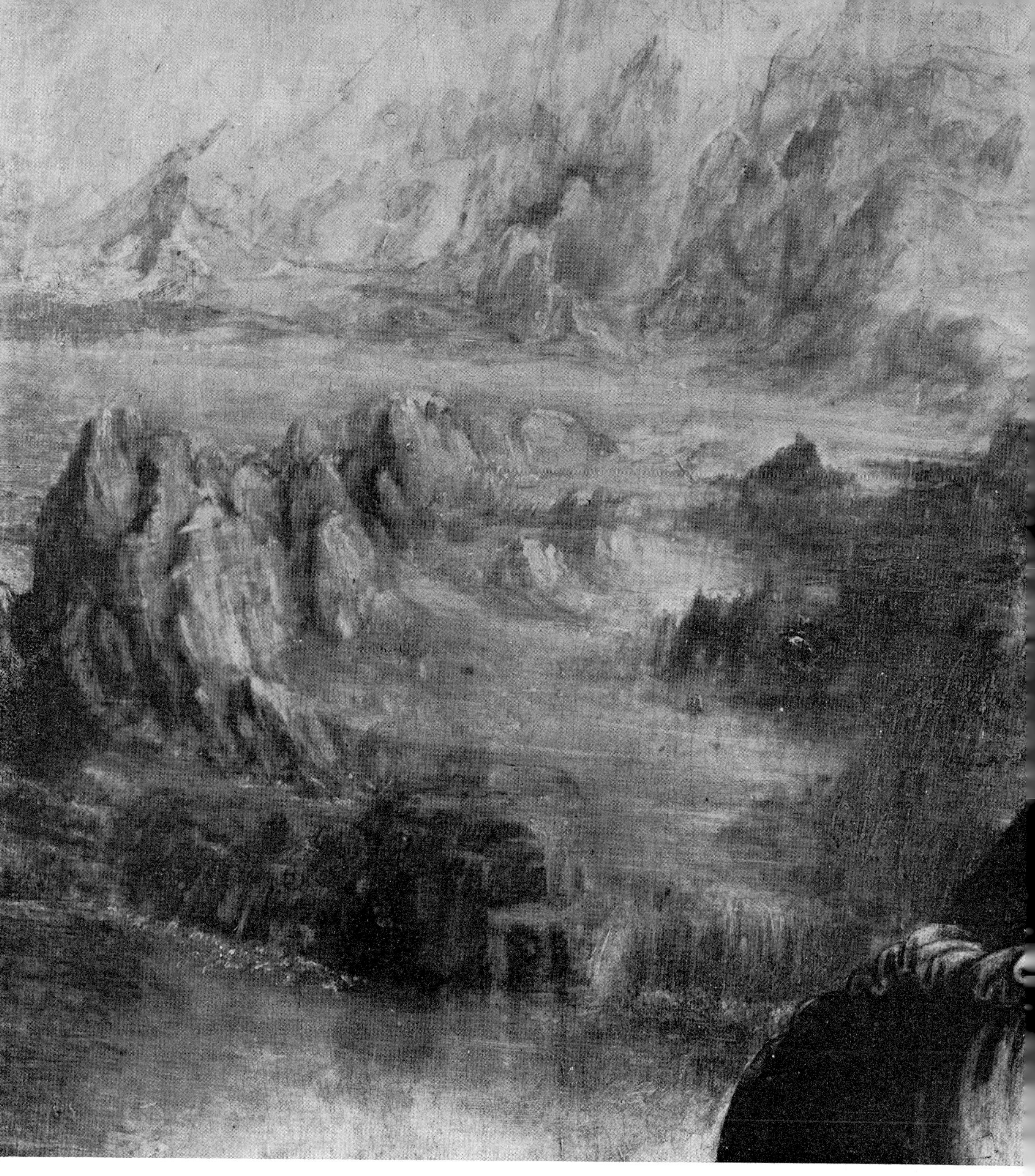

85. LEONARDO DA VINCI (1452–1519): *Rocky Mountains*. Detail from Plate 128

Fields, roads, walls and buildings—most landscapes in Renaissance painting are places where men dwell and build and cultivate the soil, where the spectator would feel at home. Bellini was a poet and even when his subject was, as here, one of great tragedy, he reconciled it with lyrical passages of gentle beauty without detracting from the impact of its sadness. In Leonardo's painting the contrast is reversed: the subject is the happy one of maternal love, but his rocks are bare, forbidding and inhospitable. He was a scientist of insatiable curiosity as well as a poet, and his researches in geology and the motion of water have shaped the strange crag formations of this picture, the *Virgin of the Rocks* (Plate 80) and the *Mona Lisa* (Plate 125). All three paintings are unreal, yet are fundamentally unlike the equally unreal 'medieval' scheme of Plate 12.

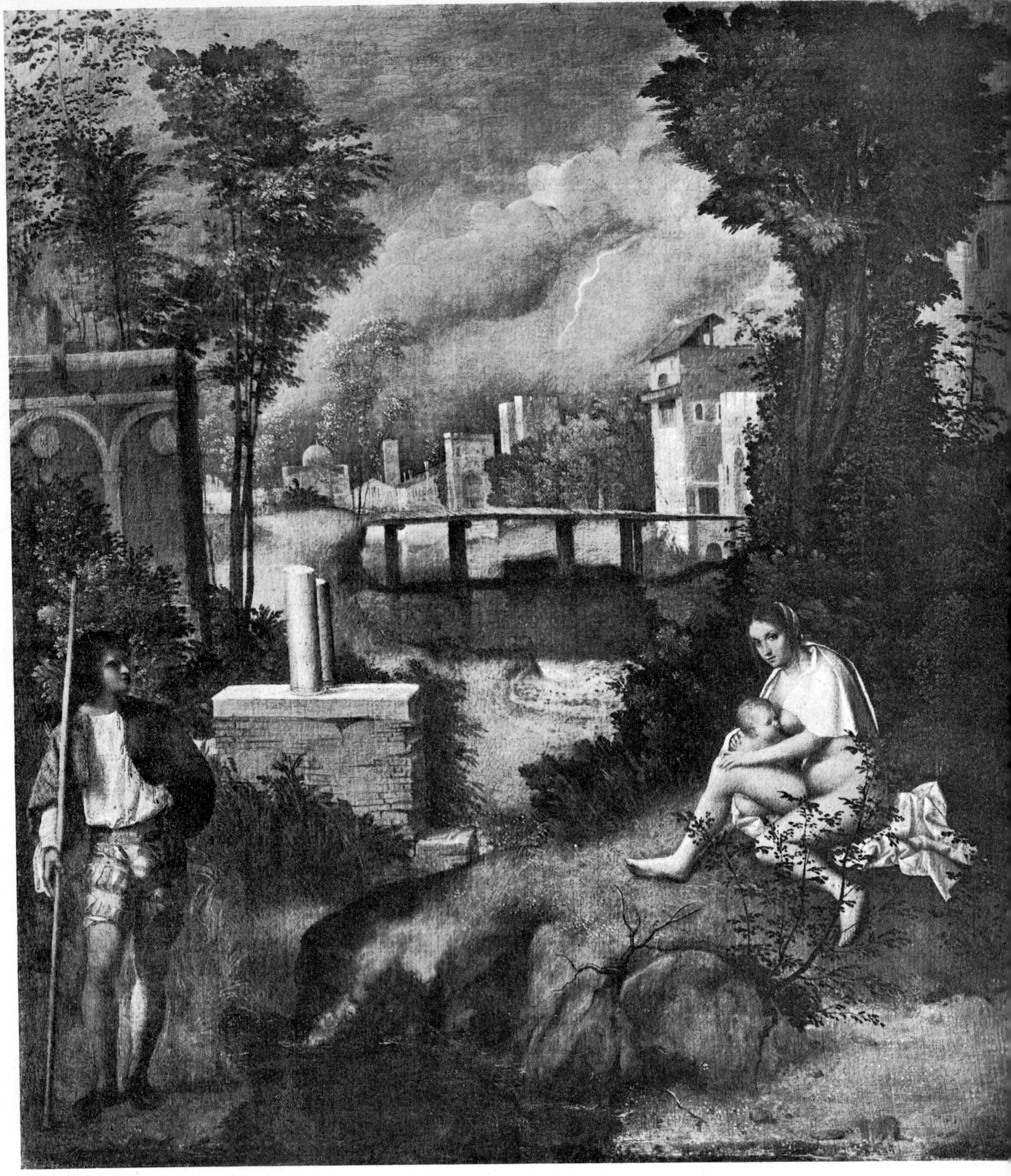

86. GIORGIONE (*c.* 1477–1510): *The Tempest.* About 1504. Canvas, $32\frac{3}{4} \times 28\frac{3}{4}$ in. Venice, Accademia

'A summer storm bursts at sunset above the towers of a little town, by which runs a stream. The bridge and grassy outcrops are reflected in the water and the thick trees are shaken by a sudden gust, the leaves glistening in the light. The figures are, as it were, caught by chance, momentarily stilled in the fleeting glare of the lightning flash.' (T. Pignatti) An early writer called the nursing mother a gipsy and the watchful young man a soldier.

7. TITIAN (*c.* 1489–1576): *Fête Champêtre*. About 1510. Canvas, 43 × $54\frac{1}{2}$ in. Paris, Louvre

The pastoral tradition, so hauntingly introduced into Venetian painting by Giorgione, was carried forward by his younger colleague Titian. In the latter's muted fantasy an elegant young man with a lute and his rustic companion pay no heed to the naked girls, one of whom holds a recorder and other seems to pour water from a jug into a well—a world of 'pre-ordained harmony' where the still summer warmth has fused dreams and reality.

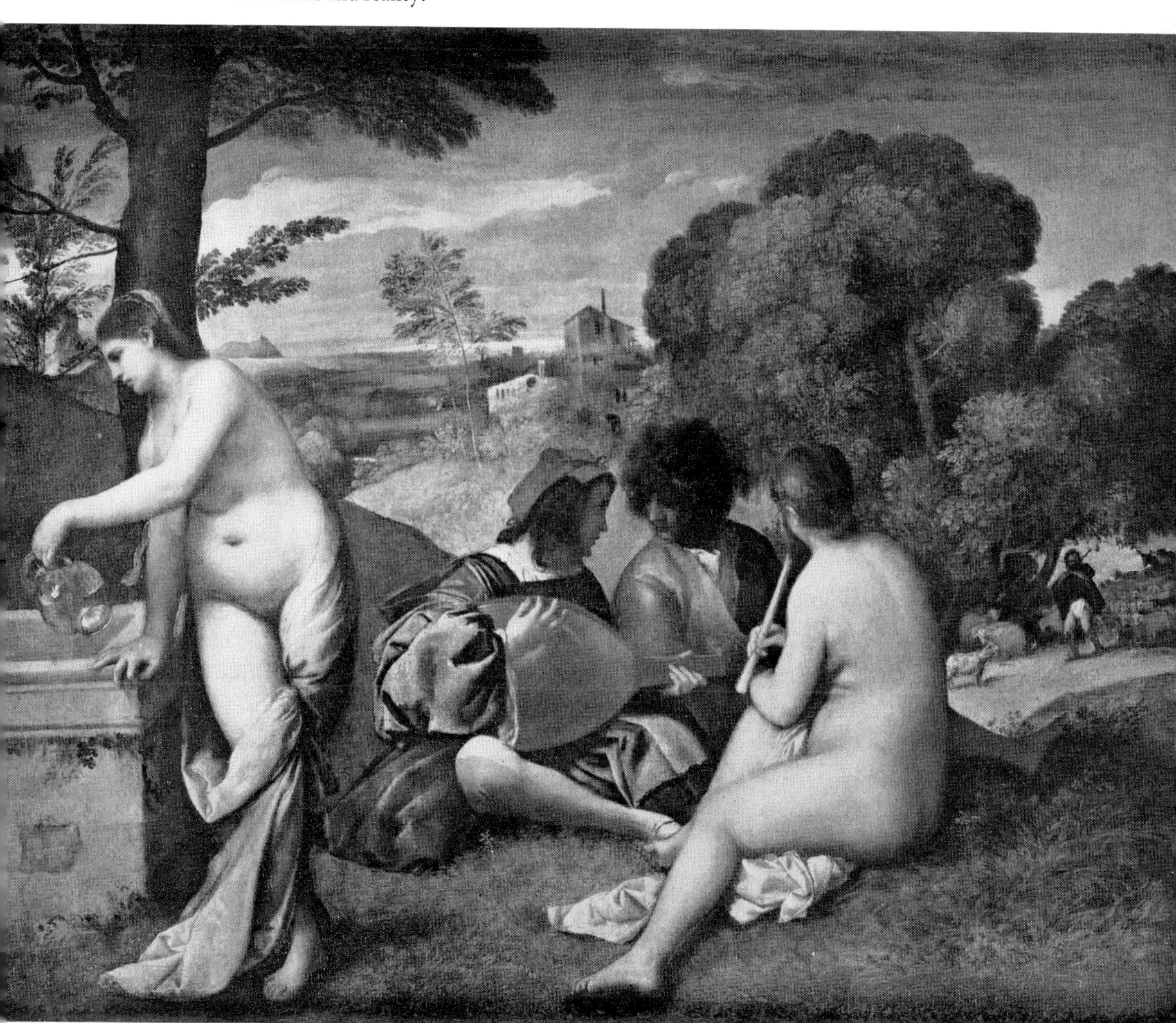

88, 89. GIORGIONE (*c.* 1477–1510): *The Adoration of the Shepherds.* 1505–10. Panel, $35\frac{3}{4} \times 43\frac{1}{2}$ in. Washington, D.C., National Gallery of Art (Samuel H. Kress Collection)

The two shepherds have come 'with all haste', their sleeves are torn and their clothes in tatters. Together with the Virgin and St. Joseph they adore their Saviour outside a rocky cave, watched by winged cherubs. The serene reverence of the figures is perfectly matched by the peaceful landscape. This romantic tract of the North Italian countryside and the closely observed plants and bushes bear out Vasari's statements that Giorgione 'fell deeply in love with the beauties of nature' and that he was so attracted by Leonardo's works, with their subtle transitions of colour and tone, that he based his own work on their style.

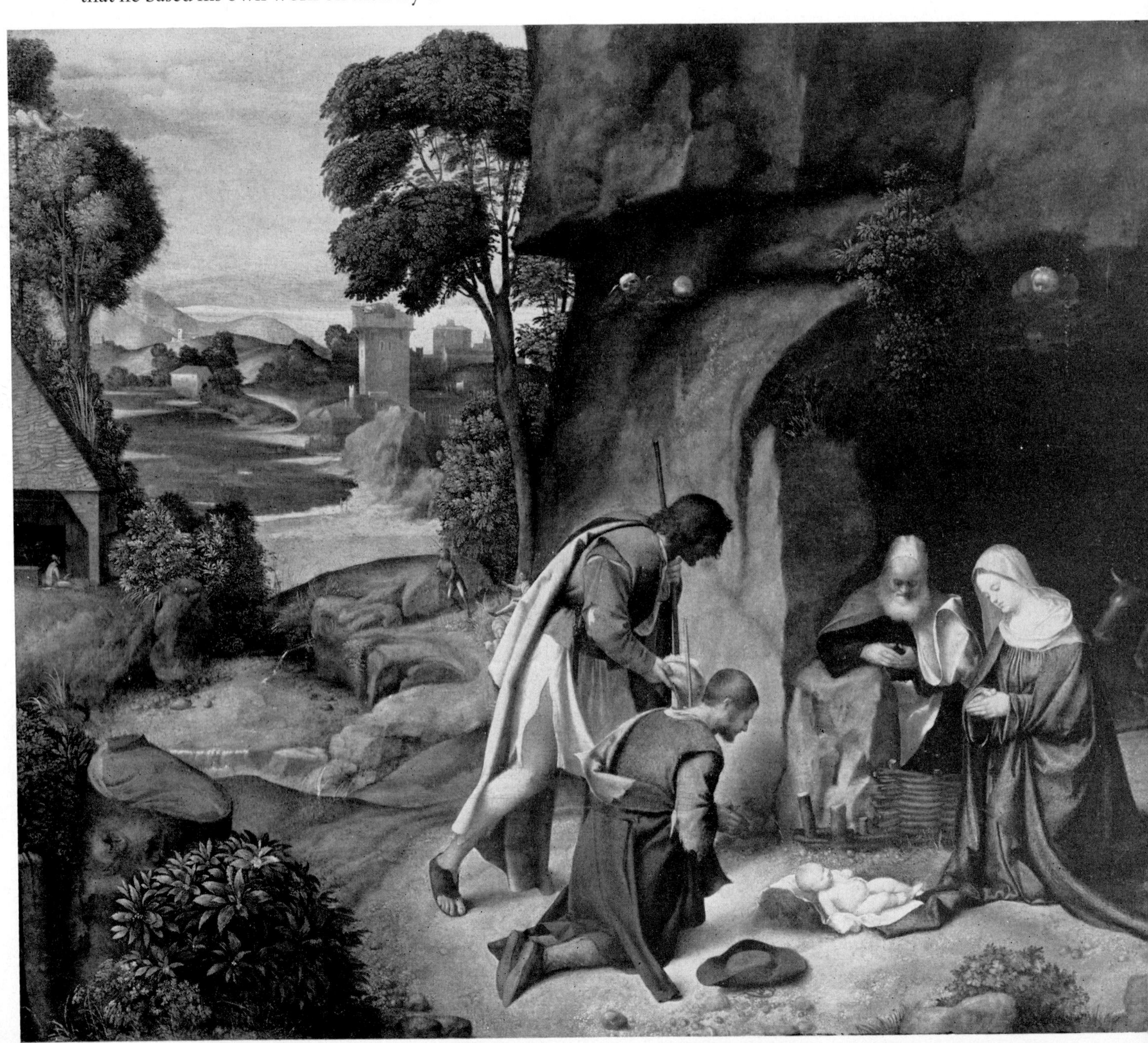

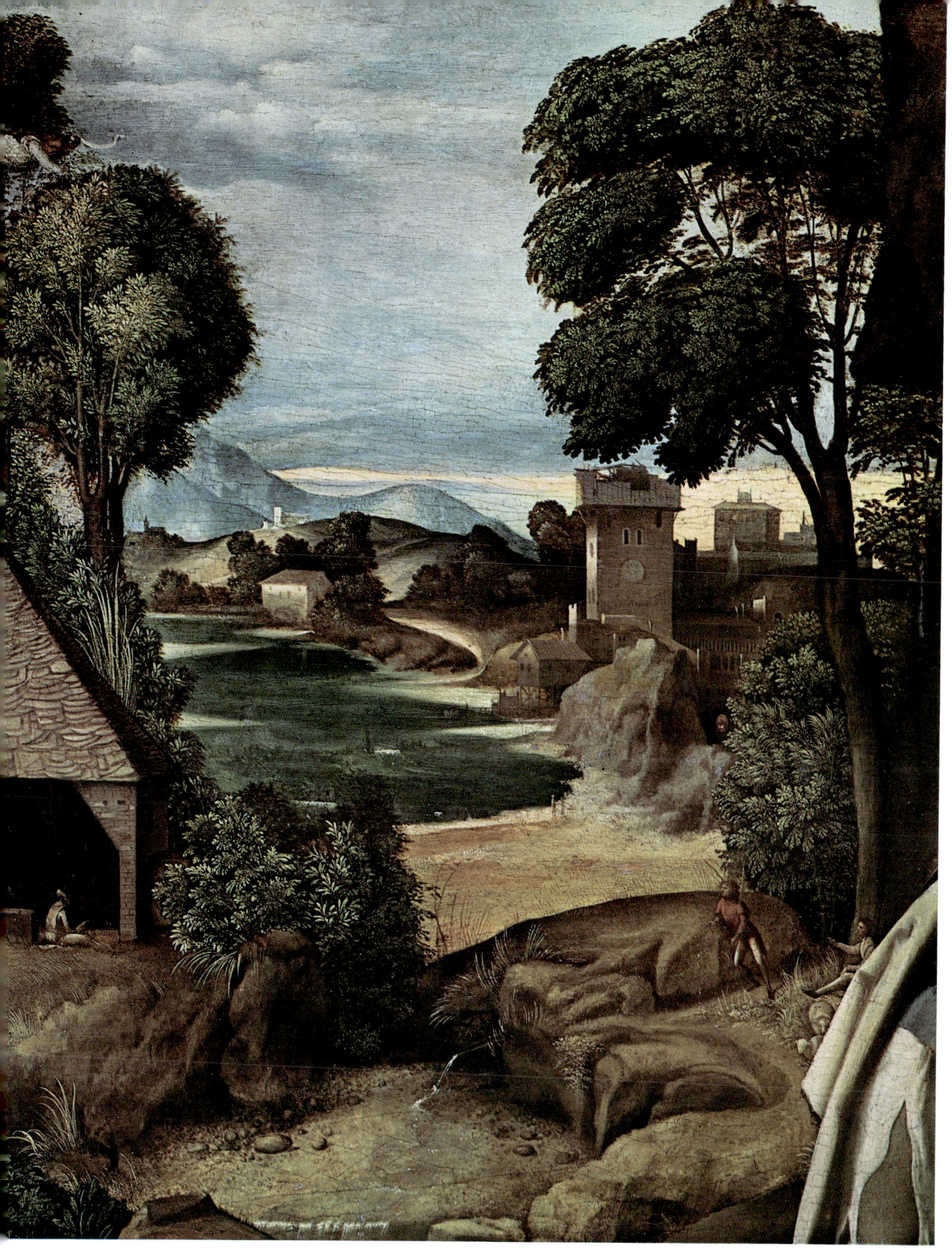

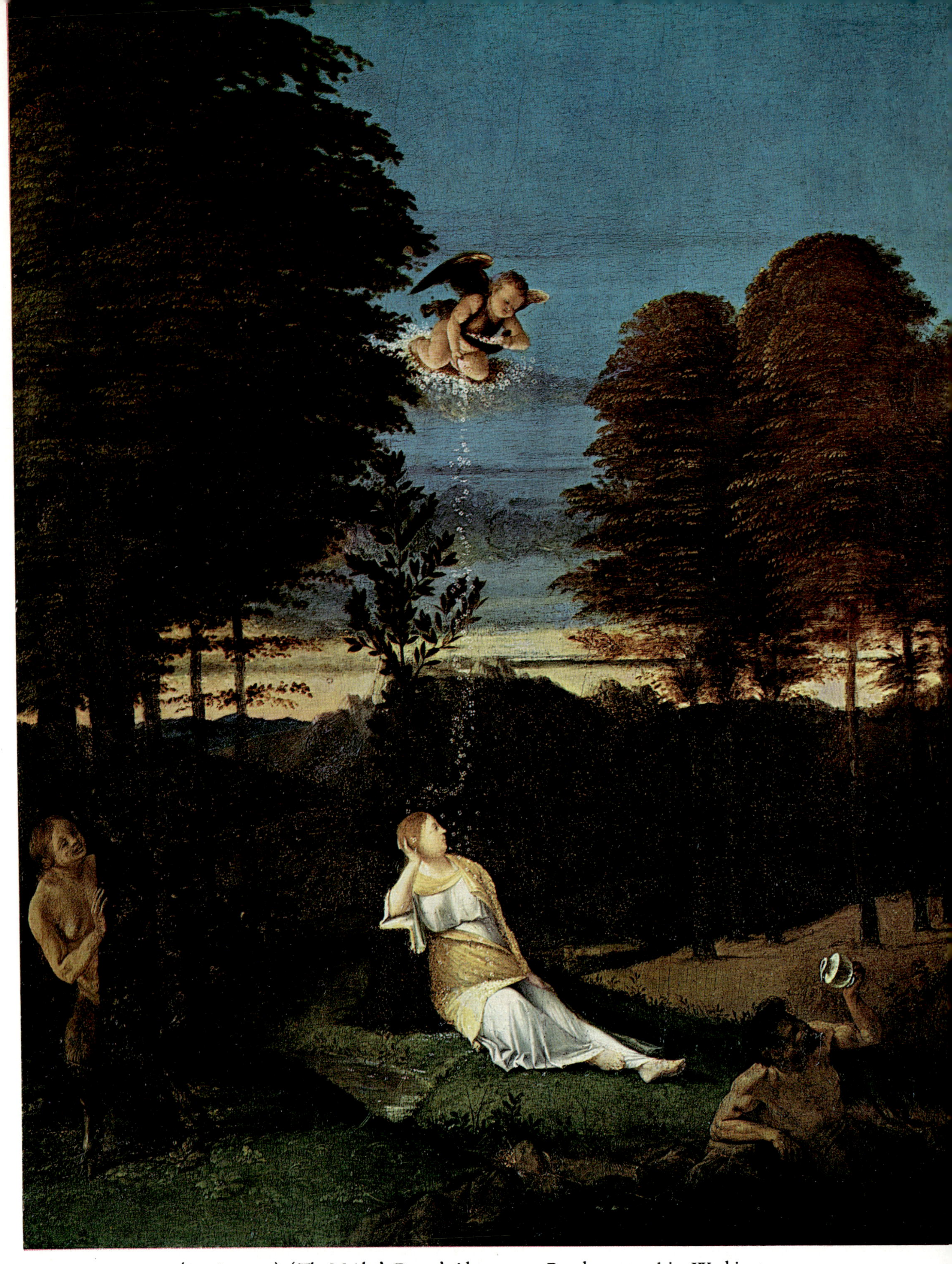

90. LORENZO LOTTO (*c.* 1480–1556): '*The Maiden's Dream*'. About 1505. Panel, 17 × 13¼ in. Washington, D.C., National Gallery of Art (Samuel H. Kress Collection)

In a pastoral landscape conjuring up a golden age, Cupid showers blossoms upon a nymph, who looks pensively to the nearby grove. A satyr couple adds a note of humour.

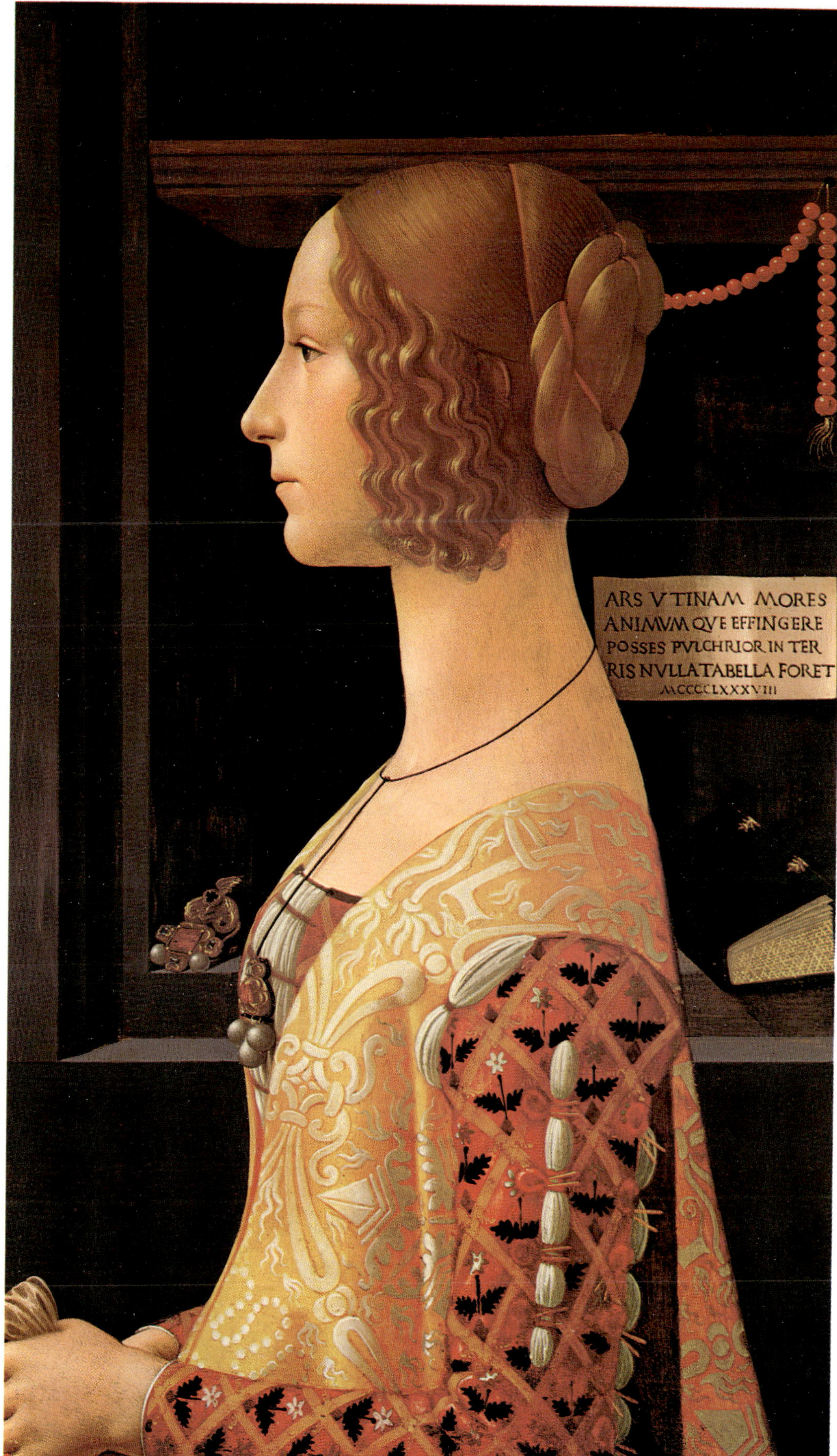

91. DOMENICO GHIRLANDAIO (1449–94): *Portrait of Giovanna Tornabuoni*. 1488. Panel, $30\frac{1}{2} \times 19\frac{1}{2}$ in. Lugano-Castagnola, Thyssen-Bornemisza Collection

The inscription, quoting the poet Martial, says: 'If art could only convey her manners and her mind there would be no lovelier picture on earth.' Giovanna died in childbirth at the age of twenty, in the same year in which this portrait was painted. See also Plate 64.

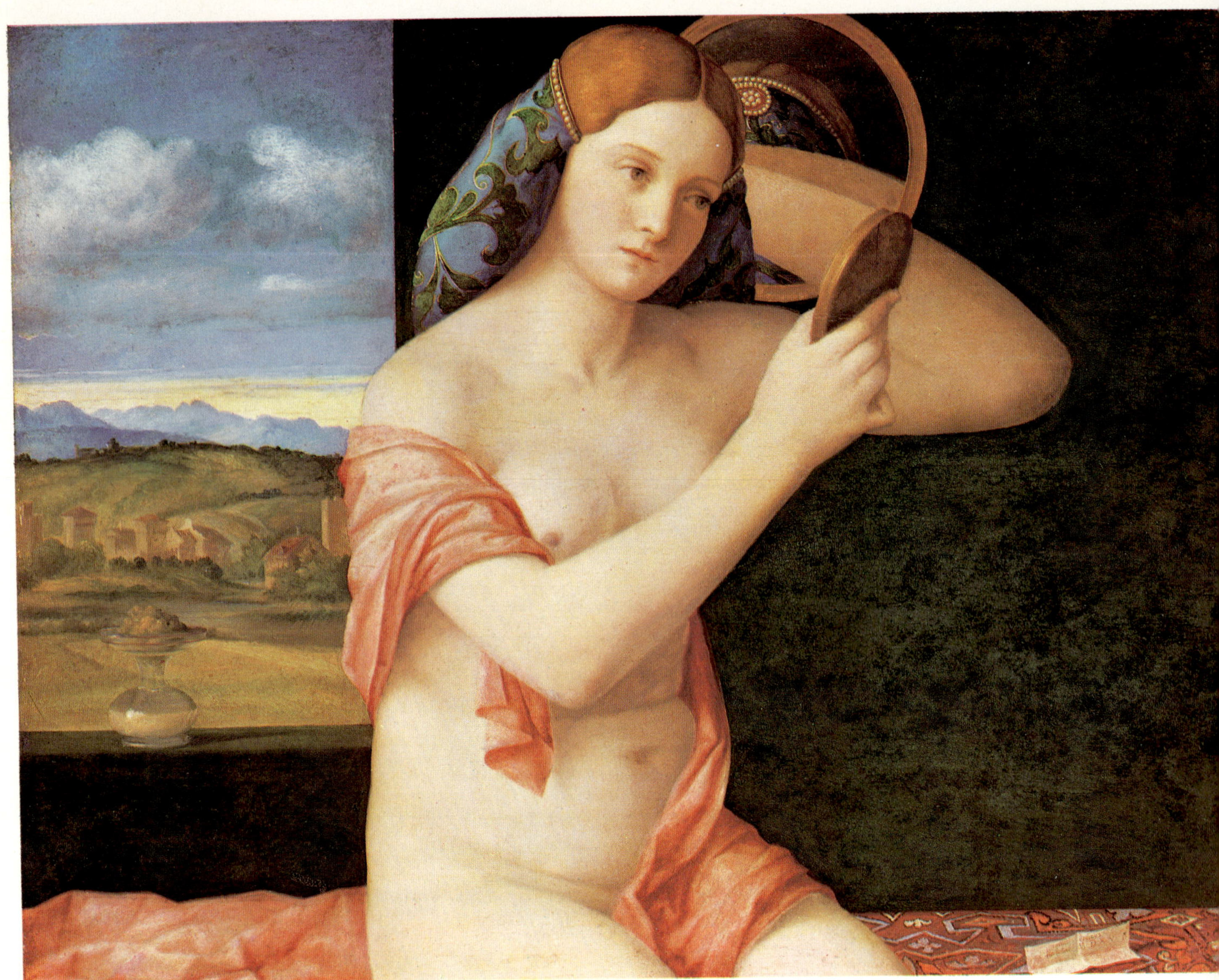

92. GIOVANNI BELLINI (*c.* 1430–1516): *Young Woman at her Toilet.* 1515. Panel, $24\frac{1}{2} \times 31$ in. Vienna, Kunsthistorisches Museum

Discreetly draped, a young woman gazes into a small hand-mirror as she adjusts her coiffure. The larger looking-glass on the wall behind her not only allows us to see her embroidered and pearl-filleted veil from the back, but also evokes the impression that, a moment before, she had been inspecting the double reflection and has just lifted her arm. The carpet, on which lies a folded letter, the crystal vase with the full-blown rose on the window-sill, and the beautiful morning landscape with the distant alpine peaks hardly divert attention from the graceful body posed in a fleeting action of youthful freshness. At the age of eighty-five, Bellini had lost none of the mastery that had given him such receptive pupils as Giorgione and Titian.

3. TITIAN (*c.* 1489–1576): *The 'Venus of Urbino.'* 1538. Canvas, 47 × 65 in. Florence, Uffizi

Among Italian Renaissance painters, Titian was perhaps the greatest master of the female nude (see also Plates 104, 172). Here the so-called Venus reclines in an elegantly paved and panelled chamber, while two maidservants open a chest to find a costume for her. 'She is wide awake and fully conscious of her charms as she gazes languidly at the spectator and rests her right arm upon a white pillow, while she lightly grasps a cluster of red roses. The dark-green curtain, the red couch spread with white sheets and the subdued light provide a muted foil for the resplendent beauty of the nude body.' (H. E. Wethey)

The pose of Venus was invented by Giorgione, but Titian's version is more full-blooded and, emotionally, coarser.

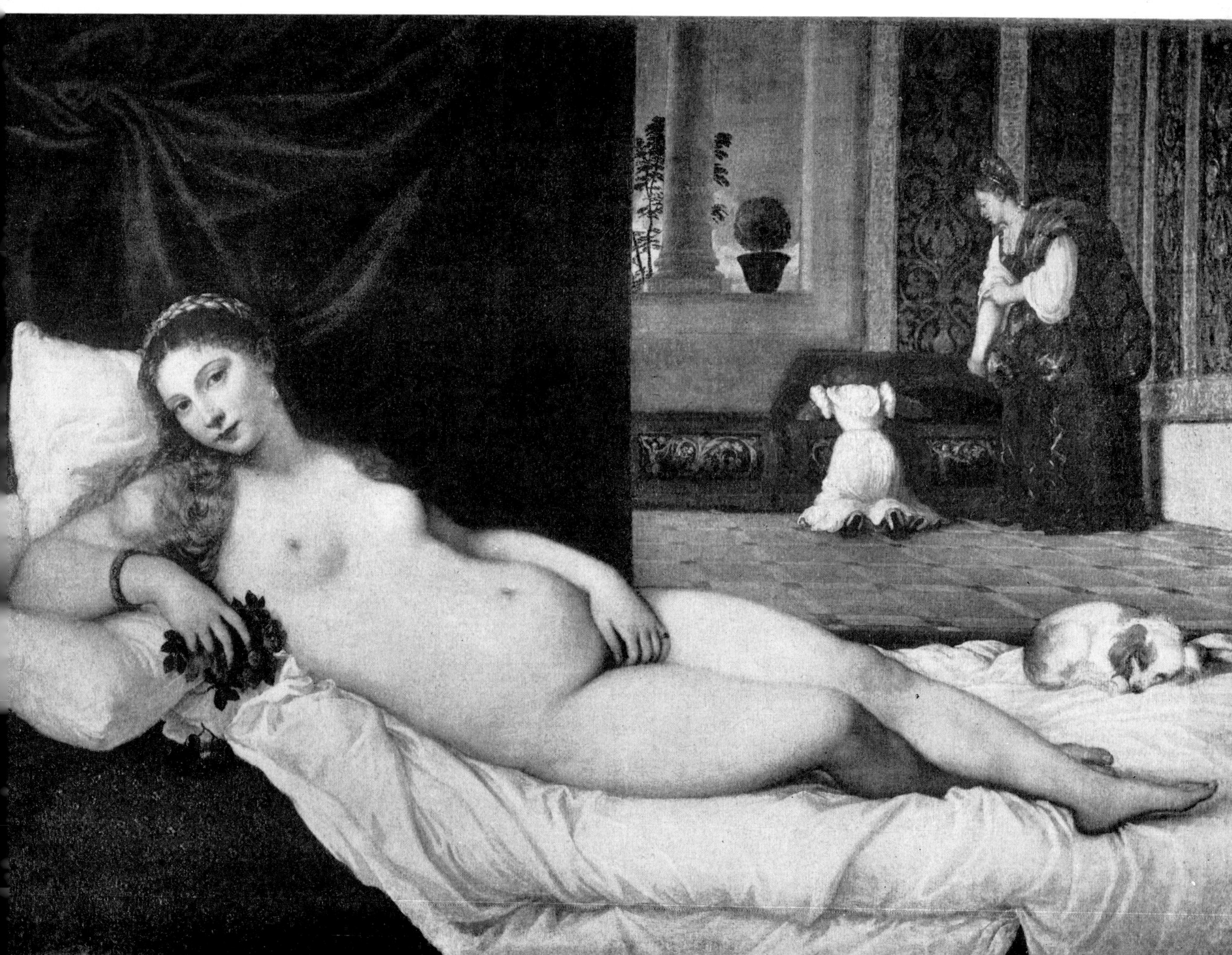

94, 95. VITTORE CARPACCIO (*c.* 1460–1523/6): *A Miracle of the Relic of the True Cross.* 1494–5. Canvas, 144 × 152 in. Venice, Accademia

On the loggia of his palace in Venice, the Patriarch of Grado heals a man possessed of devils with a relic. 'But what captivates the eye immediately is the view of Venice itself: the vista of its crowded palaces along the dark-green waters of the Grand Canal; the old wooden Rialto bridge; the maze of roof-tops and oddly-shaped chimneys, silhouetted against the light sky; the Venetians reclining in their gondolas; the gaily dressed gondoliers; the elegant youths and worthy patricians in the narrow streets. Only few of them pay attention to the white-clad brethren who, in solemn procession, bearing candles and banners, have carried the relic and now wait at the entrance to the palace, while a small group of chosen brothers are allowed to witness the miracle.' (J. Lauts)

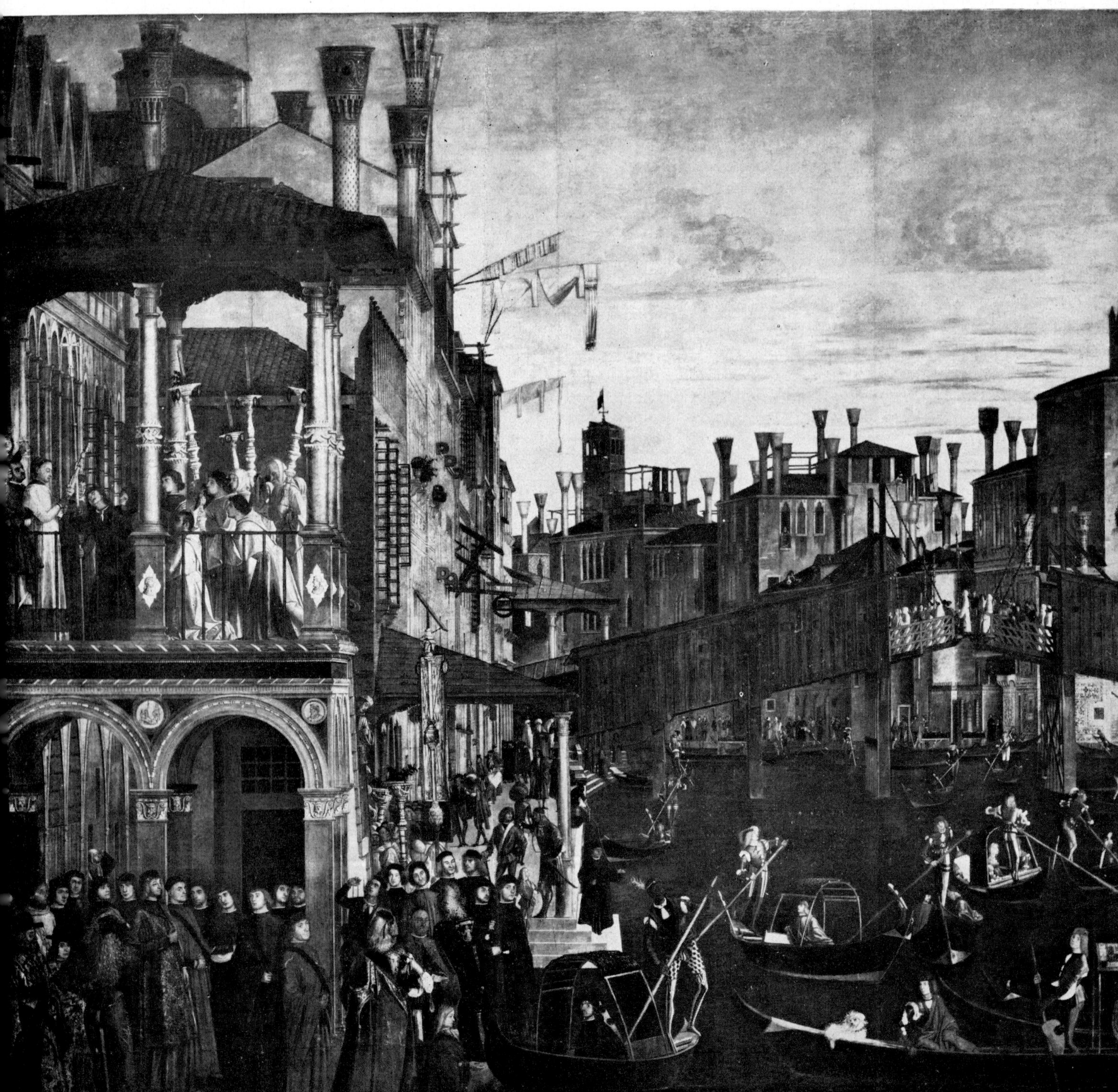

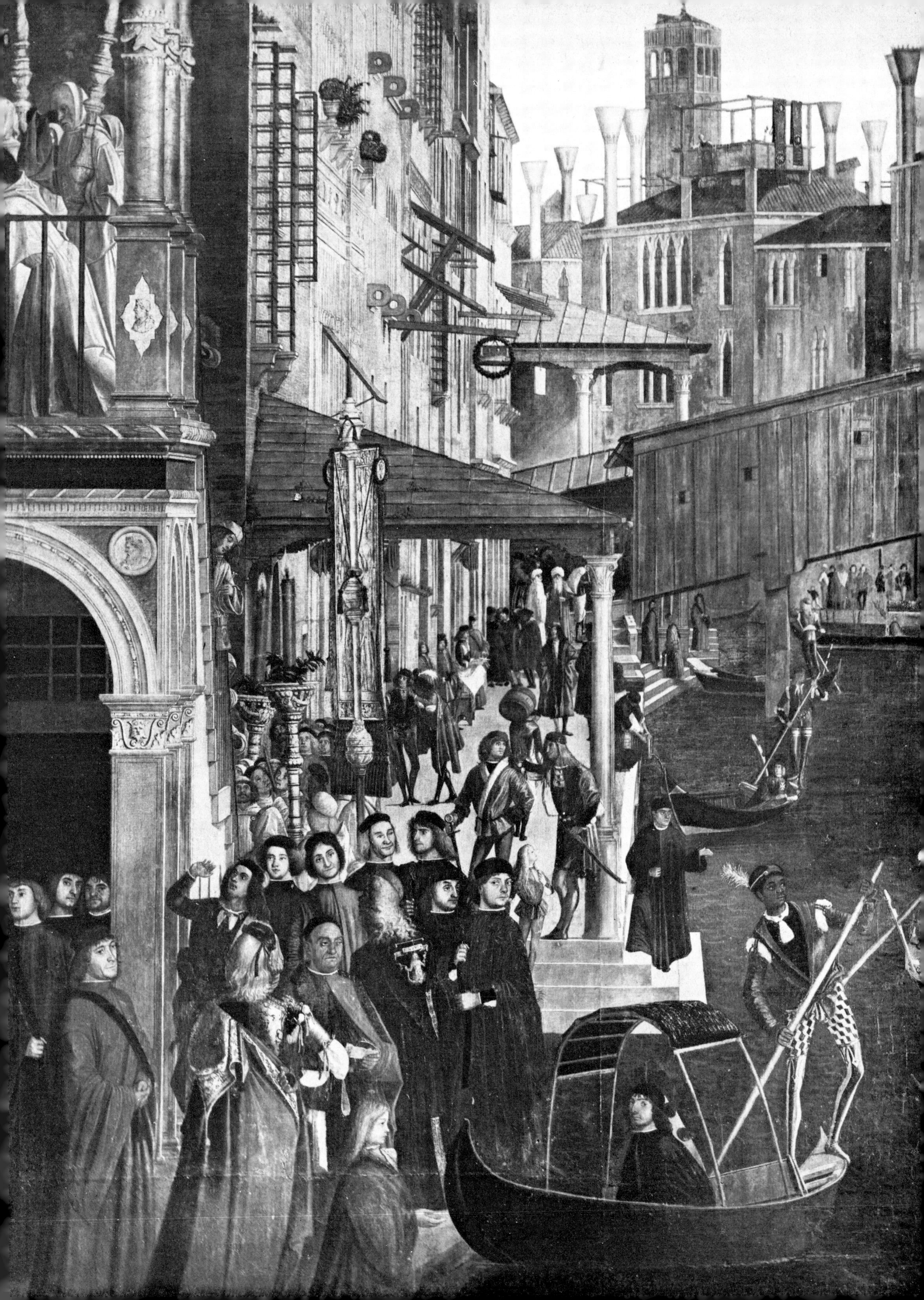

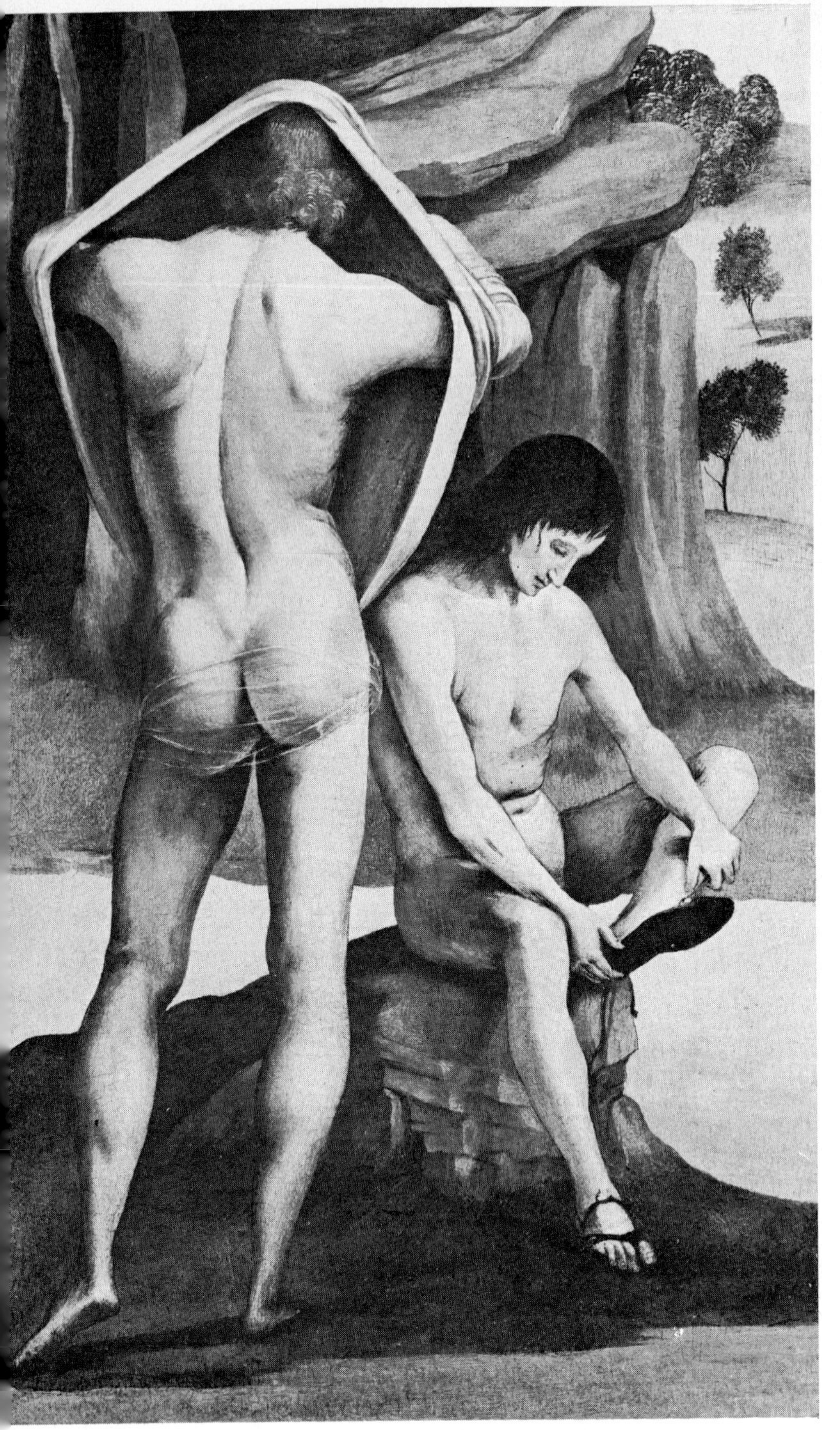

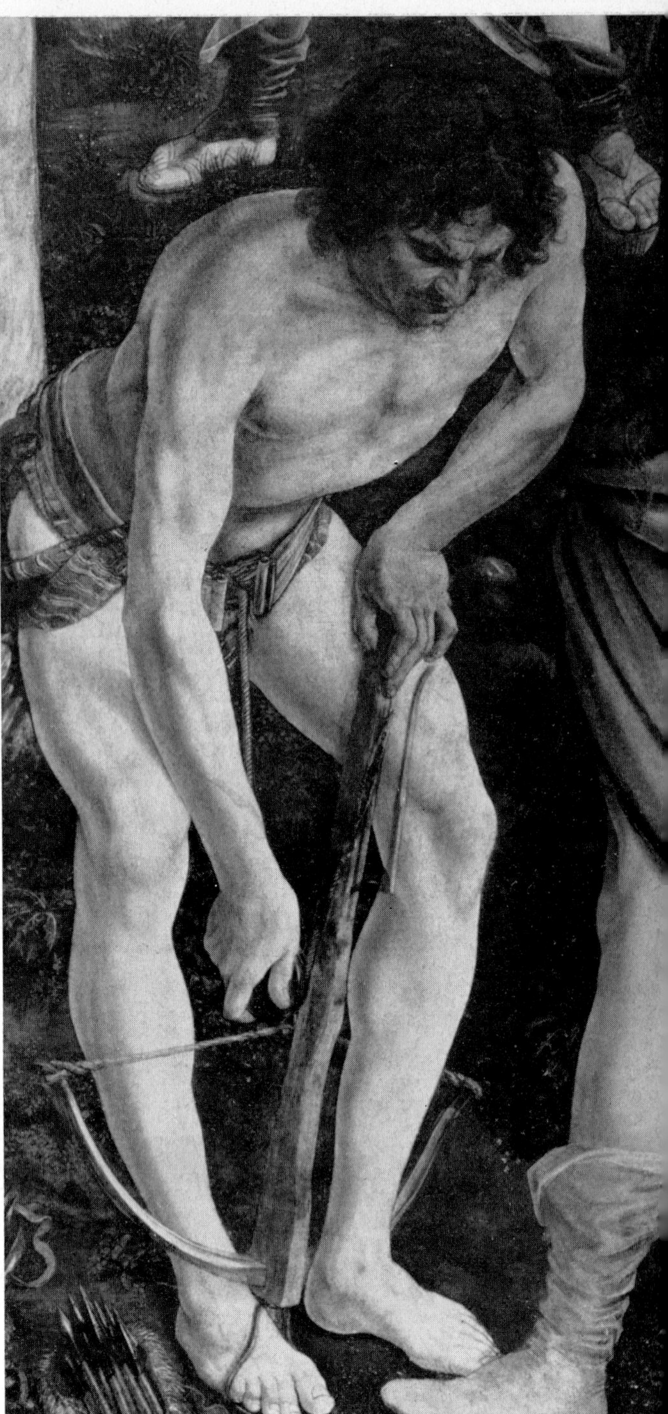

96. LUCA SIGNORELLI (*c.* 1441–1523): *Two Nudes*. Fragment from a *Baptism of Christ*. 1498. Panel, $26\frac{3}{4} \times 16\frac{1}{2}$ in. Toledo, Ohio, Museum of Art (Gift of Edward Drummond Libbey)

97. ANTONIO POLLAIUOLO (*c.* 1432–98): *An Archer*. Detail from Plate 50

The rediscovery of classical statuary gave a special impetus to the rendering of the nude male body. Italian sculptors and painters began to explore its structure and, helped by anatomical studies such as those of Leonardo, represented complicated poses and movements with a mastery which was later to be taught, as a routine, in the life classes of Academies. Pollaiuolo (like the greatest master of the male nude, Michelangelo) was both sculptor and painter. His athletic archer strains every muscle to bend the bow. Signorelli's nudes, although more relaxed, are as carefully posed in the act of undressing.

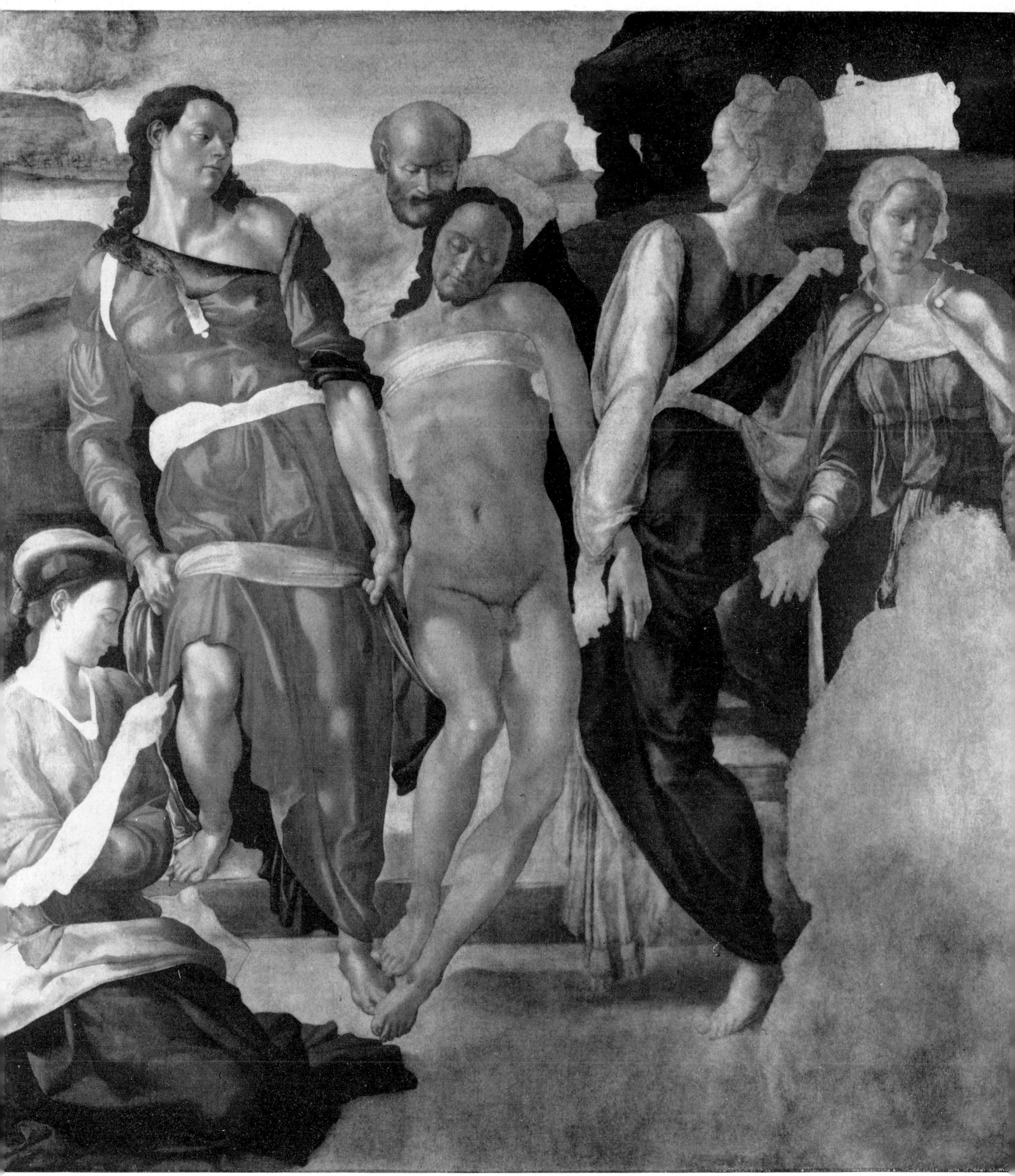

. MICHELANGELO (1475–1564): *The Entombment*. Unfinished. After 1505. Panel, 64 × 59 in. London, National Gallery

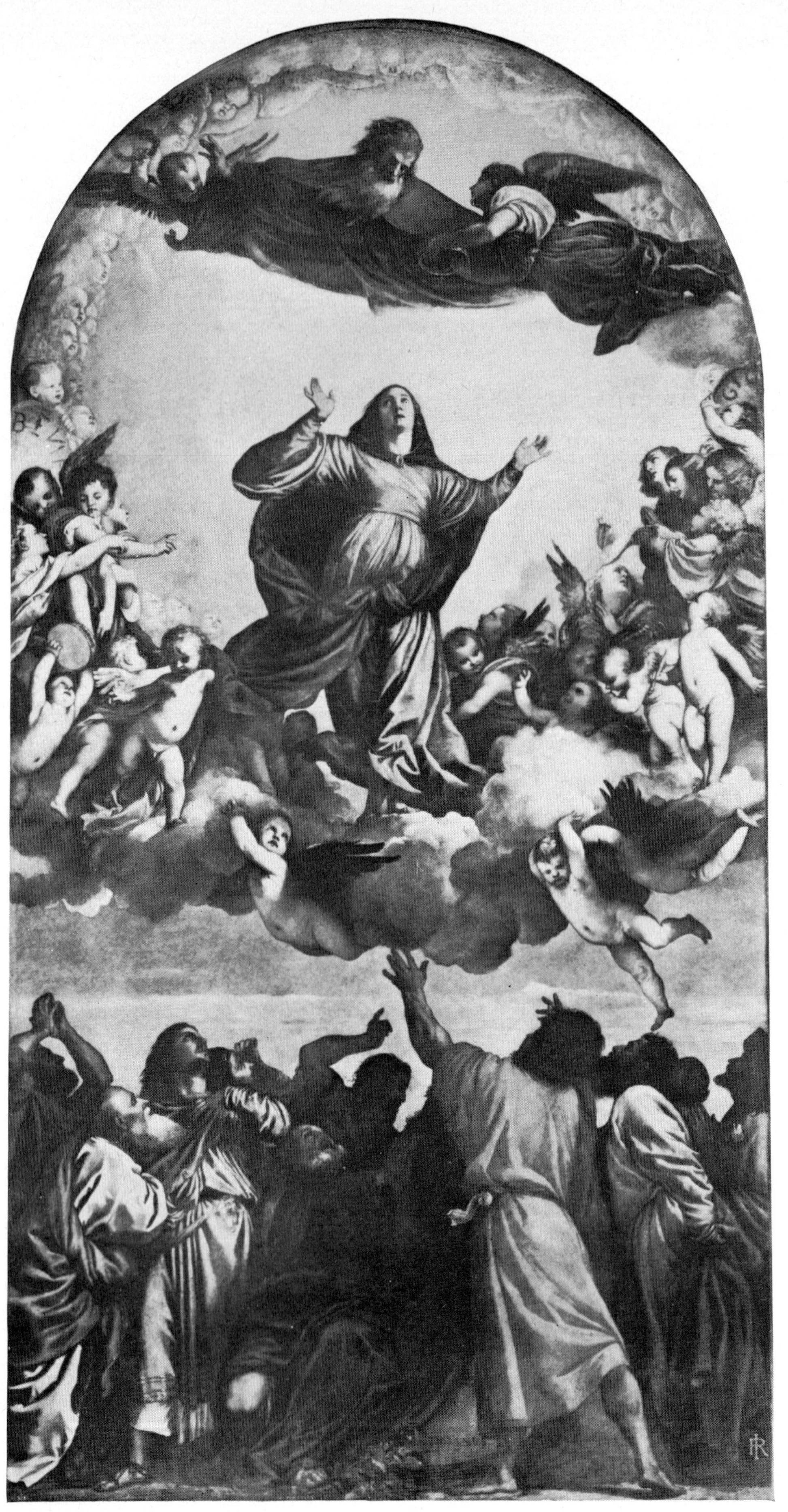

99. TITIAN (*c.* 1489–1576): *The Assumption of the Virgin.* 1516–18. Panel, 272 × 142 in. Venice, Santa Maria dei Frari

This huge altarpiece, a dramatic composition of unsurpassed solemnity, dominates the high altar of the Franciscan church in Venice. The Church had long taught that, immediately on her death, the mother of Christ was taken up, body and soul, into heaven, and Titian has given this belief its grandest expression. The astonished Apostles, and we ourselves, witness her soaring from earth, surrounded by an angelic choir, towards the Father, who is about to crown her as Queen of Heaven.

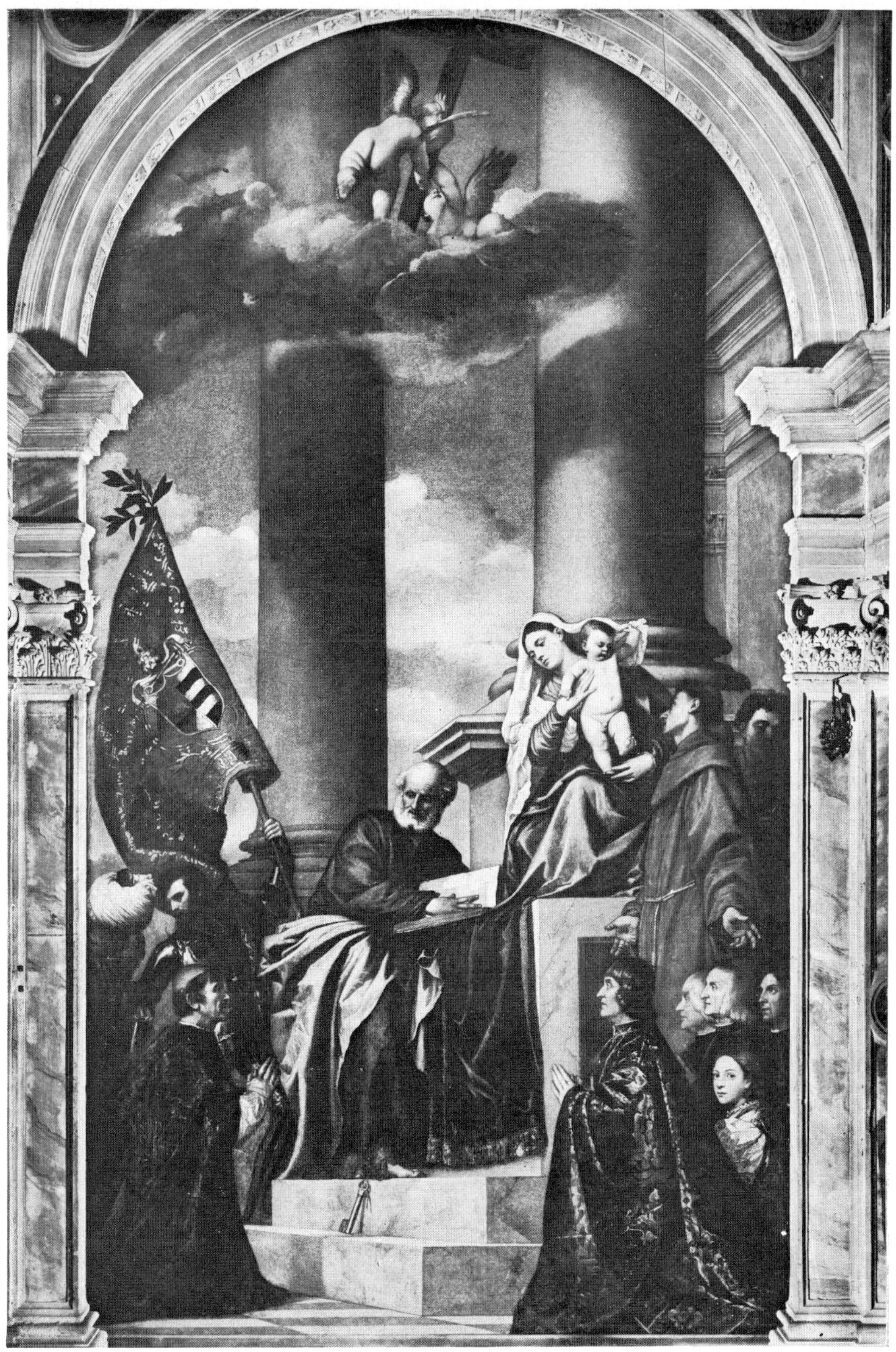

100. TITIAN (*c.* 1489–1576): *The Virgin and Child with SS. Peter, Francis and Anthony, Adored by Members of the Pesaro Family*. 1519–26. Canvas, 191 × 106 in. Venice, Santa Maria dei Frari

This altarpiece commemorates a victory of bishop Jacopo Pesaro over the Turks, and shows him, with his battle standard and a turbaned prisoner behind him, kneeling before the Virgin and Child. St. Peter, his key on the steps below him, expresses the gratitude of the Church for Jacopo's defence against the Infidel, while St. Francis invokes the Child's blessing on the other members of the bishop's family, a group which foreshadows Titian's mastery as a portraitist (see Plates 120, 148).

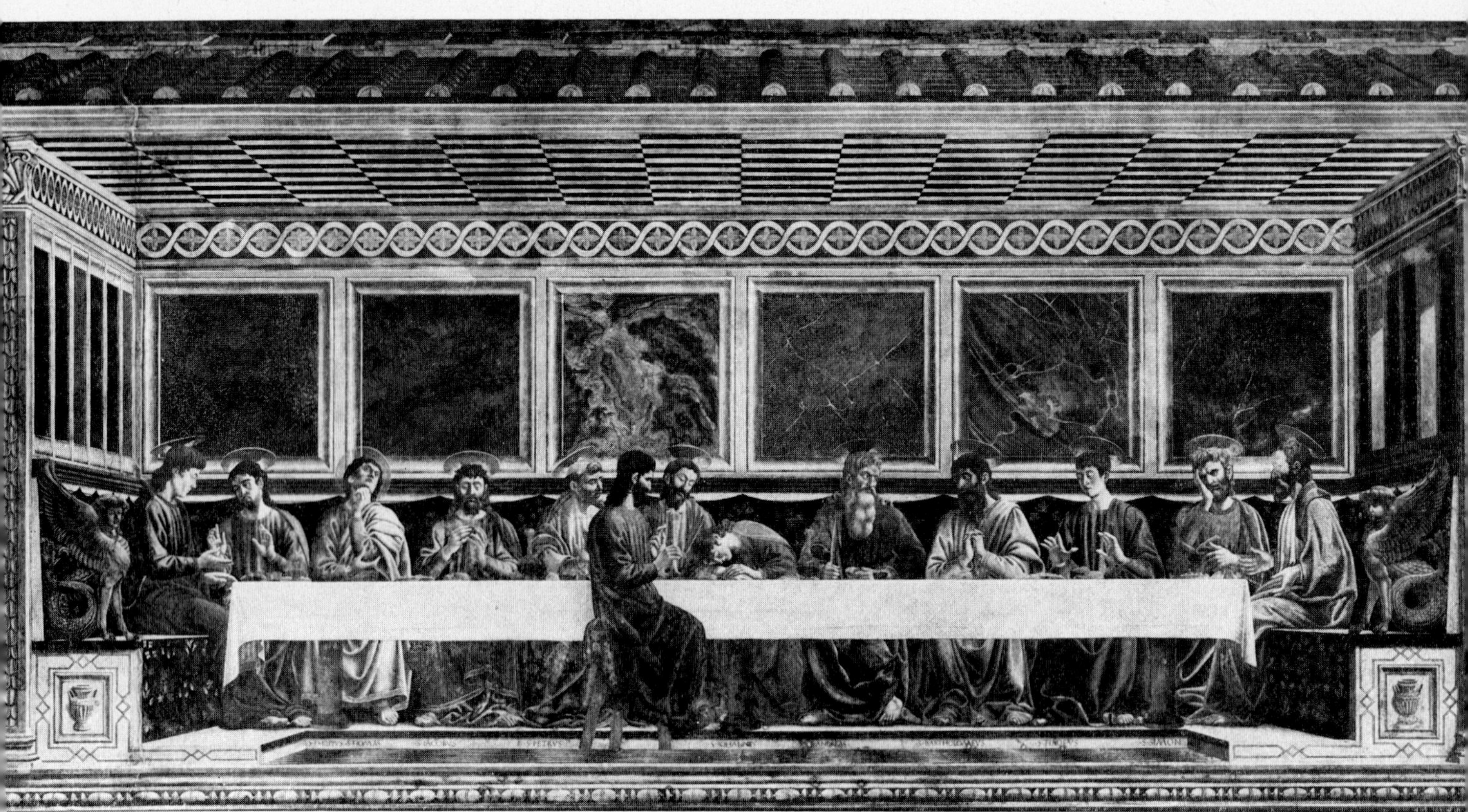

101. ANDREA DEL CASTAGNO (*c.* 1421?–57): *The Last Supper*. 1445–50. Fresco. Florence, Cenacolo di Santa Apollonia

Christ and the twelve Apostles have assembled for their last meal before the Passion. In the centre of the group St. John, the beloved disciple, leans his head on Christ's arm: St. Peter sits at Christ's right hand. Nine other Apostles are absorbed in their thoughts as if trying to gauge the import of the moment while Judas, separated from them and seated on the near side of the table, meditates treachery as he holds the bread. The restrained calm of the figures and the sharply modelled draperies give the group a plasticity which is in perfect keeping with the elaborate setting, a fantastic hall decorated with variegated marble of gleaming splendour. The impression of stability conveyed by the parallels of the architecture and the row of heads throws the central group into relief.

102. LEONARDO DA VINCI (1452–1519): *The Last Supper*. About 1495–8. Wall-painting, 165 × 360 in. Milan, Santa Maria delle Grazie

'Verily I say unto you, One of you which eateth with me shall betray me' (Mark 14:18). In choosing to depict the Apostles' reaction to these words of Christ, Leonardo created a dramatic and revolutionary composition. The Apostles are profoundly disturbed, some have risen, and they ask Christ and one another whom he can have meant. Judas, no longer, as was traditional, isolated from the rest, recoils as he hears his betrayal foretold. He, Peter and John, form the group of three at Christ's right. The perspective of the plain architecture with tapestry hangings converges upon Christ's head, where the spectator's eyes may find rest. The table is laden with bread, like the tables in the Dominican refectory from which the monks would have gazed up at these over life-size figures—but this is the Bread of Life, which they saw Christ instituting as the Eucharist. Although the painting began to decay even while Leonardo was still alive, and had to undergo numerous restorations to save it from complete ruin, it achieved immediate fame and has continued to evoke admiration as one of the supreme masterpieces of Italian Renaissance art.

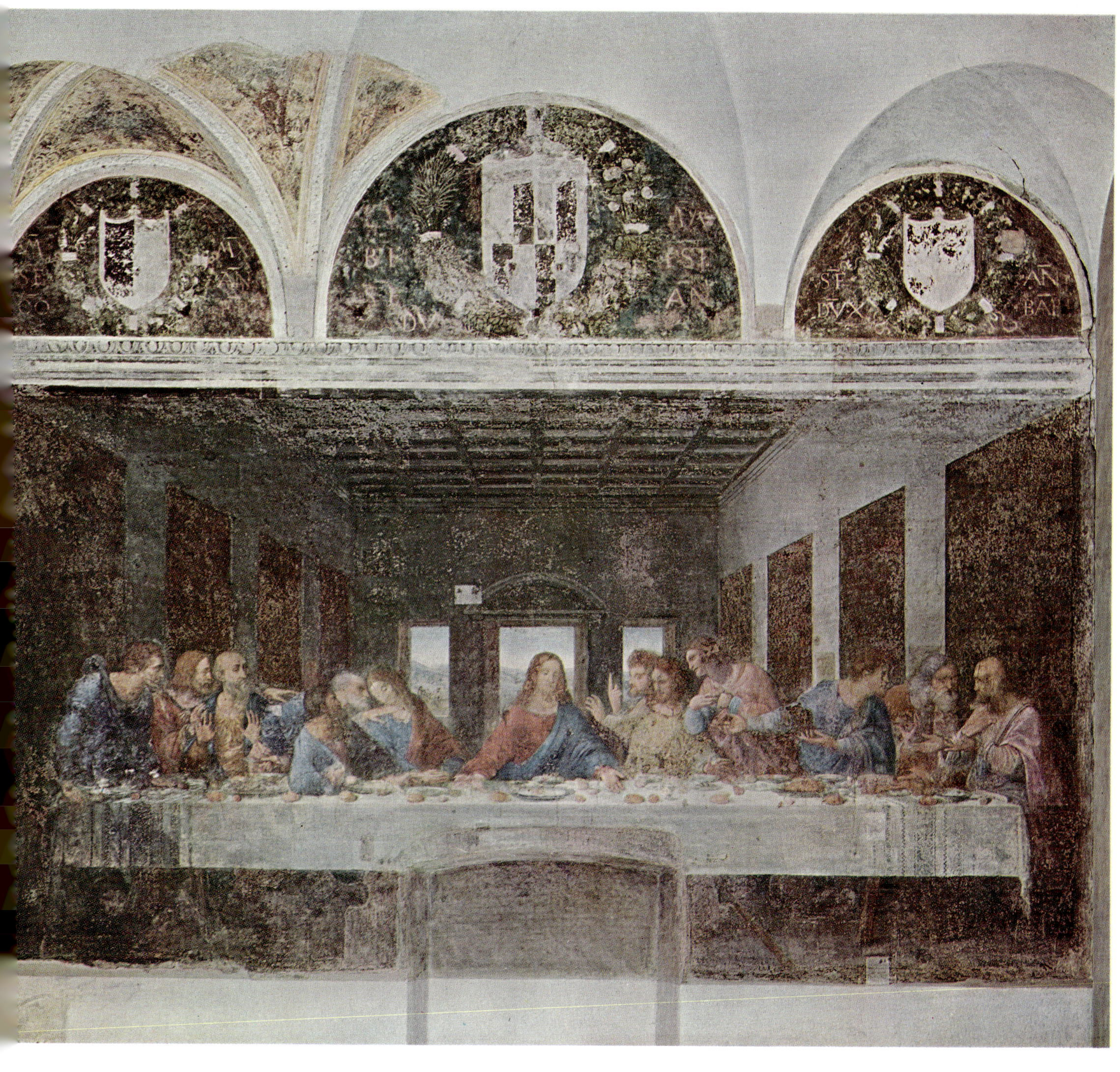

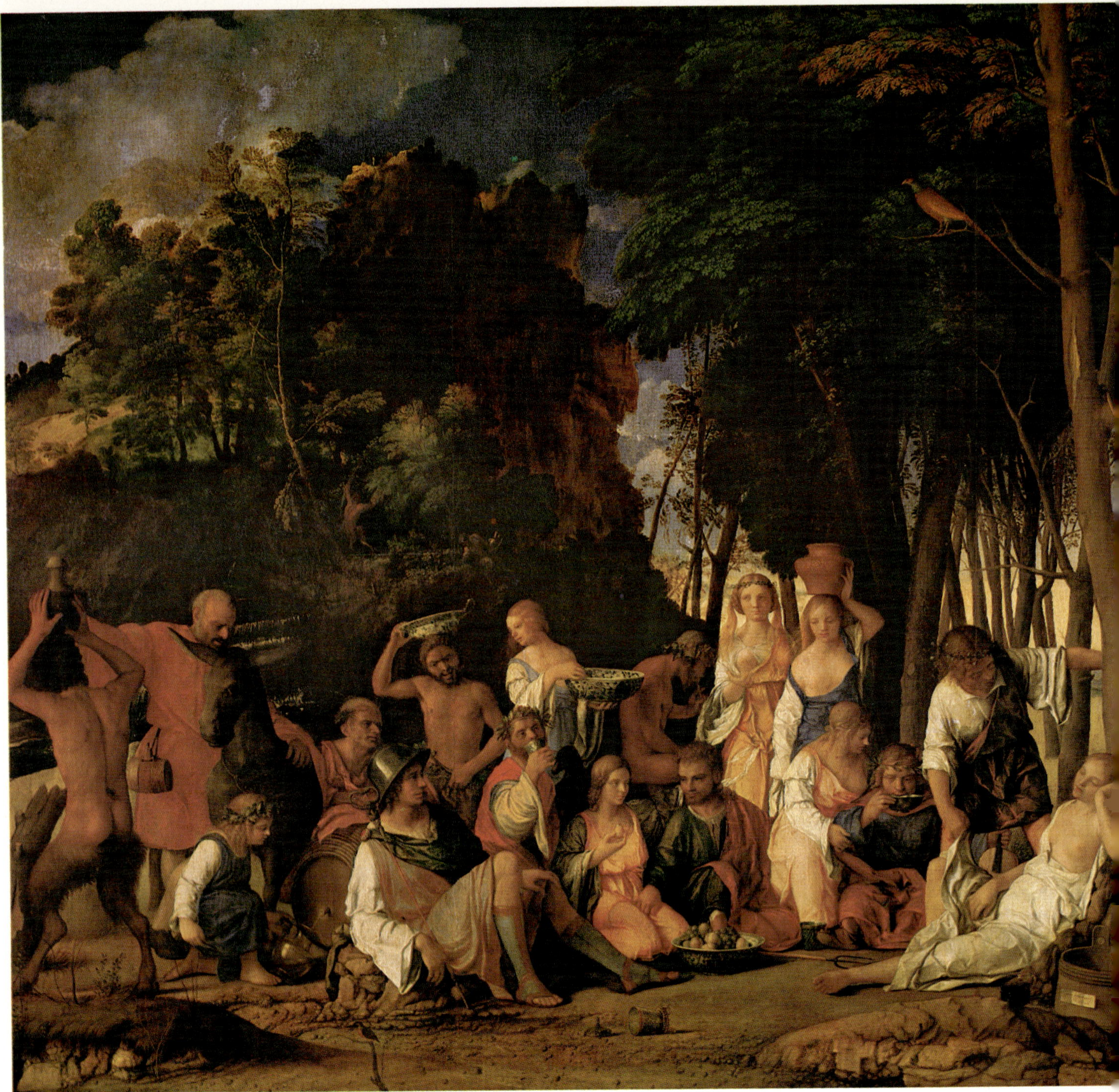

103. GIOVANNI BELLINI (*c.* 1430–1516): *The Feast of the Gods.* 1514. Canvas, 67 × 74 in. Washington, D.C., National Gallery of Art (Widener Collection)

This, the first of four mythological pictures commissioned by the Duke of Ferrara for a small room in his castle, was painted when Bellini was over eighty. It is a satire on the Olympian gods, who have become uncouth rustics in appearance and behaviour. Among the drunken and lascivious group are, from the left, a satyr, Silenus, the young Bacchus, Mercury with his wand, Jupiter crowned with a wreath, Cybele and Neptune, Ceres and Apollo, and at the right, Priapus uncovering a nymph. Some ten years after Bellini had completed the *Feast of the Gods*, Titian repainted most of the landscape background to harmonize it with the three mythological pictures (see Plate 104 opposite) he himself had painted in the meantime for the same room.

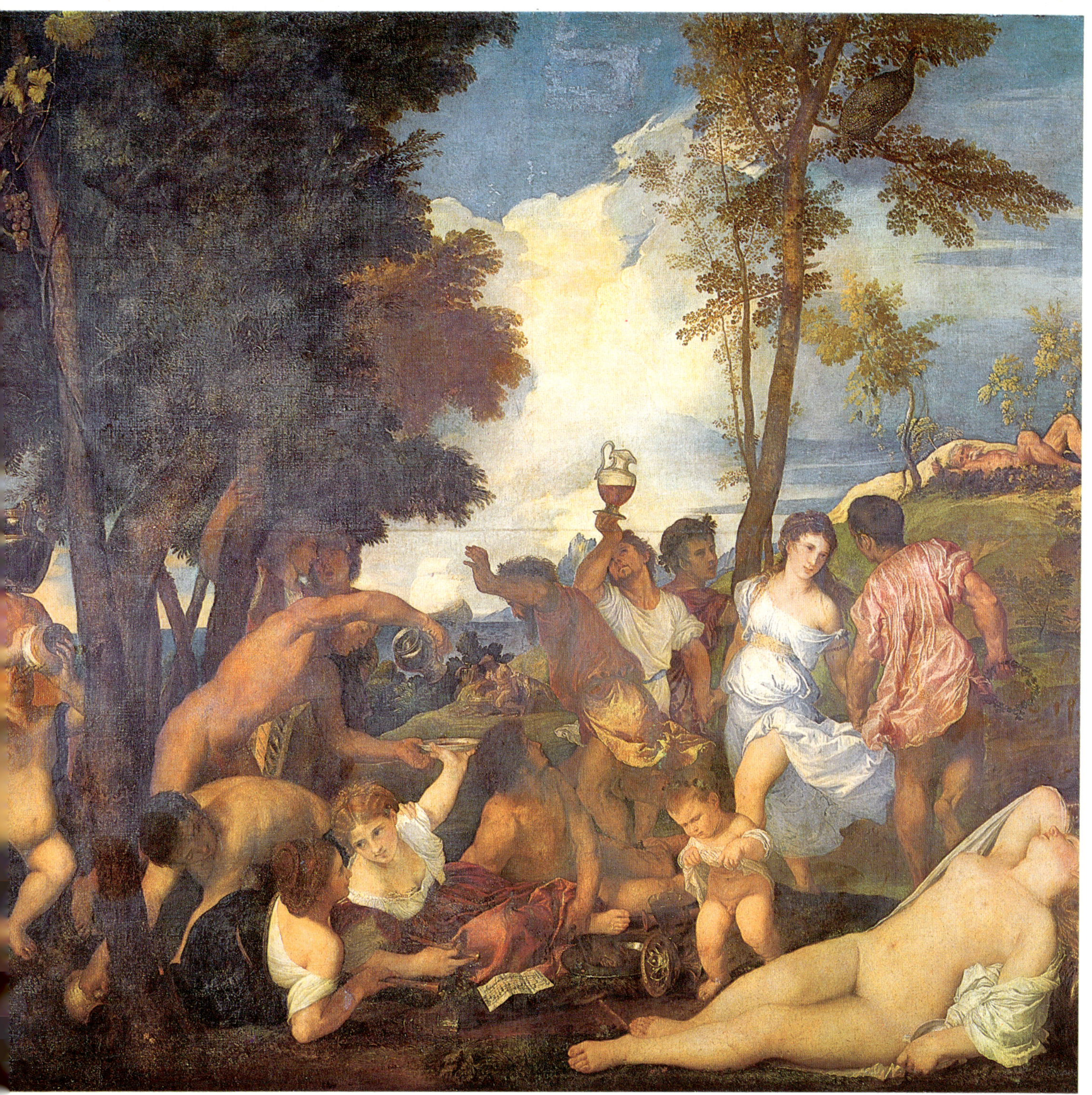

104. TITIAN (*c.* 1489–1576): *Bacchanal* (*'The Andrians'*). About 1520. Canvas, 69 × 76 in. Madrid, Prado

Here Titian has taken the ancient story of the island of Andros, where Dionysus made the rivers flow with wine, and shows the exuberance of swaying revellers drinking their fill. The sleeping Ariadne, a sensuous nude overcome with wine, has been deserted by her lover, Dionysus, whose ship is seen sailing away in the distance. The tune which the two reclining girls play on their recorders is inscribed on the sheet of music; it sums up the theme of the picture: 'He who drinks and does not drink again knows not what drinking is.'

105. MICHELANGELO (1475–1564): *The Creation of Adam*. 1511. Ceiling fresco. Vatican, Sistine Chapel

Like an electric spark, life has leapt from hand to hand, from the Creator to his image. Man is about to rise, his inert body endowed with physical energy and ennobled by the gift of a mind able to perceive his Maker. In his mantle God enfolds beings that were before man. The ideal that Florentine sculptors and painters had long been striving for has assumed final shape and meaning in Adam's body, re-created by an artist who was both sculptor and painter: spiritual significance expressed through physical beauty.

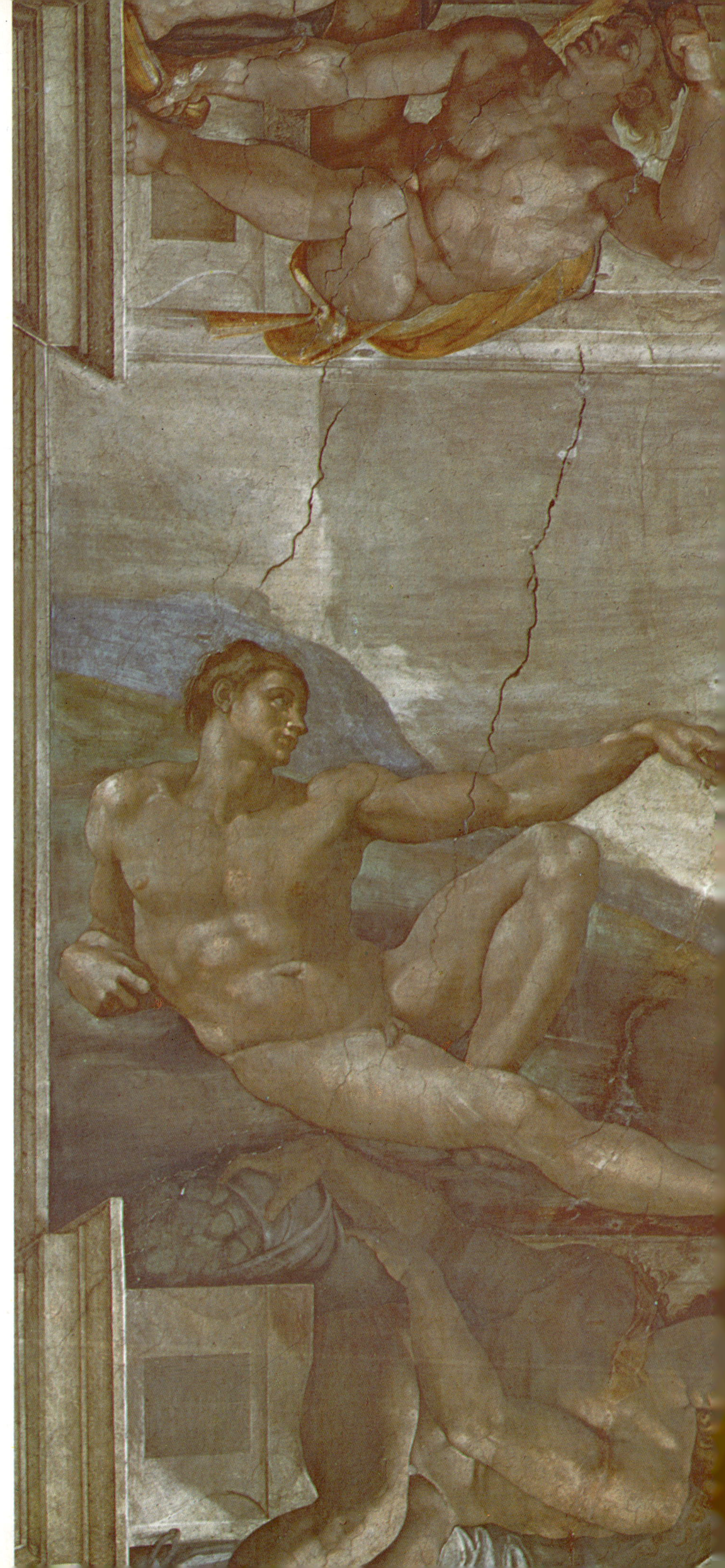

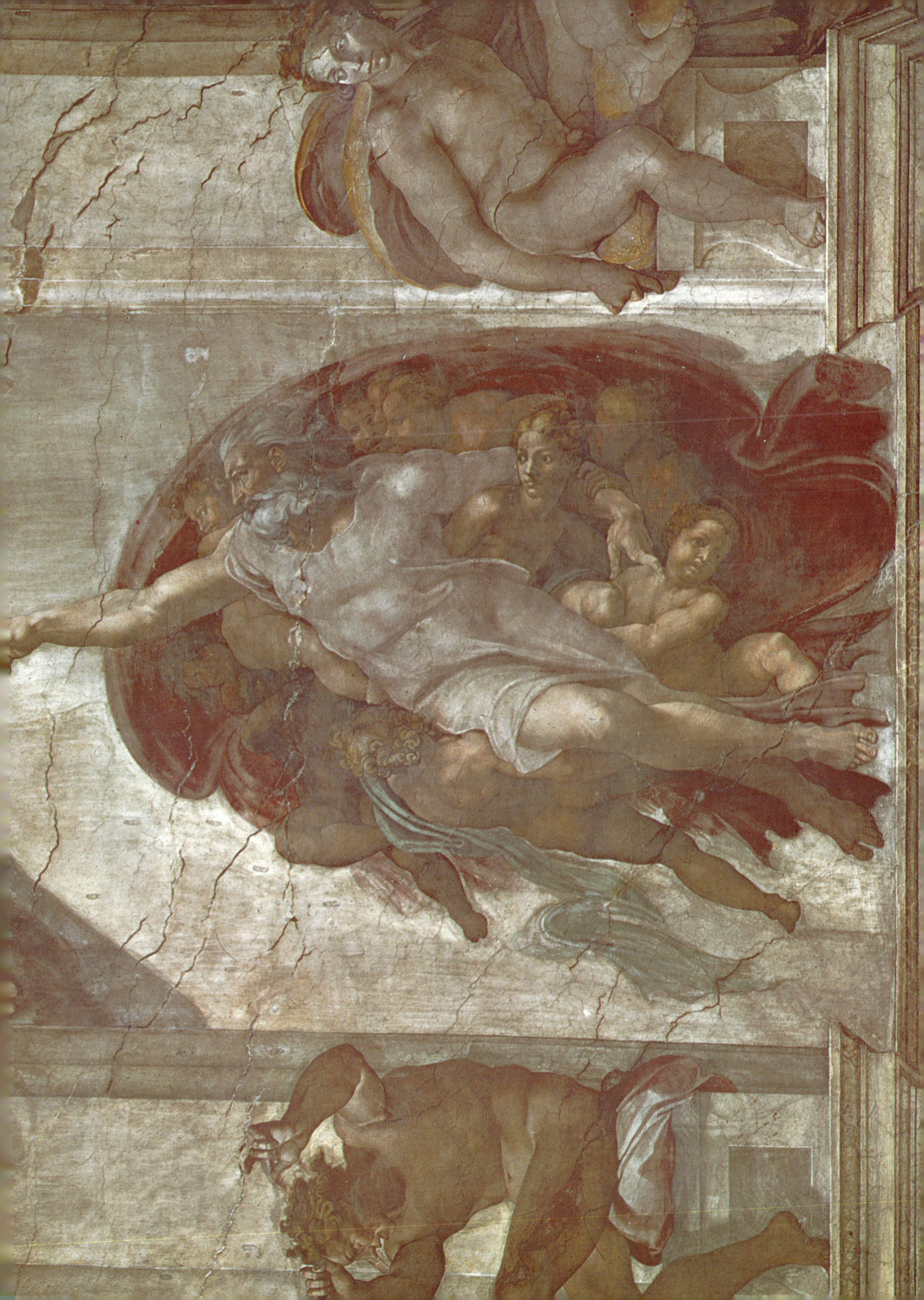

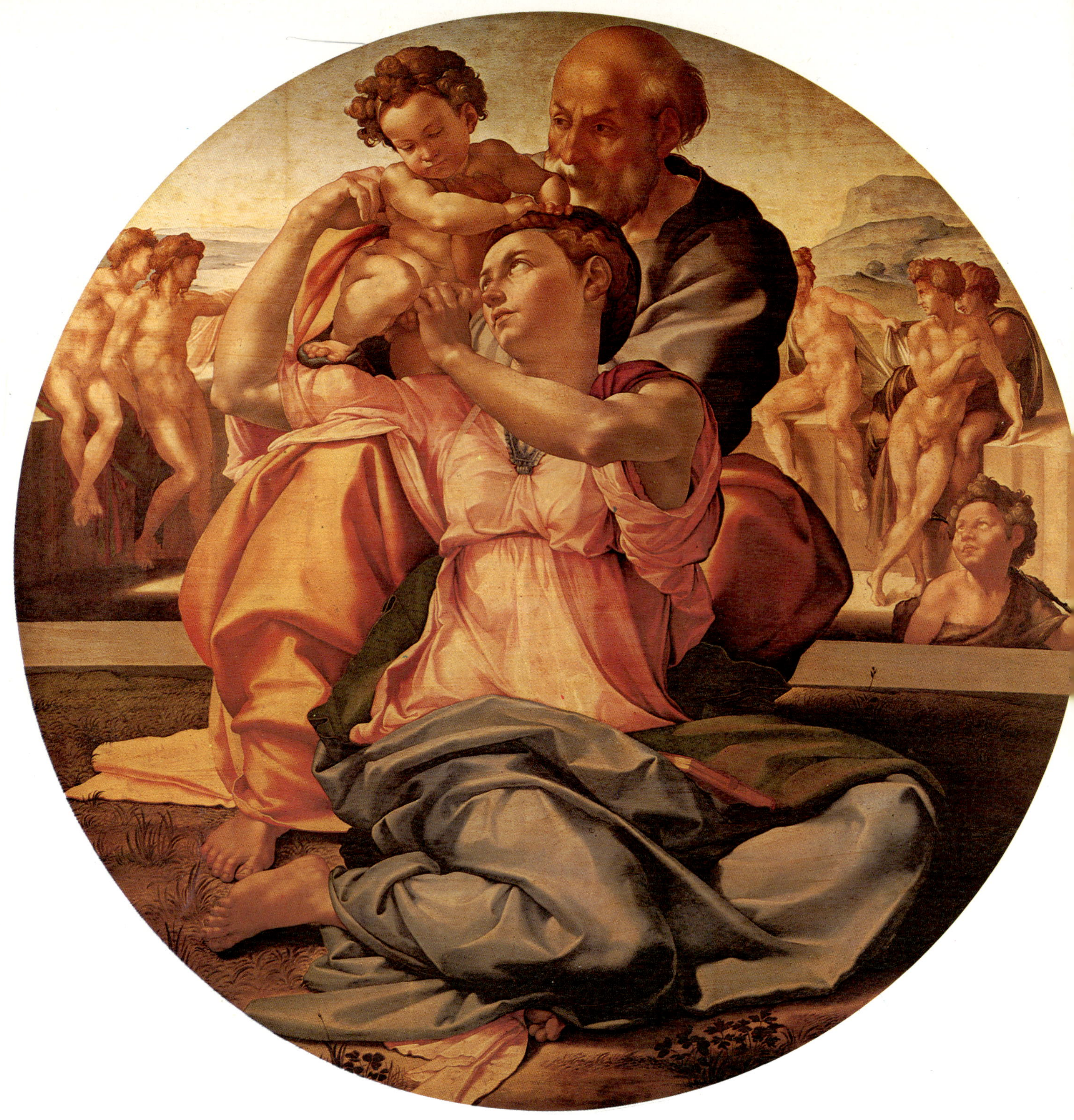

106. MICHELANGELO (1475–1564): *The Holy Family* (‘*Doni Madonna*’). 1504–5. Panel, $47\frac{1}{4}$ in. diameter. Florence, Uffizi

The Virgin, squatting on the ground, takes the Child from St. Joseph. The strangely contorted postures are defined by the clean contours. ‘Sculptural’ modelling and the nudes in the background prefigure the frescoes on the Sistine ceiling (Plates 105, 109). By contrast, Raphael’s serene picture (opposite), almost contemporary with Michelangelo’s picture, has the relaxed intimacy of a maternal idyll.

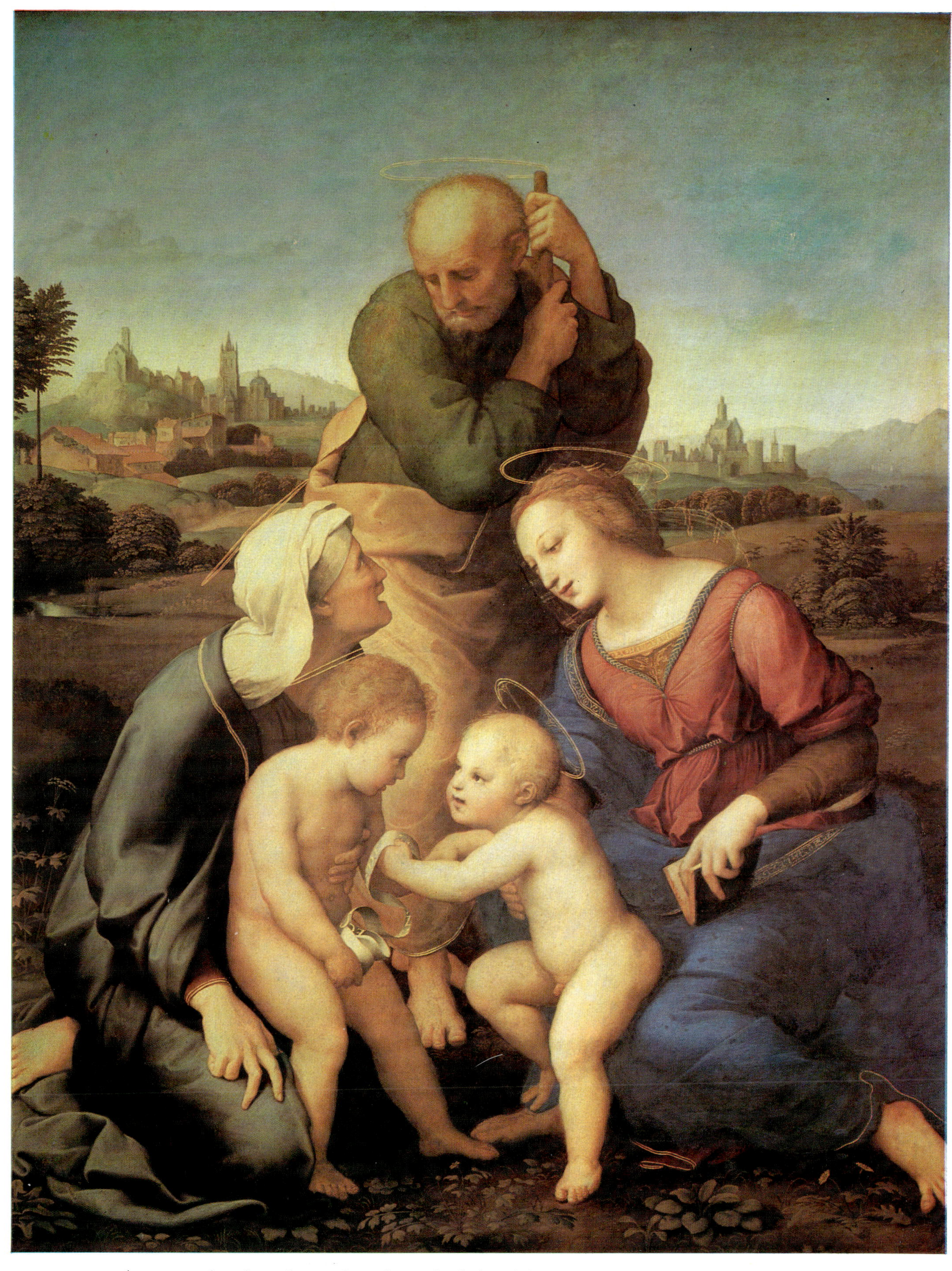

107. RAPHAEL (1483–1520): *The Holy Family with St. Elisabeth and the young St. John Baptist.* 1505–7. Panel, 51½ × 42 in. Munich, Alte Pinakothek

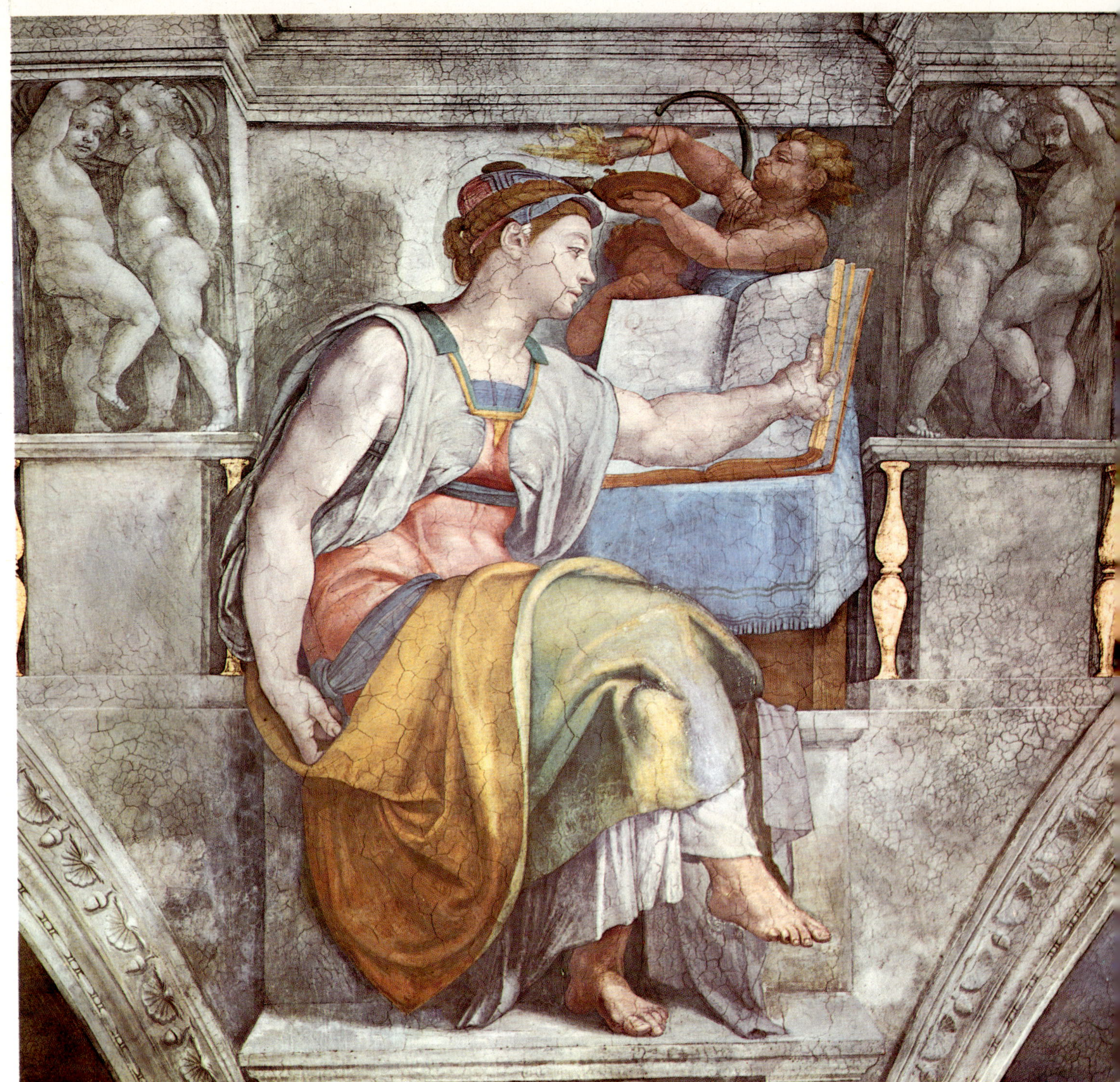

108. MICHELANGELO (1475–1564): *The Erythraean Sibyl.* 1509–12. Detail of the ceiling frescoes (Plate 109). Vatican, Sistine Chapel

The nine narrative scenes from Genesis on the Sistine ceiling are surrounded by a wealth of other figures in an interlocking scheme of unrivalled boldness and variety. The triangular spandrels alternate with colossal figures of five sibyls and seven prophets. The sibyls were wise women of antiquity, who were believed to have foretold the birth of Christ and so earned a place in Christian iconography. In depicting them, Michelangelo caught 'moments of spiritual life, inspiration itself, contemplative soliloquy and deep, silent thought'. The compactness of the figures (compare also Plate 106) can be related to Michelangelo's activities as a sculptor.

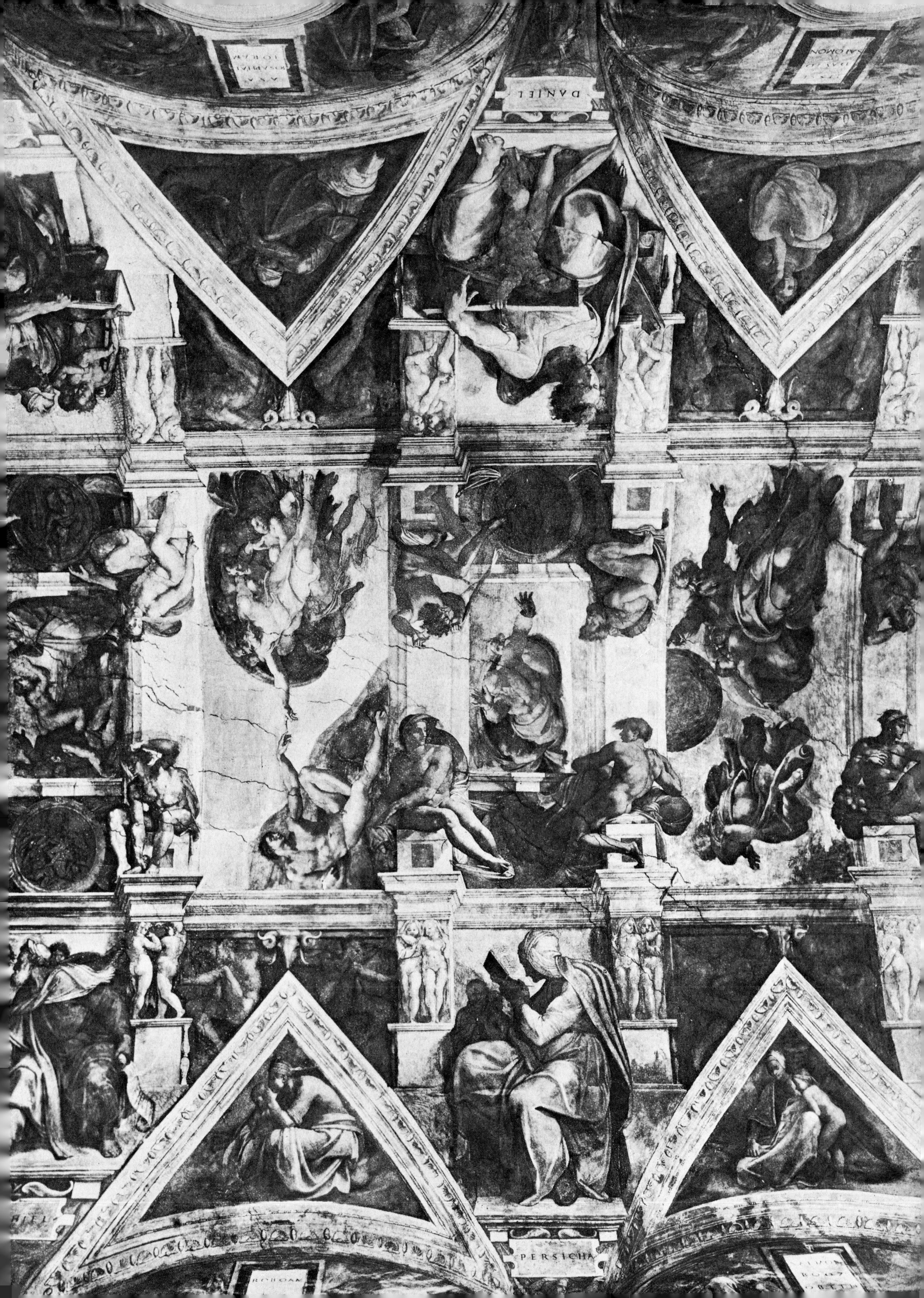
DANIEL
PERSICHA

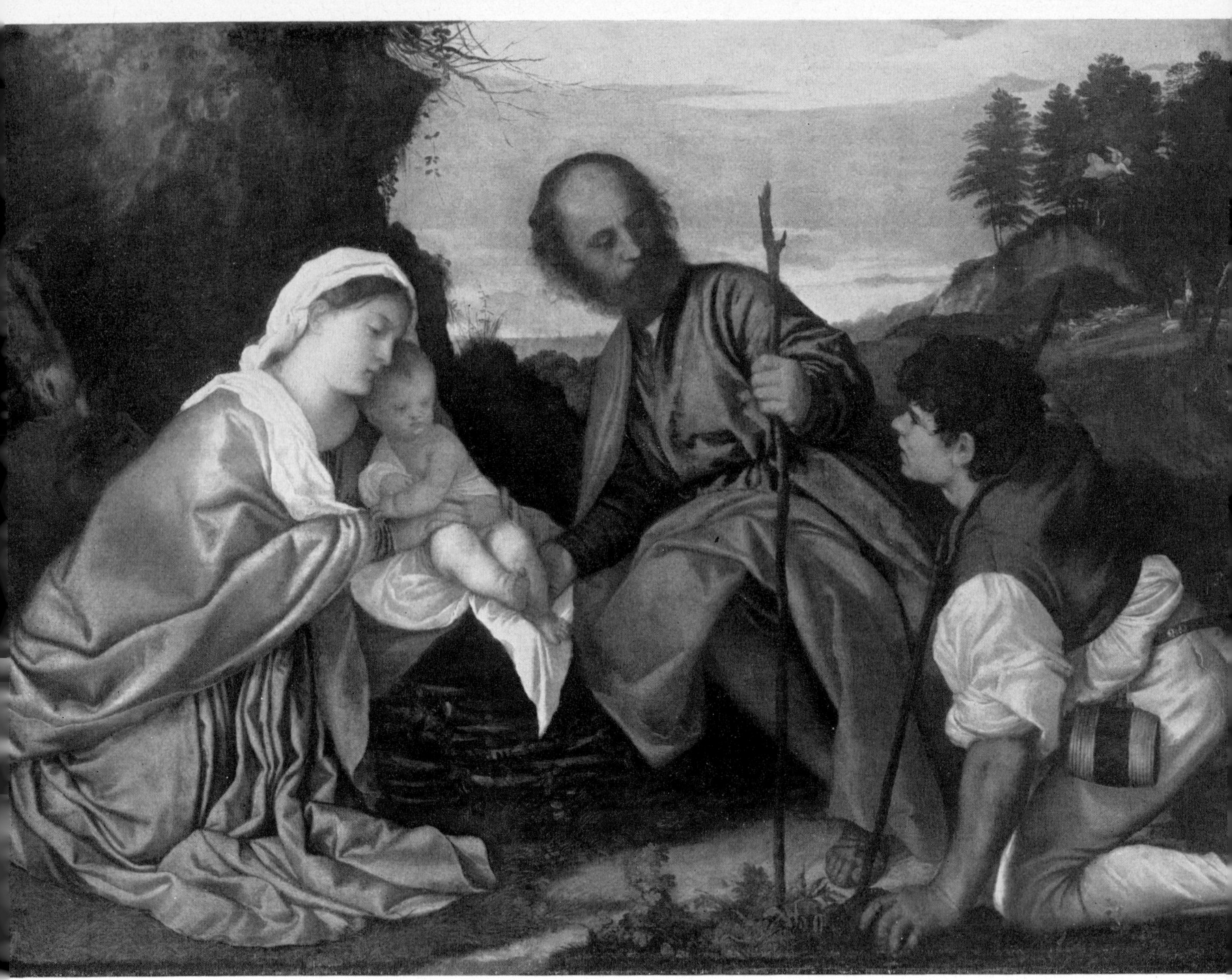

110. TITIAN (*c.* 1489–1576): *The Holy Family with a Shepherd.* About 1510. Canvas, 39 × 54¾ in. London, National Gallery

111. RAPHAEL (1483–1520): *The Sistine Madonna.* About 1513. Canvas, 104½ × 77 in. Dresden, Gemäldegalerie

On the high altar of the Benedictine church in Piacenza, where Raphael's picture remained for mor than two centuries, it must have seemed like a vision seen in a window: the curtains appear to have been drawn back to reveal the Virgin and her divine Child gazing earnestly at the spectator. Her majestic, but far from rigid figure, clothed in a billowing mantle, rests firmly on the floating clouds, while the two saints seem to sink into them. On the left, with his papal mitre at his feet, is St. Sixtus, who has given the picture its name. He has the features of Pope Julius II (see also Plate 119), who commissioned the picture from Raphael. On the right is St. Barbara, with her attribute, a tower, jus visible behind her right shoulder. The former gazes up intently at the Child and points outwards to command our reverence, the latter reaches inwards and looks down at the two cherubs leaning on the fictive ledge. As in the *Holy Family* (Plate 107), Raphael has used many subtle contrasts of pose and lighting in the creation of this masterpiece.

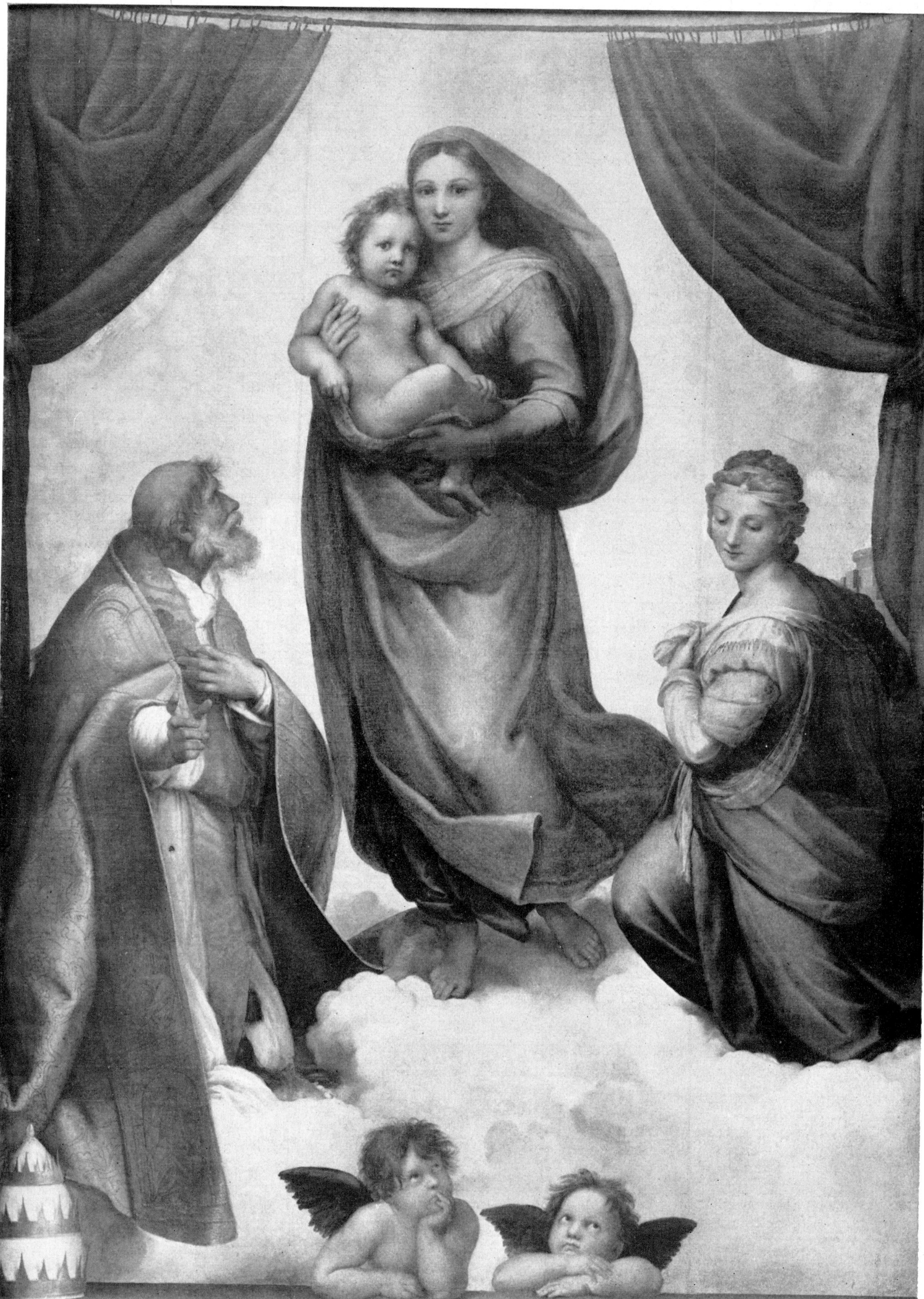

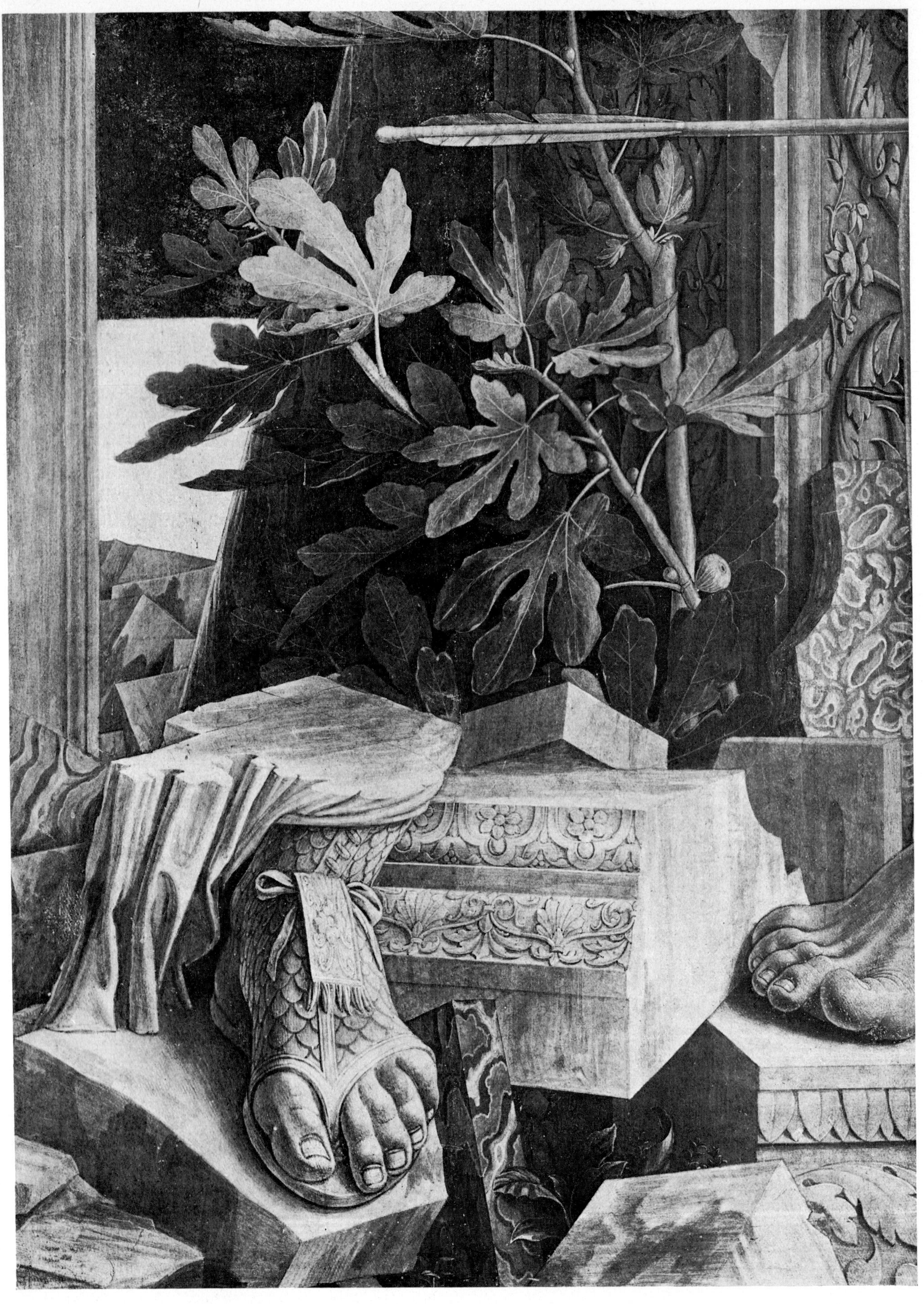

112. ANDREA MANTEGNA (*c.* 1430–1506): *Fragments of Antique Sculpture*. Detail from Plate 49

113. VITTORE CARPACCIO (*c.* 1460–1523/6): *Fragments of Antique Sculpture*. Detail from Plate 78

Broken remnants of ancient statues and reliefs were being unearthed in increasing numbers and were eagerly sought by collectors. Like surviving Roman buildings, monuments and coins, they were studied by humanists as witnesses to Roman civilization and artistic achievement, and they served the Renaissance artist in several ways: as models from which he could learn to draw what his predecessors had carved; as objects which would add authenticity to scenes set in ancient times (and that included most biblical and other religious subjects), and as symbols of the overthrow of paganism.

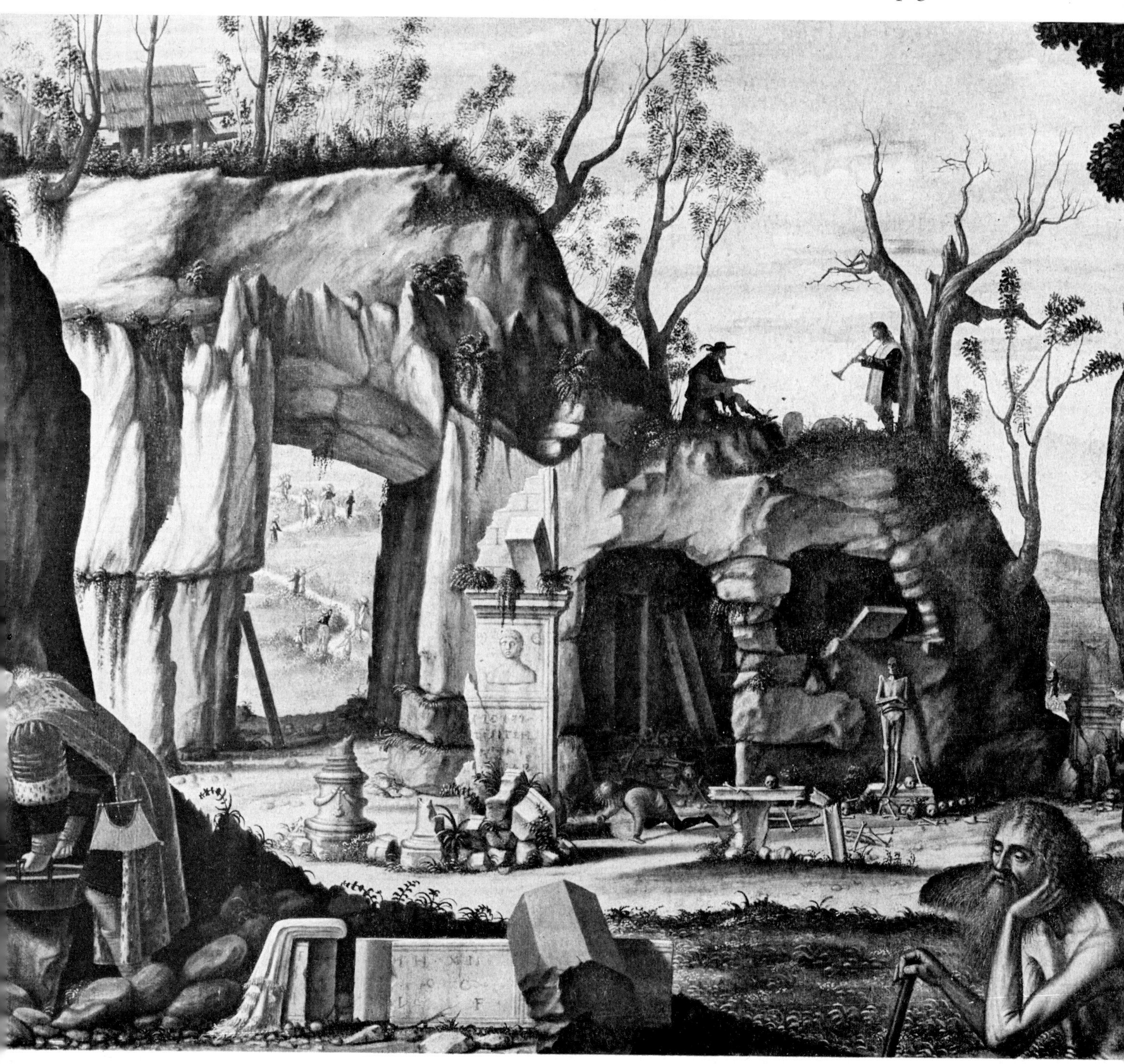

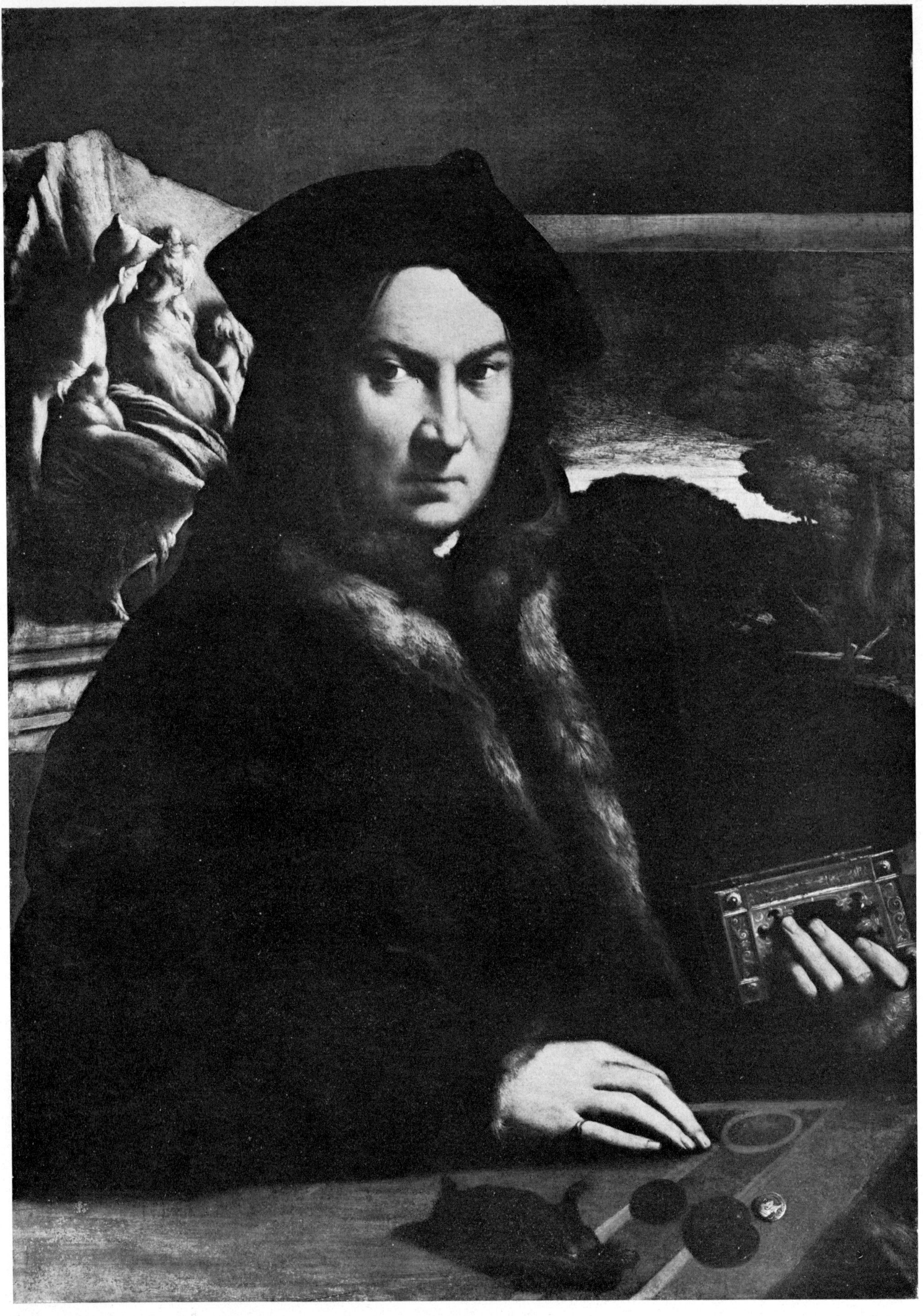

114. PARMIGIANINO (1503–40): *Portrait of a Gentleman*. About 1523. Panel, 35 × 25¼ in. Private collection, on loan to the National Gallery, London

115. LORENZO LOTTO (*c.* 1480–1556): *Portrait of Andrea Odoni*. 1527. Canvas, 40½ × 46 in. Royal Collection. Copyright reserved

Lotto's sitter was a famous Venetian antiquarian and collector of ancient sculpture. In this lively and informal portrait he proudly shows off a statuette of Diana of Ephesus, and is surrounded by diverse pieces of classical statuary, among which a group of Hercules and Antaeus can be identified. Collections of antiquities—coins, gems and inscriptions as well as sculptures—were not confined to Popes and princes, but were built up also by scholars and connoisseurs, who laid the foundation of classical archaeology.

Lotto's portrait is documented soon after it was painted, being described in 1532: 'the half-length portrait in oil of this Messer Andrea, contemplating antique marble fragments, is by the hand of Lorenzo Lotto.' And we know that it hung in Odoni's bedroom, together with furniture painted by a pupil of Titian.

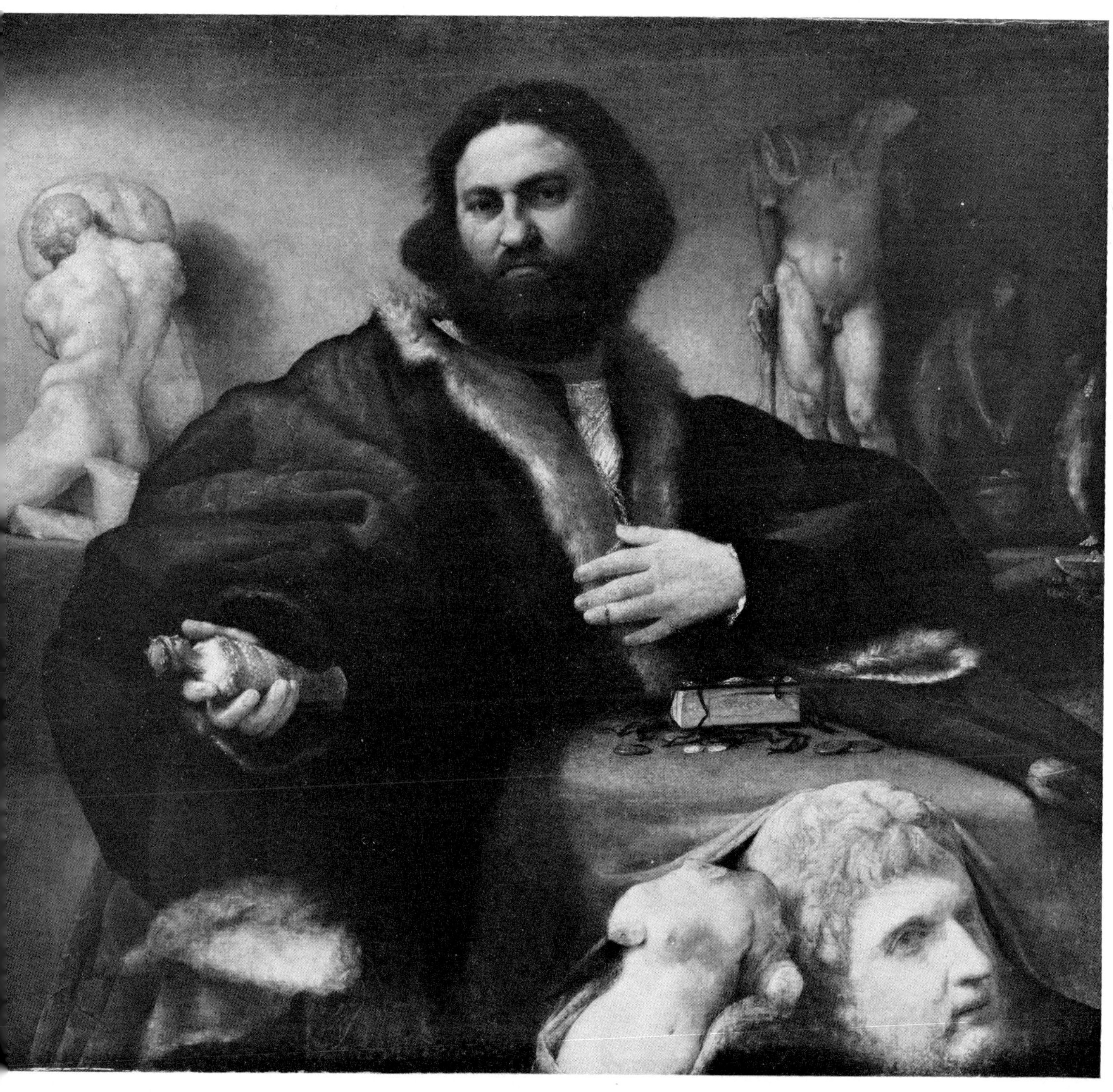

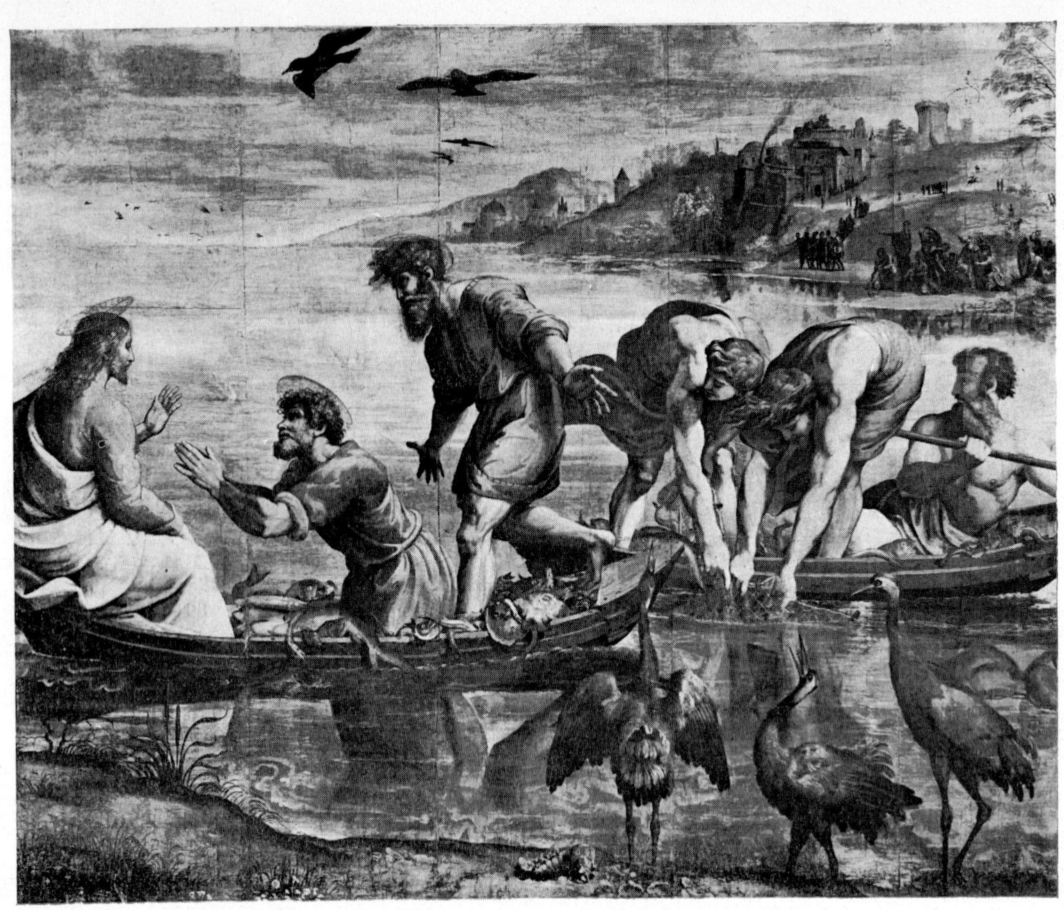

116. RAPHAEL (1483–1520): *The Miraculous Draught of Fishes*. 1515–16. Cartoon, 125½ × 157 in. Royal Collection (on permanent loan to the Victoria and Albert Museum)

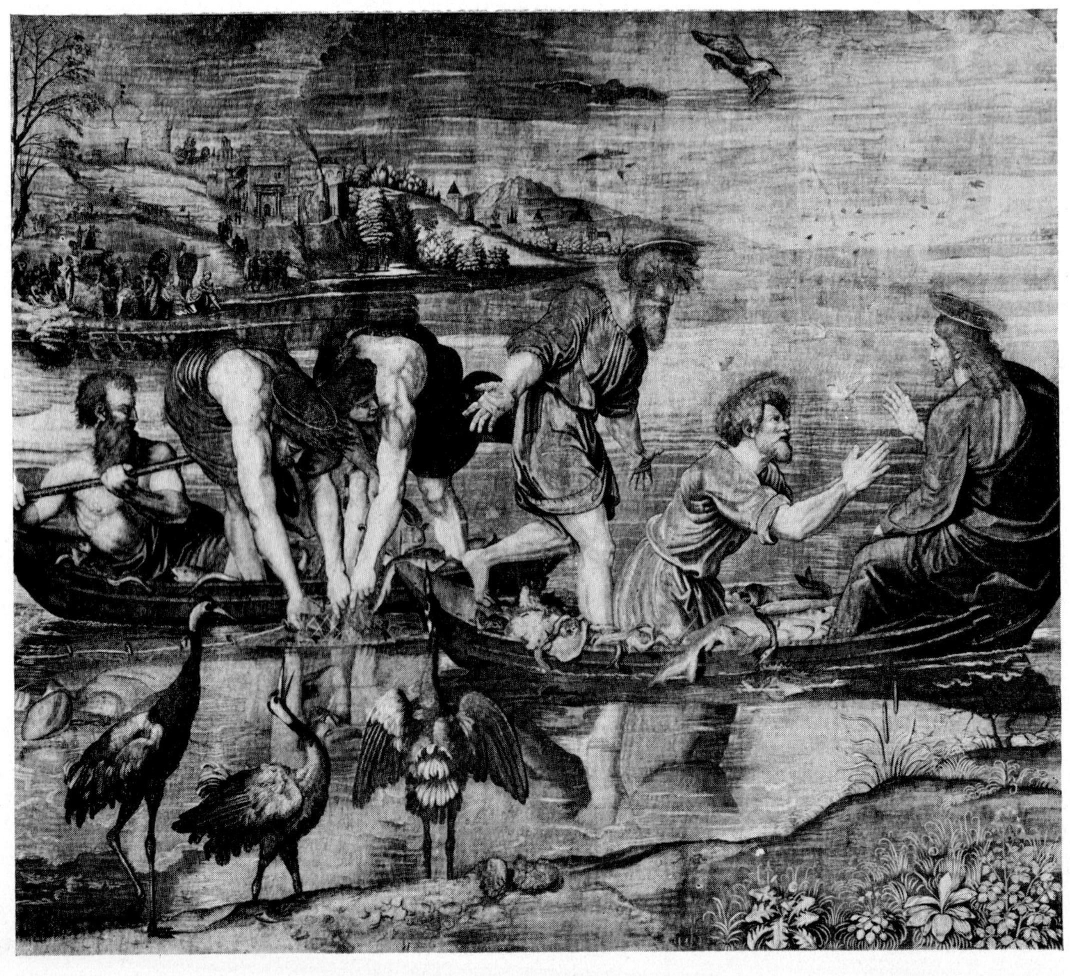

117. After RAPHAEL: *The Miraculous Draught of Fishes*. 1517–18. Tapestry, about 134 × 161 in. Vatican, Pinacoteca

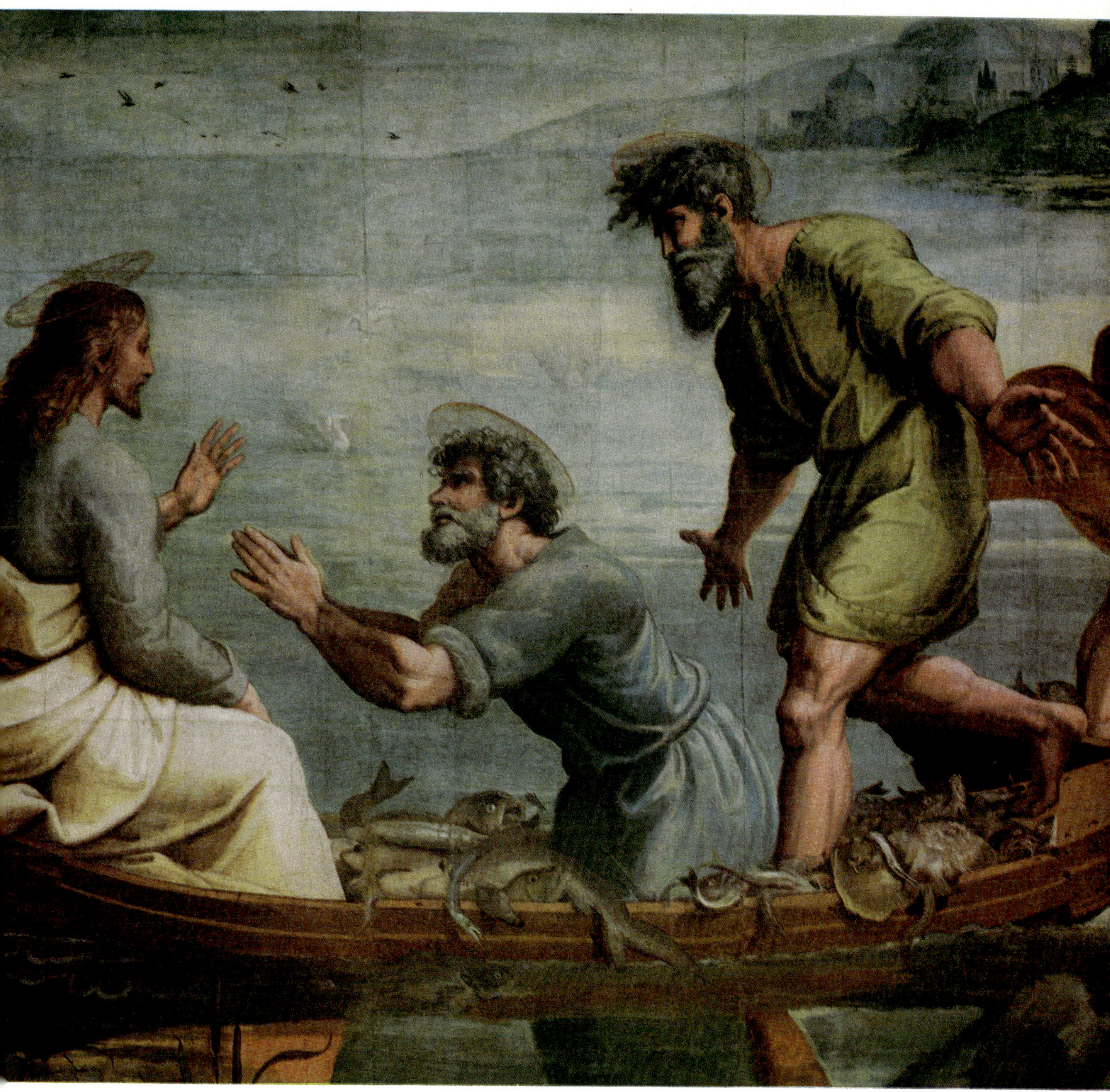

118. RAPHAEL (1483–1520): *The Miraculous Draught of Fishes*. Detail from Plate 116

Pope Leo X commissioned Raphael to prepare full-size designs (called cartoons) for ten tapestries, which were to decorate the Sistine Chapel of the Vatican. The subjects, taken from the lives of St. Peter and St. Paul, were to make clear the divine mission of the two Apostles and thus to prove the primacy of papal authority. The cartoons were sent to a Flemish weaver's workshop and copied, in reverse, on the looms. The *Draught of Fishes* represents a miracle related by St. Luke: how the fishermen on the lake of Gennesaret, having toiled in vain, cast their nets again into the deep at Christ's command and were rewarded with a catch so large that their net broke and their boat began to sink. Then—and this is the moment shown here—St. Peter fell down humbly at Christ's knees and Christ said to him: 'From henceforth thou shalt catch men.' In the distance is an idealized view of Rome, and in the foreground three great cranes wade in the lake. The still-life of heaped deepwater fishes in Peter's boat points to the nature of the miracle.

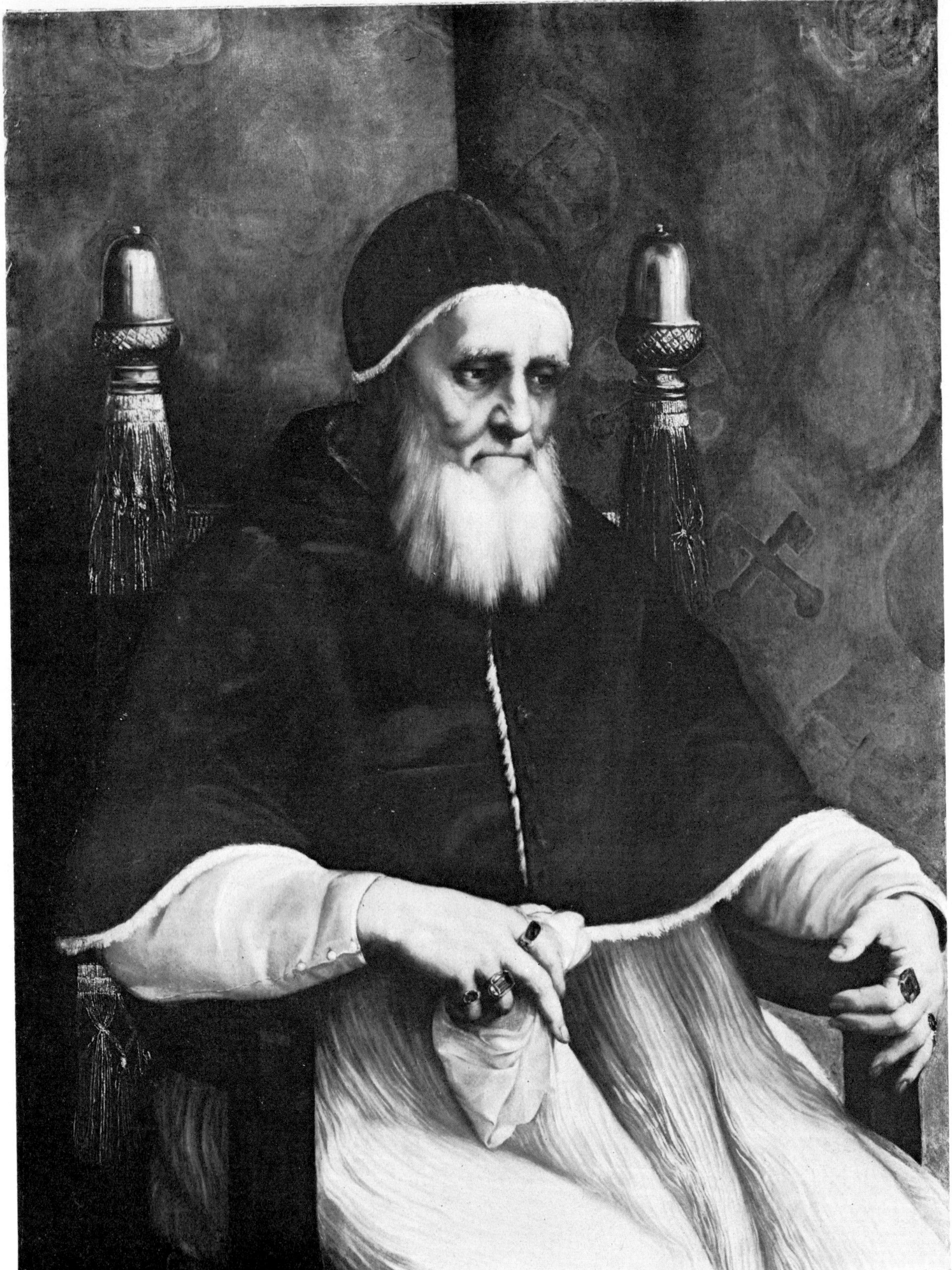

119. RAPHAEL (1483–1520): *Portrait of Pope Julius II.* 1511–12. Panel, $42\frac{1}{2} \times 31\frac{3}{4}$ in. London, National Gallery

Julius, who reigned from 1503 to 1513, was a generous patron of artists. Among the works he commissioned were his own tomb and the paintings on the Sistine Chapel ceiling (Plates 4, 105, 108, 109) by Michelangelo, and Raphael's early frescoes in the Vatican (Plates 33, 121–124). In 1506 he laid the cornerstone of the new Basilica of St. Peter's, of which Raphael was appointed architect under Julius's successor. Raphael portrayed him also in the *Expulsion of Heliodorus* (Plate 33), in the '*Disputa*' (Plate 123), and in the Sistine Madonna (Plate 111). The National Gallery panel was only recently recognized as the original version from Raphael's own hand.

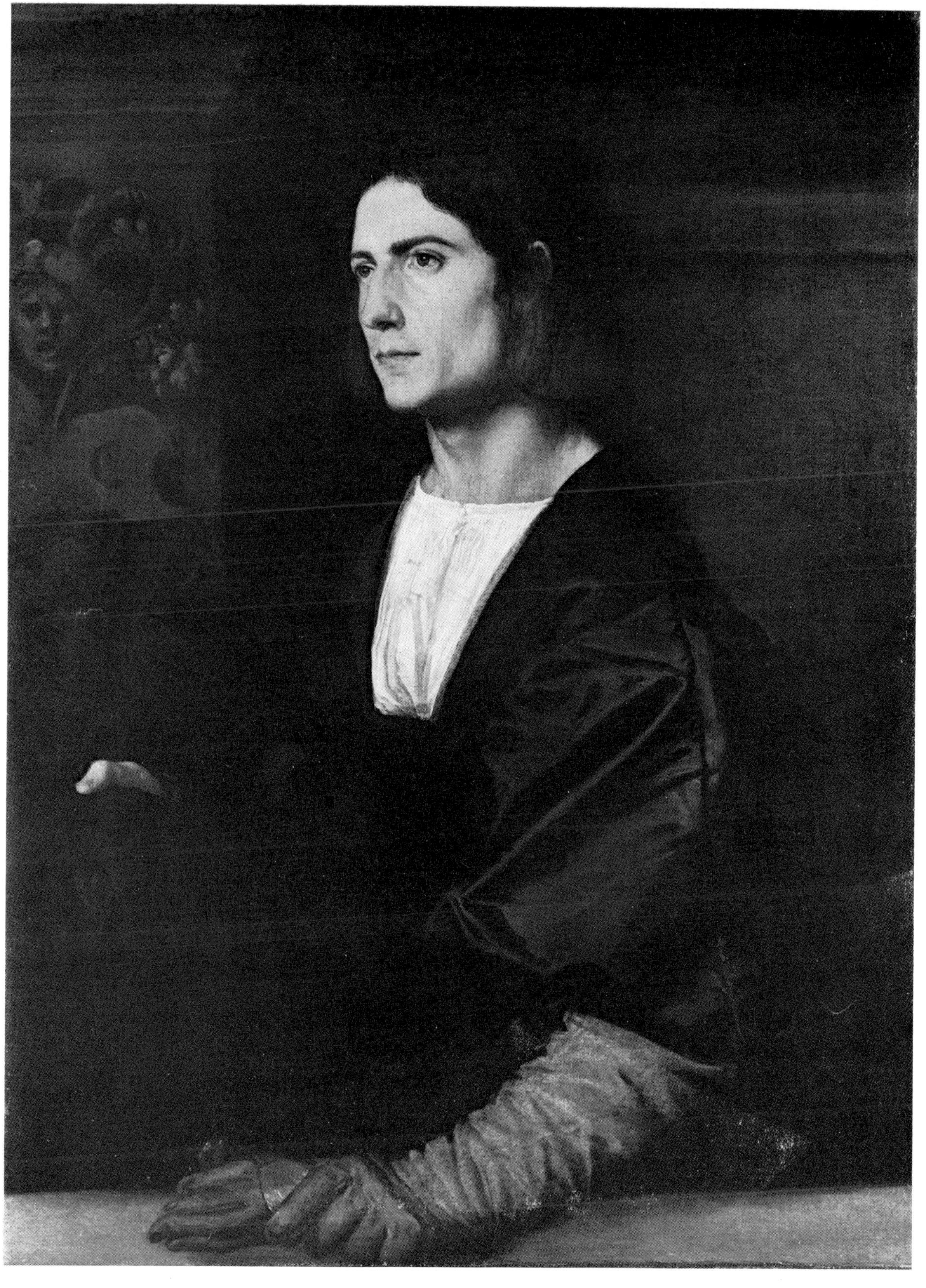

120. TITIAN (*c.* 1489–1576): *Portrait of a Young Man*. 1512–15. Canvas, 43½ × 37 in. Garrowby Hall, Earl of Halifax

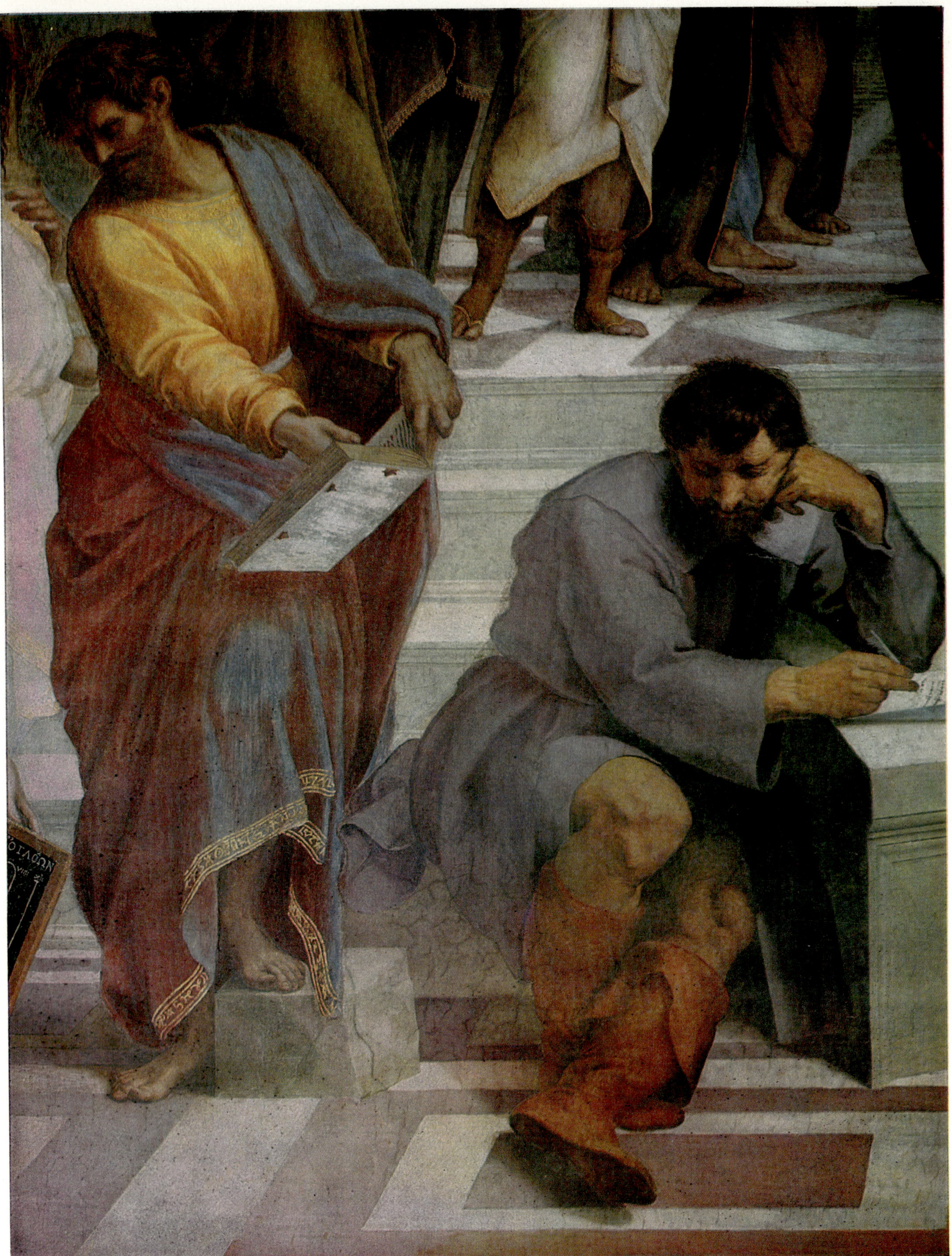

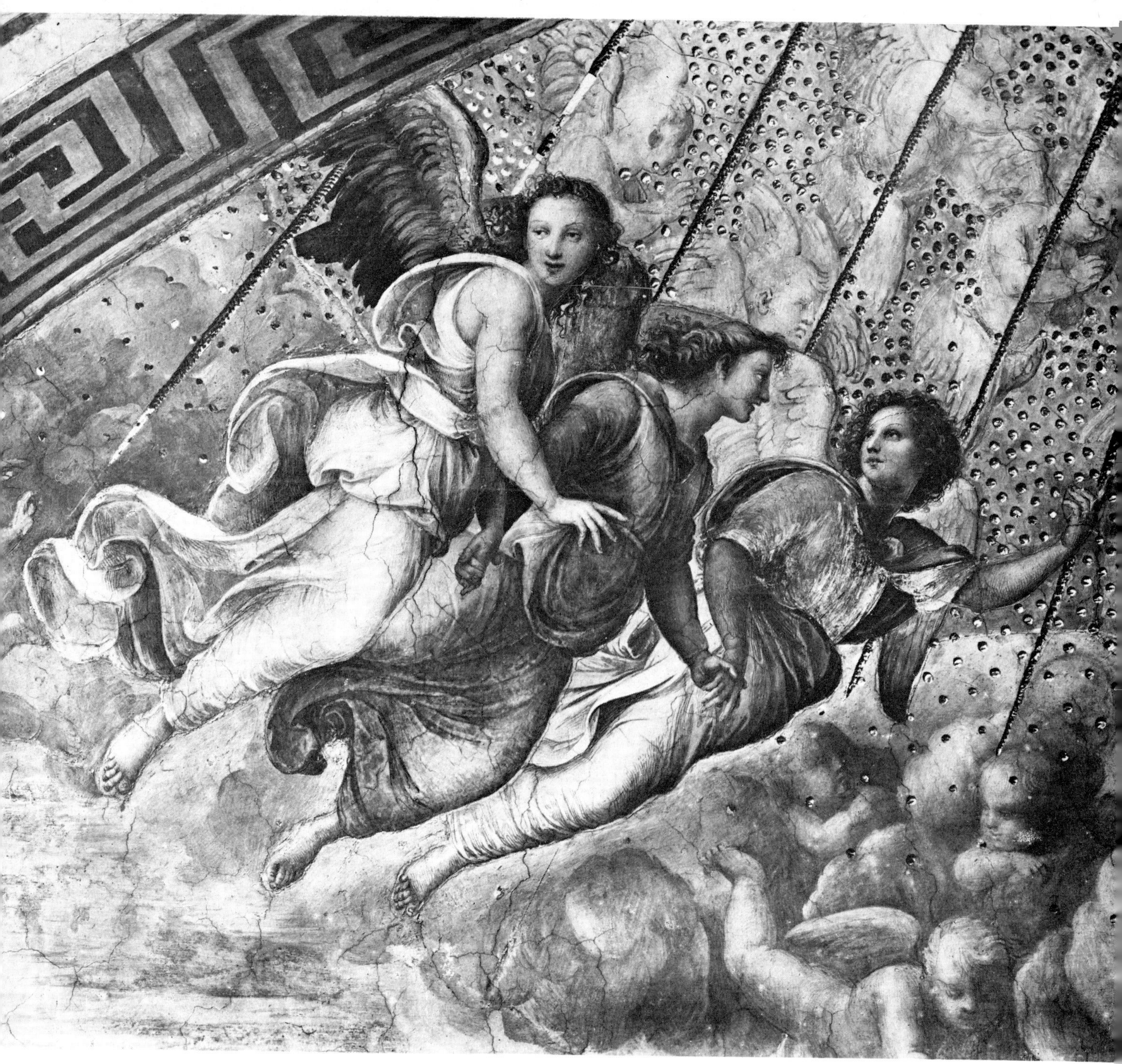

122. RAPHAEL (1483–1520): *Angels and Putti*. Detail from Plate 123

121. RAPHAEL (1483–1520): *Two Philosophers*. Detail from Plate 124

Few of the figures in *The 'School of Athens'* have been identified. Various names have been assigned to the standing man on the left of this detail. The seated man has long been thought to represent the Ionian philosopher Heraclitus, but recently it has been suggested that he may be a portrait of Michelangelo, shown as a thinker and a poet, while the large block of stone may refer to his eminence as a sculptor. The posture of the figure certainly seems to recall the prophets on Michelangelo's ceiling frescoes in the Sistine Chapel (Plate 109).

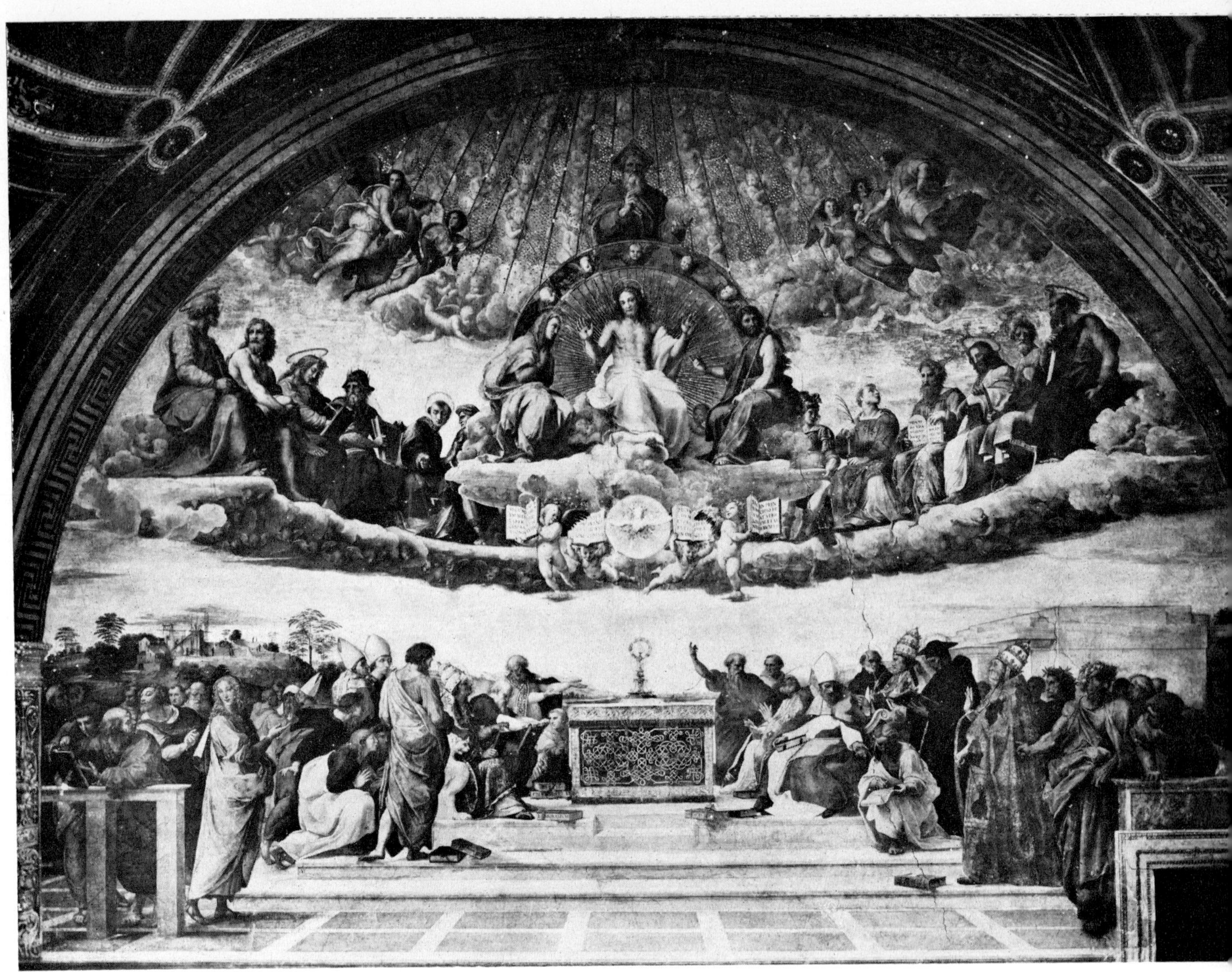

123. RAPHAEL (1483–1520): *The 'Disputa.'* 1509–10. Fresco. Vatican Palace, Stanza della Segnatura

The subject is obscured rather than clarified by the traditional title. What is represented is the divine affirmation of a central doctrine of the Catholic Church: the Real Presence in the Sacrament of the Altar. The persons of the Trinity are silhouetted against gold discs, which signify the transcendental world which they inhabit. The Father, blessing, holds the globe of the world, the Son displays the wounds of his sacrifice on the Cross. The dove of the Holy Ghost sends down golden rays upon the Eucharist and so affirms its true nature as defined by the bishops and theologians on earth. God the Father is flanked by six angels, Christ by the Virgin and the Baptist, and the Dove by the four gospels held up by *putti*. On the bank of clouds are twelve of the elect. Four Fathers of the Church are seated beside the altar: Gregory (a portrait of Pope Julius II) and Jerome on the left, Augustine and Ambrose on the right. Few of the other bystanders have been identified, but the traditional portrait of Dante is readily recognized.

124. RAPHAEL (1483–1520): *The 'School of Athens.'* 1509–11. Fresco. Vatican Palace, Stanza della Segnatura

This title was invented even later than that of the fresco on the opposite wall (opposite). The subject can be summed up as 'The Pursuit of Knowledge', and this search is exemplified in portrait groups of philosophers who had laid the foundations of the natural and moral sciences. Only three can be identified with certainty: the aged Plato and his pupil Aristotle, each carrying one of his own books, in the centre, framed by the farthest archway; and further left, Socrates, his head resembling ancient portraits and counting on his fingers in a dialectical argument. The thoughtful expressions are appropriate to the pioneers of rational study and speculation, and this realm of intellectual endeavour reflects the vigorous humanism of the papal city. But however imposing, the philosophers have to compete for our attention with the truly gigantic structure in which they are assembled. The invention of this architecture is said to be due to Bramante, who was then designing the new St. Peter's next to the Vatican Palace.

The 'Disputa' and *The 'School of Athens'* have theology and philosophy for their subjects. The other two walls are devoted to law and poetry, and all four, together with related ceiling frescoes, form a tightly coherent scheme of decoration, which is perhaps the greatest witness to Raphael's genius as a thinker and artist.

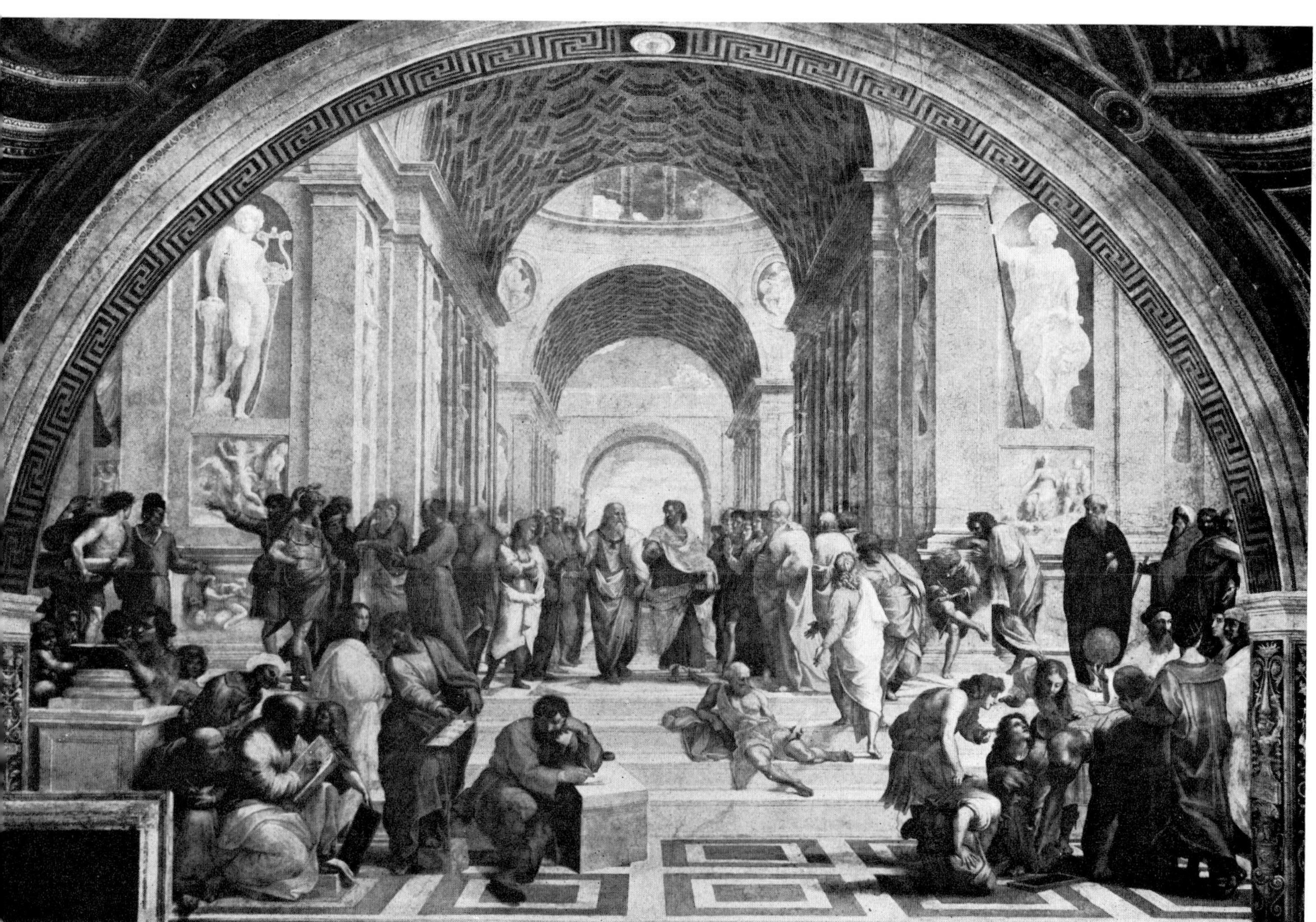

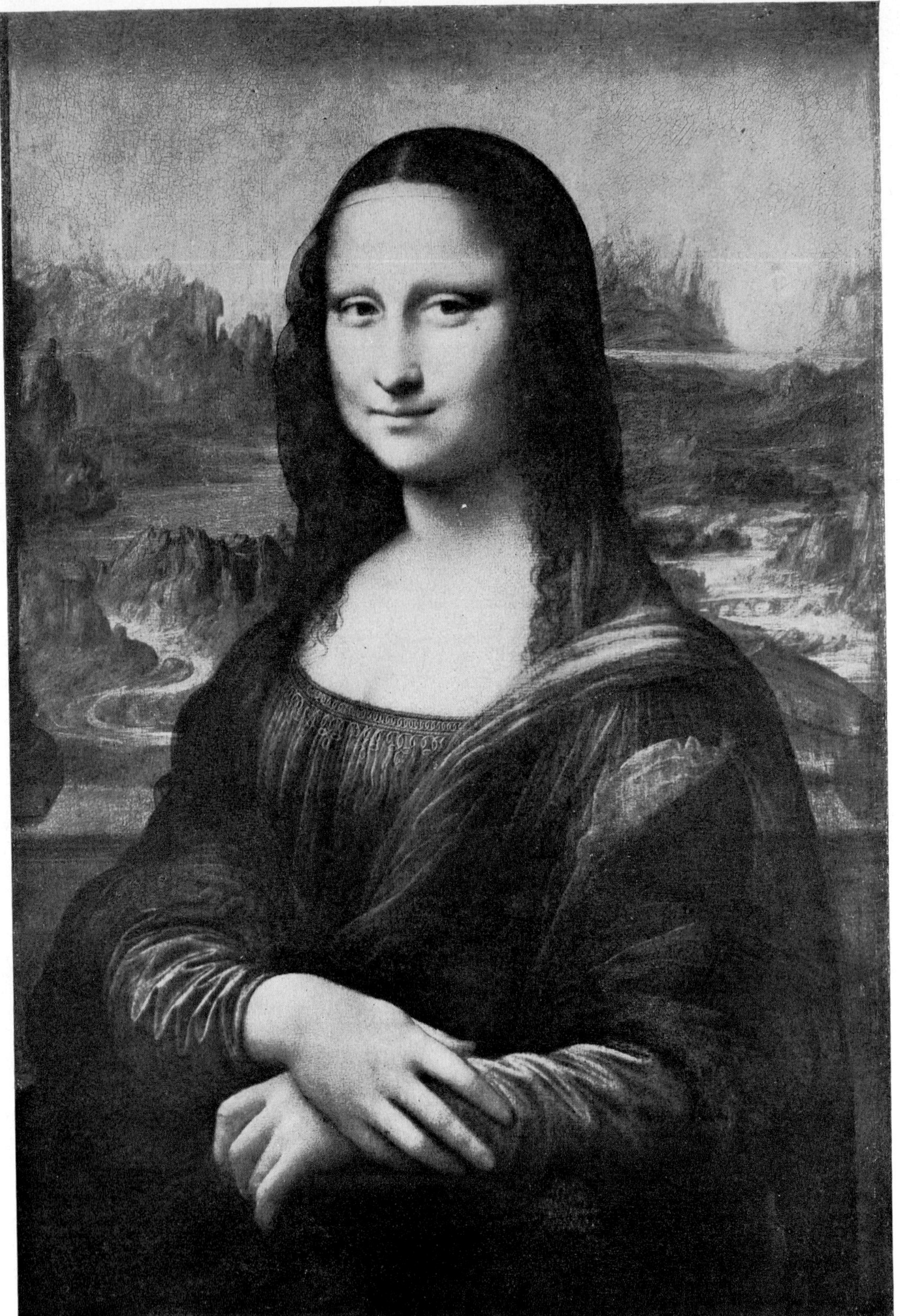

125. LEONARDO DA VINCI (1452–1519): *Portrait of Mona Lisa.* 1503. Panel, $30\frac{1}{2} \times 21$ in. Paris, Louvre

Two masterpieces of portraiture: Leonardo's enigmatic sitter, at ease yet uncommunicative in gesture and expression, dressed with simple elegance, unadorned, poised above a dream landscape of winding streams and jagged mountains; Raphael's lady, whose head, 'classical in structure and realized with breathtaking simplicity, is placed like a jewel in a setting of unrestrained and almost wilful elaboration. Hither and thither run the folds of the white gold-embroidered sleeve. . . . A diaphanous veil forms a niche behind the head.' (J. Pope-Hennessy)

126. RAPHAEL (1483–1520): *Portrait of a Woman.* 1512–13. Canvas, $33\frac{1}{2} \times 25\frac{1}{4}$ in. Floren[ce], Pitti Gallery

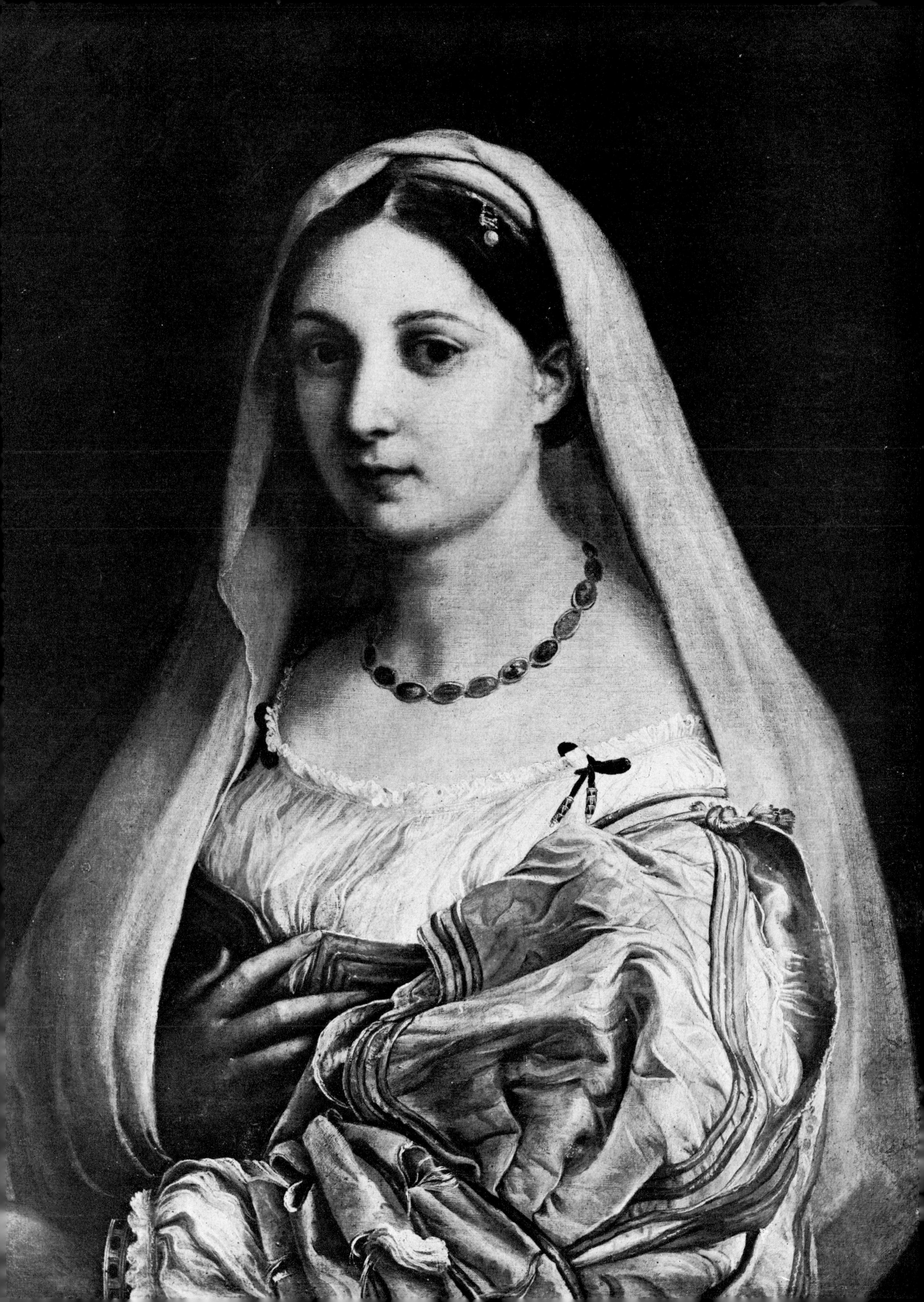

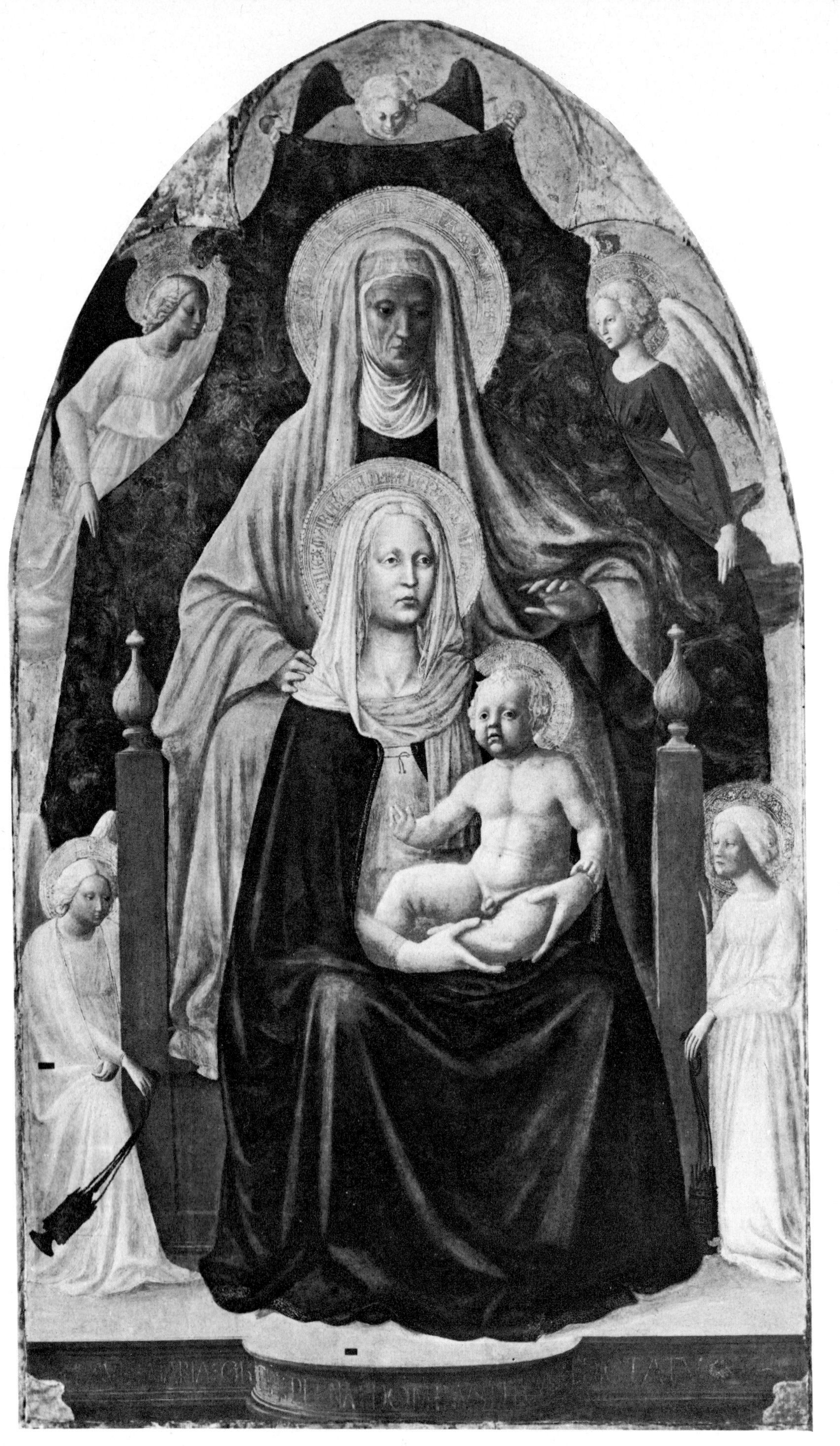

127. MASACCIO (1401–c. 1428): *The Virgin and Child with St. Anne.* 1420–4. Panel, 69 × 40½ in. Florence, Uffizi
The Virgin with her mother and her divine son was long a popular theme in Florentine painting. The composition of Masaccio's group derives from the hieratic imagery of Byzantine art, but its stiffness is softened by an incipient realism, which endows even so austere a composition with tenderness and humanity. The background is still fully in the medieval tradition; three of the angels were contributed by Masolino.

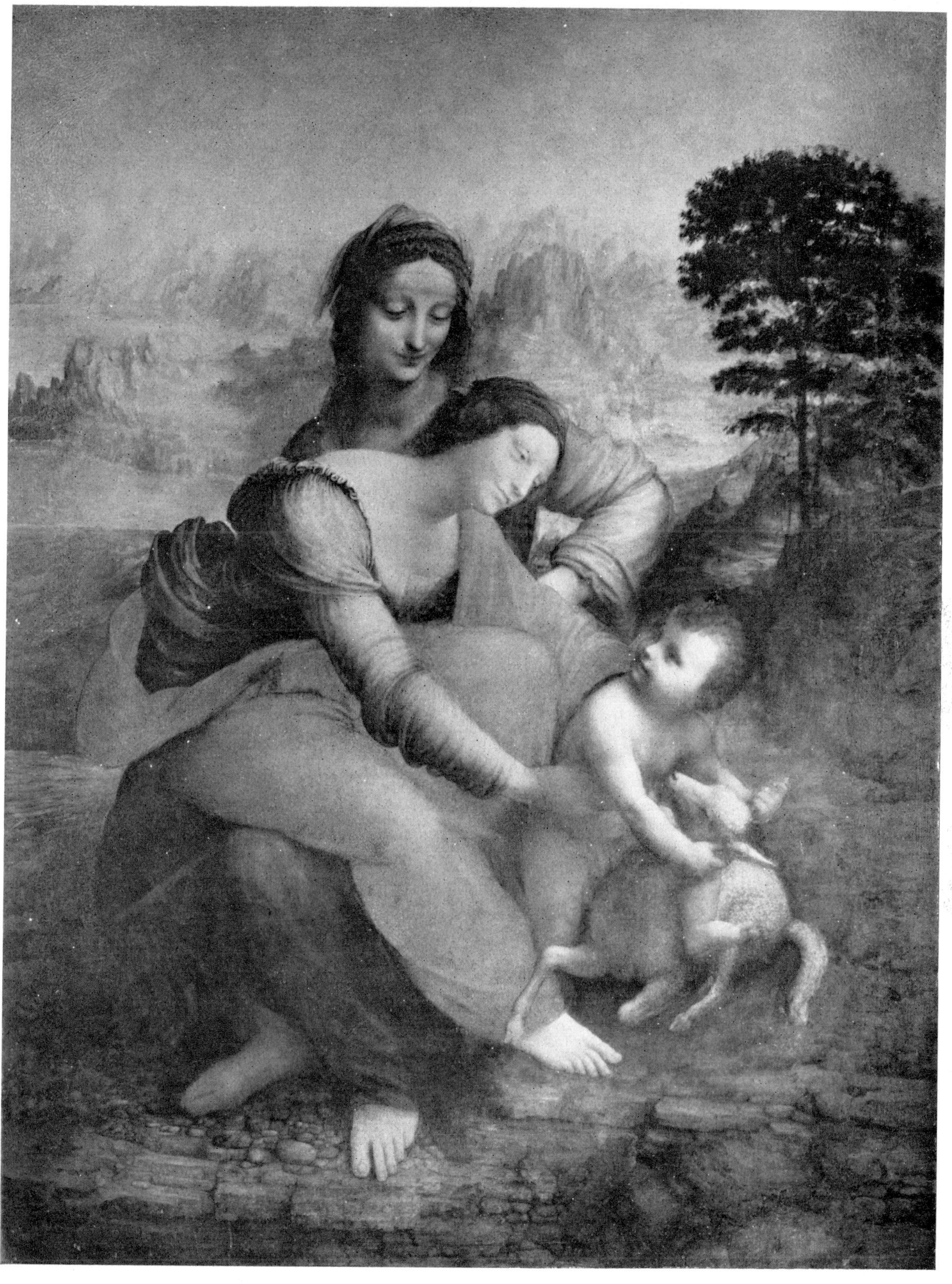

128. LEONARDO DA VINCI (1452–1519): *The Virgin and Child with St. Anne*. About 1510. Panel, 67 × 51 in. Paris, Louvre

A smiling celebration of maternal love, set in a living landscape: the Virgin, seated on her mother's lap, gently pulls the Child, who plays with the sacrificial lamb.

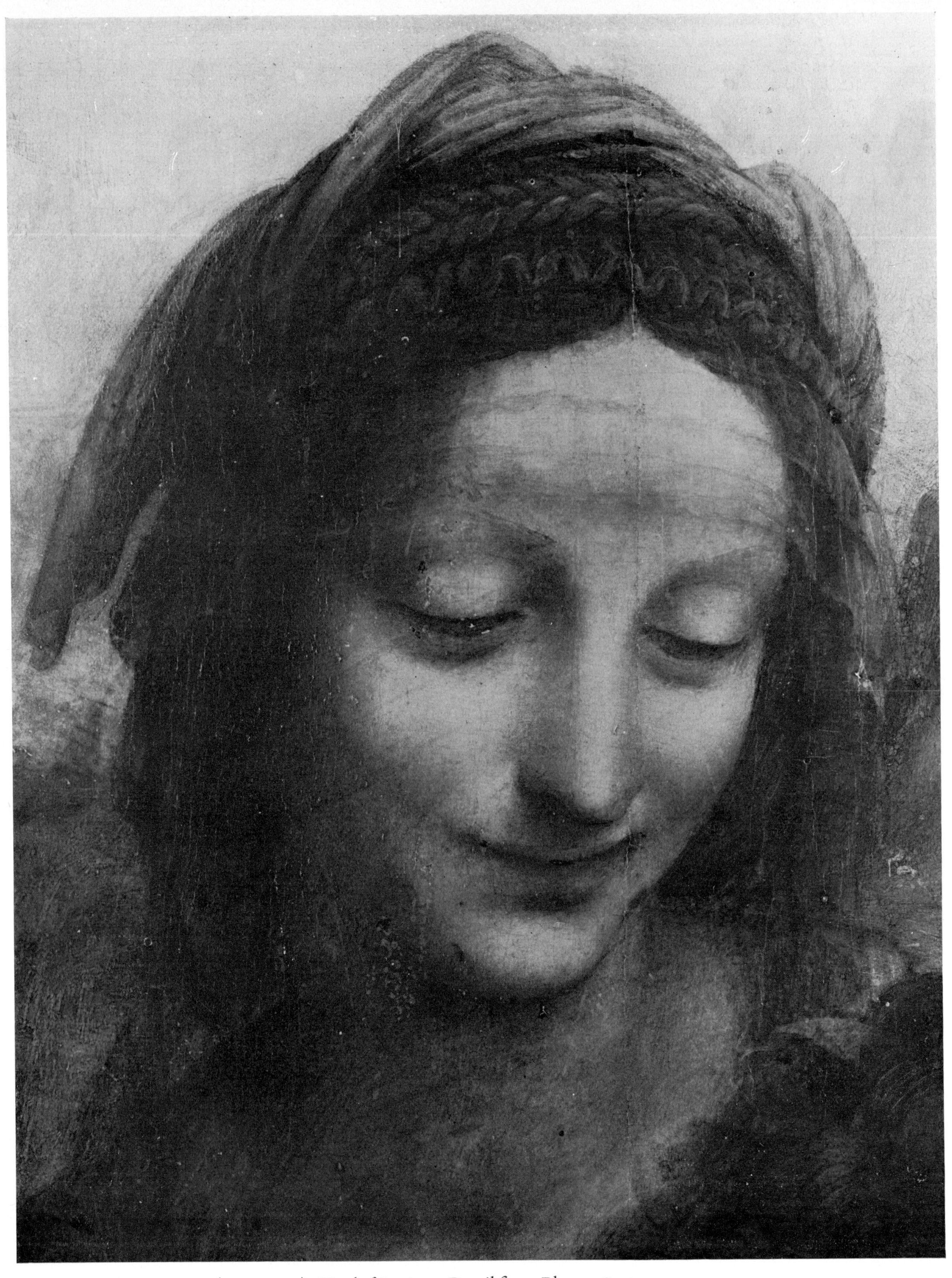

129. LEONARDO DA VINCI (1452–1519): *Head of St. Anne*. Detail from Plate 128

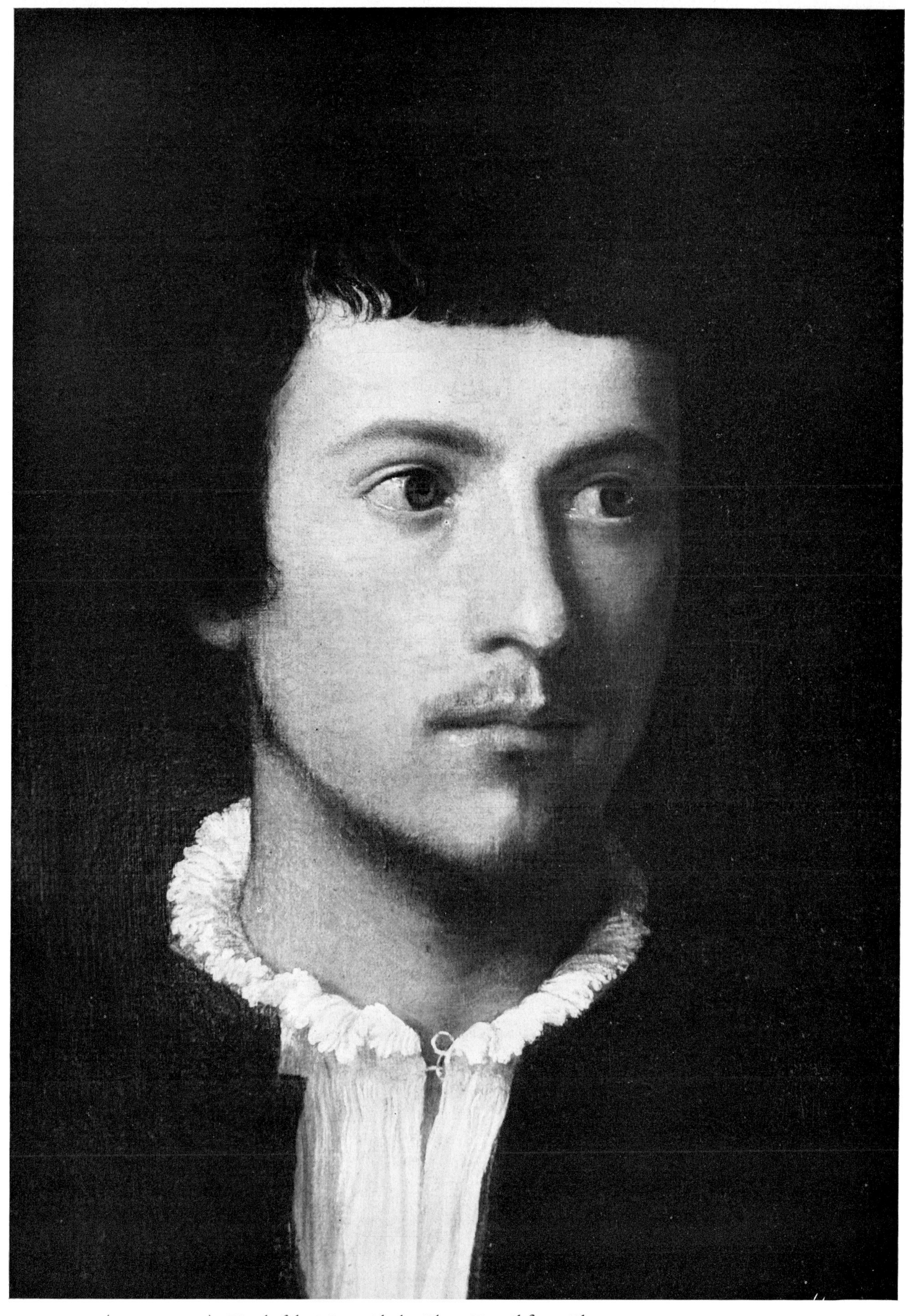

130. TITIAN (*c.* 1489–1576): *Head of the Man with the Glove*. Detail from Plate 136

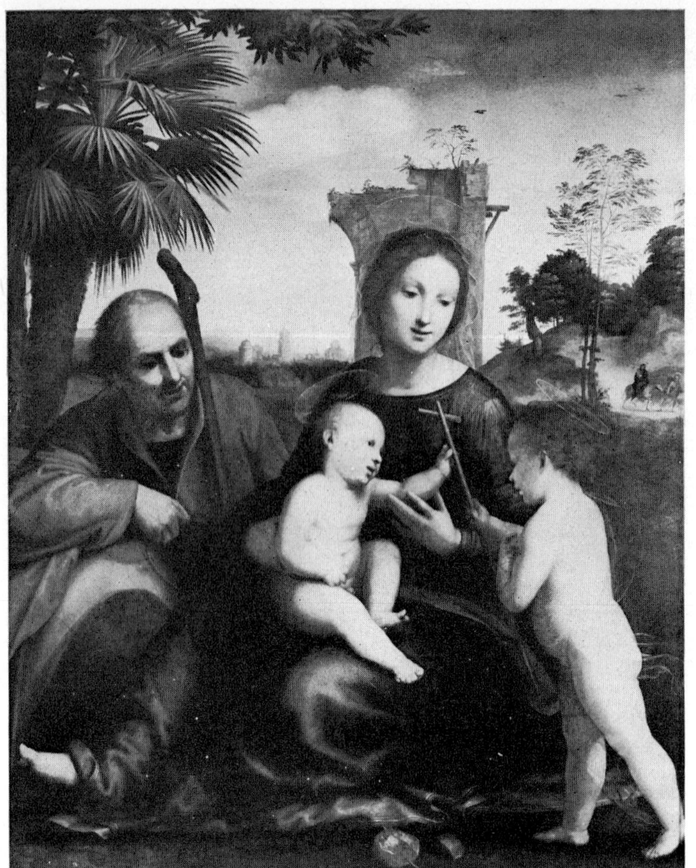

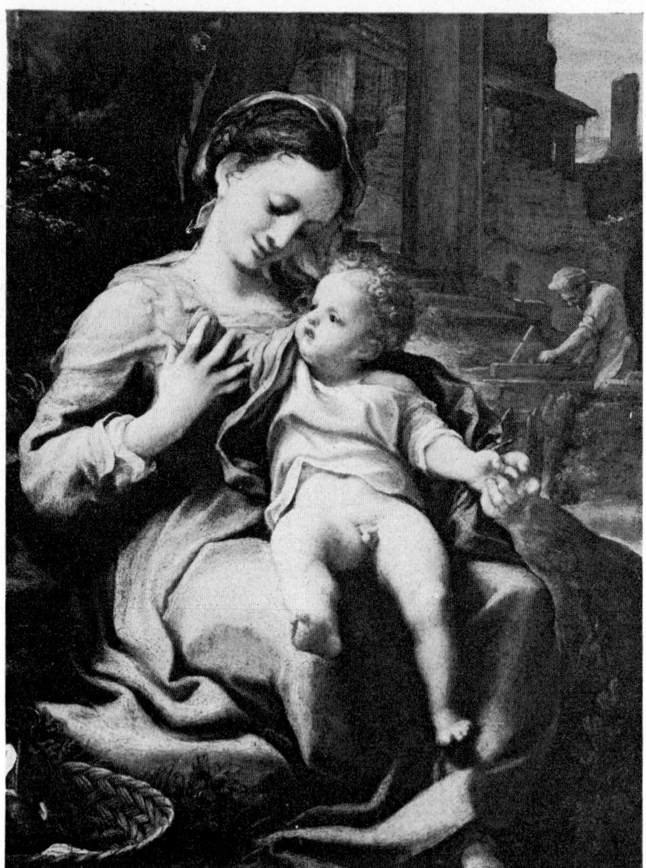

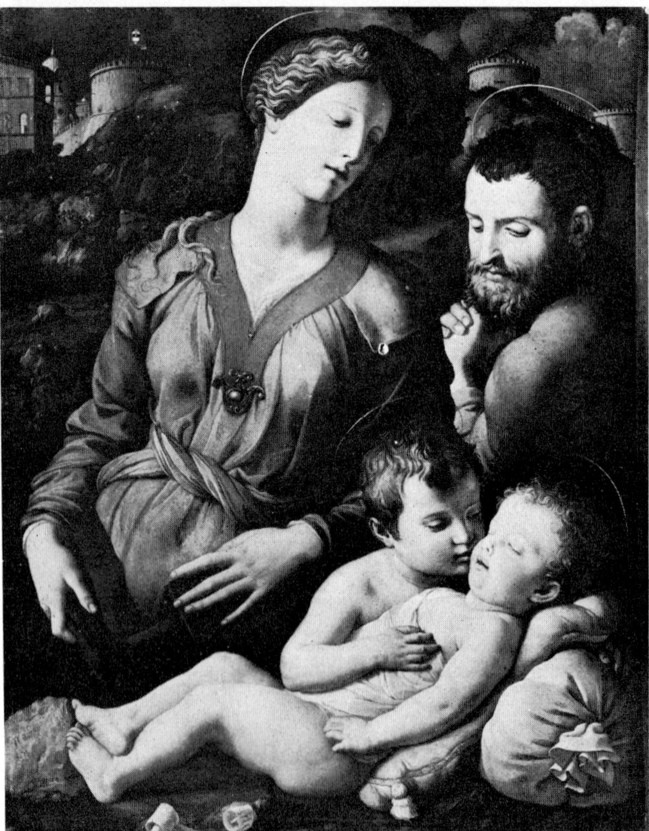

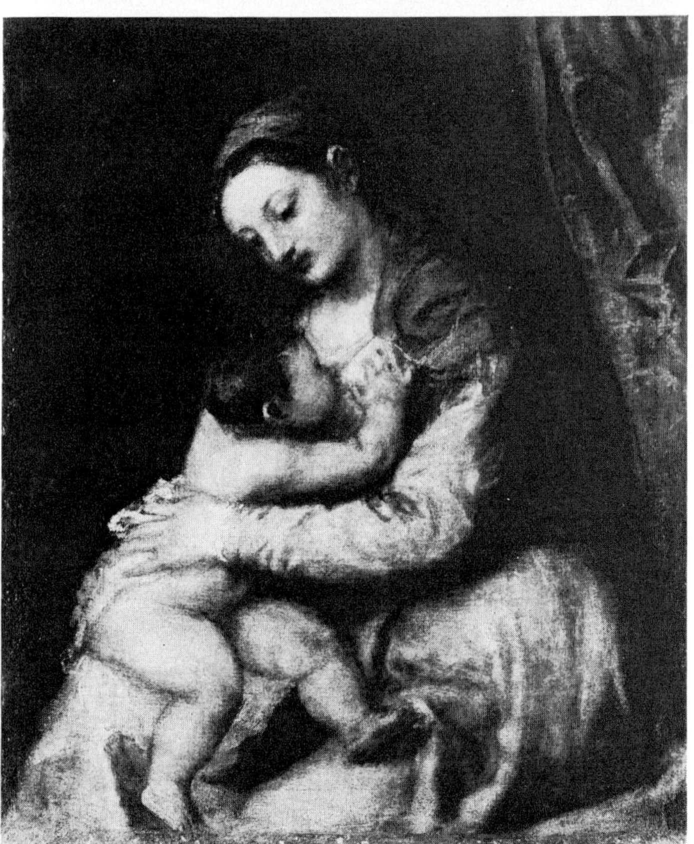

131. FRA BARTOLOMMEO (1474?–1517): *The Holy Family with the young St. John Baptist.* About 1509. Panel, 51 × 42 in. England, Private Collection

132. CORREGGIO (*c.* 1494–1534): *The Holy Family* ('*The Madonna of the Basket*'). About 1522. Panel, $13\frac{1}{4}$ × 10 in. London, National Gallery

133. BRONZINO (1503–72): *The Holy Family.* About 1540. Panel, 46 × 35 in. Florence, Uffizi

134. TITIAN (*c.* 1489–1576): *Madonna and Child.* About 1570. Canvas, $29\frac{3}{4}$ × 25 in. London, National Gallery

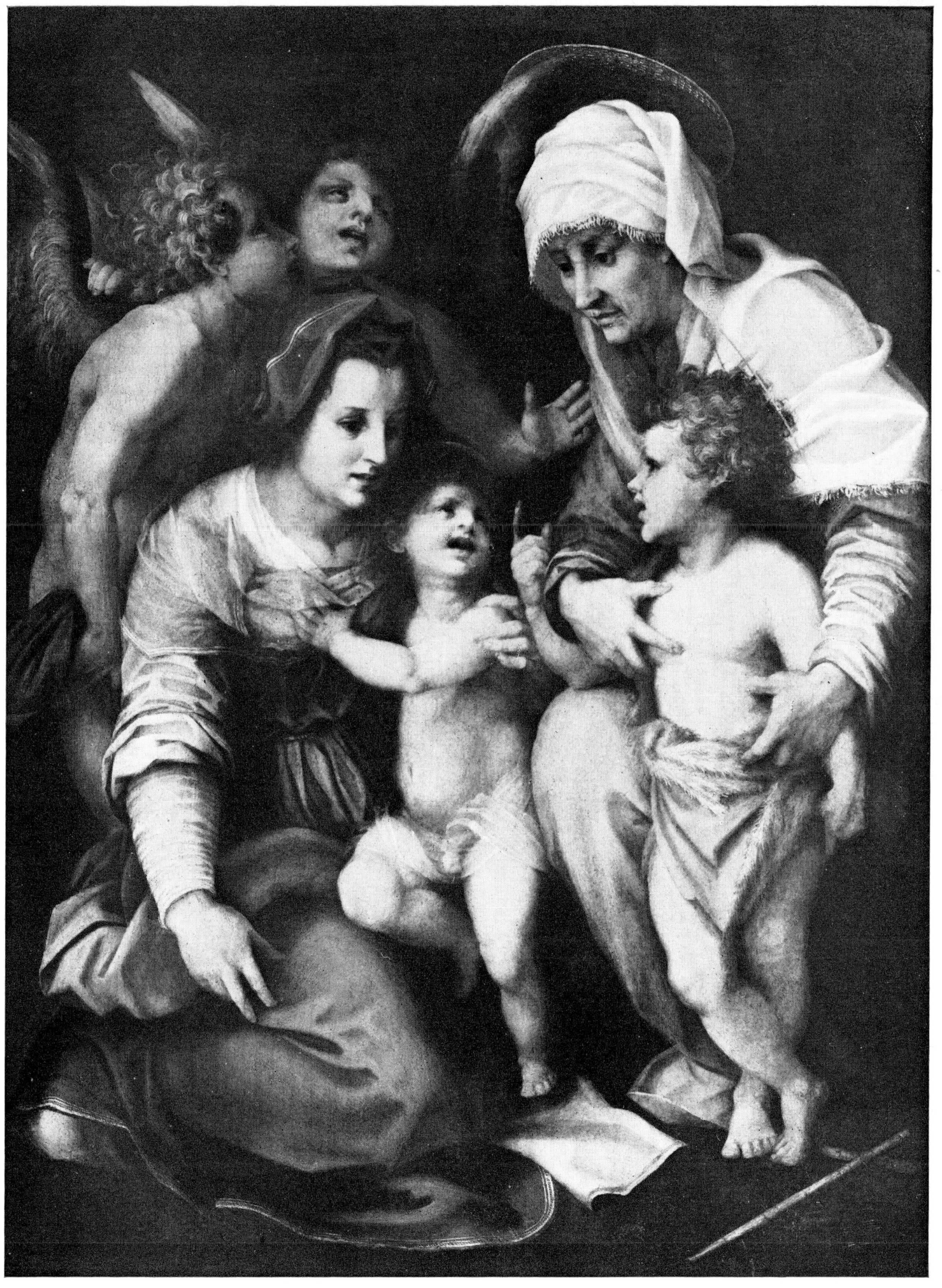

135. ANDREA DEL SARTO (1486–1530): *The Virgin and Child with St. Elisabeth and St. John Baptist.* 1515–18. Panel, $55\frac{1}{2} \times 41\frac{3}{4}$ in. Paris, Louvre

The theme of motherhood, so deeply embedded in Christian art as a symbol of the Incarnation, strikes a chord of emotion that vibrates beyond the religious sphere. Even today, our image of the Madonna is a creation of the Renaissance artist, who depicted her in huge altarpieces (Plates 69, 100, 111, 139) and smaller devotional pictures, alone with her child or accompanied by angels, saints or donors.

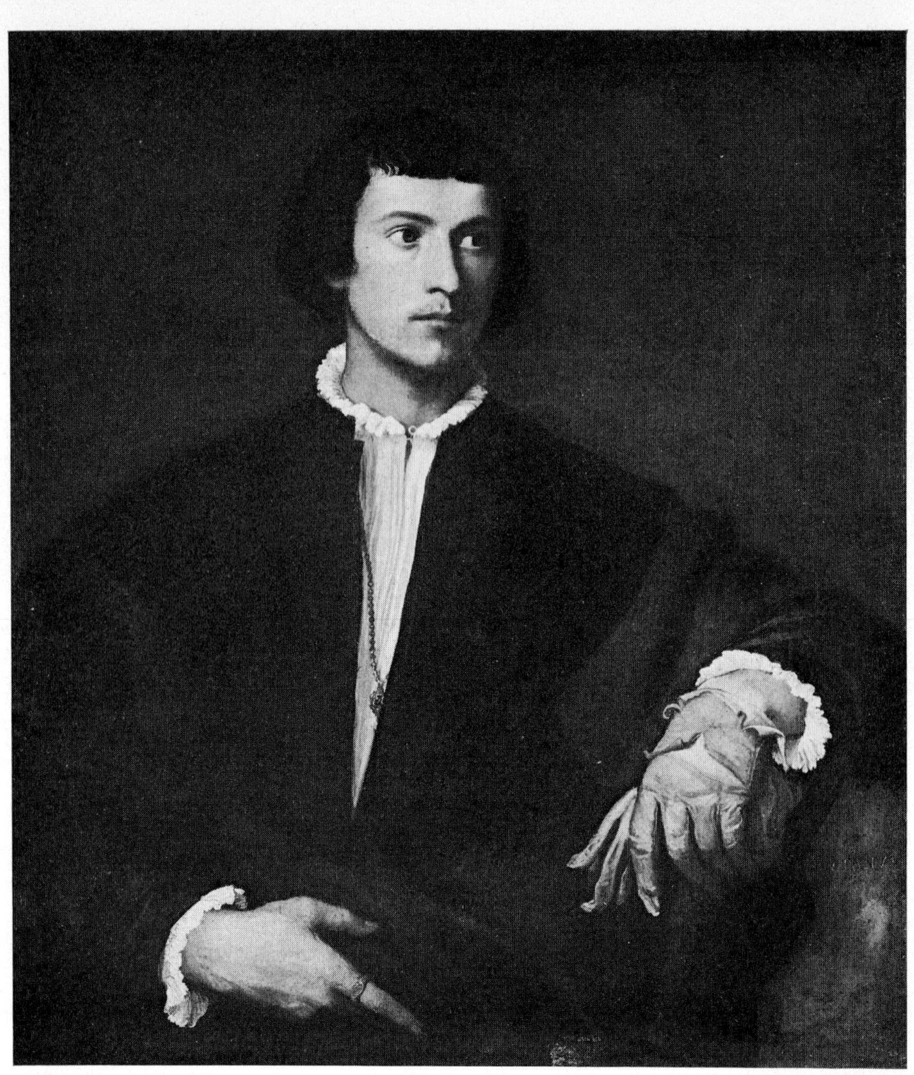

136. TITIAN (*c.* 1489–1576): *Portrait of a Man Holding a Glove*. 1520–2. Canvas, $39\frac{1}{2} \times 35$ in. Paris, Louvre

Titian was the main pioneer of the High Renaissance portrait in Venice. Building on the example of Bellini (see Plate 54), he enlarged the scale of portraiture, abolished the idea of the ledge or sill, and often played down detail of costume to increase the visual emphasis on the head. He was also fond of extending the silhouette of the figure sideways by showing an arm leaning on a pedestal.

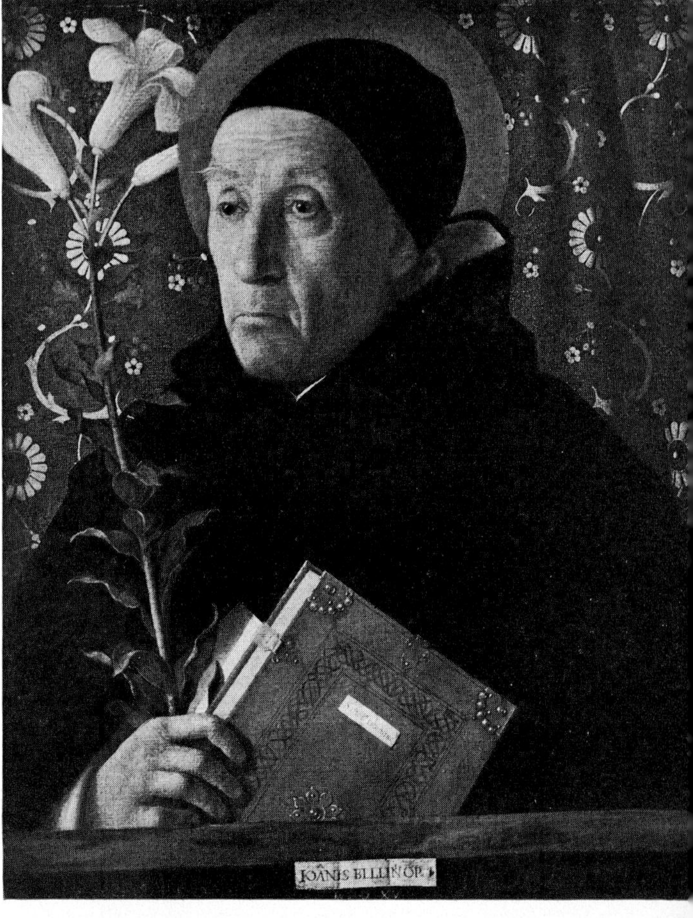

137. GIOVANNI BELLINI (*c.* 1430–1516): *St. Dominic*. 1515. Canvas, $24\frac{3}{4} \times 19\frac{1}{2}$ in. London, National Gallery

Painted when the artist was about eighty-five years old, the picture shows the saint clad in the black habit of the Order which he founded and holding a stalk of lilies, the emblem of purity, and a volume containing the Dominican Rule. It is believed to be a portrait of a Fra Teodoro of Urbino.

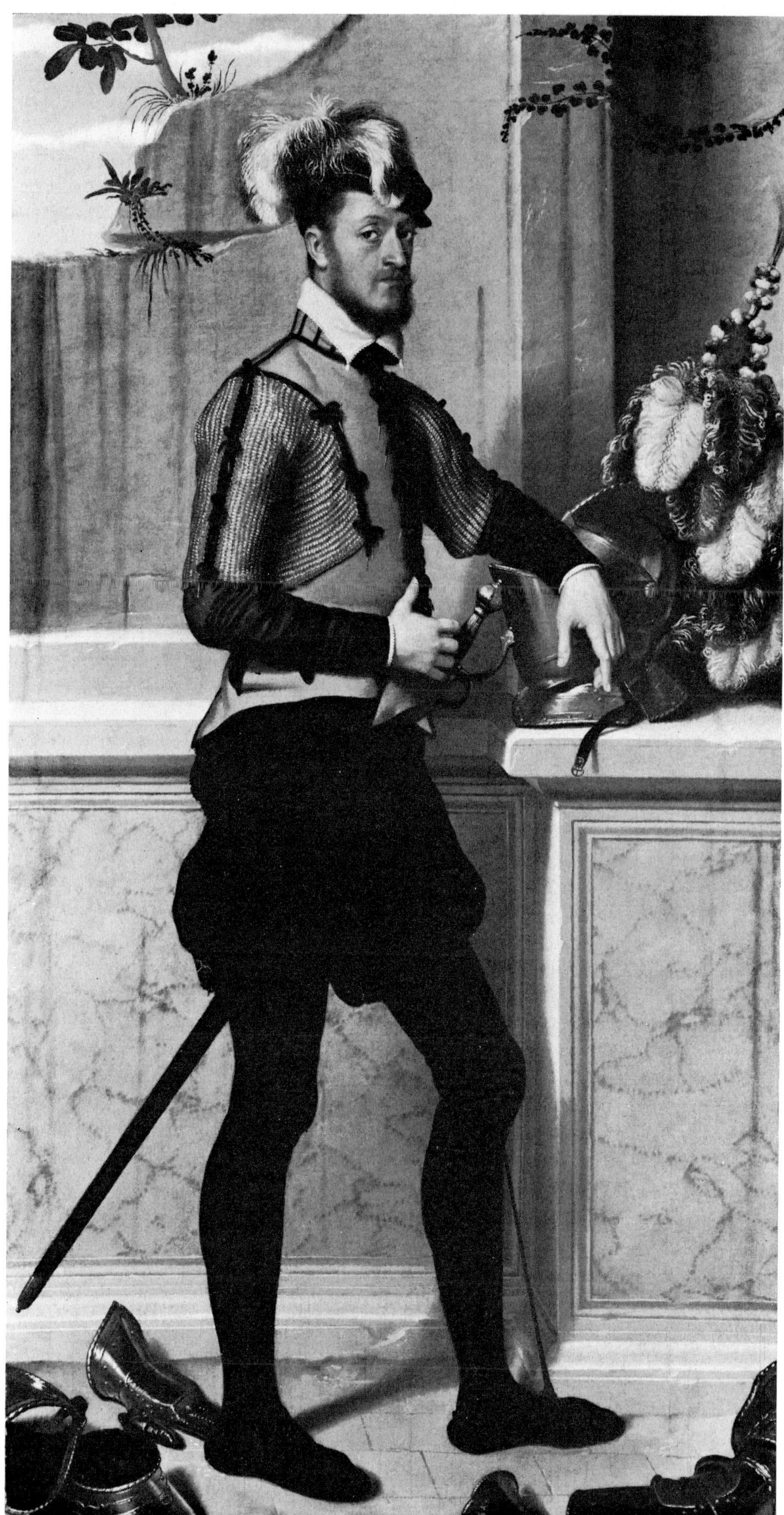

138. GIOVANNI BATTISTA MORONI (*c.* 1525–78): *Portrait of a Gentleman.* About 1554–9. Canvas, $79\frac{1}{2} \times 43\frac{3}{4}$ in. London, National Gallery.

The armour liberally scattered over floor and parapet mark him out as a soldier, although he now wears a fashionable costume and carries only his sword. On the parapet lies his helmet with a gorgeously plumed top-piece. 'The metal brace worn from his left knee to his left foot is apparently an attempt to counter the condition known as "drop-foot".' (Cecil Gould) He may have been a member of the Avogadro family of Brescia. Moroni's portraits are invariably proficient but they lack the force and power of Titian's images. One is much more aware of the separate details, of costume and setting, in Moroni's work.

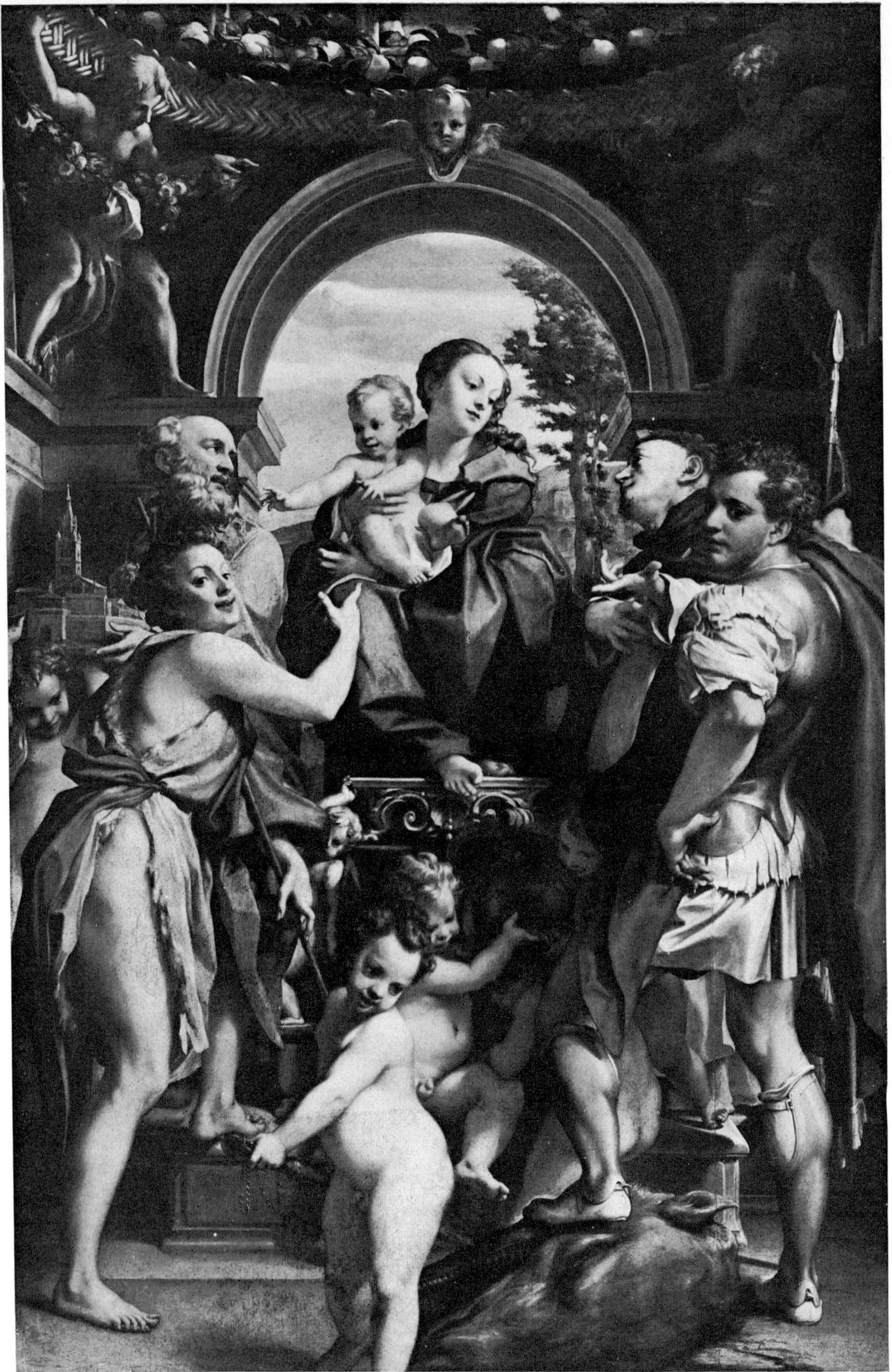

139. CORREGGIO (*c.* 1494–1534): *The Virgin and Child Enthroned with St. John the Baptist, St. Geminianus, St. Peter Martyr and St. George.* 1532. Panel, 112 × 75 in. Dresden, Gemäldegalerie

The Virgin's throne is placed so high, and the viewpoint so low, that she seems strangely hunched compared to the tall, standing saints. The device of silhouetting the main figure or group in the centre is not new, nor is the way in which the foreground figures hide those behind (compare Plates 102 and 124). But here this overlapping has become a dominant principle of composition and testifies to the rise of Mannerist design.

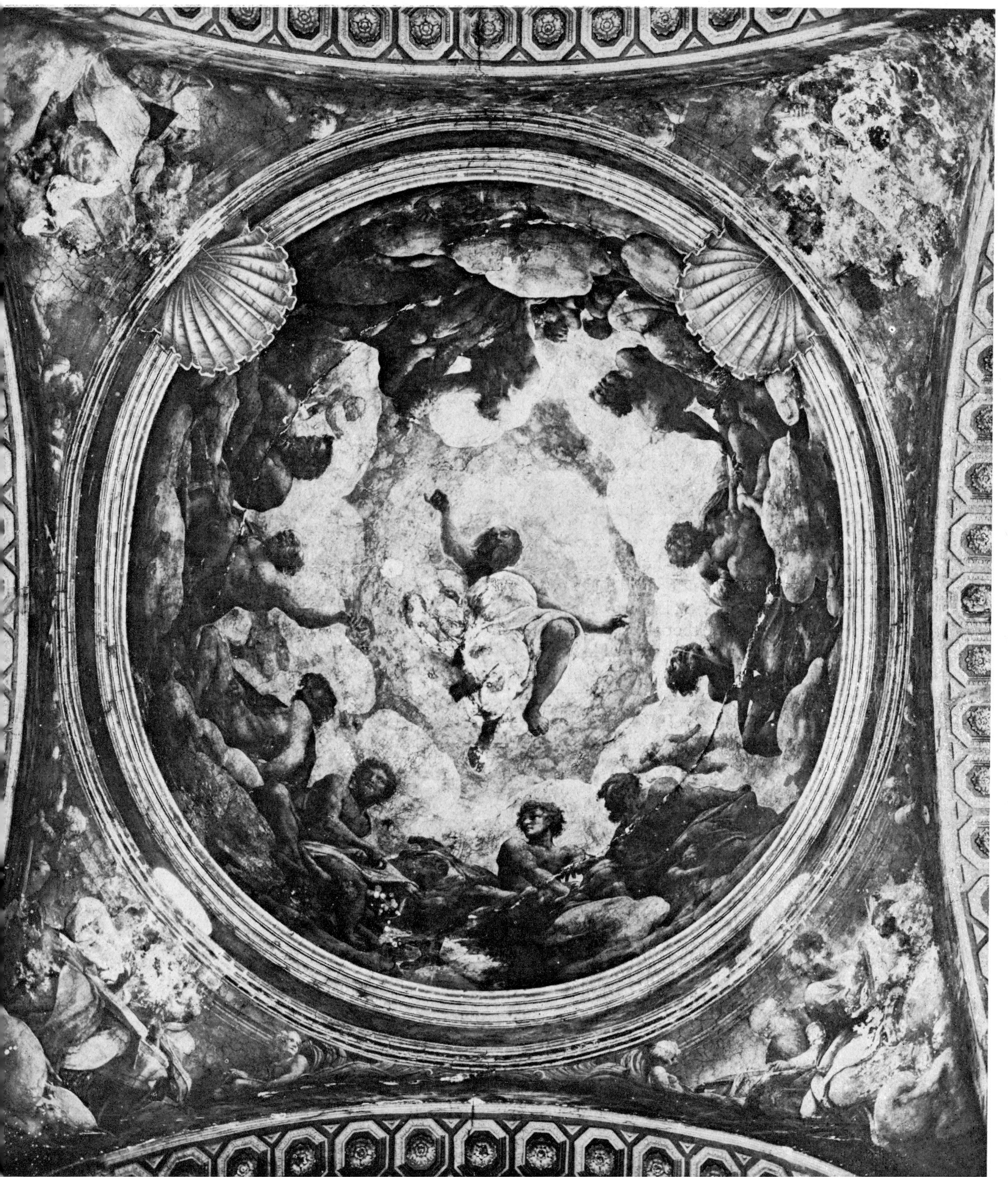

140. CORREGGIO (*c.* 1494–1534): *The Ascension*. 1520–3. Cupola fresco. Parma, San Giovanni Evangelista

141, 142. TITIAN (*c.* 1489–1576): *The Three Ages of Man.* 1512–15. Canvas, 34 × 57 in. Duke of Sutherland Collection, on loan to the National Gallery of Scotland, Edinburgh

'Infancy, maturity and old age are symbolized by the two sleeping babies, by the mature couple, and by the old man, who holds two skulls. The pair of infants will reach fulfilment as young lovers, but they too must die, as the two skulls held by Old Age remind us. The dead tree trunk, another symbol of death, is being supported by the winged Cupid to prevent death from overtaking the babies. . . . Although an allegory, the *Three Ages* is primarily concerned with youth and the passionate nature of young lovers. The girl's blonde beauty and calm restraint provide a foil to the man's dark colouring and latent energy. The attitude of his powerful body, his tousled hair, and the expression of his face project the fiery nature of youth in love. The girl gazes fondly into his eyes. Her crown of myrtle, the "symbol of everlasting love", points up the situation. He holds a recorder in his right hand; she, with the fingers of both hands placed upon the keys of her two recorders, appears to pause after playing them.' (H. E. Wethey)

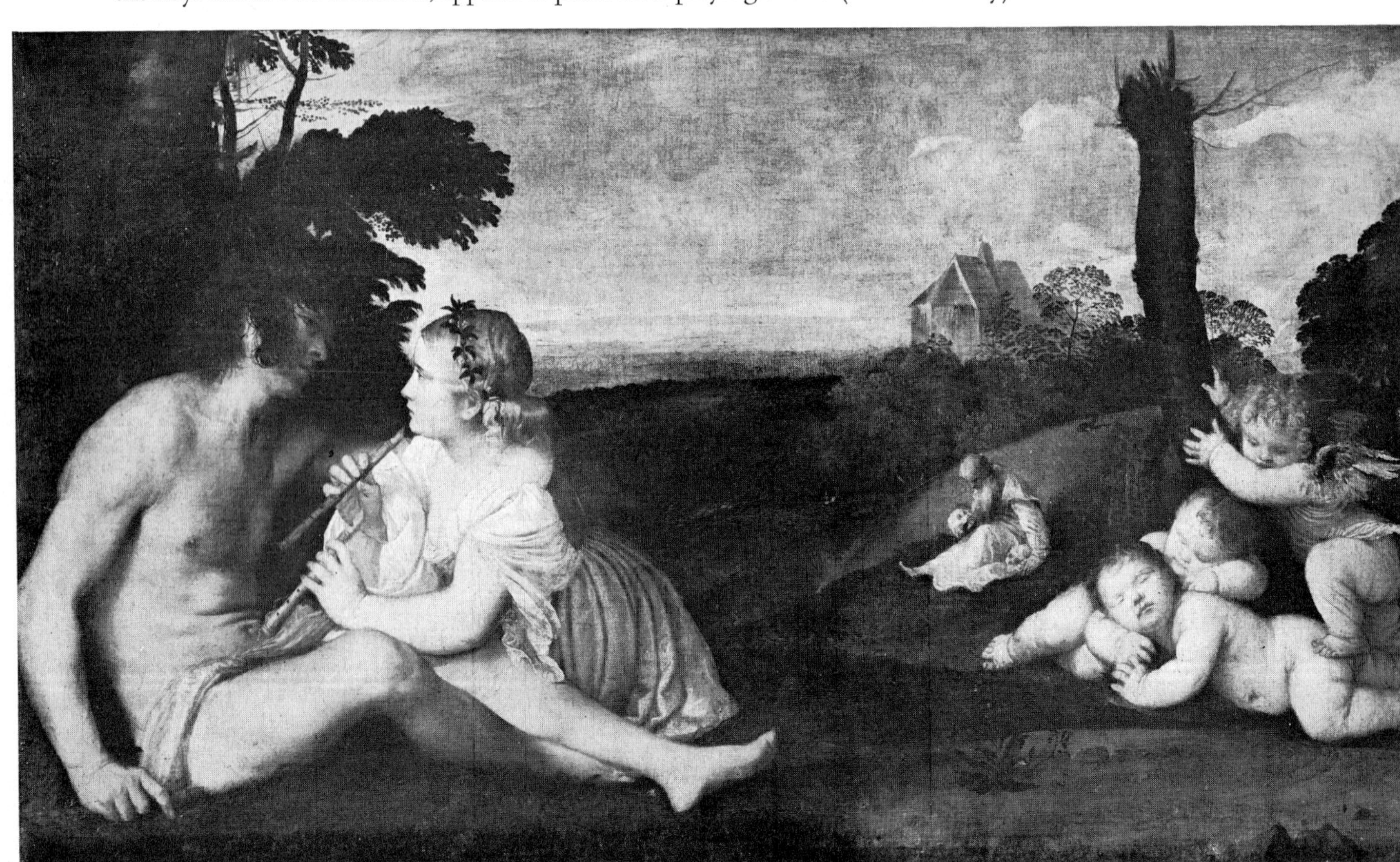

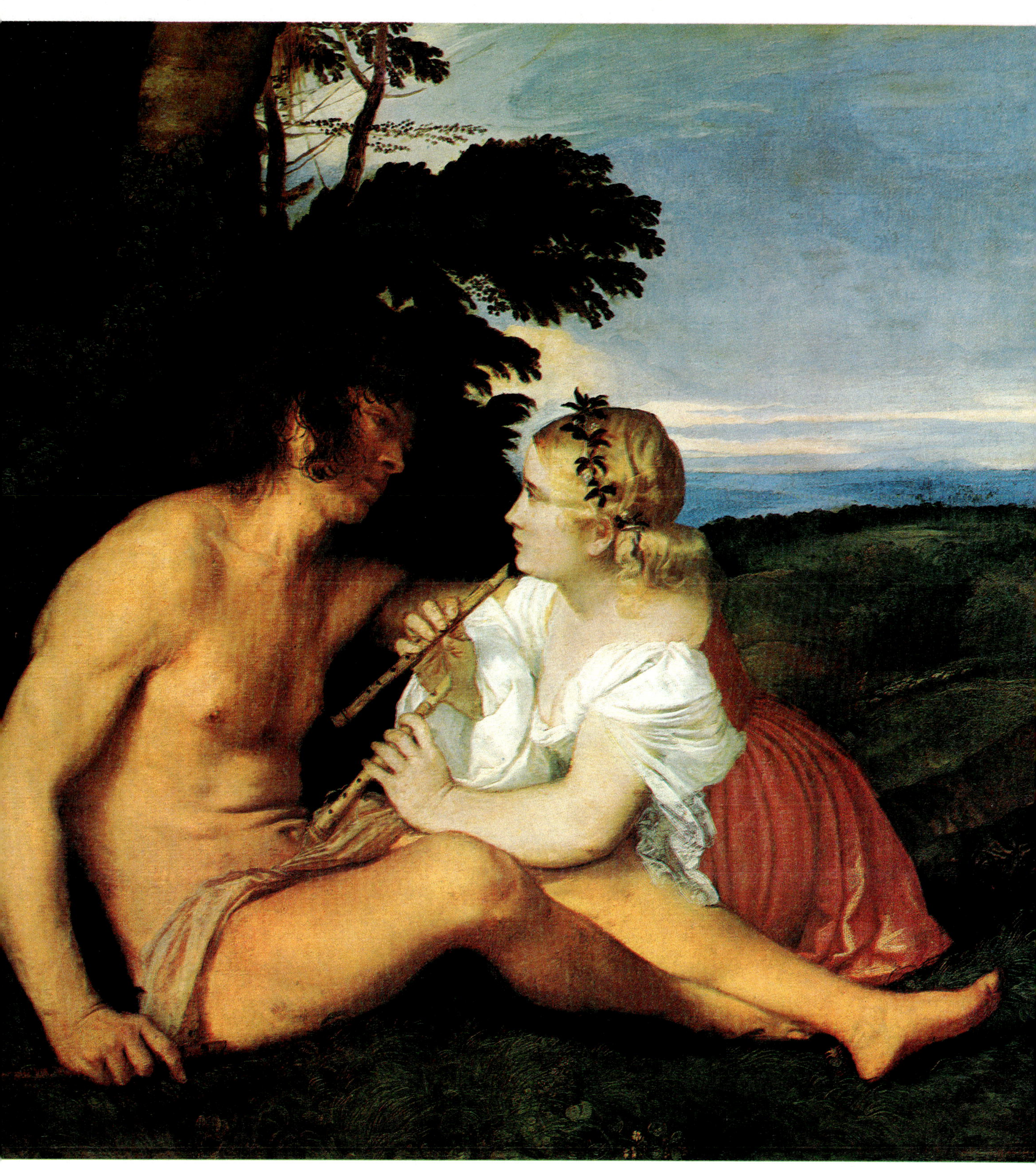

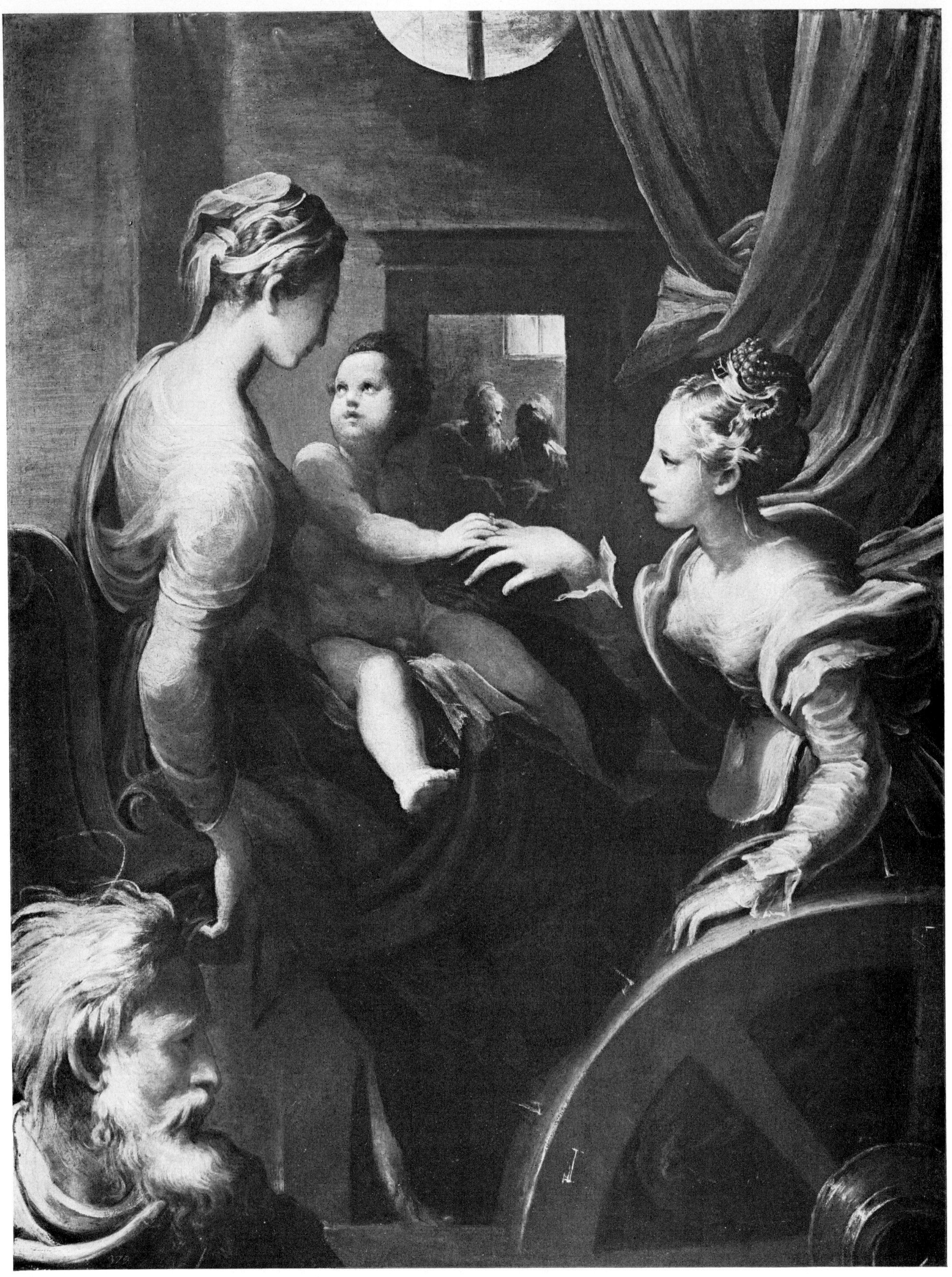

143. PARMIGIANINO (1503–40): *The Mystic Marriage of St. Catherine*. About 1530. Panel, $29\frac{1}{4} \times 22\frac{1}{2}$ in. London, National Gallery

A very good example of Parmigianino's more intimate type of devotional image. The elongated figures (look at the Virgin Mary's neck), air of elegance and ambiguous space are characteristic of his style. The wheel was the attribute of St. Catherine, a fourth-century Christian martyr.

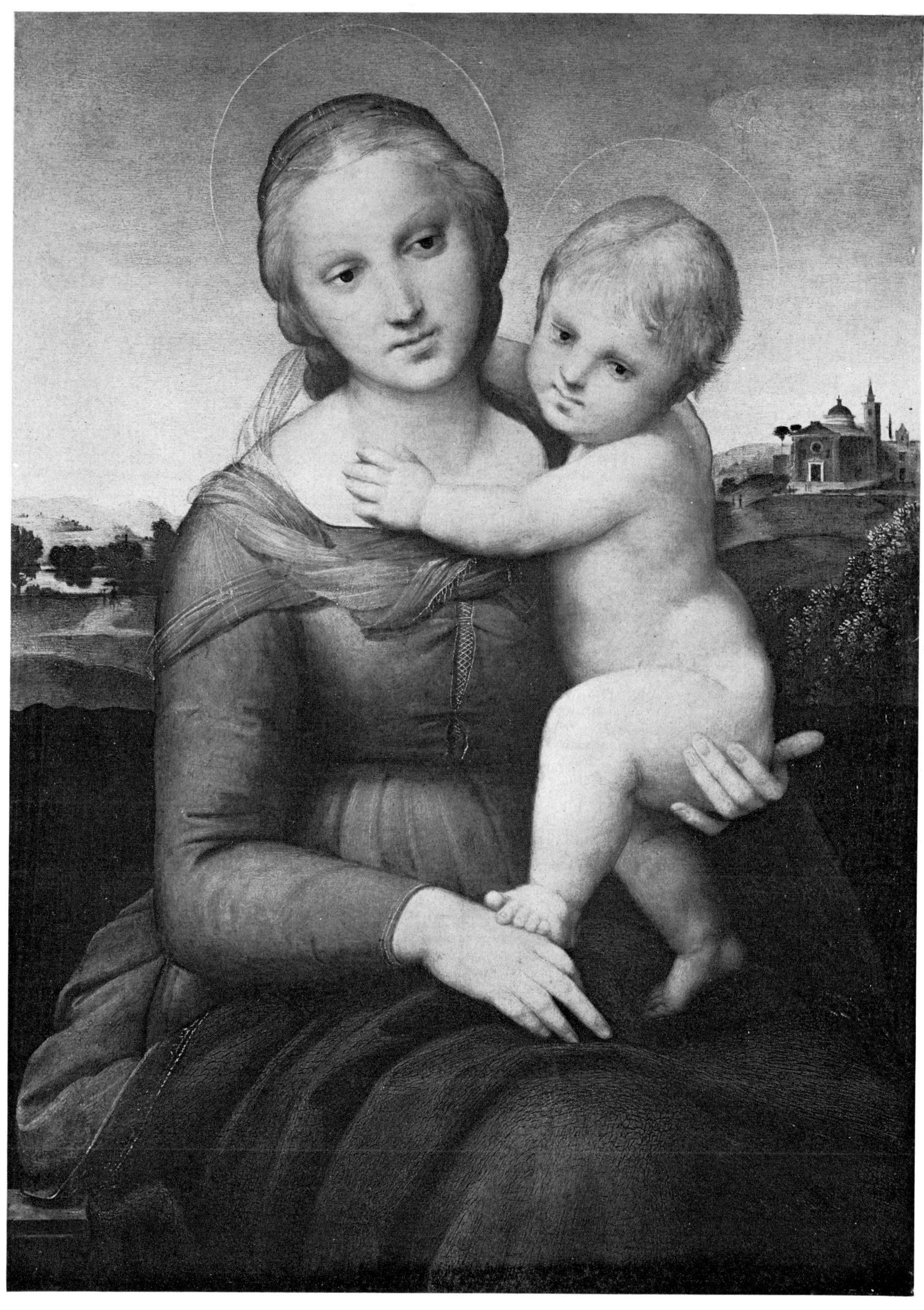

144. RAPHAEL (1483–1520): *The Virgin and Child*. 1508. Panel, $31\frac{3}{4} \times 22\frac{3}{4}$ in. Washington, D.C., National Gallery of Art (Mellon Collection)

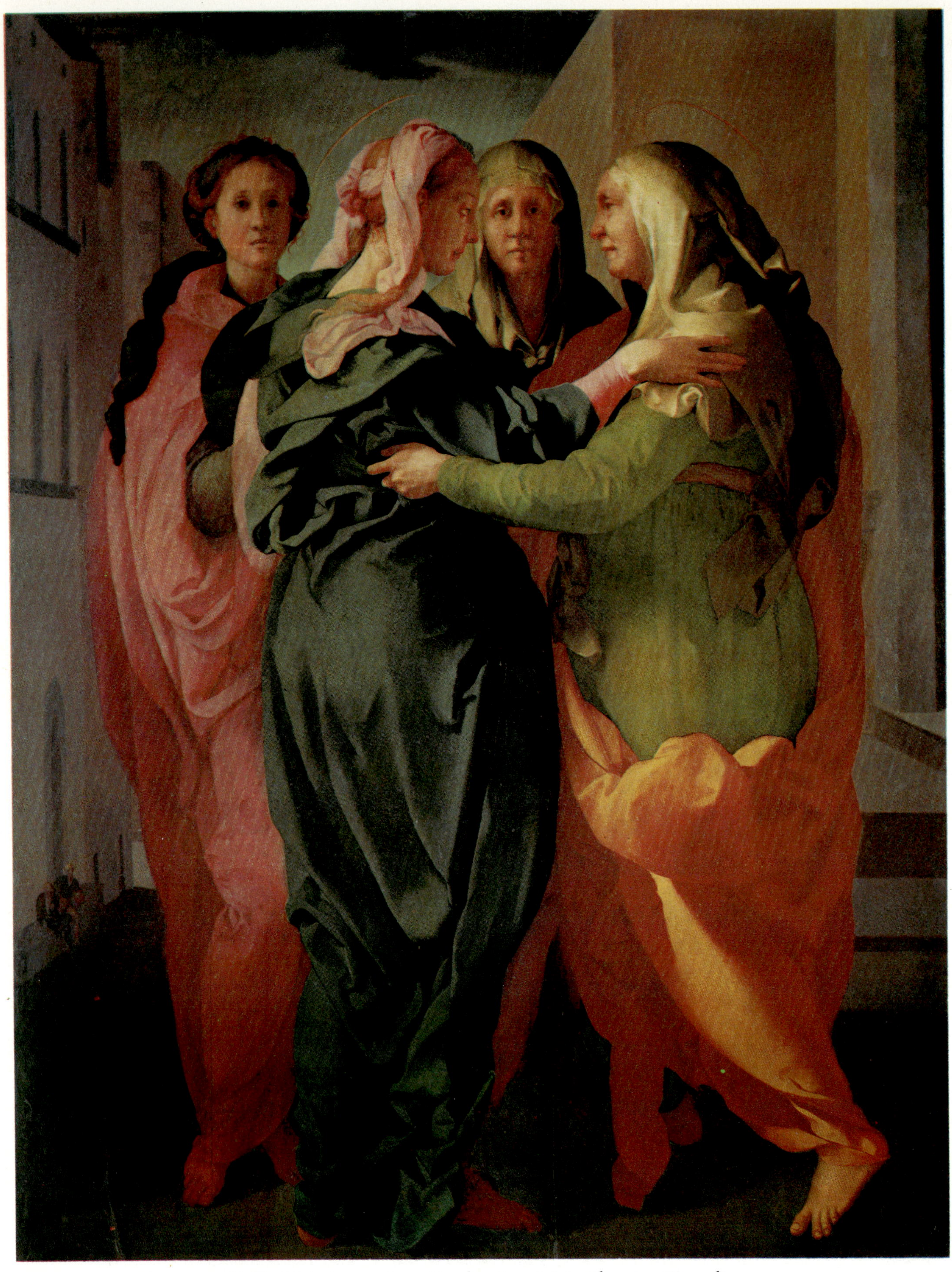

145. PONTORMO (1494–1557): *The Visitation*. 1528–30. Panel, $79\frac{1}{2} \times 61\frac{1}{2}$ in. Florence, Pieve di Carmignano

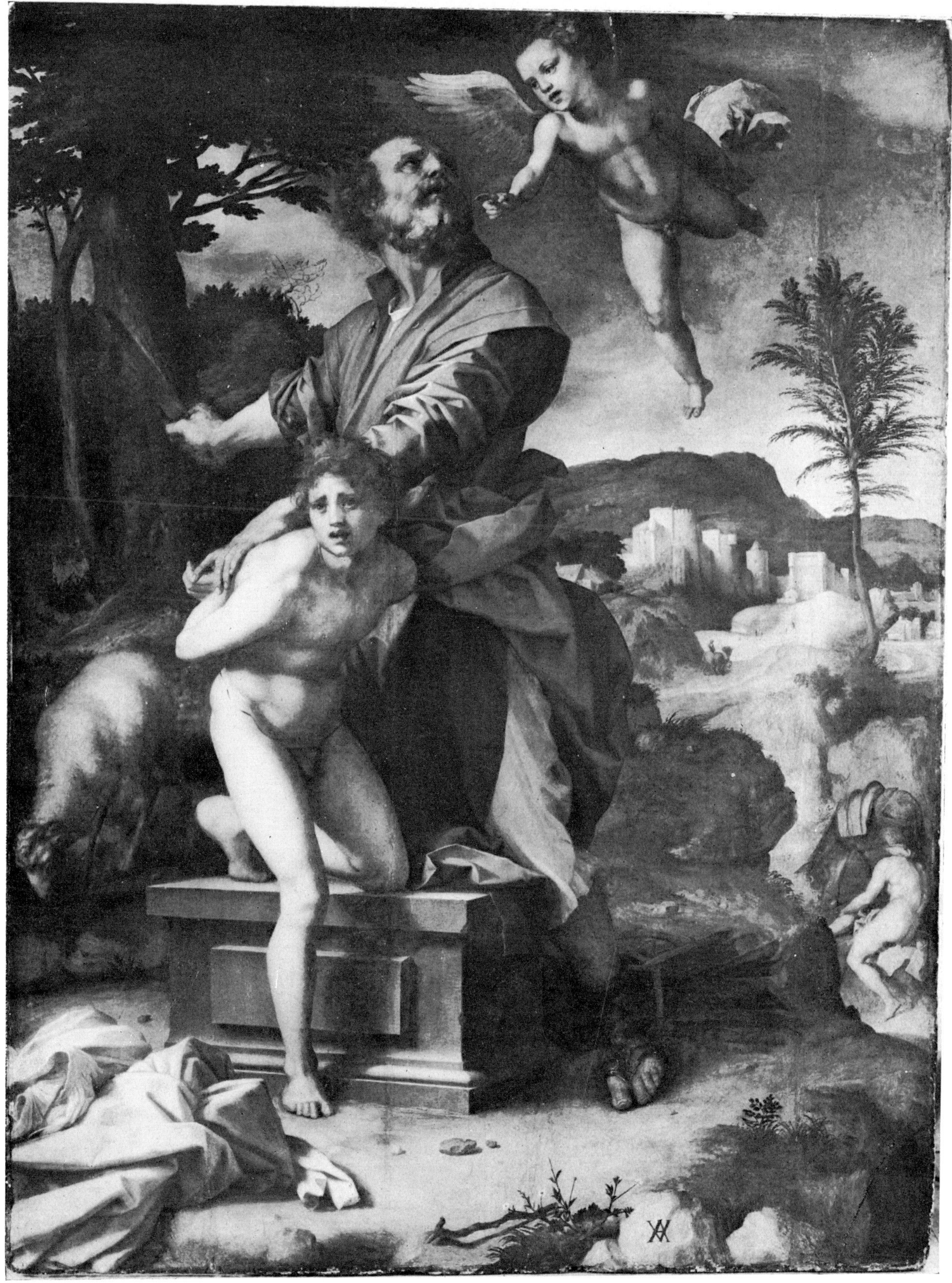

146. ANDREA DEL SARTO (1486–1530): *The Sacrifice of Isaac.* About 1529. Panel, 85 × 63½ in. Dresden, Gemäldegalerie

Andrea del Sarto was one of the most important Florentine masters of the High Renaissance; and his position was greatly improved by the defection to Rome of both Raphael and Michelangelo. His actual style was more painterly, with more attention paid to colour, and modelling in terms of colour, than had been customary in Florence. His figures are simpler and more monumental, and the overall effect of his pictures much less decorative, than the religious pictures of the previous generation. Sarto concentrated on religious subjects, in both oil and fresco, but he was also an excellent portrait painter.

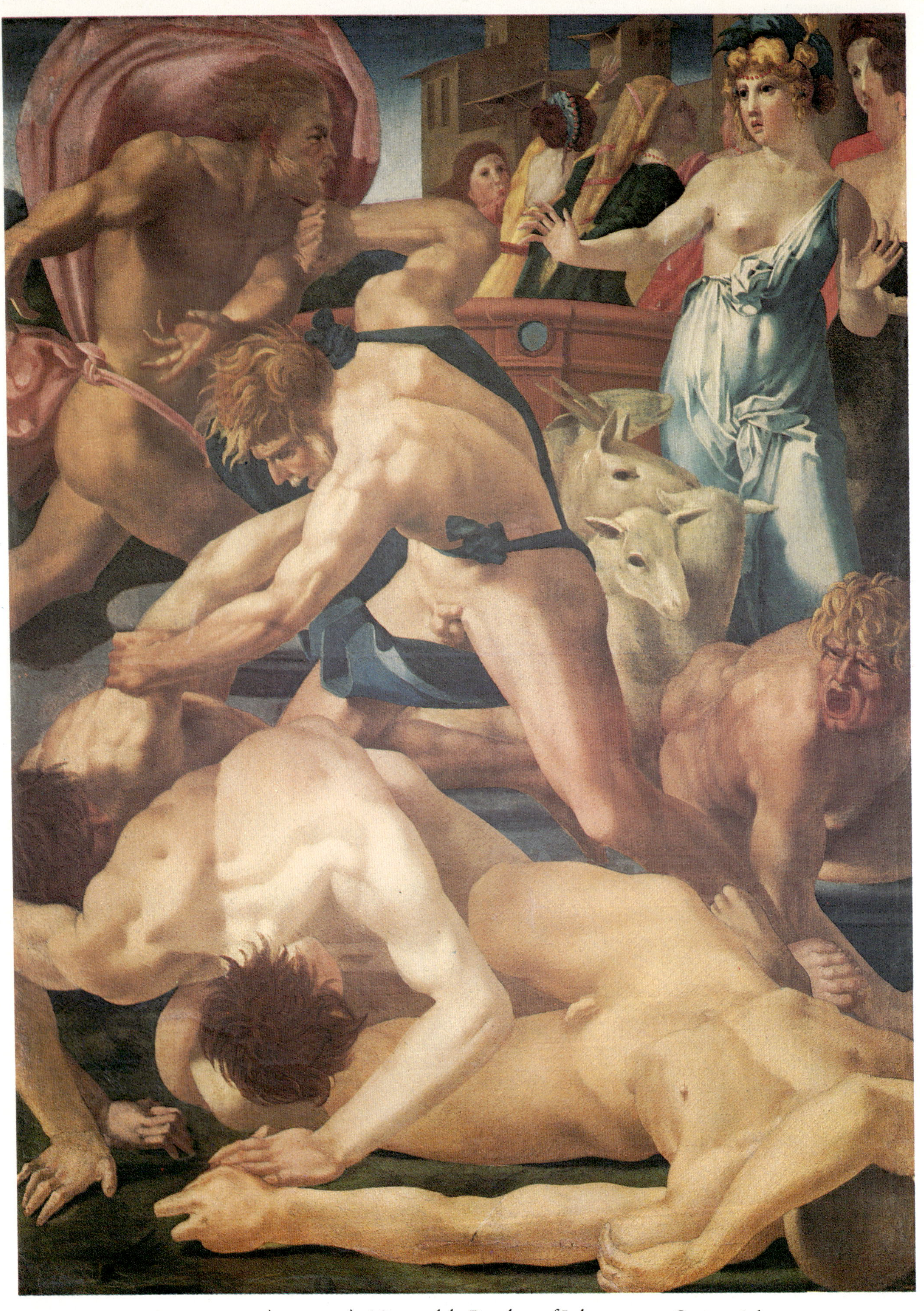

147. GIOVANNI BATTISTA ROSSO (1494–1540): *Moses and the Daughters of Jethro*. 1523–4. Canvas, $63\frac{1}{4} \times 46\frac{1}{4}$ in. Florence, Uffizi

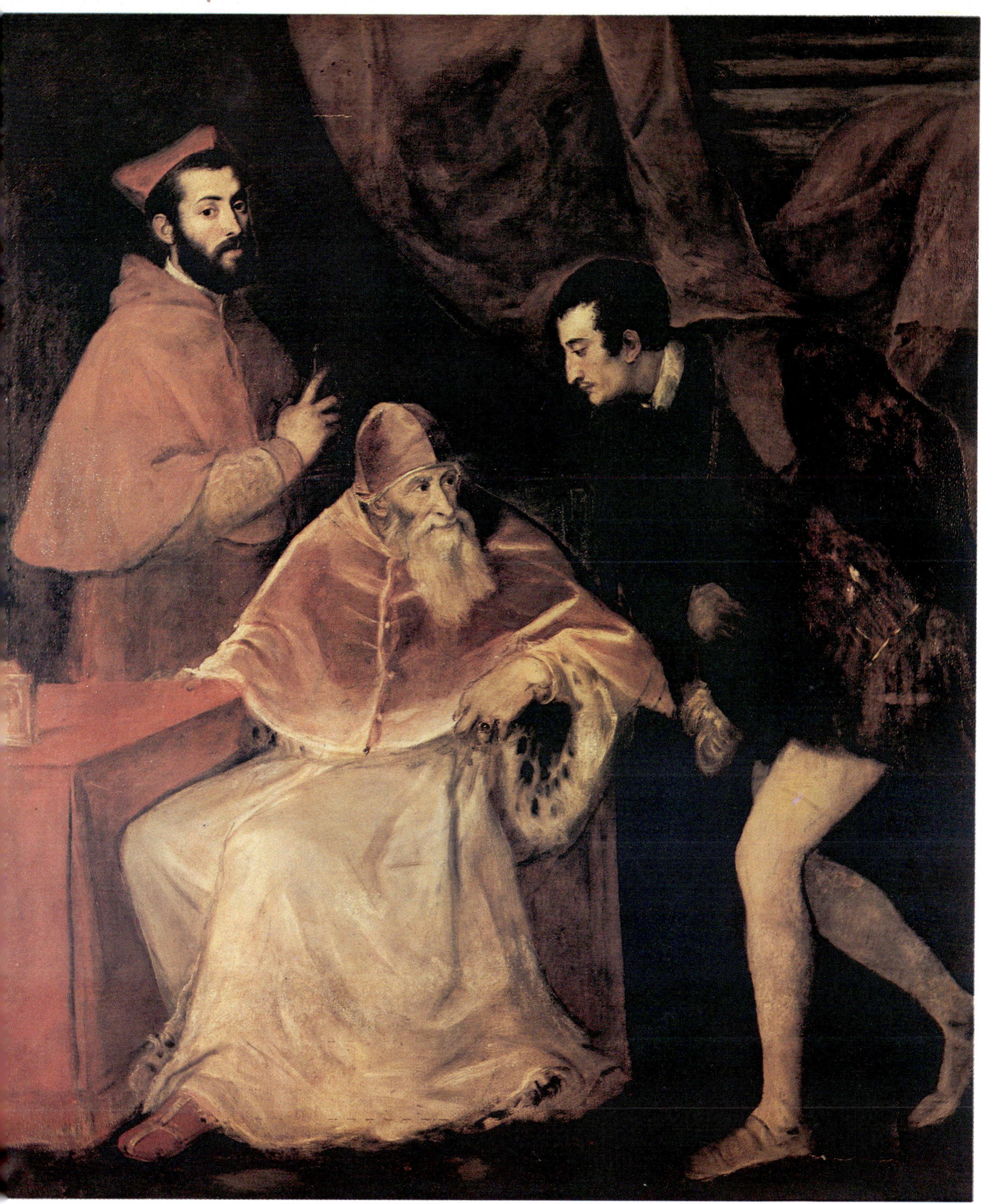

148. TITIAN (*c.* 1489–1576): *Pope Paul III with his Grandsons, Alessandro and Ottaviano Farnese.* 1545–6. Canvas, 79 × 68 in. Naples, Galleria Nazionale di Capodimonte

Paul III gave employment to the two greatest artists of his time: he commissioned three portraits of himself from Titian and three large frescoes in the Vatican from Michelangelo (Plates 162, 163), whom he also appointed architect of St. Peter's. He had been married and was the grandfather of the two dignitaries whom Titian portrayed with him. In this uneasy family conference, the crafty expressions and stage-managed poses are matched by a sultry tonality.

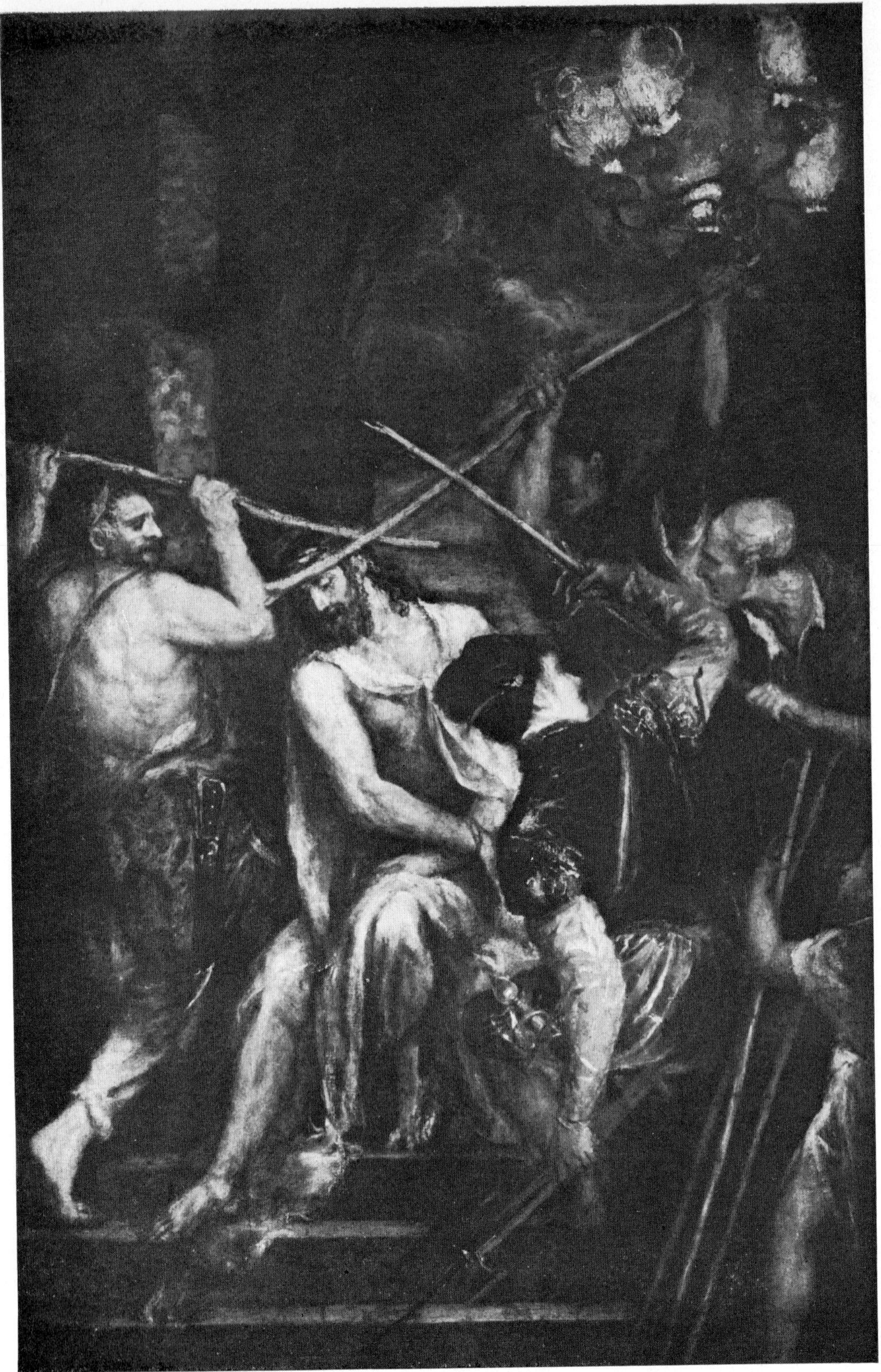

149. TITIAN (*c.* 1489–1576): *The Crowning with Thorns.* About 1570–6. Canvas, 82 × 70 in. Munich, Alte Pinakothek

Titian, like many other great artists, grew fond of certain visual ideas and compositions and would repeat them over the years. Thus, the *Crowning with Thorns* in Munich is a reworking of a composition of the 1540s now in the Louvre. But the differences are of course vital. The new version is a night scene, and thus more dramatic, and the style has become very free. The brushwork is broken and impressionist. The Munich canvas, among Titian's greatest achievements, is above all a masterpiece of old age, daring, personal, retaining all the power of the earlier design but transforming it into a vision that is deeply felt and ultimately mysterious.

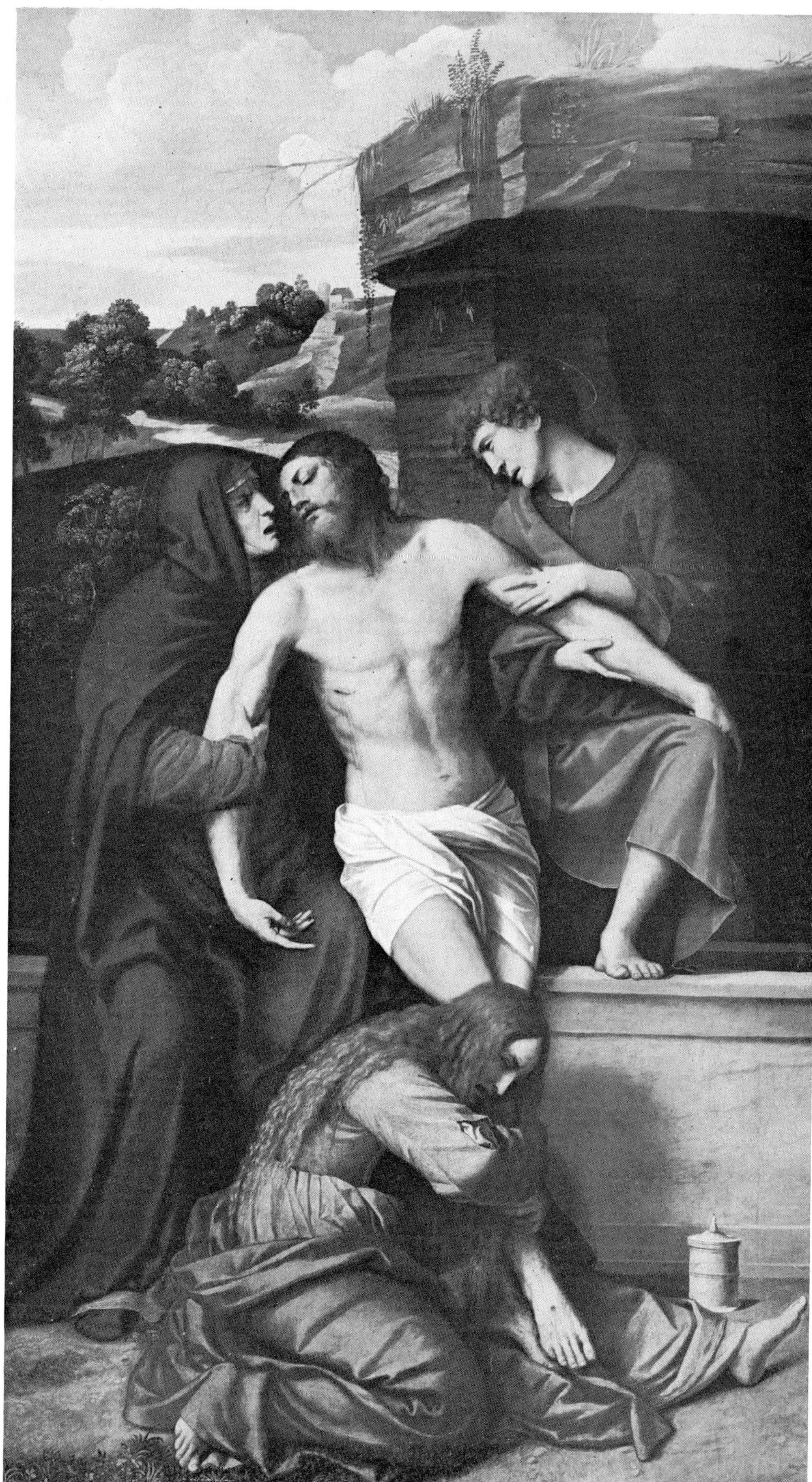

150. MORETTO DA BRESCIA (*c.* 1498–1554): *The Lamentation for Christ*. 1520–30. Panel, 69 × 38¾ in. Washington, D.C., National Gallery of Art (Samuel H. Kress Collection)

The limp body of the dead Christ is supported, on the edge of the sepulchre, by his grief-stricken mother and the beloved disciple, St. John the Evangelist, and his legs are clasped by the distraught Mary Magdalene—all three mourners had stood under the Cross (John 19:25–7). On the ground is the alabaster box of ointment with which Mary had anointed Christ's feet in token of her repentance (Luke 7:37–8). The serene landscape in the distance is a foil to the sorrowful scene.

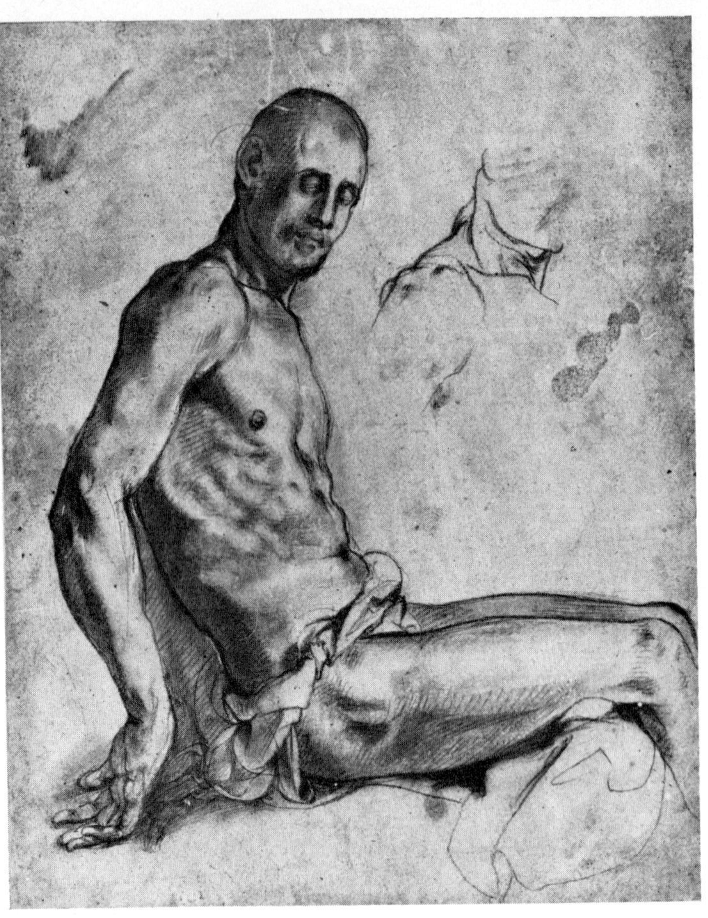

151. *Study for the Body of Christ*. Red chalk, 14×11 in. Florence, Uffizi

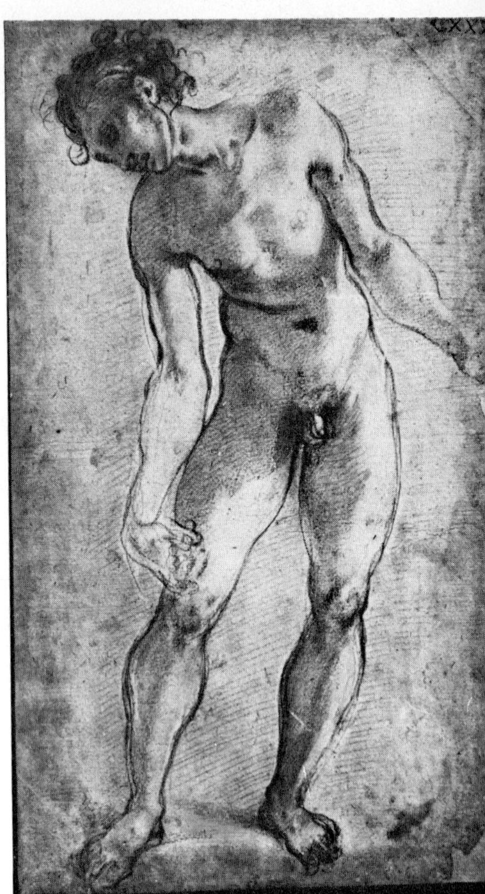

152. *Study for St. John the Evangelist*. Black chalk, $15\frac{1}{2} \times 8\frac{1}{2}$ in. Florence, Uffizi

153. *Study for a Self-portrait*. Red chalk, $6 \times 4\frac{1}{4}$ in. Florence, Uffizi

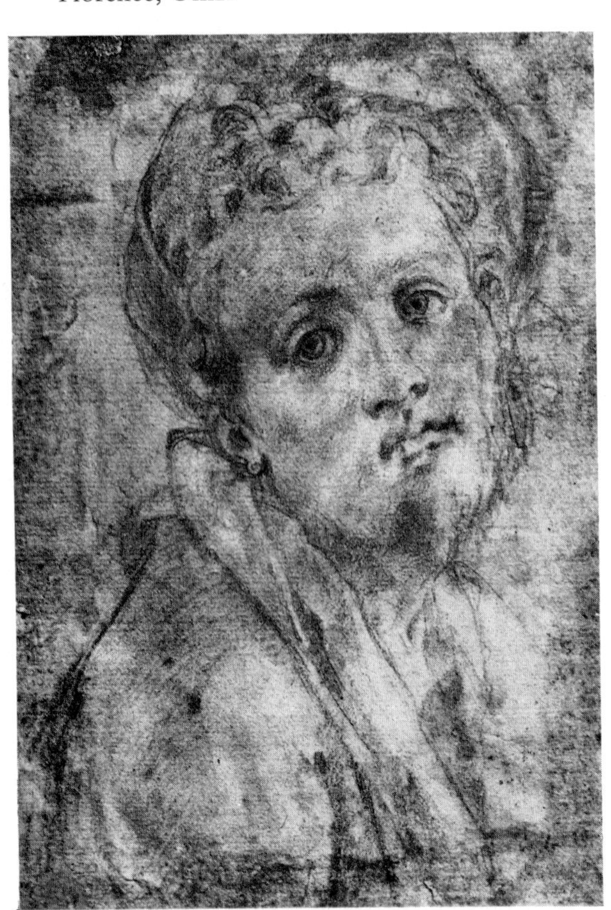

154. *Study for a Composition*. Black chalk, $15\frac{1}{2} \times 11$ in. Oxford, Christ Church Library

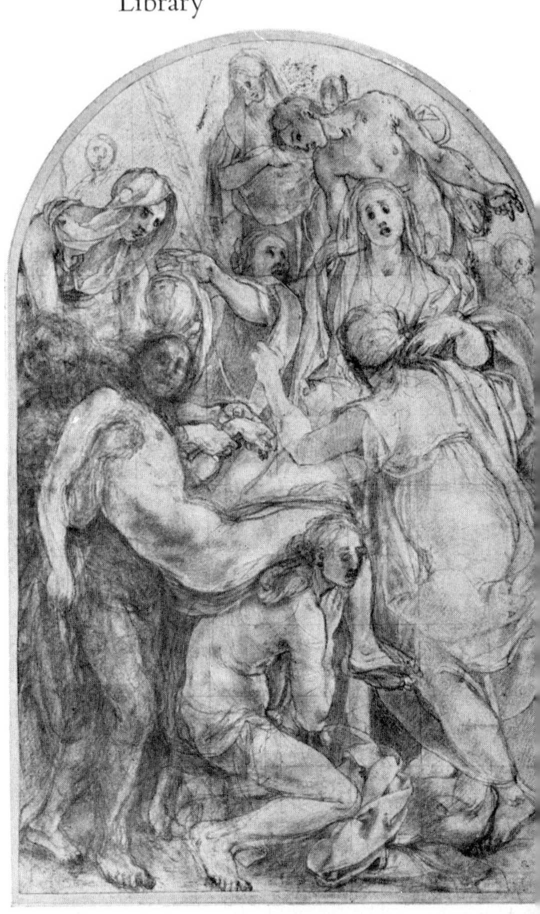

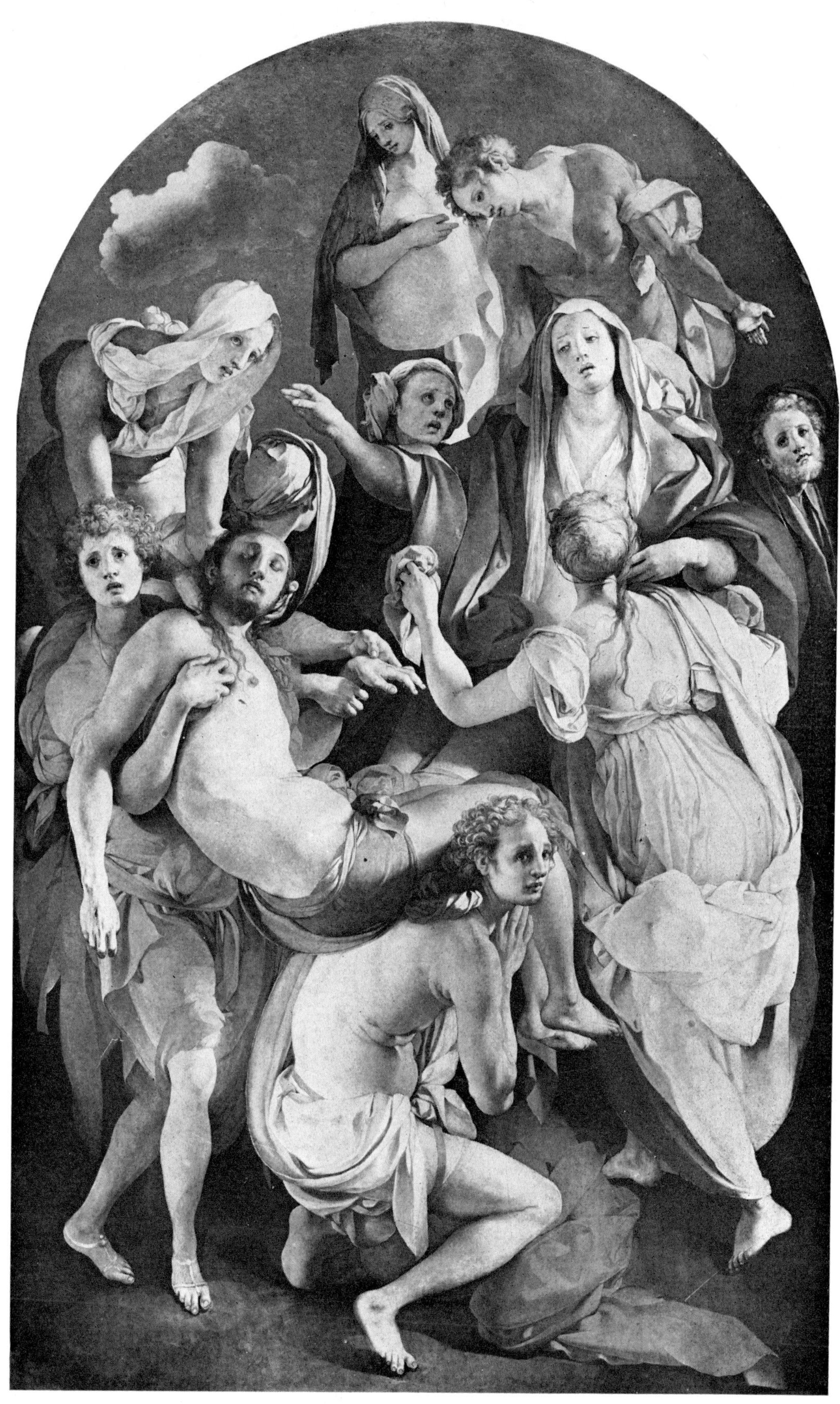

155. PONTORMO (1494–1557): *The Deposition*. 1525–8. Panel, 123 × 75 in. Florence, Santa Felicita

'One of the central pictures in the development of early Mannerism', in which 'the crowding and agitation of the figures powerfully reinforce the direct emotional effect of the sharp, pale colours.' (P. Murray)

51–4. PONTORMO (1494–1557): Four Studies for the *Deposition* (right)

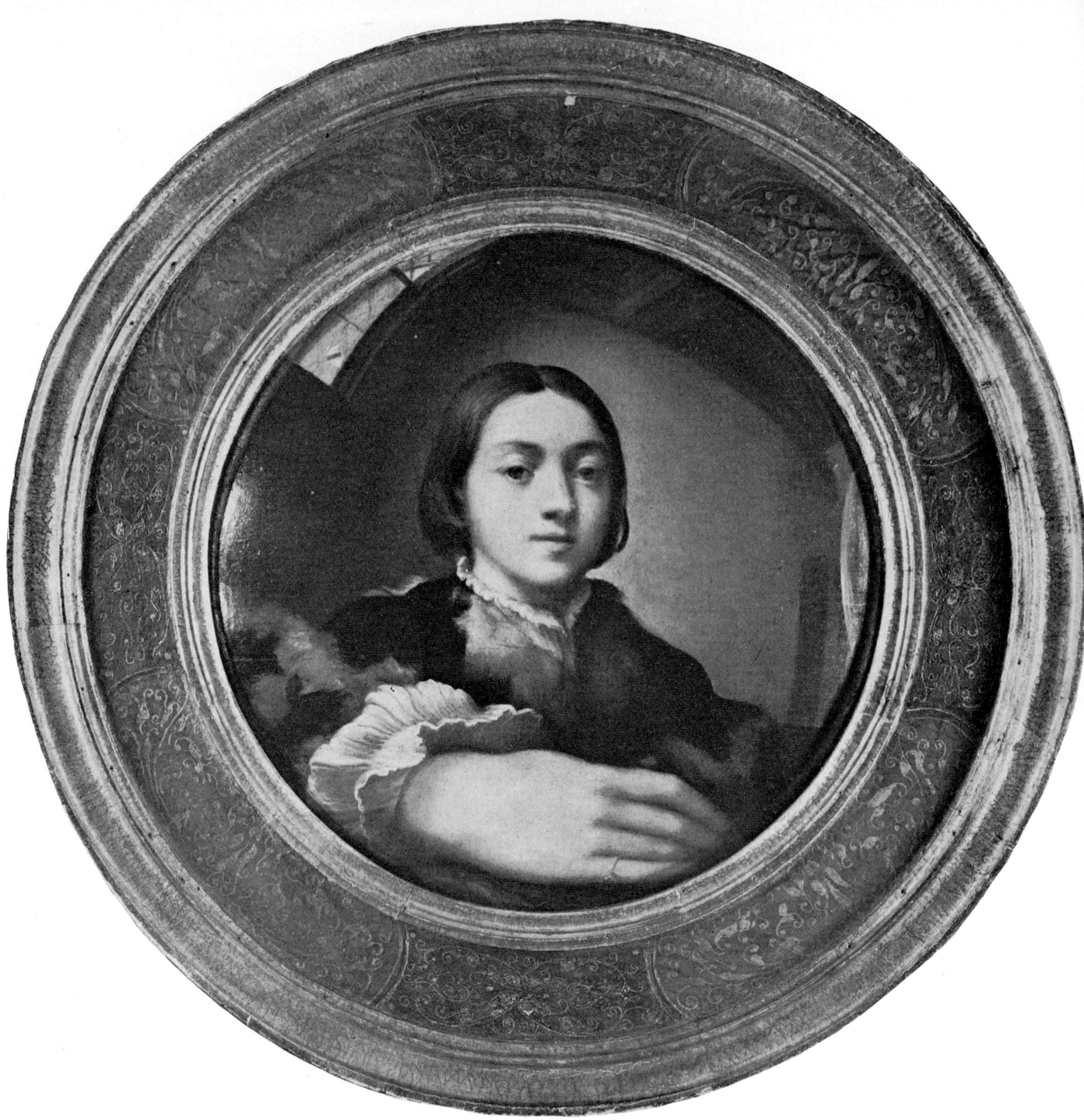

156. PARMIGIANINO (1503–40): *Self-portrait.* 1523–4. Panel, 9½ in. diameter. Vienna, Kunsthistorisches Museum

'He set himself one day to make his own portrait, looking at himself in a convex barber's mirror. He had a ball of wood made by a turner and, dividing it into half, so as to make it the same in size and shape as the mirror, set to work to paint on it all that he saw in the mirror, and particularly his own self. Now, whatever is near the mirror is magnified and whatever is at a distance is diminished, and hence he made the hand engaged in drawing rather large, as the mirror showed it.' (Vasari)

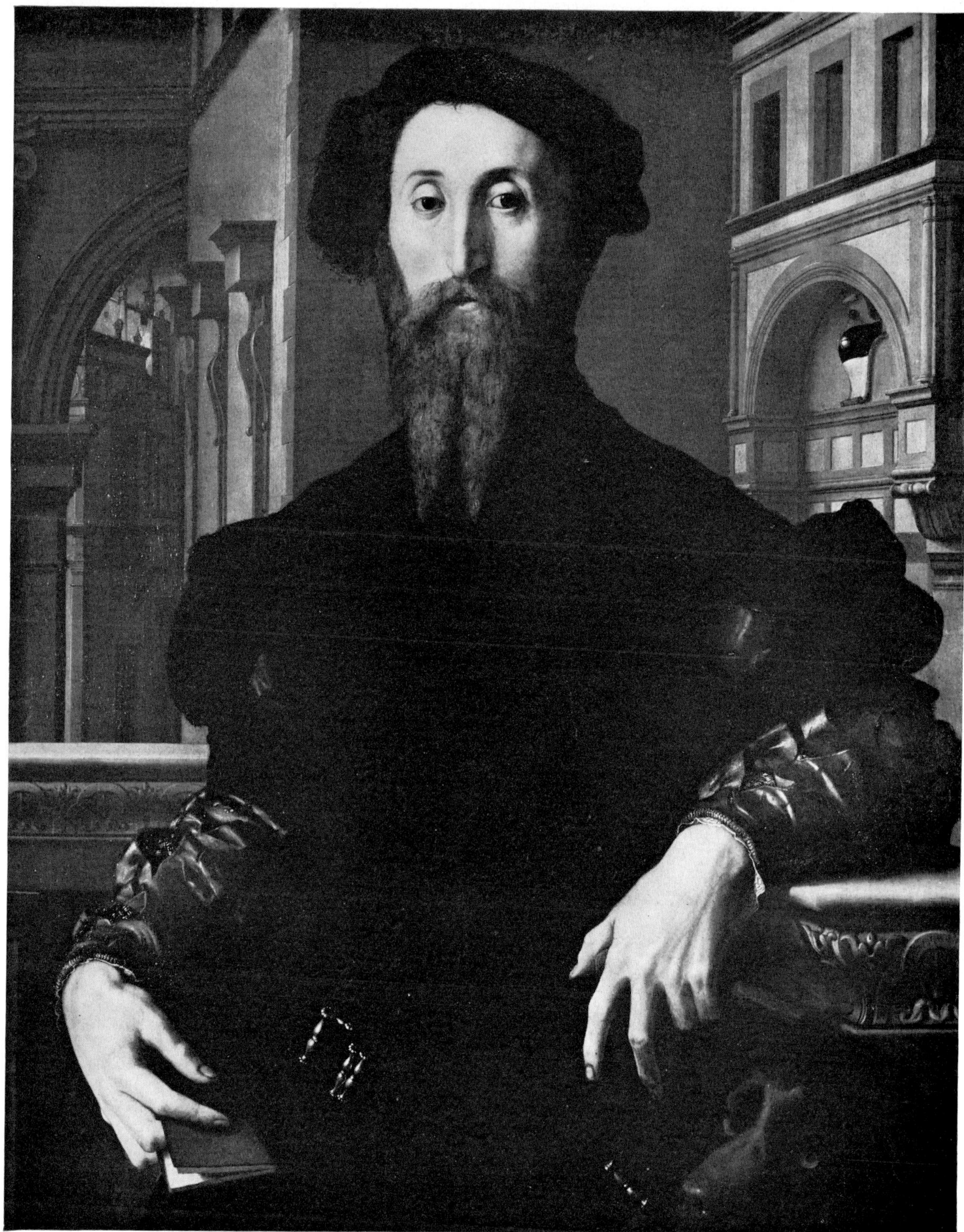

157. BRONZINO (1503–72): *Portrait of Bartolomeo Panciatichi*. About 1540. Panel, 41 × $33\frac{1}{2}$ in. Florence, Uffizi

Stately and grave, but somewhat lifeless, the sitter leans against the corner of a sculptured parapet, with his dog beside him. The skilful use of perspective in the background mitigates the static effect. Both this portrait and the *Allegory* (Plate 160) are particularly fine examples of Bronzino's meticulous, polished and deliberately rather cold art, which was greatly admired by the Florentine court.

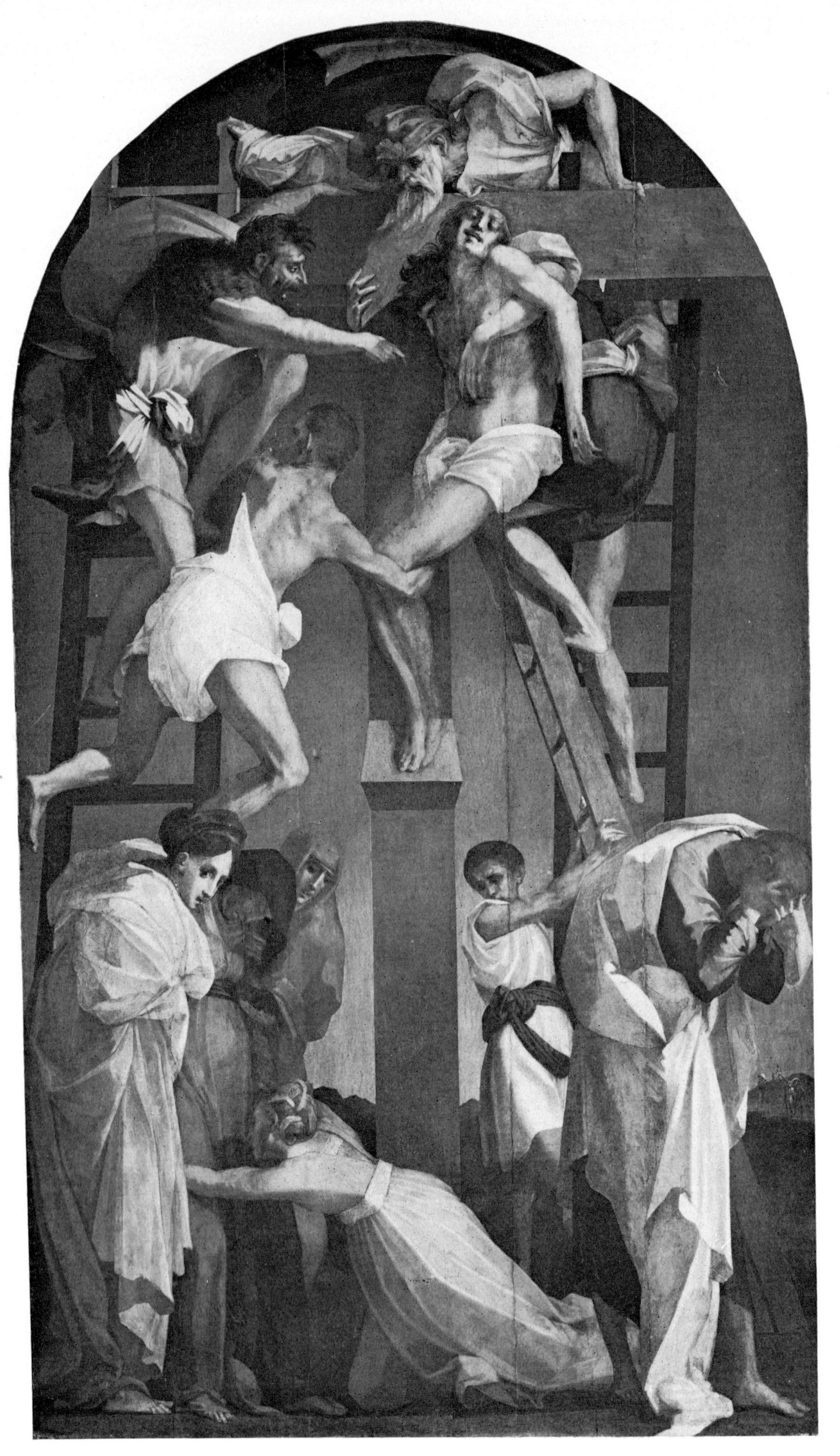

158. GIOVANNI BATTISTA ROSSO (1494–1540): *The Deposition*. 1521. Canvas, 85 × 49 in. Volterra, Pinacoteca

The gymnastic poses and dramatic gestures of the four helpers above contrast with the more muted grief of the three Maries, Mary Magdalene and St. John below, to make this a masterpiece of impassioned visual rhetoric. One ladder is leaning against the front of the Cross, another against its back; the third, seen from below, is held steady by a man standing on it and half-hidden by Christ's body. A comparison with Plate 20 shows how far Florentine art had moved in eighty years.

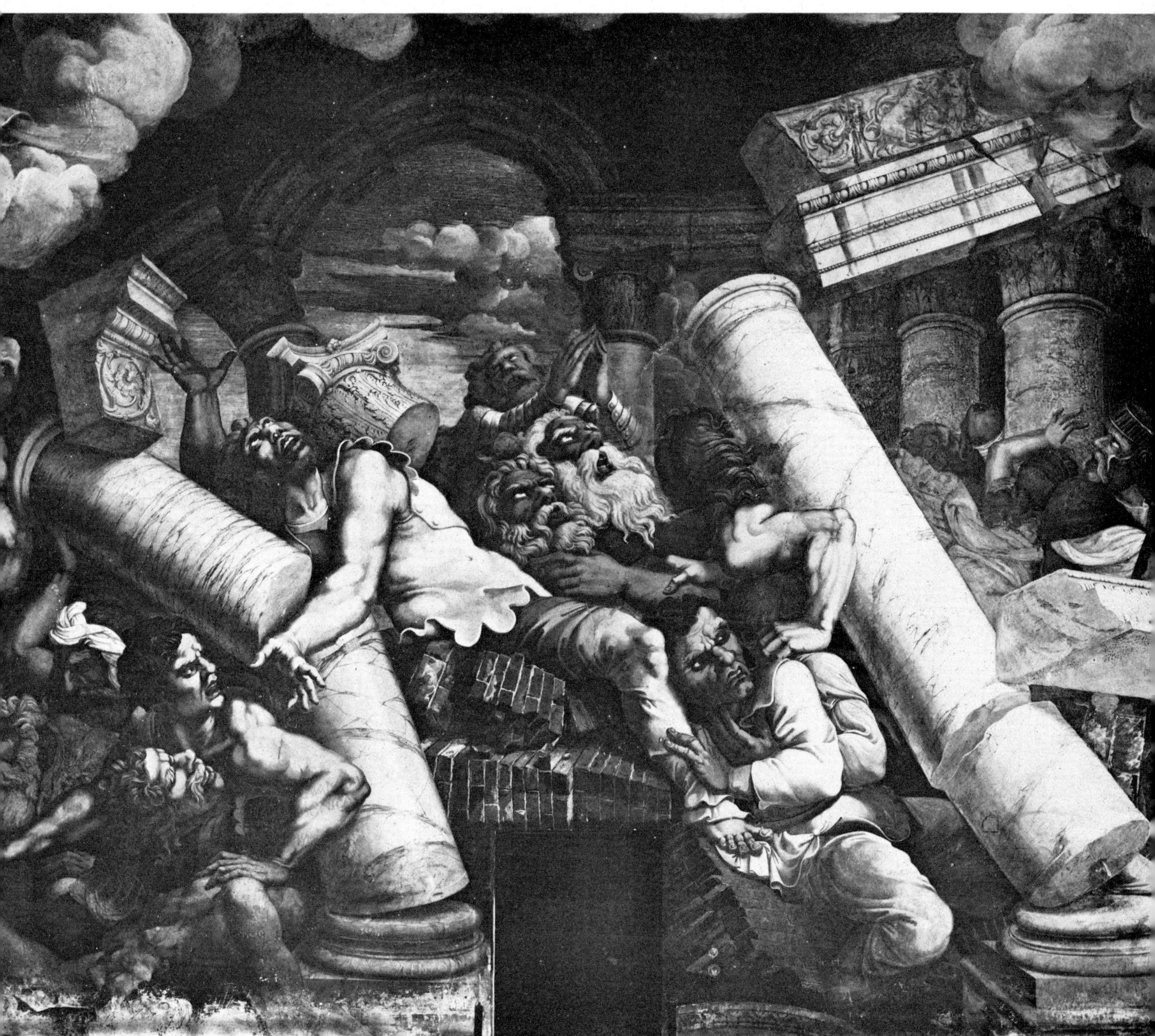

159. GIULIO ROMANO (*c.* 1499–1546): *The Fall of the Giants.* 1532–4. Fresco. Detail. Mantua, Palazzo del Tè

'*The Fall of the Giants*, occupying the whole of one room, is a piece of brutal illusionism deliberately designed to overwhelm the spectator, who finds himself involved in the crushing of the giants by the thunderbolts of Jove in the sky above. The whole of the room is painted from floor to ceiling to increase the illusion, and Vasari tells us that the flames in the fireplace were intended to add to the effect of general destruction.' (P. Murray) 'That rare Italian master, Julio Romano' (Shakespeare, *The Winter's Tale*, V. ii) was the chief assistant of Raphael and later was court-painter to the Duke of Mantua for over twenty years.

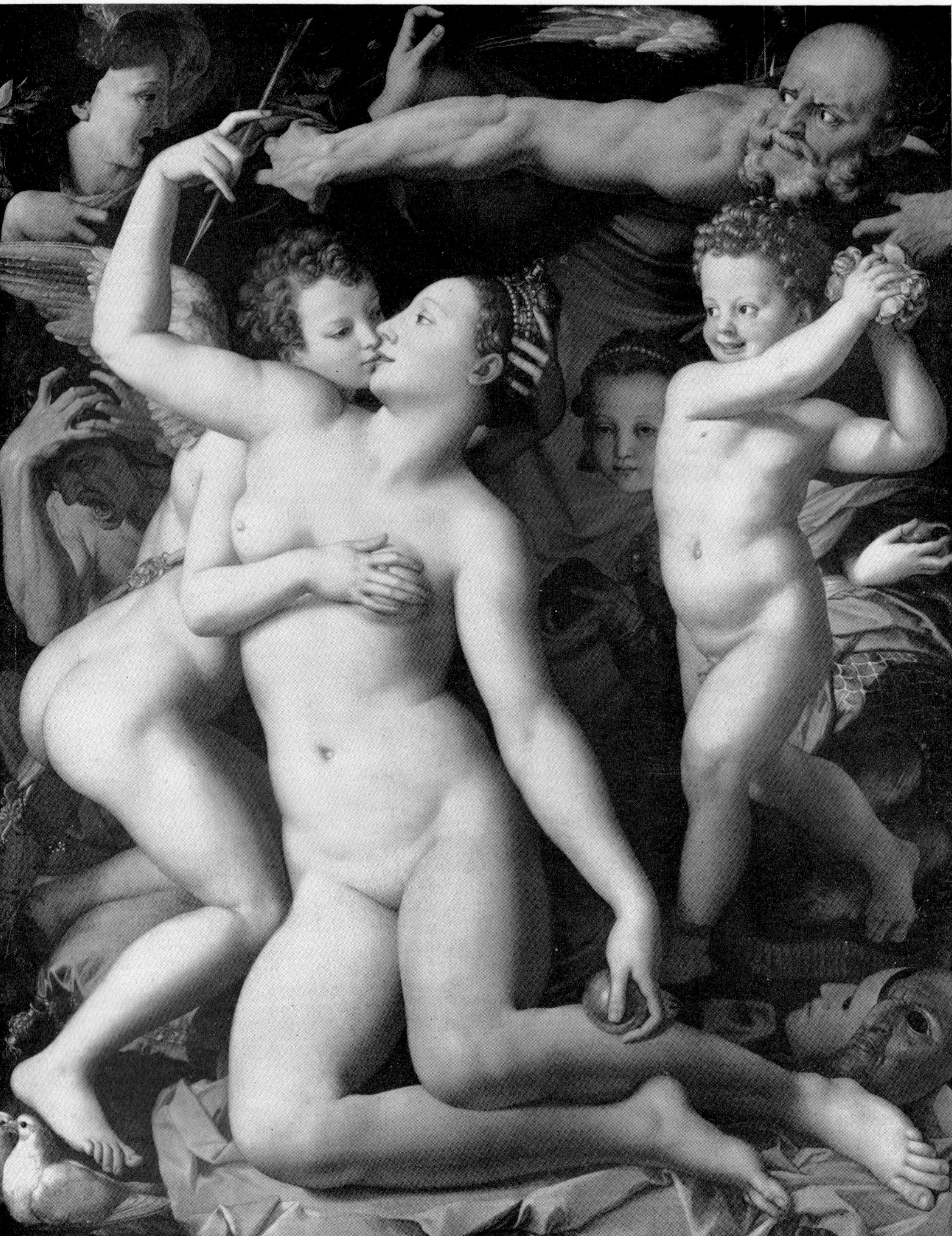

160. BRONZINO (1503–72): *An Allegory*. About 1545–6. Panel, $57\frac{1}{2} \times 45\frac{3}{4}$ in. London, National Gallery

Rarely has a serious moral message been wrapped up in such attractive nakedness, but here Truth (top left) and Time (with wings and hour-glass) have drawn back the curtain to warn us against the delights of purely sensual love. While Cupid, a pair of doves underfoot, caresses Venus, who holds his arrow and her golden apple, smiling Pleasure has rose blooms in store for them. But already Jealousy tears her hair and Deceit (as persuasively attractive as Satan in Plate 19 and Calumny in Plate 55) holds a scorpion's sting ready in one hand while offering a honeycomb with the other. The two masks reinforce the involved meaning, which met the humanist's penchant for the personification of abstract ideas.

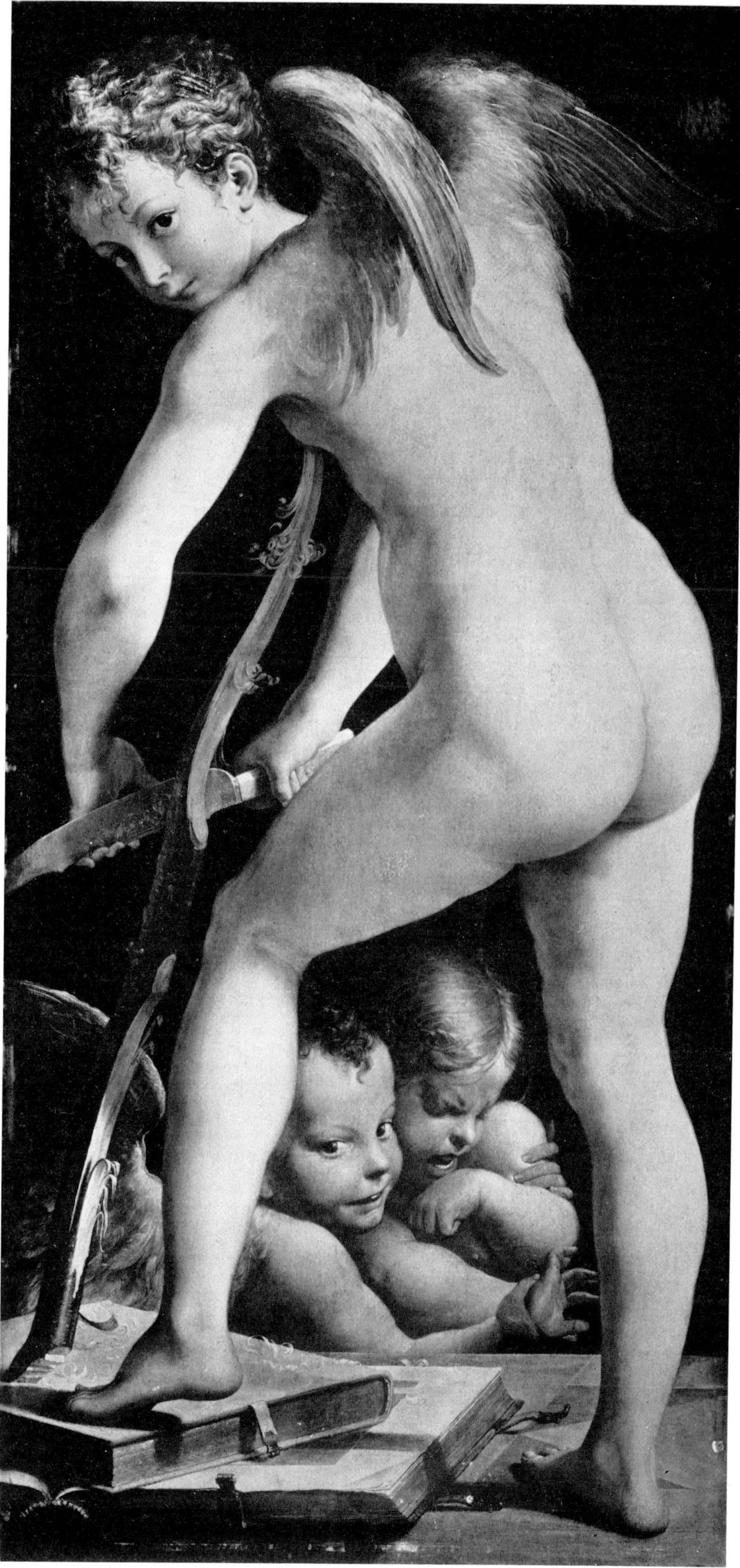

161. PARMIGIANINO (1503–40): *Cupid Carving a Bow*. 1533–4. Panel, $53\frac{1}{2} \times 25\frac{3}{4}$ in. Vienna, Kunsthistorisches Museum

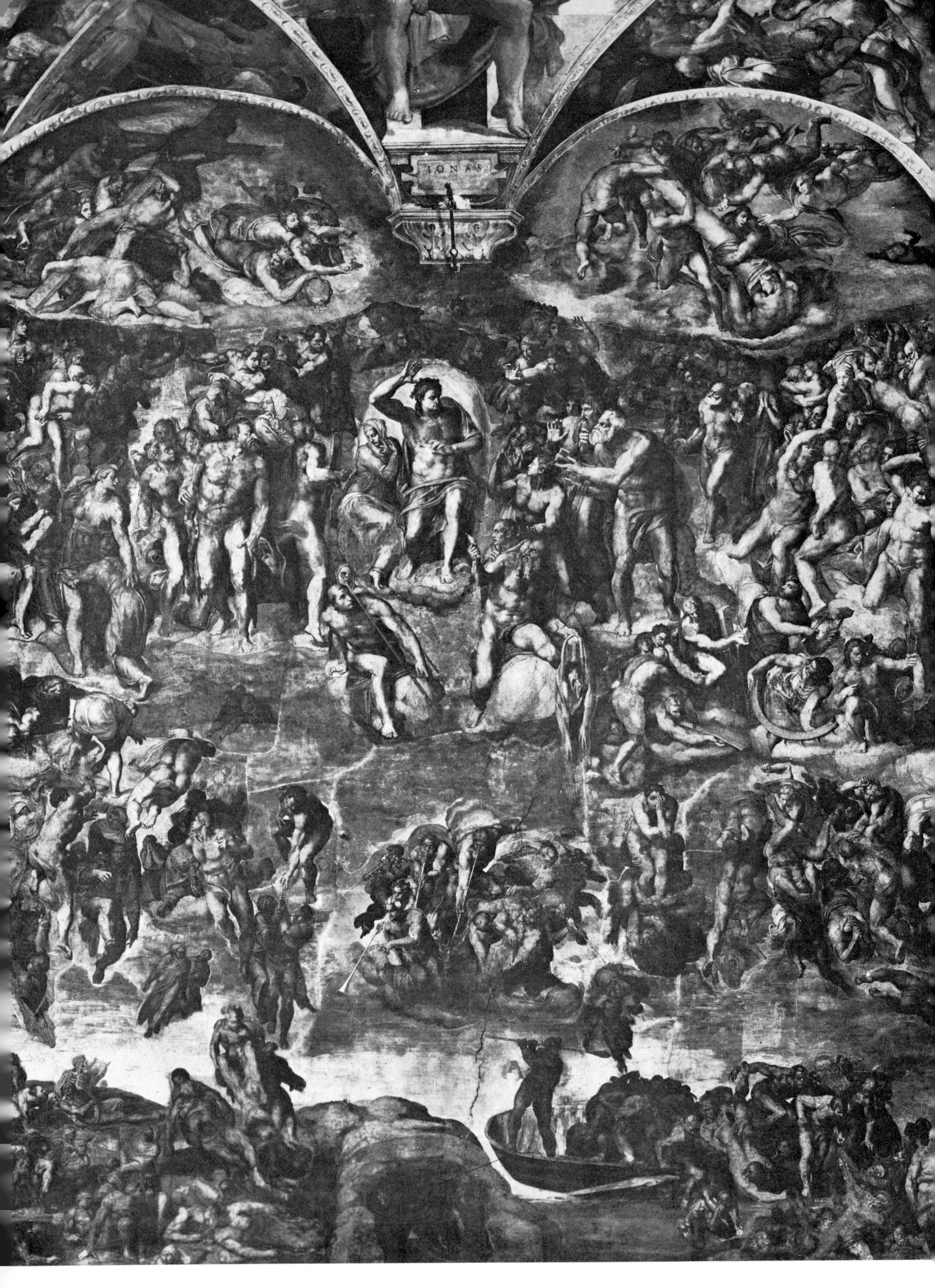
IONAS

162. MICHELANGELO (1475–1564): *The Last Judgement.* 1542–5. Fresco. Vatican, Sistine Chapel, altar wall

As angels trumpet the day of doom, the Righteous rise from their graves and ascend to heaven, while the Unrighteous are dragged down to hell by devils, a multitude of floating and writhing bodies on the threshold of eternity. Above the judge are borne the instruments of his Passion.

163. MICHELANGELO (1475–1564): *The Conversion of Saul.* 1542–5. Fresco. Vatican, Cappella Paolina

On the road to Damascus, Saul, a persecutor of the disciples, is blinded by a heavenly light. He submits to Christ's command and receives his grace. His companions 'stood speechless, hearing a voice, but seeing no man.' (Acts 9:7)

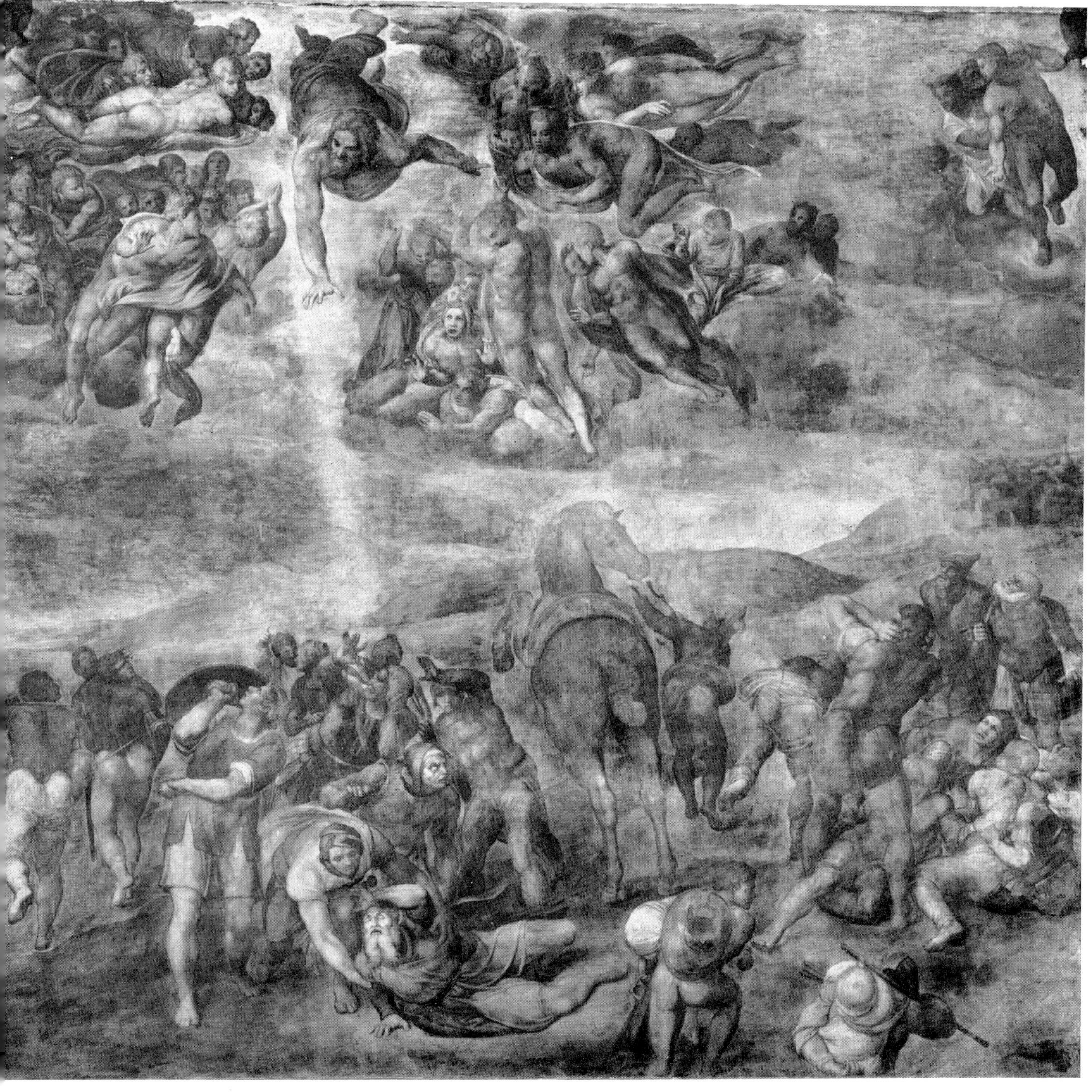

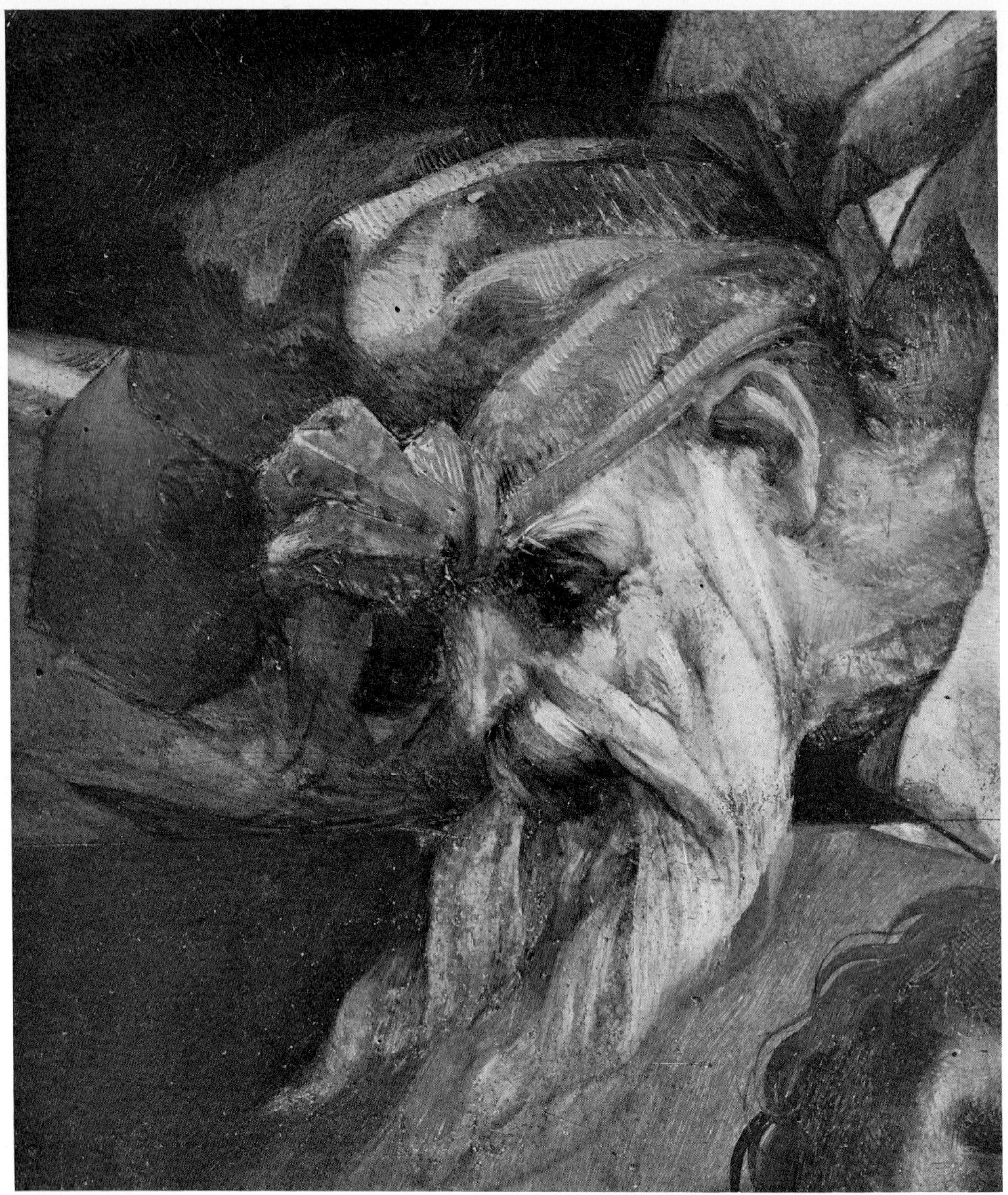

164. GIOVANNI BATTISTA ROSSO (1494–1540): *Head of Nicodemus*. Detail from Plate 158

165. MICHELANGELO (1475–1564): *Head of Saul*. Detail from Plate 1

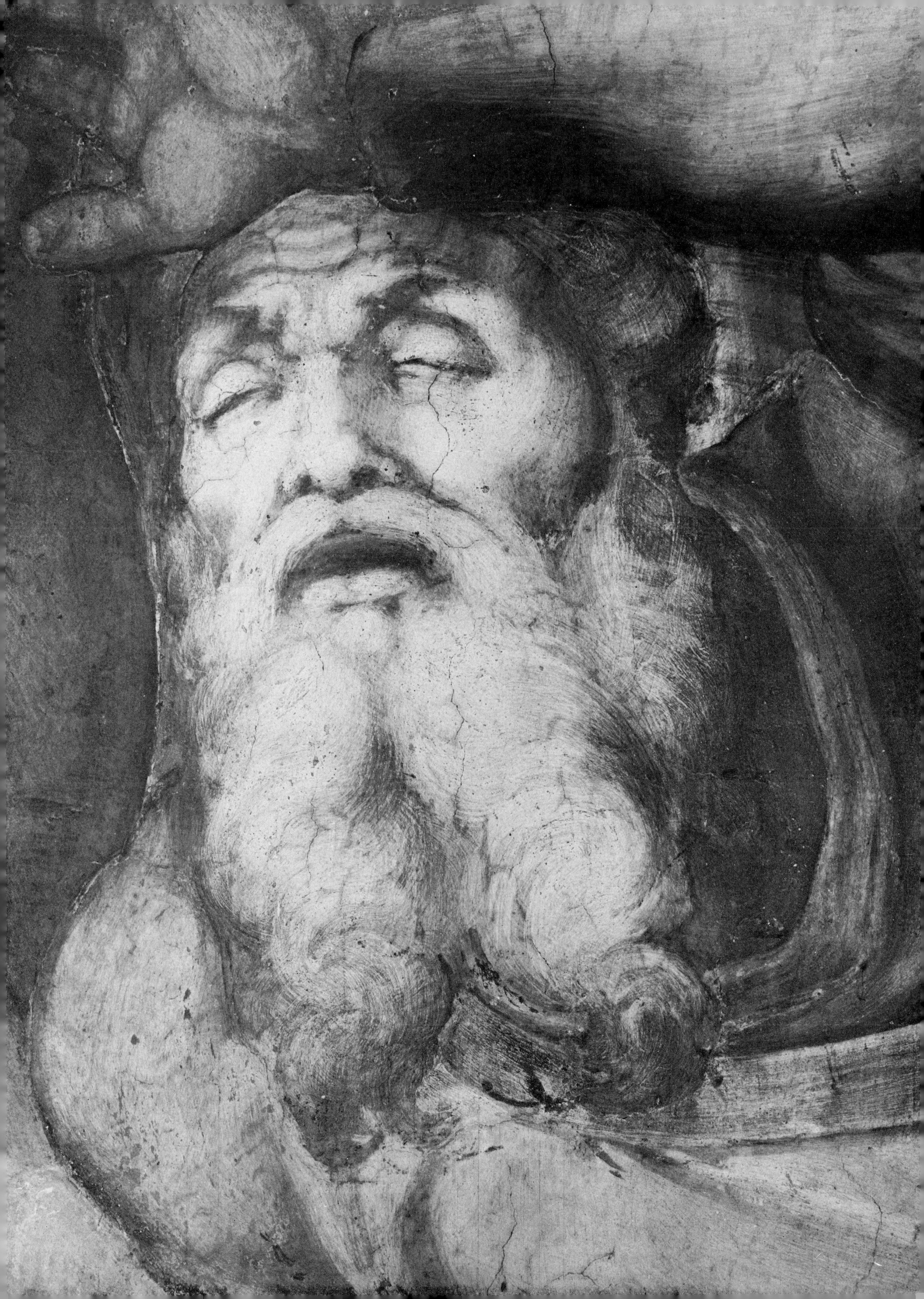

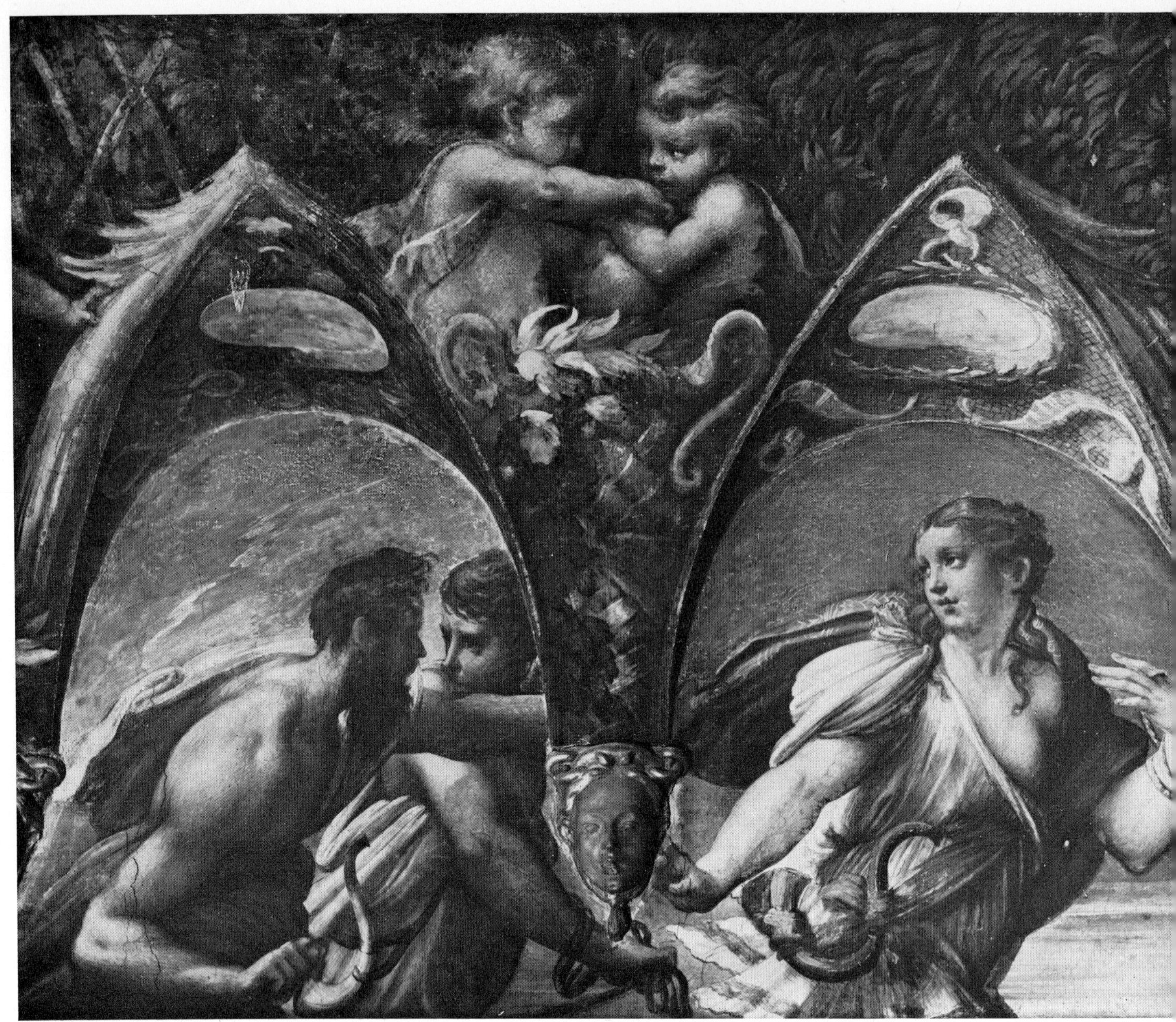

166. PARMIGIANINO (1503–40): *Diana and Actaeon*. About 1523. Fresco. Fontanellato, Castello Sanvitale

This is a detail from a small frescoed room in which the coving is decorated with scenes from the legend of Diana and Actaeon. The frescoes show how well Parmigianino maintained the delicacy and elegance of his vision even in fresco, a less subtle medium than oils.

167. PARMIGIANINO (1503–40): '*The Madonna of the Long Neck*'. 1535. Panel, 85 × 52 in. Florence, Uffi

In this strange picture, the artist has elongated all the bodies and crammed five angels' heads into a small space. He has taken care not to define distances between the topless column and the foregrou nor to make clear where the Virgin is seated, but leaves us to interpret all the spatial relations.

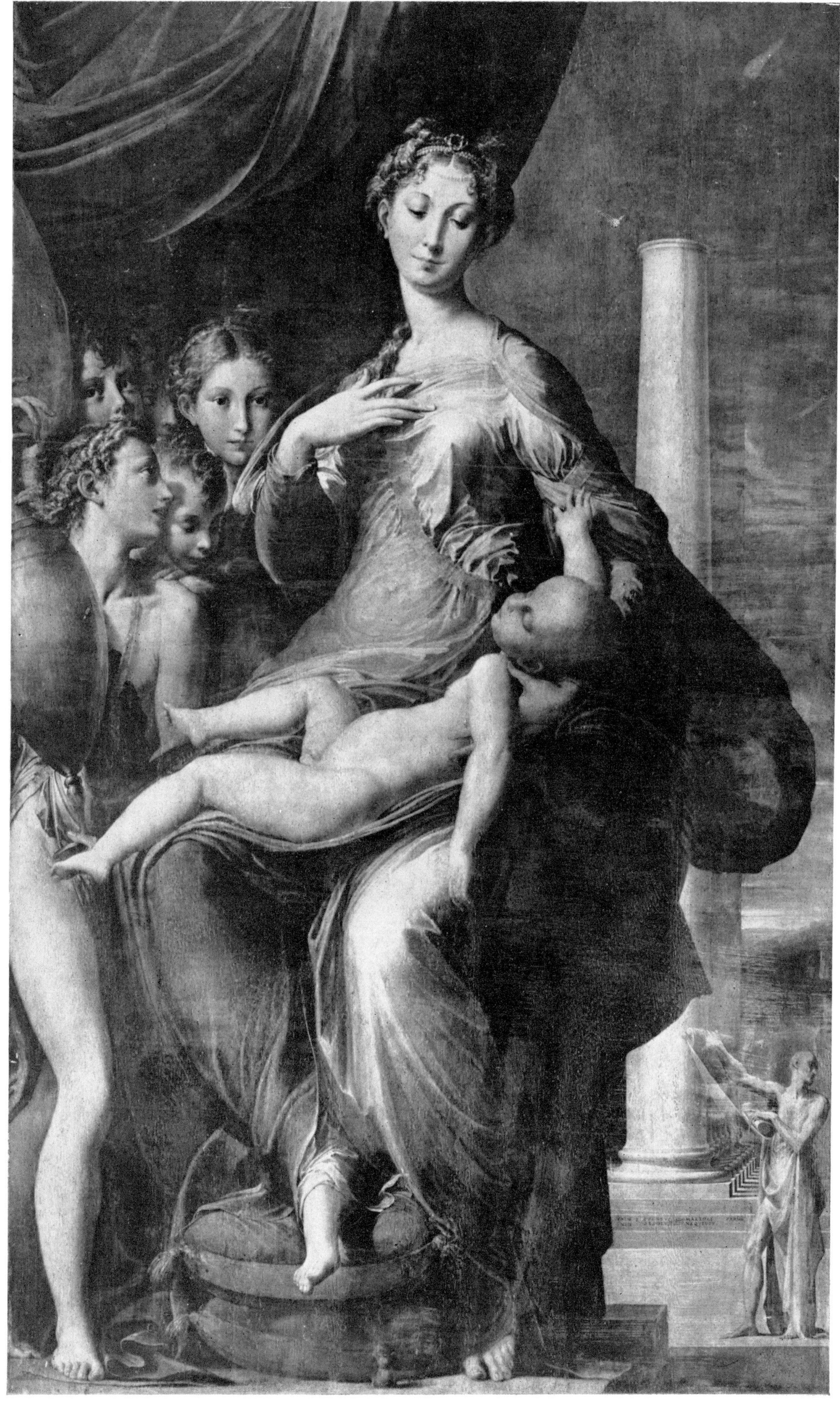

168, 169. PAOLO VERONESE (*c.* 1528–88): *The Family of Darius before Alexander*. About 1575–80. Canvas, 93 × 187 in. London, National Gallery

After the battle of Issus, Alexander the Great and his bosom friend, Hephaestion, visited the family of his defeated enemy, Darius. Unfortunately, Darius's mother mistook Hephaestion for Alexander, but the latter magnanimously forgave her. As the most prominent figure in the picture is the young man with outstretched arms, he is probably Hephaestion, and Alexander the one in armour to whom he points with his left hand. The balustrade behind the principal group and the colonnade with spectators in the background reflect the style of Venetian architecture of the artist's time and are reminiscent of a slightly earlier picture by Veronese (Plate 178).

This has always been one of Veronese's most famous and admired works and—unlike some of his very large canvases—entirely from his own hand. This type of picture, which represents Venetian painting at its most sumptuous, was an important influence on later Venetian masters, such as Sebastiano Ricci and Tiepolo.

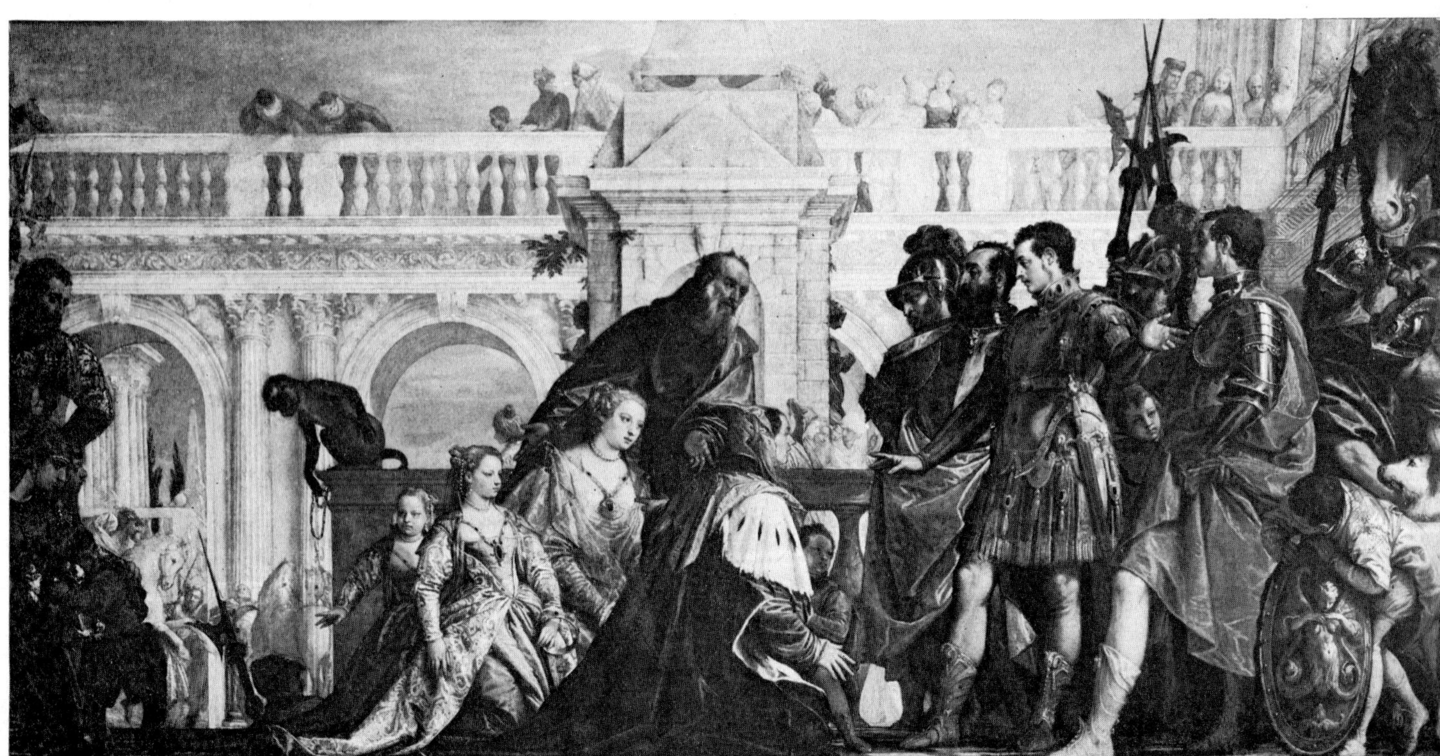

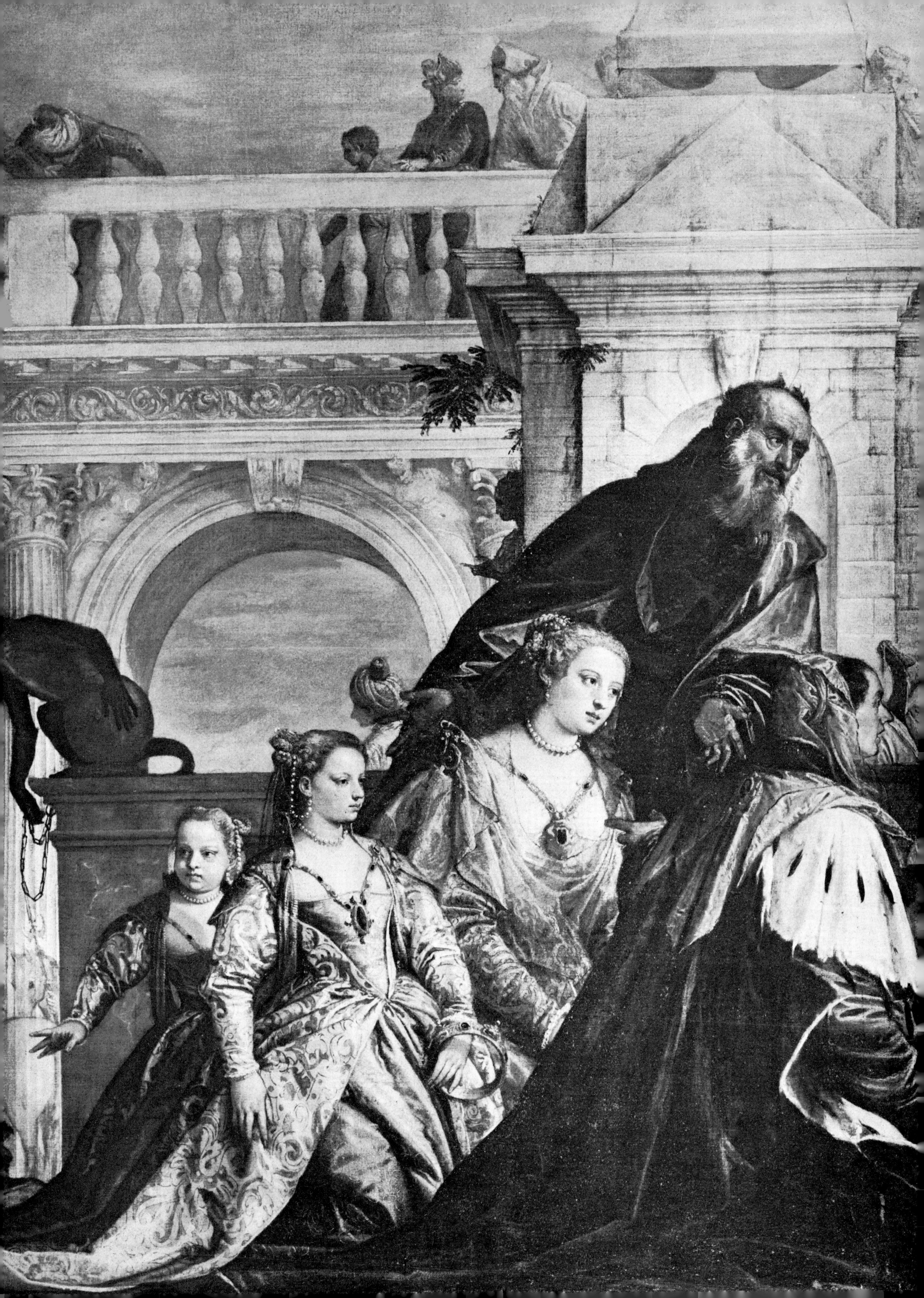

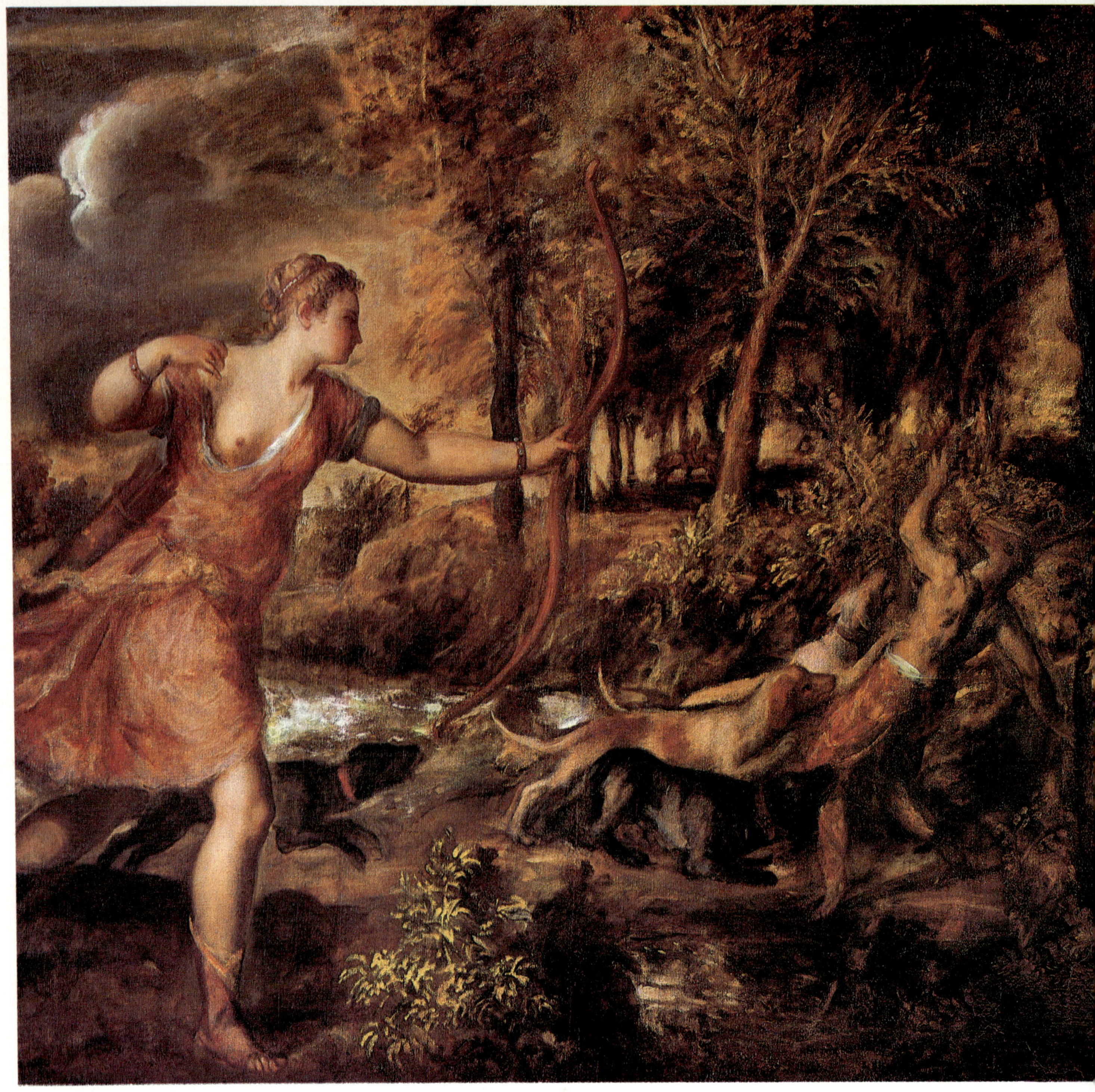

170. TITIAN (*c.* 1489–1576): *The Death of Actaeon.* 1562–6. Canvas, 70¼ × 78 in. London, National Gallery

This is the sequel to Plate 172. To punish Actaeon for his presumption (however unintentional), Diana turns him into a stag, to be torn to pieces by his own pack of hounds. Here his head is beginning to change shape as antlers sprout from it and already the baying pack mistake him for a quarry and jump up at him. Titian has treated the story with some freedom and invented the vengeful goddess aiming an arrow at him. Her Olympian figure and the shady sun-flecked forest are the aged Titian's supreme response to the inspiration of antiquity (see Plates 87, 104). Both Actaeon pictures were among several mythological compositions commissioned from him by the gloomy king of Spain, Philip II.

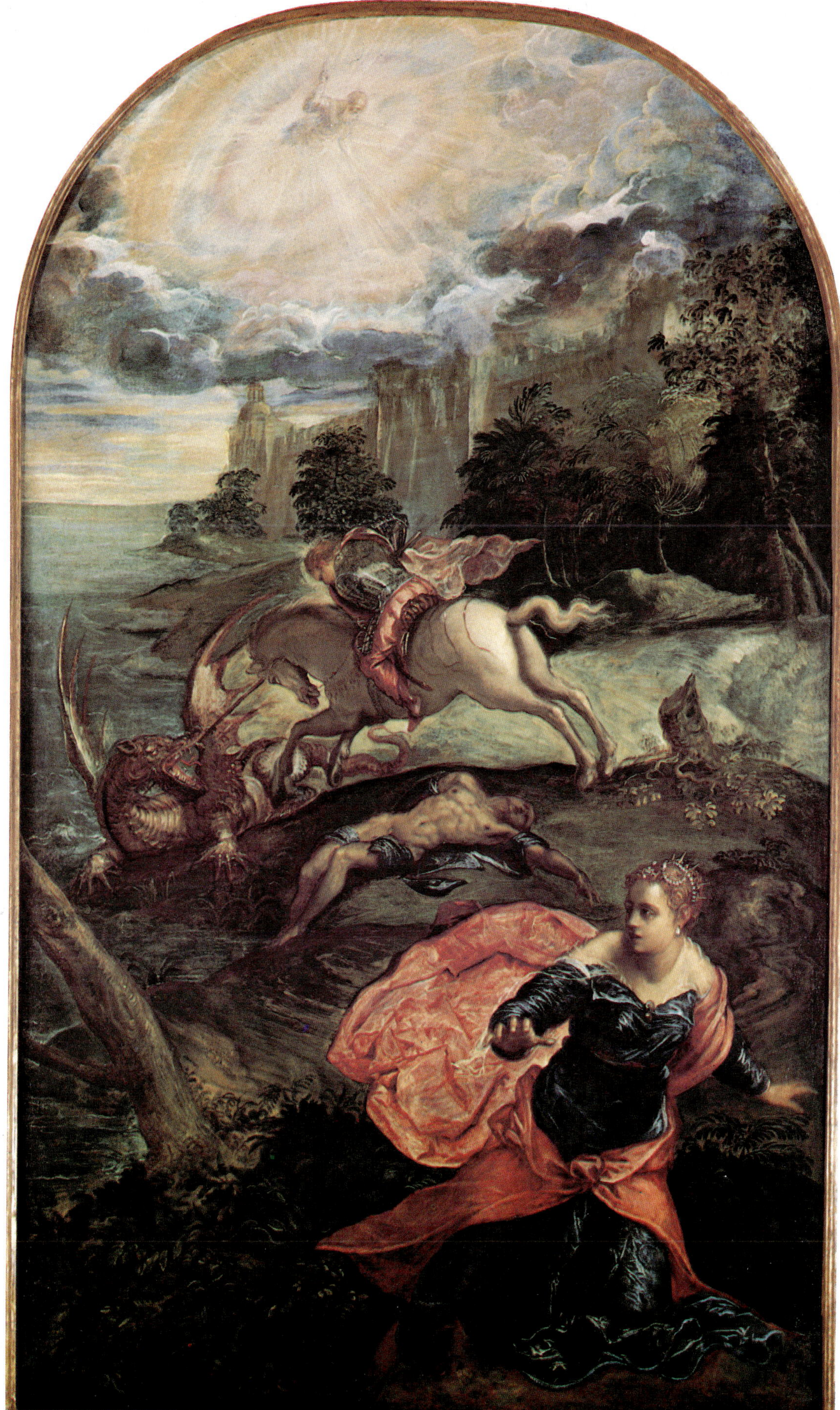

171. JACOPO TINTORETTO (1518–94): *St. George and the Dragon*. About 1560. Canvas, 62 × $39\frac{1}{2}$ in. London, National Gallery

An old legend related that a dragon which terrorized the coast of Asia Minor was slain by St. George, a Roman soldier. In this dramatic fantasy the monster has dispatched one victim, but the king's daughter escapes, as the saint, on a galloping charger, transfixes its jaws. The billowing draperies suggest the speed of onrush and flight.

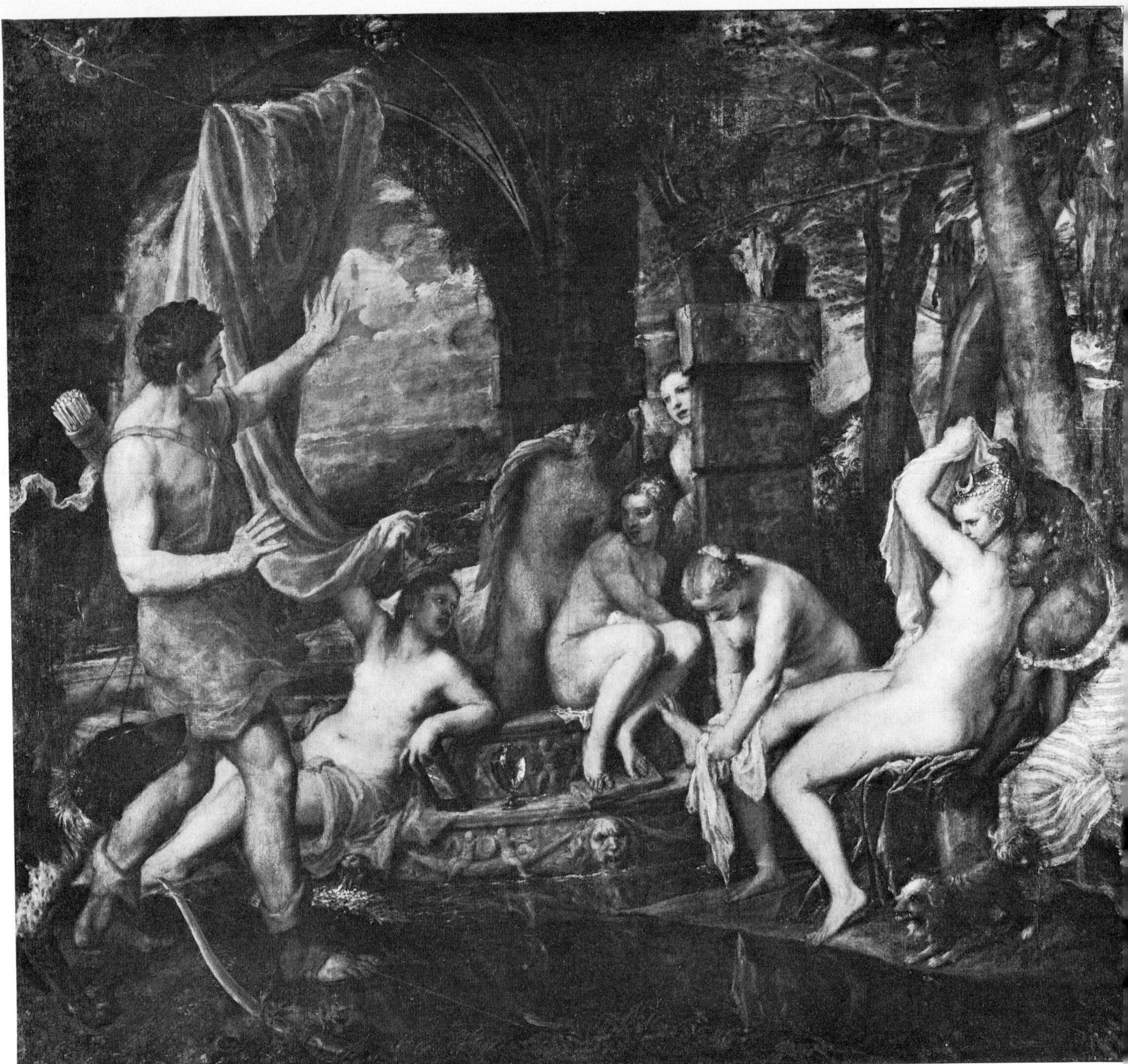

172. TITIAN (*c.* 1489–1576): *Diana and Actaeon.* About 1559. Canvas, 74 × 80 in. Duke of Sutherland Collection, on loan to the National Gallery of Scotland, Edinburgh

The subject is taken from Ovid's *Metamorphoses*, a book that enjoyed very wide popularity and furnished Renaissance and later artists with numerous stories from Greek mythology. Diana, the goddess of the chase, accompanied by her nymphs, had come to a rocky grotto to bathe in a pool. While she was drying herself after the bath, the hunter Actaeon happened to enter the grotto and saw her naked. Titian's picture, one of his later masterpieces, shows Actaeon's astonishment at the unexpected sight of the crescent-crowned goddess, who recoils and tries to cover her emblems of godhead with a veil, while her black attendant and the nymphs shrink back in fright.

173. DOSSO DOSSI (died 1542): *Circe and her Lovers in a Landscape*. About 1525. Canvas, $39\frac{1}{2} \times 53\frac{1}{2}$ in. Washington, D.C., National Gallery of Art (Samuel H. Kress Collection)

In Homer's *Odyssey* Circe is a sorceress who lives in a palace on an island and turns all who approach into lions, wolves and pigs. Dosso's interpretation seems to be more dependent on later adaptations of the myth in Italian epic poetry: some of the animals that play an important part in the *Odyssey* are missing and instead of her magic wand the sorceress displays an inscribed tablet and a book opened on a page depicting a horoscope. The romantic landscape and the dreamy mood of suspended action are reminiscent of the Venetian style of the previous generation (Plates 79, 86–88, 90).

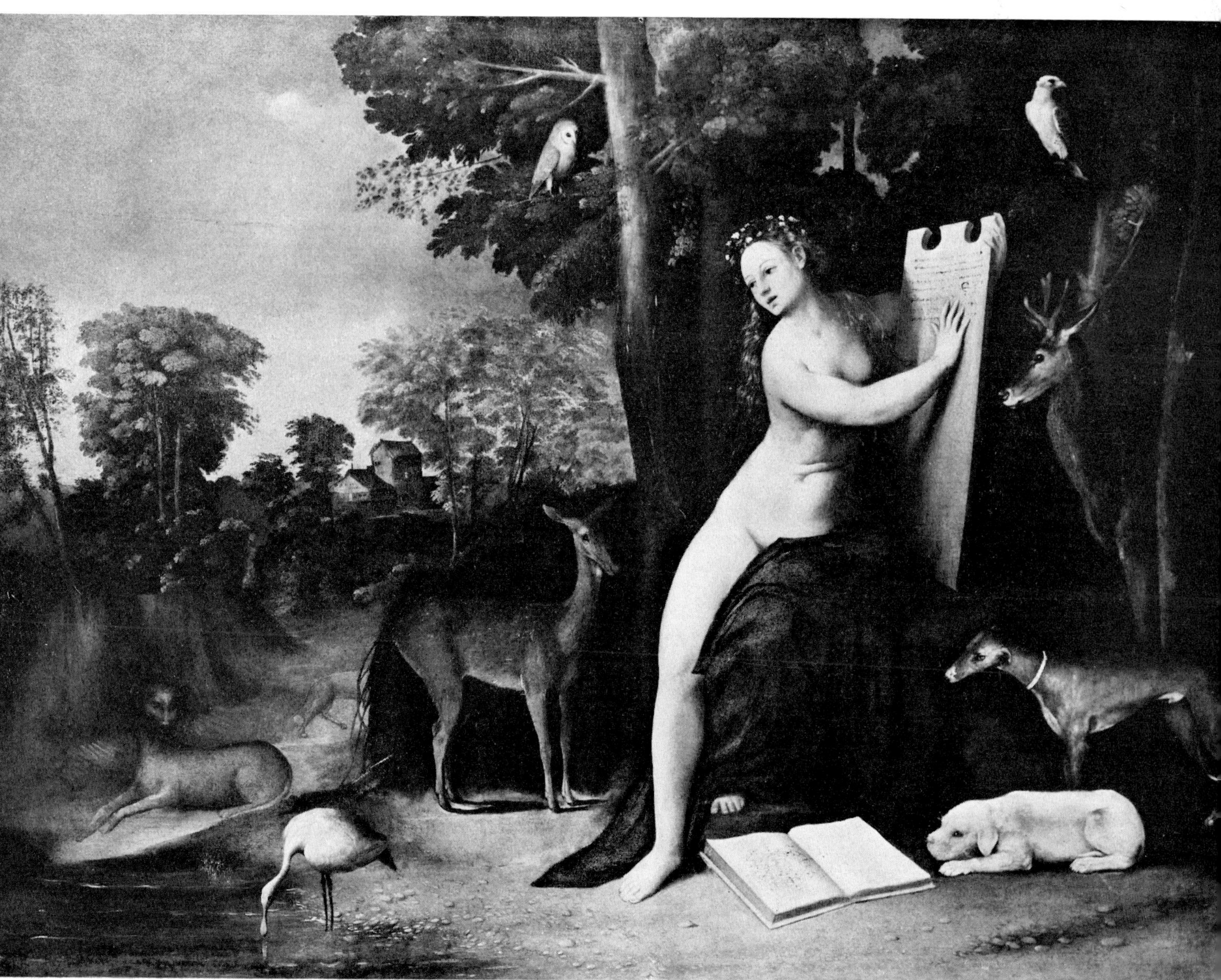

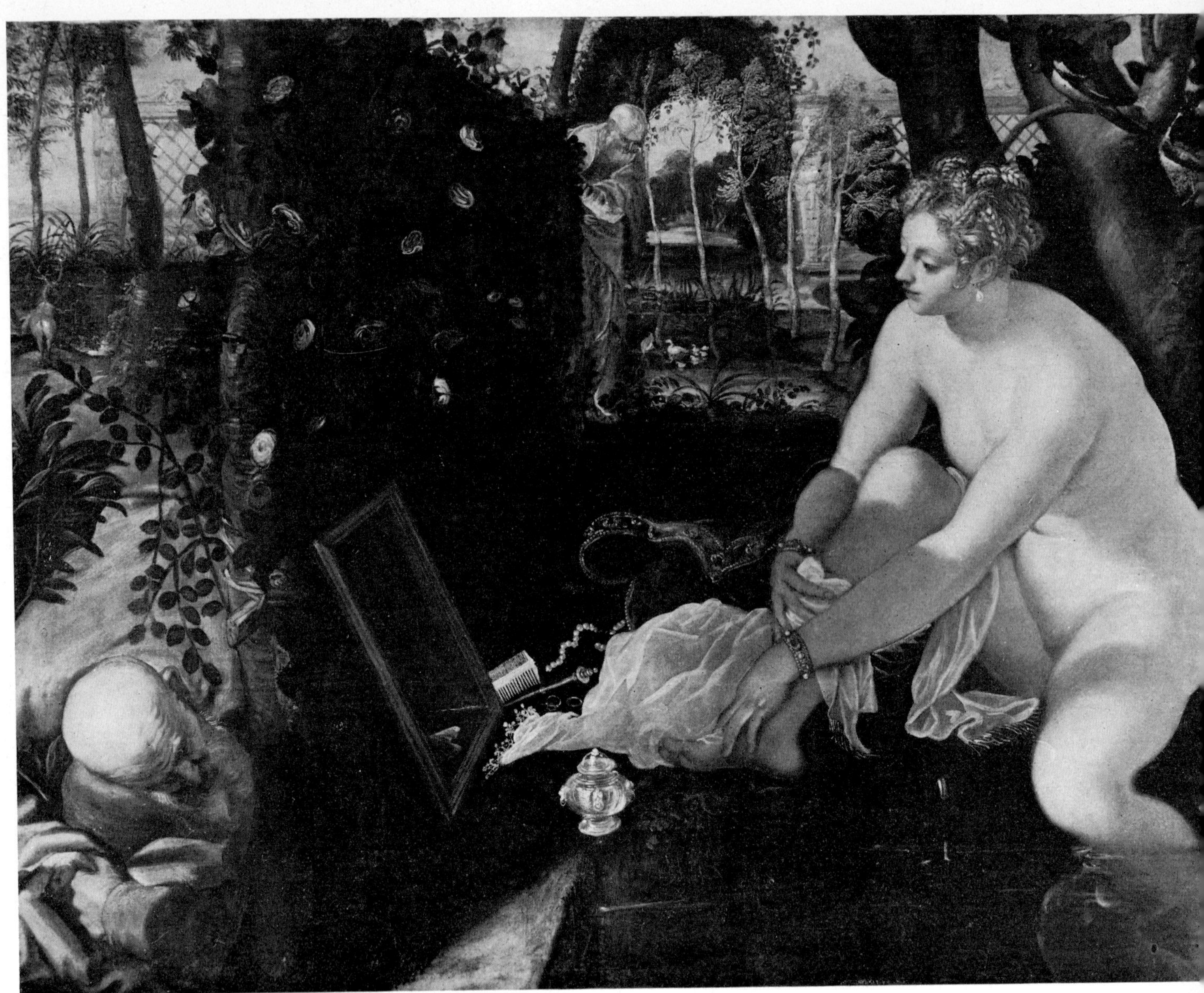

174. JACOPO TINTORETTO (1518–94): *Susannah and the Elders*. 1560–5. Canvas, $57\frac{3}{4} \times 76\frac{1}{4}$ in. Vienna, Kunsthistorisches Museum

An apocryphal addition to the Book of Daniel tells of Susannah, 'exceeding delicate and beautiful to behold', who is unjustly accused by two wicked elders of committing adultery with a young man in her husband's orchard and whose innocence is proved by a 'wise young judge'. Tintoretto has used the story for a somewhat less high-minded purpose—that of showing a young woman at her toilet (see Plate 92). Susannah, at her bath in a rock pool, is drying her leg with a fringed towel and gazing in a mirror, with her jewellery and toilet requisites scattered on the ground, while the elders steal out from behind the rose bushes.

175. TITIAN (*c.* 1489–1576): *Diana and her Attendant*. Detail from Plate 1

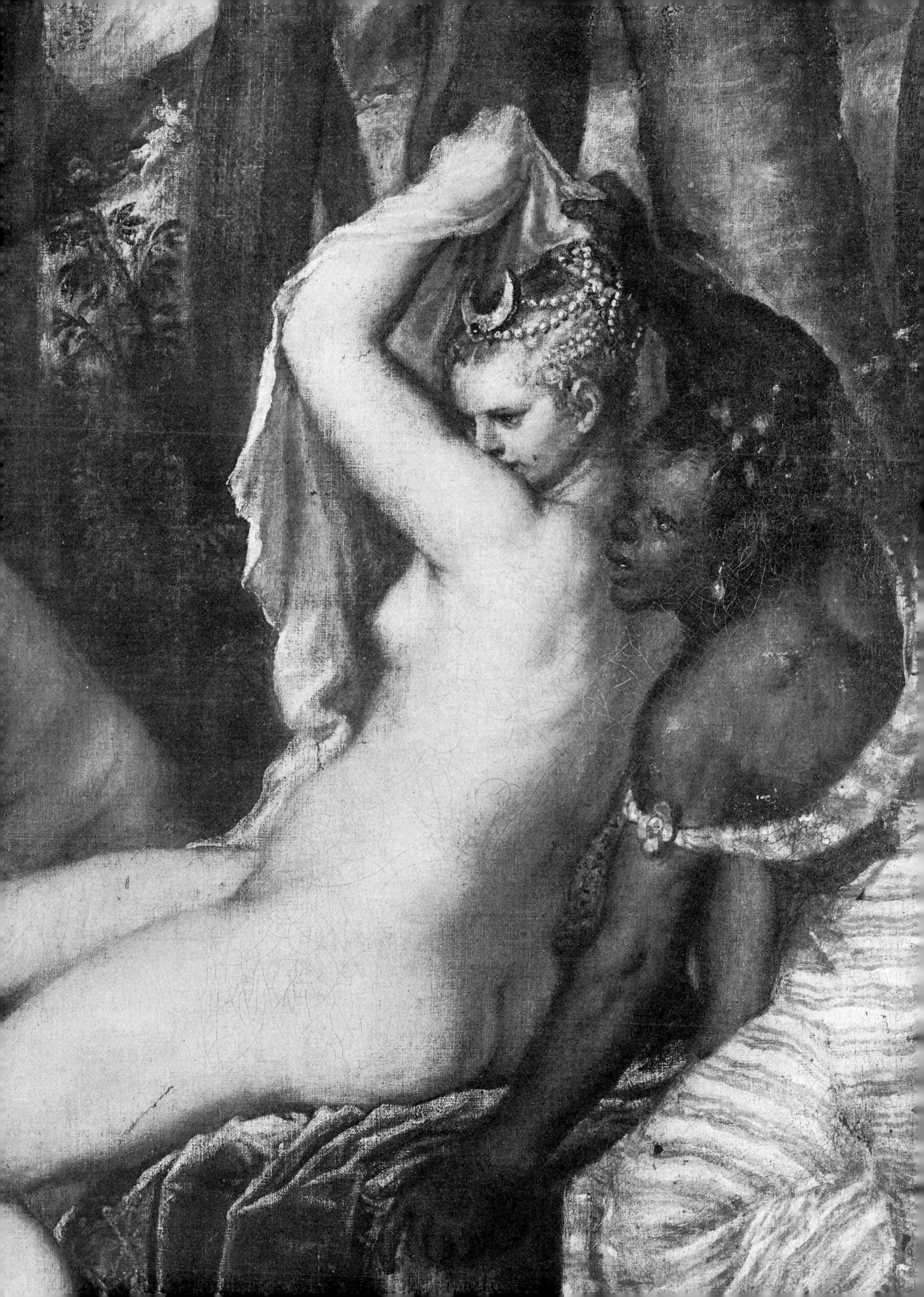

177. BACCHIACCA (1495–1557): *The Gathering of the Manna*. 1545–55. Panel, 44 × $37\frac{1}{2}$ in. Washington, D.C., National Gallery of Art (Samuel H. Kress Collection)

Like Tintoretto (Plate 174), Bacchiacca has adapted a biblical story (Exodus 16:11–18) to his own ends. These children of Israel are gathering the manna (and, at the left, the quails) in fertile Italian hill country, few of them paying heed to the commands of Moses. The painter has turned the miracle into a pretext for depicting a delightful variety of costumes, precious vessels, genre scenes and exotic animals, among them a giraffe; leopards, gazelles and a porcupine.

176. JACOPO BASSANO (*c.* 1510–92): *The Flight into Egypt*. 1540–50. Canvas, 49 × $74\frac{3}{4}$ in. Los Angeles, Norton Simon Collection

A lovely angel guides the Holy Family away from the threat of Herod's massacre, the aged Joseph walking barefoot and the Virgin and Child riding on the ass. As usual Bassano combined the biblical scene with the everyday life of his time: a countryman with rolled-up sleeves and trousers releases chickens from a basket; another, seen from the back, carries a pole and a recorder, and a younger man drinks from a small cask. Tumbledown farm buildings lead the eye to the distant mountains.

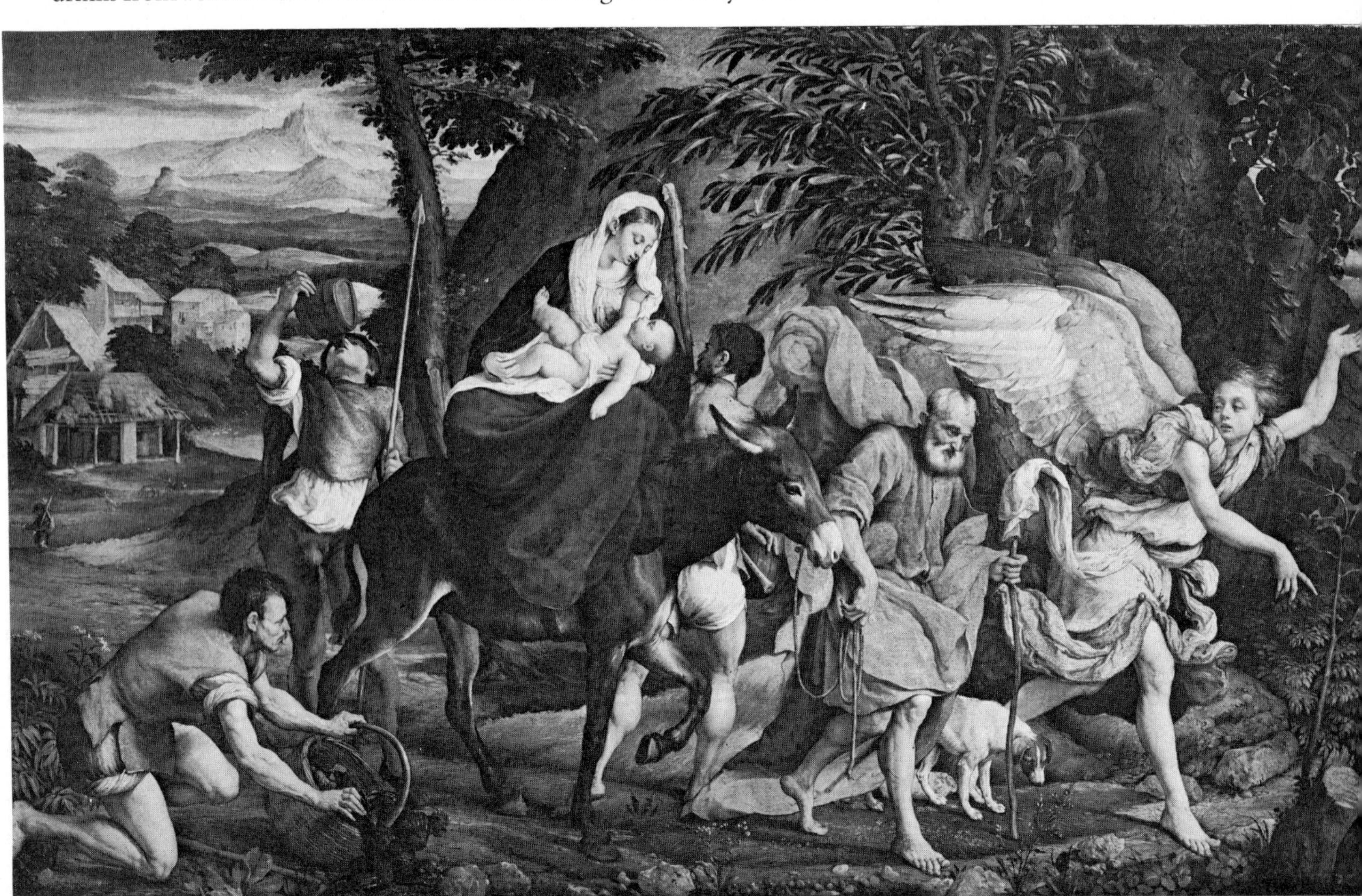

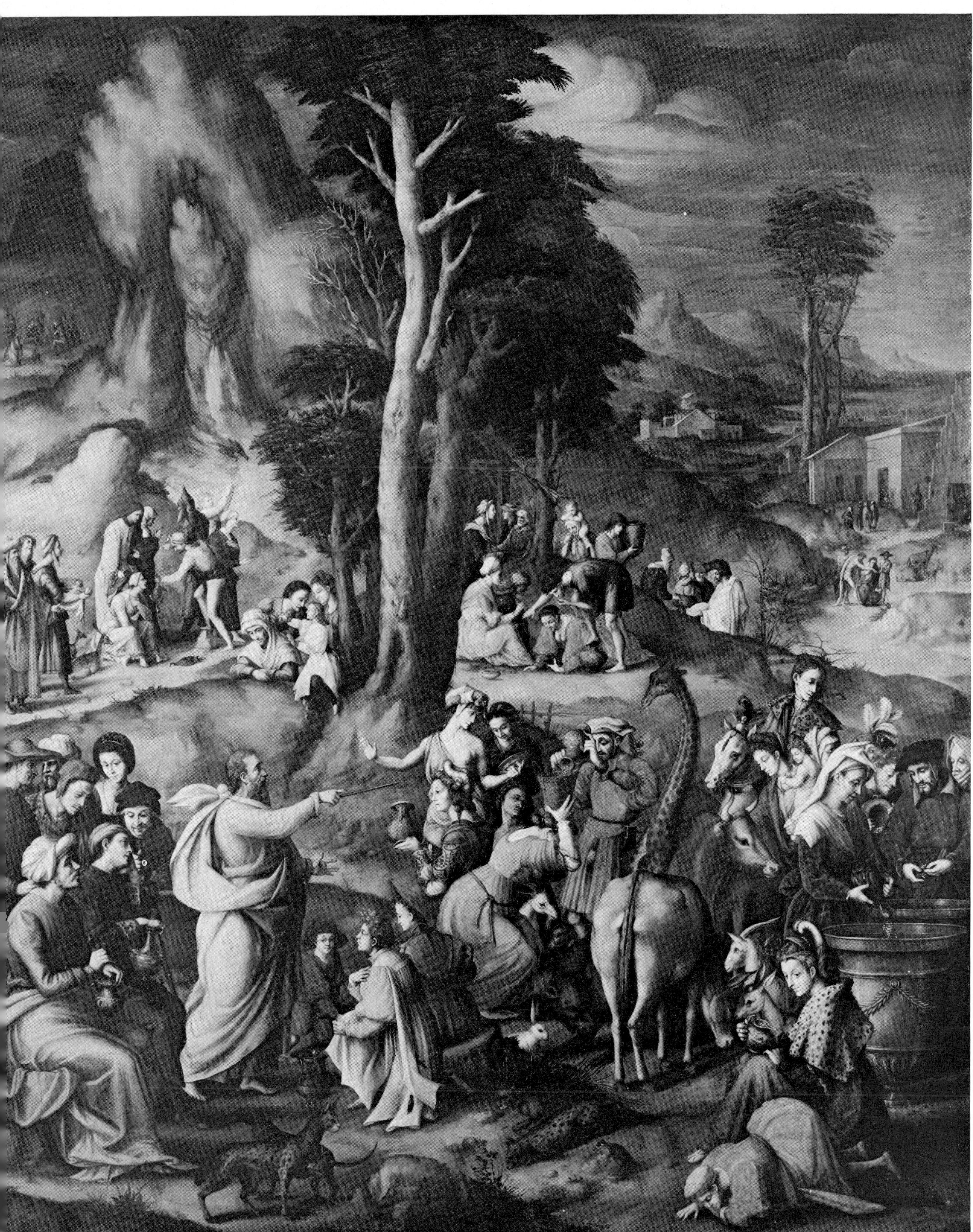

178, 179. PAOLO VERONESE (*c.* 1528–88): *The Feast in the House of Levi*. 1573. Canvas, 216½ × 503¼ in. Venice, Accademia

'And Levi made him a great feast in his own house: and there was a great company of publicans and of others that sat down with them' (Luke 5:29). Once again (as in Plates 174 and 177) the biblical subject is treated as little more than a peg on which the artist can hang what really interests him: Venetian pageantry of his own time. Indeed, so free was his treatment of the sacred text that he was summoned before the Inquisition, which had been re-invigorated by the Counter-Reformation programme of the Council of Trent. Asked to justify the unscriptural intruders in the picture—jesters, dwarfs and soldiers—he asserted the painter's right to be guided by purely artistic considerations and to allow his imagination full play. What the Inquisitors objected to is what most appeals to the taste of our more secular age: the colourful bustle of the banquet with Christ and other guests in animated conversation, waiters, entertainers, and two Turks climbing up a column, all framed between the Corinthian columns of tall arches giving a view of fashionable buildings such as those that Palladio was then designing in Venice.

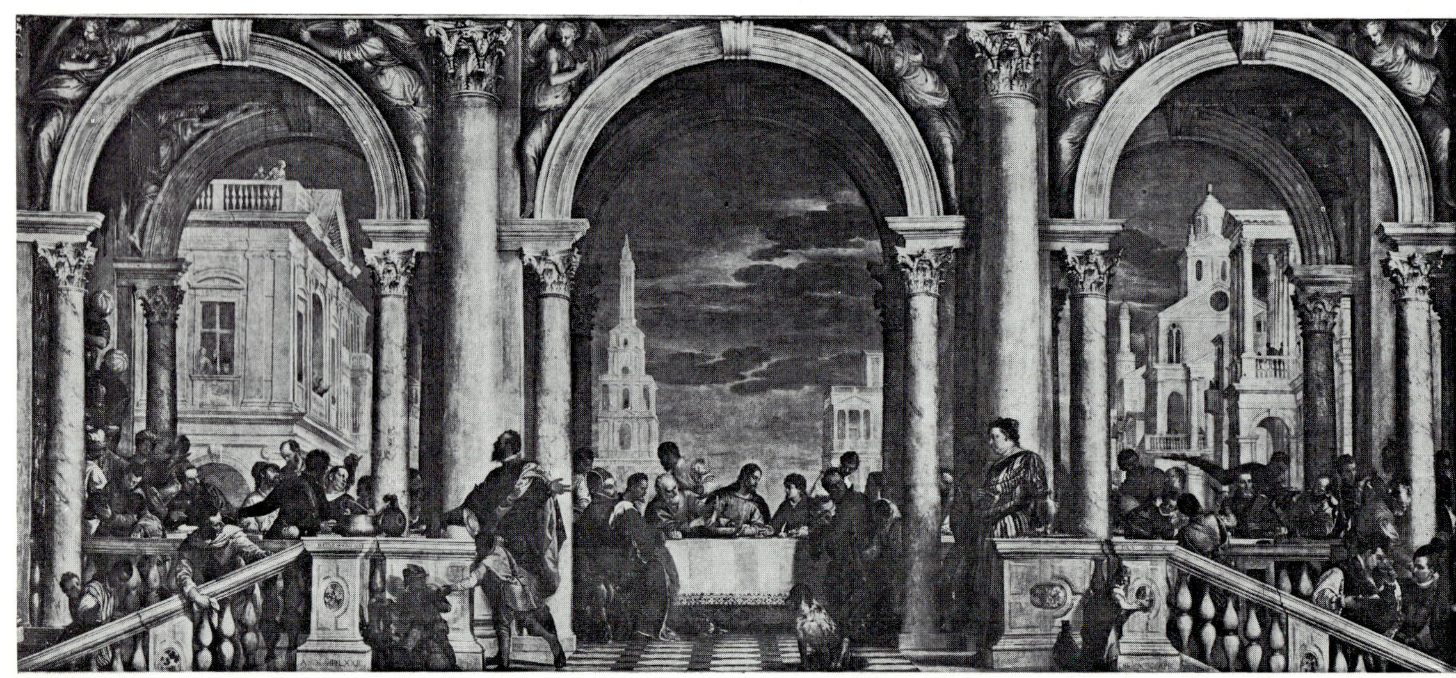

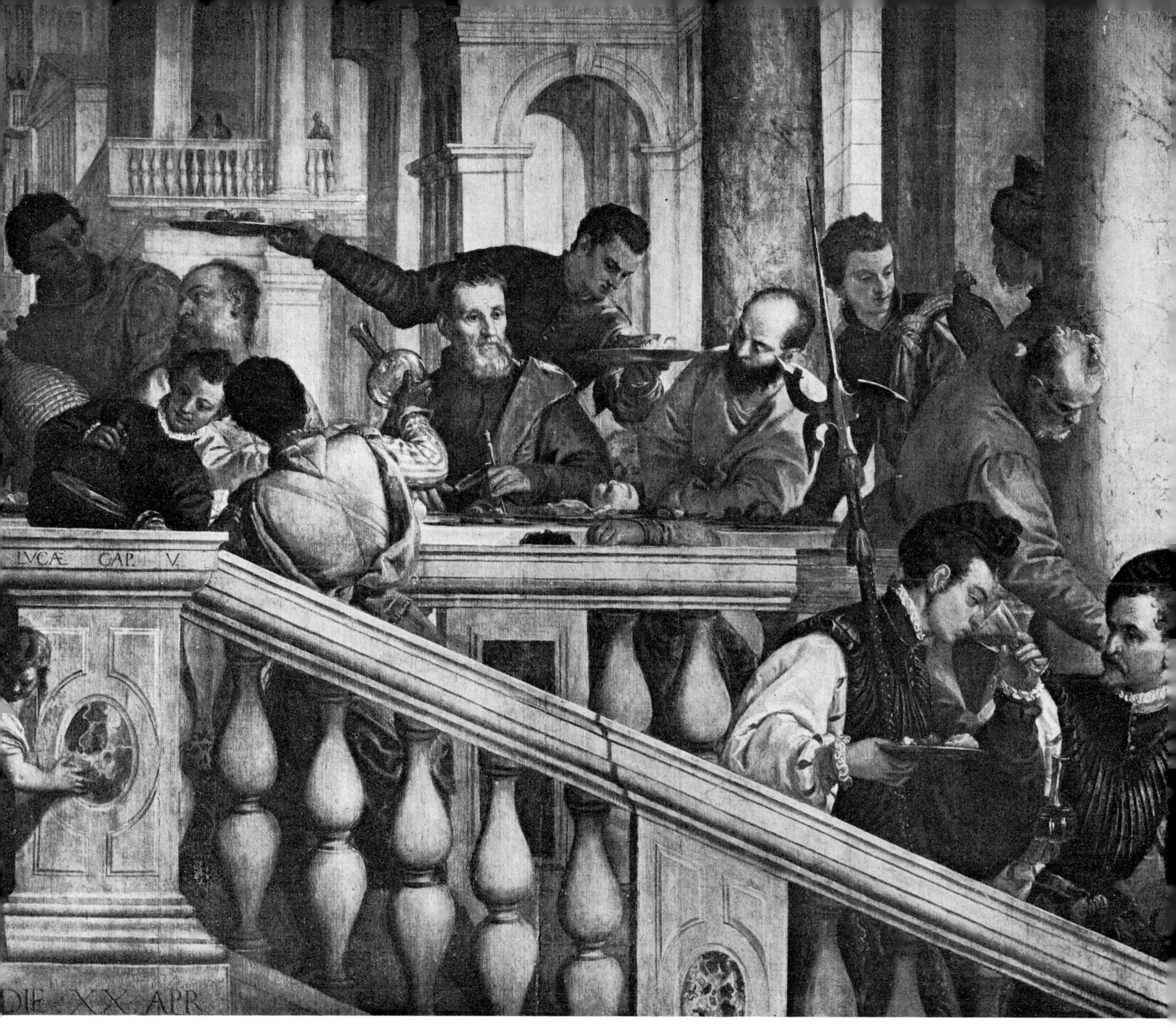
LVCAE CAP. V.
DIE XX APR

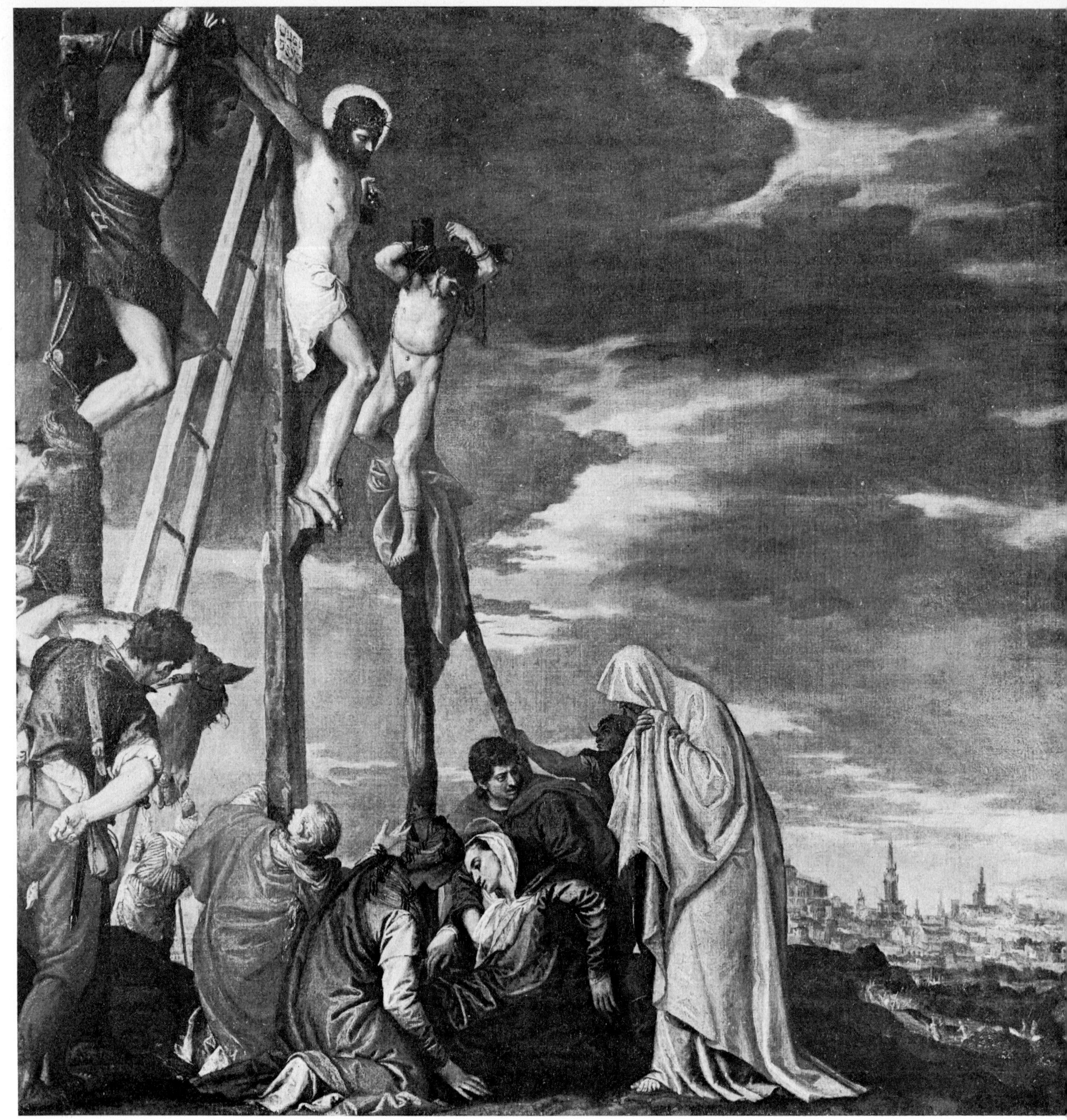

180. PAOLO VERONESE (*c.* 1528–88): *Calvary*. About 1570. Panel, 40 × 40 in. Paris, Louvre

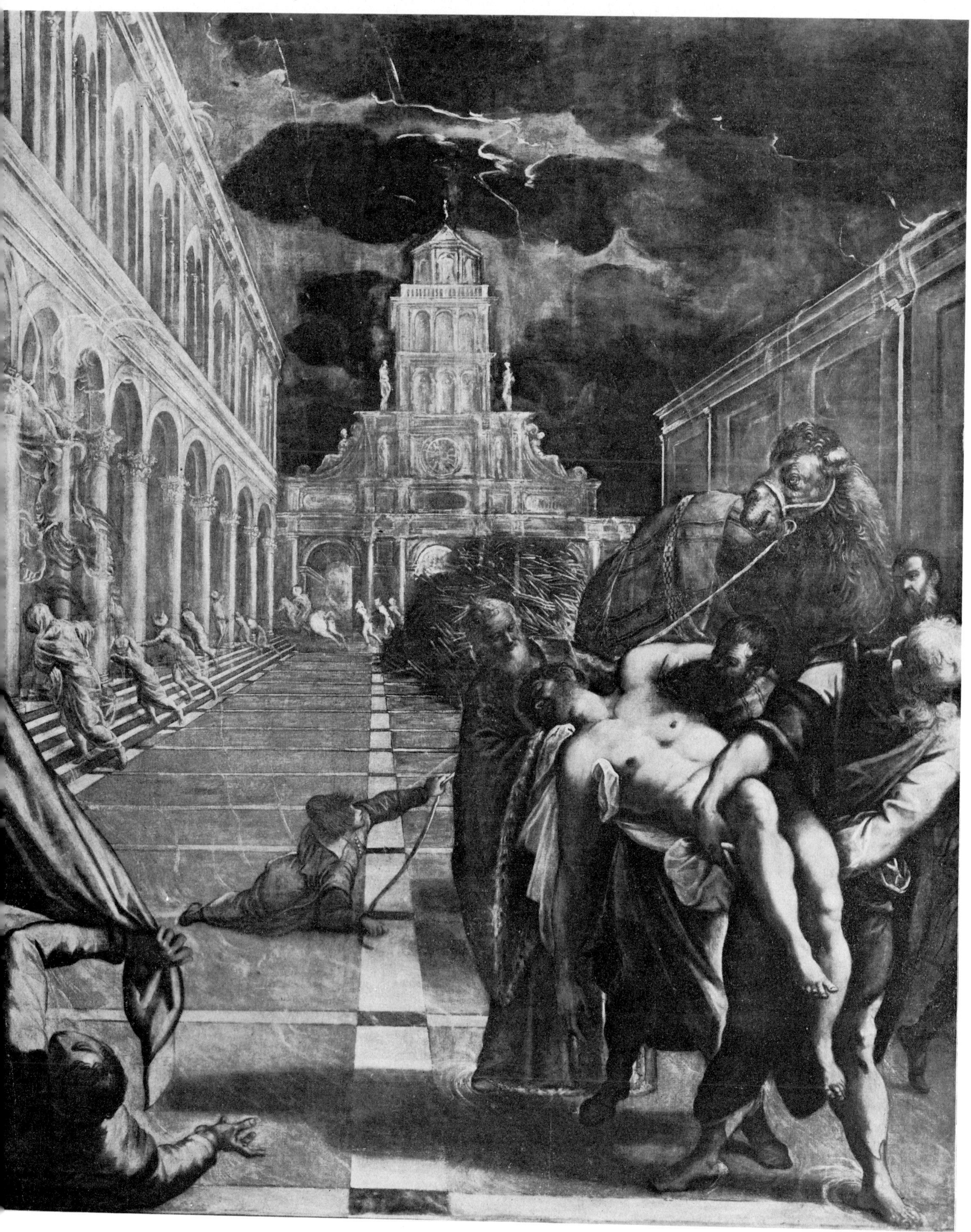

31. JACOPO TINTORETTO (1518–94): *The Removal of the Body of St. Mark from Alexandria*. 1562–6. Canvas, 166 × 124½ in. Venice, Accademia

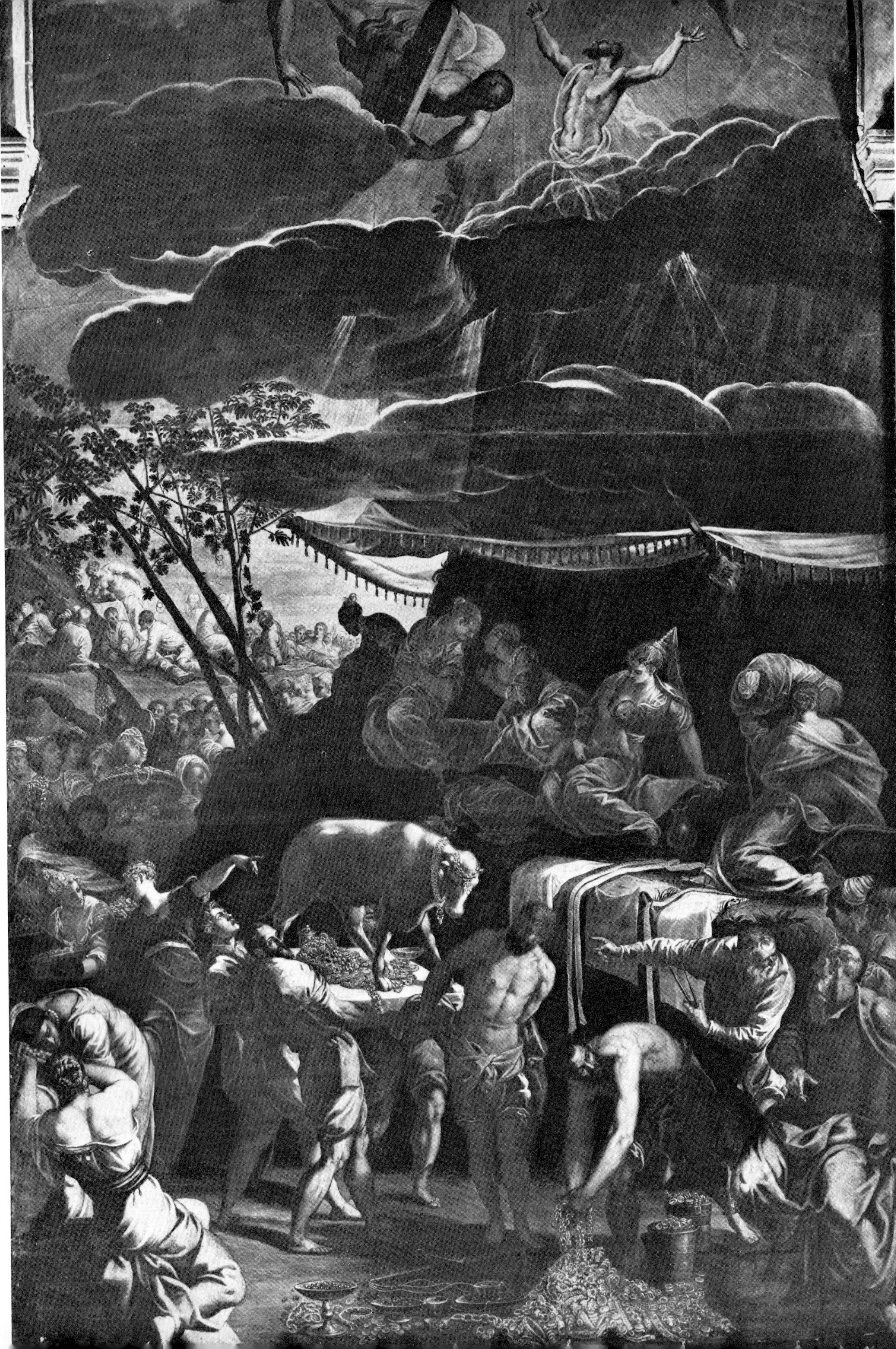

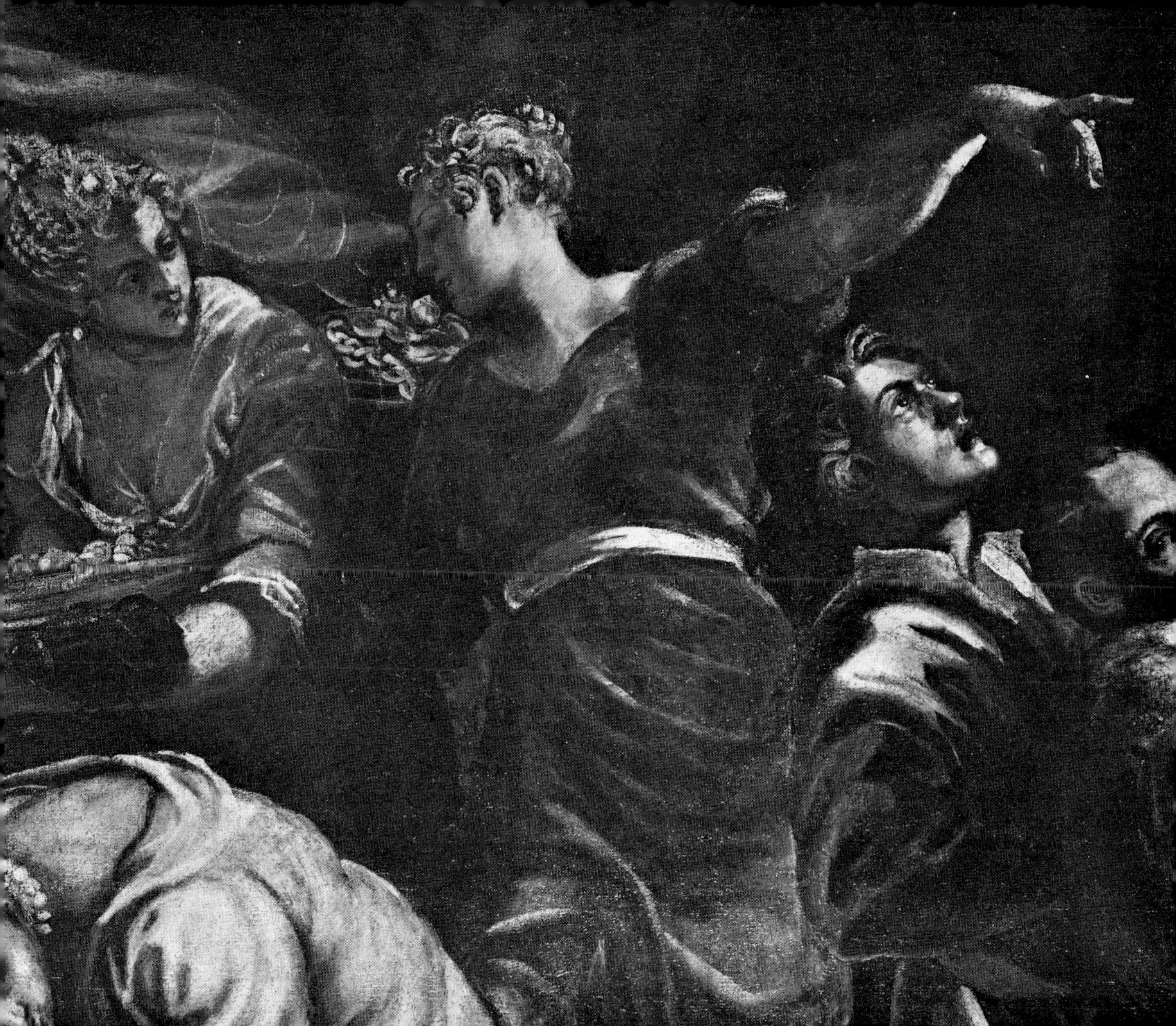

83. JACOPO TINTORETTO (1518–94): *Women Carrying Jewels.* Detail from Plate 182

82. JACOPO TINTORETTO (1518–94): *The Adoration of the Golden Calf.* About 1560. Canvas, 57 × 22¾ in. Detail. Venice, Madonna dell'Orto

When Moses delayed coming down from Mount Sinai the Israelites became impatient. 'And Aaron said unto them, Break off the golden earrings, which are in the ears of your wives, of your sons, and of your daughters, and bring them unto me. . . . And he received them at their hand, and fashioned it with a graving tool, after he had made it a molten calf: and they said, These be thy gods, O Israel . . .' (Exodus 32:3–4) The golden calf has been set up, but there is still plenty of jewellery left, heaped up in the foreground, filling bowls and buckets to the brim, and the women at the left are bringing still more. The children of Israel are all intent upon their idol, except for one who looks up and sees Moses high up on the mountain pleading with God to forgive them their idolatry.

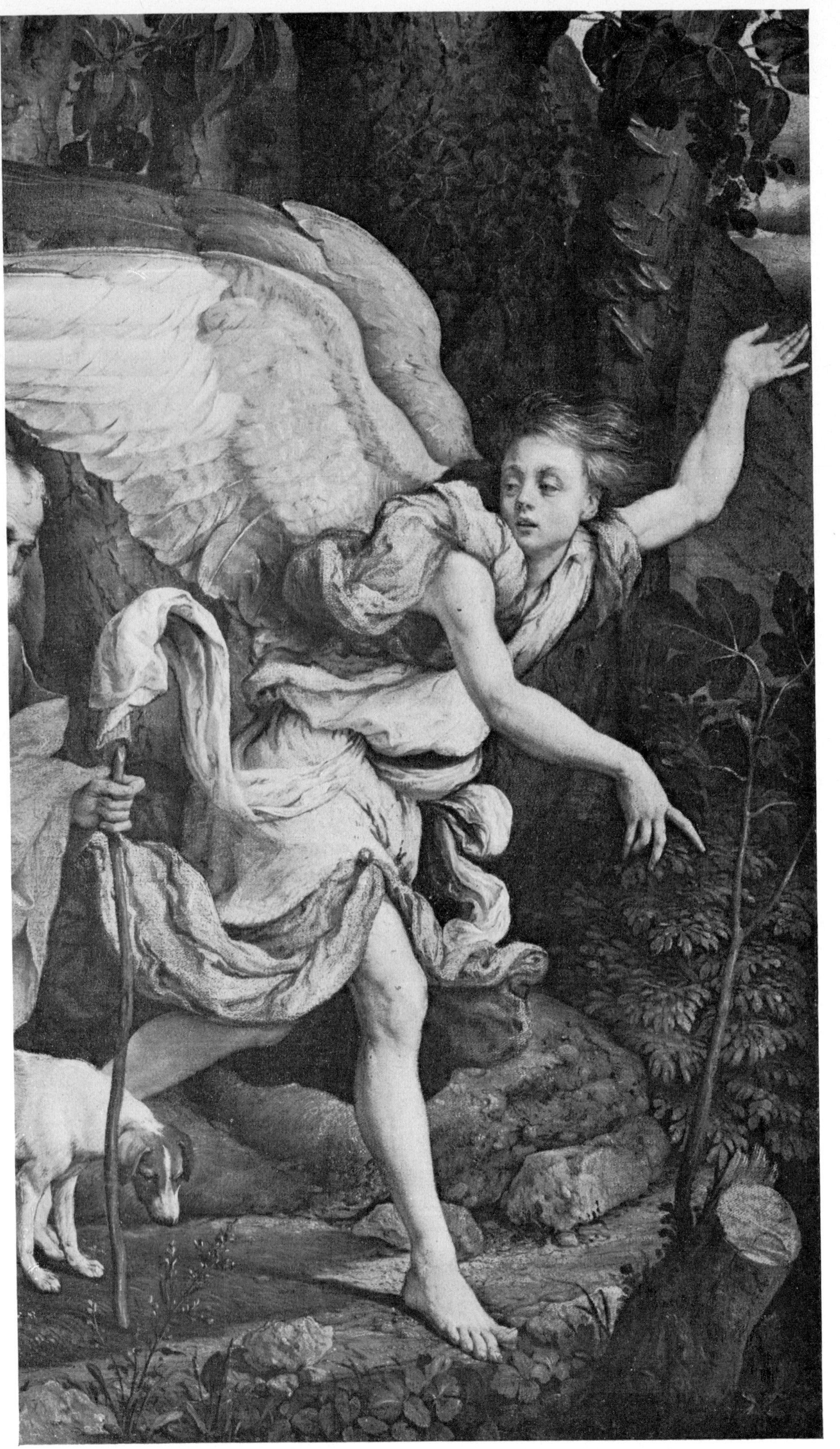

184. JACOPO BASSANO (*c.* 1510–92): *Angel*. Detail from Plate 176
Dressed in swirling drapery the angel strides ahead of the Holy Family and gestures to them to make haste. His windswept hair and the folds of his robe, freely billowing as if arrested in mid-air, impart to his pose a sense of urgency.

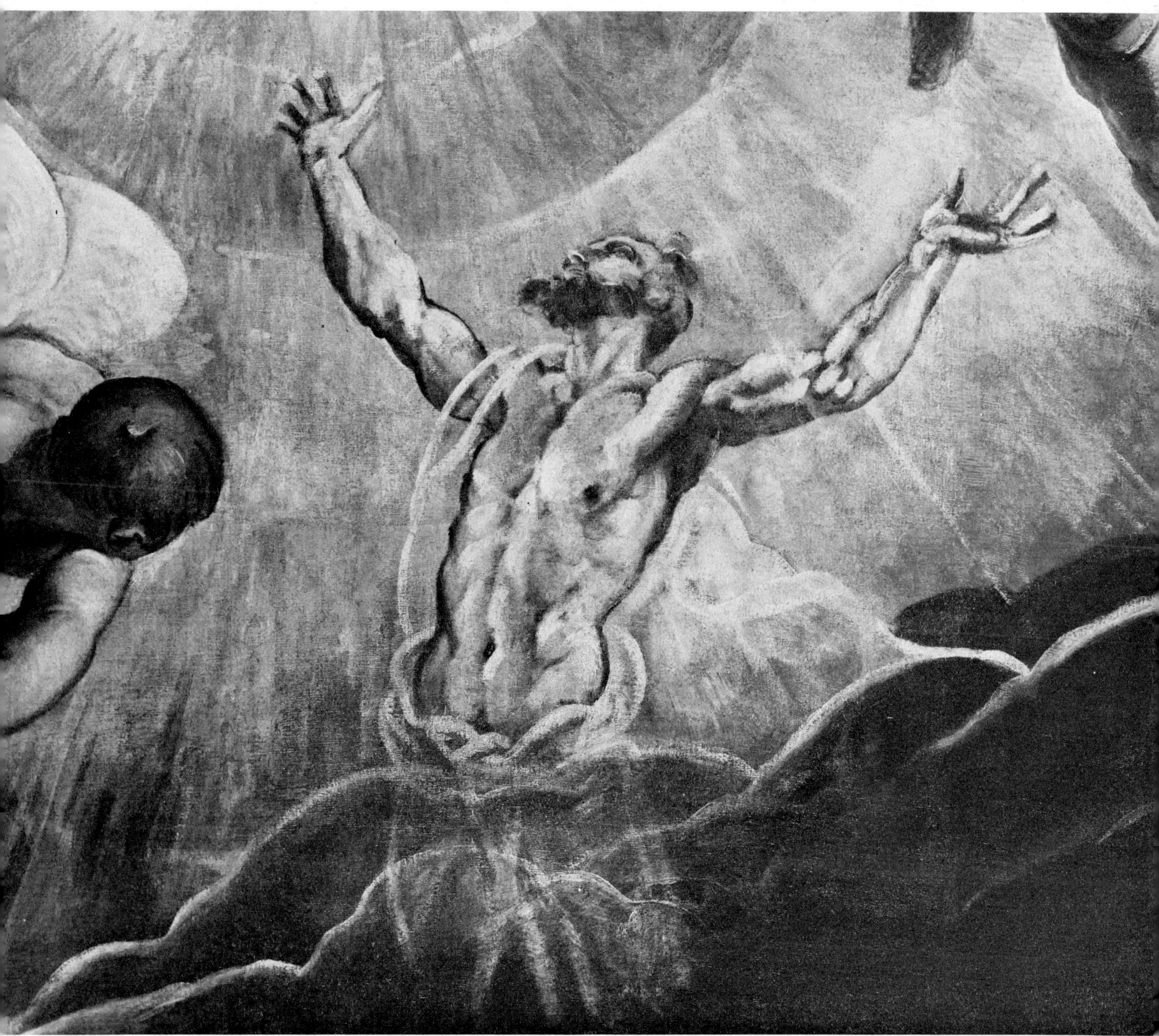

85. JACOPO TINTORETTO (1518–94): *Moses*. Detail from Plate 182

As the rays of divine omnipotence seek out the transgressors down below, Moses has bared his gaunt body like a penitent ascetic and beseeches the Almighty to deal mercifully with his people.

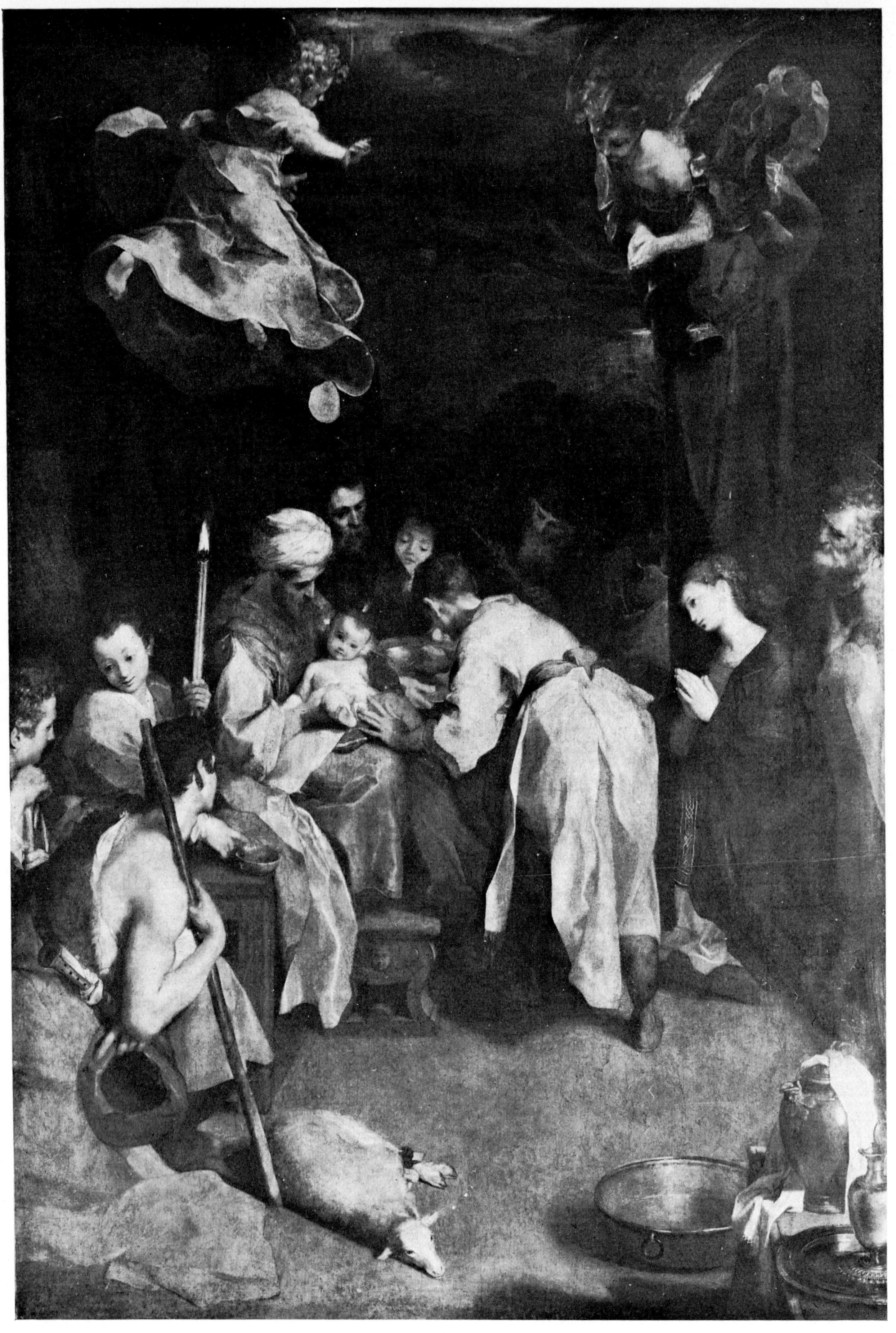

186. FEDERICO BAROCCI (*c.* 1535–1612): *The Circumcision*. 1590. Canvas, 147 × 100 in. Paris, Louvre

87. GIAN GIROLAMO SAVOLDO (active *c.* 1508–40): *Portrait of a Soldier*. About 1525. Canvas, 36 × 48 in. Paris, Louvre

Dressed in an ample costume, the soldier leans back, in a relaxed, informal posture, with pieces of armour scattered around him. In this picture we see an example of Savoldo's preoccupation with light and its effect on tonal values.

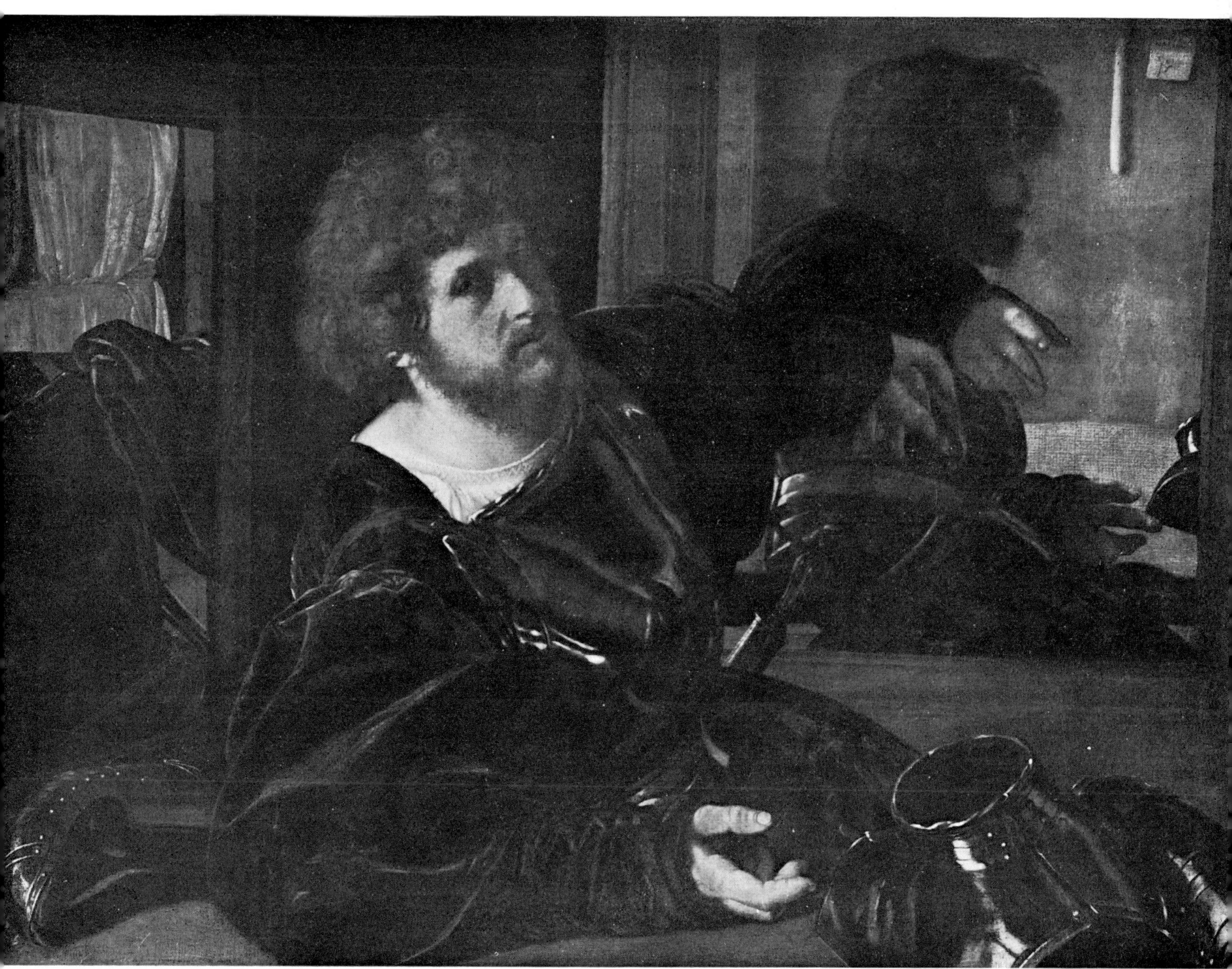

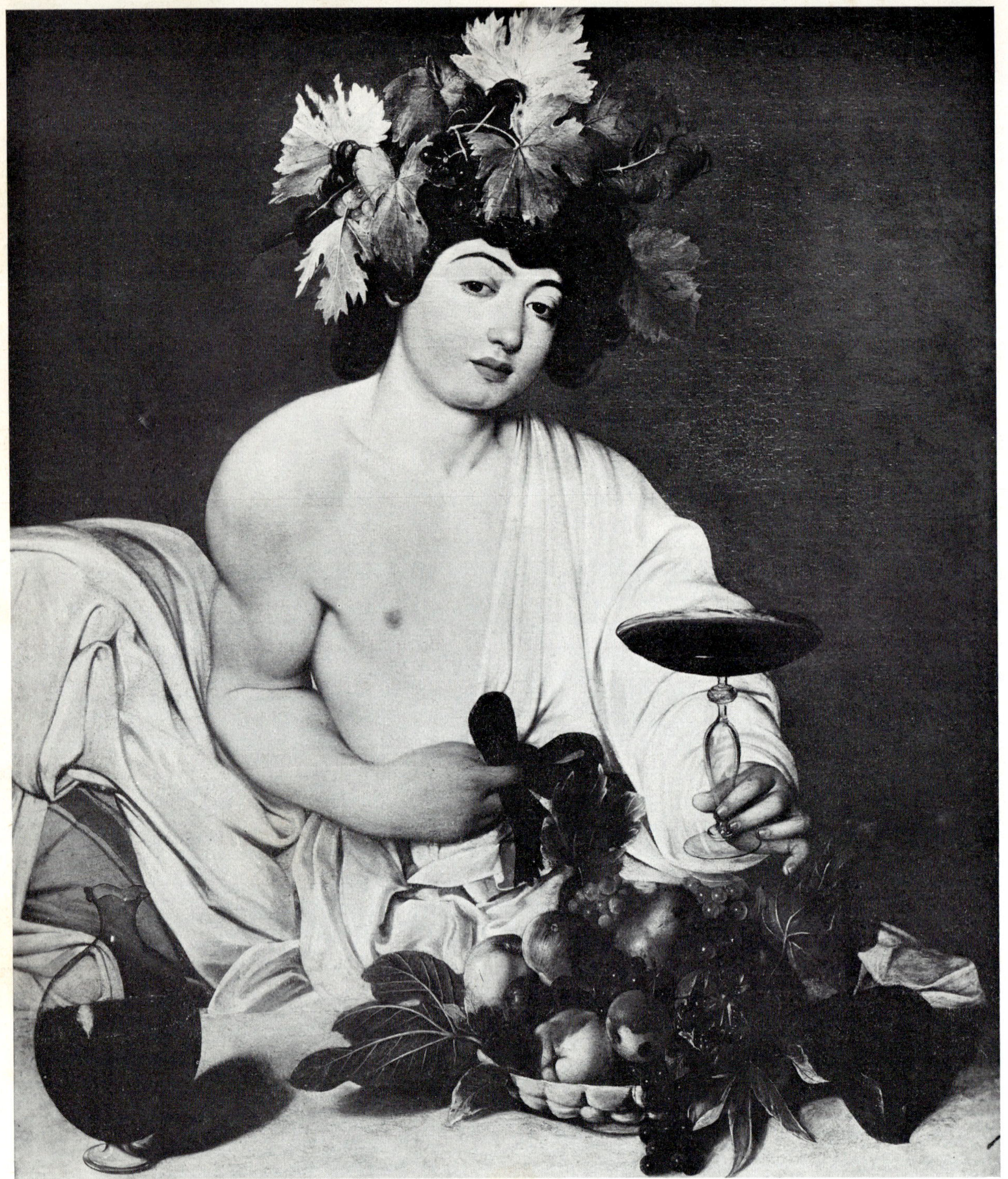

188. CARAVAGGIO (1573–1610): *The young Bacchus*. 1593. Canvas, $38\frac{1}{2} \times 33\frac{1}{2}$ in. Florence, Uffizi

A peasant in the guise of a Greek god—and indeed it was not long before Caravaggio painted peasants as Apostles and other sacred figures, to the great scandal of the faithful. Fruit, vine leaves and goblet are painted with sparkling fidelity and even this youthful work points to the future in the unashamed use of still-life as its dominating feature. But it was painted some years before Caravaggio became the great innovator whose harsh realism and dramatic lighting abandoned every pretence of seeking dignity or following well trodden paths.

Biographical Notes

Andrea del Sarto

Born in Florence in 1486, the son of Angiolo, a tailor (*sarto*), Andrea was first apprenticed to a goldsmith and was then taught for several years by Piero di Cosimo. He studied the cartoons of Leonardo and Michelangelo, and was deeply influenced by the style of the former.

His earliest work is the *Noli Me Tangere* (Florence, Uffizi), dated about 1510. The same year saw the decoration of the entrance to the church of SS. Annunziata, which he frescoed with the *Miracles of San Filippo Benizzi.*

In 1511 he began the decoration, in *terra verde,* of the Chiostro degli Scalzi: the first scene he painted was the *Baptism of Christ,* and the last, in 1526, the *Birth of St. John the Baptist.* During these years his style developed and matured (Plate 135), eventually reaching that masterly fusion of colour, balance, and subtlety with a faultless rhythm and reflective awareness, which finds its best expression in the *Madonna of the Harpies,* painted in 1517 for the nuns of San Francesco and now in the Uffizi. In 1518, invited to the French court by François I, he painted a portrait of the dauphin and the *Charity,* now in the Louvre. When, the following year, the king sent him to Florence to buy works of art, he failed to return to France. He resumed the decoration of the Chiostro degli Scalzi, while at the same time trying his hand at a historical fresco, *Caesar Receiving Tribute* (Poggio a Caiano, 1521). His *Deposition* (Florence, Palazzo Pitti) was painted in 1524 and the *Madonna del Sacco* (Florence, Chiostro dei Morti) in 1525. His style became exaggerated and Manneristic in some of his later works, such as the *Assumption of the Virgin* (Florence, Palazzo Pitti), painted in 1530. His portraits, however, were always penetrating and earnest, revealing much of the personality of both the artist and the sitter. He died in Florence in 1530.

Angelico, Fra

Guido di Pietro, called also Fra Giovanni da Fiesole and widely known as Fra (or Beato) Angelico, was born at Vicchio, in the Mugello near Florence, in about 1399. His art must be seen in the light of two historical factors: first, his efforts to continue the tradition of Trecento painting, with its close links between art and religion; and secondly, the influence of the new trends which began to appear around 1425–30.

At an early age, Guido entered the Dominican convent at Fiesole and probably took his vows in 1408, although some scholars prefer the years 1418–20. During the Great Schism, the Dominicans, feeling in sympathy with the cause of Gregory XII, had to retire to Foligno to escape the hostility of a Florence aligned with Alexander V. In 1418 the friars were allowed to return to Fiesole, and in 1449 Fra Giovanni became prior of the convent.

His earliest work seems to be an *Annunciation,* now lost, probably painted in 1432. The following year he was working on the altarpiece commissioned by the Linen Guild (*Madonna dei Linaiuoli,* Florence, Museo di San Marco), an imposing work clearly showing the influence of the new Florentine approach to problems of space, light, colour and perspective. This style continued in two altarpieces painted before 1440, one for San Domenico, Cortona, and the second for San Domenico in Perugia.

Three works in the Museo di San Marco, datable to the years around 1438–40 and illustrating the theme of the *Sacra Conversazione,* show an even more solid organization of space; the *Coronation of the Virgin* (Paris, Louvre) and the *Annunciation* (Cortona, Museo del Gesù), thought to be from the same period, show an intense appreciation of rhythm; while *The Deposition from the Cross* (Plate 20), with its landscape, its figures and its architectural decor, is one of the artist's most ambitious works. Sometime after 1436 he undertook the decoration of the Convent of San Marco: the frescoes he painted there, notably *The Transfiguration of Christ* (Plate 41), with the help of many assistants, are among his best known and most widely admired works of art.

In 1447 he went to Rome to paint the *Lives of St. Stephen and St. Laurence* in a chapel in the Vatican, and it is thought that one of the assistants who accompanied him was Benozzo Gozzoli. While in the south, he painted a *Last Judgement* in the Chapel of San Brizio, Orvieto. He died in Rome in 1455 and was buried in the Dominican church of Santa Maria sopra Minerva. Little is known of his early training, which was probably as a miniaturist and illuminator and gave him a certain affinity with Lorenzo Monaco and Masolino. After 1430, however, he strongly felt the influence of Masaccio's frescoes in the Cappella Brancacci; the Linaiuoli altarpiece, on the other hand, shows a sculptural style close to Ghiberti, while architectural features contribute to the firm composition of the Cortona *Annunciation*. Here Fra Angelico created a model much repeated by himself and his followers: a loggia with slender columns recalling the style of Michelozzo, a perspective framing the figures and expanding the space around them, an obvious concern with the effects created by the even diffusion of light.

Fra Angelico's greatest influence was on the school of Perugia: the sweetness and grace of his style were here emphasized and deeply affected the work of Perugino himself.

Antonello da Messina

Born probably in 1430, and trained in Naples, Antonello is known to have spent some time in Milan, where he may have come into contact with Petrus Christus and the van Eyck tradition. In 1456 he was back in Naples; his *Salvator Mundi* (London, National Gallery) bears the date 1465, the earliest on any of his pictures. The *Ecce Homo* (New York, Metropolitan Museum) is dated 1470 and the *Polyptych of San Gregorio* (Messina, Museo Nazionale) 1473. In these works the image of piety acquires a new intensity from an increased concentration on the human face. During the same period, Antonello painted a series of remarkable male portraits: the *Portrait of a Condottiere* (Plate 52) is signed and dated 1475, the *Portrait of a Man* (Turin, Trivulzio Collection) 1476. Others are in Cefalù, Pavia (Museo Malaspina) and New York (Metropolitan Museum); only one of them (in Berlin, dated 1478) has a landscape as a background.

Antonello probably spent some time in Rome during the years 1465–73 and he was certainly in Venice in 1475–6, where he executed a large altarpiece for San Cassiano, fragments and copies of which are in Vienna (Kunsthistorisches Museum). He is documented as dying in Messina in 1479.

The Northern influence acquired in Milan is discernible in the naturalism and the articulation of space and figures of the *Crucifixion* (Sibiu, Rumania) and of the *St. Jerome in his Study* (Plate 62). From the Northern masters he also learnt the technique of painting in oil, which gives his pictures their exquisite finish.

The Flemish tradition was abandoned with such works as the *Christ Crucified* (Plate 42), the *Virgin of the Annunciation* (Palermo, Galleria Nazionale), all showing a new monumentality achieved through a masterly use of perspective, light and space. This new style culminated in his later works, the most outstanding ones being the *Polyptych of San Gregorio*, the Syracuse *Annunciation*, the San Cassiano altarpiece and the *St. Sebastian* (Dresden, Gemäldegalerie).

Bacchiacca

Francesco d'Ubertino Verdi was born in March 1495 in Florence, where he died in 1557. According to Vasari he was a pupil of Perugino and a friend of Andrea del Sarto. In 1515–20 he painted *Benjamin Brought before Joseph* and *Joseph Receiving his Brothers* (both London, National Gallery); the panels were meant for a room which was to contain paintings by Andrea del Sarto, Francesco Granacci and Jacopo Pontormo, and show a definite taste for the singular and the rare: the overhanging rocks create a complex and uncertain space in relation to the architecture and the colour is subtle and changing.

About 1525 Bacchiacca went to Rome, where he met Giulio Romano and Benvenuto Cellini. Back in Florence he produced cartoons for tapestries representing the *Months* (1552–3) and *Grotesques* (1549), all in the Uffizi. The cartoons clearly show how his style developed from the Florentine naturalist tradition to become pure Mannerism.

Baldovinetti, Alesso

Born about 1426 in Florence, where he died in 1499, Alesso Baldovinetti became a pupil of Domenico Veneziano and an associate of Andrea del Castagno and Piero della Francesca in the church of San Egidio. In 1453 he was commissioned to decorate with mosaics the soffits above the north door in the Baptistry, and in 1455 those over the Door of Paradise. In 1454 he worked with Castagno in the Ospedale di Santa Maria Novella, where he painted an

Inferno. Among his best works are the *Nativity* (1460–2) for the cloister of the SS. Annunziata, the *Annunciation* (1466), the figures of Prophets, Evangelists and Doctors of the Church executed for San Miniato, and the *Trinity with St. Benedict and St. Giovanni Gualberto* (1470), now in the Galleria dell'Accademia. His better known works, however, are the Madonnas (*Virgin and Child*, Paris, Louvre; *Nativity*, Florence, Annunziata), which are characterized by a striking simplicity and a remarkable sensitivity in their calm features and luminous landscapes.

Barocci, Federico

Born in Urbino around 1535, Barocci died there in 1612. He probably served an apprenticeship in Rome, where he is known to have been again during the years 1560–3. Details of his style indicate that he studied Correggio, from whom he derived his shadowy contours and the delicately mannered grace of his figures. He strove to achieve unusual harmonies and bold effects, but his intimate compositions have a slightly affected charm (*Rest on the Flight into Egypt*, 1573, Vatican Museum). Barocci's great religious works, such as the *Martyrdom of St. Vitalis* (1580–3, Milan, Brera) and *The Circumcision* (Plate 186), are enlivened by an amazing treatment of space and by a delicate attention to fashionable accessories. Barocci's spatial dynamism and his shimmering colours have contributed to his standing as an important forerunner of the Rococo.

Bartolommeo, Fra

Baccio della Porta, born in Florence probably in 1474, became a Dominican in 1500 and assumed the name by which he is best known. He was an apprentice with Cosimo Rosselli and his earliest work, and the portrait of *Savonarola* (1514–17, Florence, Museo di San Marco), shows a severe and restrained style. In 1499 he began a fresco of the *Last Judgement* (Florence, Museo di San Marco) and in 1504 he was commissioned to execute the *Vision of St. Bernard* (Florence, Accademia). After a short stay in Venice, he began to paint large compositions of mystical dialogues, such as the *Marriage of St. Catherine* (Paris, Louvre, and Florence, Uffizi). His last works are often marred by grandiloquence (*Madonna della Misericordia*, 1515, Lucca, Pinacoteca) or by an obvious imitation of Raphael filtered through Andrea del Sarto (*Salvator Mundi*, 1516, Florence, Palazzo Pitti); some of them also show the intervention of his assistant Giuliano Bugiardini, particularly the *Pietà* of 1516–17, now in the Palazzo Pitti, Florence. He died in 1517.

Bassano, Jacopo

Born in about 1510 at Bassano, near Venice, Jacopo was the son of a village artist, from whom he received his training. Around 1534 he was in Venice, where he met Lorenzo Lotto, Palma il Vecchio and Titian, and studied the work of Parmigianino. The most representative works of this period are the *Samson* (*c.* 1538, Dresden, Gemäldegalerie), the *Adoration of the Shepherds* (*c.* 1550, Royal Collection) and the *Beheading of the Baptist* (*c.* 1550, Copenhagen, Nationalmuseet).

Around 1560 his manner became emotional and his colours darker: the influence of El Greco and Tintoretto further developed this style. Among the most notable works of this time are *Susanna* (Nîmes, Musée des Beaux-Arts), the *St. Jerome* (Venice, Accademia), the *Martyrdom of St. Laurence* (Belluno, Duomo) and *St. Paul Preaching* (Marostica, Sant' Antonio). His last works, in which he was helped by his sons, Francesco il Giovane and Leandro, were typical products of the family atelier and greatly contributed to the popularity of luminism in painting.

Bellini, Giovanni

Probably born around 1430, Giovanni, also called Giambellino, was the younger son of Jacopo Bellini, a well known Venetian painter. His early years are obscure but his name appears on an altarpiece painted, together with his father and elder brother Gentile, in 1460. Throughout the 1460s the three worked together, producing large canvases for the Scuola di San Giovanni and the Scuola di San Marco.

Giovanni's first major commission came in 1470: *Noah's Ark* and the *Deluge* for the Scuola Grande di San Marco. However, these pictures were probably never executed because the same commission was given to Bartolommeo Montagna in 1482.

Giovanni developed his personal style in his Madonnas: the early ones, the *Correr Madonna*, the *Davis Madonna*, and the *Crespi Madonna* recall Byzantine icons, but the colours are bright and the landscapes and skies luminous. Mantegna's influence appeared about 1465–70 in the *Madonna* now in Berlin (Staatliche Museen), and the *Transfiguration* (Venice, Museo Correr). Before then, probably in 1464, he painted a series of vigorous panels devoted to the theme of the Passion: the *Blood of the Redeemer* (London, National Gallery), the *Pietà degli Avogadori* (Venice, Doge's Palace), the *Crucifixion* (Venice, Museo Correr), the *Dead Christ* (Milan, Museo Poldi-Pezzoli) and the *Christ Blessing* (Paris, Louvre). *The Agony in the Garden* (Plate 45), painted in about 1465, is similar to Mantegna's but expresses a new kind of spirituality, which achieved yet greater results in a *Pietà* painted around 1470 and now at the Brera. In his later altarpieces (for the Carità, for SS. Giovanni e Paolo and for San Francesco at Pesaro), Giovanni showed the influence of Antonello da Messina and a masterly control of the technique of oil painting: gradually his style developed in an effort to achieve a harmonious structure of space, tonal effects and chromatic unity; his perspective often created a two-way movement of light and the landscapes became a serene celebration of the real world.

Giovanni's extraordinary vitality made him receptive, in old age, to the ideas of Giorgione and Titian. His portrait of *Doge Leonardo Loredan* (Plate 54), dated 1503–4, shows his sensitivity to these artists' fresh spirit and colour effects; in the altarpiece of San Zaccaria, painted around 1505, he made use of deep contrasts between light and shadow and exploited the harmonies between distinct colour and diffuse tonality. This style became deeper and sharper in the *Baptism of Christ* (Vicenza, Santa Corona) dated about 1502, and in two Madonnas, one in Rome (Galleria Borghese) and the other, called *Madonna degli Alberelli,* in Venice (Accademia).

The Bellini workshop dominated the development of Quattrocento art in Venice: all three were alive to the problems of the day, but Giovanni knew best how to assimilate and 'Venetianize' the new trends and influences he encountered during his long career. Mantegna's dryness and severity grew softer and Antonello lent a new intuition of space structured by light. Giovanni, by concentrating on tonal unity, prepared that background of artistic maturity which made possible the reforms of Giorgione and Titian. He died in Venice in 1516.

Botticelli, Sandro

The son of Mariano Filipepi, Sandro was born in Florence about 1445 and died there in 1510. He had three brothers: the eldest, Giovanni, gave him his nickname (*botticello* meaning small barrel); the second, Simone, was a goldsmith's apprentice with whom Sandro trained; and the third, an ardent follower of Savonarola, profoundly affected Sandro with his moral convictions. Sandro probably studied painting with Fra Filippo Lippi, but by 1470 he had his own workshop where, in 1472, Filippo Lippi's son Filippino went to work as his assistant. The influence of Andrea del Verrocchio and, at a later stage, of Antonio Pollaiuolo, is apparent in his youthful works, but by the mid-1470s his style had become highly personal. One of his earliest paintings, dated 1470, is the allegory of *Fortitude* (Florence, Uffizi), which displays the linear vigour of Pollaiuolo; another, *Judith with the Head of Holofernes* (Uffizi), combines fullness of form with richness of tone. In 1475 Giuliano de' Medici commissioned him to execute a banner depicting Pallas (Uffizi) for a tournament, and in 1476–7 Cosimo de' Medici and his family were portrayed as the magi in *The Adoration of the Magi* (Uffizi), which was painted for Santa Maria Novella. To the same period belong several portraits, outstanding for the precision and strength of the drawing as well as for the discernment of the sitter's personality.

Botticelli's unique position in Florentine society and particularly his close association with the Medici are revealed by the allegorical works he was commissioned to paint for the Medici villas: '*La Primavera*' (Plates 71, 72), dated around 1477–8, and *The Birth of Venus* (Plate 38) of about 1485–90. The panel of *Mars and Venus* (Plates 75, 76), dated 1483–5, is also stylistically close to the two better known works.

In 1480, Botticelli painted *St. Augustine*, a fresco for the church of Ognissanti, in which strength and masculinity are striking features. In 1481 he travelled to Rome to contribute scenes from the lives of Christ and Moses to the frescoes of the Sistine Chapel. Back in Florence he contributed frescoes, now destroyed, to Lorenzo's Villa dello Spedaletto and painted a series of allegories, one of which, *The Calumny of Apelles* (Plate 55), is a testimony to his scholarly leanings. He was also in demand for religious works and produced the *St. Barnaba* altarpiece (Uffizi), the *Coronation of the Virgin* (*c.* 1488–90, Uffizi), the *Madonna of the Magnificat* (*c.* 1485, Uffizi), the *Madonna of the Pomegranate* (1487, Uffizi), the *Madonna with Angels* (1490s, Milan, Ambrosiana): the increasing melancholy of these works seems to indicate the beginning of the religious crisis which was to upset his life and influence his art. The two *Pietàs* painted in the early 1490s (Milan, Museo Poldi-Pezzoli, and Munich, Arte Pinakothek) show the effects of Botticelli's reaction to Savonarola, while his increasing sensitivity towards contemporary afflictions appears in *La Derelitta* (Rome, Galleria Pallavicini), the *Mystic Nativity* (London, National Gallery) and the *Mystic Crucifixion* (Cambridge, Mass., Fogg Art Museum), all painted between 1490 and 1497.

Botticelli's supreme achievement as a draughtsman is the series of illustrations on parchment for Dante's *Divina Commedia*, executed before 1497 and now divided between Berlin and the Vatican Library.

Bronzino

Agnolo di Cosimo, the official portraitist to the Florentine ducal court, was born in Florence in 1503 and died there in 1572. Cold, refined, impeccably cultured, with a high level of technical proficiency, Bronzino learnt the controlled Tuscan technique of drawing as an apprentice to Raffaellino del Garbo, but he owes his most influential training to Jacopo da Pontormo, with whom he worked at the Certosa di Val d'Ema in 1522–5. In 1530, expelled from Florence, he entered the court of Guidobaldo II, duke of Urbino; he painted a portrait of the duke (Florence, Pitti) and decorated the Villa Imperiale near Pesaro. In 1532 he was back in Florence, working with Pontormo at Poggio a Caiano. In 1539 he began the decoration of the chapel of Eleonora da Toledo in the Palazzo Vecchio and followed this with a large number of portraits: *Cosimo I de' Medici* (1545), *Eleonora da Toledo and her son Giovanni* (*c.* 1545), *Bartolomeo Panciatichi* (Plate 157), all in the Uffizi.

The *Pietà* executed for Eleonora's chapel and now in Besançon, Musée des Beaux-Arts, shows a rather affected style; similarly exaggerated is the *Allegory* (Plate 160). After Pontormo's death in 1557, Bronzino continued the fresco work in San Lorenzo and completed Pontormo's *Martyrdom of San Lorenzo* in 1569. His last piece, the *Trinity* for the Cappella dei Pittori in SS. Annunziata, dates from 1571. The main interest in Bronzino's work is the overall conception and brilliant brushwork of his portraits, which analyse human character with unusual power; their construction is well balanced and the direct light has a precise value and a precise role. The play of cold tones is as calculated as in Lorenzo Lotto, but here combined with a vigorous contour. He was closely studied and greatly admired by Ingres and other stylists in portraiture.

Caravaggio

Michelangelo Merisi was born at Caravaggio, Lombardy, in 1573. After a brief apprenticeship, he went to Rome at the age of about sixteen. Around 1597 he was commissioned to do a series of paintings for the Contarelli Chapel in San Luigi dei Francesi: the first to be executed was *St. Matthew and the Angel*, followed by *The Calling of St. Matthew* and *The Martyrdom of St. Matthew*. To roughly the same period probably belong the *Bacchus* at the Galleria Borghese, Rome, the *Young Bacchus* at the Uffizi (Plate 188), and the *Medusa*, also at the Uffizi. Early works are fairly traditional (*Rest on the Flight into Egypt*, Rome, Galleria Doria Pamphili; the *Fortune-teller*, Paris, Louvre) and contrast with the artistic revolution which was first expressed in the paintings for San Luigi dei Francesi and which was based on his highly original treatment of light and his realistic rendering of features and details.

Close in date and style to the Contarelli works are the canvases in the Cerasi Chapel at Santa Maria del Popolo, executed in 1600–1: the *Crucifixion of St. Peter* and the *Conversion of St. Paul*.

Caravaggio's life at this time was as troubled as his art was revolutionary; a series of involvements in brawls, fights and other outrageous behaviour led in 1606 to the murder of a man and his flight to Naples. Before leaving Rome he completed the most moving of his religious paintings, the *Deposition* (Vatican, Museum), probably the *David* (Rome, Galleria Borghese) and the *Death of the Virgin* (Paris, Louvre). While in Naples, Caravaggio painted the *Flagellation* (San Domenico Maggiore) and the *Seven Works of Mercy* (Monte della Misericordia).

In July 1608 he went to Malta, where he executed his masterpiece of this period, the *Beheading of St. John the Baptist* (Valletta, Cathedral). Shortly afterwards he moved to Sicily, where he painted a *Burial of St. Lucy* (Syracuse, S. Lucia) and an *Adoration of the Shepherds* (Messina, Museo Nazionale). From here he tried to return to Naples but was forced to move on to Porto Ercole, where he caught malaria and died in July 1610.

Caravaggio's highly controversial and powerful style had a profound effect on many major artists of the seventeenth and eighteenth centuries.

Carpaccio, Vittore

Born about 1460 in Venice, where he died in 1523/6, Carpaccio probably travelled to Dalmatia and the Near East and returned to Venice sometime before 1490. His earliest dated work is the *Arrival of St. Ursula in Cologne* (1490), the first of a large series of paintings for the Scuola di Santa Orsola, Venice, completed in 1498 and now in the Accademia.

From 1502 to 1508 he executed a series of panels on the *Lives of Sts. George, Jerome and Tryphonius* for the Scuola di San Giorgio degli Schiavoni. Dating from the same period are the *Preparations for the Entombment of Christ* (*c.* 1505, Berlin, Staatliche Museen), the *St. Thomas Altarpiece* (1507, Stuttgart, Staatsgalerie), the *Presentation in the Temple* (1510, Venice, Accademia) and *St. Vitale on Horseback* (1514, Venice, San Vitale). These were followed in 1514 by a *St. Roch and Donor* (Bergamo, Galleria dell'Accademia), and in 1515 by the *Martyrdom of the Ten Thousand* (Venice, Accademia). His last recorded works are a *St. Paul* (1520, Chioggia, San Domenico) and organ shutters for the cathedral at Capodistria.

Carpaccio's early style was influenced by the *vedute* of Gentile Bellini, to which he brought a new sense of narrative and atmosphere, particularly in his cycles for the Venetian *Scuole*. Widely known among these is the *Legend of St. Ursula*, in which the individual scenes have the colourful and picturesque setting of Venetian festivals.

Carpaccio was also interested in portraiture: several contemporary faces appear in his processions, and the panel of the *Two Courtesans* (*c.* 1510, Venice, Museo Correr), together with the *Portrait of a Young Knight* (1510, Lugano, Thyssen Collection), are proofs of his ability in this field. Carpaccio was always remarkably competent at arranging the necessary setting, whether it be a landscape, an interior or architecture, and combined the love of form characteristic of the Quattrocento with a Venetian fascination for the opulent and the picturesque.

Castagno, Andrea del

Andrea di Bartolo di Bargilla was born at Castagno, near Florence, about 1421. He probably worked with Fra Filippo Lippi and studied Masaccio before executing the frescoes in the Palazzo del Podestà which depict the hanged adversaries of Cosimo de' Medici. These were painted in 1440; in 1442 he was in Venice to decorate the apse of San Zaccaria. Back in Tuscany, he painted a fresco of the *Madonna and Child with Saints* (1443, Florence, Contini Bonacossi Collection) and, between 1445 and 1450, he decorated the monastery of Santa Apollonia with *The Last Supper* (Plate 101) and three scenes from the Passion. The well known series of *Famous Men and Women*, now in the refectory of Santa Apollonia, was also executed about this time. In 1454 he turned to the SS. Annunziata, where he painted *St. Julian*, a *Trinity* and *Lazarus, Martha and the Magdalen* (the latter now lost). In 1456, the year before he died of the plague, he decorated the cathedral at Florence with an equestrian portrait of *Niccolò da Tolentino* (Plate 30) as a pendant to Paolo Uccello's painting of Sir John Hawkwood.

Correggio

Antonio Allegri was born about 1494 at Correggio, near Reggio Emilia, and he died there in 1534. Many details of his life and career are still unknown. An early group of works attributed to him suggests the influence of Mantegna softened by a delicate *sfumato* which was probably derived from Lorenzo Costa and Leonardo da Vinci. His first authenticated altarpiece is the *Madonna with St. Francis* (1514–15, Dresden, Gemäldegalerie); a series of half-length figures of the Virgin (London, Royal Collection, and Milan, Castello Sforzesco) are attributed to the years 1514–17 and show the same care in imparting a rhythmic movement to softly modelled forms.

In 1517–18 he was probably in Rome, where he saw the paintings of Raphael and Michelangelo. Back in Parma he produced some of his greatest works. Begun in 1520, the cupola of San Giovanni Evangelista dispenses with all accessory decoration and creates a stable and luminous composition. The cupola of the cathedral, dedicated to the *Assumption of the Virgin* (1524–30), adopts and amplifies the theme of praise of the human body in the flowing lines of the angels.

Correggio's compositions show a predilection for sweeping diagonals (*Madonna della Scodella*, *c.* 1530, Parma, Pinacoteca), a floating rhythm (*Deposition*, *c.* 1522, Parma, Pinacoteca) and complex compositions. From this period date such works as the *Adoration of the Shepherds* (*c.* 1525, Dresden, Gemäldegalerie), the *Madonna with St. Jerome* (*c.* 1525, Parma, Pinacoteca) and *The Virgin and Child Enthroned with St. John the Baptist, St. Geminianus, St. Peter*

Martyr and St. George (Plate 139). In the early 1530s he painted a series of mythological canvasses: *Leda and the Swan* (Berlin, Staatliche Museen), *Jupiter and Io* (Vienna, Kunsthistorisches Museum), *Danae* (Rome, Galleria Borghese) and *Jupiter and Antiope* (Paris, Louvre).

The repercussions of Correggio's art can be felt in the work of Parmigianino, Barocci, Lodovico Carracci, and, at the beginning of the nineteenth century, of Pierre-Paul Prud'hon.

Crivelli, Carlo

Born in Venice about 1435, Carlo Crivelli's last work is dated 1493 and he died in the same year. In 1457 he went to Dalmatia and returned sometime after 1465. In 1468 he was at Massa Fermana, where he painted the polyptych with the *Madonna between Four Saints*; in 1473, in Ascoli Piceno, he completed an altarpiece for the Cathedral (and two for San Domenico), the thirteen parts of which have been reassembled and are now in the National Gallery, London, under the name of the Demidoff Altarpiece. *The Annunciation with St. Emidius* (London, National Gallery) is dated 1486; the *Coronation of the Virgin* (Milan, Brera) was executed in 1493 and marks the end of his career.

Crivelli also painted small devotional panels, like the *Madonna and Child* of the Ancona Museum and the *Virgin and Child* of the Metropolitan Museum, New York.

Domenico Veneziano

Born around 1410 in Venice, Domenico died in Florence in 1461. His life and work are very imperfectly documented, and a number of doubtful attributions have been made. In 1438 he wrote from Perugia to Piero di Cosimo de' Medici asking for a recommendation; the following year he is known to have been paid by the Ospedale di Santa Maria Novella for a series of frescoes, now lost, painted in the choir of San Egidio: in the record of payment, Piero della Francesca is mentioned as one of his assistants. *The St. Lucy Altarpiece* (Plate 10) is thought to date around 1445: the *Madonna* is in the Uffizi while pieces from the predella are dispersed in various museums. About 1445 he painted scenes from the lives of St. Francis and St. John the Baptist in Santa Croce, but only one of them survives.

The *Carnesecchi Tabernacle*, a fresco painted around 1440 and transferred on to canvas in 1852, is in the National Gallery, London, while the tondo with the *Adoration of the Magi*, attributed to Domenico, is in the Staatliche Museen, Berlin. Also attributed to him are a series of portraits now in Washington, New York and Boston.

Dosso Dossi

Giovanni di Lutero was born around 1490 in Ferrara, where he died in 1542. His early style was influenced by Giorgione and Titian: he introduced Giorgionesque romanticism to the school of Ferrara, enriching it with the energetic effects learnt from Titian. His bright atmosphere and warm contrasts are as evident in his *Madonna and Saints* (Modena, Cathedral; Rome, Galleria Nazionale), as in the allegorical and mythological scenes which became his speciality. The *Witches* (Rome, Galleria Borghese; Washington, D.C., National Gallery of Art), the *Rustic Idylls* (New York, Metropolitan Museum), the *Argonauts* (Washington, D.C., National Gallery of Art), and the *Apollo with Musical Instruments* (Rome, Galleria Borghese) are characterized by lyrical landscapes and a lively fantasy.

Ercole de' Roberti

One of the three most important artists of the Ferrarese Quattrocento, Roberti was born around 1450. He owes much to Cosimo Tura and to his teacher Francesco del Cossa, but his own originality is already apparent in the frescoes of *The Months*, painted in 1470 in the Palazzo Schifanoia.

Around 1472 he was in Bologna, where he worked with Cossa on the *Griffoni Altarpiece* (Vatican Museum), painting the predella with the *Miracles of St. Vincent Ferrer*. This was followed by *St. John the Baptist* (Berlin, Staatliche Museen) and by the altarpiece of the *Virgin and Child Enthroned with Four Saints* which he painted in 1480 (Milan, Brera). This shows a new sense of colour harmony, balance of light and elegance of line, without the sharpness of the previous works.

Also around 1480 Roberti painted the portraits of *Giovanni II Bentivoglio* and his wife *Ginevra Bentivoglio* (Washington, D.C., National Gallery of Art); but his major works were the frescoes for the Garganelli Chapel in San Pietro, Bologna, which have disappeared. After 1480 he painted a number of small panels, including the *Gathering of the Manna* (London, National Gallery), the *Pietà* (Plate

44) and the *Way to Calvary* (Dresden, Gemäldegalerie). He returned to Ferrara in 1486, where he succeeded Tura as the official artist of the Este family. He died in 1496, presumably in Ferrara.

Gentile da Fabriano

Born around 1370 at Fabriano, in the Marches, Gentile is first recorded in Venice in 1408, where he painted frescoes, now destroyed, for the Palazzo Ducale. He was in Florence from 1422 to 1425, then in Siena, and in 1427 he decorated San Giovanni in Laterano, Rome, with frescoes, destroyed in the seventeenth century. Most of his work has been lost: from what is left, Gentile is clearly revealed as one of the leading painters of the International Gothic style of the early fifteenth century. He borrowed animal and flower motifs from manuscript illumination and added agility and elegance of line, a courtly refinement and an exquisite romantic atmosphere.

The most characteristic example of his art is the altarpiece of *The Adoration of the Magi* (Plate 6), painted in 1423 and now in the Uffizi (predella in Paris, Louvre); aristocratic silhouettes, elaborate detail, magic pageantry and indifference to realism are the main features of Gentile's charm, which survived long after his death in 1427.

Ghirlandaio, Domenico

The son of Tommaso Bigordi, Domenico was born in 1449 in Florence, where he died in 1494. He set up a workshop with his two brothers and the three soon achieved considerable fame with a style skilfully popularizing the art of Alesso Baldovinetti and Fra Filippo Lippi. The first dated work (1475) is the series of frescoes in the chapel of Santa Fina (San Gimignano, Collegiata); these were followed by commissions for the cathedrals of Pisa and Luca, and by the *St. Jerome*, painted in 1480 for Ognissanti, Florence. In the same year, Domenico executed the *Last Supper* in the refectory. In 1481–2 he contributed the *Resurrection* (lost) and *Christ Calling St. Peter and St. Andrew* to the Sistine Chapel. Back in Florence, he decorated the Sala dei Gigli in the Palazzo Vecchio and the Sassetti Chapel in Santa Trinita with the *Life of St. Francis* and the *Adoration of the Shepherds* (1485), and the choir of Santa Maria Novella with scenes from the *Life of the Virgin* (Plate 64) and the *Life of St. John the Baptist* (1486–90).

Among his best works are *The Visitation* (Paris, Louvre), the *Portrait of Giovanna Tornabuoni* (Plate 91) and the *Portrait of an Old Man and a Boy* (Plate 53).

Giorgione

Born around 1477 near Treviso, Giorgio Barbarelli died in Venice in 1510. Little is known about his career and the catalogue of his work is incomplete and conjectural. A document dated 1508 refers to the frescoes for the facade of the Fondaco dei Tedeschi, Venice, while in 1510 Isabella d'Este inquired about a nocturne left by the recently deceased painter. In 1568 Vasari described Giorgione's career as developing from an apprenticeship with Giovanni Bellini and the discovery of Leonardo.

About twenty paintings are attributed to him: *The Trial of Moses* and *The Judgement of Solomon* in the Uffizi; the *Boy with a Flute* (London, Royal Collection) and the *Boy with an Arrow* (Vienna, Kunsthistorisches Museum), the *Holy Family* in Washington and *The Adoration of the Magi* in the National Gallery in London. A later group, dated after 1500, comprises the *Judith* in the Hermitage, Leningrad; the altarpiece of the *Madonna with Sts. Francis and Liberale*, dated 1504 and still in the cathedral of Castelfranco Veneto; *The Adoration of the Shepherds* (Plates 88, 89); the *Laura* of 1506 (Vienna, Kunsthistorisches Museum), the *Portrait of a Man* (San Diego, Fine Arts Gallery), *The Tempest* (Plate 86), the *Three Philosophers* (Vienna, Kunsthistorisches Museum), the *Madonna Reading* (Oxford, Ashmolean Museum), the *Portrait of a Man* (Berlin, Staatliche Museen), the *Sleeping Venus* (Dresden, Gemäldegalerie) and possibly the *Fête Champêtre*. Probably his last works are the *Portrait of an Old Woman* (Venice, Accademia) and *Christ Carrying the Cross* (Venice, Scuola di San Rocco).

When Giorgione began to paint with Bellini, Venetian art had moved away from Mantegna's plasticity to a vision dominated by colour and light. Giorgione's work soon reveals Bellini's and Leonardo's influence in his sensitive landscapes, softening contours and vibrant atmosphere. He had a predilection for twilights and sunsets, overcast skies, flashes of light suddenly bursting through the clouds. His vision was both realistic and dreamlike, a fusion possibly culminating in the *Fête Champêtre*. He left many canvases unfinished: these were completed by Sebastiano del Piombo, Palma il Vecchio and Titian, all painters who were deeply influenced by his style.

Giotto

Giotto was born, perhaps in 1266 or less probably in 1276, at Colle di Vespignano, near Florence. Vasari called him the founder of modern painting; he is said to have been a pupil of Cimabue and was probably strongly influenced by Nicola and Giovanni Pisano. In his art, for the first time, human beings convey deep emotions: his simple, monumental figures are set in a space which adds the force of naturalism to the Christian message they express.

The frescoes depicting the *Life of St. Francis* in the basilica of San Francesco at Assisi have long been attributed to him, but this is now often contested on the grounds of stylistic differences between this cycle and the decoration of the Arena Chapel, Padua (Plate 2).

The Arena frescoes were probably begun soon after 1305 and finished by 1309–10. They include a *Last Judgement*; scenes from the life of St. Joachim and St. Anne, and from the life and passion of Christ; an *Annunciation* and allegorical figures of the Virtues and Vices. The paintings exemplify Giotto's use of simple architectural forms as compositional elements (*The Meeting of Joachim and Anne at the Golden Gate*), the sculptural quality of his figures and the deep emotions expressed both in their features and by their volumes (the *Lamentation over Christ*).

The same artistic elements are obvious in the later frescoes in Santa Croce, Florence, where he decorated the Bardi Chapel with scenes from the life of St. Francis and the Peruzzi Chapel with scenes from the lives of St. John the Baptist and St. John the Evangelist.

But Giotto's art was not limited to frescoes. Before 1300 he was in Rome, working for Cardinal Stefaneschi; dating from this period and attributed to him are fragments of a mosaic and of a fresco and the *Stefaneschi Altarpiece* in the Vatican Museum. Among his few signed works are the three altarpieces in the Louvre, in Bologna, and in Santa Croce, while the *Ognissanti Madonna* (Florence, Uffizi), the *Dormition of the Virgin* (Berlin, Staatliche Museen) and the *Crucifix* in Santa Maria Novella are attributions. Before his death in 1337, he had also begun work on the Campanile next to the cathedral in Florence.

Giovanni di Paolo

Born probably in 1399 and active in Siena between 1420 and 1482, Giovanni's name is mentioned for the first time in 1423. Influenced by Sassetta and Gentile da Fabriano, he soon became one of the masters of Sienese Quattrocento. His style is characterized by violent colours and a vigorous interpretation of reality which gives his paintings a dream-like quality.

His main works are a *Madonna and Child with Angels* (1426, Castelnuovo Berardenga, Propositura); a polyptych of the *Madonna and Child with Saints* dated 1445 (Florence, Uffizi); a *Presentation of Christ in the Temple* (1447–9, Siena, Pinacoteca); the *Miracle of St. Nicholas of Tolentino*, a panel from a predella dated around 1455 and now in the Museum of Art at Philadelphia; the *Last Judgement* in the Pinacoteca at Siena, painted around 1460–5; the *Six Scenes from the Life of St. John the Baptist* in the Art Institute at Chicago, and *The Annunciation* (Plate 14).

Giulio Romano

Both Mannerist painter and architect, Giulio Pippi was born in Rome in about 1499 and died in Mantua in 1546. Raphael's favourite pupil, he executed cartoons for the Sala dell'Incendio in the Vatican; he also contributed paintings to the decoration of the Loggia di Psiche in the Villa Farnesina, and had a hand in some of Raphael's paintings. In 1524 he arrived in Mantua, where he worked mainly as an architect, giving the city its cathedral and various palaces, including the Palazzo del Tè built between 1525 and 1535. The apartments of this palace are decorated with frescoes and oil paintings, all the work of Giulio Romano and his pupils; the story of Psyche is illustrated in the hall, amorous scenes in the upper rooms, and the famous *Fall of the Giants* (Plate 159), a triumph of illusionistic Mannerism, in a room in the south-east wing.

His decorative style was propagated by Francesco Primaticcio and probably influenced Rubens.

Gozzoli, Benozzo

Born in Florence in about 1421, Gozzoli was a goldsmith's apprentice before he joined Lorenzo Ghiberti at work on the Baptistry doors. He later became assistant to Fra Angelico and travelled with him to Rome and Orvieto. In 1459 the Medici commissioned him to decorate the chapel of their Florentine palace (Palazzo Medici-Riccardi) with frescoes which are Gozzoli's most imaginative work: *The Journey of the Magi* (Plate 13).

These frescoes were followed by some less imaginative works: altarpieces (*Virgin and Child Enthroned among Angels and Saints*, 1461, London, National Gallery); the decoration of the church of Sant' Agostino and of the Palazzo del Popolo at San Gimignano; frescoes in the Camposanto at Pisa representing scenes from the Old Testament.

He died in Pistoia in 1497. His workshop had helped to spread a bright, decorative kind of painting in Tuscany and Umbria which reflected the taste of the 1460s but which by the end of the century was already viewed with indulgence.

Leonardo da Vinci

One of the most famous figures of the Renaissance—artist, scientist, inventor—Leonardo was born at Vinci in 1452. Around 1469 he joined Verrocchio's workshop and, according to tradition, distinguished himself by painting the left-hand angel in his master's *Baptism of Christ* (*c.* 1475, Florence, Uffizi) as well as a small *Annunciation*, now in Paris (Louvre).

A series of *Madonnas*, now in Munich (Alte Pinakothek) and Leningrad (Hermitage), are dated 1477–8; to a slightly earlier date belong the *St. Jerome* in the Vatican and the *Portrait of Ginevra de'Benci* in Washington (National Gallery). The most famous work of this period is, however, *The Adoration of the Magi*, begun in 1481 and left unfinished (Plate 63).

In 1482 Leonardo left Florence for the court of Ludovico il Moro in Milan. Here he first worked on studies for an equestrian statue of Francesco Sforza, but never executed it. In April 1483 the Confraternity of the Immaculate Conception commissioned a painting for the church of San Francesco: *The Virgin of the Rocks* (Paris, Louvre); three years later Leonardo started work on a copy of this picture, which is now in London (Plate 80). During these years he also painted two portraits, the *Lady with an Ermine* (1483, Cracow, Czartoryski Collection) and the *Portrait of a Musician* (*c.* 1485, Milan, Ambrosiana).

In 1495 he began work on the fresco of *The Last Supper* for the Refectory of Santa Maria delle Grazie, which he finished in 1498 (Plate 102). During these Milanese years he became deeply involved in problems of architecture and began to write numerous theoretical treatises, including his *Treatise on Painting*.

In February 1500, Leonardo was in Mantua, and two months later in Venice to plan the city's defences against the Turks. At the end of April he arrived back in Florence. In October 1503 he was commissioned to execute a fresco, of which only drawings remain, of the *Battle of Anghiari* for the Palazzo Vecchio. Around the same time he probably started work on the *Portrait of Mona Lisa* (Plate 125) and on the cartoon of *The Virgin and Child with St. Anne* (Plates 85, 128, 129), which he finished about 1510.

In 1506, Leonardo went back to Milan with Charles d'Amboise. There he undertook the monument to the *condottiere* Trivulzio, which again he left unfinished when, in 1512, he left Milan to follow Giuliano de'Medici to Rome. At Giuliano's death in 1515 he left for Amboise at the invitation of François I; as engineer to the king he drew up plans for the castle of Romorantin. He died at Le Clos-Lucé in May 1519.

As painter and sculptor Leonardo owed his technique to Verrocchio; although his genius already shows in *The Adoration of the Magi*, it was under the influence of new surroundings, in Milan, that he began to emerge in all his stature. In *The Virgin of the Rocks*, in the St. Anne cartoon, in his portraits (*Ginevra de'Benci*, *La Belle Ferronnière*), traditional subjects were given a personal interpretation and his suggestive *sfumato* technique made its first appearance. The compositions were carefully arranged according to geometrical rules. Landscapes were given a new life and portraits a new physiological and psychological reality, the result of years of meditation, research and experiments.

Leonardo's influence showed itself in Lorenzo di Credi and Piero di Cosimo, Giovanni Boltraffio, Ambrogio de' Predis and Bernardino Luini; without him Raphael and Andrea del Sarto would probably not have achieved such a high degree of artistic discipline.

Lippi, Filippino

Filippino was probably born in 1457 at Prato, where his father, Fra Filippo Lippi, was at the time chaplain in the convent of Santa Margherita. He trained first with his father and then, from 1472, with Botticelli, whom he accompanied to Volterra in 1483 to decorate the Medici's Villa Spedaletto. Ten years later he worked in another Medici villa, at Poggio a Caiano. After Volterra, he turned to the Brancacci Chapel, where he painted frescoes of St. Peter and St. Paul; to the same period belongs the *Vision of St. Bernard*, a masterpiece now in the church of the Badia.

Between 1487 and 1502 he was engaged in the decoration of the Strozzi Chapel in Santa Maria Novella (the *Story of St. Philip and St. John*). In Rome, where he went in 1488, he painted allegories in the Caraffa Chapel, Santa Maria sopra Minerva.

Some of his best known works include the *Adoration of the Magi* (1496, Florence, Uffizi), the *Marriage of St. Catherine* (1501, Bologna, San Domenico) and *St. Sebastian* (1503, Genoa, Palazzo Bianco). He understood better than anyone the grace of Botticelli, which he combined with Flemish naturalism, Masaccio's solemnity and Leonardo's liveliness. He died in Florence in 1504.

Lippi, Fra Filippo

Born in Florence probably in 1406, Fra Filippo joined the Carmelites at the age of eight, took orders in 1421 and was first recorded as a painter in 1431. In 1434 he was in Padua, where he painted the *Virgin of Humility* (Milan, Castello Sforzesco). In 1437 he returned to Florence, where he was soon considered a master. To this early period belong the *Virgin and Child* (Tarquinia, Museum) and the *Virgin Surrounded by Angels and Saints* (Paris, Louvre). In 1442 he was appointed rector and abbot of the parish of Legnaia, near Florence; datable to this period are the *Annunciation* in San Lorenzo, Florence, the *Coronation of the Virgin* (Florence, Uffizi), and the Bartolini Tondo: a *Virgin and Child with Scenes from the Life of the Virgin* (Florence, Palazzo Pitti), which shows his mastery in the organization of space and in the decorative use of colour and lines. In 1452 Fra Filippo was in Prato working on the frescoes in Santo Stefano. These took twelve years to complete and show how he could employ elaborate perspective and strong compositional organization, although he never accepted the importance attached by his contemporaries to spatial and plastic values.

In 1456 Fra Filippo was chaplain at the convent of Santa Margherita and painted a large altarpiece for its chapel (Prato, Museum). Here he also met the nun Lucrezia Buti, who was to become the mother of his son Filippino. A year later, the Medici, always his faithful patrons, commissioned a triptych for the King of Naples. Although famous mainly for his Virgins, Filippo Lippi painted several Nativities: two are now in the Uffizi and one is in the Staatliche Museen in Berlin. His last work was the decoration of the apse of Spoleto Cathedral with frescoes which included a grandiose *Coronation of the Virgin*. He died in Spoleto in 1469.

Lotto, Lorenzo

Moody, unconventional and restless, Lotto, one of the great portraitists of the Renaissance, was probably born in 1480 in Venice. His early works include the portrait of *Bishop Bernardo de'Rossi* (1505, Naples, Museo di Capodimonte), the *Assumption of the Virgin* (1506, Asolo, Cathedral), the *St. Jerome in the Wilderness* (1506, Paris, Louvre), and the *Recanati Polyptych* (1508, Recanati, Pinacoteca).

Invited to Rome in 1509 to contribute to the decoration of the Vatican Stanze, he had to leave when Raphael took over. He then settled in Bergamo, where he painted a large altarpiece of the *Virgin Enthroned with Ten Saints* (1521, Santo Spirito), a *Madonna and Child* (1521, San Bernardino), and the usual *Marriage of St. Catherine* (1523, Accademia Carrara), a sensitive painting where the figures are arranged on receding planes and along oblique lines. The same taste for popular illustration appears in the frescoes for the Oratorio Guardi in Trescore, near Bergamo.

Overshadowed by Titian, he painted very little between 1524 and the late 1530s; he had to abandon his grand style for a more direct manner, as in the *Madonna of the Rosary* (1539, Cingoli, San Domenico) and the *Madonna with Saints* (1546, Ancona, Santa Maria della Piazza). In 1550 he retired to Loreto, where he painted the *Assumption of the Virgin* (1550, Ancona, Pinacoteca) and where he died.

Lotto's portraits are less uneven; they show the smooth technique, straightforward lighting and bold effects of Giovanni Bellini and Alvise Vivarini, together with velvety tonalities of greys and browns and a melancholic, dreamy undertone. The best known are the *Young Man in a Striped Coat* (1526, Milan, Castello Sforzesco), *Andrea Odoni* (Plate 115), and the *Old Man with a Blond Beard* (1542, Milan, Brera).

Mantegna, Andrea

Born in 1430 or 1431, Mantegna's name appears on the Paduan registers for the first time in 1441; he is mentioned as the apprentice and adopted son of Francesco Squarcione, painter and archaeologist. Between 1448 and 1456 he painted the Ovetari Chapel in the Church of the Eremitani, but these early frescoes are badly damaged. During these years he also executed an altarpiece for St. Luke's Chapel in Santa Giustina, a *St. Eufemia* (Naples, Museo di Capodimonte), and *The Agony in the Garden* (Plate 46).

His marriage to Jacopo Bellini's daughter brought him close to those Venetian artists whose influence he was already feeling. One of his best known works, the *San Zeno Altarpiece*, was painted in 1456–9 (predella panels in the Louvre and in the Tours Museum); about the same time he painted the *St. Sebastian* (Vienna, Kunsthistorisches Museum) and several Madonnas.

In 1459 he was called to Mantua by Ludovico Gonzaga and became court painter; his activities during the following years are crowned by the famous frescoes in the 'Camera degli Sposi' in Mantua's Palazzo Ducale (Plates 47, 48, 51), executed in 1473–4, and by the large paintings of the *Triumph of Caesar* (Royal Collection). The *Dead Christ* (Milan, Brera) was painted in 1455–6, and *The Martyrdom of St. Sebastian* (Plate 49, 112) in about 1474. After two short stays in Rome in 1484 and 1488 he continued to paint for the Gonzaga (*Madonna della Vittoria*, 1495, Paris, Louvre) as well as for Isabella d'Este in Ferrara; for the princess's study he painted the *Parnassus* (1497), *Minerva Expelling the Vices from the Grove of Virtue* (1501) and *Comus*, both of them now in the Louvre. He died in Mantua in 1506. Squarcione gave Mantegna his taste for antiquities, and his works show his admiration for a kind of severe, archaeological humanism; his landscapes are often reconstructions of classical architecture, his figures are heavily sculpted and perspective is used to give impressive views from unusual angles. The *St. Luke Altarpiece* suggests some knowledge of Piero della Francesca in its colouring, while in the one painted for San Zeno the interest in antiquity and sculptural modelling predominates. Andrea del Castagno's style is echoed in the *Dead Christ*, and Benozzo Gozzoli was probably at the back of his mind while he was decorating the Camera degli Sposi, although the daring *trompe-l'œil* perspective used here anticipates Bramante, Correggio, Veronese and Tiepolo. A friend of humanists, Mantegna set religious themes and the lives of saints against a background of Roman history, and developed a whole system of ornaments inspired by Greek and Roman reliefs and medals. Through his engravings, in which he excelled, his influence spread throughout Northern Italy and was felt by Vivarini, Giovanni Bellini, the Ferrarese, and Crivelli in the Marches.

Masaccio

Tommaso di Giovanni was born at San Giovanni Valdarno in 1401 and died probably in 1428. Together with Donatello and Filippo Brunelleschi, he was the exponent of that 'heroic' art which flourished in fifteenth-century Florence in opposition to the International Gothic, represented mainly by Ghiberti and Gentile da Fabriano.

The only known date in his life is 1422, the year he joined the Guild. He inherited the tradition of Giotto and his influence was mainly felt through his frescoes in the Brancacci Chapel in Santa Maria del Carmine, Florence (Plate 3).

This famous cycle, begun by Masolino and Masaccio in the mid-1420s, was finished much later by Filippino Lippi. The attribution of the earlier frescoes to either Masaccio or Masolino is a question of style but is by now largely agreed upon. Vasari described an altarpiece, painted by Masaccio in Pisa in 1426; this was later dismembered, but the main panel, a Madonna, has been identified with the one in the National Gallery, London. Other panels have been found in Pisa, Naples (here is the famous *Crucifixion*, in which the emotional drama expressed by the Virgin, Mary Magdalene and St. John is intensified by the plain gold background), Berlin and Vienna. This polyptych can therefore be used as an authenticated example of Masaccio's mature style and compared with the Brancacci frescoes. The scenes safely attributed to Masaccio are *Adam and Eve being Expelled from Paradise* (Plate 18), *The Tribute Money* (Plates 7, 22), *St. Peter Enthroned*, *St. Peter Healing the Sick by his Shadow* and *St. Peter Giving Alms*, together with parts of the *Raising of the Praetor's Son*, which was finished by Lippi.

Most art historians attribute to Masaccio the *Baptism of the Neophytes*, in which a few see the hand of Masolino in the head of St. Peter. The problem of the relationship between the two artists is complicated by the fact that, in some works attributed to Masolino, Masaccio's influence is unmistakable. One of Masolino's altarpieces is now divided between Naples and London: here one of the panels, *St. Jerome and St. John the Baptist*, is very close to Masaccio's style and attributed to him by many authorities.

Other works now safely attributed to Masaccio are the recently discovered San Giovenale triptych, dated 1422 and representing the *Virgin and Child* on a throne with two angels and four saints; *The Virgin and Child with St. Anne* (Plate 127), painted between 1420 and 1424 together with

Masolino, who contributed three angels and the background; and the splendid fresco of *The Holy Trinity* in Santa Maria Novella, Florence (Plates 5, 8). Masaccio's art is one of rugged, austere realism; his severe figures are arranged in a strictly controlled space and lit by a consistent fall of light; the elements of the compositions are subordinated to geometrical and mathematical systems of perspective which turn the picture into a continuation of the real world.

Masaccio's rejection of charming details and embellishments contributed to his lack of popularity among his contemporaries; Michelangelo was probably the first to understand him, as he was the first to realize the true spirit of Giotto's art.

Masolino

Born Tommaso di Cristoforo Fini in 1383, according to Vasarti, Masolino worked for Ghiberti and was apprenticed to the painter Starnina. His first known work is the Gothic *Madonna* (Bremen, Kunsthalle), dated around 1423. During the following two years he worked with Masaccio on the frescoes in the Carmine, Florence, and began the frescoes in San Clemente, Rome. In September 1425 he left for Hungary; on his return two years later he finished the San Clemente frescoes and executed a polyptych for Santa Maria Maggiore, Florence.

In 1432 he worked on a fresco of the *Virgin and Child with Angels* at Todi, and was at Castiglione Olona at about the same time, where he possibly painted the life of St. John the Baptist in the Baptistry and the life of the Virgin in the Collegiata. He died in Florence probably sometime after 1432. Although influenced by Masaccio during the two years they worked together, Masolino's style has its roots in the Gothic art of fourteenth-century Tuscany, as has the work of Gentile da Fabriano and Fra Angelico.

Master of the Barberini Panels, The

One refers by this name to the unknown painter who, about 1470, executed two panels long housed in the Barberini Collection in Rome. The panels represent the *Birth of the Virgin* (now in New York, Metropolitan Museum) and the *Presentation of the Virgin in the Temple* (Boston, Museum of Fine Arts).

Stylistically, the panels show a fondness for spacious perspectives and architectural settings of almost theatrical flavour. On the basis of these features, it has been suggested by some art historians that the painter of the panels might be identified with Giovanni Angelo de Camerino, who was active in the Marches and was associated with artistic circles in Urbino and Perugia.

The Annunciation (Plate 9) is also credited to this painter, and it has been suggested that it was a youthful work, painted some twenty years earlier than the two Barberini panels.

Melozzo da Forli

Michelozzo degli Ambrogi, born in 1438 in Forlì where he died in 1494, was one of the most active of Piero della Francesca's pupils and worked mainly in Rome, Urbino and Loreto. His frescoes for the church of San Marco, Rome, painted around 1465–70, represent the *Redeemer*, *St. Mark the Pope* and *St. Mark the Evangelist*; in SS. Apostoli he painted the *Ascension* (*c.* 1480, Rome, Palazzo del Quirinale) and *Angel Musicians* (Vatican Museum); and *The Inauguration of the Vatican Library*, painted in 1477 and considered a masterpiece of spatial organization and forceful modelling of figures, is also now in the Vatican Museum (Plate 66). Melozzo is known to have contributed to the decoration of the study of Federigo da Montefeltro in the Ducal Palace at Urbino, although it is difficult to separate his share from that of Pedro Berruguete and Justus of Ghent.

With the frescoes for the sacristy of San Marco at Loreto, Melozzo's influence, the last expression of the Quattrocento principles of Piero della Francesca, spread throughout central Italy.

Michelangelo

Born at Caprese in 1475, Michelangelo Buonarroti began his artistic career as an apprentice to Ghirlandaio. He soon joined the informal school run by the sculptor Bertoldo di Giovanni in the Medici gardens, where a large collection of ancient sculpture was gathered; and, by going to live in Lorenzo's palace, he came under the influence of humanists and scholars like Pico della Mirandola and Angelo Poliziano, who introduced him to Neoplatonism. He was drawn to Pollaiuolo's anatomical research and impressed by Jacopo della Quercia and Donatello. Between 1496 and 1501 he was in Rome, where he executed his first *Pietà* (St. Peter's).

Back in Florence for four years, he produced the *David* and the *Bruges Madonna* as well as painting the '*Doni Madonna*' (Plate 106) and preparing the cartoon for the *Battle of Cascina*, a fresco commissioned for the Palazzo Vecchio.

In 1504 Pope Julius II entrusted him with a project for his tomb, only to change his mind in 1506 (the tomb was eventually finished in 1542–5). In 1508 Michelangelo was commissioned to paint the ceiling of the Sistine Chapel: over the following four years, he painted 343 figures within compartments marked by a network of illusionistic frames; they all centre on the theme of the history of humanity between The Creation and Noah and include the Prophets and Sibyls (Plates 4, 105, 108, 109). After 1512 he returned for a while to sculpture (*Moses*, 1516, Rome, San Pietro in Vincoli; *Bound Slaves*, Florence, Accademia, and Paris, Louvre) and his final visit to Florence between 1516 and 1534 was largely occupied with the funerary chapel for the Medici in the New Sacristy of San Lorenzo; the project included a statue of the Virgin and the two tombs of Giuliano de'Medici, Duke of Nemours, and Lorenzo de'Medici, Duke of Urbino.

In Rome, under Pope Paul III, Michelangelo resumed painting with *The Last Judgement* (Plate 162) on the wall behind the altar in the Sistine Chapel. This was followed by two more frescoes, the *Crucifixion of St. Peter* and *The Conversion of Saul* (Plates 163, 165) in the Cappella Paolina.

The last period of his life was devoted to his interest in architecture, an interest already manifested in his designs for the façade of San Lorenzo in Florence (never realized) and for the Bibliotheca Laurenziana, also in Florence, which, although begun in 1524 by Michelangelo, was completed by Ammanati in 1560. In Rome his style achieved an austere majesty in the plans for the Piazza del Campidoglio; he was also an architect of St. Peter's (1546–64), supervising the erection of the tribunes and designing the dome.

His two last works are the *Pietà Rondanini* (1556–64, Milan, Castello Sforzesco) and the *Pietà di Palestrina* (*c.* 1556, Florence, Accademia), both expressions of despair and reminiscent of medieval German art. Michelangelo died in Rome in 1564.

During his lifetime, Michelangelo had witnessed the deep cultural changes which had swept over Italy since the days of the humanist court of Lorenzo de'Medici. After Lorenzo's death, that intellectual world had been threatened by the fulminations of Savonarola. Luther's Reformation had further shaken the most confident aspirations of humanism and probably affected Michelangelo's religious and spiritual outlook. His art, although fixed in the Renaissance, shared in the new feelings of profound unrest, anticipating the Baroque in its dynamic rhythms and in its expression of power, suffering and passion.

Moretto da Brescia

Born around 1498, Moretto (Alessandro Bonvicino) became, with Girolamo Romanino and Savoldo, one of the leading Brescian painters of the sixteenth century. He combined the Venetian tradition with the Lombard heritage of Foppa and Lotto in his innumerable religious paintings and portraits. His altarpieces are classical in composition, his figures austere and realistic (*St. Justina, c.* 1530–5, Vienna, Kunsthistorisches Museum; *Madonna with St. Elizabeth and Two Donors*, 1541, Berlin, Staatliche Museen).

His portraits show the same firmness of features and a skilful use of the texture and colours of fabrics (*Portrait of a Gentleman*, 1526, London, National Gallery; *Portrait of a Woman*, *c.* 1535–40, Vienna, Kunsthistorisches Museum).

The quiet strength of his outlines and the peaceful spirituality of his art represent a visual contrast to the experiments of contemporary Venetian painters; his style, particularly as expressed in his portraits, was continued by his pupil Giovanni Battista Moroni.

Moretto died in Brescia in 1554.

Moroni, Giovanni Battista

A pupil of Moretto da Brescia, Moroni was born around 1525 near Bergamo and died in 1578. In Bergamo he spent most of his career mainly executing altarpieces (*Coronation of the Virgin*, 1576, Bergamo, Sant' Alessandro della Croce).

His best work, however, consists of the large quantity of portraits which show a conception of portraiture quite unlike the rather monotonous traditional one. His paintings, which were praised by Titian himself, usually show the sitter at half-length (*Antonio Navagero*, 1565, Milan, Brera; *Portrait of a Tailor, c.* 1570, London, National Gallery), or full-length, such as the *Portrait of a Gentleman* (Plate 138). His compositions are simple but expressive, his execution is free from pre-occupation with details, his colours sober with silvery tones or based on an interplay of blacks, greys and whites. While the psychological insight remains superficial, a delicate melancholy gives Moroni's works the charm and poetry which made them famous.

Parmigianino

Francesco Mazzola, called Parmigianino, was born in Parma in 1503, and is one of the best known Mannerist painters. At first influenced by Correggio, he later turned to Domenico Beccafumi and Giovanni Pordenone; during his stay in Rome in 1524 he came into contact with Raphael, Michelangelo and Sebastiano del Piombo. All these influences were gradually fused into a highly personal art, in which the virtuosity acquired during the early period (*Self-portrait* [Plate 156]) highlighted an imagination increasingly divorced from reality. In 1527 he went to Bologna, where he stayed until 1531. His most important works of this period include *St. Roch with a Donor* (1527, Basilica of San Petronio), *The Madonna of the Rose* (1528–30, Dresden, Gemäldegalerie), and the *Madonna with St. Zacharias, St. Mary Magdalene and St. John* (*c.* 1530, Florence, Uffizi), all of which demonstrate his powerful and elegantly rhetorical style.

Back in Parma, he executed the frescoes in Santa Maria della Steccata and, probably in 1535, the famous *Madonna of the Long Neck* (Plate 167), in which the virtuosity of his elegant lines and unusual forms is carried to the extreme.

During the last years of his life (he died in 1540) Parmigianino seemed to opt for greater austerity (*Madonna with St. Stephen and St. John the Baptist*, 1538–40, Dresden, Gemäldegalerie).

Parmigianino also painted some remarkable portraits (*Gian Galeazzo Sanvitale*, 1524, and *Lady with a Fur*, also called *Anthea*, 1535–37, both in Naples, Museo di Capodimonte). His style, widely appreciated, influenced such painters as Primaticcio and Niccolò dell'Abbate, and, in openly clashing with Michelangelo's, was at the heart of all subsequent Mannerist works.

Perugino, Pietro

Perugino (his real name was Pietro Vannucci) was born around 1445 in Umbria, where he died in 1523. Little is known about his early years except that in 1472 he was in Florence working with Andrea del Verrocchio. Back in Perugia in 1473 he painted panels of the *Life of St. Bernardino*; his first signed work is *St. Sebastian*, a fresco executed in 1478 in the parish church of Cerqueto. In 1481 he worked in the Sistine Chapel, assisted by Pintoricchio: his contribution, which made him famous, is the *Delivery of the Keys to St. Peter*. Among his numerous works, one should mention the *Virgin and Child Enthroned* (1491–2, Paris, Louvre), the *Madonna and Saints* (1497, Fano, Santa Maria Nuova), the *Nativity* (1481, Rome, Villa Albani), *Christ in the Garden of Olives* (Florence, Uffizi), the *Pietà* (Florence, Palazzo Pitti), the *Crucifixion* (Florence, Santa Maria Maddalena), and an altar triptych (London, National Gallery). In 1550 he decorated with Raphael the audience chamber of the Collegio del Cambio in Perugia, and in 1503 he was employed by Isabella d'Este. His style is characterized by clearly organized space and harmonious composition, and the influence of his work on Raphael's development is apparent from paintings such as the Sistine fresco.

Piero della Francesca

Born sometime before 1420 at Borgo San Sepolcro, where he spent most of his life (he died there in 1492), Piero was rediscovered by modern art historians after three centuries of obscurity. He is now considered a major Quattrocento painter.

He appears for the first time in 1439 when, with Domenico Veneziano, he painted frescoes in the Cappella Maggiore of the Church of Sant' Egidio in Florence. After 1442 he was active in Tuscany as well as Ferrara, Rimini and Urbino; in 1445 the Confraternity of Mercy at Borgo San Sepolcro commissioned him to paint an altarpiece, later finished by his assistants: the central panel, the *Madonna della Misericordia*, almost certainly entirely by him, is now in the Museo Comunale. To the same period belong *The Baptism of Christ* (Plate 34) and *St. Jerome with Donor* (Venice, Accademia); some art historians believe that *The Flagellation of Christ* (Plate 29) was painted between 1445 and 1450, as he is known to have spent part of this time at the court of Federigo da Montefeltro; other scholars ascribe it to a later period.

Some time before 1450 he worked for Lionello d'Este at Ferrara, but the frescoes painted there have been destroyed. In 1451 Piero was in Rimini, where he painted a fresco in the Tempio Malatestiano depicting Sigismondo Malatesta with his patron saint. He moved then to Arezzo, where, in the church of San Francesco, he left the famous cycle of frescoes on *The Legend of the True Cross*, by far the most important work of his career (Plate 31). He finished them before 1459, as during this year he was in Rome working for Pius II and in Santa Maria Maggiore. Back in Umbria, he executed a *Virgin and Child between Saints* (Perugia, Galleria Nazionale), the '*Madonna del Parto*' (Plate 35) and the *Resurrection of Christ* (Plate 25); to these years also belong a polyptych for the Augustine convent of Borgo and the St. Julian fresco recently discovered in the church of Sant' Agostino. In 1465 he visited Urbino and it was probably then that he painted the portraits of *Federigo da Montefeltro, Duke of Urbino, and his wife, Battista Sforza* (Plates 58, 59). Piero's last visits to Urbino occurred in 1474 and 1478, when he painted the *Senigallia Madonna* (Urbino, Galleria Nazionale), a *Nativity* (London, National Gallery), and the altarpiece for the church of San Bernardino (Milan, Brera). To Federigo da Montefeltro he also dedicated his treatise *De Prospectiva Pingendi*, written before 1482 and now in the Museo Bodoniano at Parma. Two later treatises occupied his final years. Piero's formative training before his stay in Florence is a matter of conjecture; during the Florentine period, however, he found himself in direct contact with the work of artists absorbed in the problems of space and perspective. In Ferrara, he met Mantegna and probably Rogier van der Weyden, whose influence may be discovered in the domestic interior of the *Senigallia Madonna*. Piero's art, however, remained always solidly anchored to the conception of space and colour developed through his contacts with the Tuscan school. This is particularly apparent in the architectural setting and rhythmic perspective of *The Flagellation of Christ* (Plate 29), in the masterly balance between light and colour, between figures and structural details, in the rhythms and emotional power of gestures and features which are characteristics of the Arezzo frescoes.

Piero di Cosimo

Born about 1462 in Florence, where he died after 1515, Piero studied with Cosimo Rosselli, whom he assisted in his work in the Sistine Chapel. His life and work are scantily documented and his eclectic style shows the influence of Pollaiuolo, Leonardo, Signorelli and Raphael. He was attracted by mythological themes (*Death of Procris*, London, National Gallery; *Story of Prometheus*, Strasbourg, Musée des Beaux-Arts; and Munich, Alte Pinakothek). His masterpiece is *Mars and Venus* (Plate 73), in which he delights in the details of a dreamy landscape.

His religious paintings show Leonardo's influence in the use of *sfumato: Immaculate Conception* (Florence, Uffizi), *Madonna and Child Reading a Book* (Stockholm, Royal Palace), *Madonna and Child with a Book and a Dove* (Paris, Louvre). Piero's portraits have an extraordinary immediacy: *Giuliano da Sangallo* (Amsterdam, Rijksmuseum), *Simonetta Vespucci* (Chantilly, Musée Condé).

Pisanello, Antonio

Born in Pisa in about 1395, Antonio Pisano was trained in Verona; in 1415–20 he worked with Gentile da Fabriano in Venice and in 1431–2 he was in Rome to finish Gentile's frescoes in San Giovanni in Laterano. His portrait of Emperor Sigismund (1432, Paris, Louvre) made him famous and sought after by the courts of Milan, Rimini, Naples, Mantua and Ferrara. In spite of a large collection of drawings, mainly in the Louvre, Pisanello's art is only scantily represented as few of his works survive. Among his portraits, the best known are *Lionello d'Este* (*c.* 1441, Bergamo, Accademia Carrara) and the *Princess of the House of Este* (*c.* 1443, Louvre): both are profiles against a floral background. Two frescoes are also extant: *The Annunciation* (*c.* 1426, Verona, San Fermo), elegant and graceful, and his masterpiece, *St. George and the Princess* (1433–8, Verona, Santa Anastasia), epitomizing the richness of his imagination. Although the most brilliant representative of the courtly, Gothic art, Pisanello avoided stylization and picturesque superficiality by his precise and realistic rendering of details and features.

Pollaiuolo, Antonio

Born around 1432 in Florence, where he died in 1498, Antonio began his artistic career as a goldsmith, but little is known of his early activity in this field.

In 1466 he was commissioned by the Merchants' Guild to prepare the cartoons for twenty-seven tapestries depicting the life of St. John the Baptist; although strongly influenced by Andrea del Castagno, his style is here predominantly neo-Gothic. His later portraits of gentlewomen (Berlin, Staatliche Museen; Milan, Museo Poldi-Pezzoli) already show a new conception of space, a new vitality and harmony. These characteristics are more clearly exemplified by such works as the *Danza dei Nudi* (Arcetri), *David* (Berlin, Staatliche Museen), *Hercules and the Hydra* (London, British Museum) and *Hercules and Antaeus* (Florence, Uffizi), all dated between 1470 and 1475.

To the same period belongs his masterpiece in the National Gallery, London, *The Martyrdom of St. Sebastian* (Plates 50, 83, 97), which he is said to have painted with his brother Piero (*c.* 1441–96).

Pontormo

Jacopo Carucci was born at Pontormo, near Empoli, in 1494 and died in Florence in 1557. One of the most sensitive representatives of Mannerism, he worked under Mariotto Albertinelli and became Andrea del Sarto's assistant in 1512. His first works, *Madonna with Four Saints* (1514) and *The Visitation* (1515–16), both in SS. Annunziata in Florence, show Andrea's influence. Later he derived from Leonardo and Piero di Cosimo a taste for elegant contour and unusual motifs and attitudes.

In 1520, Pontormo worked in the hall of the Medici villa at Poggio a Caiano, where he painted lively pastoral scenes in the lunettes; between 1522 and 1525 he decorated the Certosa at Galluzzo with a cycle depicting the Passion. *The Deposition* (Plates 151–5), painted in 1525–8 in light cool tones of mauve, pink, and green, with undulating figures arranged in an effective composition, is probably a masterpiece of Pontormo's style.

As a portraitist he created a new type of painting—smooth, elongated and unquiet. The *Gem Engraver* (*c.* 1516, Paris, Louvre), *Alessandro de' Medici* (*c.* 1525, Lucca, Pinacoteca Nazionale) and the *Portrait of an Old Lady* (1550–6, Vienna, Belvedere) are remarkable for their colour, the emphasis on the features, and well illustrate Pontormo's remarkable technique. In the famous *Visitation* (Plate 145) the central group stands out through its sharp foreshortening. In his later years, under Michelangelo's influence, Pontormo tried to give greater breadth to his compositions and the contrast between the delicate faces of his figures and their muscular bodies grew more marked. This is particularly evident in the surviving sketches made for his last frescoes for the choir of San Lorenzo; the frescoes have been destroyed but the sketches show compositions of gigantic bodies and twisted forms uncontrolled by any decorative scheme.

Raphael

Raffaello Sanzio was born in Urbino in 1483, the son and pupil of Giovanni Santi. In 1500 he worked with Perugino at the Cambio, Perugia, and with Evangelista di Pian di Meleto on an altarpiece for Città di Castello. To this period belong the *Three Graces* (1500, Chantilly, Musée Condé) and the *Knight's Dream* (1500, London, National Gallery). The *Marriage of the Virgin* (1504, Milan, Brera), influenced by Perugino, the *Coronation of the Virgin* (1503, Vatican Museum) and the *Crucifixion* (1503, National Gallery) already show the development of a highly personal style: clear, well balanced compositions and a subtle draughtsmanship. Another work of this period is the *Madonna and Child Enthroned with Saints* (*c.* 1504, New York, Metropolitan Museum).

In 1504 Raphael went to Florence and discovered the work of Leonardo, whose influence is evident in such works as the *Madonna del Granduca* (1505, Florence, Palazzo Pitti), the *Madonna in the Meadow* (1505, Vienna, Kunsthistorisches Museum), *La Belle Jardinière* (1507, Paris, Louvre) and the *Madonna del Baldacchino* (1507–8, Palazzo Pitti), in which he adopted Leonardo's *sfumato* as well as his pyramidal composition.

Towards the end of 1508 Pope Julius II invited him to decorate the Vatican Stanze. Perugino, Signorelli and others had already started work there. Raphael first decorated the Stanza della Segnatura, which he completed in 1511, with frescoes depicting *The 'Disputa'* (Plates 122, 123), *The 'School of Athens'* (Plates 121, 124), *Parnassus* and the *Law*. He then turned to the Stanza d'Eliodoro, finished in 1514, where he painted episodes from Jewish and Christian history: *The Expulsion of Heliodorus from the Temple* (Plate 33), the *Liberation of St. Peter*, *Leo I Halting Attila before Rome*, and the *Mass at Bolsena*.

Commissions also came from Roman noblemen: for Sigismondo de'Conti he painted the *Madonna di Foligno* (*c.* 1511, Vatican Museum), for Agostino Chigi he decorated the Villa Farnesina with the fresco of *Galatea* (1511–12) and scenes from the *Story of Psyche* (painted, on Raphael's design, by Giulio Romano). To this period also belong the *Madonna della Sedia* (1514–15, Palazzo Pitti) and *The Sistine Madonna* (Plate 111). In 1514, after Bramante's death and Michelangelo's departure, Leo X placed Raphael in charge of all projects in Rome: the supervision of the architectural works at the Vatican, the decoration of the Vatican Logge and the execution of ten cartoons for tapestries to be placed in the Sistine Chapel. In the same year he also started work on the Stanza dell'Incendio, where he was greatly helped by Giulio Romano, being himself occupied with the tapestry cartoons (Plates 116–18). In the Logge, his contribution was limited to general supervision, as by this time he was busy with architectural commissions. In 1520, at the height of his career, he died, aged thirty-seven.

Perugino was the source of Raphael's luminous tones and spacious calm settings, to which he later added Leonardo's harmony and portrait techniques. Nor was he indifferent to Michelangelo's work, as is clear from the *Entombment* (1507, Rome, Galleria Borghese), the *Fire in the Borgo* (*c.* 1516, Vatican, Stanza dell'Incendio) and the *Sibyls* (1514, Rome, Santa Maria della Pace). At the same time he showed the influence of Venetian painting, particularly that of Sebastiano del Piombo and Titian, above all in portraits such as *La Donna Velata* (1514–16, Florence, Pitti). A truly humanist artist, Raphael provided the Italian Renaissance with its classical framework.

Rosso, Giovanni Battista

Born in Florence in 1494, Giovanni Battista di Jacopo probably worked with Andrea del Sarto, but he soon developed a highly individualistic temperament. One of his early works, the *Assumption of the Virgin* (1517, Florence, SS. Annunziata), reveals the influence of Dürer and shows a radical departure from the Renaissance ideals in the strange expressions of the faces and the voluminous drapery. These characteristics reappear in the *Madonna with Four Saints* (1518, Florence, Uffizi), heightened by eccentric colouring, and in the *Madonna with Two Saints* (1521, Villamagna).

Rosso's stylistic maturity is reached in *The Deposition* (Plates 158, 164), painted as a nocturnal event: the extraordinary treatment of light, the abstract angularity of the figures, the strangeness of colouring and expressions enhance the painting's unreal atmosphere. This development is continued in the *Marriage of the Virgin* (1523, Florence, San Lorenzo) and in the frescoes painted in Santa Maria della Pace during a stay in Rome in 1524–7. After a visit to Venice, he went to Fontainebleau, where he did some paintings and stucco decorations. According to Vasari, he committed suicide in Paris in 1540; but in fact it is more likely that he died a natural death.

Sassetta

Stefano di Giovanni di Consolo da Cortona, first called Sassetta in a document dated 1752, was born about 1392 in either Siena or Cortona.

In 1426 he had already finished a polyptych for the Compagnia della Lana, and in 1428 his name appears in the 'Register of Sienese Painters'. Between 1430 and 1432 he painted the *Madonna della Neve* for Siena Cathedral; his altarpiece for San Domenico at Cortona is dated around 1433, and in 1437 he was commissioned to execute a polyptych for the church of San Francesco at Borgo San Sepolcro. He died in April 1450.

All his altarpieces are now dismembered and the parts scattered in museums and private collections.

Sassetta's art continued the style and ideals of the Sienese school of the Trecento; his paintings show the influence of such artists as Simone Martini and Lippo Vanni, the Flemish miniature painters, and, among his Florentine contemporaries, Masolino and Paolo Uccello.

Savoldo, Gian Girolamo

Little is known about Savoldo, who was born in Brescia, possibly around 1480, and died after 1540. In 1508 he was incribed in the guild of Florentine Painters and another document shows him in Venice in 1521; he was probably in Milan from 1529 to 1535. His few surviving works contrast with the Venetian manner; in his portraits he continues the poetic mood of Giorgione: *Portrait of a Man* (1510, Milan, Brera), *Portrait of a Knight* (Washington, National Gallery). His religious paintings include a *Nativity* (1527, Royal Collection). *The Adoration of the Shepherds* (1540, Venice, San Giobbe), which shows a preoccupation with light and its transformation of tonal values, is undoubtedly a result of Flemish influence, particularly that of Jan van Eyck. His *oeuvre* also includes a *Tobias and the Angel* (*c.* 1540, Rome, Galleria Borghese), where the realistic figures and landscape are bathed in an amber atmosphere, and an altarpiece for the church of Santa Maria in Organo at Verona. His refined lyricism won him only a modest reputation during his lifetime.

Signorelli, Luca

Born around 1441 at Cortona, Luca became a pupil of Piero della Francesca, whose influence can be seen in his

St. Paul (1474, Città di Castello, Pinacoteca Comunale) and the three *Madonnas* in Boston, Oxford and Rome. Later Signorelli met the Pollaiuolo brothers and saw Filippo Lippi's work at Prato. In 1482 he contributed the *Testament and Death of Moses* to the Sistine Chapel; in this fresco, as in his *Adoration of the Magi* (1484, Paris, Louvre), he shows his gift for strong compositions.

In 1490 he painted a *Madonna* (Florence, Uffizi) for Lorenzo de'Medici; this was followed by the *Holy Family* (1491, Uffizi), an *Annunciation* (1491, Volterra, Pinacoteca Comunale), a *Circumcision* (*c.* 1492, London, National Gallery) and a *Visitation* (Berlin, Staatliche Museen). His best works are the frescoes in the monastery at Asciano and in Orvieto Cathedral, which were executed between 1497 and 1508. Between 1509 and 1513 he worked in Rome, but a change of taste forced him to retire to Cortona, where he died in 1523.

Tintoretto, Jacopo

The leading representative of Venetian Mannerism, Jacopo Robusti was born in Venice in 1518 and died there in 1594. He probably trained with Bonifazio Veronese, Andrea Schiavone or Paris Bordone, as their influence can be traced through the various stages of his art. Except for a brief visit to Mantua in 1580, he never left Venice, where he was mainly engaged on large-scale commissions from the Republic and the local confraternities. Tintoretto's first works are the *Last Supper* (1547, Venice, Santa Marcuola) and *St. Mark Rescuing a Slave* (1548, Venice, Accademia), both well within the Venetian tradition. In two later works, *Christ Washing the Disciples' Feet* (Madrid, Prado) and *St. Augustine Healing the Plague-stricken* (Vicenza Museum), Tintoretto displayed a striking use of perspective and a dramatic effect of light, colour and forms. His powerful conception of the human body is given full expression in the three paintings of the *Miracles of St. Mark*, executed between 1562 and 1566.

In 1566, he began work on the cycle for the Scuola di San Rocco, which occupied him for the next twenty-three years. The paintings illustrate scenes from the *Life of Christ* and the *Life of the Virgin* and represent the peak of the artist's visionary achievement: he used light and colour to give emphasis to his figures and swirling movement to his crowds.

After San Rocco, Tintoretto was engaged on a series of paintings for the Palazzo Ducale: much of his earlier work there had been destroyed in a fire in 1577. In 1581 he began to decorate the ceiling in the Sala del Senato with the *Triumph of Venice as Queen of the Seas*, finished in 1584, and in 1588 he painted the huge *Paradise* in the Sala del Maggior Consiglio, a masterpiece of orchestration and compositional virtuosity. Although most of his output consisted of large religious works, Tintoretto has also left a number of mythological subjects (*Mars and Venus Surprised by Vulcan*, Munich, Alte Pinakothek) and portraits (*Jacopo Soranzo*, Venice, Accademia; *Alvise Cornaro*, Florence, Palazzo Pitti). In this particular field, he remained faithful to the Venetian tradition, adding greater brilliance and deeper intensity to Titian's style and contrasting the severe faces of his sitters with their sombre costumes and backgrounds. Tintoretto was the embodiment of Venice's cultural energy: a feeling of irresistible power, drawn from the *terribilità* of Michelangelo, contributed to the humanity and grandeur of his art, which transcended the Renaissance and anticipated the Baroque.

Titian

Tiziano Vecelli was born at Pieve di Cadore, near Belluno, around 1489 and died in Venice in 1576. He was apprenticed to the Venetian Sebastiano Zuccato, who later sent him to work with Gentile Bellini. From the Bellini workshop, Titian moved on to become Giorgione's assistant, until he left Venice and arrived in Padua in 1510. In the two or three years he spent there, Titian executed three frescoes on the *Miracles of St. Anthony of Padua* (Scuola del Santo).

Back in Venice, he opened his own workshop and was soon taking up a series of religious commissions. Among these early works are *The Assumption of the Virgin* (Plate 99), the *Virgin Appearing to St. Francis, St. Aloysius and a Donor* (1520, Ancona, Pinacoteca), a polyptych for SS. Nazaro e Celso in Brescia and the *'Pesaro Madonna'* (Plate 100). Giorgione's influence during this period, however, can be best seen in a series of mythological paintings, such as *Flora* (1515, Florence, Uffizi) and the *Sacred and Profane Love* (*c.* 1515, Rome, Galleria Borghese). Around 1530, Titian was working for Duke Federico II of Mantua, for whom he painted the *Virgin with the Rabbit* (Paris, Louvre). In the same year Cardinal Ippolito de'Medici invited him to Bologna to paint a first portrait of Charles V, now lost: the second portrait, now in the Prado, was executed in 1532–3. This commission resulted in his appointment as court-painter to the Holy Roman Emperor.

Other portraits of the period include *Cardinal Ippolito de' Medici* (1533, Florence, Palazzo Pitti), *Francesco Maria della Rovere* and *Eleonora Gonzaga* (1536–8, Uffizi), *Alfonso d'Avalos* (1536, Paris, de Ganay Collection). To the year 1538 belongs *The 'Venus of Urbino'* (Plate 93), one of the finest achievements of his maturity.

During the early 1540s, Titian decorated the ceiling of Santa Maria della Salute with biblical subjects and continued his successful activity as a portrait painter with such works as *Pietro Bembo* (Washington, D.C., National Gallery of Art), *Pope Paul III* (Naples, Galleria Nazionale di Capodimonte), and *Pietro Aretino* (Florence, Palazzo Pitti).

In 1545 Titian left for Rome, and during his stay in the Vatican he painted *Pope Paul III with his Grandsons, Alessandro and Ottaviano Farnese* (Plate 148) and *Danae* (both in Naples, Galleria Nazionale di Capodimonte).

Three years later he was invited by Charles V to Augsburg to execute a number of portraits, including two of the emperor himself: on one of them Charles V was portrayed in an armchair (Munich, Alte Pinakothek), in the other on horseback (Madrid, Prado). More court portraits followed during a second visit to Augsburg in 1550–1, for instance, *King Philip II of Spain* (Madrid, Prado). Over the next twenty years, Titian found a most assiduous patron in Philip II, who commissioned from him both sacred paintings and erotic mythological compositions.

Titian's art moved along a double path: on the one hand, his religious compositions gradually developed from the Renaissance serenity and balance which he had derived from Giorgione and Bellini, to his mature dramatic style echoing both Raphael and Michelangelo. On the other, his portraits, always characterized by clarity and refinement, became richer and more sumptuous, setting a style which was greatly to influence portrait painters in centuries to come.

Tura, Cosimo

Tura was born in Ferrara before 1431 and became official painter of the d'Este dukes, for whom he is thought to have executed portraits, religious paintings, cartoons for tapestries, embroideries, sculpture, gold and silver ornaments, and furniture. Very little of this remains in Ferrara: a *St. George and the Dragon* and an *Annunciation* (1468–9, Museo della Cattedrale), two fragments of an altarpiece, and the frescoes in the Palazzo Schifanoia, painted around 1469–71 with other artists. Other paintings attributed to him include the *Roverella Polyptych* (*c.* 1474), divided between London, Paris, Rome and San Diego; the *St. Anthony of Padua* (1484, Modena, Galleria Estense); the *Madonna with St. Jerome and a Saint* (Ajaccio, Musée Fesch); and the *Pietà* (Venice, Museo Correr), influenced by Rogier van der Weyden. Tura evolved an original style in which graphic sharpness and the fantasy of the Gothic tradition are fused with plastic strength. He is considered the founder of the Ferrarese school, which derived from him a strange and disturbing poetry. He died in 1495.

Uccello, Paolo

Born around 1397 in Florence, where he died in 1475, Uccello was a painter, mosaicist, decorator and expert in marquetry. He was mentioned in June 1407 as being apprenticed to Lorenzo Ghiberti, with whom he remained until 1414 or 1415. In 1425 he went to Venice, where he was employed as a master mosaicist in San Marco, but by January 1431 he had returned to Florence. Between 1431 and 1450 he decorated the Chiostro Verde in Santa Maria Novella, Florence, with frescoes representing the *Creation of Animals and Creation of Adam*, the *Creation of Eve and the Fall of Man*, the *Deluge* (Plates 26, 28) and *Noah's Sacrifice and Drunkenness of Noah*. In 1436 he painted the equestrian portrait of *Giovanni Acuto* (Sir John Hawkwood) in the cathedral, and in 1443 he provided four cartoons for the stained-glass circular windows of the cupola. To the 1440s also probably belong the frescoes in San Miniato al Monte and the panel of the *Founders of Florentine Art* (Paris, Louvre, attributed to Uccello). Living in Padua between 1445 and 1448, he introduced the monumental Tuscan style with paintings which are now lost.

Uccello's most famous works, the three panels illustrating the *Battle of San Romano in 1432*, were painted around 1457 for a room in the Palazzo Medici-Riccardi in Florence and are now in the Uffizi, Louvre, and National Gallery in London (Plate 32). In 1468, in Urbino, he painted an altarpiece with the *Legend of the Profanation of the Host* (later completed by Justus of Ghent). One of his last works was the *Hunt* (Oxford, Ashmolean Museum). Uccello's point of departure was Masaccio's monumentality, to which he added a wealth of naturalistic details, often influenced by Pisanello.

Uccello attributed great importance to perspective and demonstrated its applications in the San Miniato frescoes, in *Giovanni Acuto* and in the *San Romano* panels, in which, however, he delights above all in the creation of detailed sceneries and fanciful backgrounds.

Veronese, Paolo

Paolo Caliari was born probably in 1528 in Verona and died in Venice in 1588. He first studied with Giovanni Caroto, from whom he derived his transparent colours and bright tonalities. He later added to these elements the influences of Titian, Giulio Romano and Parmigianino.

Among his earliest works are two altarpieces now in Verona and Mantua. Veronese settled in Venice in 1553 and only left once, in 1560, to go to Rome. His first works in the Republic were three ceiling frescoes for the Palazzo Ducale. In 1555 he was commissioned to paint the *Coronation of the Virgin* for the Sacristy of San Sebastiano, a marvellous piece of virtuosity in its perspectives, light colours and bright highlights. The *trompe-l'oeil* effects are repeated in the *Life of Esther* (1556) and the *Life of St. Sebastian* (1558) painted in the choir.

In 1562 he decorated the Sala del Maggior Consiglio in the Palazzo Ducale, and began the series of large canvases of sacred festivities: the *Marriage at Cana* (1562, Paris, Louvre), the *Feast in the House of the Pharisee* (*c.* 1572, Louvre), *The Feast in the House of Levi* (Plates 178, 179). Rejecting Tintoretto's dramatic effects, Veronese developed his own kind of illusionism, in which buildings, landscapes and architectural devices cover entire walls. In his religious compositions, crowds of figures are highlighted and stretch across the canvas in splendid costumes and settings (the *Adoration of the Magi*, 1573, London, National Gallery; the *Mystic Marriage of St. Catherine*, *c.* 1575, Venice, Accademia). Already in 1560 he had begun painting the allegorical *tondi* for the Libreria Vecchia; later he produced one of the finest and best contrived works of the time, clearly anticipating the Baroque, the *Triumph of Venice*, a fresco for the Sala del Maggior Consiglio, where he had started working in 1562. Around 1575 he painted the *Family of Darius before Alexander* (Plates 168, 169), in which the masses converge to emphasize the essential elements in the scene; their equilibrium shows an unequalled virtuosity, which develops into an almost Baroque intensity in such works as the *Annunciation* of the Rosary Chapel in San Zanipolo, painted in the mid-1560s.

To the late 1570s belong a series of large mythological canvases, such as the *Mars and Venus* (New York, Metropolitan Museum). In his last works (*St. Pantaleon Healing a Sick Boy*, 1587, Venice, San Pantaleone) his tone becomes more serious, with a pathos that had become increasingly noticeable in his late style. Many of his last paintings were finished by his brother and his two sons.

From the Mannerists, Veronese had learnt a facile draughtsmanship and an unconventional compositional treatment without losing his attachment to clarity of colour and form. Although later influenced by Tintoretto and Titian, he retained his own palette, his preference for a cold atmosphere and a more transparent light in which the forms stand out against a lighter shadow.

His contribution to painting was a sumptuous, serenely balanced yet rather superficial, style of decoration, and a gift for scenography equalled only by Tiepolo.

Verrocchio, Andrea

Andrea di Michele Cioni, called Andrea del Verrocchio, was born in Florence in about 1435. Sculptor, painter and goldsmith, he showed exceptional versatility even among Florentine artists of the Renaissance. He painted banners for the tournaments of Lorenzo de'Medici and Giuliano de' Medici, executed a bronze candelabrum for the Palazzo Vecchio, designed fountains, and in 1472 he completed the marble sarcophagus for Piero and Giovanni de'Medici in the old sacristy of San Lorenzo. In 1478–83 he worked on the marble cenotaph to Niccolò Forteguerri, now, unfinished, in the cathedral at Pistoia; at the same time he executed the sculptural group of *Christ and St. Thomas* (Florence, façade of Or San Michele). He had also reinterpreted one of Donatello's main themes in his *David* (1473–5, Bargello) and turned to a second, the equestrian statue, with his *Monument to Bartolomeo Colleoni* (1479–88), which he executed for Venice: unfortunately he died in Venice in 1488 and the statue was completed by Alessandro Leopardi in 1496.

Verrocchio's *œuvre* as a painter is more difficult to establish. His *Madonnas* (Berlin, Staatliche Museen; London, National Gallery; New York, Metropolitan Museum) have all been attributed to the various artists who worked in his studio. His most famous painting is the *Baptism of Christ* (after 1470, Florence, Uffizi), in which Leonardo's hand can be recognized in the head of the angel on the left. However, his style appears to better advantage in the *Madonna and Child with St. Donatus and St. John the Baptist* (*c.* 1485, Pistoia, Cathedral), which is characterized by the simplicity of composition and the remarkable strength of the figures. Another masterpiece is one of the two Madonnas in Berlin. All Verrocchio's compositions are classical, harmoniously balanced, and the clothes and tints are treated with Flemish precision. Probably his greatest contribution to art was achieved within his workshop, in which he taught such artists as Leonardo, Giovanni Rustici, Perugino, Lorenzo di Credi and Francesco Botticini.

Short Bibliography

NO ATTEMPT is made here to offer a guide to the vast literature about individual painters.

Frederick Hartt, *A History of Italian Renaissance Art* (Thames and Hudson, London, 1970), is an alert and well written survey which covers sculpture and architecture as well as painting and stresses the interaction between the arts. Another dimension is added by Peter and Linda Murray, *The Art of the Renaissance* (Thames and Hudson, London, 1963), as this includes the painting of Northern Europe. I am directly indebted at several points to Michael Baxandall, *Painting and Experience in Fifteenth-century Italy* (Oxford University Press, London, 1972), and to Peter Burke, *Tradition and Innovation in Renaissance Italy* (Collins, London, 1974); the first investigates the relationship between style and everyday experience, the second that between painters and society. D. S. Chambers, *Patrons and Artists in the Italian Renaissance* (Macmillan, London, 1971), prints and comments on contracts for paintings. Eve Borsook, *The Mural Painters of Tuscany* (Phaidon, London, 1960), extends an important aspect of this book; Michael Levey, *Early Renaissance*, and John Shearman, *Mannerism* (both Penguin, Harmondsworth, 1967), discuss painting in the context of literature and music as well as of the fine arts, as does Michael Levey's *High Renaissance* (Penguin, Harmondsworth, 1975). S. J. Freedberg, *Painting in Italy, 1500–1600* (Penguin, Harmondsworth, 1971), carries the history of painting richly to our chronological limit. Vasari's account of the lives of many of the painters illustrated here is translated by George Bull in *Vasari, Lives of the Artists* (Penguin, Harmondsworth, 1965), and there is much additional biographical insight in Rudolf and Margot Wittkower, *Born under Saturn* (Weidenfeld and Nicolson, London, 1963). Changing approaches to portraiture are investigated by John Pope-Hennessy's *The Portrait in the Renaissance* (Phaidon, London, 1966), and the same author's *Raphael* (Phaidon, London, 1970) traces the way in which a complex finished painting was derived from preliminary studies. Outstanding among works devoted to the ideas expressed in Renaissance paintings are: Erwin Panofsky, *Studies in Iconology* (Oxford University Press, New York, 1939), Edgar Wind, *Pagan Mysteries in the Renaissance* (Faber, London, 1958), and E. H. Gombrich, *Symbolic Images: Studies in the Art of the Renaissance* (Phaidon, London, 1972).

For biographical material Lucia Wildt has drawn upon *The Earlier Italian Schools* by Martin Davies, *The Sixteenth-Century Italian Schools* and *The Sixteenth-Century Venetian School*, both by Cecil Gould, in the series of catalogues produced by the National Gallery, London.

Acknowledgements

THE FOLLOWING plates are reproduced by gracious permission of Her Majesty the Queen: 115, 116, 118.

The publishers are grateful to all museums, institutions and private collectors who have given permission for works of art in their possession to be reproduced.

Photographs have been kindly supplied by the following:

Alinari: 2, 3, 4, 6, 7, 8, 18, 19, 20, 22, 23, 24, 25, 29, 30, 31, 33, 47, 51, 53, 58, 59, 61, 72, 77, 79, 87, 93, 94, 95, 100, 101, 109, 117, 122, 123, 125, 126, 127, 130, 135, 139, 140, 152, 153, 155, 159, 162, 166, 167, 179, 182, 187, 188

Bayerische Staatsgemäldesammlungen, Munich: 149

Caisse Nationale des Monuments Historiques, Paris: 52

Christ Church, Oxford: 154

Deutsche Fotothek, Dresden: 146

Istituto Centrale del Restauro, Florence: 21

Kunsthistorisches Museum, Vienna: 156, 161

Metropolitan Museum of Art, New York: 15

National Gallery of Art, Washington D.C.: 9, 12, 14, 88, 144, 150, 173, 177

National Gallery, London: 11, 32, 34, 36, 37, 40, 42, 43, 45, 46, 50, 54, 57, 60, 62, 67, 76, 80, 83, 84, 97, 98, 110, 114, 119, 132, 134, 137, 138, 143, 160, 168, 169

National Galleries of Scotland, Edinburgh: 39, 141

Phaidon Archive: 1, 10, 13, 16, 17, 27, 35, 38, 41, 44, 48, 55, 64, 65, 66, 68, 69, 70, 71, 73, 74, 81, 85, 86, 89, 90, 91, 92, 96, 99, 102–108, 111, 112, 118, 120, 121, 124, 129, 133, 142, 145, 147, 148, 157, 163, 165, 170, 171, 174, 176, 178, 181, 183, 184, 185

Photographie Giraudon, Paris: 49, 128, 180, 186

Royal Academy of Arts, London: 131

The Fitzwilliam Museum, Cambridge: 56

Index